W9-AGJ-565

Property of J.L.S
7/30/03 My
Barnes & Noble

Cabling: The Complete Guide to Network Wiring

Cabling: The Complete Guide to Network Wiring

David Groth
Jim McBee

SYBEX®

San Francisco • Paris • Düsseldorf • Soest • London

Associate Publishers: Guy Hart-Davis, Neil Edde
Contracts and Licensing Manager: Kristine O'Callaghan
Acquisitions & Developmental Editors: Maureen Adams,
Brenda Frink
Editor: Sally Engelfried
Senior Production Editor: Lisa Duran
Associate Production Editor: Molly Glover
Technical Editor: Art Brieva
Book Designer: Kris Warrenburg Design
Graphic Illustrator: Eric Houts for EPIC
Electronic Publishing Specialist: Kris Warrenburg Design
Proofreaders: Laurie O'Connell, Laura Schattschneider, Suzanne
Stein, Camera Obscura, Nathan Whiteside
Indexer: Ted Laux
Cover Designer: Calyx Design
Cover Illustrator: Richard Miller, Calyx Design
Color Insert: Kris Warrenburg Design, Jennifer Hines Design,
Gareth Hopson Photography, Judith Hibbard

SYBEX and the SYBEX logo are trademarks of SYBEX Inc. in the
USA and other countries.

TRADEMARKS: SYBEX has attempted throughout this book to
distinguish proprietary trademarks from descriptive terms by following the capitalization style used by the manufacturer.

The author and publisher have made their best efforts to prepare
this book, and the content is based upon final release software
whenever possible. Portions of the manuscript may be based upon
pre-release versions supplied by software manufacturer(s). The
author and the publisher make no representation or warranties of
any kind with regard to the completeness or accuracy of the contents herein and accept no liability of any kind including but not
limited to performance, merchantability, fitness for any particular
purpose, or any losses or damages of any kind caused or alleged
to be caused directly or indirectly from this book.

Copyright © 2000 SYBEX Inc., 1151 Marina Village Parkway,
Alameda, CA 94501. World rights reserved. No part of this publication may be stored in a retrieval system, transmitted, or repro-
duced in any way, including but not limited to photocopy,
photograph, magnetic or other record, without the prior agreement and written permission of the publisher.

Library of Congress Card Number: 00-102078

ISBN: 0-7821-2645-6

Manufactured in the United States of America

10 9 8 7 6 5 4 3 2 1

*For my wife, my daughter, my family,
and my friends.*
—D.G.

*This book is dedicated to my family
(Mom, Dad, sisters, cousins, and aunts).
Over a distance of thousands of miles and many
years, you still influence my actions every day.
We are all products of our environment when we
grow up; mine was great!*
—J.M.

ACKNOWLEDGMENTS

This book has been a long time in the making. First and foremost, I would like to acknowledge my coauthor, Jim McBee, for the excellent work he has done on this project. He should be proud of his efforts and it shows in the quality of this book. Also, we would like to acknowledge the other behind-the-scenes people that helped to make this book, starting with Dan Whiting of Border States Electric Supply in Fargo, ND, for all the reference material and pictures he and his company provided. His expertise was invaluable in the making of this book. Thanks, Dan! We would also like to thank photographer Steve Sillers for taking many of the pictures that can be found throughout this book.

This book would not exist without Sybex Acquisitions and Developmental Editor Maureen Adams. Thanks for bringing Jim and me together and thanks to Sybex Acquisitions and Developmental Editor Brenda Frink for managing this project. Additionally, I would like to recognize Editor Sally Engelfried for editing this book and Production Editors Lisa Duran and Molly Glover for managing the production of this book. Also, I would like to recognize the rest of the Sybex staff for all their hard work on this book, including (but not limited to) Eric Houts, the graphic illustrator; Judith Hibbard, Jennifer Hines, and Gareth Hopson for their work on the color insert; all of the proofreaders—Laurie O'Connell, Laura Schattschneider, Suzanne Stein, Camera Obscura, and Nathan Whiteside; the indexer Ted Laux; and EPS Kris Warrenburg who spent time and effort making both the book and the color insert look good.

Finally, I would like to recognize my wife, daughter, family, and friends, without whom I couldn't do any of this and for whom I do this.

—*David Groth*

At the Spring 1999 Networld+InterOp, David Groth, Maureen Adams from Sybex, and I sat down and talked about the need for a book about network cabling that was targeted towards IT professionals and people just starting out with cabling.

A year later, after many missed trips to the gym, a forgotten diet, sleepless nights, forsaken weekends, long phone calls, hundreds of hours of reading, neglected friends, and some very sore fingers, the manuscript is completed and in your hands.

And quite a year it has been! I consider myself to be a network infrastructure person. I have managed many cabling installations, and hubs, switches, routers, and servers are part of the domain in which I dwell. I learned a lot of new things working on this book. Best of all, though, I met many telecommunications professionals along the way who deserve special mention. A big thank you to coauthor David Groth, who spent the better part of a year letting me bounce ideas off him, responding to my e-mails, and returning my calls; I don't know how he found time to write!

David Barnett, RCDD, deserves a book of his own. Over the past year, the ever-patient David has worked right along with us, researching, reading, and contributing material for the tools and connectors section, as well as the appendices of this book. He reviewed many pages, answered questions, and cleared up many myths surrounding cabling.

Special thanks also goes to Janice Boothe, RCDD (and her awesome www.wiring.com Web site), and Mike Holt for their knowledge of codes. Paul Lucas, RCDD, of Paul's Cabling tolerated my nonstop questions and provided many great stories and experiences. Kudos to Matt Bridges for his assistance with components. Jeff Deckman gave his vital insight and input to the Request for Proposal (RFP) chapter; his cooperative approach to working with vendors will help many people successfully deploy telecommunications infrastructures. Charles Perkins drew from his years of field experience to help with the case studies.

A picture is worth a thousand words, and I can say more than a few thousand good words about some of the companies that provided the pictures that help make this book easier to follow. These include IDEAL DataComm, The Siemon Company, MilesTek, Ortronics, Jensen Tools, and Erico.

Others that reviewed portions of the book and provided feedback include Maureen McFerrin, Randy Williams, RD Clyde, John Poehler, and David Trachsel. Jeff Bloom and the folks at Computer Training Academy (where I teach Windows NT, TCP/IP, and Exchange courses) are always outstandingly patient when I take on a project like this.

A big thanks to my friends for remembering who I am after I emerge from this project. Finally, the consummate professionals at Sybex always leave me in awe of their skills, patience, and insight.

—Jim McBee

CONTENTS AT A GLANCE

CONTENTS

PART II   Network Media and Connectors

7 Copper Cable Media   283

INTRODUCTION

Welcome to the incredibly complex world of premises data communications cabling. This introduction serves to tell you a little about how this book came about and how you can use it to your best advantage.

Not only does cabling carry the data across your network, it can also carry voice, serial communications, alarm signals, video, and audio transmissions. In the past, people took their cabling systems for granted. However, over the last few years, the Information Technology world has begun to understand the importance of a reliable and well designed structured cabling system. Over the past five years, there has been an explosion in the number of registered structured cabling installers. With the increase in complexity of today's LANs, the number of people that need to know the basics of cabling has increased accordingly.

We had a great time writing this book. In the yearlong process of researching, writing, and editing it, we met many consummate professionals in the cabling business. Many distributors, manufacturers, and cabling contractors provided us with feedback, tips, and in-the-field experiences.

During the research phase of the book, we continually reviewed newsgroups, cabling FAQ, and other Internet resources to find out what people wanted to know about cabling. We polled Information Technology managers, help desk staff, network designers, cable installers, and system managers to find out what they wanted to know about their cabling system. The result is this book.

About This Book

This book contains chapters that cover topics that run the gamut of cabling, including:

- An introduction to data cabling

- Information on cabling standards and how to choose the correct ones

- Cable system and infrastructure constraints

- Cabling system components

- Tools of the trade

- Copper cable, fiber optic, and unbounded media

- Wall plates and cable connectors

- Cabling system design and installation

- Cable connector installation

- Cabling system testing and troubleshooting

- Creating Request for Proposals (RFPs)

- Cabling case studies

In addition to these chapters, there is a cabling dictionary at the end of the book that you can use to look up the terms that you don't know or aren't clear on, as well as three other appendices that include other resources to look at for cabling information, tips on how to get your Registered Communications and Distribution Designer (RCDD) certification, and information for the home cabler. Finally, there is a 32-page insert with color pictures of various cabling products and installations that can show you what the items look like in their "natural environment."

Who Is This Book For?

If you are standing in your neighborhood bookstore browsing through this book, you may be asking yourself who should buy it. The procedures in this book are illustrated and written in English rather than "technospeak." That's because we, the authors, designed this book specifically to help unlock the mysteries of the wiring closet, cable in the ceiling, wall jacks, and other components of a cabling system. Cabling can be a confusing topic for many of us; it has its own language, acronyms, and standards. We designed this book with the following types of people in mind:

- Information Technology (IT) professionals who can use this book to gain a better understanding and appreciation of a structured cabling system

- IT managers who are preparing to install a new computer system

- Do-it-yourselfers who need to install a few new cabling runs in their facility and want to get it right the first time

- New cable installers who want to learn more than just what it takes to pull a cable through the ceiling and terminate it to the patch panel

How to Use This Book

To understand the way this book is put together, you must learn about a few of the special conventions we used. Following are some of the items you will commonly see.

Italicized words indicate new terms. After each italicized term, you will find a definition.

TIP
Tips will be formatted like this. A tip is a special piece of information that can either make your work easier or make an installation go more smoothly.

NOTE
Notes are formatted like this. When you see a note, it usually indicates some special circumstance to make note of. Notes often include out-of-the-ordinary information about working with a telecommunications infrastructure.

WARNING
Warnings are found within the text whenever there is a technical situation that arises that may cause damage to a component or cause a system failure of some kind. Additionally, warnings are placed in the text to call particular attention to a potentially dangerous situation.

KEY TERMS
Key Terms are used to introduce a new word or term that you should be aware of. Just as in the worlds of networking, software, and programming, the world of cabling and telecommunications has its own language.

Sidebars

This special formatting indicates a sidebar. *Sidebars* are entire paragraphs of information that, although related to the topic being discussed, fit better into a standalone discussion. They are just what their name suggests: a sidebar discussion.

Cabling @ Work Sidebars

These special sidebars are used to give real-life examples of situations that actually occurred in the cabling world.

This book also contains a glossary of the terms used throughout this book. It can be found in Appendix A. Additionally, there is a 32-page color insert that will allow you to view certain items in color.

Keep an eye out for these special items within the text as you read.

Enjoy

Have fun reading this book—we've had fun writing it. We hope that it will be a valuable resource to you and will answer at least some of your questions on LAN cabling. As always we love to hear from our readers; you can reach David Groth at dgroth@corpcomm.net. Jim McBee can be reached at jmcbee@somorita.com.

PART I

Cabling Technology and Components

chapter 1

Introduction to Data Cabling

- The Golden Rules of Data Cabling

- Cable Design

- Data Communications 101

- Cabling Performance

" **D**ata cabling! It's just wire. What is there to plan?" the newly minted, programmer-turned-MIS director commented to Jim at a company where he had been contracted to help them move their 750-node network to a new location. During their initial conversation, the director had a couple of other insights:

- He said that the walls were not even up in the new location, so it was too early to be talking about data cabling.

- To save money, he wanted to pull the old Category 3 cabling and move it to the new location. ("We can run 100Base-TX on the old cable.")

- He said not to worry about the voice cabling and the cabling for the photocopier tracking system; someone else would coordinate the cabling for those systems.

Jim shouldn't have been too surprised by the ridiculous nature of these questions and comments. Too few people truly understand the importance of a reliable, standards-based, and flexible cabling system. Fewer people still understand the challenges that present themselves when building a high-speed network. Some of the technical problems associated with building a cabling system to support a high-speed network are comprehended only by electrical engineers. And many people believe that there should be a separate type of cable in the wall for each application (PCs, printers, terminals, copiers, etc.).

Data cabling has come a long way in the past 15 years. This chapter discusses some of the basics of data cabling, including topics such as:

- The golden rules of data cabling

- The importance of reliable cabling

- The legacy of proprietary cabling systems

- The increasing demands on data cabling to support higher speeds

- Cable design and materials used to make cables

- Types of communications media

- Limitations that cabling imposes on higher speed communications

- The future of cabling performance

You are probably thinking to yourself right now that all you really want to know how to do is install some cable to support a few 10Base-T workstations. Words and phrases such as attenuation, crosstalk, twisted pair, modular connectors, and multimode optical fiber cable may be completely foreign to you. Just as the world of PC LANs and WANs has its own industry buzzwords, so does the cabling business. In fact, you may hear such an endless stream of buzzwords and foreign terminology that you'll wish you had majored in electrical engineering in college.

Golden Rules of Data Cabling *- Add This to Admin. manual*

Emphasizing our own personal Golden Rules of data cabling list is a great way to start this chapter and the book. Over the years we have become cabling evangelists. If your cabling is not designed and installed properly, you will have problems that you can't even imagine. We have come up with a list of rules to consider when planning structure-cabling systems.

- Networks never get smaller or less complicated.

- Build one cabling system that will accommodate voice and data.

- Always install more cabling than you currently require. Those extra outlets will come in handy someday.

- Use structured cabling standards when building a new cabling system. Avoid anything proprietary!

- Quality counts! Use the highest quality cabling and cabling components. Cabling is the foundation of your network; if the cabling fails to perform, nothing else will matter.

- Don't scrimp on installation costs. Even quality components and cable must be installed correctly; poor workmanship has trashed more than one cabling installation.

- Plan for higher speed technologies than are commonly available today. Just because 1000Base-T Ethernet seems unnecessary today does not mean it won't be a requirement in five years.

- Documentation, while dull, is a necessary evil that should be taken care of while you're setting up the cabling system. If you wait, more pressing concerns may cause you to ignore its importance later.

The Importance of Reliable Cabling

We cannot stress enough the importance of reliable cabling. Two recent studies presented some statistics that vindicated our sometimes evangelical approach to data cabling. These studies gave us three important facts about data cabling:

- Data cabling typically accounts for less than 10 percent of the total cost of the network infrastructure.

- The life span of the typical cabling system is upwards of 16 years; cabling is the second most long-lived asset you may have (the first being the actual shell of the building).

- Nearly 70 percent of all network-related problems are due to poor cabling techniques and cable component problems.

These statistics emphasize the importance of reliable cabling and the relatively low cost of installing the proper cabling infrastructure in the first place.

NOTE   If you have installed the proper Category or grade of cable, the majority of cabling problems is usually related to patch cables, connectors, and termination techniques. The permanent portion of the cable (the part that is in the wall) is usually not the problem unless it was damaged during installation.

Of course, these were facts that we already knew from our own experiences. We have spent countless hours troubleshooting cabling systems that were nonstandard, badly designed, poorly documented, and shoddily installed. We have seen many dollars wasted on the installation of additional cabling and cabling infrastructure support that should have been part of the original installation.

Regardless of how you look at it, cabling is the foundation of your network. It must be reliable!

The Cost of Poor Cabling

note and document these problems

The costs that result from poorly planned and poorly implemented cabling systems can be staggering. A company that had recently moved into a new office space reported to us that they were going to use the existing cabling, which was supposed to be Category 5 cable. Almost immediately, 100Mbps Ethernet network users began reporting intermittent problems when they were working on the network.

These problems included exceptionally slow access times when reading e-mail, saving documents, and using their sales database. Other users reported that applications running under Windows 98 and Windows NT were locking up, which often caused them to have to reboot their PC.

After many months of investigation and network annoyances, the company finally had the cable runs tested. Many cables did not even meet the minimum requirements of a Category 5 installation, while other cabling runs were installed and terminated poorly.

> **WARNING**
>
> Often network managers mistakenly assume that data cabling either works or it does not work and there is no in-between. This is not the case. Cabling *can* cause intermittent problems.

Is the Cable to Blame?

How often is this the case?

Can faulty cable cause the intermittent problems that the above company was experiencing? Contrary to popular opinion, it certainly can. In addition to being vulnerable to outside interference from sources such as electric motors, fluorescent lighting, elevators, cellular phones, copiers, and microwave ovens, there are other problems that cabling can have.

These problems usually revolve around substandard components (patch panels, connectors, and cable) and poor installation techniques, and they can subtly manifest themselves as performance problems in the form of dropped or incomplete packets. These lost packets cause the network adapters to have to time-out and retransmit the data.

Robert Metcalfe (inventor of Ethernet, founder of 3Com, columnist for *InfoWorld*, industry pundit, and Jim's personal hero) helped coin the term *drop-rate magnification*. Drop-rate magnification is used to describe how dropping a few packets can cause significant network problems. Metcalfe estimates that a 1 percent drop in Ethernet packets can correlate to an 80 percent drop in bandwidth. Modern network protocols that send multiple packets and expect only a single acknowledgement (such as TCP/IP and Novell's IPX/SPX) are especially susceptible to this since a single dropped packet may cause an entire stream of packets to have to be retransmitted.

Dropped packets (as opposed to packet collisions) are more difficult to detect because they are "lost" on the wire. When data is lost on the wire, the data is transmitted properly but, due to problems with the cable, the data never arrives at the destination or it arrives in an incomplete format.

You've Come a Long Way, Baby! The Legacy of Proprietary Cabling Systems

In the old days, cabling was often unstructured, and standards were noticeably absent. Unfortunately, that legacy still lingers in many places. Early cabling systems were unstructured, proprietary, and often worked only with a specific vendor's equipment. Early data cabling systems were designed and installed for mainframes; these were a combination of thicknet cable, twinax cable, and terminal cable (RS-232). Since, back then, there were no cabling standards to follow, you simply had to ask the vendor which cable type should be run for a specific type of host or terminal. This may seem like an ideal solution since the vendor is specifying the exact cable that will support their equipment. Unfortunately, this cable could often only be used for that specific host or terminal type or for that specific vendor's equipment.

PC LANs came on the scene in the mid-1980s; these systems usually consisted of thicknet cable, thinnet cable, or some combination of the two. These cabling systems were also limited to only certain types of hosts and network nodes.

As PC LANs became popular, some companies demonstrated the very extremes of data cabling. Looking back, it's surprising to think that the ceilings, walls, and floor trenches could hold all the cable that was necessary to provide connectivity to each system used. As one company prepared to install a 1,000-node PC LAN, they were shocked to find all the different types of cabling systems in use. Each of these cabling systems was wired to a different wiring closet or computer room and included the following:

- Wang dual coaxial cable for Wang word processing terminals

- IBM twinax cable for IBM 5250 terminals

- Twisted-pair cable containing one or two pairs that were used by the digital phone system

- Thick Ethernet from the DEC VAX to terminal servers

- RS-232 cable to wiring closets connecting to DEC VAX terminal servers

- RS-232 cable from certain secretarial workstations to a proprietary NBI word processing system

- Coaxial cables connecting a handful of PCs to a single NetWare server

Some users had two or three different types of terminals sitting on their desks and, consequently, two or three different types of wall plates in their offices or cubicles. Due to the cost of cabling each location, the locations that needed certain terminal types were the only ones that were cabled with the cables that supported those terminals. If users moved, and they frequently did, new cables often had to be pulled.

The new LAN was based on a twisted-pair Ethernet system that used unshielded twisted-pair cabling called Synoptics Lattisnet, which was a precursor to the 10Base-T standards. Due to budget considerations, when the LAN cabling was installed, this company often used spare pairs in the existing phone cables. When extra pairs were not available, additional cable was installed. Networking standards such as 10Base-T were but a twinkle in the IEEE's (Institute of Electrical and Industrial Engineers) eye, and guidelines such as the TIA/EIA-568-A Cabling Standard were not yet formulated (see the next section for more information on TIA/EIA-568-A). Companies deploying twisted-pair LANs had little guidance, to say the least.

Much of the cable that was used at this company was sub-Category 3, meaning that it did not meet the minimum Category 3 performance requirements. Unfortunately, since the cabling was not even Category 3, once the 10Base-T specification was approved, many of the installed cables would not support 10Base-T cards on most of the network. This meant that three years into this company's network deployments, they had to rewire much of their building.

KEY TERMS   **Applications and Cabling**   Often, you will see the term *application* used when referring to cabling. If you are like me, you think of an application as a software program that runs on your computer. However, when discussing cabling infrastructures, an application is the technology that will take advantage of the cabling system. Applications include telephone systems (analog voice and digital voice), Ethernet, Token Ring, ATM, ISDN, and RS-232.

Proprietary Cabling Is a Thing of the Past

At the same company, they had at least seven different types of cables running through the walls, floors, and ceilings. Each of these cables met only the standards dictated by the vendor that required that particular cable type.

As early as 1988, the computer and telecommunications industry yearned for a versatile standard that would define cabling systems and make the practices used to build these cable systems consistent. Many vendors attempted to define their own standards for various components of a cabling system. Communications product distributor Anixter (www.anixter.com) codeveloped and published a document called *Cable Performance Levels* in 1990. This document provided a purchasing specification for communication cables that attempted to create a standard by which cabling performance could be measured. Folks who have been in the networking industry for a few years will remember cables often being referred to as Level 1, Level 2, or Level 3 cables. Anixter continues to maintain the Anixter levels program; it is currently called Anixter Levels Channel (ALC).

The Need for a Comprehensive Standard

Twisted-pair cabling in the late 1980s and early 1990s was often installed to support digital or analog telephone systems. Early twisted-pair cabling (Level 1 or Level 2) often proved marginal or insufficient for supporting the higher frequencies and data rates required for network topologies such as Ethernet and Token Ring. Even when the cabling did marginally support higher speeds of data transfer (10Mbps), the connecting hardware and installation methods were often still stuck in the "voice" age, which meant that connectors, wall plates, and patch panels were designed to support voice applications only.

The Anixter Cables Performance Levels document only described performance standards for cables. A more comprehensive standard had to be developed to outline not only the types of cables that should be used, but also the standards for deployment, connectors, patch panels, and more.

A consortium of telecommunications vendors and consultants worked in conjunction with the American National Standards Institute (ANSI), Electronic Industries Association (EIA), and the Telecommunications Industry Association (TIA) to create a standard originally known as the Commercial Building Telecommunications Cabling Standard or ANSI/TIA/EIA-568-1991. This standard has been revised and updated several times and is now simply known as ANSI/TIA/EIA-568-A or just TIA/EIA-568-A; it is discussed at length in Chapter 2, "Cabling Standards." An updated version of this standard is expected to be released in mid-2000 and will be called TIA/EIA-568-B.

Cabling and the Need for Speed

The past few years have seen some tremendous advances not only in networking technologies, but also the demands placed on those networking technologies. In the past 15 years, we have seen the emergence of standards for 10Mb Ethernet, 16Mb Token Ring, 100Mb FDDI, 100Mb Ethernet, 155Mb ATM (Asynchronous Transfer Mode), 655Mb ATM, 1Gb Ethernet, and 2.5Gb ATM. Network technology designers are already planning technologies that may support data rates of more than 10Gbps, such as 10Gb ATM and 10Gb Ethernet.

The average number of nodes on a network segment has decreased dramatically while the number of applications and the size of the data transferred has increased dramatically. Applications are becoming more complex and the amount of network bandwidth required by the typical user is increasing. Is the bandwidth provided by some of the new ultra-high speed network applications (such as 1Gb Ethernet) required today? Maybe not, but there is no doubt that networks and applications will require such throughput in the future.

Cabling @ Work: The Increasing Demands of Modern Applications

A perfect example of the increasing demands put on networks by applications is a law firm that eight years ago was running typical office automation software applications on their LAN. The average document that they worked on was about four pages in length and 12KB in size. This firm also used electronic mail; a typical e-mail size was no more than 500 bytes. Other applications included a couple of small dBase III databases, a terminal emulation application that was used to connect to the firm's IBM minicomputer, and a few Lotus 1-2-3 users. The actual size of data files transferred was relatively small, and the average 10Base-T network segment size was about 100 nodes per segment.

Today, the same law firm is still using their existing 10Base-T and finding it increasingly insufficient for their ever-growing data processing and office automation needs. Their average document length is still around four pages in length, but, thanks to the increasing complexity of modern word processing software and their own templates, the average document is nearly 50KB in size!

Even simple e-mail messages have grown in size and complexity. An average, simple e-mail message size is now about 1.5KB, and, with the new message technologies that allow the integration of inbound/outbound faxing, an e-mail message with a six-page fax attached has an average size of 550KB. Further, the firm integrated the voice mail system with the e-mail system so that inbound voice mail is automatically routed to the user's mailbox. The average 30-second voice mail message is about 150KB.

The firm also implemented an imaging system that scans and stores many documents that previously would have taken up physical file space. Included in this imaging system are litigation support documents, accounting information, and older client documentation. A single-page TIF file can vary in size (depending on the complexity of the image) from 40 to 125KB.

Additional software applications that are used by the users include a client/server document management system, a client/server accounting system, and several other networked programs that they only dreamed about eight years before. Most of the firm's attorneys make heavy use of the Internet, often visiting sites that provide streaming audio and video.

Today, their average switched segment size is less than 36 nodes per segment, and the segments are switched to a 100Mbps backbone. Even with these small segment sizes, they are finding congestion on many segments. While they would like to begin running 100Base-TX Ethernet to the desktop, they are finding that their Category 3 cabling does not support 100Base-TX networking.

Continued on next page

When this firm installs their new cabling system to support their next generation network applications, you can be sure that they will want to choose their cabling infrastructure and network application carefully to ensure that their needs for the next 10 to 15 years will be accommodated.

Does the fact that software applications and data are putting more and more of a demand on the network have anything to do with data cabling? You might think that it's more of an issue related to network interface cards, hubs, switches, and routers, but the fact is that as data rates increase, the need for higher levels of performance on the cable also increases.

Cable Design

Whether you are a network engineer, cable installer, or network manager, a good understanding of the design and components of data cabling is important. Do you know what types of cable can be run above the ceiling? What do all those markings on the cable mean? Can you safely untwist a twisted-pair cable? What is the difference between shielded and unshielded twisted-pair cable? What is the difference between single-mode and multimode fiber optic cable?

All of these are important questions to which you need to know the answer—not only when designing or installing a cabling system, but also when working with an existing cabling system.

The U.S. National Electrical Code (NEC) Article 800 defines five levels of cable for use with LAN cabling and telecommunications:

- Plenum use
- Riser
- General purpose
- Residential use
- Under-carpet cable

Cables are rated based on their flammability, heat resistance, and how much visible smoke (in the case of plenum cable) they generate when exposed to a flame. A plenum cable is certified for use in both the *riser* (a connecting path between two floors of a building) as well as the *plenum* (air duct spaces usually above a false ceiling). Plenum cable can be substituted for any of the other levels of cabling. You should consult the manufacturer or examine the cable markings to make sure of the grade of cable you are using.

Cable Jackets

The best place to start looking at cable design is to look at what is on the outside. Each type of cable (twisted-pair, fiber optic, or coaxial) will have different designs with respect to the cable covering or the jacket.

KEY TERMS   **Jacket and Sheath**   The cable's *jacket* is the plastic outer covering of the cable; this holds true for both UTP and STP cables. The *sheath* includes not only the jacket of the cable, but also any outside shielding (such as braided copper or foil) that may be surrounding the inner wire pairs. With UTP cables, the sheath and the jacket refer to the same thing. With ScTP and STP cables, the sheath includes the outer layer of shielding.

One of the most common materials used in the cable jacket is *polyvinyl chloride (PVC)*; UTP cables in the United States are almost exclusively jacketed with PVC, regardless of the flame rating of the cable. PVC was commonly used in early LAN cables as an insulator and as material for jackets, but the dielectric properties of PVC are not as desirable as other substances (such as FEP) that can be used for higher frequency. Figure 1.1 shows a cutaway drawing of a UTP (unshielded twisted pair) cable.

Other substances that are commonly used in cable jackets include ethylene-chlorotrifluoroethylene (ECTFE or HALAR). ECTFE, however, does not have the required dielectric properties for insulation.

KEY TERM   **Slitting Cord**   Inside some UTP cable jackets is a nylon or polyester string that is called the *slitting cord or slitting string*. The purpose of this cord is to assist with slicing the jacket back for removal. Some cable installers love them; others find them a nuisance.

FIGURE 1.1:

Cutaway drawing of a
UTP cable showing
insulated wire pairs,
slitting cord, and jacket

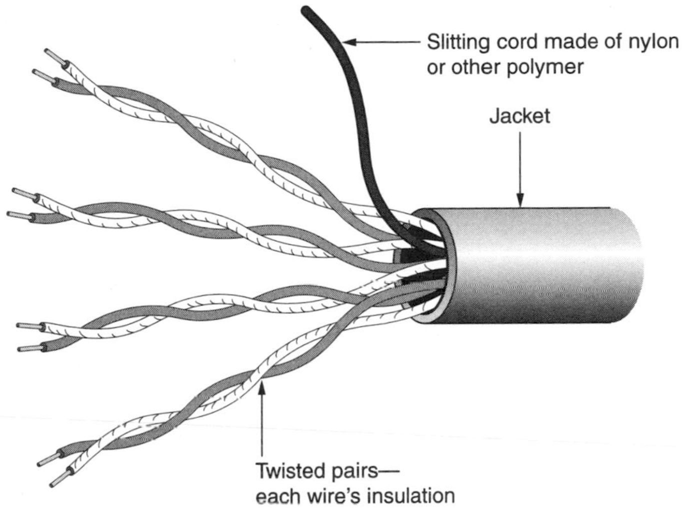

Slitting cord made of nylon
or other polymer

Jacket

Twisted pairs—
each wire's insulation
is color coded.

Plenum

Depending on whom you ask, you will get two entirely different definitions of plenum. According to building engineers, construction contractors, and air conditioning people, the *plenum* (shown in Figure 1.2) is the space between the false ceiling (a.k.a. drop-down ceiling) and the structural ceiling. This space is used for air circulation, heating ventilation, and air conditioning (HVAC). Occasionally, building engineers, contractors, and air conditioning people will also refer to the space between a false floor (such as a raised computer room floor) and the structural floor referred to as the plenum. The plenum and the HVAC equipment in the plenum are often used to ventilate many parts of the building.

Cable design engineers refer to plenum as a type of cable that is rated for use in the plenum spaces (below the floor or above the false ceiling) of a building. Those of us who have to work with building engineers, cabling professionals, and contractors must be aware of both definitions of plenum.

FIGURE 1.2:

The plenum space
and a riser

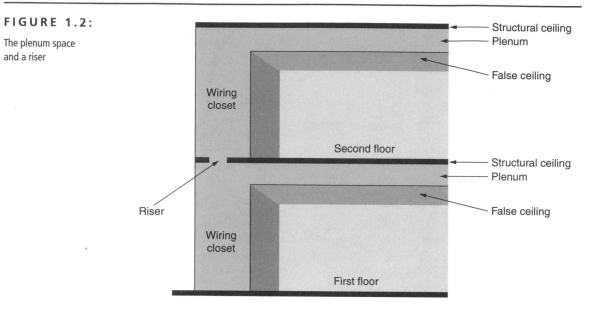

In most environments, we use the plenum space to hold data and voice cable. Ordinary cable often produces toxic fumes in the event of a fire, but plenum cable is made of materials that are more resistant to flames and produce less smoke when burning. Naturally, cable not certified to be used in the plenum is called *nonplenum cable*. Often, local city codes or building management will require that plenum cable be used in plenum spaces.

Regardless of whether plenum cable is required or not, it is a good idea to use it to lessen the likelihood of dangers associated with a fire. Cable manufacturers usually sell both plenum and nonplenum cable.

Riser

The *riser* is a vertical shaft used to route cable between two floors. Often, this is nothing more complicated than a hole (core) that's drilled in the floor and allows cables to pass through. However, a hole between two floors (or with cable in it) introduces a new problem. Remember the fire disaster movie *The Towering Inferno*? In it, the fire spread from floor to floor through the building cabling. This should not happen nowadays, because building codes require that cable be rated properly if they're going to pass through the riser. This means that the riser cable must have certain fire-resistant qualities.

NOTE   The National Electrical Code permits plenum cable to be used in the riser, but it
does not allow riser cable to be used in the plenum.

Building codes usually also require that the riser be fireproofed in some way. This usually entails placing fireproof material in the riser after the cables have been put in place. Inserting fireproof material into riser spaces is called firestopping. Techniques for firestopping are discussed in Chapter 12, "Cabling System Design and Installation."

Cable Markings

Have you picked up a twisted pair or fiber optic cable and examined the outside jacket? If you have, you will notice a lot of markings on the cable that may or may not make any sense to you. Unfortunately, there is no standard for cable markings, so identifying them is hit or miss. For cables manufactured for use in the United States and Canada, these markings identify a number of different things, including:

- Cable manufacturer and manufacturer part number

- Category of cable (e.g., UTP)

- NEC/UL flame tests and ratings

- CSA flame tests

- "Length remaining markers" so you can see how many feet of cable remains on a spool or in a box (included by some cable manufacturers such as Superior Essex [www.superioressex.com])

For a list of definitions of these markings, see the section "Common Abbreviations."

Since there is no standard for cable markings, not all cables will have the same markings. Here is an example of one cable's markings:

```
000750 FT 4/24 (UL) c(UL) CMP/MPP VERIFIED (UL) CAT 5 SUPERIOR
ESSEX COBRA 2319 H
```

These markings identify the following information about this cable:

- 000750 FT means that there is 750 feet remaining on the spool.

- 4/24 identifies the cable as having four pairs of 24 AWG wire.

- (UL) indicates that the cable is UL listed.

- c(UL) indicates that the cable is UL listed to Canadian requirements in addition to U.S. requirements.

- CMP/MPP means cable multipurpose plenum (CMP) and multipurpose plenum (MPP) and indicates that the cable can be used in plenum spaces. This is the NEC flame/smoke rating.

- VERIFIED CAT 5 means that the cable has been verified by the UL as being Category 5–compliant (and TIA/EIA-568-A–compliant).

- SUPERIOR ESSEX is the manufacturer of the cable.

- COBRA is the cable brand (in this case, a Category 5e–plus cable, which means it exceeds the requirements for Category 5).

- 2319 is the date of manufacturer in Julian format. In this case, it is the 231st day of 1999.

- H indicates the SUPERIOR ESSEX manufacturing plant.

Some manufacturers may also include their "E-file" number. This number can be used when calling the listing agency (such as the UL) to trace the manufacturer of a cable, regardless of what is printed on the cable jacket.

NOTE   Note that cables marked with CMR (communications riser) and CMG (communications general) must *not* be used in the plenum spaces.

Common Abbreviations   So that you can better decipher the markings on cables, here is a list of common markings and what they mean:

NFPA   The National Fire Protection Association

NEC   The National Electrical Code that is published by the NFPA once every three years

UL   The Underwriters Laboratories

CSA   The Canadian Standards Association

PCC   The Premises Communications Cord standards for physical wire tests defined by the CSA

Often, you will see cables marked with UL-910, FT-4, or FT-6. The UL-910 is a UL flame test, and the FT-4 and FT-6 are CSA flame tests. These tests do *not* cover the type or volume of toxic combustion products (smoke and fumes); they only cover performance on a flame-spread test.

NEC Fire Ratings   The NFPA's NEC publishes a series of cable ratings that cover flame testing for low-voltage, metallic communications cables. These are published in NEC Articles 725 and 800. Article 800 deals with data communications cables, which are considered to be higher-grade ratings. Table 1.1 lists Article 800's codes, the meaning of the code, and which cables can be substituted for a particular cable. In general, any higher-grade cable can be substituted for any lower-grade cable.

NOTE   More details on the National Electrical Code are given in Chapter 4, "Cable System and Infrastructure Constraints."

TABLE 1.1:   NEC Article 800 Communication Cable Codes and Their Meanings

Code	Meaning	Allowable Substitution
MPP	Multipurpose plenum cable	No substitutions
MPR	Multipurpose riser cable	MPP
MP	Multipurpose general purpose cable	MPP, MPR
MPG	Multipurpose general purpose cable	MPP, MPR
CMP	Communications cable plenum	MPP
CMR	Communications cable riser	MPP, CMP, MPR
CM	Communications general purpose cable	MPP, CMR, MPG, MP
CMG	Communications general purpose cable	MPP, CMR, MPG, MP
CMX	Communications cable limited use	CMG, CM, MPP, CMR, MPG, MP
CMUC	Communications under-carpet wire and cable	No substitutions

NEC Article 725 describes low voltage and signaling cable such as those used with telephone systems. Table 1.2 lists Article 725's codes and their meanings.

TABLE 1.2:   NEC Article 725 Remote Signaling and Power Limited Circuit Cable Codes

Code	Meaning	Allowable substitutions
CL3P	Class 3 plenum	MPP, CMP, FPLP
CL3R	Class 3 riser	CL3P, MPR, CMR, FPLR
CL3	Class 3	CL3P, CL3R, MP, MPG, CM, FPL, PLTC
CL3X	Class 3 limited use	CL3P, CL3R, CL3, MP, MPG, CM, CMG, FPL, PLTC, CMX
CL2P	Class 2 plenum	CL3P
CL2R	Class 2 riser	CL3P, CL2P, CL3R
CL2	Class 2	CL3P, CL3R, CL2P, CL2R, CL3, CM, CMG, MP, MPG
CL2X	Class 2 limited use	CL2, CL3P, CL3R, CL2P, CL2R, CL3, CL3X, CMX, CM, CMG, MP, MPG

NEC Article 770 covers fiber optic cables. Table 1.3 shows the common codes used with fiber optic cables.

TABLE 1.3:   NEC Article 770 Fiber Optic Cable Codes

Marking	Description	Allowable Substitutions
OFNP	Nonconductive optical fiber plenum cable	No substitutions
OFCP	Conductive optical fiber plenum cable	OFNP
OFNR	Nonconductive optical fiber riser cable	OFNP
OFCR	Conductive optical fiber riser cable	OFNP
OFNG	Nonconductive optical fiber general purpose cable	OFNP
OFCG	Conductive optical fiber general purpose cable	OFNP
OFN	Nonconductive optical fiber general purpose cable	OFNP, OFNR, OFCG
OFC	Conductive optical fiber general purpose cable	OFNP, OFNR, OFCG

NOTE There is no standard for the jacket color. Manufacturers can make the jacket any color they care to. There are at least a dozen different colors in which Category 5 cable can be ordered, including hot pink. Colors like hot pink and bright yellow don't function any differently than plain gray cables, but they sure are easier to spot when you are up in the ceiling! Many cable installers will pick a different color cable based on the jack position or patch panel the cable is going to so that they are easier to identify quickly.

Wire Insulation

Inside the cable jacket are the wire pairs. The material used to insulate these wires must have excellent dielectric properties, which means that it must not conduct electricity. Refer back to Figure 1.1 for a diagram of the wire insulation.

KEY TERM **Dielectric** A material that has good *dielectric* properties is a poor conductor of electricity. Dielectric materials are used as insulation.

There is a variety of insulating materials including polyolefin (polyethylene and polypropylene), fluorocarbon polymers, and even PVC. The manufacturer chooses the materials based on the material cost, flame test ratings, and desired transmission properties. Materials such as polyolefin are cheap and have great transmission properties, but they burn like crazy, so they must be used in combination with material that has better flame ratings.

The most common materials used to insulate the wire pairs in Category 5 and greater cables are fluorocarbon polymers. Pre-Category 5 cable will most likely use other insulation materials. There are a couple of different varieties of fluorocarbon polymers:

- Fluorinated ethylene-propylene (FEP)
- Polytetrafluoroethylene (PTFE or TFE)

These polymers were developed by DuPont and are also sometimes called by their trademark, Teflon. The most commonly used and most desirable of these materials is FEP. Over the past few years, the popularity of plenum-grade cables has often exceeded the supply of available FEP. Unfortunately, this means that plenum-grade cable is often sold at a premium, so many manufacturers use less desirable materials in some of their cables.

The practice of using a different insulation material for one or even two of the wire pairs is not uncommon. Often, polyethylene (PE) is substituted for insulation on one of the pairs of wire.

TIP

> When purchasing cables, inquire as to whether or not other insulation material has been used for wire insulation. Cables that use FEP exclusively are considered safer in the event of a fire.

Insulation Colors

The insulation around each wire in a UTP cable is color-coded. These are standardized color codes that help the cable installer to make sure each wire is connected correctly with the connecting hardware. Each pair of wires is assigned a specific color; one wire in the pair is colored solid using that color, and the other wire is white with a strip of the assigned color. Sometimes, neither wire will be completely solid; instead, one wire will have a small stripe of white and the other wire will be mostly white with a small stripe of the associated color. These are often a little more difficult to quickly identify.

Table 1.4 lists the color codes for a four-pair UTP cable. The stripe (or secondary) color for four-pair cable is always white. Pair 1, for example, is read (if you are reading them out loud) White-blue/Blue.

TIP

> The solid color is also sometimes called the *ring* or *primary* color, and the stripe color is sometimes called the *tip* or *secondary* color. For more information on insulation colors, see Chapter 7, "Copper Cable Media."

TABLE 1.4:   Color Codes for Four-Pair UTP Cable

Pair Number	Solid Color (Primary)	Stripe Color (Secondary)
1	Blue	White
2	Orange	White
3	Green	White
4	Brown	White

Table 1.5 lists the color codes found in a binder group (a group of 25 pairs of wires) in larger capacity cables. The 25-pair cable is not often used in data cabling, but it is frequently used for voice cabling for backbone and cross-connect cable. Every pair in a 25-pair is identified by a combination of five primary (solid or tip) and five secondary (stripe or ring) colors.

TABLE 1.5: Color Codes for 25-Pair UTP Binder Groups

Pair Number	Solid Color	Stripe Color
1	Blue	White
2	Orange	White
3	Green	White
4	Brown	White
5	Slate	White
6	Blue	Red
7	Orange	Red
8	Green	Red
9	Brown	Red
10	Slate	Red
11	Blue	Black
12	Orange	Black
13	Green	Black
14	Brown	Black
15	Slate	Black
16	Blue	Yellow
17	Orange	Yellow
18	Green	Yellow
19	Brown	Yellow

Continued on next page

TABLE 1.5 CONTINUED: Color Codes for 25-Pair UTP Binder Groups

Pair Number	Solid Color	Stripe Color
20	Slate	Yellow
21	Blue	Violet
22	Orange	Violet
23	Green	Violet
24	Brown	Violet
25	Slate	Violet

Waiter! There's Halogen in My Cable!

Much of the cable that is currently in use in the United States and elsewhere in the world contains halogens. A *halogen* is a nonmetallic element, such as fluorine, chlorine, iodine, or bromine. When exposed to flames, substances made with halogens give off toxic fumes when they burn that quickly harm the eyes, nose, lungs, and throat. Further, these fumes and their associated smoke can make evacuating a building more difficult.

Did you notice that some of the halogen elements (fluorine and chlorine) are elements commonly found in cable insulation and jackets? Even when cables such as PVC cables are designed to be flame-resistant, any cable, when exposed to high enough temperatures, will melt and burn. PVC cables contain chlorine, which emits toxic fumes when burned. If these cables are exposed to water when they begin to burn (such as from a sprinkler system), corrosive acids that may further endanger people in the building or existing equipment will form.

Many different manufacturers are now making low-smoke, zero-halogen (LSZH or LS0H) cables. These cables are designed to emit no toxic fumes and produce little or no smoke when exposed to flames. Tunnels, enclosed rooms, aircraft, and other minimum-ventilation areas are prime spots for the use of LSZH cables. This is because halogen cables will release less smoke and hazardous fumes in areas that are more difficult to escape from quickly.

Continued on next page

Some safety advocates are calling for the use of LSZH cables in the plenum space as well. Review your local building codes to determine if you can use LSZH cable. Many governments around the world have already standardized zero-halogen cables. However, the United States is lagging behind on this effort. This is principally due to arguments that plenum cable already generates a low enough smoke environment to safely evacuate a building.

The other advantage of LSZH cable is that it does not emit corrosive acids when burned and thus will not harm equipment. Many opponents of LSZH cable reason that if an area of the building is on fire, the equipment is going to be damaged by flames before it is damaged by corrosives from a burning cable.

We don't expect that LSOH cables will take over anytime soon, but there is a movement to define a "smoke-limited" type cable in the next version of the NEC (Article 800).

Twists

When you slice open many types of copper-based communications cables, you will notice that the individual pairs of wire are twisted around one another. On first thought, you may not realize just how important these twists are.

TIP   Did you know that even a wire pair that is untwisted more than half of an inch can adversely affect the performance of the entire cable?

Twisted-pair cable is any cable that contains a pair of wires that are wrapped or twisted around one another between 2 and 12 times per foot—and sometimes even greater than 12 times per foot (as with Category 5 and higher). The twists help to cancel out the electromagnetic interference (EMI) generated by high speed data communication over the wire. This interference can cause problems for adjacent wire pairs, which is called *crosstalk*. Crosstalk and the effects of crosstalk are discussed in the section "Hindrances to High Speed Data Transfer" later in this chapter.

Cables commonly used for patch cables and for horizontal cabling (patch panel to wall plate) typically contain four pairs of wire. The order in which the wires are crimped or punched down can be very important.

TIP   Companies such as Panduit (www.panduit.com) have developed termination tools and patch cables that all but eliminate the need to untwist cables more than a tiny amount.

Twisted-pair cable comes in two primary flavors: unshielded twisted pair and shielded twisted pair. These are described in the section "Twisted Pair," later in this chapter and in further detail in Chapter 7.

Wire Gauge

Copper wire diameter is most often measured using a unit called AWG (American Wire Gauge). Contrary to what your intuition may tell you, as the AWG number gets smaller, the wire diameter actually gets larger; thus, AWG 24 wire is smaller than AWG 22 wire. Larger wires are useful because they have more physical strength and lower resistance. However, the larger the wire diameter, the more copper is required to make the cable. This makes the cable heavier, harder to install, and more expensive.

The cable designer's challenge is to use the lowest possible diameter wire (reducing costs and installation complexity) while at the same time maximizing the wire's capabilities to support the necessary power levels and frequencies.

Category 5 UTP is always 24 AWG; IBM Type 1A is typically 22 AWG. Table 1.6 shows common AWG sizes along with the corresponding diameter, area, and weight per kilometer.

TABLE 1.6:   American Wire Gauge Diameter, Area, and Weight Values

AWG	Nominal Diameter Inches	Mm	Circular Mil. Area	Area sq. mm	Weight Kg/Km
10	.1019	2.60	10380	5.262	46.78
11	.0907	2.30	8234	4.172	37.09
12	.0808	2.05	6530	3.309	29.42
13	.0720	1.83	5178	2.624	23.33
14	.0641	1.63	4107	2.081	18.50

Continued on next page

TABLE 1.6 CONTINUED: American Wire Gauge Diameter, Area, and Weight Values

AWG	Nominal Diameter Inches	Mm	Circular Mil. Area	Area sq. mm	Weight Kg/Km
15	.0571	1.45	3260	1.650	14.67
16	.0508	1.29	2583	1.309	11.64
17	.0453	1.15	2050	1.307	9.219
18	.0403	1.02	1620	0.8226	7.313
19	.0359	0.912	1200	0.6529	5.807
20	.0320	0.812	1020	0.5174	4.600
21	.0285	0.724	812.1	0.4105	3.649
22	.0253	0.643	640.4	0.3256	2.895
23	.0226	0.574	511.5	0.2581	2.295
24	.0201	0.511	404.0	0.2047	1.820
25	.0179	0.455	320.4	0.1623	1.443
26	.0159	0.404	253.0	0.1288	1.145
27	.0142	0.361	201.5	0.1021	0.9077
28	.0126	0.320	159.8	0.08097	0.7198
29	.0113	0.287	126.7	0.06425	0.5712
30	.0100	0.254	100.5	0.05097	0.4531
32	.0080	0.203	63.2	0.03203	0.2847
34	.0063	0.160	39.8	0.02014	0.1790
36	.0050	0.127	25.0	0.01267	0.1176
38	.0040	0.102	15.7	0.007968	0.07084

The dimensions in Table 1.6 were developed over 100 years ago. Since that time, the purity and, therefore, the resistance of copper has improved due to better copper processing techniques. Copper used in today's cables is more conductive and has less resistance than in cable manufactured in the past. The standards have a waiver on the actual dimensions of a wire. The real concern is not the dimensions of the wire, but how it performs. The AWG standard indicates that a 24 AWG wire will have a diameter of .0201 inches, but based on the performance of the material, the actual diameter of the wire may be slightly less or slightly more (but usually less).

Solid Conductors versus Stranded Conductors

Category 5 cable that is used as horizontal cable (permanent cable or cable in the walls) has a solid conductor, as opposed to patch cable and cable that is run over short distances, which usually has a stranded conductor. Stranded-conductor wire consists of many smaller wires interwoven together to form a single conductor.

TIP   Connector types (such as patch panels and modular jacks) for solid-conductor cable are different than they are for stranded-conductor cable. Stranded-conductor cables will *not* work with IDC-style connectors found on patch panels and 66-style punchdown blocks.

Though stranded-conductor wire is more flexible, solid-conductor cable has much better electrical properties than stranded-conductor because stranded-conductor wire is subject to as much as an additional 20 percent attenuation (loss of signal).

KEY TERM   **Core**   The *core* of the cable is anything found inside the sheath. This is usually just the insulated twisted pairs, but it may also include a slitting cord and the shielding over individual twisted pairs in an STP cable. People incorrectly refer to the *core* of the cable when they mean the *conductor*.

This phenomenon is called *skin effect*. At higher frequencies (the frequencies used in LAN cables), the signal current concentrates on the outer portion of the wire. Since stranded-conductor wire has a less-defined outer surface (due to the multiple strands involved), attenuation is increased. Higher attenuation numbers are less desirable.

Most cabling standards recommend using solid-conductor wire in the horizontal or permanent portion of the link, but the standards allow for the use of stranded-conductor wire in patch cables where flexibility is more important. We know of several Category 5 installations that have used stranded-conductor wires for their horizontal links. While we consider this a poor practice, here are some important points to keep in mind if you choose to use a mixture of these cables:

- Stranded-conductor wire requires different connectors.
- Stranded-conductor wires don't work as well in punch-down blocks designed for solid conductor cables.
- You must account for reduced horizontal link distances.

Cable Length

The longer the cable, the less likely the signal will be carried completely to the end of the cable. Cable design engineers are now measuring two additional performance parameters of cable, the propagation delay and the delay skew. Both of these parameters are related to the speed at which the electrons can pass through the cable and the length of the wire pairs in cable. These are discussed in the section "You Can't Go That Fast: Cable Limitations" later in this chapter.

Cable Length versus Wire Length   A Category 5 cable has four pairs of wire. By design, each of the four pairs of wires is twisted in such a fashion so that the wire pairs are slightly different lengths. Therefore, signals that were transmitted simultaneously on two different pairs of wire will arrive at slightly different times. The *wire length* is the length of the individual pair of wires, whereas the *cable length* is the total length of the actual cable containing all the wire pairs.

Part of a modern cable tester's feature set is the ability to perform wire length tests. Here is a list of the wire lengths of a cable whose cable length is 137 feet from the wall plate to the patch panel. As you can see, the actual wire length is longer due to the twists in the wire.

Pair	Distance
1-2	145 ft
3-6	143 ft
4-5	141 ft
7-8	142 ft

Warp Factor One, Please

Light travels almost 300,000,000 meters per second in a perfect vacuum. This is faster than those of us who are not physicists can imagine. If traveling at the speed of light were possible, it would take a mere 8.5 seconds to reach the sun from Earth. In a fiber optic cable that is one kilometer long, data can travel from start to finish in about 3.3 microseconds (0.0000033 seconds).

Data does not travel through copper cabling quite as fast. One of the ways that the speed of data through a copper cable is measured is in relation to how fast an electron can travel through the cable. This value is called the Nominal Velocity of Propagation (NVP) and is expressed as a percentage of the speed of light. The value for most cables is between 60 and 90 percent. The cable manufacturer specifies this value as part of the cable's design.

Take, for example, a cable that Jim recently measured using a hand-held cable tester. The NVP for this cable was 67 percent and the cable was 90 meters long. An electron will travel through this cable at a speed of about 200,000,000 meters per second. An electron can travel from one end of this cable to another in 450 nanoseconds (0.00000045 seconds).

Types of Communications Media

There are four major types of communications media (cabling) available for data networking today: unshielded twisted pair, shielded twisted pair, coaxial, and fiber optic cable. An additional variety of twisted-pair cable called screened twisted pair has recently appeared on the scene; this is a hybrid of shielded and unshielded twisted pair.

Twisted-Pair Cable

By far the most economical cabling installed today is twisted-pair wiring. Not only is the cost of twisted-pair wiring cheaper than other media, installation is simpler and the tools required to install it are not as costly. Unshielded twisted pair (UTP) and shielded twisted pair (STP) are the two primary varieties of twisted pair on the market today, but screened twisted pair (ScTP) is emerging and will become more common in the future.

Unshielded Twisted Pair (UTP)   Though it has been used for many years in telephone systems, unshielded twisted pair (UTP) for LANs first became common in the late 1980s with the advent of Ethernet over twisted-pair wiring and the 10Base-T standard. UTP is cost effective and simple to install.

> **NOTE**   An interesting historical note: Alexander Graham Bell invented and patented twisted-pair cabling and an optical telephone in the 1880s. During that time, Bell offered to sell his company to Western Union for $100,000, but they refused to buy.

UTP cabling typically has only an outer covering (jacket) consisting of some type of nonconducting material. This jacket covers one or more pairs of wire that are twisted together. In this chapter, as well as throughout much of the rest of the book unless specified otherwise, assume that UTP cable is a four-pair cable. Four-pair cable is the most commonly used cable in network installations today. The characteristic impedance of UTP cable is 100 ohms plus or minus 15 percent, though 120-ohm UTP cable is sometimes used in Europe and is allowed by the ISO/IEC 11801 cabling standard.

A typical UTP cable is shown in Figure 1.3. This simple cable consists of a jacket that surrounds four twisted pairs. Each 24 AWG wire is covered by an insulation material that has good dielectric properties.

FIGURE 1.3:

UTP cable

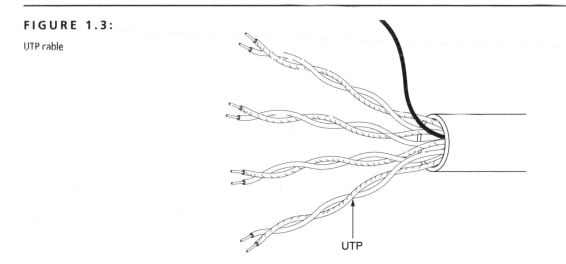

UTP

UTP cabling seems to generate the lowest expectations of these cabling types, but it is also the most commonly used. This is mostly due to the cost and ease of installation of UTP. With every new generation of UTP cable that is rolled out, network engineers think they have reached the limits of the UTP cable's bandwidth and capabilities. However, cable manufacturers continue to extend the capabilities of simple UTP cabling. During the development of 10Base-T and a number of proprietary UTP Ethernet systems that were released prior to 10Base-T, critics said that UTP would never support data speeds of 10Mbps. Later, the skeptics said that UTP would never support data rates at 100Mbps. In July 1999, the IEEE approved the 1000Base-T standard, which allows Gigabit Ethernet to run over Category 5 cable!

Not All UTP Is Created Equal!

Though two cables may look identical, their supported data rates can be dramatically different. Older UTP cables that were installed to support telephone systems may not even support 10Base-T Ethernet. To help consumers choose the right cable (and components) for the right application, the Telecommunications Industries Association and the Electronic Industries Association (TIA/EIA) developed a standard called the Commercial Building Telecommunications Cabling Standard, or TIA/EIA-568-A. This is the most recent version of the standard; a new version of it is expected to be released in mid-2000.

This standard has been updated over the years and currently defines five categories of UTP cable. These are as follows:

Category 1 This type of cable usually supports frequencies of less than 100KHz. Common applications include analog voice telephone systems.

Category 2 This cable type supports frequencies of up to 4MHz. It's not commonly installed except in installations that use twisted-pair ArcNet and Apple LocalTalk networks.

Category 3 This type of cable supports data rates up to 20MHz. This was the most common variety of UTP for a number of years starting in the late 1980s. Common applications include 4Mbps UTP Token Ring, 10Base-T Ethernet, 100Base-T4, and digital and analog telephone systems.

Category 4 This cable was designed to support frequencies of up to 16MHz. It has never been widely popular and was infrequently used since it was only marginally less expensive than Category 5 cable. Common applications include 16Mbps UTP Token Ring.

Continued on next page

Category 5   Currently, the most common cable installed. It is designed to support frequencies of up to 100MHz. Applications include 100Base-TX TP-PMD (FDDI over copper), 155Mbps ATM over UTP, and (thanks to sophisticated encoding techniques), it supports 1000Base-T Ethernet. To support 1000Base-T applications, the installed cabling system must pass performance tests specified by TSB-95.

Category 5e (Enhanced Category 5)   Category 5e was introduced with the arrival of the TIA/EIA-568-A.5 version of the cabling standards. Performance specifications for Category 5e cabling have been tightened up, but it is still designed to support only frequencies up to 100MHz. Applications are the same as those for Category 5 cabling.

There are other TIA/EIA categories in development that will support even higher frequencies than 100MHz; among these are Category 6 and Category 7 cabling.

The cabling standards are discussed in more detail in Chapter 2. Additional information on copper media can be found in Chapters 7 and 9.

Shielded Twisted Pair (STP)   Shielded twisted-pair (STP) cabling was first made popular by IBM when they introduced their Type classification for data cabling. Though more expensive to purchase and install than UTP, STP offers some distinct advantages. The current TIA/EIA-568-A cabling standard permits IBM Type 1A horizontal cable, which supports frequency rates of up to 300MHz. STP cable is also much less susceptible to outside electromagnetic interference (EMI) due to the fact that all cable pairs are well shielded.

Some STP cabling uses a woven copper-braided jacket, such as IBM Types 1 and 1A cable. This jacket provides considerably more protection than the UTP jacket. Inside the woven copper jacket, STP consists of twisted pairs of wire (usually two pairs) wrapped in a foil shield. Some STP cables have only a foil shield around the wire pairs. The bottom line of STP is the fact that individual wire pairs are shielded. Figure 1.4 shows a typical STP cable. The wire used in STP cable is 22 AWG (just a little larger than the 24 AWG wire used by UTP LAN cables) and has an impedance of 150 ohms, plus or minus 10 percent.

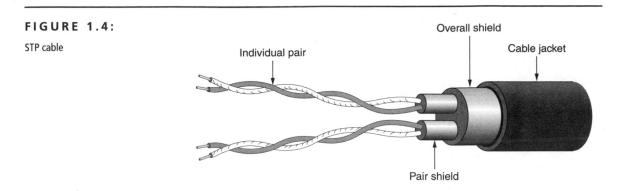

Simply installing STP cabling does not guarantee that you will improve a cable's immunity to EMI or reduce the emissions from the cable. There are several critical conditions that must be met to achieve good shield performance:

- The shield must be continuous along the whole link.

- All components must be shielded. No UTP patch cords can be used.

- The shield must fully enclose the cabling along the whole link. No exposed surface of conductors without shielding can be used.

- The shield must be grounded at both ends of the link, and the building grounding system must conform to grounding standards (such as TIA/EIA-607).

If one of these conditions is not satisfied, shield performance will be badly degraded. For example, tests have shown that if the shield continuity is broken, the emissions from a shielded cabling system increase as much as 20dB on the average.

Screened Twisted Pair (ScTP)   One of the interesting developments over the past few years is screened twisted-pair (ScTP) cabling, a hybrid of STP and UTP cable. ScTP cable contains four pairs of 24 AWG, 100-ohm wire (see Figure 1.5) surrounded by a foil shield or wrapper and a drain wire for bonding purposes. ScTP is also sometimes called foil twisted-pair (FTP) cable because the foil shield surrounds all four conductors. This foil shield is not as large as the woven copper-braided jacket used by some STP cabling systems such as IBM Types 1 and 1A. ScTP cable is essentially STP cabling that does not shield the individual pairs; the shield may also be smaller than some varieties of STP cabling.

The foil shield is the reason ScTP is less susceptible to noise. In order to implement a completely effective ScTP system, however, the shield continuity must be maintained throughout the entire channel. This includes patch panels, wall plates, and patch cords. Yes, you read this correctly; the continuity of not only the wires, but also the shield must be maintained through connections. Like STP cabling, the entire system must be bonded to ground at each end of each cable run, or you will have created a massive antenna.

FIGURE 1.5:

ScTP cable

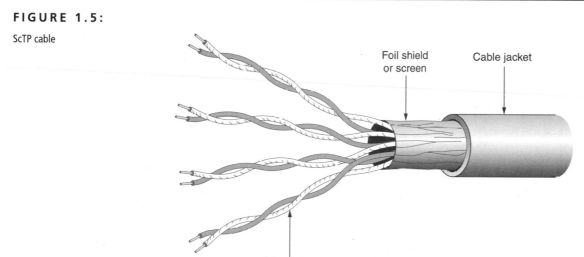

Standard eight-position modular jacks (commonly called RJ-45s) do not have the ability to do this. This means that special mating hardware, jacks, patch panels, and even tools must be used to install and use an ScTP cabling system. There are many manufacturers of ScTP cable and components—just make sure to follow all installation guidelines.

ScTP is recommended for use in environments that have abnormally high ambient electromagnetic interference, such as hospitals, airports, or government/military communications centers. Initially, there was disagreement among customers and vendors as to the value of an ScTP system since some tests indicate that UTP noise immunity and emissions characteristics are comparable with ScTP cabling systems. Often, the decision to use ScTP simply boils down to whether you want the warm and fuzzy feeling of knowing that there is that extra shield in place.

Though the TIA is currently working on a standard that will incorporate the use of ScTP, there is no current standard. This means that a number of vendors have introduced their own ScTP products. These products are proprietary and often don't interact with other vendor's components. If you choose to use an ScTP solution prior to the standards being developed for it, you should use all cable and components from a single vendor.

Should You Choose Unshielded, Shielded, Screened, or Optical Fiber Cable?

This is one of the questions that many network managers and cabling infrastructure systems designers face. Often the decision is very cut and dried, but sometimes it is not.

For typical office environments, UTP cable will be always be the best choice. Most offices don't experience anywhere near the amount of electromagnetic interference necessary to justify the additional expense of installing shielded twisted-pair cabling.

Environments such as hospitals and airports may benefit from a shielded or screened cabling system. The deciding factor seems to be the external field strength. If the external field strength does not exceed three volts per meter (V/m), good quality UTP cabling should work without any problems. If the field strength exceeds three V/m, shielded cable will be a better choice.

However, many cabling designers feel that if the field strength exceeds three V/m, fiber optic cable is a better choice. Further, these designers will argue for the additional bandwidth and security of fiber optic cable.

While everyone has an opinion on the type of cable that we should be installing, it is true that the only cable type that won't be outgrown quickly is optical fiber.

Optical Fiber Cable

As late as 1993, it seemed that in order to move toward the future of desktop computing, businesses would have to install fiber optic cabling directly to the desktop. Copper cable (UTP) performance continues to be surprising, however. Fiber optic cable is discussed in more detail in Chapter 10, "Fiber Optic Media."

NOTE
Fiber versus fibre: are these the same things? Yes, just as the words color (U.S. spelling) and colour (British spelling) are the same thing. Fiber and fibre are the same thing, but your spell checker will probably ask you about fibre.

Although for most of us, fiber to the desktop is not yet a practical reality, fiber optic cable is touted as the ultimate answer to all our voice, video, and data transmission needs and continues to make inroads in the LAN market. Some distinct advantages of fiber optic cable include:

- Transmission distances can be much greater than copper cable.

- Potential bandwidth is dramatically higher than copper.

- Fiber optic is not susceptible to outside EMI or crosstalk interference, nor does it generate EMI or crosstalk.

- Fiber optic cable is much more secure than copper cable because electrical monitoring equipment cannot be used to eavesdrop on the data being transmitted through a fiber optic cable.

NOTE
Fiber optic cable can easily handle data at speeds above 1Gbps; in fact, it has been demonstrated as handling data rates exceeding 200Gbps!

Since the late 1980s, LAN solutions have used fiber optic cable in some capacity. Recently, a number of ingenious solutions that allow both voice and data to use the same fiber optic cables have been put on the market.

Fiber Optics Comes of Age (and Affordability)

Fiber optic cable used to be much harder to install than copper cable. In addition, the cost of the cable alone is usually somewhat more expensive than that of copper, and precise installation practices must be followed at all times.

However, in the past few years, the cost of an installed fiber optic link has dropped and is often only 10 to 15 percent more than the cost of a UTP link. Better fiber optic connectors and installation techniques have contributed to make fiber optic systems even easier to

Continued on next page

install. Installers experienced with both fiber optic systems and copper systems will tell you that when using the newest fiber optic connectors and installation techniques, fiber optic cable is easier to install than UTP.

The main hindrance to using fiber optics all the way to the desktop in lieu of UTP or STP is that the electronics (workstation network interface cards and hubs) are still significantly more expensive.

Fiber optic cable uses a strand of glass or plastic to transmit data signals through using light; the data is carried in light pulses. Unlike the transmission techniques used by its copper cousins, optical fibers are not electrical in nature. Plastic core cable is easier to install and cheaper than glass core, but plastic cannot carry data as far as glass.

NOTE   Light is transmitted through a fiber optic cable using light emitting diodes (LEDs) or lasers. With newer LAN equipment designed to operate over longer distances such as 1000Base-LX, lasers are commonly being used.

A fiber optic cable (shown in Figure 1.6) consists of a jacket (sheath), protective material, and the optical fiber portion of the cable. The optical fiber portion of the cable consists of a core (typically 62.5 microns in diameter, but it can also be 8.3 or 50 microns) that is smaller than a human hair, which is surrounded by a cladding. The cladding (typically 125 micrometers in diameter) is surrounded by a coating, buffering material, and, finally, a jacket. The cladding provides a lower refractive index in order to cause reflection within the core so that light waves are transmitted through the fiber.

There are two varieties of fiber optic cable that are commonly used in LANs and WANs today: single-mode and multimode. The mode can be thought of as bundles of light rays entering the fiber; these light rays enter at certain angles.

KEY TERM   **Dark Fiber**   No, this is not a special new type of fiber cable. When telecommunications companies and private businesses run fiber optic cable, they never run the exact number of pairs of fiber that they need. That would be foolish. Instead, they run two or three times the amount of fiber that they currently require. The spare pairs of fiber are often called *dark fiber* because they are not currently in use. Telecommunications companies often lease out these extra pairs to other companies.

Single-pair fiber optic cable

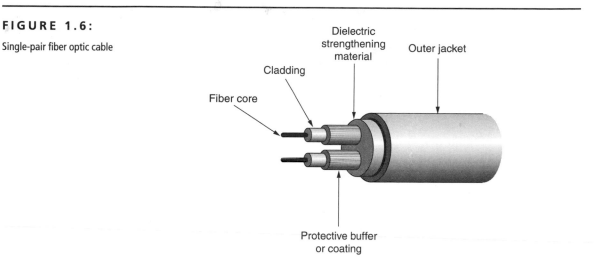

Single-Mode Fiber Optic Cable   *Single-mode fiber* (SMF) (sometimes called monomode) optic cable is most commonly used by telephone companies and in data installations as backbone cable. Single-mode fiber optic cable is *not* used as horizontal cable to connect computers to hubs. The light in a single-mode cable travels straight down the fiber (as shown in Figure 1.7) and does not bounce off the surrounding cladding as it travels. Typical single-mode wavelengths are 1310 and 1550 nanometers.

Prior to using single-mode fiber optic cable, make sure that the equipment you are using supports it. The equipment that uses single-mode fiber typically uses lasers to transmit light through the cable.

Single-mode fiber optic
cable

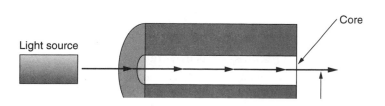

Multimode Fiber Optic Cable   *Multimode fiber* (MMF) optic cable is usually the fiber optic cable that is used with networking applications such as 10Base-FL, 100Base-F, FDDI, ATM, and other applications that require optical fiber cable for use as horizontal cable and backbone cable. Multimode cable allows more than one mode of light to propagate through the cable. Typical wavelengths of light used in multimode cable are 850 and 1300 nanometers.

There are two types of multimode fiber optic cable: step index or graded index. Step index multimode fiber optic cable indicates that the refractive index between the core and the cladding is very distinctive. The graded index fiber optic cable is the most common type of multimode fiber, but the core contains many layers of glass; each has a lower index of refraction as you go outward from the core of the fiber. Both types of multimode fiber permit multiple modes of light to travel through the fiber simultaneously (see Figure 1.8).

FIGURE 1.8:

Multimode fiber optic cable
(graded index multimode)

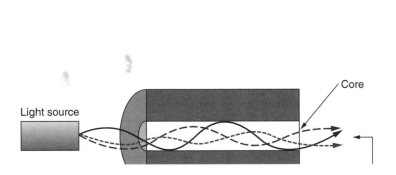

The typical multimode fiber optic cable consists of two strands of fiber (duplex); the core is 62.5 microns (micrometers) in diameter, and the cladding is 125 microns in diameter (this is often simply referred to as 62.5/125-micron). The newest version of the TIA/EIA-568 standard also recognizes the use of 50/125-micron multimode fiber optic cable.

Coaxial Cable

At one time, *coaxial cable* was the most widely used cable type in the networking business. However, it is falling by the wayside in the data networking arena, except for those of us that are lucky enough to have cable modem Internet service. Coaxial (or just coax) cable is difficult to run and is generally more expensive than twisted-pair cable. In defense of coaxial cable, however, it provides a tremendous amount of bandwidth and is not as susceptible to outside interference. At least for the foreseeable future, cable TV (CATV) will continue to be delivered over coax. Although we commonly use it to connect our televisions to our VCRs, we will probably soon see fiber optic or twisted-pair interfaces to televisions and VCRs.

Coaxial cable comes in many different flavors, but the basic design is the same for all types. Figure 1.9 shows a typical coaxial cable; at the center is a solid (or sometimes stranded) copper core. The core is surrounded by some type of insulation material, such as TFE or PVC. The insulation is shielded by either a sleeve or braided wire mesh and the whole thing is covered by a jacket.

FIGURE 1.9:

Typical coaxial cable

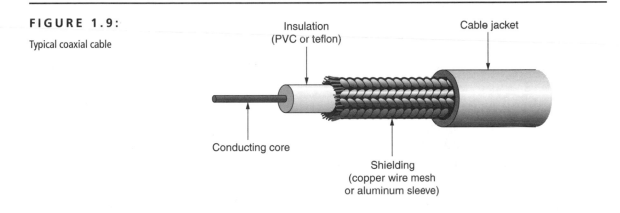

The shielding shown in Figure 1.9 protects the data being transmitted through the core from outside electrical noise and keeps the data being transmitted through the cable from generating significant amounts of interference. Coaxial cable works well in environments where high amounts of interference are common. For example, a few years ago, Jim installed coaxial cable in a power plant because in some areas the Category 3 cable was not reliable.

There are a number of varieties of coaxial cable available on the market. You pick the coaxial cable that is required for the application; unfortunately, coaxial cable installed for Ethernet cannot be used for an application such an ArcNet. Some common types of coaxial cable are listed in Table 1.7.

TABLE 1.7:   Common Coaxial Cable Types

Cable	Description
RG-58 /U	50-ohm coaxial cable with a solid core. Commonly called *thinnet* and used with 10Base-2 Ethernet and some cable TV applications.
RG-58 A/U	50-ohm coaxial cable with a stranded core. Also known as *thinnet*. Used by 10Base-2 Ethernet and some cable TV applications.
RG-58 C/U	Military specification version of RG-58 A/U
RG-59U	75-ohm coaxial cable. Used with Wang systems and some cable TV applications.
RG-62U	93-ohm coaxial cable. Used with IBM cabling systems and ArcNet.

Data Communications 101

To fully understand some of the limitations involved when working with data communications and network cabling, some basic terms must be understood. Unfortunately, vendors, engineers, and network managers serve up high tech and communications terms as if they were balls in a tennis match. Worse, they often misuse these terms or don't even fully understand what they mean.

One common term is *bandwidth*; does it mean maximum frequency or maximum data rate? Other terms are thrown around as if you had a Ph.D. in Electrical Engineering, including *impedance*, *resistance*, and *capacitance*.

Our favorite is the use of *decibels*. We always thought they were used to measure sound, but that's not necessarily true when it comes to data communications. For the next few pages, we will take you through a crash course in Data Communications 101 and get you up to speed on these and other terms and how they can affect cabling.

Frequency versus Data Rate

One of the things about cabling that is initially confusing is the fact that cables are often rated in hertz rather than bits per second. Network engineers are more concerned with how much data can be pushed through the cable than with the frequency at which that data is traveling.

Frequency (bandwidth) is the number of cycles that are completed per unit of time and is generally expressed in *hertz* (cycles per second). Figure 1.10 shows a cycle that took one second to complete; this is hertz. Data cabling is typically rated in kilohertz (KHz) or megahertz (MHz). In Figure 1.10, for a cable rated at 100MHz, the cycle would have to complete 100,000,000 times in a single second! The more cycles per second, the more interference the cable generates (crosstalk) and the more susceptible to data loss (attenuation) the cable is.

FIGURE 1.10:

1 cycle every second or 1 hertz

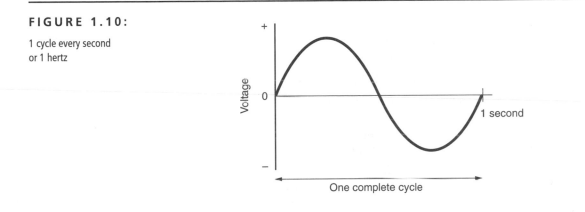

The *data rate* (or information capacity) is defined as the number of bits per second that move through a transmission medium.

With traditional cabling, there is a fundamental relationship between the number of cycles per second (frequency or bandwidth) that a cable can support and the amount of data that can be pushed through the cable (information capacity or data rate.) For example, Category 5 (and Category 5e) cables are rated at 100Mhz. To implement a 100Base-TX network, you must be using Category 5 cabling since the cable must support a frequency of 100MHz. During each digital cycle, a single bit is pushed through the cable.

This would seem to be a good way to think of the relationship between information rate and cable bandwidth. However, the IEEE recently approved the 803.3ab standard (1000Base-T); this standard covers running Gigabit Ethernet over Category 5 cabling! Does this mean that a Category 5 cable can operate at frequencies up to 1GHz?

No, up to this point, cable manufacturers have only been able to design UTP cables that support frequencies of up to 350Mhz; shielded twisted-pair cabling and fiber optic cabling can support higher bandwidths. So how do they manage to deliver data at 1Gbps across a Category 5 cable whose maximum bandwidth is 100MHz? The next section gives you the answer.

The Secret Ingredient: Encoding

10Base-T and 100Base-TX networks use only two of the four pairs of wire in the Category 5 cable. One solution to the question of how to achieve higher data rates would be to use the additional pairs and multiple data pairs, split the data up, and transmit it on the multiple pairs simultaneously. But even if all four pairs were used for transmission, this would still give only a fraction of the necessary data rate necessary to achieve 1Gbps.

Consider the example in Figure 1.11 of a street that permits one car to pass a certain stretch of road each second. Let's say that our desired capacity for this particular part of the street is three cars per second. To increase the capacity of this thoroughfare, we could increase the number of lanes handling traffic to three lanes. But to achieve 1Gbps data rates on Category 5 rated cabling, the cable would have to have 20 pairs of wire (10 transmit pairs and 10 receive pairs) instead of the current four pairs. This is not a practical solution.

FIGURE 1.11:

Street that allows one car
to pass each second

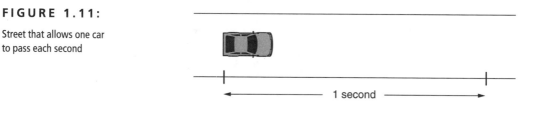

Only a single car can pass through each second.

Instead of increasing the number of lanes available, sophisticated encoding (multiplexing) techniques are used to send more bits of data over the wire during each cycle. In Figure 1.12, the rules for our street has changed. Cars are spaced together or encoded so that multiple cars can move through the street each second (during each cycle). Further, the street shown in Figure 1.12 is bidirectional; this means that cars travel one way for an instant and then travel back the other way the next instant. No single wire pair (or lane, in the analogy) is dedicated to just being a transmit or receive pair.

**NOTE**   Even with sophisticated encoding techniques, for Gigabit Ethernet to work over Category 5 cabling, all four pairs must be used.

FIGURE 1.12:

Street that allows multiple cars through during each cycle

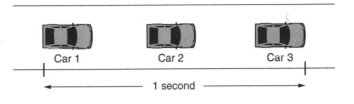

Allows three cars to pass through each second. That's encoding!

Opposition to Data Flow (Loss of Signal Energy)

In copper wiring, a signal loses energy during its travel because of electrical properties at work in the cable. The opposition to the flow of current through a cable or circuit is expressed as *impedance*. Impedance is a combination of resistance, capacitance, and inductance and is expressed in ohms; a typical UTP cable is rated at between 100 and 120 ohms. All Category 3, 4, 5, and 5e cables used in the United States are rated at 100 ohms.

Impedance values are useful when testing the cable for problems, shorts, and mismatches. There are three possible impedance readings that a cable tester could show to indicate a possible problem:

- An impedance value that is not between 100 and 120 ohms indicates that a mismatch in the type of cables or components has occurred. This might mean that an incorrect connector type has been installed or an incorrect cable type has been cross-connected into the circuit.

- An impedance value of zero indicates that the cable is open or that it has been cut somewhere.

- An impedance value of infinity indicates that the cable has been short-circuited.

Two important factors in the impedance of a cable are resistance and capacitance. *Resistance* acts as a hindrance to the signal and thus restricts the flow of electrons through the cable and causes some of the signal energy to be absorbed by the cable. This energy is dissipated as heat, but the amount of heat generated by LAN cabling is negligible due to the low current and voltage levels. The longer the cable, the more resistance it offers. Materials such as copper, gold, and silver offer low resistance and are used as conductors. Materials that have very high resistance are known as dielectrics and are used as insulation for conductors.

Capacitance is the electrical property that occurs when a cable has more than one wire and the wires are placed close together. Electrons on the wires will interfere with one another, which will in turn create an electrostatic charge. This charge will cause the cable to resist changes in the circuit's voltage.

What a Difference a dB Makes!

Let's say that we are comparing cable performance. A manufacturer says that the attenuation (power loss) for a cable with a length of 90 meters (operating at 100MHz) is 20dB. What does this mean? Would you be surprised to learn that the signal strength has dropped by a factor of 100? That's right, if you apply an input power level of five watts, the output level will be .05 watts! For every 3dB of attenuation, it's a 50 percent loss of power!

To give you a quick summary, low decibel values of attenuation are desirable since that means that less of the signal is lost on its way to the receiver. Higher values of crosstalk (NEXT, ELFEXT, etc.) and return loss are desirable because that means that less signal has been measured on adjacent wires.

This may be all you ever wanted to know about decibels (dB). If you want to know more, read further through this section to get the technical details.

Digging a Little Deeper into Decibels

You may think of a decibel (dB) in terms of audible noise. When referring to the domain of sound, a decibel is not actually a specific unit of measurement but rather is used to express a ratio of sound pressure.

However, the decibel is also commonly used when defining attenuation, crosstalk, and return loss. Just as with sound, when referring to communications and electrical transmission performance, the decibel is a ratio rather than a specific measurement. The decibel value is independent of the actual input and output voltage or power and is thus considered a generic performance specification.

Understanding what the decibel numbers are telling you is important when comparing one cabling media or performance measurement with another.

Decibels 101   The *bel* part of decibel was named after Alexander Graham Bell, the inventor of the telephone. A *decibel* is a tenfold logarithmic ratio of power (or voltage) output to power (or voltage) input. Keep in mind that the decibel is indicating a power ratio, not a specific measurement. The decibel is a convenient way to reflect the power loss or gain, regardless of the actual values.

NOTE   For measurements such as attenuation, NEXT, ELFEXT, ACR, and return loss, the decibel value is always negative since it represents a loss, but often the negative sign is taken out when the measurement is written. The fact that the number represents a loss is assumed to be understood.

Cable testers as well as performance specifications state, for example, attenuation in decibels. Let's say, for example, that you measure two cables of identical length and determine that the attenuation is 15dB for one cable and 21dB for the other. Naturally, you know that since lower attenuation is better, the cable with an attenuation of 15dB is better than the 21dB value because it will lose less signal over the cable's length. But how much better? Would you be surprised to learn that even though the difference between the two cables is only 6dB, there is 50 percent more attenuation of voltage or amperage (power is calculated differently) on the cable whose attenuation was measured at 21dB?

To fully appreciate the performance specifications that a decibel represents, you have to understand how the numbers are calculated.

Decibels and Power   When referring to power (watts), decibels are calculated in this fashion:

$$dB = 10 * \log_{10} (P1/P2)$$

P1 indicates the measured power, and P2 is the reference power (or input power).

To expand on this formula, let's look at an example. Our reference power level (P2) is 1.0 watt. The measured power level (P1) on the opposite side of the cable is .5 watts. This means that through this cable, 50 percent of the signal was lost due to attenuation. Now, plug these values into the power formula for decibels. This yields a value of –3dB. What does this mean?

Every 3dB of attenuation translates into 50 percent of the signal power being lost through the cable. Lower attenuation values are desirable since this means that a higher power level is arriving at the destination.

Every 3dB of return loss translates into 50 percent of the signal power being reflected back to the source. Higher decibel values for return loss are desirable since this indicates that *less* power is being returned to the sender.

Every 3dB of NEXT translates into 50 percent of the signal power being allowed to couple to adjacent pairs. Higher decibel values for NEXT (and other crosstalk values) are desirable since higher values indicate that less power is coupling with adjacent pairs.

An increase of 10dB means a tenfold increase in the actual measured parameter. Table 1.8 shows the logarithmic progression of decibels with respect to power measurements.

TABLE 1.8: Logarithmic Progression of Decibels

Decibel Value	Actual Increase in Measured Parameter
3dB	2
10dB	10
20dB	100
30dB	1,000
40dB	10,000
50dB	100,000
60dB	1,000,000

Decibels and Voltage   Most performance specifications and cable testers typically reference voltage ratios, not power ratios. When referring to voltage (or amperage), decibels are calculated slightly differentlt than for power. The formula is

$$dB = 20 * \log_{10} (P1/P2)$$

P1 indicates the measured voltage or amperage, and P2 is the reference (or output) voltage (amperage). This makes the decibel numbers slightly different when discussing voltage. Substituting a reference value of 1.0 volt for P2 and .5 volts for P1 (the measured output), we get a value of –6dB. What does this mean?

- Every 6dB of attenuation translates into 50 percent of the voltage being lost to attenuation. Lower decibel attenuation values are desirable since this means that a higher voltage level is arriving at the destination.

- Every 6dB of return loss translates into 50 percent of the voltage being reflected back to the source. Higher decibel values for return loss are desirable since this indicates that *less* voltage is being returned to the sender.

- Every 6dB of NEXT translates into 50 percent of the voltage coupling to adjacent wire pairs. Higher decibel values for NEXT (and other crosstalk values) are desirable since higher values indicate that less power is coupling with adjacent pairs.

Table 1.9 represents various decibel levels and the corresponding voltage and power ratios. Notice in Table 1.9 that (for the power ratio) if a cable's attenuation is measured at 10dB, only one-tenth of the signal transmitted will be received on the other side.

TABLE 1.9: Decibel Levels and Corresponding Power and Voltage Ratios

dB	Voltage Ratio	Power Ratio
1	1	1
-1	.891	.794
-2	.794	.631
-3	.707	.500
-4	.631	.398
-5	.562	.316
-6	.500	.250
-7	.447	.224
-8	.398	.158

Continued on next page

TABLE 1.9 CONTINUED: Decibel Levels and Corresponding Power and Voltage Ratios

dB	Voltage Ratio	Power Ratio
-9	.355	.125
-10	.316	.100
-12	.250	.063
-15	.178	.031
-20	.100	.010
-25	.056	.003
-30	.032	.001
-40	.010	.000
-50	.003	.000

Applying a Knowledge of Decibels

Now that you have a background on decibels, let's take a look at the specified channel performance for Category 5 versus the proposed channel performance for Category 6 cable at 100Mhz.

Media Type	Attenuation	NEXT	Return Loss
Category 5	24	27.1	8.0
Category 6	20.9	39.9	12.0

For the above values to be meaningful, you need to look at them with respect to the actual percentage of loss. For this example, we use voltage. If you take each decibel value and solve for the P1/P2 ratio using this formula, you would arrive at the following values:

```
Ratio = 1 / (Inverse log10(dB/20))
```

Media	Remaining Signal Due to Attenuation	Allowed to Couple (NEXT)	Signal Returned (NEXT)
Category 5	6.3%	4.4%	39.8%
Category 6	9.0%	1%	25.1%

Existing cable standards allow a transmission to lose 99 percent of its signal but still be received properly. In the Category 5 cable example, only 6.3 percent of the voltage is received at the destination. For an Ethernet application operating at 2.5 volts of output voltage, the measured voltage at the receiver would be about .16 volts for Category 5 cable and .23 volts for Category 6 cable.

Using the techniques above for reversing the decibel calculation, you can better compare the performance of any media.

You Can't Go That Fast: Cable Limitations

The amount of data that even simple unshielded twisted-pair cabling can transfer has come a long way over the past dozen or so years. In the late 1980s, many experts felt that UTP cabling would never support data rates greater than 10Mbps. Today, data rates of 1.2Gbps and higher are supported over cable lengths approaching 100 meters! And UTP may be able to support even greater data rates in the future.

Let's look back at the MIS Director that mistakenly assumed that "it is just wire." He might be right—what is the big deal? Shouldn't data cabling be able to support even higher data rates?

Have you tried to purchase data grade cable recently? Have you ever tested a cable run with an even mildly sophisticated cable tester? A typical cabling catalog can have over 2,000 different types of cables! You may have come away from the experience wondering if you needed a degree in electrical engineering in order to understand all the terms and acronyms. The world of modern cabling has become a mind-boggling array of communications buzzwords and engineering terms.

Who knew that data cabling had become so sophisticated?! As the requirements for faster data rates emerges, the complexity of the cable design increases. As the data rates increase, the magic that happens inside a cable becomes more and more mysterious, and the likelihood that data signals will become corrupt while traveling at those speeds also increases.

Ah! So it is not that simple after all! As data rates increase, electrical properties of the cable change, signals become more distorted, and the distances that a signal can travel decrease. Designers of both 1000Base-T (Gigabit Ethernet) and the cables that can support frequencies greater than 100Mhz have found electrical characteristics that they did not have to contend with at lower frequencies and data rates. These additional electrical characteristics manifest themselves as different types of crosstalk and arrival delay of electrons on different pairs of wires.

Hindrances to High Speed Data Transfer

Electricity flowing through a cable is nothing more than electrons moving through the cable. In order for a signal to be received properly by the receiver, enough electrons must make it all the way through the cable from the sender to the receiver. As the frequency employed on a cable (and consequently the potential data rate) increases, a number of phenomena occur that hinder the electron's travel through the cable (and, consequently, the transfer of data.)

These phenomena are important to not only the person who has to specify what cable to purchase, but also the person who tests and certifies the cable to be good. As the networking technologies get more and more complex, additional phenomena are added to mix.

The current specifications for Category 5 cabling outline a number of these phenomena and the maximum (or minimum) acceptable values that a cable can meet and still be certified as Category 5 compliant.

External Interference

One hindrance to transmitting data at high speed is the possibility that the signals (electrons) traveling through the cable will be acted upon by some outside force. Though the designer of any cable, whether it's twisted pair or coaxial, attempts to compensate for this, external forces are beyond the cable designer's control. All electrical devices, including cables with data flowing through them, generate electromagnetic interference (EMI). Low power devices and cables supporting low bandwidth applications do not generate enough of an electromagnetic field to make a difference. Some equipment generates radio-frequency interference; you may notice this if you live near a TV or radio antenna and you own a cordless phone.

Set Your Cell Phones to Stun

At the beginning of each Microsoft technical class that Jim teaches, he asks his students to set their cell phones and pages on stun (silent ring or vibrate mode). Even so, in almost every class, at least one student complains that their computer monitor is sometimes unreadable or "jumping around." The cause: their cell phone was placed under the monitor and is ringing. Anytime the phone is ringing, it interferes with a nearby electrical device.

Devices and cables that use lots of electricity can generate EMI that can interfere with data transmission. Consequently, cables should be placed in areas where they will avoid these devices. Some common sources of EMI in a typical office environment include:

- Motors
- Heating and air conditioning equipment
- Fluorescent lights
- Laser printers
- Elevators
- Electrical wiring — *Placing Electrical & data on the same pole*
- Televisions
- Some medical equipment

NOTE   Talk about electromagnetic interference! An MRI (magnetic resonance imaging) machine, which is used to look inside the body without surgery or x-rays, can erase a credit card from 10 feet away.

When running cabling in a building, avoid running the cable within a few feet of these devices. Never install data cabling in the same conduit as electrical wiring.

In some cases, even certain types of businesses and environments have high levels of interference, including airports, hospitals, military installations, and power plants. If you are installing cabling in one of these types of environments, consider using cables that are properly shielded, or use fiber optic cable.

Attenuation

As electrons travel through a cable, some of the electrons don't make it all the way to the end of the cable; this results in a loss of signal. This loss of signal is known as *attenuation*. The longer the cable, the more signal loss there will be. In fact, past a certain point, the data will no longer be transmitted properly because the signal loss will be too great. Attenuation is measured in decibels (dB); the lower the attenuation value, the more of the original signal is received (in other words, the lower the better). Figure 1.13 illustrates the problem that attenuation causes in LAN cabling.

FIGURE 1.13:

The signal deteriorates as it travels between a node on a LAN and the hub.

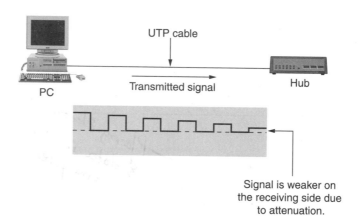

UTP cable

Transmitted signal

PC

Hub

Signal is weaker on the receiving side due to attenuation.

Attenuation on a cable will increase as the frequency used increases. The same exact cable will have a dramatically higher attenuation value at 100MHz than it did at 1Mhz. A 100-meter cable may have a measured attenuation of less than 2dB at 1MHz, but measure an attenuation greater than 20dB at 100MHz!

Higher temperatures increase the effect of attenuation. For each higher degree Celsius, attenuation is typically increased 1.5 percent for Category 3 cables and 0.4 percent for Category 5 cables. Attenuation values can also be increased by 2 to 3 percent if the cable is installed in metal conduit.

Signal strength is the strongest at the transmitter and, due to attenuation, weakest at the receiver. When the signal arrives at the receiver, it must still be recognizable to the receiver. Attenuation values for cables are very important.

Attenuation values are different for different categories of cables and the frequencies employed. In general, the better designed (i.e., more expensive) the cable is, the less attenuation it will experience. Table 1.10 lists maximum attenuation values for various UTP cable types. Note that many of these values were updated by the TIA/EIA in 2000. As of April 2000, only Categories 5 and 5e will be considered a standard; Categories 6 and 7 are proposed standards. (Category 5e was included as part of the TIA/EIA-568-A.5 standard that was released in Fall 1999.)

TABLE 1.10: Maximum Attenuation Values at Various Frequencies

Cable Type	Frequency (MHz)	Maximum Attenuation (dB)
Category 5	100	21.6
Category 5e	100	21.6
Category 6	100	21.7
Category 6	250	36.0
Category 7	100	20.8
Category 7	250	54.1

Cabling and Standards

Maximum acceptable values of attenuation, minimum acceptable values of crosstalk, and even cabling design issues—who is responsible for making sure that there are standards published? Though this varies from country to country, in the United States, the predominant standards organization supervising data cabling standards is the TIA/EIA (Telecommunications Industries Association/Electronic Industries Association). The standard that covers Category 5 cabling, for example, is TIA/EIA-568-A, which is part of the guideline for building structured cabling systems. These standards are not rigid like an Internet RFC but are refined as needed via through addendum. The TIA/EIA-568-A document dictates the performance specifications for cables and connecting hardware. Chapter 2 discusses common cabling standards in more detail.

Crosstalk

As electrons travel through a cable, some of them may leave the wire they are moving along and land on an adjacent wire. The higher the frequency, the greater the likelihood that some electrons will "jump the fence" to an adjacent wire (see Figure 1.14). This is known as *crosstalk*. Electrons may also leave the wire completely and cause electromagnetic interference for other devices. There are two types of crosstalk: near-end crosstalk and far-end crosstalk. Crosstalk is measured in decibels; the higher the crosstalk value, the better the connection.

FIGURE 1.14:

Crosstalk

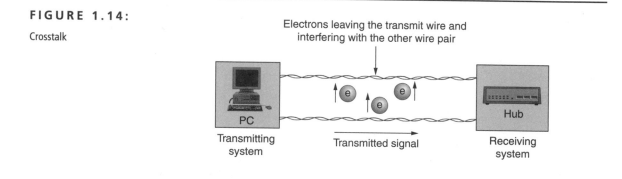

Electrons leaving the transmit wire and interfering with the other wire pair

PC
Transmitting system

Transmitted signal

Hub
Receiving system

Wait a Minute! Higher Crosstalk Values Are Better?

When crosstalk values are measured, the value is considered a loss. Often, the negative sign is left out because of this. When looking for desirable crosstalk values, remember that larger numbers are better. Does this make sense to you? It sure confused us the first time we heard it.

To make sense of it, think about what crosstalk is measuring. Crosstalk is measured on adjacent pairs of wire with respect to the signal traveling through the reference pair. It is measuring the amount of signal that is allowed to "leak" over to adjacent wires. The higher the crosstalk value, the less signal has leaked to an adjacent pair. Thus, higher crosstalk values are better.

Table 1.11 shows the minimum crosstalk values for a couple of different types of crosstalk and crosstalk performance measurements; this includes ELFEXT pair-to-pair (pp), ELFEXT power sum (ps), and NEXT power sum (ps), which are discussed later in this chapter. Crosstalk values for Category 5, 5e, and 6 are shown for the basic link (end-to-end), whereas the Category 7 numbers are for the channel (permanent equipment). Currently, Categories 6 and 7 are still standards in development.

TABLE 1.11: Minimum Acceptable Crosstalk Values for Various Cable Types at Various Frequencies

Cable Type	Frequency	NEXT pp	NEXT ps	ELFEXT pp	ELFEXT ps
Category 5	100	29.3	N/A	17.0	14.4
Category 5e	100	32.3	29.3	20.0	17.0
Category 6*	100	41.9	39.3	25.2	22.2
Category 6*	250	35.4	32.7	17.2	14.2
Category 7*	100	39.9	37.1	N/A	N/A
Category 7*	600	51.0	48.0	N/A	N/A

*Proposed performance requirements as of mid-2000

KEY TERMS   **Channel Link and Basic Link**   The *channel link* is defined as the entire cable from host to network equipment, including patch cables, patch panel equipment, and cross-connects (if permitted). This is in contrast to the *basic link*, which defines only the permanent portion of the cabling system, excluding patch cords and cross-connects. Patch cords and cross-connects are not included in the basic link.

Near-End Crosstalk (NEXT)   As electrons leap from the wire they are on due to crosstalk and land on adjacent wires, the electrons may return back in the direction of the sender. If the crosstalk occurs far enough from the sender, the signal may have attenuated enough so that it is not noticeable once it returns to the sender. This is called *near-end crosstalk* (NEXT) because the signal returns to the near end. NEXT is measured on wires adjacent to the wire on which the signal is being transmitted and can interfere with signals being transmitted from the remote side of the link on adjacent wires. NEXT is most common within 20 to 30 meters (60 to 90 feet) of the transmitter. Figure 1.15 illustrates near-end crosstalk.

FIGURE 1.15:

Near-end crosstalk (NEXT)

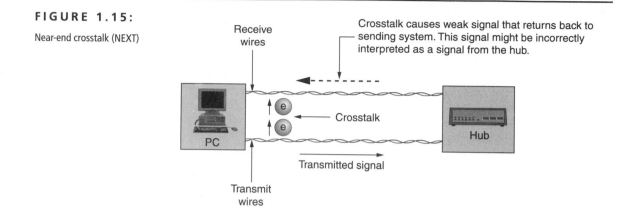

Crosstalk on poorly designed or poorly installed cables is a major issue with technologies such as 10Base-T and 100Base-TX. However, as long as the cable is installed correctly, NEXT is less of an issue when using 1000Base-T because the designers implemented technologies to help with NEXT cancellation. NEXT cancellation techniques with 1000Base-T are necessary since all four pairs are employed for both transmitting and receiving data.

> **NOTE**
>
> Cables that have had their twists undone (untwisted) can be problematic because the twists are what help cancel crosstalk. Twists are normally untwisted at the ends near the patch panels or connectors when the cable is connected. On the receiving pair of wires in a cable, the signal that is being received at the end of the cable will be the weakest. If the wires on adjacent transmit pairs are untwisted, this will cause a greater amount of crosstalk than normal and can interfere with the received signal. A cable should never have the wire pairs untwisted more than half an inch.

Far End Crosstalk (FEXT)   Some of the electrons that leap from the wire may land on an adjacent wire and continue to travel toward the receiver (the far end). *Far-end crosstalk* (FEXT) is similar to NEXT except that it is measured at the opposite end of the wire from where the signal was sent. Due to attenuation, the signals on the far end of the transmitting wire pair are much weaker than the signals on the near end.

FEXT is rarely measured, but it is used to derive equal level far-end crosstalk (ELFEXT) (discussed later in this chapter). More FEXT will be seen on a shorter cable than a longer one since the signal at the receiving side has had less distance over which to attenuate.

Attenuation to Crosstalk Ratio (ACR)

Attenuation to crosstalk ratio (ACR) is an indication of how much larger the received signal is when compared to the NEXT (crosstalk or noise) on the same pair. As a signal travels down a wire away from the transmitter, it is attenuated and is at its weakest when it arrives at the receiver. FEXT affects the far end of the wire and thus will affect the signal most adversely when it is at its weakest point. NEXT is most noticeable at the near end of the wire, closest to the transmitter.

ACR is also sometimes referred to as the *signal-to-noise ratio* (SNR). The "gap" between the cable's attenuation and NEXT is also considered to be the cable's useable bandwidth. Technically, SNR also incorporates not only "noise" that has been generated by the data transmission itself, but also outside interference. These two values are usually almost identical except in environments with high levels of EMI.

KEY TERM   **Headroom**   Since ACR represents the minimum gap between attenuation and crosstalk, the *headroom* represents the difference between the minimum ACR and the actual ACR performance values.

The differential between the crosstalk (noise) and the attenuation (loss of signal) is important because it assures that the signal being sent down a wire is stronger at the receiving end than any interference that may be imposed by crosstalk.

Figure 1.16 shows the relationship between attenuation and NEXT as the frequency approaches 100MHz. Notice that as the frequency increases, the NEXT values get lower and lower while the attenuation values get higher and higher. The margin or gap between the attenuation and NEXT lines is the ACR. The values used in Figure 1.16 are the attenuation and NEXT values for the channel link found in the TSB-67 bulletin for testing Category 5 cable. The values used to create Figure 1.16 are taken from TSB-67 and are shown in Table 1.12. Notice that for the channel link, the minimum ACR value at 100MHz is just over 3dB.

FIGURE 1.16:

Attenuation to crosstalk ratio for a Category 5 channel link

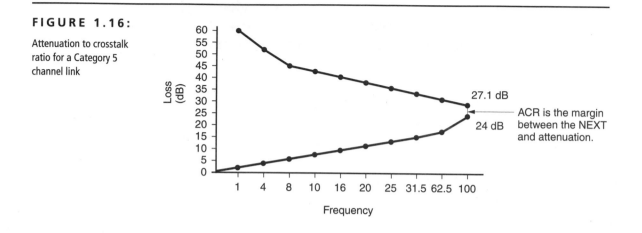

TABLE 1.12: Attenuation and NEXT Values for a Category 5 Channel Link from TSB-67

Frequency (MHz)	Attenuation	NEXT
1	2.5	60
4	4.5	50.6
8	6.3	45.6
10	7	44
16	9.2	40.6
20	10.3	39
25	11.4	37.4
31.25	12.8	35.7
62.5	18.5	30.6
100	24	27.1

ACR is especially important to "two-pair" network applications, such as 10Base-T and 100Base-TX. Even though 10Base-T and 100Base-TX operate over Category 5 cabling, both only use two pairs of wire to carry the signal. One pair of wire is used to carry the signal in each direction. The expected or desired signal at the receiving end of the cable has to account for attenuation, so the desired signal is the transmitted signal less the amount of signal lost due to attenuation.

The undesired signal (noise) is the total amount of noise as a result of crosstalk (NEXT) and the external interference from sources such as electromagnetic interference. Solving problems relating to ACR usually means troubleshooting NEXT because, short of replacing the cable, the only way to improve attenuation is to use shorter cables.

UTP Cabling and Newer LAN Technologies

Due to the complex modulation technology used by 1000Base-T Ethernet, the TIA has recently specified additional cabling performance specifications. The original testing specification (TSB-67) did not include these performance characteristics, which include power sum and pair-to-pair crosstalk measurements, delay skew, return loss, and ELFEXT. Some of these newer performance characteristics are important from the perspective of crosstalk. While crosstalk is important in all technologies, faster technologies such as 1000Base-T use all four pairs in parallel for transmission; thus, 1000Base-T is more sensitive to crosstalk.

The TIA/EIA has released an updated specification called TSB-95 that specifies additional testing and performance parameters required to certify a cable to support higher speed installations such as 1000Base-T.

Return Loss

Some of the electrons that are sent on their way through a cable may hit an impedance mismatch or imperfection in the wire and be reflected back to the sender. This is known as *return loss*. If the electrons travel a great distance through the wire before being bounced back to the sender, the return loss may not be noticeable because the returning signal may have dissipated (due to attenuation) by the time it returns to the sender. If the signal echo from the bounced signal is strong enough, it can interfere with ultra-high speed technologies such as 1000Base-T. Table 1.13 shows the current maximum acceptable values for return loss.

TABLE 1.13:   Return Loss Values

Cable Type	Frequency (MHz)	Return Loss (dB)
Category 5	100	8
Category 5e	100	10
Category 6	100	12
Category 6	250	8
Category 7	100	14.1
Category 7	600	8.7

Equal Level Far-End Crosstalk (ELFEXT)

Equal level far-end crosstalk (ELFEXT) is the unwanted crosstalk coupling between cabling pairs measured at the end of the cable that is opposite to the end of the signal source. ELFEXT is calculated, not measured. It is calculated by subtracting the attenuation of the pair causing the crosstalk from the far-end crosstalk (FEXT); this pair induces in an adjacent pair. This measures the ratio of disturbance to the level of the desired signal; this is another indication of signal-to-noise ratio.

Each pair-to-pair combination is measured since the attenuation on each pair will be slightly different. The value represents the ratio between the strength of the noise due to crosstalk from end signals compared to the strength of the received data signal. Another way to think of ELFEXT is to think of it as far-end ACR.

If the ELFTEXT value is very high, it may indicate excessive attenuation or that the far-end crosstalk is higher than expected.

Pair-to-Pair and Power Sum Crosstalk

When implementing networking technologies that use more than one pair of wires at a time, additional crosstalk factors come into play. Though these are not part of the original Category 5 testing specification, they have become important recently due to the availability of cables that exceed Category 5 specifications and applications that use more than a single pair simultaneously.

Pair-to-Pair Crosstalk   The first of these technologies is *pair-to-pair crosstalk* measurements. When implementing applications such as 1000Base-TX, more than one wire pair in a single cable will be used simultaneously; thus, crosstalk that each pair induces on each other pair must be within specified limits. Figure 1.17 shows a cutaway drawing of a simple four-pair cable. Pair-to-pair crosstalk measurements must be taken between each of the pair combinations to ensure that it meets specifications. Notice that in Figure 1.17, wire pair 4 will generate crosstalk that affects the other three wire pairs. A tester will have to measure 12 separate pair-to-pair crosstalk measurements to account for all pair-to-pair combinations.

FIGURE 1.17:

Cutaway of a UTP cable showing pair-to-pair crosstalk

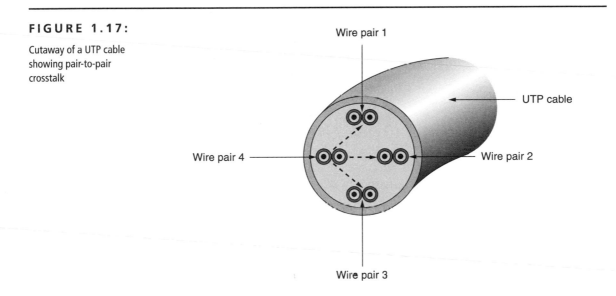

Wire pair 4 will generate crosstalk that will affect the other three pairs of wire in the cable.

Refer back to Table 1.11 for current TIA pair-to-pair crosstalk specifications for Category 5, Enhanced Category 5, Category 6, and Category 7 cables.

Power Sum Crosstalk   *Power sum crosstalk* must also be taken into consideration for cables that will support technologies that use more than one wire pair in parallel. Power sum crosstalk is the measurement of crosstalk that all the other wire pairs place on a pair of wires when all four pairs are active simultaneously. Figure 1.18 shows a cutaway of a four-pair cable. Notice that the crosstalk from pairs 2, 3, and 4 all affect pair 1. The sum of this crosstalk must be within specified limits. Since each pair affects each other pair, this measurement will have to be made four separate times, once for each wire pair.

FIGURE 1.18:

Power sum crosstalk

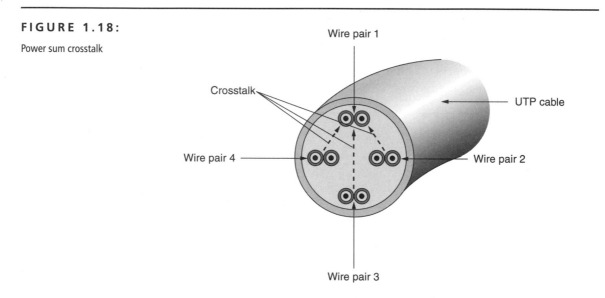

Crosstalk from pairs 2, 3, and 4 will affect pair 1.

Refer back to Table 1.11 for the power sum crosstalk specifications for Category 5, Enhanced Category 5, Category 6, and Category 7 cable. These numbers are subject to change as the proposed standards are further refined.

Propagation Delay

Electrons travel through a cable at a constant speed that is expressed as a percentage of light speed. This percentage is called NVP (Nominal Velocity Propagation) and for UTP cables is usually between 60 and 90 percent. The manufacturer of the cable controls the NVP value. The difference between the time at which a signal starts down a network cable and the time at which it arrives on the other side is the *propagation delay* of the link. Table 1.14 shows the maximum propagation delay for various cable types.

TABLE 1.14: Maximum Propagation Delay for Various Cable Types

Cable Type	Maximum Propagation Delay
Category 5	548 nsec
Category 5e	548 nsec
Category 6	548 nsec
Category 7	504 nsec

Delay Skew

Delay skew is a phenomenon that occurs as a result of each set of wires being different lengths (as shown in Figure 1.19). This is because the individual wire pairs in the cable are all slightly different lengths. Signals transmitted on two or more separate pairs of wire will arrive at slightly different times since the wire pairs are slightly different lengths. Cables that are part of a Category 5, 5e, or 6 installation cannot have more than a 50ns delay skew. Cables that are part of the proposed standard Category 7 cannot have a delay skew of larger than 20ns. Channels that have a delay skew of more than 50ns cannot successfully support 1000Base-T because the data streams cannot remain synchronized. Since 10Base-T and 100Base-TX only use a single pair for transmitting, delay skew is not an issue.

FIGURE 1.19:

Delay skew for four-pair operation

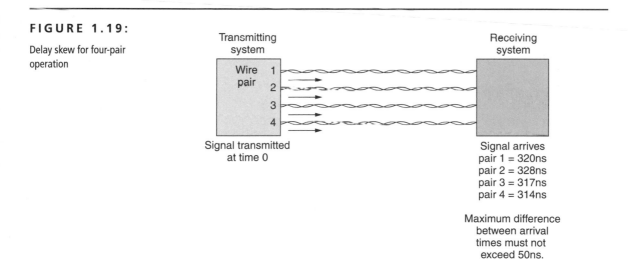

The Future of Cabling Performance

In the near future, we will see the ratification of the Category 6 and Category 7 standards. The draft of Category 6 cabling already includes some additional performance characteristics that are not found in Category 5 or TSB-95, including ELFEXT loss and FEXT loss.

In the not-too-distant future, we may also be running 10Gbps Ethernet to the desktop over twisted-pair cable. Some pundits claim that it will never happen, but some of them were the ones who claimed that 10Mbps Ethernet would never operate over twisted-pair. And somewhere, someone in a think tank is already dreaming up Category 8 standards. As materials and manufacturing techniques improve, who knows what types of performance future twisted pair cabling may offer?

Cabling Standards

Use this chapter to create information management templates
For Hardware/cabling
— System · documentation
— Labeling system
— records management
— contracts
— process tracking forms
— database applications
— Monitoring · service features
— Creating proposal specifications
— should be included in systems
administration manual (Training)

In the past, companies often had several cabling infrastructures since no single cabling system would support all of a company's applications. Cabling standards are important not only for consumers, but also for vendors and cabling installers. Vendors must clearly understand how to design and build products that will operate on a standard cabling system. Cable installers need to understand what products can be used, proper installation techniques and practices, and how to test installed systems.

This chapter covers some of the important topics related to cabling standards.

Structured Cabling and Standards

Typical business environments and requirements change quickly. Companies restructure and reorganize at alarming rates. In some companies, the average employee changes work locations once every two years. At one company that Jim worked for, during his two-year tenure he changed offices five times. Each time, his telephone, both networked computers, a VAX VT-100 terminal, and a networked printer had to be moved. The data and voice cabling system had to be able to support these reconfigurations in the work environment quickly and easily. Earlier cabling designs would not have easily supported this business environment.

Until the early 1990s, cabling systems were proprietary, vendor-specific, and lacked flexibility. Some of the downsides of pre-1990 cabling systems included:

- Vendor-specific cabling locked the customer into a proprietary system.

- Upgrades or new systems often required a completely new cabling infrastructure.

- Moves and changes often necessitated major cabling plant reconfigurations. Some coaxial and twinax cabling systems required that entire areas (or the entire system) be brought down in order to make changes.

- Applications and devices from other vendors would not work over another vendor's cabling system.

- Companies often had several cabling infrastructures that had to be maintained for their various applications.

- Troubleshooting proprietary systems was time consuming and difficult unless you were intimately familiar with that system.

Cabling has changed a lot over the years. Cabling installations have emerged from proprietary, vendor-specific installations to flexible, open solutions that can be used by many vendors and applications. This change is the result of the adaptation of standards-based, structured cabling systems. The driving force behind this acceptance is due not only to customers, but also to the cooperation between many telecommunications vendors and international standards organizations.

A properly designed *structured cabling* system is based around components or wiring units. An example of a wiring unit is a floor of an office building, as shown in Figure 2.1. All the work locations on that floor are connected to a single wiring closet. Each of the wiring units (floors of the office building) can be combined together using backbone cables as part of a larger system.

FIGURE 2.1:

Typical small office with horizontal cabling running to a single wiring closet

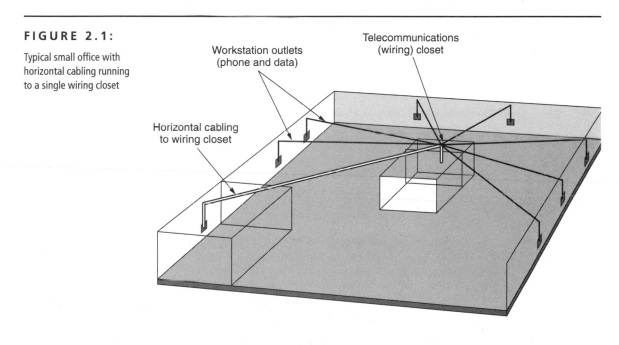

Workstation outlets (phone and data)

Telecommunications (wiring) closet

Horizontal cabling to wiring closet

TIP

A structured cabling system is not designed around any specific application but rather is designed to be generic. This permits many applications to take advantage of the cabling system.

The components used to design a structured cabling system should be based on a widely accepted standard and should allow many applications (analog voice, digital voice, 10Base-T, 100Base-TX, 16Mbps Token Ring, RS-232, etc.) to use the cabling system. The components should also adhere to certain performance specifications so that the installer or customer will know exactly what types of applications will be supported.

There are a number of standards related to data cabling. In the United States, the standard is the ANSI/TIA/EIA-568-A 1995 Standard, also known as the Commercial Building Telecommunications Cabling Standard. The TIA/EIA-568-A Standard is a standard adopted by ANSI (American National Standards Institute), but the ANSI portion of the standard name is commonly left out. In Europe, the predominant standard is the ISO/IEC 11801 Standard, also known as the International Standard on Information Technology Generic Cabling for Customer Premises.

These two standards are quite similar, although their terminology is different and the ISO/IEC 11801 standard permits an additional type of UTP cabling. Throughout much of the rest of the world, countries and standards organizations have adopted one of these standards as their own. Both of these standards are discussed in more detail later in this chapter.

Cabling Standards: A Moving Target

This chapter briefly introduces the TIA/EIA-568-A and the ISO/IEC 11801 standards, but it is not intended to be a comprehensive guide to either standard. Even as you read this book, networking vendors and standards committees are figuring out ways to transmit larger quantities of data, voice, and video over copper and fiber optic cable. As a result of these efforts, the standards and performance specifications for the standards are continually being updated. If you are responsible for large cabling systems design and implementation, you should own a copy of the relevant standards.

Most of the TIA/EIA standards mentioned in this chapter are available for purchase through Global Engineering Documents at (800) 854-7179 or on the Web at `global.ihs.com`. Global Engineering Documents sells printed versions of the TIA, EIA, ETSI, and others. The ISO/EIC Standards and ITU recommendations are available for purchase from the ITU's Web site at `www.itu.int/publications/bookstore.html`. CSA International standards documents are available from the CSA at (416) 747-4000 or on the Web at `www.csa.ca`.

Standards Organizations

If you pick up any document or catalog on data cabling, you will see acronyms and abbreviations for the names of standards organizations. If you want to know more about a particular standard, you should be familiar with the organization that publishes that particular standard. These United States–based and international organizations publish hardware, software, and physical infrastructure standards to ensure interoperability between electrical, communications, and other technology systems. Your customers and coworkers may laugh at the elation you express when you get even simple networked devices to work, but if you plug something in and breathe a silent sigh of relief when it works, you are not alone. In fact, the simple act of getting two stations communicating with one another on a 10Base-T network, for example, is a monumental achievement when you consider the number of components and vendors involved. Just think: computers from two different vendors that use Ethernet adapters may also be from different companies. These Ethernet adapters may also be connected by cable and connectors provided by another company, which in turn may be connected to a hub that was built by an additional company. Even the software that the two computers are running may come from different companies. There are dozens of other components that must work together.

The fact that anything is interoperable at all is amazing. Thankfully, there are a number of organizations around the world that are devoted to the development of standards that encourage interoperability. These organizations are often nonprofit, and the people that devote much of their time to the development of these standards are usually volunteers. These standards not only include cabling specifications, performance, and installation practices, but also the development of devices such as networking equipment like Ethernet cards. As long as the manufacturer follows the appropriate standards, their devices should be interoperable with other networking devices.

The number of organizations that provide standards is still more amazing. It might be simpler if there were only a single international organization responsible for all standards. However, if that were the case, probably nothing would ever get accomplished. Consequently, there are many organizations around the world that are responsible for development of standards. The following sections describe these organizations, but this is by no means all of the organizations that exist.

American National Standards Institute (ANSI)

Five engineering societies and three United States government agencies founded the American National Standards Institute (ANSI) in 1918 as a private, nonprofit membership organization sustained by its membership. ANSI's mission is to encourage voluntary compliance with standards and methods. ANSI's membership includes almost 1,400 private companies and government organizations in the United States as well as international members.

ANSI does not develop the American National Standards (ANS) standards, but it facilitates standards development by establishing a consensus between the members interested in developing a particular standard. ANSI promotes the use of standards developed in the United States through membership in various international organizations such as the International Organization Standards (ISO) and the International Electrotechnical Commission (IEC). ANSI was a founding member of the ISO and is one of the five permanent members of the ISO governing council and one of four permanent members on the ISO's Technical Management Board.

ANSI standards include a wide range of information technology standards such as SCSI interface standards, programming language standards, and standards for character sets. ANSI helped to coordinate the efforts of the Electronic Industries Association (EIA) and the Telecommunications Industry Association (TIA) to develop the Commercial Building Telecommunications Cabling Standard (a.k.a. ANSI/TIA/EIA-568-A), which is accepted as *the* cabling standard in the United States. TIA/EIA-568 is discussed in more detail later in this chapter. Information on and links to purchase these standards documents can be found on ANSI's Web site at www.ansi.org.

Electronics Industries Association (EIA)

The Electronics Industries Association (EIA) was established in 1924 and was originally known as the Radio Manufacturers Association. Since that time, the EIA has evolved into an organization that represents a wide variety of electronics manufacturers in the United States and abroad; these manufacturers make products for a wide range of markets for consumer, commercial, industrial, and government products. The EIA is organized along specific product and market lines that allow each EIA sector to be responsive to its specific needs. These sectors include components, consumer electronics, electronic information, industrial electronics, government, and telecommunications.

The EIA (along with the TIA) was the driving force behind the TIA/EIA-568-A Commercial Building Telecommunications Cabling Standard. More information is available on the Web at www.eia.org.

Telecommunications Industry Association (TIA)

The Telecommunications Industry Association (TIA) is a trade organization that consists of a membership of over 900 telecommunications and electronics companies that provide services, materials, and products throughout the world. The TIA membership manufacturers and distributes virtually all the telecommunication products used in the world today. TIA's mission is to represent its membership on issues relating to standards, public policy, and market development. The 1988 merger of the United States Independent Telephone Association (USTSA) and the EIA's Telecommunications Technologies Group formed the TIA.

The TIA (along with the EIA) was instrumental in the development of the TIA/EIA-568-A Commercial Building Telecommunications Cabling Standard. TIA can be found on the Web at www.tiaonline.org.

TIA Committees

In the United States (and much of the world), the TIA is ultimately responsible for the standards related to structured cabling as well as many other technological devices we use every day. If you visit the TIA Web site (www.tiaonline.org), you will find that committees develop the standards. Often, a single standard will be contributed to by a number of committees. You may find a number of abbreviations that you are not familiar with. These include:

Abbreviation Meaning/Description

SFG   Standards Formulation Groups is a committee responsible for developing standards.

FO   Fiber Optics is a committee dedicated to fiber optic technology.

TR   Technical Review is an engineering committee.

WG   Working Group is a subcommittee.

UPED   User Premises Equipment Division.

Continued on next page

Some of the TIA committees and their responsibilities include:

Committee	Functions
FO-2	Optical Communications is responsible for developing standards related to fiber optic communications and fiber optic devices.
FO-6	Fiber Optics is responsible for developing standards for fiber optic tooling and testing, connecting devices, and reliability of fiber optic connectors.
TR-29	Facsimile Systems and Equipment is responsible for the development of standards relating to faxing.
TR-30	Data Transmission Systems and Equipment develops standards related to data transmission as well as faxing.
TR-32	Personal Radio Equipment is responsible for the development of consumer-oriented products such as cordless telephones.
TR-41	User Premises Telecommunications Requirements is responsible for the standards relating to technologies such as IP telephony (VoIP or Voiceover IP), wireless telephones, caller ID, multimedia building distribution, and wireless user premises equipment.
TR-42	User Premises Telecommunications Infrastructure is responsible for standards such as the Commercial Building Telecommunications Cabling (TIA/EIA-568-B.1 or subcommittee TR-42.1), Residential Telecommunications Infrastructure (TIA/EIA-570-A or subcommittee TR-42.2), Commercial Building Telecommunications Pathways and Spaces (TIA/EIA-569-A or subcommittee TR-42.3), Telecommunications Copper Cabling Systems (TIA/EIA-568-B.2 and B.4 or subcommittee TR-42.7), Workgroup on Copper Connecting Hardware (subcommittee TR 42.2.1), and Telecommunications Optical Fiber Cabling Systems (TIA/EIA-568-B.3 or subcommittee TR-42.8). All the work by the subcommittees of TR-42 formed the TIA/EIA-568-B standard that is expected to be ratified sometime in mid-2000.

National Fire Protection Association (NFPA)

The National Fire Protection Association (NFPA) was founded in 1896 as a non-profit organization to help protect people, property, and the environment from fire damage. NFPA is now an international organization with more than 65,000 members representing over 100 countries. The organization is a world leader on fire prevention and safety. The NFPA's mission is to help reduce the risk of fire through codes, safety standards, research, and fire-related education. The NFPA can be found on the Internet at www.nfpa.org.

Though not directly related to data cabling, the NFPA is responsible for the development and publication of the National Electrical Code (NEC). The NEC is published every three years (the next NEC will be published in 2002) and covers issues related to electrical safety standards; it is not used as a design specification or an instruction manual.

There are two sections of the NEC that are relevant to data cabling, Articles 725 and 800. Many municipalities have adopted the NEC as part of their building codes and, consequently, electrical construction and wiring must meet the specifications in the NEC. While the NEC itself is not a legal document, if portions of the NEC are adopted by municipalities as part of their local building codes, those codes become laws. In Chapter 4, "Cable System and Infrastructure Constraints," we will discuss the use of the NEC when considering the restrictions that may be placed on a cabling design.

National Electrical Manufacturers Association (NEMA)

The National Electrical Manufacturers Association (NEMA) is a U.S.-based industry association that helps promote standardization of electrical components, power wires, and cables. These standards help to encourage interoperability between products that were built by different manufacturers. These standards are generally used to form the basis for ANSI standards. NEMA can be found on the Internet at www.nema.org.

Federal Communications Commission

The Federal Communications Commission (FCC) was founded as part of the U.S. government in 1934. The FCC consists of a board of seven commissioners appointed by the President; this board has the power to regulate electrical communications systems originating in the United States. These communications systems include television, radio, telegraph, telephone, and cable TV systems. Regulations relating to premises cabling and equipment are covered in FCC Part 68 rules. The FCC can be found on the Web at www.fcc.gov.

Underwriters Laboratories (UL)

Founded in 1894, Underwriters Laboratories, Inc. (UL) is a nonprofit, independent organization dedicated to product safety testing and certification. While not involved directly with cabling standards, UL works with cabling and other manufacturers to ensure that electrical devices are safe. UL tests products for paying customers; if the product passes the requirements of the standard for which the product is submitted, the UL listing or verification is granted. The UL mark of approval is applied to cabling and electrical devices worldwide. UL can be found on the Web at www.ul.com.

International Organization for Standardizations (ISO)

The International Organization for Standardizations (ISO) is an international organization of national standards bodies based in Geneva, Switzerland. The standards bodies that are members of the ISO represent over 130 countries from around the world; the United States representative to the ISO is the American National Standards Institute (ANSI). The ISO was established in 1947 as a nongovernmental organization to promote the development of standardization in intellectual, scientific, technological, and economic activities. The ISO Web site can be found at www.iso.ch.

> **NOTE**
> If the name is the International Organization for Standardizations, shouldn't the acronym be IOS instead of ISO? It should be, if ISO were an acronym—but ISO is taken from the Greek word *isos*, meaning equal.

ISO standards include standards for implementing codes for film speed, formats for telephone and banking cards, standardized freight containers, the universal system of measurements known as SI, paper sizes, and metric screw threads, just to name a few. One of the common standards that you may hear about now is the ISO 9000 Standard, which provides a framework for quality management and quality assurance.

ISO frequently collaborates with the IEC (International Electrotechnical Commission) and the ITU (International Telecommunications Union). One such result of this collaboration is the ISO/IEC 11801:1995 standard titled Generic Cabling for Customer Premises. ISO/IEC 11801 is the ISO/IEC equivalent of the TIA/EIA-568-A Standard.

International Electrotechnical Commission (IEC)

The International Electrotechnical Commission (IEC) is an international standards and conformity assessment body founded in 1906 to publish international standards relating to electrical, electronic, and related technologies. Membership in the IEC includes more than 50 countries.

There are two types of IEC members. The first type is a full member, which has voting rights in the international standards process. The second type is an associate member, which has observer status and can attend all IEC meetings.

The mission of the IEC is to promote international standards and cooperation on all matters relating to electricity, electronics, and related technologies. The IEC and the ISO (International Organization Standards) cooperate on the creation of standards such as the Generic Cabling for Customer Premises (ISO/IEC 11801:1995). The IEC can be found on the Web at www.iec.ch.

Institute of Electrical and Electronic Engineers (IEEE)

The Institute of Electrical and Electronic Engineers (IEEE, pronounced "I triple-E") is an international, nonprofit association consisting of more than 330,000 members in 150 countries. The IEEE was formed in 1963 when the American Institute of Electrical Engineers (AIEE, founded in 1884) merged with the Institute of Radio Engineers (IRE, founded in 1912). The IEEE is responsible for 30 percent of the electrical engineering, computer, and control technology literature that is published in the world today. They are also responsible for the development of over 800 active standards and have many more under development. These standards include the 10Base-x standards (such as 10Base-T, 100Base-TX, etc.) and the 802.x standards (such as 802.2, 802.3, etc.). More information can be found about the IEEE on the Web at www.ieee.org.

National Institute of Standards and Technology (NIST)

The United States Congress established the National Institute of Standards and Technology (NIST) with a number of major goals. These included assisting in the improvement and development of manufacturing technology, improving product quality and reliability, and encouraging scientific discovery. NIST is an agency of the United States Department of Commerce and works with major industries to achieve its goals.

NIST has four major programs through which it carries out its mission:

- Measurement and Standards Laboratories

- Advanced Technology Program

- Manufacturing Extension Partnership

- A quality outreach program associated with the Malcolm Baldridge National Quality Award

Though not directly related to most cabling and data standards, NIST's efforts contribute to the standards and the development of the technology based on these standards. NIST can be found on the Internet at www.nist.gov.

International Telecommunications Union (ITU)

The International Telecommunications Union (ITU), based in Geneva, Switzerland, is the standards organization formerly known as the International Telephone and Telegraph Consultative Committee (CCITT). The origins of the CCITT can be traced back over 100 years; the ITU was formed to replace it in 1993. The ITU does not publish standards per se, but it does publish recommendations. These recommendations are nonbinding standards agreed to by consensus of 1 of 14 technical study groups. The mission of the ITU is to study the technical and operations issues relating to telecommunications and to make recommendations on implementing standardized approaches to telecommunications.

The ITU currently publishes more than 2,500 recommendations, including standards relating to telecommunications, electronic messaging, television transmission, and data communications. The ITU can be found on the Internet at www.itu.int.

CSA International (CSA)

CSA International originated as the Canadian Standards Association but changed their name to reflect CSA International's growing work and influence on international standards. Founded in 1919, CSA International is a nonprofit, independent organization with more than 8,000 members worldwide; it is the functional equivalent of the UL. CSA International's mission is to develop standards, to represent

Canada on various ISO committees, and to work with the IEC when developing these standards. Some of the common standards published by CSA International include:

- CAN/CSA-T524 Residential Wiring

- CAN/CSA-T527 Bonding and Grounding for Telecommunications

- CAN/CSA-T528 Telecommunications Administration Standard for Commercial Buildings

- CAN/CSA-T529 Design Guidelines for Telecommunications Wiring Systems in Commercial Buildings

- CAN/CSA-T530 Building Facilities Design Guidelines for Telecommunications

Many cabling and data products that are certified by the United States National Electrical Code (NEC) and Underwriters Laboratories (UL) are also certified by the CSA. Cables manufactured for use in the United States are often marked with the CSA electrical and flame test ratings as well as the U.S. ratings. CSA International can be found on the Internet at www.csa.ca.

ATM Forum

Started in 1991, the ATM Forum (Asynchronous Transfer Mode) is an international, nonprofit organization whose mission is to promote and accelerate the use of ATM products and services.

Specifications developed and published by the ATM Forum include LAN Emulation (LANE) over ATM (af-lane-0021.000) and ATM Physical Medium Dependent Interface Specification for 155Mbps over Twisted-Pair Cable (af-phy-0015.000). These documents are available free of charge on the ATM Forum's Web site at www.atmforum.org.

European Telecommunications Standards Institute (ETSI)

The European Telecommunications Standards Institute (ETSI) is a nonprofit organization based in Sophia Antipolis, France. The ETSI currently consists of almost 696 members from 50 countries representing manufacturers, service providers, and consumers. The ETSI's mission is to determine and produce telecommunications standards and to encourage worldwide standardization.

The ETSI coordinates its activities with international standards bodies such as the ITU. They can be found on the Web at www.etsi.org.

Building Industry Consulting Services International (BICSI)

Though not specifically a standards organization, the Building Industry Consulting Services International (BICSI) deserves a special mention. BICSI is a nonprofit, professional organization that was founded in 1974 to support telephone company building industry consultants (BICs) that are responsible for design and implementation of communications distribution systems in commercial and multifamily buildings. Currently, the BICSI serves nearly 17,000 members from 75 countries around the world.

BICSI supports a professional certification program called the RCDD (Registered Communications Distribution Designer). People with an RCDD certification have demonstrated competence and expertise in the design, implementation, and integration of telecommunications systems and infrastructure. For more information on the RCDD program or becoming a member of the BICSI, check out their Web site at www.bicsi.org.

Occupational Safety and Health Administration (OSHA)

A division of the United States Department of Labor, the Occupational Safety and Health Administration (OSHA) was formed in 1970 with the goal of making workplaces in the United States the safest in the world. To this end, they pass laws designed to protect employees from many types of job hazards. OSHA adopted many parts of the National Electrical Code (NEC), which was not a law unto itself, giving those adopted portions of the NEC legal status. For more information on OSHA, you can find them on the Web at www.osha.gov.

ANSI/TIA/EIA-568-A Cabling Standard

In the mid-1980s, consumers, contractors, vendors, and manufacturers became concerned about the lack of standards relating to building telecommunications cabling. Up until that point, all communications cabling was proprietary and often suited only to a single purpose use. The Computer Communications Industry Association (CCIA) asked the EIA to develop a standard that would encourage structured, standardized cabling.

Under the guidance of the TIA TR-41 committee and associated subcommittees, in 1991, the TIA and EIA published the first version of the Commercial Building Telecommunications Cabling Standard, better known as ANSI/TIA/EIA-568 or simply TIA/EIA-568.

> **NOTE**
>
> Sometimes you will see the Commercial Building Telecommunications Cabling Standard referred to as ANSI/TIA/EIA-568 and sometimes just as TIA/EIA-568. You will also sometimes see the EIA and TIA transposed. The original name of the standard was EIA/TIA-568, but over the years it has been changed. The official name of the standard today (incorporating all revisions and addenda) is TIA/EIA-568-A.5 (meaning that there have been five addenda).

Over the next few years, the EIA released a number of Telecommunications Systems Bulletins (TSB) covering specifications for higher grades of cabling (TSB-36), connecting hardware (TSB-40), patch cables (TSB-40A), testing requirements for modular jacks (TSB-40A), and additional specifications for shielded twisted-pair cabling (TSB-53). The contents of these TSBs, along with other improvements, were used to revise TIA/EIA-568; this revision was released in 1995 and is called TIA/EIA-568-A. As published, the TIA/EIA-568-A takes precedence over TIA/EIA-568, TSB-36, TSB-40, TSB-40A, and TSB-53.

In fall 1999, a new addendum to the standard was released called TIA/EIA-568-A.5 that incorporates all previous additions to the "A" standard in addition to identifying Category 5e cabling and performance standards.

> **NOTE**
>
> A new revision of the entire standard is expected in mid-2000 that will incorporate all changes and many TSBs that affect the "A" version of the standard. Among other things, Category 4 cable and Category 5 cable will no longer be recommended (although they will still be recognized as valid cabling types). Category 5e will replace Categories 4 and 5 as the recommended Category of cable. This standard will be known as TIA/EIA-568-B.

> **NOTE**
>
> The Canadian equivalent of TIA/EIA-568-A is CSA T529. This standard will undoubtedly be updated to reflect the updated "B" version that is expected to be ratified in mid-2000.

Should I Use TIA/EIA-568-A or ISO/IEC 11801?

This chapter describes both the TIA/EIA-568-A and ISO/IEC 11801 cabling standards. You may wonder which standard you should follow. Though these two standards are quite similar (ISO/IEC 11801 was based on TIA/EIA-568-A), the ISO/IEC 11801 standard was developed with cable commonly used in Europe and consequently contains some references that are more specific to European applications. There is also some different terminology in the two standards.

If you are designing a cabling system that is to be used in the United States (or Canada), you should follow the TIA/EIA-568-A standard. You should know, however, that the ISO is taking the lead (with assistance from TIA, EIA, CSA, and others) in developing new cabling standards, so maybe in the future we will see only a single standard implemented worldwide that will be a combination of both standards.

TIA/EIA-568-A Purpose and Scope

The TIA/EIA-568 standard was developed and has evolved into its current form for several reasons:

- To establish a cabling standard that would support more than a single vendor application

- To provide direction of the design of telecommunications equipment and cabling products that are intended to serve commercial organizations

- To specify a cabling system generic enough to support both voice and data

- To establish technical and performance guidelines, and provide guidelines for installation of the planning and installation of structured cabling systems

The scope of the TIA/EIA-568-A standard specifies cabling that is "office-oriented." The specifications address the following:

- Subsystems of structured cabling

- Minimum requirements for telecommunications cabling

- Installation methods and practices

- Connector and pin assignments

- That the useful life of a telecommunications cabling system should exceed ten years

- Media types and performance specifications for horizontal and backbone cabling

- Connecting hardware performance specifications

- Recommended topology and distances

- The definitions of cabling elements (horizontal cable, cross-connects, telecommunication outlets, etc.)

WARNING   The TIA/EIA-568-A standard publishes two wiring patterns for use with UTP jacks and plugs. These wiring schemes indicate the order that the wire pairs should be connected to the pins in modular jacks and plugs and are known as T568A and T568B. Do not confuse these with the standards TIA/EIA-568-A and the forthcoming TIA/EIA-568-B. Both the "A" version of the standard and the "B" version of the standard include these wiring patterns. To learn more about these wiring patterns, see Chapter 9.

Subsystems of a Structured Cabling System

The TIA/EIA-568-A standard breaks down six areas of concern with relation to structured cabling. These areas are the entrance facility (building entrance), equipment room, backbone cabling, telecommunications closet, horizontal cabling, and the work area.

TIP   This chapter provides an overview of highlights of the TIA/EIA-568-A standard. It is not meant as substitute for the official standards document. Cabling professionals should purchase a full copy of the standard. The standards document (or CD-ROM version) can be purchased from Global Engineering Documents at global.ihs.com.

Interpreting Standards

Standards documents are worded using precise language that is designed to spell out exactly what is expected of an implementation using that standard. If you read carefully, you may notice that slightly different words are used when making recommendations.

If you see the word *shall* or *must* used when making a recommendation, this recommendation is a *mandatory* requirement. Words such as *should*, *may*, or *desirable* are *advisory* in nature and are not required as part of the standard.

Entrance Facility

The entrance facility (building entrance) defined by TIA/EIA-568-A specifies the point in the building where cabling interfaces with the outside world. All external cabling (campus backbone, interbuilding, antennae pathways, and telecommunications provider) should enter the building and be terminated in a single point. Telecommunications carriers are usually required to terminate within 50 feet of entering a building. The physical requirements of the interface equipment are defined in TIA/EIA-569, the Commercial Building Standard for Telecommunications Pathways. This is the standard that covers telecommunications closet design and pathways that cabling uses.

TIA/EIA-569 recommends a dedicated entrance facility for buildings with more than 20,000 usable square feet. If the building has more than 70,000 usable square feet, TIA/EIA-569 requires a dedicated, locked room with plywood termination fields on two walls. The TIA/EIA-569 standard also specifies recommendations for the amount of plywood termination fields based on the square feet in the building.

KEY TERM   **Demarcation Point**   The *demarcation point* (also called the *demarc*, pronounced dee-mark) is the point within a facility where a telecommunications circuit provided by an outside vendor such as the phone company terminates. From this point further into the customer facility, the customer provides the equipment and cabling. Maintenance and operation of equipment past the demarc is the customer's responsibility.

The entrance facility may share space with the equipment room, if necessary or possible. Telephone companies often refer to the entrance facility as the demarcation point. Some entrance facilities also house telephone or PBX (public branch exchange) equipment. Figure 2.2 shows an example of an entrance facility.

FIGURE 2.2:

Entrance facility for campus and telecommunications wiring

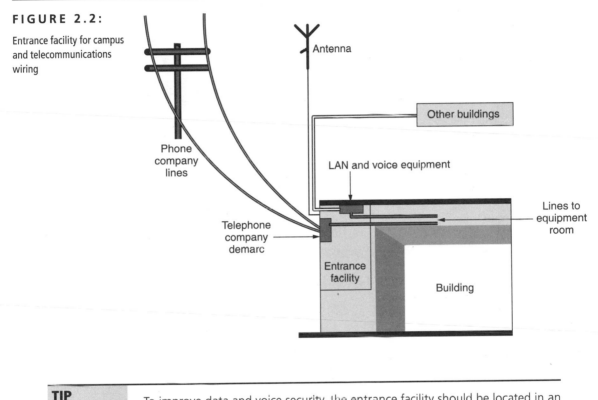

TIP

To improve data and voice security, the entrance facility should be located in an area that can be physically secured.

Equipment Room

The next subsystem of structured cabling defined by TIA/EIA-568-A is the equipment room. Equipment rooms are specified to house more sophisticated equipment than the entrance facility or the telecommunications closets. Often telephone equipment or data networking equipment such as routers, switches, and hubs are located in the equipment room. In smaller organizations it is desirable to have the equipment room located in the same center as the computer room, which houses network servers and possibly phone equipment. Figure 2.3 shows the equipment room.

FIGURE 2.3

Equipment room, backbone cabling, and telecommunications closets

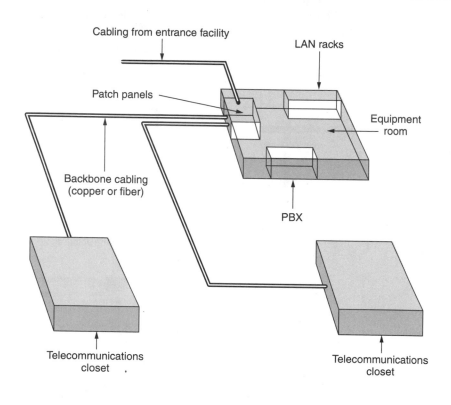

NOTE   For information on the proper design of an equipment room, refer to TIA/EIA-569.

Any room that houses telecommunications equipment, whether it's a telecommunications closet or equipment room, should be physically secured. Many data and voice systems have had security breaches because anyone could walk in off the street and gain physical access to the voice/data network cabling and equipment. Some companies go so far as to put alarm and electronic access systems on their telecommunication closets and equipment rooms.

Backbone Cabling

The third subsystem of structured cabling is called backbone cabling. (Backbone cabling is also sometimes called vertical cabling, cross-connect cabling, riser cabling, or intercloset cabling.) Backbone cabling is necessary to connect entrance facilities, equipment rooms, and telecommunications closets. Refer back to Figure 2.3 to see backbone cabling that connects an equipment room with telecommunications closets. Backbone cabling consists of not only the cables that connect the telecommunication closets, equipment rooms, and building entrance, but also the cross-connect cables, mechanical terminations, or patch cords used for backbone-to-backbone cross-connection.

KEY TERM   **Cross-connect**   A *cross-connect* is a facility or location within the cabling system that permits the termination of cable elements and the reconnection of those elements by jumpers, termination blocks, and/or cables to another cabling element (another cable or patch panel).

Backbone cabling includes:

- Cabling between equipment rooms and building entrance facilities

- In a campus environment, cabling between buildings that may connect buildings between entrance facilities

- Vertical connections between floors

TIA/EIA-568-A specifies additional design requirements for backbone cabling, some of which carry specific stipulations:

- Grounding should meet the requirements as defined in TIA/EIA-607, the Commercial Building Grounding and Bonding Requirements for Telecommunications.

- Care must be taken when running backbone cables to avoid sources of electromagnetic interference or radio frequency interference.

- No more than two hierarchical levels of cross-connects are allowed, and the topology of backbone cable will be a star topology. Each horizontal cross-connect should be connected directly to a main cross-connect or to an intermediate cross-connect that then connects to a main cross-connect. No more than one cross-connect can exist between a main cross-connect and a horizontal cross-connect. Figure 2.4 shows multiple levels of equipment closets and telecommunications closets.

- Equipment connections to the backbone should be made with cable lengths of less than 30 meters (98 feet).

- For high-speed data applications, the total maximum backbone distance should not exceed 90 meters (295 feet) over copper wiring. This distance is for uninterrupted lengths of cable (cross-connects are not allowed).

- Bridge taps are not allowed.

- Multipair cable may be used as long as it meets the minimum performance requirements such as power sum crosstalk.

FIGURE 2.4:

Star topology of equipment rooms and telecommunication closets connected via backbone cabling

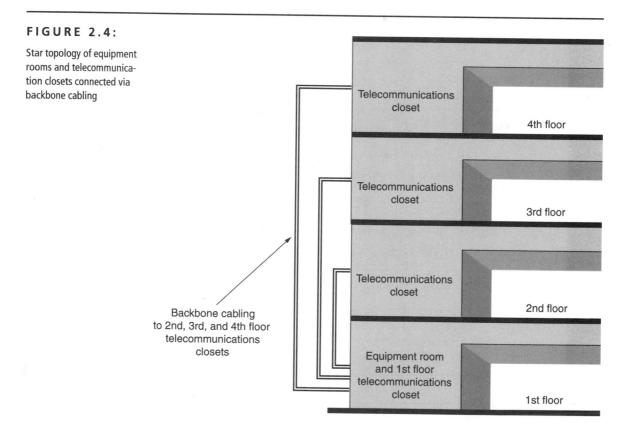

Telecommunications closet

4th floor

Telecommunications closet

3rd floor

Telecommunications closet

2nd floor

Equipment room and 1st floor telecommunications closet

1st floor

Backbone cabling to 2nd, 3rd, and 4th floor telecommunications closets

KEY TERM   **Shared Sheath**   *Shared sheath*—a single cable that supports more than one application—is permitted in TIA/EIA-568-A. This may occur, for example, when a single four-pair cable is used to support Ethernet on two of the pairs and voice or another Ethernet channel on the remaining two pairs. However, this is not advisable, since often two separate applications will have incompatible signal levels, and the crosstalk generated by one application will interfere with the signals on another pair. See Chapter 9, "Cable Connectors," for more information on devices and connections for doing this.

Recognized Backbone Media   TIA/EIA-568-A recognizes several types of media (cable) for backbone cabling. These media types can be used in combination as required by the installation. The application and the area being served will determine the quantity and number of pairs required. Table 2.1 lists the media types, applications, and maximum distances permitted for the recognized cable types.

TABLE 2.1:   Media Types, Applications, and Maximum Distances Permitted

Media	Application	Distance
100-ohm UTP (22 or 24 AWG)	Data	90 meters (295 feet)
100-ohm UTP (22 or 24 AWG)	Voice	800 meters (2,625 feet)
150-ohm STP-A	Data	90 meters (295 feet)
Single-mode 8.3/125-micron optical fiber	Data	3,000 meters (9,840 feet)
Multimode 62.5/125-micron optical fiber	Data	2,000 meters (6,650 feet)

NOTE   TIA/EIA-568-A also specifies a maximum bend radius for backbone cabling: a backbone cable should never be bent more than 10 times its outer diameter. Tight bends can damage the cable or affect the cable's performance characteristics.

KEY TERM   **Media**   The term *media* is used in the cabling business to denote the type of cabling that is being used. Media can include fiber optic cable, twisted-pair cable, coaxial cable; it can also be extended to include wireless networking.

Coaxial (50-ohm) cabling is recognized by the TIA/EIA-568-A version of the standard, but it is not recommended for new installations. With the release of TIA/EIA-568-B, coaxial cable will no longer be recognized as valid data cabling media.

Backbone Distances

Backbone distances are dependent on the application in use. High-speed data applications over UTP (Ethernet, Token Ring, ATM, FDDI, and CDDI) are much more limited in distance than lower speed applications. Low-speed applications such as voice, RS232, and IBM 3270 can travel much farther over UTP or STP cable. The actual distance will depend on the application, equipment, and manufacturer's specifications and data speed.

Telecommunications Closets

The telecommunications closet is the location within a building where cabling components such as cross-connects and patch panels are located. A telecommunications closet may also contain networking equipment such as hubs, switches, and routers. Backbone cabling equipment rooms terminate in the telecommunications closet. Figure 2.2 includes a telecommunications closet.

TIA/EIA-569 discusses telecommunications closet design and specifications and a further discussion of this subsystem can be found in Chapter 5, "Cabling System Components." TIA/EIA 569 recommends that telecommunications closets be stacked vertically between one floor and another. TIA/EIA-568-A further dictates the following specifications relating to telecommunications closets:

- Care must be taken to avoid cable stress, tight bends, staples, wrapping cable too tightly, and excessive tension. You can avoid these pitfalls with good cable management techniques.

- Use only connecting hardware that is in compliance with the standards that you want to achieve.

- Patch cables, cords, equipment cables, and work area cables are outside the scope of TIA/EIA-568-A; these items are application- (voice- or data-) specific.

- Horizontal cabling should not terminate directly to an application-specific device, but rather to a telecommunications outlet. Patch cables or equipment cords should be used to connect the device to the cabling. For example, horizontal cabling should never come directly out of the wall and plug in to a phone or network adapter.

NOTE

The entrance facility, equipment room, and telecommunications closet may be located in the same room. This room may also house telephone or data equipment. TIA/EIA-568-A does not require that these facilities be separate.

Horizontal Cabling

The next subsystem of structured cabling is *horizontal cabling*. Horizontal cabling, as specified by TIA/EIA-568-A, is the cabling that extends from the telecommunications closets to the work area and terminates in telecommunications outlets (information outlets or wall plates). Horizontal cabling includes the following:

- Cable from the patch panel to the work area
- Telecommunications outlets
- Cable terminations
- Cross-connections (where permitted)
- A maximum of one transition point

Figure 2.5 shows a typical horizontal cabling infrastructure spanning out from a telecommunications closet in a star topology. The star topology is required.

Application-specific components (baluns, repeaters) should not be installed as part of the horizontal cabling system (inside the walls). These should be installed in the telecommunication closets or work areas.

KEY TERM

Transition Point   TIA/EIA-568-A allows for one *transition point* in horizontal cabling. The transition point is the point where one type of cable connects to another, such as where round cable connects to under-carpet cable. A transition point can also be a point where cabling is distributed out to modular furniture.

FIGURE 2.5:

Horizontal cabling in a star topology from the telecommunications closet

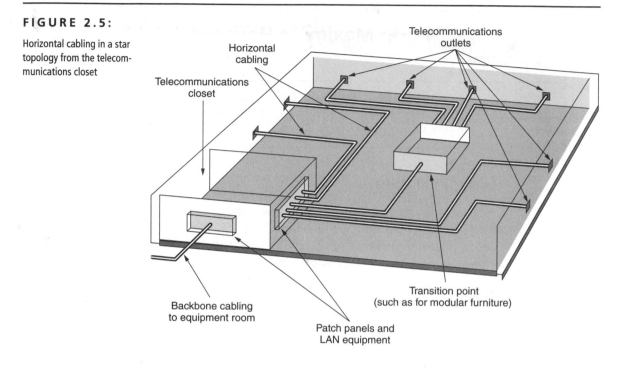

Recognized Media   TIA/EIA-568-A recognizes several types of media (cables) that can be used as horizontal cabling. Often, more than one media type will be run to a single work area telecommunications outlet, such as a UTP cable being used for voice and a fiber optic cable being used for data. The maximum distance for horizontal cable from the telecommunications closet to the telecommunications outlet is 90 meters (295 feet). Horizontal cables recognized by the TIA/EIA-568-A standard include the following:

- Four-pair, 100-ohm, 24 AWG solid conductor UTP cable

- Two-pair, 150-ohm STP cable

- Two-fiber 62.5/125-micron optical fiber

Cabling @ Work: Maximum Horizontal Cabling Distance

If you ask someone the maximum distance of cable between a network hub (such as 10Base-T) and the computer, you are likely to hear that it is 100 meters. But many people ignore the fact that patch cords are required and assume that the distance is from the patch panel to the telecommunication outlet (wall plate). This is not the case.

The TIA/EIA-568-A standard states that the maximum distance between the telecommunications outlet and the patch panel is 90 meters. The standard further allows for a patch cord at the workstation area that is up to three meters in length and a patch cord in the telecommunications closet that is up to six meters in length. (If you did the math, you figured out that the actual maximum length is 99 meters, but what's one meter between friends?) This maximum distance is the maximum distance for a structured cabling system based on TIA/EIA-568-A, regardless of the media type (twisted-pair copper or optical fiber).

The "100 meter" maximum distance is not a random number; it was chosen for a number of reasons, including the following:

- Providing a stake in the ground as far as defining transmissions distances for communications equipment designers. This distance limitation assures them that they can base their equipment designs on the fact that standards-based structured cabling systems will always present them with a maximum distance of 100 meters between the terminal and the hub in the closet. The 100 meters distance is without regard to media type.

- Providing building architects a standard by which they should place telecommunications communications closets so that no telecommunications outlet will be farther than 90 meters from the nearest wall outlet (cable distance, which is not necessarily a straight line).

- Ensuring that common technologies (such as 10Base-T Ethernet) would be able to achieve reasonable signal quality and maintain data integrity. Much of this decision was based on the timing required for a 10Base-T Ethernet workstation to transmit a minimum packet (64 bytes) to the farthest station on an Ethernet segment. The propagation of that signal through the cable had to be taken in to account.

Can a structured cabling system exceed the 100-meter distance? Sure. Good quality Category 5 or 5e cable will allow 10Base-T Ethernet to be transmitted farther than Category 3. When using 10Base-FL (10Mbps Ethernet over fiber optic cable), multimode optical fiber cable has a maximum distance of 2000 meters, so a structured cabling system that was going to support exclusively 10Base-FL applications could have much longer horizontal cabling runs.

Continued on next page

But (you knew there was a "but," didn't you?) your cabling infrastructure will no longer be based on a standard. It will support the application that it was designed to support, but it may not support others.

Further, for unshielded twisted-pair cabling, attenuation and crosstalk increase as the length of the cable increases. While attenuation and crosstalk do not drastically increase immediately above the 100-meter mark, they still do continue to increase, and your cabling system will exceed the limits that your application hardware was designed to expect. Your results will be inconsistent.

The moral of this story is don't exceed the specifications for a structured cabling system and still expect it to meet the needs of standards-based applications.

Is There a Minimum Distance for UTP Horizontal Cable?

The TIA/EIA-568-A does not specify a minimum length for UTP cabling. However there is something known as a "short link phenomenon" that occurs in cabling links that are usually less than 20 meters (60 feet) in length that usually support 100Base-TX applications. This first 20 to 30 meters of a cable is where crosstalk is the most common.

In higher speed networks such as 100Base-TX, short cables may cause the signal generated by crosstalk or return loss to be returned back to the transmitter. The transmitter may interpret these returns as collisions and cause the network not to function correctly at high speeds.

To correct this problem, try extending problematic cable runs with extra long patch cords.

Telecommunications Outlets   TIA/EIA-568-A specifies that each work area shall have a minimum of two information outlet ports. One of these is typically used for voice, and the other is typically used for data. Figure 2.6 shows a possible telecommunications outlet configuration. These telecommunications outlets go by a number of names, including information outlets, wall jacks, and wall plates. However, an information outlet is officially considered to be one jack on a telecommunications outlet; the telecommunications outlet is considered to be part of the horizontal cabling system. Chapters 9 and 10 have additional information on telecommunications outlets.

FIGURE 2.6:

Telecommunications outlet
with a UTP for voice and a
UTP/STP/fiber for data

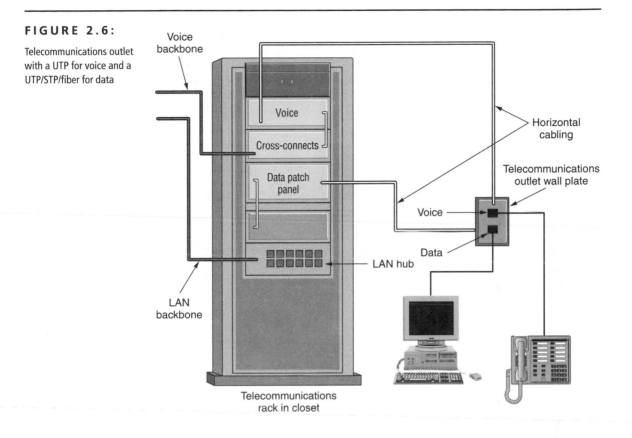

The information outlets wired for UTP should follow one of two conventions for wire pair assignments or wiring patterns; these conventions are known as T568A and T568B. They are nearly identical except for the fact that pairs 2 and 3 are reversed. There is no single correct choice for these conventions as long as the same convention is always used throughout the cabling system. T568B is much more common, but T568A is partially compatible with an older wiring scheme called USOC. Once you pick a wiring pattern, stick with it. Further, when you purchase patch panels and wall plates, you will be required to specify which pattern you are using since this equipment is usually color-coded to make installation of the wire pairs easier.

Figure 2.7 shows the T568A and T568B wire pair assignments. For more information on wiring patterns, modular plugs, and modular jacks, see Chapter 9.

Modular jack wire pattern assignments for T568A and T568B

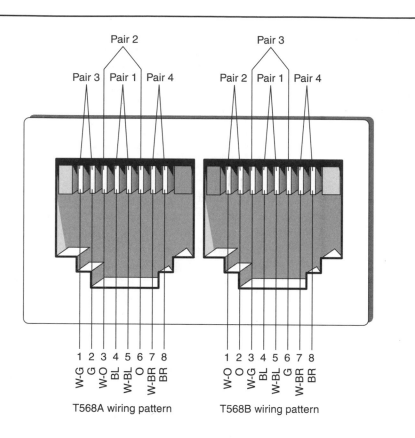

T568A wiring pattern   T568B wiring pattern

The wire/pin assignments in Figure 2.7 are assigned by wire color. The standard wire colors are shown in Table 2.2.

TABLE 2.2: Wire Color Abbreviations

Wire Abbreviation	Wire Color
W/G	White/green
G	Green
W/O	White/orange
O	Orange
W/B	White/blue

Continued on next page

TABLE 2.2 CONTINUED: Wire Color Abbreviations

Wire Abbreviation	Wire Color
B	Blue
W/Br	White/brown
Br	Brown

Though the specific application you are using may not require all the pins in the information outlet, you should make sure that all wires are terminated to the appropriate pins if for no other reason than to ensure interoperability with future applications that may use the same media. Table 2.3 shows some common applications in use today and the pins that they use.

TABLE 2.3: Application-Specific Pair Assignments for UTP Cabling*

Application	Pins 1-2	Pins 3-6	Pins 4-5	Pins 7-8
Analog voice	-	-	Tx/Rx	-
ISDN	Power	Tx	Rx	Power
10Base-T (802.3)	Tx	Rx	-	-
Token Ring (802.5)	-	Tx	Rx	-
100Base-TX (802.3u)	Tx	Rx	-	-
100Base-T4 (802.3u)	Tx	Rx	Bi	Bi
100Base-VG (802.12)	Bi	Bi	Bi	Bi
FDDI (TP-PMD)	Tx	Optional	Optional	Rx
ATM User Device	Tx	Optional	Optional	Rx
ATM Network Equipment	Rx	Optional	Optional	Tx
1000Base-T (802.3ab)	Bi	Bi	Bi	Bi

Bi = Bi-directional, Optional = May be required by some vendors
* Table courtesy of The Siemon Company (www.siemon.com)

TIP   A good structured wiring system will include documentation printed and placed on each of the telecommunications outlets.

Pair Numbers and Color-Coding   The wire pairs in a UTP cable are color-coded so that each pair of wires can be easily and quickly terminated to the appropriate pin on the connecting hardware (patch panels or telecommunication outlets). Different color codes are used depending on the types of cabling and the number of pairs of wire in each cable. With four-pair UTP cables, each pair of wire is coded with a solid colored wire (sometimes called the primary color or the ring color) and a striped colored wire (sometimes call the secondary color or the tip color) that corresponds to the solid wire. The stripe color on four-pair UTP cabling is always white.

When reading these, you identify them by their color codes, such as orange and white-orange. Table 2.4 lists the pair numbers, color codes, and pin assignments for T568A and T568B.

TABLE 2.4:   Four-Pair UTP Color Codes, Pair Numbers, and Pin Assignments for T568A and T568B

Pair Number	Color Code	T568A Pins	T568B Pins
1	Blue (B) White/blue (W/B)	B=4 W/B=5	B=4 W/B=5
2	Orange (O) White/orange (W/O)	O=6 W/O=3	O=2 W/O=1
3	Green (G) White/green (W/G)	G=2 W/G=1	G=6 W/G=3
4	Brown (Br) White/brown (W/Br)	Br=8 W/Br=7	Br=8 W/Br=7

Basic Link versus Channel Link

TIA Technical Systems Bulletin (TSB) 67 specifies test parameters for testing installed cabling. TIA/EIA-568 standards only define performance criteria for individual components, not an installed cabling system. TSB-67 defines two basic link types with respect to testing: the basic link and the channel link; these link types are commonly used in the cabling industry.

Continued on next page

The *basic link* contains only the cabling found in the walls (horizontal cabling), one transition point, the telecommunications outlet, and one cross-connect or patch panel. The basic link is assumed to be the permanent portion of the cabling infrastructure. The basic link is illustrated below.

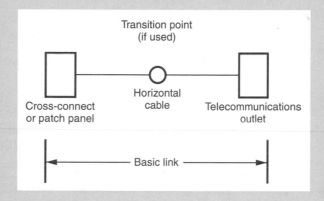

As well as the basic link, the *channel link* includes installed equipment, patch cords, and the cross-connect jumper cable; however, the channel does *not* include phones, PBX equipment, hubs, or network interface cards. Two possible channel link configurations are shown below; one is the channel link for a 10Base-T Ethernet workstation and one is for a telephone.

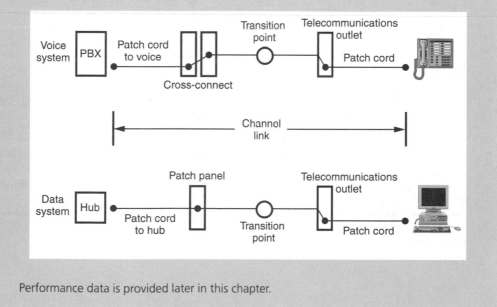

Performance data is provided later in this chapter.

Work Area

The sixth subsystem of structured cabling is the work area. The work area begins at the telecommunications area and includes components such as the following:

- Patch cables, modular cords, fiber jumpers, and adapter cables.

- Adapters such as baluns and other devices that modify the signal or impedance of the cable (these devices must be external to the information outlet).

- Station equipment such as computers, telephones, fax machines, data terminals, modems, etc.

The work area wiring should be simple and easy to manipulate. In today's business environments, changes such as moves, adds, or removal of equipment are frequent. Consequently, the cabling system needs to be easily adaptable to these changes.

Cabling @ Work: Planning for Sufficient Outlets and Horizontal Cable

Do you have enough horizontal cabling? Company XYZ (name changed to a fictional name to protect the innocent) recently moved to a new location. In their old location, they continually suffered from a lack of data and voice outlets. Users wanted phones, modems, and fax machines located in areas that no one had ever imagined. The explosion of users with multiple computers in their offices and networked printers only compounded the problem.

XYZ's director of information services vowed that this would never happen to her again. Each work area was wired with a four-port telecommunications outlet. Each of these outlets could be used for either voice or data. In the larger offices, she had telecommunications outlets located on opposite walls. Even the lunchrooms and photocopier rooms had telecommunications outlets. This foresight gives Company XYZ the ability to add many more workstations, printers, phones, and other devices that require cabling without the additional cost of running new cables. The "per-cable cost" to install additional cables later is far more expensive than installing additional cables during the initial installation.

Media and Connecting Hardware Performance

TIA/EIA-568-A specifies performance standards for unshielded twisted-pair (UTP) cabling, shielded twisted-pair (STP) cabling, and fiber optic cabling. Further, specifications are laid out for length of cable and conductor types for horizontal, backbone, and patch cables.

100-ohm Unshielded Twisted-Pair Cabling

TIA/EIA-568-A specifies three categories of UTP cable to be used with structured cabling systems. These are commonly referred to by their category number and are rated based on the maximum frequency bandwidth. These categories are found in Table 2.5, along with the ISO/IEC application class that each Category of cable will support.

TABLE 2.5:   TIA/EIA-568-A Cable Categories

Category	ISO/IEC Class	Maximum Bandwidth
Category 1	Class A	100KHz
Category 2	Class B	4MHz
Category 3	Class C	16MHz
Category 4	-	20MHz
Category 5	Class D	100MHz
Category 5e	Class E	100MHz
Category 6*	Class F	250MHz

* Under development

Ensuring a Specific Level of Cabling Performance

UTP cabling systems cannot be considered Category 3-, 4-, 5-, or 5e–compliant (and consequently certified) unless all components of the cabling system satisfy the specific performance requirements of the particular category you are planning to achieve. This includes:

- All backbone and horizontal cabling

Continued on next page

- Telecommunications outlets

- Patch panels

- Cross-connect wires and cross-connect blocks

All patch panel terminations, wall plate terminations, crimping, and cross-connect punchdowns also must follow the specific recommendations for the respective category that you are planning to achieve.

Horizontal and Backbone UTP Cabling   Characteristic impedance of horizontal and backbone UTP cables should be 100 ohms plus or minus 15 percent from 1MHz up to the maximum bandwidth supported by the cable. Table 2.6 lists the attenuation (highest permissible value) and near-end crosstalk (NEXT) (lowest permissible value) for various frequencies between 1MHz and the maximum bandwidth supported by the category of cable.

TABLE 2.6:   Horizontal Cabling Attenuation and Next Loss Per 100 Meters (328 Feet) at 20 Degrees Celsius (68 Degrees Fahrenheit)

Frequency (MHz)	Category 3 Attn/NEXT (dB)	Category 4 Attn/NEXT (dB)	Category 5 Attn/NEXT (dB)
1.0	2.4/41	2.2/56	2.0/62
4.0	5.6/32	4.3/47	4.1/53
8.0	8.5/27	6.2/42	5.8/48
10.0	9.7/26	6.9/41	6.5/47
16.0	13.1/23	8.9/38	8.2/44
20.0	-	10.0/36	9.3/42
25.0	-	-	10.4/41
31.25	-	-	11.7/39
62.5	-	-	17.0/35
100	-	-	22.0/32

The values represented for NEXT in Table 2.6 represent worst pair-to-pair cross-talk in horizontal cables. These values do not include loss and crosstalk values resulting from connections such as telecommunications outlets, cross-connects, and patch panels. TIA/EIA-568-A only specifies performance values for components. For backbone cables, the NEXT value represents the power sum NEXT.

NOTE

You may recall from Chapter 1, "Introduction to Data Cabling," that lower atten-uation numbers and higher crosstalk numbers (NEXT) are better. Pair-to-pair crosstalk and power sum NEXT are discussed in more detail in Chapter 1.

Connecting Hardware Performance Loss   Part of the TIA/EIA-568-A stan-dard is intended to ensure that connecting hardware (cross-connects, patch panels, patch cables, telecommunications outlets, and connectors) does not have an adverse effect on attenuation and NEXT. To this end, the standard specifies attenu-ation and NEXT loss for connecting hardware; the specified values are in Table 2.7.

TABLE 2.7:   Attenuation and NEXT Limits for UTP Connecting Hardware

Frequency (MHz)	Category 3 Attn/NEXT (dB)	Category 4 Attn/NEXT (dB)	Category 5 Attn/NEXT (dB)
1.0	0.4/58	0.1/65	0.1/65
4.0	0.4/46	0.1/58	0.1/65
8.0	0.4/40	0.1/52	0.1/62
10.0	0.4/38	0.1/50	0.1/60
16.0	0.4/34	0.2/46	0.2/56
20.0	-	0.2/44	0.2/54
25.0	-	-	0.2/52
31.25	-	-	0.2/50
62.5	-	-	0.3/44
100	-	-	0.4/40

Patch Cables and Cross-Connect Jumpers

TIA/EIA-568-A also specifies requirements that apply to cables used for patch cables and cross-connect jumpers. This includes recommendations for maximum distance limitations for patch cables and cross-connects, as shown here:

Cable Type	Maximum Distance
Main cross-connect*	20 meters (66 feet)
Intermediate cross-connect*	20 meters (66 feet)
Telecommunications closet	6 meters (20 feet)
Work area	3 meters (10 feet)

> *Main and intermediate cross-connects will only be used with voice and other low bandwidth applications.

The total maximum distance of the channel should not exceed the maximum distance recommended for the application that is being used. For example, the channel distance for 100Base-TX Ethernet should not exceed 100 meters.

TIP Patch cables should use stranded conductors rather than solid conductors so that the cable is more flexible. Solid-conductor cables are easily damaged if they are bent too tightly or too often.

Patch cables usually have a slightly higher attenuation than horizontal cables due to the fact that patch cables use stranded conductors rather than solid conductors. Though this increases patch cable flexibility, it also increases attenuation. Table 2.8 lists the maximum attenuation for patch cables.

TABLE 2.8: Maximum Attenuation for Patch Cables

Frequency (MHz)	Category 3 (dB)	Category 4 (dB)	Category 5 (dB)
1.0	3.1	2.6	2.4
4.0	6.7	5.2	4.9
8.0	10.2	7.4	6.9

Continued on next page

TABLE 2.8 CONTINUED: Maximum Attenuation for Patch Cables

Frequency (MHz)	Category 3 (dB)	Category 4 (dB)	Category 5 (dB)
10.0	11.7	8.3	7.8
16.0	15.7	10.7	9.9
20.0	-	12.0	11.1
25.0	-	-	12.5
31.25	-	-	14.1
62.5	-	-	20.4
100	-	-	26.4

150-ohm Shielded Twisted-Pair Cabling

Shielded twisted-pair cabling (STP) is often more desirable for data communications due to the fact that STP cabling has a sheath of shielding around all pairs of the cable, and the individual pairs of wire also often have a shield. STP cable performs extremely well in areas where electromagnetic interference (EMI) and radio frequency interference are concerns. Attenuation loss is lower for STP cable than it is for UTP cable, and NEXT performance is much better (due to the shielding). However, STP is not used as often as UTP in most environments because the cost of the cable is higher, and the hardware that takes advantage of it is often more expensive.

For STP cabling, TIA/EIA-568-A recognizes IBM type 1A for backbone and horizontal cabling and IBM type 6A for patch cables.

STP Backbone and Horizontal Cable   IBM type 1A cabling (STP-A) is recognized for use as backbone and horizontal cabling; IBM type 6A is recognized for use as patch cable. This cable is two-pair, 22 AWG solid-conductor cable with characteristic impedance of 150 ohms (plus or minus 10 percent) and is rated for frequency usage between 3MHz and 300MHz. Table 2.9 shows the performance characteristics for attenuation and NEXT for STP-A cabling.

TABLE 2.9:   Horizontal and Backbone STP-A Performance Characteristics

Frequency (MHz)	Attenuation (dB)*	NEXT (dB)
4.0	2.2	58.0
8.0	3.1	54.9
10.0	3.6	53.5
16.0	4.4	50.4
20	4.9	49.0
25	6.2	47.5
31.25	6.9	46.1
62.5	9.8	41.5
100	12.3	38.5
300	21.4	31.3

*Attenuation per 100 meters (328 feet) at 25 degrees Celsius

150-ohm STP-A Data Connectors   TIA/EIA-568-A specifies a 150-ohm STP-A data connector for connections. This unique hermaphroditic connector was originally developed by IBM and is also sometimes called the IBM data connector.

TIA/EIA specifies worst case attenuation and NEXT loss performance parameters for 150-ohm STP-A connectors as seen in Table 2.10.

TABLE 2.10:   Attenuation and NEXT Loss for 150-ohm STP-A Data Connectors

Frequency (MHz)	Attenuation (dB)	NEXT (dB)
4.0	.05	65.0
8.0	.10	65.0
10.0	.10	65.0
16.0	.15	62.4
20.0	.15	60.5

Continued on next page

TABLE 2.10 CONTINUED: Attenuation and NEXT Loss for 150-ohm STP-A Data Connectors

Frequency (MHz)	Attenuation (dB)	NEXT (dB)
25	.15	58.5
31.25	.15	56.6
62.5	.20	50.6
100	.25	46.5
300	.45	36.9

Optical Fiber Cabling

TIA/EIA-568-A includes specifications for using fiber optic cabling. The standard permits two types of fiber optic cabling: 62.5/125-micron single-mode and 62.5/125-micron multimode optical fiber. Horizontal cabling systems are specified to use multimode cable, while backbone cabling may use either multimode or single-mode optical fiber cable.

There are two widely used connectors used with fiber optic cabling systems, the ST and SC connectors. Currently installed applications that require the ST connector type are allowed, but future applications and deployments should use the 568SC-type connector. This specification was changed so that the fiber optic specifications in the TIA/EIA-568-A agree with the IEC 11801 standard used in Europe. The TIA/EIA-568-A standard does not currently recognize the new small form factor connectors such as the MT-RJ connector.

KEY TERM   **Fiber "Modes"**   Fiber optic cable is referred to as either single-mode or multimode fiber. The term *mode* refers to the "bundles" of light that enter the fiber optic cable. Single-mode fiber optic cable uses only a single mode of light to propagate through the fiber cable, while multimode fiber allows multiple modes of light to propagate. In multimode fiber optic cable, the light bounces off the cable walls as it travels through the cable, which causes the signal to weaken more quickly.

Multimode Optical Fiber Cable   Multimode fiber optic is most often used as horizontal cable. Multimode cable permits multiple modes of light to propagate through the cable and thus lowers cable distances and has a lower available bandwidth. Devices that use multimode fiber optic cable typically use light emitting diodes (LEDs) to generate the light that travels through the cable; however, higher bandwidth network devices such as Gigabit Ethernet are now using lasers with multimode fiber optic cable. TIA/EIA-568-A recognizes two-fiber (duplex) 62.5/125-micron multimode fiber; TIA/EIA-568-A also recognizes 50/125-micron multimode fiber optic cable. Table 2.11 shows the maximum permitted attenuation at the commonly used wavelengths.

TABLE 2.11: Performance of Multimode Optical Fiber Cable Used for Horizontal or Backbone Cabling

Wavelength (nm)	Maximum Attenuation (dB/km)	Minimum Bandwidth (MHz-km)
850	3.75	160
1300	1.5	500

Single-Mode Optical Fiber Cable   Single-mode optical fiber cable is commonly used as backbone cabling; single-mode fiber is also usually the cable type used in phone systems. Light travels through single-mode fiber optic cable using only a single mode, meaning it travels straight down the fiber and does not "bounce" off the cable walls. Since only a single mode of light travels through the cable, single-mode fiber optic cable supports higher bandwidth and longer distances than multimode fiber optic cable. Devices that use single-mode fiber optic cable typically use lasers to generate the light that travels through the cable.

TIA/EIA-568-A recognizes 62.5/125-micron, 50/125-micron, and 8.3/125-micron single-mode optical fiber cables. TIA/EIA-568-A states that the maximum backbone distance using single-mode fiber optic cable is 3,000 meters (9,840 feet), and the maximum backbone distance using multimode fiber is 2,000 meters (6,560 feet). Table 2.12 shows the maximum attenuation for single-mode fiber at common wavelengths.

TABLE 2.12: Performance of Single-Mode Optical Fiber Cable Used for Backbone Cabling

Wavelength (nm)	Maximum Attenuation (dB/km)
1310	.5
1550	.5

Optical Fiber and Telecommunications Closets   The TIA/EIA-568-A standard specifies some required features of telecommunications closets that must be adhered to, in order to be standards-compliant. These are the required features:

- The telecommunications outlet(s) must have the ability to terminate a minimum of two fibers into 568SC couplings.

- The telecommunications outlet must provide a means of securing fiber and maintaining a minimum bend radius of 30 millimeters to prevent damage to the fiber.

- The telecommunications outlet must be able to store at least one meter of two-fiber (duplex) cable.

- The telecommunications outlet supporting fiber cable must be a surface mount box that attaches on top of a standard 4"×4" electrical box.

The "B" Version Is Coming

Sometime in mid-2000, the TIA TR42.1 committee (with help from other subcommittees) will ratify the TIA/EIA-568-B version of the Commercial Building Telecommunications Cabling Standard. A lot has changed since the "A" version of the standard was developed. Even though addenda and telecommunications systems bulletins have been issued to keep the standard current, the standard needs to be updated to reflect the changing world. The new "B" version has been broken into three sections.

Part 1: General Requirements

Part 1 addresses issues such as cabling distances (horizontal and backbone), media selection, open office cabling, installation practices, field test practices, work area connections, and telecommunication and equipment rooms. This section will incorporate the content from the "A" version of the standard as well as all addenda to the "A" version, TSB-67, TSB-72, TSB-75, and TSB-95.

Part 2: Twisted-Pair Media

Part 2 covers the electrical and mechanical requirements for twisted-pair cables, patch cables, connectors, component testing, field tester requirements, and testing methods. It will draw from the previous version of the standard as well as from TSB-67 and TSB-95.

Continued on next page

Expect Category 4 and Category 5 cable to disappear from the recommended media list (they will be recognized, but not recommended); Category 5e cable will take the place of Category 5 cable. Category 5e cable has been a standard media type since fall 1999 when addendum #5 was added to the "A" version of the standard. Do not expect Category 6 cable to appear in the standard until later in 2000 or early 2001. Category 7 cabling is being worked on by the ISO and will probably be adopted by the EIA once the ISO has the kinks worked out.

Part 3: Optical Fiber Media

Part 3 of the standard covers the use of optical fiber cables, including fiber optic testing, field performance testing, cable types, patch cables, and connectors. Do not expect to see the small form factor war be settled with this standard, as the standards committee does not feel that these connectors are mature enough to be incorporated in to the standard.

Telecommunications Systems Bulletins

Periodically, the TIA publishes Telecommunications Systems Bulletins (TSBs) for the purpose of making recommendations or providing information or guidance relating to a particular host standard. TSBs are not considered standards as they specify no mandatory requirements. They merely provide guidance or additional information for the existing standards. Some of the TSBs are later incorporated into updated versions of the standards.

The TIA has released a number of TSBs relating to the TIA/EIA-568-A version of the standard to provide additional information and guidance when implementing the standard. Two key TSBs are TSB-67 and TSB-95, which relate to field testing of cabling.

TSB-67

TIA published TSB-67 for the purpose of providing guidelines for testing UTP cabling systems. TSB-67 (a.k.a. "Transmission Performance Specifications for Field Testing UTP Cabling Systems") defines a number of performance parameters and specifies the minimum or maximum acceptable parameters for these performance parameters.

Further, TSB-67 provides two additional definitions that define the types of cabling links:

Basic link Includes the horizontal cable (up to 90 meters), telecommunications outlets, or a transition point and one horizontal cross-connect (or patch panel). The basic link is assumed to be the permanent portion of the link.

Channel link Includes all components of the basic link plus patch cables and additional cross-connects.

Table 2.13 shows the maximum attenuation and minimum NEXT loss performance parameters for the basic link.

TABLE 2.13: Basic Link Attenuation and NEXT Loss

Frequency (MHz)	Attenuation (Maximum)			NEXT Loss (Minimum)		
	Cat 3	Cat 4	Cat 5	Cat 3	Cat 4	Cat 5
1	3.2	2.2	2.1	40.1	54.7	60.0
4	6.1	4.3	4.0	30.7	45.1	51.8
8	8.8	6.0	5.7	25.9	40.2	47.1
10	10.0	6.8	6.3	24.3	38.6	45.0
16	13.2	8.8	8.2	21.0	35.3	42.3
20	-	9.9	9.2	-	33.7	40.7
25	-	-	10.3		-	39.1
31.25	-	-	11.5	-	-	37.6
62.5	-	-	16.7	-	-	32.7
100	-	-	21.6	-	-	29.3

Table 2.14 shows the maximum attenuation and the minimum NEXT loss for the channel link. The channel link numbers include losses that are a result of cross-connects and patch cables.

TABLE 2.14: Channel Link Attenuation and NEXT Loss

Frequency (MHz)	Attenuation (Maximum)			NEXT Loss (Minimum)		
	Cat 3	Cat 4	Cat 5	Cat 3	Cat 4	Cat 5
1	4.2	2.6	2.5	39.1	53.3	60.0
4	7.3	4.8	4.5	29.3	43.3	50.6
8	10.2	6.7	6.3	24.3	38.2	45.6
10	11.5	7.5	7.0	22.7	36.6	44.0
16	14.9	9.9	9.2	19.3	33.1	40.6
20	-	11.0	10.3	-	31.4	39.0
25	-	-	11.4	-	-	37.4
31.25	-	-	12.8	-	-	35.7
62.5	-	-	18.5	-	-	30.6
100	-	-	24.0	-	-	27.1

TSB-95

The TIA has subsequently published TSB-95 (a.k.a. "Additional Transmission Performance Guidelines for 100-ohm Four-Pair Category 5 Cabling") to provide guidance for testing existing cabling systems to ensure that they will support high-speed, duplex applications such as Gigabit Ethernet. TSB-95 is considered a complement to TSB-67; it provides additional performance characteristics for equal level far-end crosstalk (ELFEXT), return loss (RL), delay, and delay skew. Chapter 1 describes these performance parameters in detail.

TSB-95 is targeted towards installed cabling systems. It does not provide performance parameters for connectors and cable, only for the basic link and the channel link. If you are planning to install a new cabling system, the performance characteristics that are part of TSB-95 are included in the latest version of the TIA standards.

TSB-75

The TIA published TSB-75 (a.k.a. "Open Office Cabling Index") to provide additional specifications for horizontal cabling in office environments that use modular furniture and moveable partitions. TIA/EIA-568-A provides no allowances for offices that can be "rearranged;" it assumes that once a cable is placed, it is stationary. In modern office areas, this is not necessarily practical since work areas often consist of cubicles and moveable walls.

TSB-75 defines horizontal cabling methodologies that permit the use of multiuser telecommunication outlets and/or consolidation points. TSB-75 uses two terms relating to open office cabling that may be of interest:

> **MuTOA** Multiuser telecommunications outlet assembly, which is an outlet that consolidates telecommunications jacks for many users into one area.

> **CP** Consolidation point, which is an intermediate interconnection scheme that allows horizontal cables that are part of the building pathways to extend to telecommunication outlets in open office pathways such as modular furniture. The ISO/IEC 11801 refers to the CP as a transition point (TP).

Library Problem

If you are planning on using modular furniture or moveable partitions, check with the vendor of the furniture or partitions to see if they provide pathways within their furniture for data cabling. Further, ask what type of interface they may provide or require to your existing cabling system. You will have to plan for connectivity to their furniture in your wiring scheme.

Cabling vendor The Siemon Company and modular furniture manufacturer DRG have teamed up to build innovative modular future with built-in cable management that is compliant with TSB-75 and the TIA/EIA-568 standards. This furniture system is called MACsys; you can find more information about the MACsys family of products on the Web at www.siemon.com/macsys/.

ANSI/TIA/EIA-569-A

Though the TIA/EIA-569-A standard describes the subsystems (entrance facility, equipment room, backbone cabling, telecommunications closets, horizontal cabling, and the work area) of a structured cabling system, the TIA has published a more thorough document called TIA/EIA-569-A Commercial Building Standard for Telecommunications Pathways and Spaces standard.

The purpose of the TIA/EIA-569-A standard is to provide a flexible and standardized support system for a structured cabling system and to provide the detail necessary to design and build these facilities. It does this by providing the detail required to build these pathways and support spaces in both single- and multitenant buildings.

> **NOTE** This standards document is especially important since often network managers, architects, and even cable installers don't give enough forethought to the spaces and infrastructure that will support structured cabling systems or data communications equipment.

On first glance at the TIA/EIA-569-A standard, you may feel that there is a lot of repetition. TIA/EIA-569-A, however, defines pathways and spaces that are used by a commercial cabling system and the details of those pathways. The elements defined include:

- Entrance facility
- Equipment room
- Main terminal space
- Telecommunications closets
- Horizontal pathways
- Backbone pathways
- Work areas

> **NOTE** When planning telecommunications pathways and spaces, make sure you allow for future growth.

TIA/EIA-569-A provides some common design considerations for the entrance facility, equipment room, and telecommunications closets with respect to construction, environmental considerations, and environmental controls:

- The door (without sill) should open outward, slide sideways, or be removable. It should be fitted with a lock and be a minimum of 36 inches (.91 meters) wide by 80 inches (2 meters) high.

- Electrical power should be supplied by a minimum of two dedicated 120V 20A nominal, nonswitched AC duplex electrical outlets. Each of these outlets should be on separate branch circuits. The equipment room may have additional electrical requirements based on the telecommunications equipment that will be supported there (LAN servers, hubs, phone switches [PBXs], UPS systems, etc.).

- Sufficient lighting should be provided (500 lx or 50-foot candles). The light switches should be located near the entrance door.

- Grounding should be provided and used per TIA/EIA-607 (the Commercial Building Grounding and Bonding Requirements for Telecommunications standard) and the NEC or local code, whichever takes precedence.

- These areas should not have false (drop) ceilings.

Other TIA/EIA-569-A recommendations include:

- Slots and sleeves that penetrate firewalls or that are used for riser cables should be firestopped per the applicable codes.

- Separation of horizontal and backbone pathways from sources of electromagnetic interference (EMI) must be maintained per NEC Article 800.52.

- Metallic raceways and conduits should be grounded.

Based on our own experiences, we recommend:

- Equip each telecommunications closet, the entrance facility, and the equipment room with electrical surge suppression and UPS (uninterruptible power supply) that will supply that area with at least 15 minutes of standby AC power in the event of a commercial power failure.

- Equip these areas with standby lighting that will last for at least an hour if the commercial power fails.

- Make sure that these areas are sufficiently separated from sources of EMI such as antennas, medical equipment, elevators, motors, and generators.

- Keep a flashlight or chargeable light in an easy-to-find place in each of these areas in the event the commercial power fails and the battery operated lights run down.

NOTE   For full information, consult the TIA/EIA-569 standard, which may be purchased through Global Engineering Documents on the Web at `global.ihs.com`.

Entrance Facility

The entrance facility is the location in the building where cables from outside enter the building. This includes phone cables from a telecommunications provider, antenna cables, and cables from a campus-wide backbone. The location of the entrance facility is usually either on the first floor or in the basement of a building and must take into consideration the requirements of the telecommunications services required and other utilities that may need to use this facility (CATV, water, and electrical power).

TIA/EIA-569-A specifies the following design considerations for an entrance facility:

- When security, continuity, or other needs dictate, an alternate entrance facility may need to be provided.

- One wall at a minimum should have 3/4" (20 mm) thick A-C plywood.

- It should be a dry area that is not subject to flooding or moisture.

- It should be as close to the actual entrance pathways (where the cables enter the building) as possible.

- Equipment not relating to the support of the entrance facility should not be installed.

NOTE   The entrance facility should not double as a storage room or janitor's closet.

Main Terminal Space

The main terminal space is a facility that is commonly a shared space in a multi-tenant building. The main cross-connects exist in this room. These rooms are generally a combination of an equipment room and a telecommunications closet, though the TIA/EIA specifies that the design for a main terminal space follow the design considerations laid out for an equipment room. Customer equipment may or may not be located in this room. However, our opinion is that it is not desirable to locate your own equipment in a room that is shared with other tenants of a building. One reason for this is that you may have to be given permissions from the building manager to gain access to this facility.

Equipment Room

The equipment room is described as being a centralized space where all backbone cabling terminates, as well as the location of phone system equipment and, possibly, computer equipment. Considerations to think about when designing an equipment room include the following:

- Environmental controls must be present to provide HVAC 24 hours per day, seven days per week. Temperature range (64–75 degrees Fahrenheit or 18–24 degrees Celsius) should be maintained, along with 30–55 percent relative humidity. An air filtering system should be installed to protect pollution and contaminants such as dust.

- Seismic and vibration precautions should be taken.

- Minimum height of the ceiling should be 8 feet (2.4 meters).

- Minimum door requirements are the same for equipment rooms as they are for telecommunications closets and the entrance facility, but a double door is recommended.

- The entrance area to the equipment room should be large enough to provide delivery of large equipment.

- The room should be above water level to minimize danger of flooding.

- The backbone pathways should terminate in the equipment room.

- The entrance facility and equipment room functions may be combined into a single room in a smaller building.

Cabling @ Work: Bad Equipment Room Design

One company we are familiar with spent nearly a million dollars designing and building a high-tech equipment room, complete with raised floors, cabling facilities, power conditioning, backup power, and HVAC. The room was designed to be a showcase for their voice and computer systems. The day equipment started arriving, much of the HVAC and air conditioning equipment could not be moved into the room because there was not enough clearance in the hallway outside of the computer room to move the equipment into the room. Several walls had to be torn out (including the wall of an adjacent tenant) to move the equipment into the room.

Another company located their equipment room in a space that used to be part of a telecommunications closet. The space had core holes drilled to the floor above, but the holes had not been filled in after the previous tenant vacated the property. The company on the lower floor installed their computer equipment but did not have the core holes filled. A few months later, a new tenant had a contractor fill the holes. The contractor's workers poured nearly a ton of concrete down the core and on top of the computer equipment in the room below before someone realized that the hole was not filling up.

Many organizations have experienced the pain of flooding from above. One company's computer room was directly below the bathrooms on the floor above. An overflowing toilet (combined with a stopped-up drain) caused hundreds of gallons of water to spill down into the computer room. Don't let this kind of disaster occur in your equipment rooms!

Compare to Work you have seen – how secure →

Telecommunications Closets

The telecommunications closet (a.k.a. wiring closet) is one of the basic units of structured cabling. These rooms are where the horizontal structured cabling originates. Horizontal cabling is terminated in patch panels or termination blocks and then uses horizontal pathways to reach work areas. The telecommunications closet may also contain networking equipment such as LAN hubs, switches, routers, and repeaters.

Here are some design considerations suggested by the TIA/EIA-569-A:

- Each floor of a building should have at least one telecommunications closet, depending on the distance to the work areas. The closets should be close enough to the areas being served so that the horizontal cable does not exceed a maximum of 90 meters (as specified by the TIA/EIA-568-A standard).

- Environment controls are required to maintain a temperature that is the same as adjacent office areas. Positive pressure should be maintained in the telecommunications closets, and there should be a minimum of one air change per hour (or per local code).

- Ideally, closets should "stack" on top of one another in a multifloor building. Backbone cabling (sometimes called vertical or riser cable) between the closets merely goes straight up or down.

- Two walls of the telecommunications closet must have 3/4-inch (20 mm) A-C plywood mounted on the walls. This plywood should be 8 feet (2.4 meters) high.

- The room and equipment installed in the room should take into consideration vibration and seismic requirements.

- Conduit between two closets on the same floor must be interconnected with a minimum of one 78(3) trade-size conduit or equivalent pathway. 78(3) trade-size conduit has a sleeve size of 78 mm or 3 inches.

Shake, Rattle, and Roll

A company that Jim worked for was using metal racks and shelving in the equipment rooms and telecommunications closets. The metal racks were not bolted to the floors or supported from the ceiling. During the 1989 San Francisco earthquake, these racks all collapsed forward, taking with them hubs, LAN servers, tape units, UPSs, and disk subsystems. If you live in an area that is prone to earthquakes, make sure that seismic precautions are taken.

Horizontal Pathways

The horizontal pathways are the paths that horizontal cable takes between the wiring closet and the work area. The most common place that horizontal cable is routed is in the plenum, which is the space between the structural ceiling and the false (or drop) ceiling. The plenum is also where the air conditioning ducts call home.

NOTE   Cable installers often install cable directly across the upper portion of false ceiling. Many people consider this to be poor installation practice since this means cable may also be draped across fluorescent lights, power conduits, and air conditioning ducts. Some local codes may not permit communications cable to be installed without conduit or some other type of pathway.

The most common types of horizontal pathways are conduit and trays (or wireways). *Trays* are either metal or plastic structures that the cable is laid into as it is installed. These can be rigid or flexible. *Conduit* can be metal or plastic tubing that is usually rigid but can also be flexible (in the case of fiber optic cable, this is sometimes called *inner duct*). Both conduit and trays are designed to keep the cable from resting on top of the false ceiling or being exposed if the ceiling is open. Other types of horizontal pathways include the following:

- Access floor, which is found in raised floor computer rooms. The tile for these floors rests on pedestals, and each tile can be removed with a special tool. Some manufacturers make cable management systems that can be used in conjunction with access floors.

- Under floor or trenches, which are in concrete floors. These trenches are usually covered with metal and can be accessed by pulling the metal covers off.

- Perimeter pathways, which are usually some type of plastic or metal system designed to mount on walls, floors, or ceilings and contains one or more cables. Many vendors make raceway equipment (see Chapter 5 for more information).

When designing or installing horizontal pathways, here are some considerations to keep in mind:

- Horizontal pathways are not allowed in elevator shafts.

- Make sure that the pathways will be able to support the weight for the amount of cable you plan to run and that they meet seismic requirements.

- Horizontal pathways should be grounded.

- Horizontal pathways should not be routed through areas that are not going to be dry.

KEY TERM   **Drawstring**   A *drawstring* is a small nylon cord that is inserted into a conduit when the conduit is installed and assists with pulling cable through the conduit later. Larger conduits will have multiple drawstrings.

Backbone Pathways

Backbone pathways provide paths for backbone cabling between the equipment room, telecommunications closets, main terminal space, and entrance facility. The TIA suggests in TIA/EIA-569-A that the wiring closets be "stacked" on top of one another from one floor to another so that cables can be routed straight up through a riser. TIA/EIA-568-A defines a couple of types of backbone pathways:

Ceiling pathways   Allow the cable to be run loosely though the plenum

Conduit pathways   Have the cable installed in a metallic or plastic conduit

Tray pathways   Are the same types of trays that are used for horizontal cabling

KEY TERMS   **Sleeves, Slots, and Cores**   *Sleeves* are circular openings that are cut in walls, ceilings, and floors; a *slot* is the same thing but rectangular in shape. A *core* is a circular hole that is cut in a floor or ceiling and is used to access the floor above or below. Cores, slots, and sleeves that are cut through a floor, ceiling, or wall that is designed as a firestopping wall must have firestopping material inserted in the hole after the cable is installed through it.

Some considerations to think about when designing backbone pathways include the following:

- Intercloset conduit must be 78(3) trade size (3-inch or 78 mm sleeve).

- Backbone conduit must be 103(4) trade size (4-inch or 103 mm sleeve).

- Firestopping material must be installed where a backbone cable penetrates a fire wall (a wall designed to stop or hinder fire).

- Trays, conduits, sleeves, and slots need to penetrate at least one inch (25 mm) into telecommunication closets and equipment rooms.

- Backbone cables should be grounded per local code, the NEC, and TIA/EIA-607.

- Backbone pathways should be dry and not susceptible to water penetration.

Work Areas

The work area is the area where the horizontal cable terminates at the wall outlet (telecommunications outlet). This is the area where the users and telecommunications equipment connect to the structured cabling infrastructure. TIA/EIA-569-A recommendations for work areas include the following:

- A power outlet should be nearby but should maintain minimum power/telecommunications separation requirements (see NEC Article 800-52 for specific information).

- Each work area should have at least one telecommunications outlet box. TIA/EIA-568-A recommends that each telecommunications outlet box have a minimum of two outlets (one for voice and one for data).

- For voice applications, the PBX control center, attendant, and reception areas should have independent pathways to the appropriate telecommunications closets.

- Furniture needs should be taken into consideration.

- The minimum bend radius of cable should be exceeded at the opening in the wall.

TIA/EIA-569 also makes recommendations for wall openings for furniture pathways.

ANSI/TIA/EIA-607

The TIA defines a standard called the TIA/EIA-607 Commercial Building Grounding and Bonding Requirements for Telecommunications Standard. The purpose of this standard is to cover grounding and bonding to support a telecommunications system. This standard should be used in concert with Article 250 and Article 800 of the NEC. TIA/EIA-607 does *not* cover building grounding; it only covers the grounding of telecommunications systems.

TIA/EIA-607 specifies that the telecommunications ground must tie in with the building ground. Each telecommunications closet must have a telecommunications grounding system, which commonly consists of a "telecommunications bus bar." This bus bar is tied back to the building grounding system. All shielded cables, racks, and other metallic components should be tied into this bus bar.

TIA/EIA-607 specifies that the minimum ground wire size must be a 6 AWG wire, but depending on the distance that the ground wire must cover, it may be up to 3/0 AWG (a pretty large copper wire!). Ground wire sizing is based on the distance that the ground wire must travel; the further the distance, the larger the wire must be. TIA/EIA-607-A supplements (and is supplemented by) the NEC. For example, Article 800-33 specifies that telecommunications cables *entering* a building be grounded as near as possible to the point at which it enters the building.

TIP   When protecting a building with a building ground, don't overlook the need for lightning strike protection. Network and telephone components are often destroyed by a lightning strike. See NEC Article 780 for more information.

Grounding is one of the most commonly overlooked components during the installation of a structured cabling system. An improperly grounded communications system, even though it supports low voltage applications, can result in, well, a shocking experience. Time after time we have heard stories of telecommunications cabling systems that were improperly grounded (or not grounded at all) that have generated mild electrical or throw-you-off-your-feet shocks; they have even resulted in some deaths.

Grounding is not a subject to be undertaken by the do-it-yourselfer or an occasional cable installer. A professional electrician *must* be involved. They will know the best practices to follow, where to ground components, which components to ground, and the correct equipment to be used. Further, electricians must be involved when a telecommunications bus bar is tied into the main building ground system.

WARNING   Grounding to a water pipe may not provide you with sufficient grounding as many water systems now tie in to PVC-based (plastic) pipes.

Cabling @ Work: An Example of Poor Grounding

One of the best examples we can think of that illustrates poor grounding practices was a very large building that accidentally had two main grounds installed. A building should only have one main ground, yet in this building each side had a ground. A telecommunications backbone cable was then grounded to each main ground.

Under some circumstances, a ground loop formed that caused this cable to emit electromagnetic interference at specific frequencies. This frequency just so happened to be used by air traffic control beacons. When the building cable emitted signals on this frequency, it caused planes to think they were closer to the airport than they really were. One plane almost crashed as a result of this poorly grounded building. The FAA (Federal Aviation Administration) and the FCC (Federal Communications Commission) closed the building and shut down all electrical systems for weeks until the problem was eventually found.

ANSI/TIA/EIA-570-A

ANSI, the EIA, and the TIA published TIA/EIA-570-A, or the Residential and Light Commercial Telecommunications Cabling Standard, to address the growing need for "data-ready" homes. Just a few years ago, only the most serious of us geeks would have admitted to having a network in our homes. Today, more and more homes have small networks that consist of two or more home computers, a cable modem, and a shared printer. Even apartment buildings and condominiums are being built or remodeled to include data outlets; some apartment buildings and condos even provide direct Internet access.

The TIA/EIA-570-A standard provides standardized requirements for residential telecommunications cabling for two grades of information outlets: basic and multimedia cabling. This cabling is intended to support applications such as voice, data, video, home automation, security/alarm systems, environmental controls, and intercoms. The TIA/EIA-570-A standard specifies two grades of information outlets for residential cabling:

Grade 1   Intended to support basic telephone and video services. The standard recommends using one four-pair Category 3 or 5 UTP cable (Category 5 preferred) and one RG-6 coaxial cable.

Grade 2 Intended to support enhanced voice, video, and data service. The standard recommends using two four-pair Category 5 cables and two RG-6 coaxial cables. One Category 5 cable is used for voice and the other for data. One RG-6 cable is for satellite service and the other is for a local antenna or cable TV connection.

The standard further dictates that a central location within a home or multi-tenant building be chosen at which to install a central cabinet or wall-mounted rack to support the wiring. This location should be close to the telephone company demarcation point and near the entry point of cable TV connections. Once the cabling system is installed, you can use it to connect phones, televisions, computers, cable modems, and EIA-6000–compliant home automation devices.

> **TIP**
>
> The TIA/EIA-570-A standard does not require the use of plenum cable in residential cabling, but we recommend you use it anyway. Flames and smoke are spread much more quickly by nonplenum cable.

Other TIA/EIA Standards and Bulletins

The TIA/EIA alliance publishes additional standards and bulletins relating to data and voice cabling as well as performance testing. Table 2.15 shows many of these standards and bulletins, as well as some new standards that were developed and then incorporated into the TIA/EIA-568 standards.

TABLE 2.15: TIA/EIA Standards and Bulletins (and Standards Incorporated into TIA/EIA-568)

Standard	Description
TIA/EIA-569-A	*Commercial Building Standards for Telecommunications Pathways and Spaces* This standard specifies design and construction practices within and between buildings to support telecommunications media and equipment. Specific standards are included for areas through which telecommunications equipment media are installed.
TIA/EIA-606	*Administration Standard for the Telecommunications Infrastructure of Commercial Buildings* Specifies standard methods for labeling telecommunications infrastructure equipment such as pathways, spaces, and media-dependent applications. This includes specifications for labels, color coding, and data recording. This standard was incorporated into TIA/EIA-568-A in 1995.

Continued on next page

TABLE 2.15 CONTINUED: TIA/EIA Standards and Bulletins (and Standards Incorporated into TIA/EIA-568)

Standard	Description
TIA/EIA-607	*Commercial Building Grounding and Bonding Requirements for Telecommunications* This standard covers planning, design, and implementation of grounding systems to support multivendor and multiproduct environments.
TIA/EIA TSB-36	*Additional Cable Specifications for Unshielded Twisted-Pair Cables* This standard was incorporated into TIA/EIA-568-A in 1995 and is included in the "B" version as well. It provides performance characteristics for high performance UTP cabling and is primarily targeted towards cable manufacturers.
TIA/EIA TSB-40A	*Additional Transmission Specifications for Unshielded Twisted-Pair Connecting Hardware* This standard was incorporated into TIA/EIA-568-A in 1995 and is included in the "B" version as well. It provides transmission performance requirements for UTP connecting hardware for Category 3, 4, and 5 cable. Connecting hardware includes outlets, patch panels, transition connectors, and cross-connect blocks.
TIA/EIA TSB-53A	*Additional Specifications for Shielded Twisted-Pair (STP) Connecting Hardware* Provides transmission performance characteristics for STP connecting hardware. In 1995, this TSB was incorporated in to TIA/EIA-568-A and is included in the "B" version as well.
TIA/EIA TSB-67A	*Transmission Performance Specifications for Field Testing of UTP Cabling Systems* This bulletin provides test methods, performance parameters and minimum requirements for testing of Category 3, 4, and 5 cabling and related connecting hardware.
TIA/EIA TSB-72	*Centralized Optical Fiber Cabling Guidelines* Specifies guidelines and connecting hardware requirements for fiber optic cabling systems supporting centralized equipment located within a telecommunications closet or equipment room. This bulletin was incorporated into TIA/EIA-568-A and is included in the "B" version as well.
TIA/EIA TSB-95	*Additional Transmission Performance Guidelines for 100-ohm Four-Pair Category 5 Cabling* Defines additional performance characteristics that should be tested above and beyond the parameters specified in TSB-67. These are to be used with existing Category 5 cabling systems to ensure they will support Gigabit Ethernet systems.

As requirements and cabling changes, standards are updated and new TSBs are issued. Table 2.16 shows some of the emerging standards and TSBs.

TABLE 2.16:   Emerging Standards and Bulletins

Standard	Description
TIA/EIA-568-A.5	*Performance Specifications for Category 5E Channels* This is the updated version of TIA/EIA-568-A. It defines new performance categories (such as delay skew and ELFEXT) for Category 5e cabling.
TSB-96	*Field Certification of Installed Category 5 Channels and Level II-E Test Equipment* Specifies additional performance categories for field testing of Category 5 and 5e cabling required to support Gigabit Ethernet (1000Base-T). It introduces new testing parameters such as ELFEXT, return loss, propagation delay, and delay skew. This bulletin will also specify tighter requirements for a new level of field test equipment (Level II-E).
TIA/EIA 526-14	*Optical Power Loss Measurements of Installed Multimode Fiber Cable Plant* Specifies guidelines and procedures for measuring optical loss between two passively connected points of a multimode fiber optic cabling plant. This standard specifies light sources, test jumpers, calibration, accuracy, interpretation of results, and documentation.
TIA/EIA 526-7	*Measurement of Optical Power Loss of Installed Single-Mode Fiber Cable Plant* Specifies guidelines and procedures for measuring optical loss between two passively connected points of a single-mode fiber optic cabling plant.
Category 6	*Transmission Performance Specifications for Four-Pair 100-ohm Category 6 Cabling* Specifies components such as cabling and connecting hardware and defines basic link and channel definitions for Category 6 channels and Level III field tester requirements. Ratification is not expected before late 2000 or early 2001.
Category 7	*Transmission Performance Specifications for Four-Pair 100-ohm Cabling at Bandwidth up to 600Mhz* Work has just begun creating a specification for Category 7 cabling running at 600Mhz. This standard will require different connecting hardware and a different cable design. Interestingly, TIA is not directly involved in this standard, but will probably adopt whatever standard the ISO comes up with. No realistic time frame can be established for ratification since so much work needs to be done on this cable standard, but it will be sometime in 2001 or later.

If you want to keep up on the latest TIA/EIA standards and the work of the various committees, visit the TIA Web site at `www.tiaonline.org/standard/sfg` and go to the TR-42 committee page.

ISO/IEC 11801

The International Organization Standards (ISO) and the International Electrotechnical Commission (IEC) publish a standard called ISO/IEC 11801; ISO/IEC 11801 is predominantly used in Europe. This standard was released in 1995 and is similar in many ways to the TIA/EIA-568 standards, upon which it is based. However, there are a number of differences in terminology and some slightly different specifications. Table 2.17 shows the common codes and elements of an ISO/IEC 11801 structured cabling system.

TABLE 2.17: Common Codes and Elements Defined by ISO/IEC 11801

Element	Code	Description
Building distributor	BD	A distributor in which building-to-building backbone cabling terminates and where connections to interbuilding or campus backbone cables are made.
Building entrance facilities	BEF	Location provided for the necessary electrical and mechanical services necessary to support telecommunications cabling entering a building.
Campus distributor	CD	Distributor location from which campus backbone cabling originates.
Equipment room	ER	Location within a building dedicated to housing distributors and specific equipment.
Equipment room	FD	A distributor used to connect between horizontal cable and other cabling subsystems or equipment.
Horizontal cable	HC	Cable from the floor distributor to the telecommunications outlet.
Telecommunications closet	TC	Cross-connection point between backbone cabling and horizontal cabling. May house telecommunications equipment, cable terminations, cross-connect cabling, and data networking equipment.
Telecommunications outlet	TO	The point where the horizontal cabling terminates on a wall plate or other permanent fixture. This provides interface to the work-area cabling.
Transition point	TP	The location in horizontal cabling where a change of cable form takes place, such as from round to under-carpet cable.
Work-area cable		Connects equipment in the work area (phones, computers, etc.) to the telecommunications outlet.

Some of the differences between TIA/EIA-568-A and ISO/IEC 11801 include:

*   ISO/IEC 11801 provides allowances for two additional media types for use with backbone and horizontal cabling, 120-ohm UTP cable and 50/125-micron multimode optical fiber.

*   The transition point term is much broader with ISO/IEC 11801, which includes not only transition points such as under-carpet cable to round cable (as defined by TIA/EIA-568-A), but also consolidation point connections.

*   ISO/IEC 11801 specifies a maximum patch cable and cross-connect length of five meters (16.4 feet).

Some terminology differences between TIA/EIA-568-A and ISO/IEC 11801 include:

*   The ISO/IEC 11801 definition of the campus distributor (CD) is similar to the TIA/EIA-568-A definition of a main cross-connect (MC).

*   The ISO/IEC 11801 definition of a building distributor (BD) is equal to the TIA/EIA-568-A definition of an intermediate cross-connect (IC).

*   The ISO/IEC 11801 definition of a floor distributor is defined by TIA/EIA-568-A as the horizontal cross-connect (HC).

Classification of Applications and Links

ISO/IEC 11801 defines classes of applications and links based on the type of media that is being used and the frequency requirements. The original 11801 standard defines four classes of applications for copper and one for fiber optic cabling. The ISO/IEC 11801 specifies the following classes of applications and links:

Class A   Voice and low frequency rate applications up to 100kHz

Class B   Low speed data applications operating at frequencies up to 1MHz

Class C   Medium speed data applications operating at frequencies up to 16MHz

Class D   High-speed applications operating at frequencies up to 100MHz

Optical Class   Applications where bandwidth is not a limiting factor

These applications are then cross-referenced based on the category of cabling that will support them and the maximum permissible distances. Table 2.18 illustrates the categories, classes, and permissible distances.

TABLE 2.18: Maximum Distances for Classes of Application and Categories of Cable

Media	Class A	Class B	Class C	Class D	Optical
Category 3	2km	200m	100m	-	-
Category 4	3km	260m	150m	-	-
Category 5	3km	260m	260m	100m	-
150-ohm shielded cable	3km	400m	250m	150m	-
Multimode optical fiber	-	-	-	-	2km
Single-mode optical fiber	-	-	-	-	3km

Distances include allowances for patch cables, jumpers, and equipment connections. The basic link specification for Class C applications on Category 3 cable and Class D applications on Category 5 cable is 90 meters.

Anixter Cable Performance Levels Program

The networking industry is rapidly changing; new technologies are released every few months, and updates to existing technologies occur almost constantly. Such rapid change in the industry is not conducive to clear, sweeping standards. Standards can take years to ratify; often by the time a standard can be agreed upon and published, it is no longer useful to those that are rapidly deploying leading edge technologies.

If you have picked up a catalog of cabling components recently, you have probably seen twisted-pair cabling products promising performance (lower attenuation values and higher crosstalk and return loss values) better than Category 5 cabling. Some of these cable products call themselves category 5 plus, category 6, category 7, or other such names—note that "category" is in lowercase. The TIA has working groups in the process of revising the TIA/EIA standards all the time and many of these "better than Category 5" cable types will eventually become standards.

The problem is that they are not currently standards. A vendor that advertises category 6 or category 7 performance is really not giving you any further data to compare other types of cables from other vendors. Differentiating these products becomes nearly impossible.

NOTE

> Don't confuse the TIA/EIA Categories (with a capital "C") with Anixter Cable Performance Levels. Though they are quite similar, cabling products that are classified for a specified Anixter Level meet or exceed standards put forth by standards organizations.

For this reason, Anixter (`www.anixter.com`), a worldwide distributor of communications products and cable, developed the Anixter Cable Performance Levels program (also called ALC or Anixter Levels Channel) . The initial document was published in 1989 and defined three levels of cable performance for twisted-pair cabling. Anixter tested and categorized the products that they sold, regardless of the manufacturer, so that customers can properly choose products and compare products between vendors. These levels included:

Level 1   Minimum quality cable required for telephone voice-grade applications

Level 2   Minimum quality cable required to support low speed (less than 1.2Mbps) data communications such as mainframe and minicomputer terminals

Level 3   Minimum quality cable required to support 10Mbps Ethernet and 4/16Mbps Token Ring

These cable types were defined three years prior to the first ANSI/TIA/EIA-568 standard, which defined Category 1, 2, and 3 cabling. When the first iteration of TIA/EIA-568 was released in 1991, vendors were already making promises of higher performance and better cabling. To meet these needs, Anixter added two new levels:

Level 4   Minimum quality cable required to support applications operating at a frequency of up to 20MHz, which would include passive 16Mbps Token Ring.

Level 5 Minimum quality cable required to support applications operating at frequencies up to 100MHz. The original intent of Level 5 was to provide a copper version of Fiber Distributed Data Interface (FDDI).

Anixter no longer maintains Levels 1 through 4, since the performance requirements for those levels are specified by the TIA/EIA-568-A Categories and ISO/IEC 11801 standards. However, Anixter's Level 5 specification exceeds the new Category 5e performance specifications.

ALC: Looking Forward

By 1997, there were newer networking technologies on the horizon. At that time, the need for better twisted-pair cable performance was becoming evident. To complicate matters even further, there were over 150 different constructions of Category 5 cabling. Some of these Category 5 cables performed half as well as others.

To further help customers compare cable technologies that would exceed Category 5 standards, two additional levels of performance have been specified in the Anixter Levels 97 program. The Level 5 specification was also updated. The performance levels specified by the ALC 97 program include the following:

Level 5 Minimum cable performance required to handle frequencies up to 200MHz

Level 6 Minimum cable performance required to handle frequencies up to 350MHz

Level 7 Minimum cable performance required to handle frequencies up to 400MHz

NOTE In order for a vendor's cables or components to be categorized as part of the Anixter Levels Program, Anixter must test the components in their own lab, the manufacturer must use only virgin materials, and the manufacturer must be ISO 9000 registered.

What About Components?

We would like to put forth a word of caution here that will be reiterated throughout this book. If you are requiring Level 5, 6, or 7 performance from your cabling infrastructure, choosing the correct level of cable is only a small part of the decision. Anixter further tests and certifies components (patch panels, wall plates, patch cables, connectors, etc.) to be used with the cabling.

The components used must also be certified to the same level as the cable. Further, we recommend that you use components from the same manufacturer as the cable you are purchasing. (Some cable and component manufacturer is going to love us for saying that!) Finally, solid installation practices must be followed to get the performance you are expecting.

Other Cabling Technologies

Over the years, a number of vendor-specific systems were widely adopted and came to be considered de facto standards. Some of these are still widely used today. As a customer, one of the things that makes a proprietary cabling system attractive is that there is only one company to name in the law suit. (That was a poor attempt at humor.) Seriously, when a single company is responsible for the components and installation as well as the cable, you can be assured that the cabling infrastructure as a whole should function as promised.

Complications arise when vendors and competing technologies need to be integrated together. Though some of these systems may lock the customer into a single vendor solution, the advantages of that single vendor solution may be attractive. Some of the more popular vendor solutions include:

- The IBM Cabling System
- Lucent Technologies SYSTIMAX
- Digital Equipment Corporation's DECconnect
- NORDX/CDT Integrated Building Distribution System

The focus of this book is centered on the TIA/EIA-568-A standards, but the above standards deserve mentioning and are briefly discussed in the following pages.

The IBM Cabling System

In the early 1980s, specifications for cabling and structure were even more rare than they were in the late 1980s. In an attempt to encourage a single standard for cabling, in 1984 IBM developed its own cabling system called the *IBM Cabling System*. Though we personally disliked working with the IBM Cabling System, we do respect the fact that IBM was way ahead of the rest of the industry in promoting a standard cabling system. IBM cabling is still in wide enough use to deserve a mention here.

The original IBM Cabling System defined a number of different components, including:

- Cable types
- Data connectors
- Face plates
- Distribution panels

IBM Cable Types

The IBM Cabling System defines cables as Types rather than Categories or Levels. There are seven types of cable defined by the IBM Cabling System.

Type 1A   Type 1A cabling (originally known simply as Type 1) is the only cable type that was adopted as part of the TIA/EIA-568-A standard. Type 1A cable was designed to support 4- and 16Mbps Token Ring, but has been improved to support FDDI over copper and video applications operating at frequency rates of up to 300MHz. The ISO is currently working on a specification that will allow STP cable to operate at frequencies up to 600MHz.

Type 1A (shown in Figure 2.8) cabling consists of two pairs of twisted-pair wire (22 AWG). The wire impedance is 15 ohms, plus or minus 10 percent. Each wire is insulated and the wire pair is twisted; each pair is then encased in additional shielding. Both pairs are then encased in additional shielding. This design results in less attenuation and significantly better NEXT performance. The same type of cable can be used for horizontal cabling as well as patch cabling.

Type 2A   Type 2A cabling (originally known simply as Type 2) is essentially the same cable as IBM Type 1A. Type 2A is also shown in Figure 2.8; the difference is that in addition to the shielded twisted-pair of Type 1A, there are four pairs of unshielded twisted-pair cable outside the main shield. These additional pairs are Category 3–compliant and can be used for applications that do not require shielded twisted cable, such as voice applications.

FIGURE 2.8:

IBM Cabling System Type 1A and Type 2A cabling

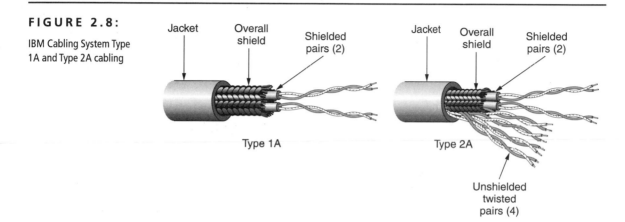

Type 1A   Type 2A

Type 3   Type 3 cable is voice grade, unshielded twisted-pair cable. It consists of four solid, unshielded twisted-pair 22 AWG or 24 AWG pairs. The twisted pairs have a minimum of two twists per foot and impedance of 100 ohms through a frequency range of 256KHz to 2.3MHz. Do not confuse Type 3 with Category 3, because the performance specifications are different.

Type 5   Type 5 cable consists of two 62.5/125-micron multimode fibers in an optical cable. IBM has also used 50/125- and 100/140-micron fiber optic cable, but since 62.5/125-micron is the de facto standard for FDDI and is included in both the TIA/EIA-568-A and ISO/IEC 11801 standards, it is more desirable. Three connector types are specified, SMA, ST, and SC connectors.

Type 6   Type 6 cable consists of two twisted-pair cables with one shield. The wires are 26 AWG stranded cable with an impedance of 150 ohms, plus or minus 10 percent. Designed to be used as station or patch cable up to a 30-meter maximum.

Type 8   Type 8 cable is designed for use under carpeting. The cable is housed in a flat jacket and consists of two shielded twisted-pair 22 AWG cables with an impedance of 100 ohms. Type 8 cable is limited to 50 percent of the distance that can be used with Type 1A cable.

Type 9 Type 9 cable is similar to Type 6. It consists of two 26 AWG wire pairs twisted together and then shielded. The wire core can be either stranded or solid, and the impedance is 150 ohms, plus or minus 10 percent. The advantage of using Type 9 is that it has a smaller diameter and accepts eight-position modular jack connectors (a.k.a. RJ-45). Though Type 9 was designed to be used to connect from the wall plate to the station adapter, it can be used as horizontal cabling as well.

IBM Data Connector

The most unique component of the IBM Cabling System is the IBM connector. The IBM connector (or simply data connector) is neither a male connector nor a female connector, but rather hermaphroditic. Two identical connectors can be connected to each other.

This data connector is used in patch panels, hubs, and wall plates. The beauty of this connector is that it eliminated the need for complementary male and female connectors. The data connector (shown in Figure 2.9) is commonly used with IBM Token Ring MAUs.

FIGURE 2.9:

IBM data connector

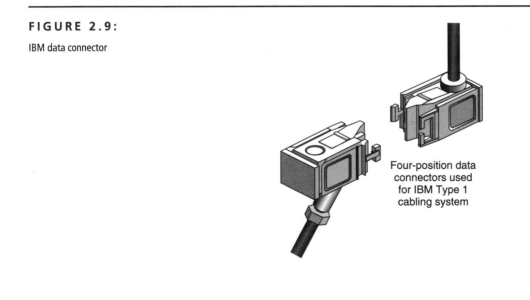

Four-position data connectors used for IBM Type 1 cabling system

Lucent SYSTIMAX SCS Cabling System

The Bell Labs subsidiary of Lucent Technologies (formerly AT&T) developed the *SYSTIMAX SCS (Structured Connectivity Solutions) Cabling System*. Calling SYSTI-MAX SCS Cabling System a proprietary solution would be a stretch, since the SYSTIMAX is based on the TIA/EIA-568 standards.

Lucent has developed a number of structured connectivity solutions that include copper and fiber media. These modular solutions incorporate Lucent cabling and components as well as Lucent cable management and patch panels. Lucent has solutions that can provide up to 622Mbps over copper.

Since Lucent is providing a single-vendor solution for all components, it is much easier for them to take a holistic approach to cable performance and reliability. Rather than looking at the performance of individual components, the SYS-TIMAX designers look at performance optimization for the entire channel.

For further information about the SYSTIMAX SCS Cabling System, check them out on the Web at www.lucent.com/netsys/systimax.

Digital Equipment Corporation DECconnect

Digital Equipment Corporation designed the DECconnect system to provide a structured cabling system for their customers. DECconnect consists of four different types of technologies and five different cable types (listed in Table 2.19). DECconnect never caught on as a widely used cabling system for Local Area Networking and voice applications, though we still see it at customers with VAXs.

TABLE 2.19: DECconnect Applications and Cable Types

Application	Cable Type	Connector Type
Voice	Four-pair UTP	RJ-45
Low-speed data (terminals)	Two-pair UTP	Modified, keyed RJ-45
Network	50-ohm coax	BNC
Network	62.5/125-micron fiber	ST or SMA
Video	75-ohm coax	F-Type

One of the downsides of the DECconnect system was the variety of cable types that had to be run. If you had locations that required a terminal, PC with Ethernet, and a PBX telephone, you would possibly have to run three separate types of horizontal cable to a single wall plate. With modern structured cabling systems such as the TIA/EIA-568-A standard, a single cable type could be used, though three cables must still be run.

NORDX/CDT Integrated Building Distribution System

The Integrated Building Distribution System (IBDN) originated with Northern Telecom (Nortel) and is now sold by NORDX/CDT. The IBDN system is similar to the Lucent SYSTIMAX SCS system and TIA/EIA-568-A. When used within the guidelines of the TIA/EIA-568-A, IBDN is standards-compliant. For more information on IBDN, see the NORDX/CDT Web site at www.nordx.com.

Choosing the Correct Cabling

Technically, when you begin the planning stages of a new cabling installation, you should not have to worry about the types of applications that will be used. The whole point of structured cabling standards such as TIA/EIA-568-A and ISO/IEC 11801 is that they will support almost any networking or voice application in use today.

Still, it is a good idea to have an understanding of the networking application you are cabling for and how that can affect the use of the cabling system. Further, since cabling that's related to data also connects to various types of network devices, it is a good idea to have an understanding of the networking hardware that is used in common installations.

Topologies

The network's *topology* refers to the physical layout of the nodes and hubs that make up the network. Choosing the right topology is important because the topology affects the type of networking equipment, cabling, growth path, and network management.

Today's networking architectures fall into one of three categories:

- Star
- Bus
- Ring

Topologies are tricky because some networking architectures appear to be one type of technology but are in reality another. Token Ring is a good example of this since Token Ring uses *hubs* (MAUs). All stations are connected centrally to a hub so it appears to be a star topology, but in reality it is still a ring topology. Often two topology types will be used together to expand a network.

NOTE   Ethernet and Token Ring are sometimes mistakenly referred to as topologies, but they are actually network architectures.

Star Topology

When implementing a *star topology*, all computers are connected to a single centrally located point. This central point is usually a hub. All cabling used in a star topology is also run from the point where the network nodes are located back to a central location. Figure 3.1 shows a simple star topology.

FIGURE 3.1:

Star topology with a central hub

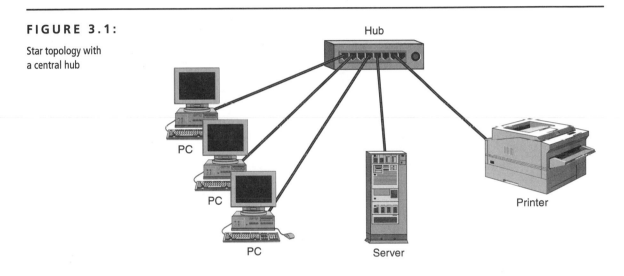

NOTE   A hub by any other name would still be a hub. In the early days of UTP Ethernet, the Ethernet equipment manufacturer Synoptics called their hubs "concentrators." IBM still refers to their STP hubs sometimes as MAUs or MSAUs (multistation access units) and their UTP hubs as CAUs or CSAUs. Still other manufacturers and users refer to a hub as a repeater because it repeats the signal it receives to all nodes.

From the perspective of cabling, the star topology is the most common and is also the easiest to cable. The TIA/EIA-568-A and ISO/IEC 11801 standards assume that the network architecture uses a star topology. If a single node on the star fails or the cable to that node fails, then only that single node fails. However, if the hub fails, then the entire star fails.

Killing an Entire Star Topology

While a single node failure cannot usually take down an entire star topology, situations occur in which it can. In some circumstances, a node fails and causes interference for the entire star. In other cases, shorts in a single cable can send disruptive electrical signals back to the hub and cause the entire star to cease functioning. Of course, failure of the hub will also affect all nodes in a star topology.

Bus Topology

The *bus topology* is the simplest network topology. Also known as a linear bus, all computers are connected to a contiguous cable or a cable that is joined together to make it contiguous. Figure 3.2 illustrates a bus topology.

FIGURE 3.2:

Bus topology

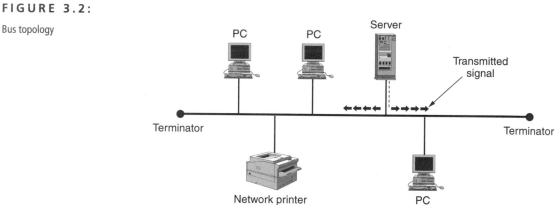

Ethernet is a common example of a bus topology. Each computer determines when the network is not busy and transmits data as needed. Computers in a bus topology only listen for transmissions from other computers; they do not repeat or forward the transmission on to other computers.

The signal in a bus topology travels to both ends of the cable. To keep the signal from bouncing back and forth on the cable, both ends of the cable in a bus topology must be terminated. A component called a *terminator*, essentially nothing more than a resistor, is placed on both ends of the cable. The terminator absorbs the signal and keeps it from bouncing; this is referred to as *maximum impedance*. If either terminator is removed or if the cable is cut anywhere along its length, all computers on the bus will fail to communicate.

Coaxial cabling is most commonly used in true bus topology networks such as thin/thick Ethernet. However, 10Base-T Ethernet still functions as if it were a bus topology even though it is wired as a star topology.

Ring Topology

A *ring topology* requires that all computers be connected in a contiguous circle, as shown in Figure 3.3. There are no ends to the ring and there is no hub. Each computer in the ring receives signals (data) from its neighbor, repeats the signal, and passes it along to the next node in the ring. Since the signal has to pass through each computer on the ring, a single node or cable failure can take the entire ring down.

FIGURE 3.3:

Ring topology

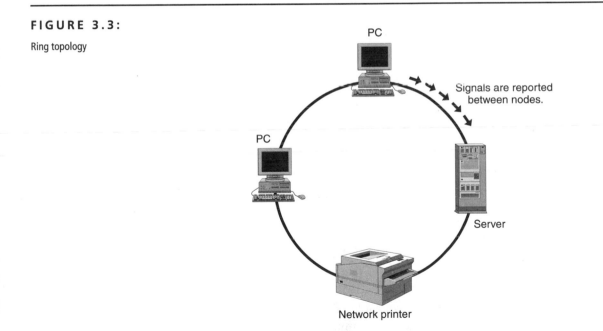

A true ring topology is a pain in the neck to install cable for because it is difficult to expand a ring over a large physical area due to the fact that the cable has to remain in a circle. Token Ring is a ring topology. Even though Token Ring stations may be connected to a central MAU (and thus appear to be a star topology), the data on the Token Ring travels from one node to another. It passes though the MAU each time.

UTP, Optical Fiber, and Future-Proofing

The common networking technologies today (Ethernet, Token Ring, FDDI, and ATM) can all use either UTP or optical fiber cabling, and IT professionals are faced with the choice of which cable media to choose. MIS managers and network administrators hear a lot about "future-proofing" their cabling infrastructures. If you believe the hype from some cabling vendors, installing their particular cable and components will guarantee that you won't have to ever update your cabling system again. However, you should keep in mind that in the early 1990s, network managers thought they were future-proofing their cabling system when they installed Category 4 cabling rather than Category 3 cabling.

Today, the same type of dilemma faces decision-makers trying to decide if they want Category 5, 5e, or 6 cabling and components. Add to this the additional complexity of deciding whether or not you should include optical fiber cabling. Here are some of the advantages of using optical fiber:

- It has higher potential bandwidth.
- It's not susceptible to electromagnetic interference.
- It can transmit over longer distance.
- Improved termination techniques and equipment make it more desirable.
- Cable, connectors, and patch panels are now cheaper than they used to be.
- It's valuable in situations where EMI is especially high.
- It offers better security (because the cable cannot be spliced or monitored).

Though optical fiber cable has come of age, there are still some reasons that you may want to consider remaining with UTP cabling. Some reasons for doing this include the following:

- Fiber optic cable installation is 10 to 15 percent more expensive than an equivalent Category 5e installation.

- Networking hardware (network interface cards and hubs) is two to three times more expensive than UTP-based hardware.

- Higher bandwidth requirements are not an issue for you.

- Cable security concerns are not a valid issue for you.

- You have no EMI interference.

When considering optical fiber cable, remember that you are trying to guarantee that the cabling system will not have to be replaced for a very long time, regardless of future networking technologies that may appear. Some questions you should ask yourself when deciding if fiber optic is right for you include:

- Do you rent or own your current location?

- If you rent, how long is your lease, and will you be renewing your lease when it is up?

- Are there major renovations planned that would cause walls to be torn out and rebuilt?

If you will be occupying your present space for longer than five years and you want to guarantee that your cabling infrastructure will be future-proofed, optical fiber may be the right choice for your horizontal cabling. Don't forget to take into consideration the higher cost of networking hardware prior to making any decisions.

Network Architectures

The TIA/EIA-568-A cabling standard covers almost any possible combination of cable necessary to take advantage of the current network architectures that can be found in today's business environment. These network architectures include Ethernet, Token Ring, Fiber Distributed Data Interface (FDDI), Asynchronous Transfer Mode (ATM), and 100VG-AnyLAN. Understanding the different types of cable that these architectures can take advantage of is also important.

Ethernet

Ethernet is the most mature and common of the network architectures. According to technology analysts IDC (International Data Corporation), Ethernet is used in over 80 percent of all network installations.

In some form or fashion, Ethernet has been around for over 30 years. A predecessor to Ethernet was developed by the University of Hawaii (called, appropriately, the Alohanet) to connect geographically dispersed computers. This radio-based network operated at 9,600Kbps and used an access method called CSMA/CD (Carrier Sense Multiple Access/Collision Detection), in which computers "listen" to the cable and transmit data if there is no traffic. If two computers transmit data at exactly the same time, the nodes must detect that a "collision" has occurred and retransmit the data. Extremely busy CSMA/CD-based networks can become very slow when collisions become excessive.

In the early 1970s, Robert Metcalfe and David Boggs, scientists at Xerox's Palo Alto Research Center (PARC), developed a cabling and signaling scheme that used CSMA/CD and was loosely based on the Alohanet. This early version of Ethernet used coaxial cable and operated at 2.94Mbps. Even early on, Ethernet was so successful that Xerox (along with Digital Equipment Corporation and Intel) updated it to support 10Mbps. Ethernet was the basis for the IEEE 802.3 standard for CSMA/CD networks.

NOTE   Ever seen the term *DIX*? Or DIX connector? DIX is an abbreviation for Digital, Intel, and Xerox. The DIX connector is also known as the AUI (attachment unit interface), which is the 15-pin connector that you see on older Ethernet cards and transceivers.

Over the past 25 years, despite stiff competition from more modern network architectures, Ethernet has survived and flourished. In the past 10 years alone, Ethernet has been updated to support speeds of 100Mbps and 1000Mbps; currently researchers are planning 10Gbps Ethernet!

Ethernet has evolved to the point that it can be used on a number of different cabling systems. Table 3.1 lists some of the Ethernet technologies. The first number in an Ethernet designator indicates the speed of the network, the second portion (the *base* portion) indicates baseband, and the third indicates the maximum distance or the media type.

TABLE 3.1:   Cracking the Ethernet Designation Codes

Designation	Description
10Base-2	10Mbps Ethernet over thinnet coaxial cable (RG-58) with a maximum segment distance of 185 meters (they rounded up and call it 10Base-2 instead of 10Base185).
10Base-5	10Mbps Ethernet over thick (50-ohm) coaxial cable with a maximum segment distance of 500 meters.
10Base-36	10Mbps. This is actually a broadband implementation of Ethernet with a maximum segment length of 3,600 meters.
10Base-T	10Mbps Ethernet over unshielded twisted-pair cable. Maximum cable length (hub to network card) is 100 meters.
10Base-FL	10Mbps Ethernet over multimode optical fiber cable. Designed for connectivity between network interface cards on the desktop and a fiber optic Ethernet hub. Maximum cable length (hub to network card) is 2000 meters.
10Base-FB	10Mbps Ethernet over multimode optical fiber cable. Designed to use a signaling technique that allows a 10Base-FB backbone to exceed the maximum number of repeaters permitted by Ethernet. Maximum cable length is 2000 meters.
10Base-FP	10Mbps Ethernet over multimode optical fiber cable designed to allow linking multiple computers without a repeater. Not commonly used. Maximum of 33 computers per segment, and the maximum cable length is 500 meters.
100Base-TX	100Mbps Ethernet over Category 5 or better UTP cabling using two wire pairs. Maximum cable distance is 100 meters.
100Base-T4	100Mbps Ethernet over Category 3 or better UTP cabling using all four wire pairs. Maximum distance using Category 3 cable is 100 meters.
100Base-FX	100Mbps Ethernet over multimode optical fiber cable. Maximum cable distance is 400 meters.
100Base-VG	More of a first cousin of Ethernet. This is actually 100VG-AnyLAN, which is described later in this chapter.
1000Base-SX	Gigabit Ethernet over multimode optical fiber cable designed for workstation to hub implementations.
1000Base-LX	Gigabit Ethernet over single-mode optical fiber cable designed for backbone implementations
1000Base-CX	Gigabit Ethernet over STP Type 1 cabling designed for equipment interconnection such as clusters. Maximum distance is 25 meters.
1000Base-T	Gigabit Ethernet over Category 5 or better UTP cable where the installation has passed performance tests specified by TSB-95. Maximum distance is 100 meters from network interface card to hub.

KEY TERMS **Baseband and Broadband**   *Baseband* network equipment transmit an unmodulated digital signal, whereas *broadband* networks modulate the signal (or convert it to analog) for transmission.

10Mbps Ethernet Systems

Why is Ethernet so popular? On a properly designed and cabled network, Ethernet is fast, easy to install, reliable, and cheap. Ethernet can be installed on almost any type of structured cabling system, including unshielded twisted pair and fiber optic cable.

10Base-5: "Standard Ethernet Cable"

The earliest version of Ethernet ran on a rigid coaxial cable that was called Standard Ethernet cable but was more commonly referred to as *thicknet*. To connect a node to the thicknet cable, a specially designed connector was attached to the cable (called a *vampire tap* or *piercing tap*).

When the connector was tightened down on to the cable, the tap pierced the jacket, shielding, and insulation to make contact with the inner core of the cable. This connector had a transceiver attached, to which a transceiver cable (or drop cable) was attached. The transceiver cable connected to the network node.

Though thicknet was difficult to work with (because it was not very flexible and was hard to install and connect nodes to), it was reliable and had a usable cable length of 500 meters (about 1640 feet). That is where the "10" and the "5" in 10Base-5 come from: *10Mbps, baseband, 500 meters.*

Though we never see new installations of 10Base-5 systems anymore, it can still be found in older installations, where it is typically used as backbone cable. 10Base-T hubs and coaxial (thinnet) cabling are attached at various places along the length of the cable. Given the wide availability of fiber optic equipment and inexpensive hubs and UTP cabling, there is virtually no reason that you would install a new 10Base-5 system today.

10Base-T Ethernet   For over 10 years, 10Base-T (the T stands for twisted pair) Ethernet has reigned as king of the network architectures. There is a good reason for this: 10Base-T Ethernet will work over any standard Category 3 or better UTP cabling, and UTP cabling is cheap to install, reliable, and easy to manage.

TIP If you are cabling a facility for 10Base-T, plan to use, at a minimum, Category 5 cable and components. The incremental price is only slightly higher than Category 3, and you will be providing a growth path to faster network technologies.

Some important facts about 10Base-T:

- The maximum cable length of a 10Base-T segment is 100 meters (328 feet) when using Category 3 cabling. Somewhat longer distances may be achieved with higher grades of equipment, but remember that you are no longer following the standards if you attempt this.

- The minimum length of a 10Base-T cable (node to hub) is 2.5 meters (about 8 feet).

- A 10Base-T network can have a maximum of 1,024 computers on it; however, performance may be extremely poor on large networks.

- For older network devices that have only AUI type connectors, transceivers can be purchased to convert to 10Base-T.

- Though a 10Base-T network appears to operate like a star topology, internally it is still a bus topology. Unless a technology like switching or bridging is employed, a signal on a single network segment will be repeated to all nodes on the network.

- 10Base-T requires only two wire pairs of an 8-pin modular jack to operate. Figure 3.4 shows the pin layout and their usage.

FIGURE 3.4:

8-pin modular jack used with 10Base-T

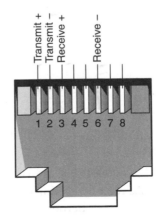

TIP   Even though 10Base-T uses only two pairs of a four-pair cable, all eight pins should be connected properly.

10Base-F Ethernet

Standards for using Ethernet over fiber optic cable existed back in the early 1980s. Originally, fiber optic cable was simply used to connect repeaters whose separation exceeded the distance limitations of thicknet cable. The original specification was called Fiber Optic Inter Repeater Link (FOIRL), which provided the ability to link two repeaters together with fiber optic cable up to 1,000 meters (3,280 feet) in length.

NOTE   Unless stated otherwise, all fiber optic devices use multimode optical fiber cable.

The cost of fiber optic repeaters and fiber optic cabling dropped greatly during the 1980s, and connecting individual computers directly to the hub via fiber optic cable became more common. Originally, the FOIRL standard was not designed with individual computers in mind, so the IEEE developed a series of fiber optic media standards. These standards are collectively known as 10Base-F. The individual specifications for 10Base-F Ethernet include the following:

10Base-FL   An updated version of the FOIRL specification that is designed to interoperate with existing FOIRL equipment. Maximum distance used between 10Base-FL and an FOIRL device is 1,000 meters, but it is 2,000 meters (6,561 feet) between two 10Base-FL devices. 10Base-FL is most commonly used to connect network nodes to hubs and to interconnect hubs. Most modern Ethernet equipment upports 10Base-FL; it is the most common of the 10Base-F specifications.

10Base-FB   A specification that describes a synchronous signaling backbone segment. This specification allows the development of a backbone segment that exceeds the maximum number of repeaters that may be used in a 10Mbps Ethernet system. 10Base-FB is available only from a limited number of manufacturers and supports distances of up to 2,000 meters.

10Base-FP   A specification that provides the capability for a fiber optic mixing segment that links multiple computers on a fiber optic system without repeaters. 10Base-FP segments may be up to 500 meters (1,640 feet), and a single 10Base-FP segment (passive star coupler) can link up to 33 computers. This specification has not been adopted by many vendors and is not widely available.

Why Use 10Base-FL?

In the past, fiber optic cable was considered expensive, but it is becoming more and more affordable. In fact, fiber optic installations are becoming nearly as inexpensive as UTP copper installations. The major point that causes some network managers to cringe is that the network equipment is also more expensive. A recent price comparison found one popular 10Base-F network interface card was more than 2.5 times more expensive than the 10Base-T equivalent.

However, fiber optic cable, regardless of the network architecture, has key benefits for many businesses. Choosing 10Base-FL allows you to take advantage of these benefits for both current use and the future:

- Fiber optic cable will make it easy to incorporate newer and faster technologies in the future.

- Fiber optic cable is not subject to electromagnetic interference, nor does it generate interference.

- Fiber optic cable cannot be tapped and is not subject to emanations, so it is more secure.

- Potential bandwidth of fiber optic cable is greater than any current or forecast copper technologies.

These facts make fiber optic cable more desirable for customers who are concerned about security, growth, or electromagnetic interference. Fiber is commonly used in hospitals and military environments.

Getting the Fiber Optic Cable Right

A number of manufacturers make equipment that supports Ethernet over fiber optic cabling. One of the most important things you will do during the planning of a 10Base-F installation is to pick the right cable and connecting hardware. Here are some pointers:

- Use 62.5/125-micron multimode fiber optic cable.

- Each horizontal run should have at least two strands of multimode fiber.

- Make sure that the connector type for your patch panels and patch cables matches the hardware you are choosing. Some older equipment uses exclusively ST connector while newer equipment uses the more common SC connector.

10Base-2 Ethernet   Though not as common as it once was, 10Base-2 is still an excellent way to connect a small number of computers together in a small physical area such as a home office, classroom, or lab. 10Base-2 Ethernet uses thin coaxial (RG-58 /U or RG-58 A/U) to connect computers together. This thin coaxial cable is also called *thinnet*.

Coaxial cable and network interface cards use a special connector called a BNC connector. This male connector (on the network interface card) is inserted into the female, and the female connector (called a T-connector) is then twisted 90 degrees to lock it into place. The T-connector allows two cables to be connected on each side of it, and the middle of the T-connector plugs into the network interface card. The thinnet cable never connects directly to the network interface card. This arrangement is shown in Figure 3.5.

FIGURE 3.5:

10Base-2 network

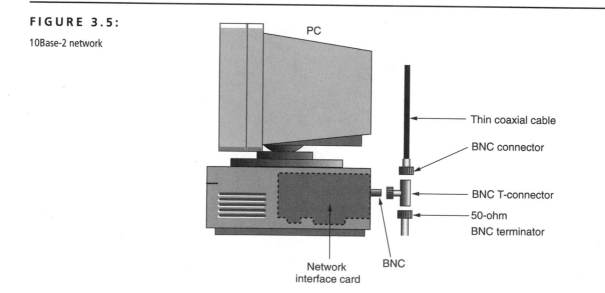

PC

Thin coaxial cable

BNC connector

BNC T-connector

50-ohm
BNC terminator

Network
interface card

BNC

NOTE   *BNC* is an abbreviation for Bayonet-Neill-Concelman. The B indicates that the connector is a bayonet-type connection, and Neill and Concelman are the inventors of the connector. You may also hear this connector called a British Naval Connector.

The TIA/EIA-568-A standard does not recommend the use of coaxial cabling, though it recognizes that coaxial cabling still exists. The next revision of the TIA/EIA-568 standard will probably remove any mention of coaxial cable. From our own experience, here are some reasons *not* to use 10Base-2:

- You plan to connect more than 10 computers on a single segment.

- Ethernet cards with thinnet (BNC) connections are not as common as they once were. Usually you have to pay extra for network interface cards with thinnet connectors.

- You want to use Ethernet switching technologies. Although switching technologies are available for thin Ethernet, they are less common and more expensive than they are for thick Ethernet.

- Your network spans more than one or two rooms or building floors.

- You are building a home network and plan to connect to the Internet using a cable modem or DSL. If that's the case, go ahead and invest in a simple 10Base-T hub.

- UTP cabling, 10Base-T hubs, and 10Base-T network interface cards are plentiful and inexpensive.

Though 10Base-2 is simple to install, there are a number of points to keep in mind if you choose to implement it:

- Both ends of the cable must be terminated.

- A cable break anywhere along the length of the cable will cause the entire segment to fail.

- The maximum cable length is 185 meters and the minimum is .5 meters.

- T-connectors must always be used for any network node; cables should never be connected directly to a network interface card.

- A thinnet network can have as many as five segments connected by four repeaters. However, only three of these segments can actually have network nodes attached. The other two segments will only connect to repeaters; these segments are sometimes called interrepeater links.

WARNING   Coaxial cables should be grounded properly (the shield on one end of the cable should be grounded, but not both ends). If a coaxial cable is not grounded properly, possibly lethal electrical shocks can be generated. Refer to TIA/EIA-607 for more information on building grounding, or talk to your electrical contractor. We know of one network manager who was thrown flat on his back when he touched a rack because the cable and its associated racks had not been properly grounded.

100Mbps Ethernet Systems

Though some critics said that Ethernet would never achieve speeds of 100Mbps, designers of Fast Ethernet proved them wrong. Two approaches were presented to the IEEE 802.3 committee. The first approach was to simply speed up current Ethernet system and use the existing CSMA/CD access control mechanism. The second was to take an entirely new access control mechanism called demand priority. In the end, the IEEE decided to create standards for both approaches. The 100Mbps version of 802.3 Ethernet is called 100Base-T Fast Ethernet, and the demand priority approach is called 100VG-AnyLAN (described later in this chapter).

There are three different approaches to cabling a Fast Ethernet system. These approaches are standardized as 100Base-TX, 100Base-T4, and 100Base-FX.

100Base-TX Ethernet   100Base-TX standard uses media physical media standards developed by ANSI that were originally defined for FDDI (ANSI standard X3T9.5). 100Base-TX requires Category 5 or better cabling but uses only two of the four pairs. The eight-position modular jack (RJ-45) uses the same pin numbers as 10Base-T Ethernet.

Though a typical installation requires the use of hubs or switches, two 100Base-TX nodes can be connected together "back-to-back" with a crossover cable; this crossover cable is made exactly the same way as a 10Base-T crossover cable. (See Chapter 9, "Cable Connectors," for more information on making a 10Base-T or 100Base-TX crossover cable.) Here are some things to keep in mind when planning a 100Base-TX Fast Ethernet network:

- All components must be Category 5 certified, including cables, patch panels, and connectors. Proper installation practices must be followed.

- The cabling system must be able to pass tests specified by TIA TSB-67. If you are planning to move to faster networking technologies (1000Base-T), make sure that the cable tester being used is testing for compliance with TSB-95.

- The maximum segment cable length is 100 meters. With higher-grade cables, longer lengths of cable may work, but proper signal timing cannot be guaranteed.

- 100Base-TX uses the same pins as 10Base-T, as shown previously in Figure 3.4.

100Base-T4 Ethernet   The 100Base-T4 standard was developed as part of the 100Base-T specification, so that existing Category 3–compliant systems could also support Fast Ethernet. The designers accomplish 100Mbps throughput on Category 3 cabling by using all four pairs of wire; 100Base-T4 requires a minimum of Category 3 cable. This can ease the migration path to 100Mbps technology.

100Base-T4 is not used as frequently as 100Base-TX, partially due to the cost of the network interface cards and network equipment. The 100Base-T4 network interface cards are generally 50 to 70 percent more expensive than 100Base-TX cards. Also, 100Base-T4 cards do not automatically negotiate and connect to 10Base-T hubs, as most 100Base-TX cards do. For this reason, 100Base-TX cards are more popular. However, 100Base-TX does require Category 5 cabling.

If you are planning to use 100Base-T4, here are some things to keep in mind:

- Maximum cable distance is 100 meters using Category 3, although distances of up to 150 meters can be achieved if Category 5 or better cable is used. Distances greater than 100 meters are not recommended, however, because round trip signal timing cannot be ensured even on Category 5 cables.

- All eight pins of an 8-pin modular jack must be wired. Older Category 3 systems often wired only the exact number of pairs (two) necessary for 10Base-T Ethernet. Figure 3.6 shows the pins that are used. Table 3.2 shows the usage of each of the pins in a 100Base-T4 connector. Either the T568A or T568B wiring patterns can be used, as long as they are used consistently.

- The 100Base-T4 specification recommends using Category 5 patch cables, panels, and connecting hardware wherever possible.

FIGURE 3.6:

8-pin modular jack wiring
pattern for 100Base-T4

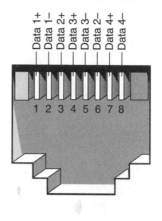

TABLE 3.2:   Pin Usage in 8-Pin Modular Jack Used by 100Base-T4

Pin	Name	Usage	Abbreviation
1	Data 1 +	Transmit +	Tx_D1+
2	Data 1 −	Transmit −	Tx_D1−
3	Data 2 +	Receive +	Rx_D2+
4	Data 3 +	Bidirectional Data 3 +	Bi_D3+
5	Data 3 −	Bidirectional Data 3 −	Bi_D3−
6	Data 2 −	Receive −	Rx_D2−
7	Data 4 +	Bidirectional Data 4 +	Bi_D4+
8	Data 4 −	Bidirectional Data 4 −	Bi_D4−

100Base-FX Ethernet   Like its 100Base-TX copper cousin, 100Base-FX uses a physical media standard that was developed by ANSI for FDDI. The 100Base-FX specification was developed to allow 100Mbps Ethernet to be used over fiber optic cable. Though the cabling plant is wired in a star topology, 100Base-FX is still a bus topology.

If you choose to use 100Base-FX Ethernet, here are some considerations to take into account:

- Cabling plant topology should be a star topology and should follow TIA/EIA-568-A or ISO 11801 recommendations.

- Each network node location should have a minimum of two strands of multimode fiber (MMF).

- Maximum link distance is 400 meters; though fiber optic cable can transmit over much farther distances, proper signal timing cannot be guaranteed at distances greater than 400 meters. If you follow TIA/EIA-568-A or ISO 11801 recommendations, the maximum horizontal cable distance should not exceed 100 meters.

- The most common fiber connector type used for 100Base-FX is the SC connector, but the ST connector and the FDDI MIC connector may also be used. Make sure you know which type of connector(s) your hardware vendor will require.

Gigabit Ethernet (1000Mbps)

The IEEE approved the first Gigabit Ethernet specification in June 1998; this was the IEEE 802.3z standard. The purpose of IEEE 802.3z is to enhance the existing 802.3 standard to include 1000Mbps operation to the then current standard, which supported 10Mbps and 100Mbps. The new standard includes specifications for media access control, topology rules, and the gigabit media independent interface. IEEE 802.3z specifies three physical layer interfaces: 1000BASE-SX, 1000BASE-LX, and 1000BASE-CX.

In July 1999, the IEEE approved an additional standard known as IEEE 802.3ab, which adds an additional Gigabit Ethernet physical layer for 1000Mbps over UTP cabling to the existing 802.3 standard. The UTP cabling, all components, and installation practices must be Category 5 or greater. The only caveat is that the Category 5 installation must meet the performance requirements outlined in Telecommunications Systems Bulletin (TSB) 95.

We are still in the early stages of Gigabit Ethernet, and we don't expect to see it deployed directly to the desktop in most organizations. The cost of Gigabit Ethernet hubs and network interface cards is too high to permit this in most environments. Only applications that demand the highest performance will actually see Gigabit Ethernet to the desktop in the first few years of its lifetime.

Initially, the most common uses for Gigabit Ethernet will be for intrabuilding or campus backbones. Figure 3.7 shows a "before and after" illustration of a simple network that has had Gigabit Ethernet deployed. Prior to deployment, the network had a single 100Mbps switch that served as a backbone for several 10Mbps and 100Mbps segments. All servers were connected to the 100Mbps-backbone switch. The 100Mbps-backbone switch may become the bottleneck.

FIGURE 3.7:

Moving to a Gigabit Ethernet backbone

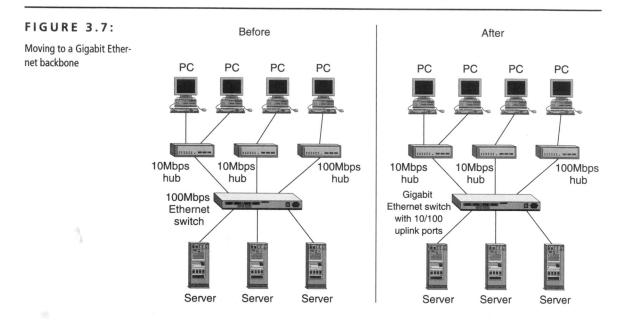

After deployment of Gigabit Ethernet, the 100Mbps-backbone switch is replaced with a Gigabit Ethernet switch. The network interface cards in the servers are replaced with Gigabit network interface cards. The 10Mbps and 100Mbps hubs connect to ports on the Gigabit switch that will accommodate 10 or 100Mbps segments. In this simple example, the bottleneck on the backbone has been relieved. The hubs that the end users connect to and the end user computers did not have to be disturbed.

TIP

To get the full usage of Gigabit Ethernet, computers that have Gigabit Ethernet cards installed should have a 64-bit PCI bus. The 32-bit PCI bus will work with Gigabit Ethernet, but it is not nearly as fast as Gigabit Ethernet. The 64-bit PCI bus can take full advantage of Gigabit Ethernet speeds.

Gigabit Ethernet and Fiber Optic Cables   Initially, 1000Mbps Ethernet was only supported on fiber optic cable. The IEEE 802.3z standard included support for three physical media options (PHYs). Each of these was designed to support different distances and types of communications. The three physical media options are

> **1000Base-SX**   Targeted to horizontal cabling applications such as to workstations and other network nodes. 1000Base-SX is designed to work with multimode fiber optic cable.

> **1000Base-LX**   Designed to support backbone type cabling such as intra-building and campus backbones. 1000Base-LX is designed to be used with single-mode fiber optic cable, though in some cases multimode fiber can be used. Check with the equipment vendor.

> **1000Base-CX**   Designed to support interconnection of equipment clusters. This specification actually uses 150-ohm STP cabling similar to IBM Type 1 cabling over distances no greater than 25 meters.

When cabling for Gigabit Ethernet using fiber, you should follow the TIA/EIA-568-A standards for 62.5/125-micron multimode fiber for horizontal cabling and 8.3/125-micron single-mode fiber for backbone cabling.

1000Base-T Ethernet   The IEEE designed 1000Base-T with the intention of supporting Gigabit Ethernet to the desktop. One of the primary design goals was to support the existing base of Category 5 cabling. Except for a few early adopters, most organizations will not quickly adopt 1000Base-T to the desktop. However, as 1000Base-T network equipment becomes more cost effective, this will change.

In July 1999, the IEEE 802.3ab task force approved IEEE standard 802.3ab, which defines using 1000Mbps Ethernet over Category 5 unshielded twisted pair cable. Unlike 10Base-T and 100Base-TX, all four pairs must be used with 1000Base-T. Since Category 5 cabling only supports frequency rates up to 100MHz, special modulation techniques had to be employed to "stuff" 1000Mbps through a cable that is only rated to 100MHz.

In 1999, the TIA issued TSB-95 to define additional performance parameters (above and beyond those specified in TSB-67) that should be performed in order to certify an existing Category 5 cabling installation for use with 1000Base-T. The additional criteria include far-end crosstalk, delay skew, and return loss. For more information on these performance criteria, see Chapter 1, "Introduction to Data Cabling."

If you are planning to deploy 1000Base-T in the future, make sure that you are using Category 5 cable and components at a minimum, that solid installation practices are used, and that all links are tested and certified using TSB-67 and TSB-95 performance criteria.

Token Ring

Developed by IBM, *Token Ring* uses a ring topology to pass data from one computer to another. A former teacher of Jim's referred to Token Ring as the Fahrenheit network architecture because more Ph.D. degrees worked on it than there were degrees in the Fahrenheit scale. Even Ethernet fans will concede that Token Ring is a superior technology.

Token Ring employs a sophisticated scheme to control the flow of data. If no network node needs to transmit data, a small packet, called the *free token*, continually circles the ring. If a node on the network needs to transmit data, it must have possession of the free token before it can create a new token ring data frame. Once the data arrives at its destination, a new free token is placed on the original network by the *transmitting* station. Then the next node on the ring can transmit data if necessary.

This scheme, called *token passing*, guarantees equal access to the ring and that no two computers will transmit at the same time. Token passing is the basis for IEEE standard 802.5. This scheme might seem pretty slow since the free token must circle the ring continually, but keep in mind that the free token is circling at speeds approaching 70 percent of the speed of light. A smaller token ring network may see a free token circle the ring up to 10,000 times per second!

NOTE   On 4Mbps Token Ring, there is always one free token circling the ring. With 16Mbps Token Ring, there are four free tokens circling the ring.

Since a ring topology is difficult to cable, IBM employs a hybrid star/ring topology. All nodes in the network are connected centrally to a hub (MAU or MSAU in IBM jargon), as shown in Figure 3.8. The transmitted data still behaves like a ring topology, traveling down each cable (called a *lobe*) to the node and then returning to the hub, where it starts down the next cable on the MAU.

FIGURE 3.8:

Token Ring hybrid star/ring topology

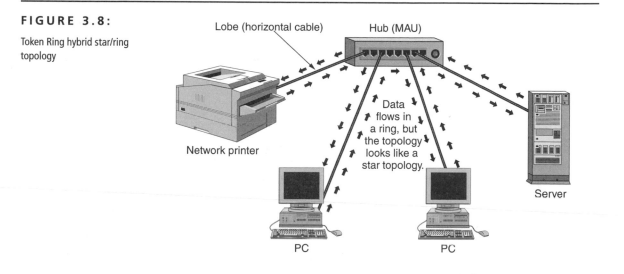

Even a single node failure or lobe cable can take down a Token Ring. The designers of Token Ring realized this and designed the MAU with a simple electromechanical switch (a relay switch) that adds a new node to the ring when it is powered on. If the node is powered off or if the lobe cable fails, the electromechanical switch disengages and the node is removed from the ring. The ring continues to operate as if the node were not there.

Token Ring operates at either 4Mbps or 16Mbps; however, a ring only operates at a single speed. Care must be taken on older Token Ring hardware to make sure that a network adapter operating at the wrong speed is not inserted into a ring because this can shut down the entire network.

Token Ring and Shielded Twisted-Pair (STP)

Token Ring originally operated on *shielded twisted-pair* (STP) cabling. IBM designed a cabling system that included a couple of types of shielded twisted-pair cables; the most common of these was IBM Type 1 cabling (later called IBM Type 1A). IBM Type 1A cabling is now specified as a valid cable type in the TIA/EIA-568-A specification.

The IBM cabling system used a unique, hermaphroditic connector that is commonly called an *IBM data connector*. The IBM data connector has no male and female components, so two IBM patch cables can be connected together to form one long patch cable.

Unless your cabling needs specifically require an STP cabling solution for Token Ring, we recommend against using STP cabling. Excellent throughput is available today with existing technologies over UTP cabling, and the only reason to implement STP today is if the environmental interference from electromagnetic interference is too great to use UTP.

Token Ring and Unshielded Twisted-Pair (UTP)

Starting around 1990, vendors started releasing *unshielded twisted-pair* solutions for Token Ring. The first of these solutions was simply to use media filters or baluns on the Token Ring network interface cards, which connected to the card's 9-pin interface and allowed a UTP cable to connect to the media filter. The balun matches the impedance between the 100-ohm UTP and the network device, which is expecting 150 ohms.

KEY TERMS   **Baluns and Media Filters**   *Baluns* and *media filters* are designed to match impedance between two differing types of cabling, usually unbalanced coaxial cable and balanced two-wire twisted pair. While baluns can come in handy, they can also be problematic and should be avoided if possible.

The second UTP solution for Token Ring was network interface cards equipped with 8-pin modular jacks (RJ-45) that supported 100-ohm cables rather than a DB9 connector.

Any cabling plant that is certified Category 3 or better should support Token Ring. However, for growth and future expansion, a minimum of Category 5 cabling and components should be used.

NOTE   A number of vendors make Token Ring network interface cards that support fiber optic cable. While using Token Ring over fiber optic cables is not common, it is possible.

Fiber Distributed Data Interface (FDDI)

Fiber Distributed Data Interface (FDDI) is a networking standard that was produced by the ANSI X3T9.5 committee in 1986. The FDDI specification defines a high-speed (100Mbps), token-passing network using fiber optic cable. In 1994, the standard was updated to include copper cable (called CDDI or Copper Distributed Data Interface). FDDI was slow to be widely adopted, but it has found a niche as a reliable, high-speed technology for backbones and applications that demand reliable connectivity.

Though at first glance FDDI appears to be similar to Token Ring, it is different from both Token Ring and Ethernet. A Token Ring node can transmit only a single frame when it gets the free token and then must wait until it has the free token again before it can transmit again. An FDDI node, once it has possession of the free token, can transmit as many frames as it can generate within a predetermined time before it has to give up the free token.

FDDI can operate as a true ring topology, or it can be physically wired like a star topology. Figure 3.9 shows a FDDI ring that consists of dual-attached stations (DAS); this is a true ring topology. A dual-attached station has two FDDI interfaces. The first is called an A port, which is used to connect the input of the primary ring and the output of the secondary ring. The second is called a B port, which is used to connect the output of the primary ring and the input of the secondary ring. Each node on the network in Figure 3.9 has an FDDI network interface card that has two FDDI attachments. This creates two rings: a primary ring and a secondary ring. Cabling for such a network would be a royal pain since the cables would have to form a complete circle.

FIGURE 3.9:

FDDI ring

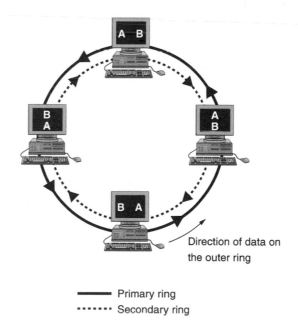

Direction of data on
the outer ring

——— Primary ring
•••••• Secondary ring

FDDI networks can also be cabled as a star topology, though they still behave like a ring topology. FDDI network interface cards may be purchased with either a single FDDI interface (*single-attached station* or *SAS*) or with two FDDI interfaces (*dual-attached station* or *DAS*). Single-attached stations must connect to a FDDI concentrator or hub. A network can also be mixed and matched, with network nodes such as workstations using only a single-attached station connection and servers or other critical devices having dual-attached station connections. This allows the critical devices to have a primary and secondary ring.

Working with FDDI, you may be introduced to some new terminology and acronyms, including the following:

MAC   The media access control responsible for addressing, scheduling, and routing data.

PHY   The physical protocol layer responsible for coding and timing of signals such as clock synchronization of the ring. The actual data speed on a FDDI ring is 125Mbps; an additional control bit is added for every four bits.

PMD   The physical layer medium responsible for the transmission between nodes. FDDI includes two PMDs: Fiber-PMD on fiber optic networks and TP-PMD on twisted-pair networks.

SMT   The station management responsible for handling FDDI ring management including ring management (RMT), configuration management (CFM), connection management (CMT), physical connection management (PCM), and entity coordination management (ECM). SMT coordinates neighbor identification, insertion, and de-insertion into the ring, fault detection, traffic monitoring, and fault detection.

Cabling and FDDI

When planning cabling for a FDDI network, practices recommended in TIA/EIA-568-A or ISO 11801 should be followed. FDDI using fiber optic cable for the horizontal links uses FDDI MIC connectors. Care must be taken to ensure that the connectors are keyed properly for the device they will connect to.

FDDI using copper cabling (CDDI) requires Category 5 cable and associated devices. Horizontal links should pass performance tests specified in TSB-67 at a minimum, though it is a also good idea to use the performance criteria specified by TSB-95.

Asynchronous Transfer Mode (ATM)

ATM (*asynchronous transfer mode*, not to be confused with automated teller machines) first emerged in the early 1990s. If networking has an equivalent of rocket science, then ATM is it. ATM was designed to be a high-speed communications protocol that does not depend on any specific LAN topology. It uses a high-speed cell-switching technology that can handle data as well as real-time voice and video. The ATM protocol breaks transmitted data up in to 53-byte "cells." A *cell* is analogous to a packet or frame, except that an ATM cell does not always contain source or destination addressing information; the ATM cell also contains no higher-level addressing and packet control information.

ATM is designed to "switch" these small cells through an ATM network very quickly. It does this by setting up a virtual connection between the source and destination nodes; the cells may go through multiple switching points before ultimately arriving at their final destination. The cells may also arrive out of order, so the receiving system may have to reassemble and correctly order the arriving cells. ATM is a connection-oriented service in contrast to most network architectures, which are broadcast-based.

Data rates are scalable and start as low as 1.5Mbps, with speeds of 25, 51, 100, 155Mbps and higher. The most common speeds of ATM networks today are 51.84Mbps and 155.52Mbps. Both of these speeds can be used over either copper or fiber optic cabling. 622.08Mbps ATM is also becoming common but is currently used exclusively over fiber optic cable. ATM supports very high speeds because it is designed to be implemented by hardware rather than software, so faster processing speeds are possible. Soon, fiber-based ATM networks will be operating at data rates of 10Gbps.

In the U.S., the standard for synchronous data transmission on optical media is *SONET* (Synchronous Optical Network); the international equivalent of SONET is SDH (synchronous digital hierarchy). SONET defines a base data rate of 51.84Mbps; multiples of this rate are known as optical carrier (OC) levels, such as OC-3, OC-12, etc. Common OC levels and their associated data rate can be found in Table 3.3.

TABLE 3.3: Common Optical Carrier Levels (OC-X)

Level	Data Rate
OC-1	51.84Mbps
OC-3	155.52Mbps
OC-12	622.08Mbps
OC-48	2.488Gbps

ATM was designed as a WAN protocol. However, due to the high speeds that it can support, many organizations are using it to attach servers (and often workstations) directly to the ATM network. To do this, a set of services, functional groups, and protocols was developed to provide *LAN emulation* (called *LANE* by the ATM folks). LANE also provides communication between network nodes attached to a LAN (such as Ethernet) and ATM-attached nodes. Figure 3.10 shows an ATM network connecting to LANs using LANE. Note that the ATM network does not have to be in a single physical location and can span geographic areas.

FIGURE 3.10:

ATM network with LAN emulation (LANE)

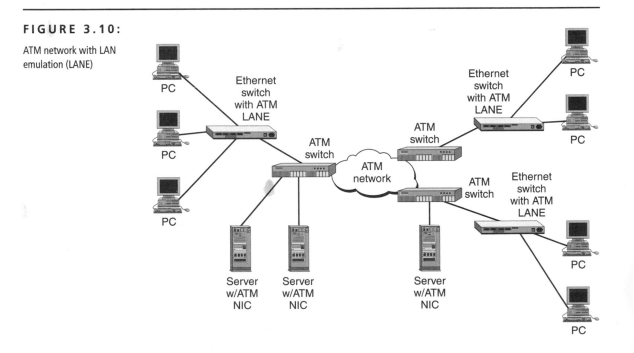

NOTE   For more information on ATM, check out the ATM Forum's Web site at www
.atmforum.org.

Cabling and ATM

What sort of cabling should you consider for ATM networks? Fiber optic cabling is still the medium of choice for most ATM installations. While ATM to the desktop is still not terribly common, we know of at least a few organizations that have deployed 155Mbps ATM directly to the desktop.

For fiber optic cable, as long as you are following the TIA/EIA-568-A standard or the ISO 11801 standard, you should not have problems. ATM equipment and ATM network interface cards use 62.5/125-micron multimode optical fiber.

If you are planning on using 155Mbps ATM over copper, plan to use Category 5 cabling. All links should pass tests specified in TSB95 and TSB67.

100VG-AnyLAN

Initially developed by Hewlett Packard, AT&T, and IBM as an alternative to other 100BaseX technologies (100Base-TX, 100Base-T4, and 100VG-AnyLAN), 100VG-AnyLAN was refined and ratified by the IEEE as IEEE standard 802.12. It combines the best of both Ethernet and Token Ring technologies and includes the following as its design goals:

- Permit the use of existing Category 3, 4, or 5 cabling.

- Provide a smooth migration path from Ethernet and Token Ring LANs and frame formats.

- Eliminate the "collisions" associated with Ethernet.

- Support a cascaded star topology of 2.5 km and more than three levels of cascading.

- Cable distances of 200 meters for UTP and 2000 meters for fiber.

- Provide fair access and bounded latency.

- Provide two levels of priority for frames: normal and high.

- Provide a low latency service through high priority to support multimedia applications.

NOTE   What does the VG stand for? Voice grade. 100VG-AnyLAN was designed to operate over a minimum of Category 3 cable.

Nodes on a 100VG-AnyLAN network can receive at any time, but they are subject to media access rules called *demand priority* when they need to transmit. Other
network technologies, such as Ethernet, Token Ring, and FDDI, implement media
access rules at the node. For example, a Token Ring node can transmit only when
it has possession of the "free token." Ethernet nodes can transmit anytime they
sense that the media is not currently in use. 100VG-AnyLAN nodes transmit only
when their hub decides that they can transmit; the node requests that the hub
allow it to transmit. This gives each node "equal" access, though simultaneous
requests are serviced in "port order" unless the node sent a high priority request
to the hub.

Unlike Token Ring and FDDI, no token passing takes place on an 100VG-
AnyLAN network. Network access is provided by the 100VG-AnyLAN hubs
rather than by a free token.

Cable and 100VG-AnyLAN

100VG-AnyLAN was designed with the idea that it would be used on UTP-based
networks. The equipment that shipped for 100VG-AnyLAN was designed for use
with Category 3, 4, or 5 cabling. Since 1994, additional media has been supported
in the form of fiber optic and STP cabling. Any cabling infrastructure designed
using the TIA/EIA-568A standards should be capable of supporting 100VG-
AnyLAN, including those using Category 3 cables.

NOTE   100VG-AnyLAN uses *all* four pairs in a Category 3, 4, or 5 cable. Therefore, all of
these pairs must be connected and wired properly.

Initially, it seemed that 100VG-AnyLAN would require Category 5 cables and
connecting hardware just like 100Base-T. However, this is not the case because
VG uses a frequency of 30MHz and employs all four pairs in the cable. If you are
wondering how 100VG-AnyLAN can use Category 3, which is rated to only 16MHz,
and Category 4, which is rated to only 20MHz, give yourself a gold star. The answer
to your question is that 100VG-AnyLAN overcomes the noise through the use of

sophisticated transceivers and runs Category 3 and Category 4 cables at 30MHz. However, the cables must meet Category 3 or 4 specifications exactly.

The cables that may be used and the maximum distances permitted are shown in Table 3.4; the distances specified in this table are not only for node-to-hub cables, but also hub-to-hub cables. The IEEE 802.12 standard specifies the cable formats that can be used within a demand priority network such as 100VG-AnyLAN.

TABLE 3.4: Cable Categories, Types, and Maximum Distances

Category	Cable Type	Maximum Distance
Category 3	4-pair UTP	100 meters
Category 4	4-pair UTP	100 meters
Category 5	4-pair UTP	200 meters
IBM Type 1A	2-pair STP	100 meters
Fiber Optic	Multimode	2000 meters

What Is Bundled Cable?   100VG-AnyLAN hubs allow a UTP cable option called bundled cable. *Bundled cable* has many twisted-pair cables within a single sheath; usually 25 pairs. Bundled cable is permitted between the nodes and the hubs but not in hub-to-hub connections. This feature was designed to allow support for older Category 3 cabling infrastructures that used bundled cable as part of their horizontal cabling.

Most new cabling installations use *unbundled cable*, meaning a single sheath that contains only four pairs of cable. The 100VG-AnyLAN hub has an option that is labeled with something like "Use Bundled Cable." You should use this option only if you are truly using bundled cable (for example, cable with 25 pairs) or it can cause a performance hit. If this option is turned on, the 100VG-AnyLAN hub ensures that only a single packet is in a sheath of cable at any given time. The hub has the capability to transmit over many pairs simultaneously, but it will not do this if the bundled option is selected.

NOTE   Can two 100VG-AnyLAN nodes be connected together without a hub (like using a crossover cable for 10Base-T)? No, 100VG-AnyLAN cards require the hub to tell them when they can transmit.

Cascading

Multiple levels of 100VG-AnyLAN hubs can be cascaded together, provided the hub's uplink port is used to connect it to the next level above. There is typically a "root" level hub with one or more child hubs. Child hubs can have only a single parent, except for the root hub, which does not need a parent. There can be up to four levels of cascaded hubs off of a single root hub (the root hub is considered the top or fifth level). This arrangement is illustrated in Figure 3.11.

NOTE   100VG-AnyLAN permits five levels of hubs to be cascaded. 100Base-X permits only two levels of hubs to be cascaded.

FIGURE 3.11:

100VG-AnyLAN cascading

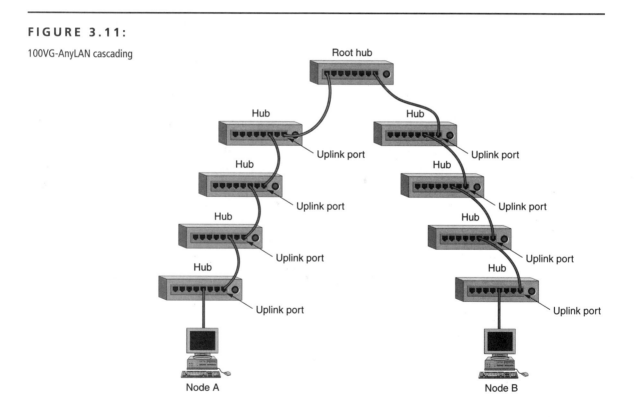

Cascading multiple hubs can build an exceptionally large network, especially given the extended cable distances that 100VG-AnyLAN allows. One limitation that this size network does impose is the maximum cable radius.

Maximum Cable Radius   100VG-AnyLAN imposes a maximum cable radius that depends on the media that is being employed. The *maximum cable radius* is the maximum distance between two nodes on the network. The maximum distance between node A and node B in Figure 3.11 is the maximum cable radius. When using Category 3, 4, or 5 cable, the maximum distance between two nodes is 2,000 meters. Figure 3.11 actually gives us 10 separate physical cable segments; assuming that each node using the maximum UTP cable length, this will reach the 2,000-meter limit.

Fiber optic 100VG-AnyLAN networks and copper/fiber combination networks have a maximum cable radius of 2,500 meters. This limitation exists due to a restriction on the maximum delay from any node to the root repeater.

Network Connectivity Devices

At this point, we've talked about many of the common network architectures that you may encounter and some of the things you may need to know relating to providing a cabling infrastructure to support them. We've looked at the products we can use to bring our communication endpoints to a central location. But are there any conversations taking place? What we need now is a way to tie everything together.

This section focuses on the rest of the pieces you need to establish seamless communication across your internetwork.

Repeaters

Nowadays, the terms *repeater* and *hub* are used synonymously, but they are actually not the same things. Prior to the days of twisted pairs networking, network backbones carried data across coaxial cable, similar to what is used for cable television.

Computers would connect into these either by BNC connectors, in the case of thinnet, or by vampire taps, in the case of thicknet. Everyone would be connected to the same coaxial backbone. Unfortunately, when it comes to electrical current flowing through a solid medium, you have to contend with the laws of physics. There exists a finite distance of electrical signals that can travel across a wire before they become too distorted. Repeaters are used to overcome this challenge.

Repeaters work at the physical layer of the OSI reference model. Their job is to simply boost an electrical signal's strength so that it can travel further across a wire. Figure 3.12 illustrates a repeater in action.

FIGURE 3.12:

Repeaters are used to boost signal strength.

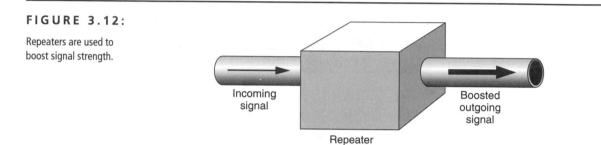

Being passive in nature, repeaters do not look at the contents of the packets flowing across the wire, nor do they alter the contents of those packets.

Theoretically, repeaters could be used to extend cables infinitely, but due to the underlying limitations of communication architectures like Ethernet's collision domains, repeaters are used to tie together a maximum of five coaxial cable segments.

Hubs

Previously, we stated that the terms *hub* and *repeater* are often used interchangeably in the age of twisted pairs networking. This is because repetition of signals is a function of repeating hubs. The semantic distinction between the two terms is that a repeater joins two backbone coaxial cables, whereas a hub joins two or more twisted-pair cables.

In twisted pairs networking, each network device is connected to an individual network cable. In coaxial networking, all network devices are connected to the same coaxial backbone. A hub eliminates the need for BNC connectors and vampire taps in order for communication to occur. Figure 3.13 illustrates how network devices connect to a hub versus coaxial backbones.

FIGURE 3.13:

Twisted pairs networking versus coaxial networking

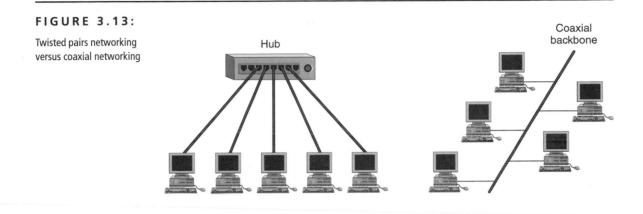

Hubs work the same way as repeaters, in that incoming signals are amplified before they are retransmitted across its ports. Like repeaters, hubs operate at the OSI physical layer, which means they do not alter or look at the contents of a packet traveling across the wire. When a hub receives an incoming signal, it amplifies it and sends it out over all of its ports. Figure 3.14 shows a hub at work.

FIGURE 3.14:

Hubs at work

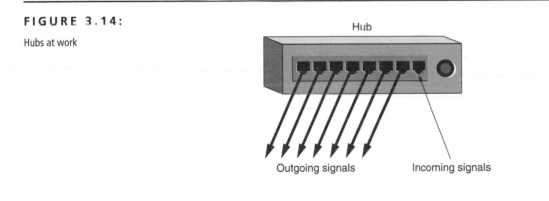

Hubs typically provide from 8 to 24 twisted-pair connections, depending on the manufacturer and model of the hub (although some hubs support several dozen ports). Hubs can also be connected to each other (cascaded) by means of BNC, AUI ports, or crossover cables to provide flexibility as our networks grow. The cost of this flexibility is paid for in performance.

As a media access architecture, Ethernet is built on carrier sensing and collision detection mechanisms (CSMA/CD). Prior to transmitting a signal, an Ethernet host first listens to the wire to determine if any other hosts are transmitting. If the wire is clear, the host transmits. On occasion, two or more hosts will sense that the wire is free and try to transmit simultaneously or nearly simultaneously. Only one signal is free to fly across the wire at a time, and when multiple signals meet on the wire, they become corrupted by the collision. When a collision is detected, the transmitting hosts wait a random amount of time before retransmitting, in the hopes of avoiding another data collision. Figures 3.15 shows a situation where a data collision is produced, and Figure 3.16 shows how Ethernet handles these situations.

FIGURE 3.15:

Ethernet data collision

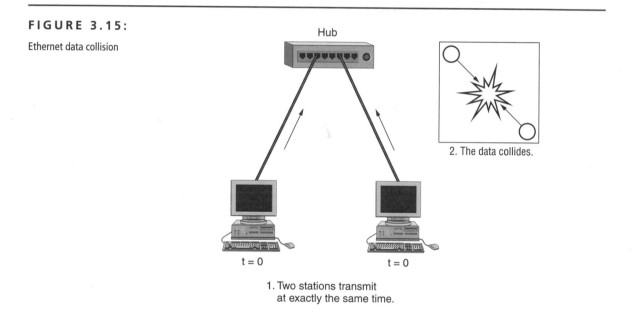

2. The data collides.

1. Two stations transmit
at exactly the same time.

So what implications does this have on performance? If you recall from our original explanation of how a hub works, when a hub receives an incoming signal, it simply passes it across all of its ports. For example, with an eight-port hub, if a host attached to port 1 transmits, the hosts connected to ports 2 through 8 will all receive the signal. Consider the following: If a host attached to port 8 wants to communicate with a host attached to port 7, the hosts attached to ports 1 through 6 will be barred from transmitting because they will sense signals traveling across the wire.

FIGURE 3.16:

How Ethernet responds to data collisions

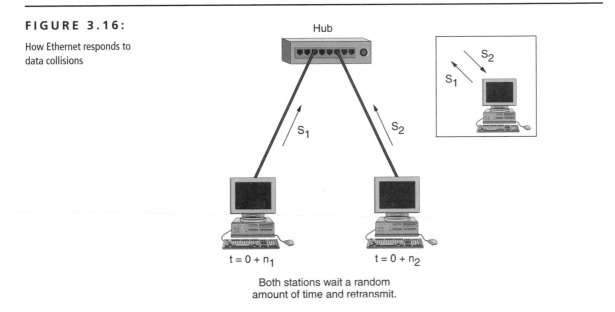

Both stations wait a random
amount of time and retransmit.

NOTE   Hubs pass incoming signals across all of their ports, preventing two hosts from transmitting simultaneously. All of the hosts connected to a hub are therefore said to share the same amount of bandwidth.

On a small scale, such as our eight-port example above, the shared bandwidth performance implications may not be that significant. However, consider the cascading of four 24-port hubs, where 96 hosts are now sharing the same bandwidth. When one host transmits, 95 others cannot. The bandwidth that our network provides is finite (limited by our cable plant and network devices). Therefore, in shared bandwidth configurations, the amount of bandwidth available to a connected host is inversely proportional to the number of hosts sharing that bandwidth. For example, if 96 hosts are connected to the same set of Fast Ethernet (100Mbps) hubs, they have only 1.042Mbps available. For Ethernet (10Mbps), the situation is even worse, with only 0.104Mbps available. All hope is not lost, however. We'll look at ways of overcoming these performance barriers through the use of switches and routers.

As a selling point, hubs are relatively inexpensive to implement.

Bridges

When we use the terms *bridge* or *bridging*, we are generally describing functionality provided by modern switches. Just like a repeater, a bridge is a network device used to connect two network segments. The main difference between them is that bridges operate at the link layer of the OSI reference model and can therefore provide translation services required to connect dissimilar media access architectures such as Ethernet and Token Ring. Because of this functionality, bridging is an important internetworking technology.

In general there are four types of bridging:

Transparent bridging   Typically found in Ethernet environments, the transparent bridge analyzes the incoming frames and forwards them to the appropriate segments one hop at a time (see Figure 3.17).

Source-route bridging   Typically found in Token Ring environments, source-route bridging provides an alternative to transparent bridging for NetBIOS and SNA protocols. In source-route bridging, each ring is assigned a unique number on the source-route bridge port. Token Ring frames contain address information, including a ring number, which the bridge analyzes to forward the frame to the appropriate ring (see Figure 3.18).

Source-route transparent bridging   An extension of source-route bridging whereby nonroutable protocols such as NetBIOS and SNA receive the routing benefits of source-route bridging and a performance increase associated with transparent bridging.

Translation bridging   Used to connect network segments with different underlying media access technologies such as Ethernet to Token Ring or Ethernet to FDDI, etc. (see Figure 3.19).

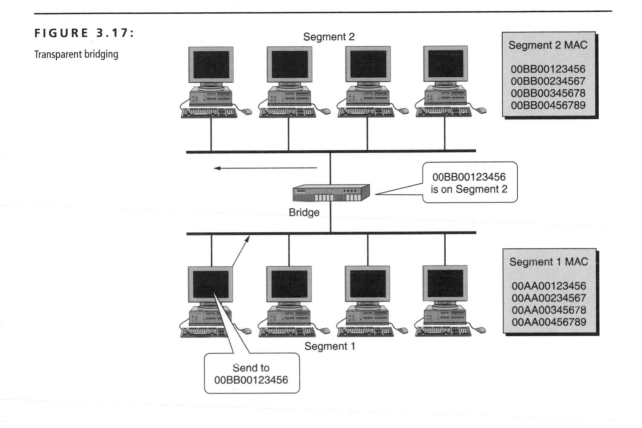

FIGURE 3.17:

Transparent bridging

FIGURE 3.18:

Source-route transparent
bridging

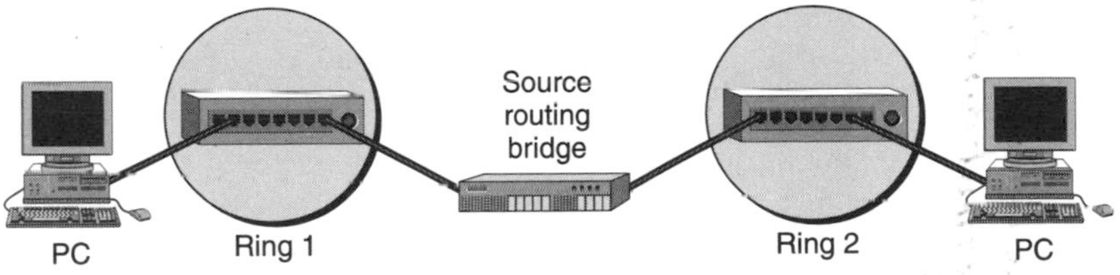

FIGURE 3.19:

Translation bridging

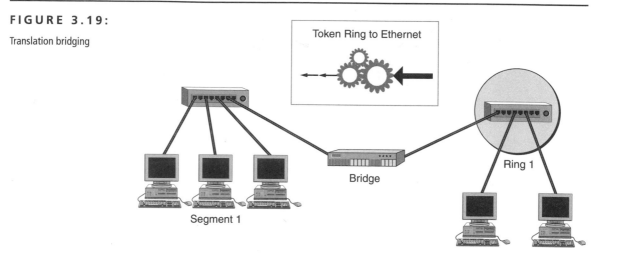

Compared to modern routers, bridges are not complicated devices; they consist of network interface cards and the software required to forward packets from one interface to another. As previously mentioned, bridges operate at the link layers of the OSI reference model, so a brief discussion of link layer communication is in order to understand how bridges work.

How are network nodes uniquely identified? In general, it's assumed that you're referring to OSI network layer protocols such as the Internet protocol (IP). When you assign an IP address to a network node, one of the requirements is that it must be unique on our network. At first, you might think this means that every computer in the world must have a unique IP address in order to communicate, but this is not the case. This is because of the Internet Assigned Numbers Authority's (IANA) specification for the allocation of private address spaces in RFC 1918. For example, Company XYZ and Company WXY could both use IP network 192.168.0.0/24 to identify network devices on their private networks. However, networks that use a private IP address specified in RFC 1918 cannot communicate over the Internet without network address translation or proxy server software and hardware.

IP as a protocol merely provides for the logical grouping of computers as networks. Since IP addresses are logical representations of groups of computers, how does communication between two endpoints occur? It turns out that communication does occur over IP.

IP as a protocol provides the rules governing addressing and routing. IP communication occurs at the link layers of the OSI reference model.

Every network interface card has a unique 48-bit address assigned to the adapter know as its MAC address. In order for two nodes to converse, one computer must first resolve the MAC address of its destination. In IP, this is handled by a protocol known as the *Address Resolution Protocol* (ARP). Once a MAC address is resolved, the frame gets built and is transmitted on the wire as a unicast frame (there is a source and destination MAC address). Each network adapter on that segment hears the frame and examines the destination MAC address to determine if the frame is destined for them. If the frame's destination MAC address matches the receiving system's MAC address, the frame gets passed up to the network layer; otherwise, the frame is simply discarded.

So how does this relate to bridging, you may ask? In transparent bridging, the bridge passively listens to all of the traffic coming across the wire and analyzes the source MAC addresses to build tables that associate a MAC address with a particular network segment. When a bridge receives a frame destined for a remote segment, it then forwards that frame to the appropriate segment so that the clients can communicate seamlessly.

Bridging is one technique that can be used to solve the shared bandwidth problem that exists with hubs. In the hub example above where we cascaded four 24-port hubs through the use of bridges, we can physically isolate each segment so that only 24 hosts are competing for bandwidth and therefore increase throughput. Similarly, with the implementation of bridges, you can also increase the number of nodes that can transmit simultaneously from one (in the case of cascading hubs) to four. Another benefit is that collision domains can be extended; that is, the physical distance between two nodes can exceed the physical limits imposed if the two nodes exist on the same segment. Logically, all of these nodes will appear to be on the same network segment.

Bridging does a lot in meeting the challenges of internetworking, but there are limits in its implementation. For instance, bridges will accommodate a maximum of seven physical segments. And although you've made more efficient use of our available bandwidth through segmentation, you can still do better with switching technologies.

Switches

Switches are the next rungs up the evolutionary ladder of bridges. In modern star topology networking, as with repeaters and hubs, when you need bridging functionality, you often run out and buy a switch. But bridging is not the only benefit of switch implementation. Switches also provide the benefit of micro-LAN segmentation, which means that every node connected to a switched port receives its own dedicated bandwidth. And with Layer-3 switching, you can further segment our network into virtual LANs.

Like bridges, switches also operate at the link layers of the OSI reference model, and, in the case of Layer-3 switches, sometimes extend into the network layer. The same mechanisms are used to build dynamic tables that associate MAC addresses with switched ports. However, where bridges implement store-and-forward bridging via software, switches implement either store-and-forward or cut-through switching via hardware, with a marked improvement of speed.

Micro-LAN segmentation is the key benefit of switches, and most organizations have either completely phased out hubs or are in the process of doing so to accommodate the throughput requirements for multimedia applications. Although switches are becoming more affordable, ranging in price from $10 per port to slightly over $20, their price may still prevent organizations from migrating to completely switched infrastructures. At a minimum, however, servers and workgroups should be linked through switched ports.

Routers

Routers are packet-forwarding devices just like switches and bridges; however, routers allow transmission of data between network segments. Unlike switches, which forward packets based on physical node addresses, routers operate at the network layer of the OSI reference model, forwarding packets based on a network ID.

If you recall from our communication digression in bridging, we defined a network as a logical grouping of computers and network devices. A collection of interconnected networks is referred to as an *internetwork*. Routers provide the connectivity within an internetwork.

So how do routers work? In the case of the IP protocol, an IP address is 32 bits long. Those 32 bits contain both the network ID and the host ID of a network device. IP distinguishes between network and host bits by using a subnet mask.

The *subnet mask* is a set of contiguous bits with values of one from left to right that IP should consider to be the address of a network. Bits used to describe a host are masked out by a value of 0 through a binary calculation process called *ANDing*. Figure 3.20 shows two examples of network IDs calculated from an ANDing process.

FIGURE 3.20:

Calculation of IP network IDs

192.168.145.27 / 24

Address:
11000000 10101000 10010001 00011011

Mask:
11111111 11111111 11111111 00000000

Network ID:
11000000 10101000 10010001 00000000

192.168.145.0

192.168.136.147 / 29

Address:
11000000 10101000 10001000 10010011

Mask:
11111111 11111111 11111111 11111000

Network ID:
11000000 10101000 10001000 10010000

192.168.136.144

NOTE   We use IP as the basis of our examples because it is the industry standard for enterprise networking; however, TCP/IP is not the only routable protocol suite. Novell's IPX/SPX and Apple Computer's AppleTalk protocols are also routable.

Routing is a core component of the IP protocol, and it turns out that all networking devices configured to use TCP/IP make some sort of routing decision. Once a destination IP address has been resolved, IP will perform an AND calculation on the IP address and subnet mask, as well as the destination IP address to your subnet mask. IP then compares the results. If they are the same, then both devices exist on the same network segment and no routing has to take place. If the results are different, then IP checks the devices routing table to see if there are explicit instructions on how to get to the destination network and forwards the frame to that address or sends the packet along to a default gateway (router).

Routers themselves are simply specialized computers concerned with getting packets from point A to point B. When a router receives a packet destined for its network interface, it examines the destination address to determine the best way to get it there. It makes this decision based on information contained within its own routing tables. Routing tables are associations of network IDs and interfaces that know how to get to that network. If a router can resolve a means to get the packet from point A to point B, it forwards to either the intended recipient or to the next router in the chain. Otherwise, the router informs the sender that it doesn't know how to reach the destination network. Figure 3.21 illustrates communication between two hosts on different networks.

FIGURE 3.21:

Host communication between internetworked segments

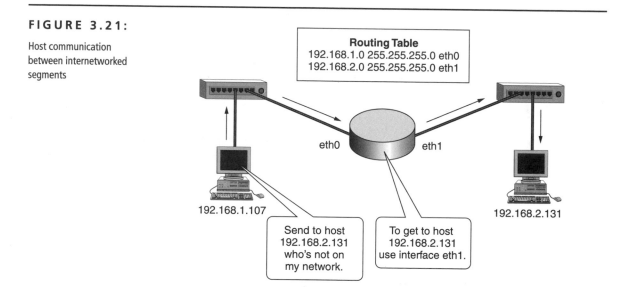

A detailed discussion on the inner workings of routers is well beyond the scope of this book, and, in fact, internetworking product vendors such as Cisco Systems offer certifications in the configuration and deployment of their products. If you are interested in becoming certified in Cisco products, Sybex also publishes excellent study guides for the CCNA and CCNP certification exams. For a more intimate look at the inner workings of the TCP/IP protocol suite, you may also be interested in *TCP/IP: 24seven*, also published by Sybex (ISBN: 0-7821-2509-3; 1999).

Cable System and Infrastructure Constraints

- What Are Codes and Where Did They Come From?

- The Federal Communications Commission

- The National Fire Protection Agency

- Underwriters Laboratories, Inc.

- The National Electrical Code

What constrains you when building a structured cabling system? Can you install cable anywhere you please? You probably already realize some of the restrictions of your cabling activities; these restrictions include installing cable too close to electrical lines and over fluorescent lights. However, many people don't realize that there are actually documents and codes that help dictate how cabling systems (both electrical as well as communications) must be designed and installed in order to conform to your local laws.

In the United States, governing bodies issue codes to protect life, health, and property. Once adopted by the local regulating authority, codes have the force of law. Standards, which are guidelines to ensure system functionality after installation, are issued to ensure construction quality.

Codes are issued or adopted by various branches of government to address minimum safety requirements. The governing body that has jurisdiction in a locality will issue codes for that locality. The codes for an area are written or adopted by and under control of the jurisdiction having authority (JHA). Sometimes these codes are called building codes or simply codes. This chapter discusses codes and how they affect the installation of communications cabling.

Where Do Codes Come From?

Building, construction, and communications codes originate from a number of different sources. Usually these codes originate nationally rather than at the local city or county level. Local municipalities usually adopt these national codes as local laws. Other national codes are issued that affect the construction of electrical and communications equipment.

Two of the predominant national code players in the United States are the Federal Communications Commission and the National Fire Protection Association. The Americans with Disabilities Act also affects the construction of cabling and communications facilities since it requires that facilities must be constructed to provide universal access.

The United States Federal Communications Commission

The United States Federal Communications Commission (FCC) issues reports and orders that govern the installation of telecommunications cabling and the design of communications devices that are built or used in the United States. The reports and orders that the FCC issues help to prevent problems relating to communications equipment; this includes providing manufacturers with guidelines for designing devices that will not interfere with the operation of other communications equipment.

The FCC Part 68 Rule provides regulations for connecting premises cabling and customer-provided equipment to the regulated networks. The FCC also publishes numerous Reports and Orders. These Reports and Orders deal with specific issues regarding communications cabling, electromagnetic emissions, and frequency bandwidths. The following is a list of some of the more important documents issued by the FCC:

Part 68 Rule (FCC Rules)   Rules governing the connection of premise equipment and wiring to the national network

Telecommunications Act 1996   Establishes new rules for provisioning and additional competition in telecommunications services

CC Docket 81-216   Rules for providing customer-owned premise wiring

CC Docket 85-229   Computer Inquiry III review of the regulatory framework for competition in telecommunications

CC Docket 86-9   Policies governing shared tenant services in commercial buildings

Part 15 (FCC Rules)   Addresses electromagnetic radiation of equipment and cables

CC Docket 87-124   FCC Docket implementing the ADA (Americans with Disabilities Act)

CC Docket 88-57   Defines the location of the demarcation point on a customer premise

Fact Sheet ICB-FC-011   Connection of one- and two-line terminal equipment to the telephone network and the installation of premises wiring

Memorandum Opinion and Order FCC 85-343   Covers the rights of users to access embedded complex wire on customer premises

---

NOTE   Most of the FCC rules, orders, and reports can be viewed on the FCC Web site at www.fcc.gov.

The National Fire Protection Association

In 1897, a group of industry professionals (insurance, electrical, architectural, and other allied interests) formed the National Association of Fire Engineers with the purpose of writing and publishing the first guidelines for the safe installation of electrical systems and providing guidance to protect people, property, and the environment from fire. The guidelines are called the National Electrical Code (NEC). This group continued to meet and update the information contained in the NEC until 1911. The National Fire Protection Association (NFPA) now sponsors the National Electrical Code. The NFPA is an international, nonprofit, membership organization representing over 65,000 members and 100 countries. The NFPA continues to publish the NEC as well as other recommendations for a variety of safety concerns.

The National Electric Code is updated by various committees and code-making panels, each responsible for specific articles in the NEC. The NEC is just one article sponsored by the NFPA, Article 70, and is offered for use in law and regulatory purposes in the interest of life and property protection.

NOTE   Information about the NFPA and many of their codes and standards can be found on the Web at www.nfpa.org. The NFPA codes can be purchased through Global Engineering Documents (global.ihs.com); major codes, such as the National Electrical Code, can be purchased through almost any bookstore.

The National Fire Protection Association (NFPA) also sponsors the following fire and safety codes relating to telecommunications. Currently, there are more than 600 NFPA fire codes and standards used in the United States and throughout the world. Some examples of these documents include the following:

NFPA 1 (Fire Prevention Code)   Addresses basic fire prevention requirements to protect buildings from the hazards created by fire and explosion.

NFPA 13 (Installation of Sprinkler Systems)   Addresses proper design and installation of sprinkler systems for all types of fires.

NFPA 54 (National Fuel Gas Code)   Provides safety requirements for fuel gas equipment installations, piping, and venting.

NFPA 70 (National Electrical Code)   Addresses proper installation of electrical systems and equipment.

NFPA 70B (Recommended Practice for Electrical Equipment Maintenance)   Provides guidelines for maintenance and inspection of electrical equipment such as batteries.

NFPA 70E (Standard for Electrical Safety Requirements for Employee Workplaces)   A basis for evaluating and providing electrical safety-related installation requirements, maintenance requirements, requirements for special equipment, and work practices. This document is compatible with OSHA (Occupational Safety and Health Administration) requirements.

NFPA 72 (National Fire Alarm Code)   Provides a guide to the design, installation, testing, use, and maintenance of fire alarm systems.

NFPA 75 (Standard for the Protection of Electronic Computer/Data Processing Equipment)   Provides requirements for computer room installations that require fire protection.

NFPA 101 (Life Safety Code)   Provides minimum building design, construction, operation, and maintenance requirements needed to protect building occupants from fire.

NFPA 262 (Standard Method of Testing for Fire and Smoke Characteristics of Wires and Cables)   Describes techniques for testing visible smoke and fire-spreading characteristics for wires and cables.

NFPA 780 (Standard for the Installation of Lightning Protection Systems)   Provides guidelines for protection of buildings, people, and special structures against lightning strikes.

NFPA 1221 (Standard for the Installation, Maintenance, and Use of Public Fire Service Communications Systems)   Provides guidance for fire service communications systems that are used for emergency notification. This guide incorporates NFPA 297 (Guide on Principals and Practices for Communications Systems).

These codes are updated every few years; the NEC, for example, is updated every three years. It was updated in 1999 and will be updated again in 2002.

You can purchase guides to the NEC that interpret the code and make it easier for the layman to understand. These guides, as well as the NEC document itself, may be purchased at almost any technical or large bookstore. You can also purchase it online from the NFPA's excellent Web site at `www.nfpa.org`.

If you are responsible for the design of a telecommunications infrastructure, a solid understanding of the NEC is essential. Otherwise, you may find your installation running into all sorts of red tape with your local municipality.

TIP

The best reference on the Internet for the NEC is the National Electrical Code Internet Connection maintained by Mike Holt; this site can be found at `www.mikeholt.com`. There is useful information there for both the beginner as well as the expert. Mike Holt is also the author of the book *Understanding the 1999 National Electrical Code*, which is an excellent reference for anyone trying to make heads or tails of the NEC.

Underwriters Laboratories

Underwriters Laboratories, Inc. (UL) is a nonprofit product safety testing and certification organization. The UL mark on electrical products indicates that the product has been tested for safety. Once a product has been tested, UL allows the manufacturer to place the UL listing mark on the product or product packaging.

KEY TERM

UL listed and UL recognized   The UL mark identifies whether a product is UL *listed* or UL *recognized*. If a product carries the *UL Listing Mark* (UL in a circle) followed by the word LISTED, an alphanumeric control number, and the product name, it indicates that the complete (all components) product has been tested to the UL's nationally recognized safety standards and found to be reasonably free of electrical shock risk, fire risk, and other related hazards. If a product carries the *UL Recognized Component Mark* (the symbol looks like a backward R and J), it means that individual components may have been tested, but not the complete product. This mark may also indicate that testing or evaluation of all the components is incomplete.

There are a number of different UL marks that you may find on a product that has been listed by the UL (all UL listing marks contain UL inside of a circle). Some of these include the following:

UL   This is the most common of the UL marks and indicates that samples of the complete product have met UL's safety requirements.

C-UL   This UL mark is applied to products that have been tested to Canadian safety requirements and will be sold in the Canadian market.

C-UL-US   This is a new listing mark that indicates compliance with both Canadian and United States requirements.

UL-Classified   This mark indicates that the product has been evaluated for a limited range of hazards or is suitable for use under limited or special conditions. Specialized equipment such as fire fighting gear, industrial trucks, and other industrial equipment carry this mark.

C-UL-Classified   This is the classification marking for products that the UL has evaluated using the Canadian standards to evaluate products for specific hazards or properties.

C-UL-Classified-US   This is the classification marking for products that meet the classified compliance standards for both the United States and Canada.

Recognized Component Mark (backwards R and J)   This is the marking for products that have been evaluated by the UL but which are designed to be part of a larger system. Examples are the power supply, circuit board, disk drives, CD-ROM drive, and other components of a computer. The Canadian designator (a C preceeding the Recognized Component Mark) is the Canadian equivalent.

C-Recognized Component   This indicates a component certified by the UL on both the United States and Canadian requirements.

International "emc-Mark"   This indicates that the product meets the electromagnetic requirements for Europe, the United States, Japan, and Australia (or any combination of the four). In the United States, this mark is required for some types of products including radios, microwaves, medical equipment, and radio-controlled equipment.

Other marks that may be found on equipment include the Food Service Product Certification mark, the Field Evaluated Product mark, the Facility Registration mark, and the Marine UL mark.

The NEC requires that a Nationally Recognized Test Laboratory (NRTL) recognize communications cables used in commercial and residential products. This recognition comes in the form of a "listed for the purpose" rating. Usually the UL is used to provide listing services, but the NEC requires that the listing be done by an NRTL, so other laboratories can provide similar services. One such alternate testing laboratory is ETL SEMKO (www.etlsemko.com).

There are over 750 UL standards and standard safety tests; some of the UL standards that are used for evaluating cabling related products include the following:

UL 444   The standard for testing multiple conductors, jacketed cables, single or multiple coaxial cables, and optical fiber cables. This test applies to communications cables that are intended to be used in accordance with the NEC Article 800 or the Canadian Electrical Code (Part I) Section 60.

UL 910   The standard for testing the flame spread and smoke-density (visible smoke) for electrical and optical fiber cables that are used in spaces that handle environmental air (that's a fancy way to say the plenum). This test does not investigate the toxicity of smoke produced, nor does it cover cable construction or electrical performance. NEC Article 800 specifies that cables that have passed this test can carry the NEC flame rating designation CMP (communications multipurpose plenum).

UL 1581   The standard for testing flame-spread properties of a cable that is designed for general purpose use or limited use. This standard contains details of the conductors, insulation, jackets, and coverings as well as the methods for preparing for testing. The measurement and calculation specifications given in chapter are used in UL 44 (Standards for the Thermoset-Insulated Wires and Cables), UL 83 (Thermoplastic-Insulated Wires and Cables), UL 62 (Flexible Cord and Fixture Wire), and UL 854 Service-Entrance Cables). NEC Article 800 specifies that cables that have passed these tests can carry the NEC flame rating designation CMG, CM, or CMX (all of which mean "communications general purpose cable").

UL 1666   The standard for testing flame propagation height for electrical and optical fiber cables that are installed in vertical shafts (the riser). This test only tests to make sure that flames will not spread from one floor to another. It does *not* test for toxicity of the products' combustion. It does not evaluate the construction for any cable or the cable's electrical performance. The NEC Article 800 specifies that cables that have passed this test may carry a designation of CMR (communications riser).

UL has an excellent Web site that has summaries of all the UL standards and provides access to their newsletters. The main UL Web site is www.ul.com; they have a separate Web site for the UL Standards Department located at ulstandardsinfonet.ul.com. UL Standards may be purchased through Global Engineering Documents on the Web at global.ihs.com.

Codes and the Law

At the state level in the United States, many public utility/service commissions issue their own rules governing the installation of cabling and equipment in public buildings. States also monitor tariffs with the service providers for the state.

At the local level, the state, county, city, or other jurisdiction having authority over the area issues codes. Most local governments issue their own codes that must be adhered to when installing communications cabling or devices in the jurisdictions under their authority. Usually, the NEC is the basis for electrical codes, but often the local code will be stricter than the NEC.

Over whom the jurisdiction has authority must be determined prior to any work being initiated. Most localities have a code office, a fire marshall, or a permitting office, which must be consulted.

The strictness of the local codes will vary from location to location and often reflects a particular geographic region's potential for disaster or experience with a previous disaster. For example:

- Some localities in California have strict earthquake codes that state that equipment and racks must be attached to buildings in a specific manner.

- In Chicago, some localities require that all cables be installed in metal conduits so that cables will not catch fire easily. This is to help prevent flame spread that some cables may cause.

- Las Vegas has strict fire containment codes, which require firestopping of openings between floors and fire walls. These opening may be used for running horizontal or backbone cabling.

WARNING   Local codes take precedence over all other installation guidelines. Ignorance of local codes could result in fines, having to reinstall all components, or the inability to obtain a Certificate of Occupancy for a building.

Localities may adopt any version of the NEC or write their own codes. Don't assume that a specific city, county, or state has adopted the NEC word for word. Contact the local building codes or construction or building permits department to be sure that what you are doing is legal.

Historically, telecommunications cable installations were not subject to local codes or inspections. However, there have been several commercial building fires during which the communications cables burned and produced toxic smoke and fumes, and when the smoke mixed with the water vapor, hydrochloric acid was produced, causing death and injury to personnel and property damage. Because of these fires, most jurisdictions having authority now issue permits and perform inspections of the communications cabling.

TIP   If a municipal building inspector inspects your cabling installation and denies you a permit (such as a Certificate of Occupancy), they must tell you exactly which codes you are not in compliance with.

The National Electrical Code

The National Electrical Code (NFPA 70) is reissued every three years. This section of this chapter provides a summary of the information in the NEC. All information contained in this chapter is based upon the 1999 edition of the NEC. Prior to installing any communications cable or devices, consult your local jurisdictions having authority to determine which codes apply to your project.

The reader is advised to become familiar with the local codes. Verify all interpretations with local code enforcement officials, as enforcement of the codes is their responsibility. If you are responsible for the design of a telecommunications infrastructure, or if you supervise the installation of such an infrastructure, you should own the official code documents and be intimately familiar with them.

The following list of NEC articles is not meant to be all-inclusive; they are a representation of some of the articles that may impact telecommunications installations.

The NEC is divided into chapters, articles, and sections. Technical material often refers to a specific article or section. Section 90-3 explains the arrangement of the NEC chapters. The NEC currently contains nine chapters; most chapters concern the installation of electrical cabling, equipment, and protection devices. The pertinent chapter for communications is Chapter 8. The rules governing the installation of communications cable differ from those that govern the installation of electrical cables; thus the rules for electrical cables as stated in the NEC do not generally apply to communications cables. Section 90-3 states this by saying that Chapter 8 is independent of all other chapters in the NEC except where they are specifically referenced in Chapter 8. This section summarizes only information from the 1999 National Electrical Code that is relevant to communications systems; the NEC sections that are missing from this chapter are not relevant to communications cabling. Much of this information refers to Chapter 8 of the NEC.

NOTE   If you would like more information about the NEC, you should purchase the NEC in its entirety or purchase a book such as the one by Mike Holt mentioned earlier in the chapter. Refer also to Mike Holt's Web site www.mikeholt.com.

NEC Chapter 1 General Requirements

NEC Chapter 1 includes definitions, usage, and definitions of spaces about electrical equipment. This content includes the following:

Article 100—Definitions   This article contains definitions for terms found in the NEC as they relate to the proper application of the NEC.

Article 110-3 (b)—Installation and Use   This is one of the articles referenced by Chapter 8. This article states that any equipment included on a list found acceptable by the local jurisdiction having authority and/or any equipment labeled that it has been tested and found suitable for a specific purpose shall be installed and used in accordance with any instructions included in the listing or labeling.

Article 110-26—Spaces about Electrical Equipment   This article calls for a minimum of three feet of clear working space around all electrical equipment to permit safe operation and maintenance of the equipment. This article is not referenced in Chapter 8, but many standards-making bodies address the need for three feet of clear working space around communications equipment.

NEC Chapter 2 Wiring and Protection

NEC Chapter 2 includes information about conductors on poles, installation requirements for bonding, and grounding.

WARNING   Grounding is important to all electrical systems. Grounding systems prevent possibly fatal electrical shock. Further information about grounding can be found in TIA/EIA-607, which is the Commercial Building Grounding and Bonding Requirements for Telecommunications standard.

The grounding information in NEC Chapter 2 that affects communications infrastructures includes:

Article 225-14 (d)—Conductors on Poles   This article is referenced in Chapter 8 and states that conductors on poles shall have a minimum separation of one foot where not placed on racks or brackets. If power cable is on the same pole as communications cables, the power cable (over 300 volts) shall be separated from the communications cables by not less than 30 inches. Historically, power cables have always been placed above communications cables on poles. This is done because communications cables placed on poles cannot inflict bodily harm to personnel working around them. Power cables, on the other hand, *can* inflict bodily harm, so they are put at the top of the pole out of the communications workers' way.

Article 250—Grounding   Covers the general requirements for the bonding and grounding of electrical service installations. Communications cables and equipment are bonded to ground using the building electrical entrance service ground. Several subsections in Article 250 are referenced in Chapter 8; other subsections not referenced in Chapter 8 will be of interest to communications personnel both from a safety stand point and for effective data transmission. Buildings not properly bonded to ground are a safety hazard to all personnel that occupy the building. Communications systems not properly bonded to ground will not function properly.

Article 250-2 (c)—Bonding of Electrically Conductive Materials and Other Equipment   Electrically conductive materials (such as communications conduits, racks, cable trays, and cable shields) that are likely to become energized in a transient high voltage situation (such as lightning striking a building) shall be bonded to ground in such a manner to establish an effective path to ground for any fault current that may be imposed.

Article 250-32—Two or More Buildings or Structures Supplied from a Common Service   This article is referenced in Chapter 8. In multibuilding campus situations, the proper bonding of communications equipment and cables in multiple buildings is governed by several different circumstances, as listed below.

> **Section 250-32 (a)—Grounding Electrode**   Each building shall be bonded to ground with a grounding electrode (such as a ground rod), and all grounding electrodes shall be bonded together to form the grounding electrode system.
>
> **Section 250-32 (b)—Grounded Systems**   In remote buildings, grounding system shall comply with either (1) or (2):
>
> **(1) Equipment Grounding Conductor**   Rules that apply where the equipment-grounding conductor is run with the electrical supply conductors and connected to the building or structure disconnecting means and to the grounding electrode conductors.
>
> **(2) Grounded Conductor**   Rules that apply where the equipment-grounding conductor is not run with the electrical supply conductors.
>
> **Section 250-32 (c)—Ungrounded Systems**   The electrical ground shall be connected to the building disconnecting means.
>
> **Section 250-32 (d)—Disconnecting Means Located in Separate Building or Structure on the Same Premises**   The guidelines for installing grounded circuit conductors and equipment grounding conductors and bonding the equipment grounding conductors to the grounding electrode conductor in separate buildings when there is one main electrical service feed to one building with the service disconnecting means and branch circuits to remote buildings. The remote buildings do not have a service disconnecting means.

Section 250-32 (e)—Agricultural Buildings or Structures   Buildings in which livestock is housed have special rules for bonding the buildings to ground.

Section 250-32 (f)—Grounding Conductor   The size of the grounding conductors per NEC Table 250-122.

Article 250-50—Grounding Electrode System   Referenced from Chapter 8. On premises with multiple buildings, each electrode at each building shall be bonded together to form the grounding electrode system. The bonding conductor shall be installed in accordance with the following:

Section 250-64 (a)   Aluminum or copper-clad aluminum conductors shall not be used.

Section 250-64 (b)   Grounding conductor installation guidelines.

Section 250-64 (e)   Metallic enclosures for the grounding electrode conductor shall be electrically continuous.

Article 250-50—(continued)   The bonding conductor shall be sized per Section 250-66; minimum sizing is listed in NEC Table 250-66. The grounding electrode system shall be connected per Section 250-70. An unspliced (or spliced using exothermic welding process or an irreversible compression connection) grounding electrode conductor shall be run to any convenient grounding electrode. The grounding electrode shall be sized for the largest grounding electrode conductor attached to it.

NOTE

Note that interior metallic water pipes shall not be used as part of the grounding electrode system. This is a change from how communications workers historically bonded systems to ground.

Section 250-50 (a)—Metal Underground Water Pipe   An electrically continuous metallic water pipe, running a minimum of 10 feet in direct contact with the earth, may be used in conjunction with a grounding electrode. The grounding electrode must be bonded to the water pipe.

Section 250-50 (b)—Metal Frame of the Building or Structure The metal frame of a building may be used as the grounding electrode, where effectively grounded.

Section 250-50 (c)—Concrete-Encased Electrode Very specific rules govern the use of steel reinforcing rods, embedded in concrete at the base of the building, as the grounding electrode conductor.

Section 250-50 (d)—Ground Ring A ground ring that encircles the building may be used as the grounding electrode conductor if the minimum rules of this section are applied.

Article 250-52—Made and Other Electrodes Where none of the structural electrodes specified in Section 250-50 is available, one or more of the electrodes specified in Section 250-50 (b) through (d) shall be used. Made electrodes are electrodes that are not an integral part of the permanent building structure. Made rods are installed for the sole purpose for bonding the structure to ground.

Section 250-52 (b)—Other Local Metal Underground Systems or Structures Underground pipes, tanks, or other metallic systems may be used as the grounding electrode. In certain situations, vehicles have been buried and used for the grounding electrode.

Section 250-52 (d)—Rod and Pipe Electrodes Rods and pipes of not less than eight feet in length shall be used. Rods or pipes shall be installed in the following manner:

(1) Electrodes of pipe or conduit shall not be smaller than $3/4$-inch trade size and shall have an outer surface coated for corrosion protection.

(2) Electrodes of rods of iron or steel shall be at least $5/8$-inch in diameter.

(3) The electrode shall be installed so that at least eight feet of length is in contact with the soil at an angle not more than 45 degrees from the vertical. The upper end of the electrode shall be below ground level or flush with the ground. All connections to the rod shall be protected against physical damage.

Section 250-52 (d)—Plate Electrodes Each plate shall be at least $1/4$-inch in thickness installed not less than $2\ 1/2$ feet below the surface of the earth.

Article 250-60—Use of Air Terminals This section is referenced in Article 800. Air terminals are commonly known as lightning rods; they must be bonded directly to ground in a specific manner. The grounding electrodes used for the air terminals shall not replace or be used in lieu of a building grounding electrode. This section does not prohibit the bonding of all systems together. FPN (fine print note) number 2: Bonding together of all separate grounding systems will limit potential differences between them and their associated wiring systems.

Article 250-70—Methods of Grounding Conductor Connection to Electrodes   This section is referenced in Article 800. All conductors must be bonded to the grounding electrode system. Connections made to the grounding electrode conductor shall be made by exothermic welding, listed lugs, listed pressure connectors, listed clamps, or other listed means. Not more than one conductor shall be connected to the electrode by a single clamp.

(1)   For indoor telecommunications purposes only, a listed sheet metal strap-type ground clamp, which has a rigid metal base and is not likely to stretch, may be used.

Article 250-92 (b)—Bonding to Other Services   An accessible means for connecting intersystem bonding and grounding shall be provided at the service entrance. This section is also referenced in Article 800, as telecommunications services must have an accessible means for connecting to the building bonding and grounding system at the entrance of the telecommunications cables into the building. The three acceptable means are

(1)   Exposed nonflexible metallic service raceways.

(2)   Exposed grounding electrode conductor.

(3)   Approved means for the external connection of a copper or other corrosion-resistant bonding or grounding conductor to the service raceway or equipment. An approved external connection is the main grounding busbar, which should be located in the telecommunications entrance facility.

Article 250-104—Bonding of Piping Systems and Exposed Structural Steel   Concerns the use of metal piping and structural steel.

> **Section 250-104 (a)—Metal Water Piping**   Referenced in Article 800. Interior metal water piping systems may be used as bonding conductors as long as the interior metal water piping is bonded to the service entrance enclosure, the grounded conductor at the service, or the grounding electrode conductor or conductors.

Article 250-119—Identification of Equipment Grounding Conductors
Equipment grounding conductors may be bare, covered, or insulated. If covered or insulated, outer finish shall be green or green with yellow stripes.

> **Section 250-119 (a)—Conductors Larger Than No. 6**   A conductor larger than No. 6 shall be permitted. The conductor shall be permanently identified at each end and at each point where the conductor is accessible. The conductor shall have one of the following:
>
> **(1)** Stripping on the insulation or covering for the entire exposed length
>
> **(2)** A green coloring or covering
>
> **(3)** Marking with green tape or adhesive labels

NOTE

The above referenced bonding and grounding minimum specifications are for the purposes of safety. Further specifications for the bonding of telecommunication systems to the building grounding electrode are in the ANSI/TIA/EIA-607 standard, which is discussed in detail in Chapter 2 of this book, "Cabling Standards."

NEC Chapter 3 Wiring Methods and Materials

NEC Chapter 3 covers wiring methods for all wiring installations. Certain articles are of special interest to telecommunication installation personnel.

Article 300-11—Securing and Supporting   This article covers securing and supporting electrical and communications wiring.

> **Section 300-11 (a)—Secured in Place**   Cables and raceways shall not be supported by ceiling grids nor by the ceiling support wire assemblies. All cables and raceways shall use an independent means of secure support and shall be securely fastened in place. This section is a new addition to the 1999 code. Currently, any wires that are supported by the ceiling assembly are "grandfathered" in and do not have to be rearranged. This means that if noncompliant ceiling assemblies existed before NEC 1999 was published, they can remain in place. New installations of cable cannot be supported by

a ceiling or the ceiling support wires; the cables must have their own independent means of secure support.

(1) Ceiling support wires may be used to support cables; however, those support wires shall not be used to support the ceiling. The cable support wires must be distinguished from the ceiling support wires by color, tags, or other means. Cable support wires shall be secured to the ceiling assembly.

Article 300-21—Spread of Fire or Products of Combustion   Installations of cable in hollow spaces such as partition walls, vertical shafts, and ventilation spaces such as ceiling areas, shall be made so that the spread of fire is not increased. Communications cables burn rapidly and produce poisonous smoke and gasses. If openings are created or used through walls, floors, ceilings, or fire-rated partitions they shall be firestopped. If a cable is not properly firestopped, a fire can follow the cable (remember the movie *Towering Inferno*?). A basic rule of thumb is this: If there is a hole, firestop it. Firestop manufacturers have tested and approved design guidelines that must be followed when firestopping any opening.

NOTE   Consult with your local jurisdiction having authority prior to installing any firestop.

Article 300-22—Wiring in Ducts, Plenums, and Other Air-Handling Spaces   This section applies to using communications and electrical cables in air ducts and the plenum.

Section 300-22 (a)—Ducts for Dust, Loose Stock, or Vapor Removal No wiring of any type shall be installed in ducts used to transport dust, loose stock, or flammable vapors or for ventilation of commercial cooking equipment.

Section 300-22 (b)—Ducts or Plenums Used for Environmental Air If cables are to be installed in a duct used to transport environmental air, the cable must be enclosed in a metal conduit or metallic tubing. Flexible metal conduit is allowed for a maximum length of four feet.

Section 300-22 (c)—Other Space Used for Environmental Air The space over a hung ceiling, which is used for the transport of environmental air, is an example of the type of space to which this section applies.

(1) Wiring Methods   Cables and conductors installed in environmental air handling spaces must be listed for the use; a plenum-rated cable must be installed in a plenum-rated space. Other cables or conductors which are not listed for use in that space shall be installed in electrical metallic tubing, metal conduit, or solid bottom metal cable tray with solid metal covers.

Section 300-22 (d)—Information Technology Equipment   Electric wiring in air-handling spaces beneath raised floors for information technology equipment shall be permitted in accordance with Article 645.

NEC Chapter 5 Special Occupancy

NEC Chapters 1 through 3 apply to residential and commercial facilities. NEC Chapter 5 deals with areas that may have special conditions to consider. These include the use of electrical and communications cabling in areas that may be subject to flammable or hazardous gas and liquids.

Article 500-1—Scope: Articles 500 through 504   Articles 500 through 504 cover the requirements for electrical and electronic equipment and wiring for all voltages in locations where fire or explosion hazards may exist. Flammable gases or vapors, flammable liquids, combustible dust, or fibers that may ignite may cause these conditions. This article includes specifications for providing all areas designated as hazardous as having proper documentation. This article further references other standards from the National Fire Protection Association, the American Petroleum Institute, and the Instrument Society of America.

NOTE   For more information on installing wiring and systems in hazardous locations see Articles 501-4 (a), 501-5 (a) and (c), 501-14, 502-4 (a), 502-14, 503-12. All of the above listed articles are referenced in Article 800.

NEC Chapter 7 Special Conditions

NEC Chapter 7 deals with low power systems such as signaling and fire control systems. Article 725 specifically deals with Classes 1, 2, and 3 remote control, signaling, and power-limited circuits.

Article 725-1—Scope   This article covers remote control, signaling, and power-limited circuits that are not an integral part of a device or appliance (for example, safety control equipment and building management systems). The article covers the types of conductors to be used, their insulation, and conductor support.

Article 760   Fire Alarm Systems   Fire alarm systems are not normally considered part of the communications infrastructure, but the systems and wiring used for fire alarm systems are becoming more and more integrated into the rooms and spaces designated for communications. As such, all applicable codes must be followed. Codes of particular interest to communications personnel are

Section 760-61 (d)—Cable Uses and Permitted Substitutions Multiconductor communications cables CMP, CMR, CMG, and CM are permitted substitutions for Class 2 and 3 general and limited use communication cable. Class 2 or 3 riser cable can be substituted for CMP or CMR cable. Class 2 or 3 plenum cable can only be substituted with CMP or MPP plenum cable. Coaxial, single conductor cable MPP (multipurpose plenum), MPR (multipurpose riser), MPG (multipurpose general), and MP (multiporpose) are permitted substitutions for FPLP (fire protective signal cable plenum), FPLR (fire protective signal cable riser), and FPL (fire protective signal cable general use) cable.

Section 760-71 (b)—Conductor Size   The size of conductors in a multiconductor cable shall not be smaller than AWG 26. Single conductors shall not be smaller than AWG 18. Standard multiconductor communications cables are AWG 24 or larger. Standard coaxial cables are AWG 16 or larger.

Article 770—Optical Fiber Cables and Raceways   The provisions of this article apply to the installation of optical fiber cables, which transmit light for control, signaling, and communications. This article also applies to the raceways that contain and support the optical fiber cables. The provisions of this article are for the safety of the installation personnel and users coming in contact with the optical fiber cables; as such, installation personnel should follow the manufacturers' guidelines and recommendations for the installation specifics on the particular fiber being installed. There are three types of optical fiber defined in the NEC:

Nonconductive   Optical fiber cables which contain no metallic members or other conductive materials. It is important for personnel to know whether or not a cable contains metallic members. Cables containing metallic members may become energized by transient voltages or currents, which may cause harm to the personnel touching the cables.

Conductive   Cables that contain a metallic strength member or other metallic armor or sheath. The conductive metallic members in the cable are for the support and protection of the optical fiber—not for conducting electricity or signals—but they may become energized and should be tested for foreign voltages and currents prior to handling.

Composite   Cables which contain optical fibers and current-carrying electrical conductors, such as signaling copper pairs. Composite cables are classified as electrical cables and should be tested for voltages and currents prior to handling. All codes applying to copper conductors apply to composite optical fiber cables.

Article 770-6—Raceways for Optical Fiber Cables   Plastic raceways for optical fiber cables, otherwise known as innerduct, shall be listed for the space it occupies; for example: a general listing for a general space, a riser listing for a riser space, or a plenum listing for a plenum space. The optical fiber occupying the innerduct must also be listed for the space. If a space is plenum, the optical fiber and the innerduct must be listed as plenum. Unlisted underground or outside plant innerduct shall be terminated at the point of entrance.

Article 770-8—Mechanical Execution of Work   Optical fiber cables shall be installed in a neat and workmanlike manner. Cables and raceways shall be supported by the building structure. The support structure for the optical fibers and raceways must be attached to the structure of the building, not attached to a ceiling, lashed to a pipe or conduit, or laid in on ductwork.

Article 770-50—Listings, Marking, and Installation of Optical Fiber Cables   Optical fiber cables shall be listed as being suitable for the purpose; cables shall be marked in accordance with NEC Table 770-51. Most manufacturers put the marking on the optical fiber cable jacket every two to four feet. The code does not tell you what type of cable to use (such as single-mode or multimode), just that the cable should be resistant to the spread of fire. For fire resistance and cable markings for optical cable, see Table 4.1.

TABLE 4.1:   Optical Cable Markings from NEC Table 770-50

Marking	Description
OFNP	Nonconductive optical fiber plenum cable
OFCP	Conductive optical fiber plenum cable
OFNR	Nonconductive optical fiber riser cable
OFCR	Conductive optical fiber riser cable
OFNG	Nonconductive optical fiber general purpose cable
OFCG	Conductive optical fiber general purpose cable
OFN	Nonconductive optical fiber general purpose cable
OFC	Conductive optical fiber general purpose cable

Section 770-50 (a)—Types OFNP and OFCP   For use in plenums, ducts, and other spaces used for handling environmental air. These cables have adequate fire resistance and low smoke producing characteristics.

Section 770-50 (b)—Types OFNR and OFCR   For use in a vertical shaft or from floor to floor. These cables have fire-resistant characteristics capable of preventing the spread of fire from floor to floor.

Section 770-50 (c)—Types OFNG and OFCG   For use in spaces that are not classified as a plenum and are for general use on the same floor. These cables are fire-resistant.

Section 770-50 (d)—Types OFN and OFC   For the same use as OFNG and OFCG cables. OFN and OFC have the same characteristics as OFNG and OFCG as well.

Article 770-52—Optical Fiber Raceways   This article defines the types of raceways that should be used in various situations.

Section 770-52 (a)—Plenum Raceways   Have adequate fire-resistant and low smoke producing characteristics. Plenum raceways must be used in plenum-rated areas. Plenum-rated cable is the only type of cable that may occupy the plenum-rated raceway.

Section 770-52 (b)—Riser Raceways   Have fire-resistant characteristics to prevent the carrying of fire from floor to floor and must be used in the riser.

Section 770-52 (c)—General Purpose Raceways   Are fire-resistant and used in general areas that are not a plenum, or they travel from floor to floor.

Section 770-52 (d)—Cable Trays   Optical fiber cables of the proper listing may be installed in cable trays with other low voltage communication, remote control, signaling, and network cables.

Article 770-53—Cable Substitutions   There is no permitted substitution for an OFNP cable, but an OFNP cable may be substituted for any other listed cable.

NEC Chapter 8 Communications Systems

NEC Chapter 8 is the section of the NEC that directly affects the design and installation of a telecommunications infrastructure.

Article 800-1—Scope   This article covers telephone, telegraph, outside wiring for alarms, paging systems, building management systems, and other central station systems.

NOTE   For the purposes of this chapter, a cable is defined as a factory assembly of two or more conductors having an overall covering.

Article 800-6—Mechanical Execution of Work   Cables and equipment shall be installed in a neat and workmanlike manner. Cables shall be supported by the building structure. Cables shall be installed in such a manner that they will not be damaged by normal building use.

Article 800-7—Hazardous Locations Cables and equipment installed in hazardous locations shall be installed in accordance with Article 500.

Article 800-10—Overhead Wires and Cables Cables entering buildings from overhead poles shall be located on the pole on different crossarms from power conductors; the crossarms for communications cables shall be located below the crossarms for power. There shall be sufficient climbing space through the communications cables in order to reach the power cables. A minimum distance separation of 12 inches must be maintained from power.

Article 800-11—Underground Circuits Entering Buildings In a raceway system underground, such as conduits, communications raceways shall be separated from electric cable raceways with brick, concrete, or tile partitions.

> **Section 800-11 (c)—Point of Entry** New to the 1999 NEC is that the addition of wiring and cables for communications shall enter a building within 20 feet of the electrical service entry point. Separate rooms should be maintained for power and communications, but the service entry rooms shall be within 20 feet of each other for grounding purposes.

Article 800-30—Circuits Requiring Primary Protectors A listed primary protector shall be provided on each circuit run partly or entirely in aerial wire and on each circuit that may be exposed to accidental contact with electric light or power. Primary protection shall also be installed on circuits in a multibuilding environment on premises where the circuits run from building to building and where there exists a lightning exposure. A circuit is considered to have lightning exposure unless one of the following conditions exists:

(1) The buildings are sufficiently high to intercept lightning (such as circuits in a large metropolitan area). Chances of lightning hitting a cable are minimal; the lightning will strike a building and be carried to ground through the lightning protection system. Furthermore, Article 800-13 states that a separation of at least six feet shall be maintained from lightning conductors; do not attach cable to lightning conductors, run cable parallel with them, or lay your cables across them. Stay as far away from the lightning protection systems as possible.

(2) Direct burial or underground cable runs of 140 feet or less with a continuous metallic shield or in a continuous metallic conduit where the

metallic shield or conduit is bonded to the building grounding electrode system. An underground cable with a metallic shield or in metallic conduit that has been bonded to ground will carry the lightning to ground prior to its entering the building. If the conduit or metallic shields have not been bonded to ground, the lightning will be carried into the building on the cable, which could result in personnel hazards and equipment damage.

(3) Areas having an average of five or fewer thunderstorm days per year with an earth resistance of less than 100 ohmmeters. There are very few areas that meet these criteria in the United States. It is strongly recommended that customers in areas that do meet these criteria install primary protection anyway. Primary protection is inexpensive compared to the people and equipment it protects. When in doubt, install primary protection on all circuits entering buildings no matter where the cables originate or how they travel.

There are several types of primary protectors that are permitted by the National Electrical Code.

Fuseless Primary Protectors   Fuseless primary protectors are permitted under the following conditions:

- Noninsulated conductors enter the building through a cable with a grounded metallic sheath and the conductors in the cable safely fuse on all currents greater than the current-carrying capacity of the primary protector. This protects all circuits in an overcurrent situation.

- Insulated conductors are spliced onto a noninsulated cable with a grounded metallic sheath. The insulated conductors are used to extend circuits into a building. All conductors or connections between the insulated conductors and the exposed plant must safely fuse in an overcurrent situation.

- Insulated conductors are spliced onto noninsulated conductors without a grounded metallic sheath. A fuseless primary protector is allowed in this case only if (1) the primary protector is listed for this purpose or (2) the connections of the insulated cable to the exposed cable or the conductors of the exposed cable safely fuse in an overcurrent situation.

- Insulated conductors are spliced onto unexposed cable.

- Insulated conductors are spliced onto noninsulated cable with a grounded metallic sheath and the combination of the primary protector and the insulated conductors safely fuse in an over-current situation.

Fused Primary Protectors   If the above requirements are not met, a fused type primary protector shall be used. The fused type protector shall consist of an arrester connected between each line conductor and ground.

The primary protector shall be located in, on, or immediately adjacent to the structure or building served. The primary protector shall be located as close as practical to the point at which the exposed conductors enter or attach to the building. In a residential situation, primary protectors are located on an outside wall where the drop arrives at the house. In a commercial building, the primary protector is located in the space where the outside cable enters the building. The primary protector location should also be the one that offers the shortest practicable grounding conductor to the primary protector to limit potential differences between communications circuits and other metallic systems.

The primary protector shall not be located in any hazardous location, nor in the vicinity of easily ignitable material.

Article 800-32—Secondary Protector Requirements   Secondary protection shunts to ground any currents or voltages that are passed through the primary protector. Secondary protectors shall be listed for this purpose and shall be installed behind the primary protector. Secondary protectors provide a means to safely limit currents to less than the current-carrying capacity of the communications wire and cable, listed telephone line cords, and listed communications equipment that has ports for external communications circuits.

Article 800-33—Cable Grounding   The metallic sheath of a communications cable entering a building shall be grounded as close as practicable to the point of entrance into the building. The sheath shall be opened to expose the metallic sheath, which shall then be grounded. In some situations, it may be necessary to remove a section of the metallic sheath to form a gap. Each section of the metallic sheath shall then be bonded to ground.

Article 800-40—Primary Protector Grounding Primary protectors shall be grounded in one of the following ways.

Section 800-40 (a)—Grounding Conductor Insulation The grounding conductor shall be insulated and listed as suitable for the purpose.

- Material. The grounding conductor shall be copper or other corrosion-resistant conductive material, either stranded conductor or solid conductor.

- Size. The grounding conductor shall not be smaller than 14 AWG (American Wire Gauge).

- Run in a straight line. The grounding conductor shall be run in as straight a line as possible.

- Physical damage. The grounding conductor shall be guarded from physical damage. If the grounding conductor is run in a metal raceway (such as conduit), both ends of the metal raceway shall be bonded to the grounding conductor.

Section 800-40 (b)—Electrode The grounding conductor shall be attached to the grounding electrode as follows:

- To the nearest accessible location on the building or structure grounding electrode system, the grounded interior metal water pipe system, the power service external enclosures, the metallic power raceway, or the power service equipment enclosure.

- If a building has no grounding means from the electrical service, install the grounding conductor to an effectively grounded metal structure or a ground rod or pipe of not less than five feet in length and 1/2-inch in diameter, driven into permanently damp earth and separated at least six feet from lightning conductors or electrodes from other systems.

Section 800-40 (d)—Bonding of Electrodes If a separate grounding electrode is installed for communications, it must be bonded to the electrical electrode system with a conductor not smaller than No. 6 AWG. Bonding together of all electrodes will limit potential differences between them and their associated wiring systems.

Article 800-50—Listings, Markings, and Installation of Communications Wires and Cables   Communications wires and cables installed in buildings shall be listed as being suitable for the purpose. Communications cables and wires shall be marked in accordance with NEC Table 800-50. Listings and markings shall not be required on a cable that enters from the outside and where the length of the cable within the building, measured from its point of entrance, is less than 50 feet. It is possible to install an unlisted cable more than 50 feet into a building from the outside, but it must be totally enclosed in rigid metal conduit. Outside cables may not be extended 50 feet into a building if it is practicable to place the primary protector closer than 50 feet to the entrance point. Table 4.2 refers to the contents found in NEC Table 800-50.

TABLE 4.2:   Copper Communications Cable Markings from NEC Table 800-5

Marking	Description
MPP	Multipurpose plenum cable
CMP	Communications plenum cable
MPR	Multipurpose riser cable
CMR	Communications riser cable
MPG	Multipurpose general purpose cable
CMG	Communications general purpose cable
MP	Multipurpose general purpose cable
CM	Communications general purpose cable
CMX	Communications cable, limited use
CMUC	Under-carpet communications wire and cable

Article 800-50—Listing Requirements for Communications Wires and Cables and Communications Raceways   Conductors in communications cables, other than coaxial shall be copper.

Section 800-50 (a)—Type CMP   Type CMP cable is suitable for use in ducts, plenums, and other spaces used for environmental air. CMP cable shall have adequate fire-resistant and low smoke producing characteristics.

Section 800-50 (b)—Type CMR   Type CMR cable is suitable for use in a vertical run from floor to floor and shall have fire-resistant characteristics capable of preventing the carrying of fire from floor to floor.

Section 800-50 (c)—Type CMG   Type CMG is for general use, not for use in plenums or risers. Type CMG is resistant to the spread of fire.

Section 800-50 (d)—Type CM   Type CM is suitable for general use, not for use in plenums or risers; it is also resistant to the spread of fire.

Section 800-50 (e)—Type CMX   Type CMX cable is used in residential dwellings. It is resistant to the spread of fire.

Section 800-50 (f)—Type CMUC   Type CMUC is a cable made specifically for under-carpet use; it may not be used in any other place, nor can any other cable be installed under carpets. It is resistant to flame spread.

Section 800-50 (g)—Multipurpose (MP) Cables   Multiconductor and coaxial cables meeting the same requirements as communications cables shall be listed and marked as MPP, MPR, MPG, and MP.

Section 800-50 (h)—Communications Wires   Wires and cables used as cross-connects or patch cables in communications rooms or spaces shall be listed as being resistant to the spread of fire.

Section 800-50 (i)—Hybrid Power and Communications Cable
Hybrid power and communications cables are permitted where both the power and communications cables are listed and rated for 600 volts minimum and are resistant to the spread of fire. These cables are allowed only in general purpose spaces, not in risers or plenums.

Section 800-50 (j)—Plenum Communications Raceway   Plenum-listed raceways are allowed in plenum areas; they shall have low smoke producing characteristics and be resistant to the spread of fire.

Section 800-50 (k)—Riser Communications Raceway   Riser-listed raceways have adequate fire-resistant characteristics capable of preventing the carrying of fire from floor to floor.

Section 800-50 (l)—General Purpose Communications Raceway
General purpose raceway has adequate fire-resistant characteristics.

Very Important

Power Limited is the key

Article 800-52—Installation of Communications Wires, Cables, and Equipment   This article defines the installation of communications wires, cables, and equipment with respect to electrical power wiring.

Section 800-52 (a)   Communications wires and cables are permitted in the same raceways and enclosures with power limited: remote-control circuits, signaling circuits, fire alarm systems, nonconductive and conductive optical fiber cables, community antenna and radio distribution systems, and low-power network powered broadband communications circuits.

Section 800-52 (c) (1)   Communications cables or wires shall not be placed in any raceway, compartment, outlet box, junction box, or similar fitting with any conductors of electrical power.

- **Other Applications**   Communications cables and wires shall be separated from electrical conductors by at least two inches, but the more separation the better. The NEC and the ANSI standards no longer give minimum power separations from high voltage power and equipment because it has been found that separation is generally not enough to shield communications wires and cables from the induced noise of high power. Concrete, tiles, grounded metal conduits, or some other form of insulating barrier may be necessary to shield communications from power.

- **Spread of Fire or Products of Combustion**   Openings around penetrations through walls, floors, ceilings, or partitions shall be firestopped using approved methods.

Knowing and Following the Codes

Knowing and following electrical and building codes is of utmost importance. If you don't, at the very least you may have problems with building inspectors. More importantly, other problems may arise from an installation that does not meet building codes that may endanger the lives of the occupants of the building.

Further, even if you are an information technology director or network manager, being familiar with the codes that affect the installation of your cabling infrastructure can help you when working with cabling and electrical contractors. Knowing your local codes can also help you when working with your local, city, county, or state officials.

chapter 5

Cabling System Components

- Components of a Structured Cabling System

- Wiring Closets

- Patch Panels and Connecting Blocks

Pick up any cabling catalog, and you will find a plethora of components and associated buzzwords that you never dreamed existed. Terms such as patch panel, wall plate, plenum, 110-block, 66-block, modular jacks, raceways, and patch cables are just a few of these terms. What does this all mean, and how are these components used to create a structured cabling system?

In this chapter, we'll provide an overview and descriptions of the inner workings of a structured cabling system so that you won't feel so confused next time you pick up a cabling catalog or work with professional cabling installers. Topics in this chapter include the following:

- Picking the right type of cable
- Fire safety and cabling products
- Cabling components in workstation areas
- Concealing cables and protecting fiber optic cable
- Telecommunications closets
- Networking components often found in a telecommunications closet

The Cable

In Chapter 2, "Cabling Standards," we discussed the various cable media that are recommended by the TIA/EIA-568-A Commercial Building Telecommunications Cabling Standard and some of the cables' performance characteristics. Rather than repeating the characteristics of available cable media such as unshielded twisted pairs and optical fiber, we'll describe the components involved in transmitting data from the work area to the wiring closet. These major cable components can be described as horizontal cable, backbone (vertical) cable, and patch cables.

Horizontal and Backbone Cables

The terms *horizontal* cable and *backbone* (sometimes called vertical) cabling have nothing to do with the cable's physical orientation toward the horizon. Horizontal cables run between a cross-connect panel in a wiring closet and a wall jack. Backbone (or vertical) cables run between wiring closets and the main cross-connect point of a building (usually referred to as the equipment room). Figure 5.1 illustrates the typical components found in a structured cabling environment, including the horizontal cable, backbone cable, telecommunication outlets, and patch cables.

FIGURE 5.1:

Typical components found in a structured cabling system

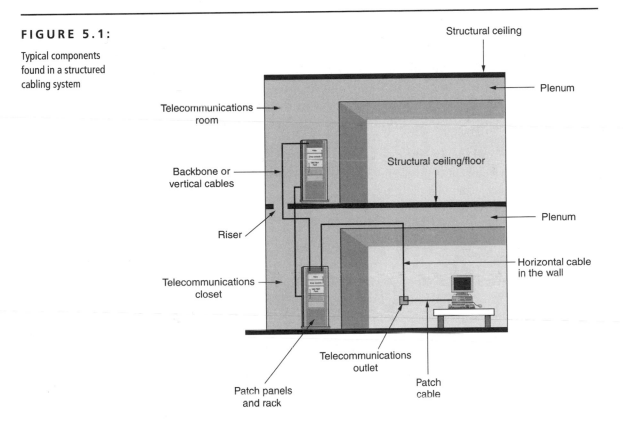

More information on horizontal and backbone cabling can be found in Chapter 2. Installing copper cabling for use with horizontal or backbone cabling is discussed in Chapter 7, "Copper Cable Media."

Horizontal Cables

Horizontal runs are usually implemented with 100-ohm four-pair unshielded twisted-pair (UTP) solid-conductor cables, as specified in the TIA/EIA-568 standard for commercial buildings. The standard also provides for horizontal cabling to be implemented using 150-ohm shielded twisted-pair (STP) cable, 62.5/125-micron multimode optical fiber, and 50-ohm coaxial cable. Coaxial cable will be dropped from the recognized media in the "B" version of the 568 standard, which is expected to be ratified by the TIA in mid-2000.

Backbone Cables

As with horizontal cables, backbone (also called *vertical* or *riser*) cables can be implemented using 100-ohm UTP, 150-ohm STP, 62.5/125-micron multimode optical fiber or 8.3/125-micron single-mode optical cable. Optical fiber is the preferred installation media because of distance limitations associated with copper wiring. Another plus for running a fiber backbone is that glass does not conduct electricity and is not subject to electromagnetic interference (EMI) like copper is. Similarly, if lightning were to strike a building in a multibuilding campus, the risk of that current being conducted between buildings across the cabling infrastructure is greatly reduced.

Modular Patch Cables

Modular patch cables (cords) are used to provide the connection between field-terminated horizontal cables to network connectivity devices such as switches and hubs. As the saying goes, a chain is only as strong as its weakest link. Because of their role in structured cable infrastructures, modular patch cords are almost always that weakest link.

Where horizontal cables contain solid conductors, patch cords are made with stranded cores to withstand the abuse of flexing and reconnecting. Although you could build your own field terminated patch cords, we strongly recommend against this practice.

The manufacture of patch cords is very exacting, and even under controlled factory conditions it is difficult to achieve and guarantee consistent transmission performance. The first challenge lies within the modular plugs themselves. The parallel alignment of the contact blades forms capacitive plate, which becomes a source of signal coupling or crosstalk. Further, the untwisting and splitting of the pairs as a result of the termination process increases the cable's susceptibility to crosstalk interference. If that weren't enough, the mechanical crimping process that secures the plug to the cable could potentially disturb the cable's normal geometry by crushing the conductor pairs. This is yet another source of crosstalk interference and a source of attenuation.

TIP
Factory terminated and tested modular cords are required to achieve consistent transmission performance. We strongly recommend using premade patch cords rather than making them yourself.

At first glance, modular patch cords may seem like a no-brainer, but it turns out that they may be the most crucial component to accurately specify. As a side note, the current TIA/EIA-568 and ISO/IEC 11801 standards provide only for electrical standards. When specifying patch cables, you may also require that your patch cords be tested to ensure that they meet the proper transmission performance standards for their category.

Pick the Right Cable for the Job

Professional cable installers and cable plant designers are called upon to interpret and/or draft cable specifications to fulfill businesses' structured cabling requirements. Anyone purchasing cable for business or home use may also be required to make a decision regarding what type of cable to use. Installing inappropriate cable could be very unfortunate in the event of a disaster such as a fire.

What do we mean by unfortunate? It is very conceivable that the cable plant designer or installer could be held accountable in court and held responsible for damages incurred as a result of substandard cable installation. Cables come in a variety of different ratings, and many of these ratings have to do with how well the cable will fare in a fire. If a poorly made or substandard cable is exposed to extreme heat and/or water from fire suppression systems, toxic fumes and liquid can be produced.

Rather than focus on performance standards, which are specified in Chapter 2, we will focus on cable jackets (sheathing) standards as they relate to fire safety.

NOTE
See the InfraTech, Inc. white paper, *Warranty Liability*, for some interesting information on warranties, cable testing, and the critical issues surrounding cabling. This white paper can be found on the Internet at www.totalcomsolution.com.

Cable Jackets

UTP cabling that conforms to the TIA/EIA-568-A standard is available; this cable is referred to as Category 3, 4, 5, or 5e cable. These cable types can be ordered with both plenum and nonplenum jackets. Manufacturers have also started shipping products that exceed Category 5e performance with the expectation that their cables will perform as Category 6 and Category 7 cables as specified in future standards; these cables also ship with plenum and nonplenum jackets.

NOTE   For specific information on the performance specifications of Categories 3, 4, 5, and 5e cabling, see Chapter 1, "Introduction to Data Cabling."

Regardless of the type of jacket on the cable, each cable Category will meet its expected transmission performance characteristics. The jackets themselves are designed to meet or exceed recommendations for combustibility. More details can be found on cable ratings (and the cable markings that identify these ratings) in Chapter 1.

Plenum

The word *plenum* is used frequently in the air conditioning, construction, and cabling industries. The plenum is an area in a building in which cable can be installed, such as a duct-way or an enclosed area within the ceiling or walls. Cable jackets are said to be plenum-rated when they meet low flame-spread and low-smoke safety performance specifications for air handling duct spaces. Plenum sheathings are typically composed of PVC with flame-retardant additives. The individual wires are typically insulated with fluorinated ethylene propylene (FEP), another flame-retarding plastic, although no standard is in place that requires this practice.

A cable that is rated as a plenum class of cable can be used in the building plenum as well as in a "riser," which is a connection between two floors of a building. Cables that are rated for use only as riser cable cannot be used in the plenum.

PVC   *PVC* stands for polyvinyl chloride, one of the earliest developed and most widely used plastics today. PVC cable is typically used within surface-mounted raceways and is not rated for use in plenum spaces unless it is contained within a separate conduit.

Local Government Codes and Building Regulations

When researching this chapter, we came across a recent white paper published by the Association of Cabling Professionals (ACP) that calls for an increased awareness of cabling for fire safety. This white paper, *Cabling for Safe Schools* (available at www.wireville.com/firesafe/w-paper.htm), gives advice for writing plenum cable specifications.

The article describes the materials used to form the cable sheathing, as well as the insulation surrounding the individual wires. When we defined plenum-grade cable, we said that the wires are usually insulated with FEP (and have been since 1976, when plenum cable was introduced). The treated PVC sheathings and FEP insulation provide a combination that far exceeds the low flame-spread and low smoke specification defined by UL. FEP is usually used with Category 5 and greater cables; lower category cables often use PVC for both the jacket and wire insulation.

In recent times, however, the laws of supply and demand have caught up with the cable manufacturing industry. Because of the explosive growth of networking, the requirements for the production of plenum cable have exceeded the available supply of FEP. To keep up with the demand, cable manufacturers have begun to substitute FEP insulation with plastics such as polyethylene, which can maintain the stringent electrical performance characteristics outlined by the TIA/EIA and NEC. However, polyethylene is nearly 10 times as combustible as FEP, so plenum cables using polyethylene wire insulation only marginally pass the fire safety standards set by UL. Cable engineers often refer to cables with a large amount of polyethylene as having a "high fuel load" because they are more likely to burn quickly, emit toxic fumes, and produce lots of visible smoke.

When drafting a specification for plenum cable, it is not enough to say Category 5 plenum cable. Insist on the installation of plenum cable with FEP insulation.

For more information on building codes, please see Chapter 4's ("Cable System and Infrastructure Constraints") examination of the government and building regulations for safety and performance as specified by the National Electric Code (NEC) and Underwriters Laboratories (UL).

Wall Plates and Connectors

Wall plates and connectors serve as the work area endpoints for horizontal cable runs. In addition to wall plates, you also have the option of installing surface and/or floor-mounted boxes in your work area. Using these information outlets or telecommunications outlets helps you organize your cables; these cables also aid in protecting horizontal wiring from end users. Without the modularity provided by information outlets, you would wind up wasting a significant amount of cable trying to accommodate all the possible computer locations within a client's work area—the excess cable would most likely wind up as an unsightly coil in a corner.

NOTE   Refer to Chapter 8, "Wall Plates," for more information on wall plates.

The drawback of information outlets is that they require you to introduce another patch cable into your cabling equation, and we've already discussed the issues regarding patch cable reliability and performance.

Wall plates and surface- and floor-mounted boxes come in a variety of colors to match your office's decor. Companies such as Ortronics, Panduit, and The Siemon Company also offer products that can be used with modular office furniture. The Siemon Company even went one step farther and integrated their telecommunications cabling system into their own line of office furniture called MACsys. Figure 5.2 shows a sample faceplate from the Ortronics TracJack line of faceplates.

To help ensure that a cable's proper bend radius is maintained, Panduit and The Siemon Company offer angled modules to snap into their faceplates. Figure 5.3 shows The Siemon Company's CT faceplates and MAX series angled modules. Faceplates with angled modules for patch cords keep the cord from sticking straight out and becoming damaged.

FIGURE 5.2:

Ortronic's TracJack
faceplates

(Photo courtesy of Ortronics)

FIGURE 5.3:

The Siemon Company's
CT faceplates and MAX
series angled modules

(Photo courtesy of The Siemon
Company)

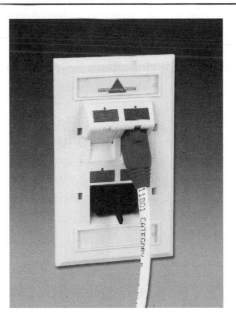

In addition to modular connectors for twisted-pair cable, connectors also exist for optical fiber, coaxial, and even audio/video cable to fulfill your organization's information needs.

Cabling Pathways

In this section, we'll look at the cabling system components outlined by the TIA/EIA-569-A Commercial Building Telecommunications Pathways and Spaces Standard for concealing, protecting, and routing your cable plant. In particular, we'll describe the components used in work areas and wiring closets and for horizontal and backbone cable runs. As you read these descriptions, you'll notice that one element they all have in common is that they must be electrically grounded per the TIA/EIA-607 Commercial Building Grounding and Bonding Requirements for Telecommunications.

Conduit

Conduit can be metallic or nonmetallic, rigid or flexible piping (as permitted by the applicable electrical code) that runs from a work area to a wiring closet. One advantage of using conduit to hold your cables is that it may already exist in your building. Assuming that there is space left, it shouldn't take long to pull your cables through it. A drawback to conduit is that it provides a finite amount of space to house cables. When drafting specifications for conduit, we recommend that you require that enough conduit be installed so that it would be only 40 percent full by your current cable needs. Conduit should only be filled to 60 percent, so this margin leaves you with plenty of room for future growth.

According to the TIA/EIA-569-A, standard conduit can be used to route horizontal and backbone cables. Firestopped conduit can also be used to connect wiring closets in multistoried buildings. Some local building codes require the use of conduit for *all* cable, both telecommunication and electrical.

Cable Trays

As an alternative to conduit, *cable trays* can be installed to route your cable. Cable trays are typically wire racks specially designed to support the weight of a cable infrastructure. Cable trays provide an ideal way to provide for the management of a large number of horizontal runs. Cables simply lie within the tray, so they are very accessible when it comes to maintenance and troubleshooting. The TIA/EIA-569-A standard provides for cable trays to be used for both horizontal and backbone cables.

Figure 5.4 shows a cable runway system that resembles ladders. This type of runway looks like a ladder that is mounted horizontally inside the plenum or over the top of equipment racks in a telecommunications closet or equipment room. In the plenum, this type of runway keeps cables from being draped over the top of florescent lights, HVAC equipment, or ceiling tiles; they are also helpful in keeping cable from crossing electrical conduit. This is especially useful near telecommunication closets and equipment rooms where there may be a large amount of horizontal cable coming together. When used in a telecommunications or equipment room, this runway can keep cables up off the floor or run them from a rack of patch panels to an equipment rack.

FIGURE 5.4:

Runway system used to suspend cables overhead

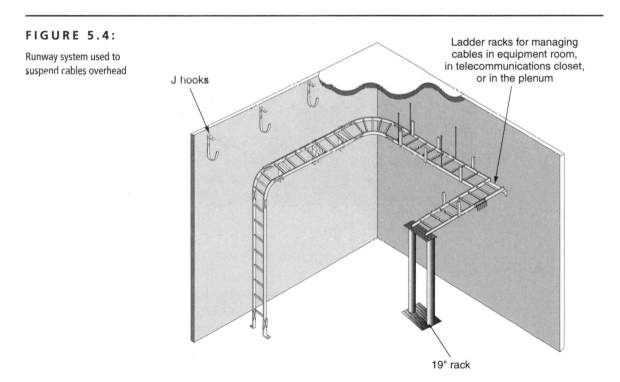

J hooks

Ladder racks for managing cables in equipment room, in telecommunications closet, or in the plenum

19" rack

Another type of cable suspension device is the CADDY CatTrax from Erico. These cable trays are flexible, easy to install, and can be installed in the plenum, telecommunications closet, or equipment room. The CatTrax (shown in Figure 5.5) also keeps cables from being laid directly onto the ceiling tile of a false ceiling or across lights and electrical conduit because it provides continuous support for cables.

FIGURE 5.5:

The CADDY CatTrax flexible cable tray from Erico

(Photo courtesy of Erico)

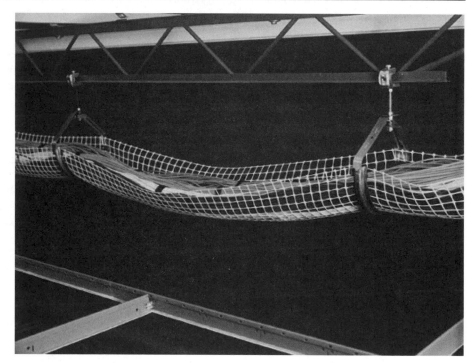

Raceways

Raceways are a special type of conduit used for surface mounting horizontal cables. Raceways are usually pieced together in a modular fashion with vendors providing connectors that do not exceed the minimum bend radius. Raceways are mounted on the outside of a wall in places where cable is not easily installed inside the wall; common uses include walls made of brick or concrete (where no telecommunications conduit has been installed). To provide for accessibility and modularity, raceways are manufactured in components (see Figure 5.6). Figure 5.7

shows a sample of a surface mount runway that is carrying a couple of different cables; this runway is hinged to allow cables to be easily installed in the runway.

FIGURE 5.6:

Surface-mounted modular raceway system

(Photo courtesy of MilesTek)

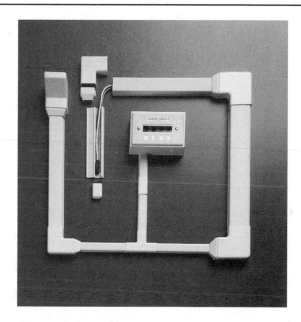

FIGURE 5.7:

Sample surface-mount runway with cables

(Photo courtesy of The Siemon Company)

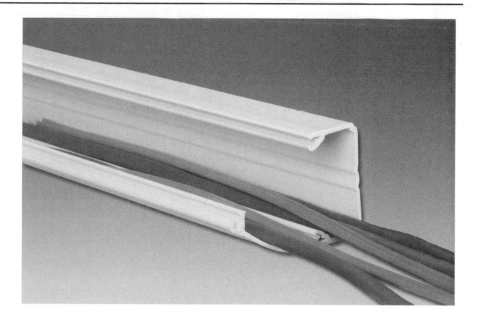

One-piece systems usually provide a flexible joint to open the raceway to gain access to cables, which can then be snapped shut. To meet your information output needs, vendors producing raceways often produce modular connectors to integrate with their raceway system.

Fiber Protection Systems

As with raceways, *fiber protection systems* (see Figure 5.8) are a special type of conduit and cable management system designed specifically to address the special protection needs of optical fiber cable. Copper and coaxial cables are often much more forgiving with respect to bend radius than are optical fiber cables. Severe bends in optical fiber cable will result in attenuation and eventual signal loss, which translates to lost data, troubleshooting, downed network connections, and lost productivity. To protect your fiber investment, we recommend that you consider investing in a fiber protection system.

FIGURE 5.8:

The Siemon Company's LightWays fiber protection system

(Photo courtesy of The Siemon Company)

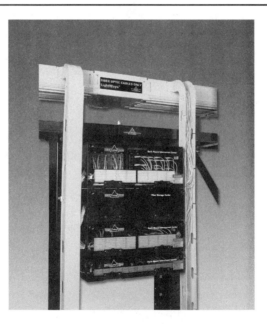

KEY TERM   **Inner Duct**   *Inner duct* is a flexible, plastic conduit system that is often used to run fiber optic cable through in order to provide an additional layer of protection.

When evaluating a prospective system, you should account for the total cost of the installation rather than the cost of materials. Ensure that it will support the weight of your cable without sagging. In addition, because your network will grow with time, you should consider how flexible the solution will be for future modifications. Will you be able to add new segments or vertical drops without having to move existing cable? The most expensive part of your system will be the labor costs associated with the installation. Does the system require special tools to install, or does it snap together in a modular fashion?

Wiring Closets

The *wiring closet* is where your network begins. Up to this point, we've described the components required to bring your end users to this common ground, the foundation of the digital nervous system. In this section, we'll cover the types of wiring closets, along with suggested design elements. From there, we'll discuss the pieces of equipment found within a typical closet. We'll conclude with a brief discussion on network devices.

A Wiring Closet by Any Other Name

Wiring closets are known by a number of names and acronyms. The TIA/EIA-568-A standard refers to wiring closets as telecommunications closets. Some cabling professionals refer to these as wiring closets, while others call them intermediate cross-connects (ICCs) or intermediate distribution frames (IDFs). These are usually remote locations in a large or multistory building.

The wiring closets are all connected to a central wiring center known by the TIA/EIA-568-A standard as an equipment room (or telecommunications room). Other cabling professionals call these the main distribution frame (MDF) or the main cross-connect (MCC); often an organization's computer room is in the same location as the MCC or MDF.

Horizontal cabling is run from telecommunications closets to the workstation areas. Backbone (or vertical) cabling runs from the telecommunications closets to the equipment rooms.

There are two types of wiring closets, *intermediate distribution frames* (IDFs) and *main distribution frames* (MDFs). Depending on the size of your organization and size of your building, you may have one or more IDFs concentrating to an MDF. IDFs are strategically placed throughout a building to provide a single point for termination from your work areas. In a multistory building, you should have at least one IDF per floor. As the distances between your end devices and IDF approach their recommended maximum limits (90 meters in the case of Category 5 installations), you should consider implementing additional IDFs. IDFs are connected to MDFs in a star configuration by either fiber or copper. As we mentioned in our discussion of backbone cabling, fiber is preferred because the distances between closets can reach to 2,000 meters. When connecting with copper, the closets must be within 800 meters of each other.

TIA/EIA Recommendations for Wiring Closets

The TIA/EIA does not distinguish between the roles of wiring closets (telecommunications closets) for its published standards. The following is a summary of the minimum standards for a telecommunications wiring closet per the TIA/EIA-569-A Commercial Building Telecommunications Pathways and Spaces Standard.

- The telecommunications closet must be dedicated to telecommunications functions.

- Equipment not related to telecommunications shall not be installed or enter the telecommunications closet.

- Multiple closets on the same floor shall be interconnected by a minimum of one 78(3) (3-inch or 78 mm opening) trade size conduit or equivalent pathway.

- The telecommunications closet must support a minimum floor loading of 2.4 kPA (50 lb/ft2).

The equipment room is used to contain the main distribution frame (the main location for backbone cabling), phone systems, power protection, uninterruptible power supplies, LAN equipment (such as bridges, routers, switches, and hubs), and possible file servers and data processing equipment. TIA/EIA-569-A provides a recommendation of a minimum of .75 square feet of floor space in the equipment room for every 100 square feet of user workstation area. You can also estimate the requirements for square footage using Table 5.1, which shows estimated equipment room square footage for an equipment room based on the number of workstations.

TIP   Further information about the TIA/EIA-569-A standard can be found in Chapter 1.

TABLE 5.1: Estimated Square Foot Requirements Based on the Number of Workstations

Number of Workstations	Estimated Equipment Room Floor Space
1 to 100	150 square feet
101 to 400	400 square feet
401 to 800	800 square feet
801 to 1,200	1,200 square feet

NOTE   The actual floor space required in any equipment room will be based on the amount of equipment that must be housed in the room. Use Table 5.1 for a base calculation, but don't forget to take into account equipment that may be in this room, such as LAN racks, phone switches, and power supplies.

The TIA/EIA further recommends that the following conditions be met in addition to the minimum standards requirements:

- There shall be a minimum of two dedicated 120V 20A nominal, non-switched, AC duplex electrical outlet receptacles, each on separate branch circuits.

- Additional convenience duplex outlets shall be placed at 1.8 m (six feet) intervals around the perimeter, 150 mm (six inches) above the floor.

- There shall be access to the telecommunications grounding system, as specified by TIA/EIA-607.

- HVAC requirements to maintain temperature that is the same as adjacent office area shall be met. A positive pressure shall be maintained with a minimum of one air change per hour or per code.

- There shall be a minimum of one closet per floor to house telecommunications equipment/cable terminations and associated cross-connect cable and wire.

- The wiring closet shall be located near the center of the area being served.

- Horizontal pathways shall terminate in the telecommunications closet on the same floor as the area served.

- The wiring closet shall accommodate seismic requirements.

- Two walls should have 20 mm (3/4 in) A-C plywood 2.4 m (8 ft) high.

- Lighting shall be a minimum of 500 lx (50-foot candles) and mounted 2.6 m (8.5 ft) above the floor.

- False ceilings shall not be provided.

- There shall be a minimum door size of 910 mm (36 in) wide and 2000 mm (80 in) high without sill, hinged to open outward or slide side-to-side or be removable, and it shall be fitted with a lock.

Although this last list is suggestions, it is our position that you should strive to fulfill as many of these requirements as possible. If your budget only allows for a few of these suggestions, grounding, separate power, and the ventilation and cooling requirements should be at the top of your list to fulfill.

TIP   Locking telecommunication closets and equipment rooms are especially important in security-conscious environments. Under some circumstances, an organization's data can be compromised if a malicious person gains physical access to your telecommunications equipment. Some organizations go so far as to put alarm systems on their telecommunications closets and equipment rooms.

Cabling Racks and Enclosures

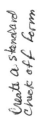

Racks are the pieces of hardware that help us to organize the presentation and management of our cabling infrastructure. Racks range in height from 39 to 84 inches in height and come in two widths, 19 and 23 inches. Nineteen-inch widths are much more commonplace and have been in use for nearly 60 years. These racks are commonly called just 19-inch racks or, sometimes, EIA racks. Mounting holes are spaced between 5/8 and two inches apart, so you can be assured that no matter who your preferred equipment vendor is, their equipment will fit in your rack. In general, there are three types of racks available for purchase: wall-mounted brackets, skeletal frames, and full equipment cabinets.

TIP
Not all racks use exactly the same type of mounting screws or mounting equipment. Make sure that you have sufficient screws or mounting gear for the types of racks that you purchase.

Wall-Mounted Brackets

For small installations and areas where economy of space is a key consideration, *wall-mounted brackets* may provide the best solution. Wall-mounted racks such as MilesTek's Swing Gate wall rack in Figure 5.9 have a frame that swings out 90 degrees to provide access to the rear panels. Wall racks such as the one featured here include wire guides to help with cable management.

FIGURE 5.9:

MilesTek's Swing Gate wall rack

(Photo courtesy of MilesTek)

Racks such as the one in Figure 5.9 are ideal for small organizations that may only have a few dozen workstations or phone outlets but are still concerned about building an organized cabling infrastructure.

TIP   When installing wall-mounted racks with swinging doors, be sure to verify that there is enough room to actually open the front panel before the rack is finally secured to the wall.

Skeletal Frames (19-Inch Racks)

Skeletal frames, like the one shown in Figure 5.10 and often called 19-inch racks or EIA racks, are probably the most common type of rack. These racks are designed and built based on the EIA-310C standards. These skeletal frames come in sizes ranging from 39 to 84 inches in height with a 22-inch base plate to provide stability. Their open design makes it easy to work on both the front and back of the mounted equipment.

FIGURE 5.10:

Skeletal frame (19-inch rack)

(Photo courtesy of MilesTek)

When installing this type of rack, you should ensure that you leave enough space between the rack and the wall to accommodate the installed equipment (most equipment is 6 to 18 inches deep). You should also leave enough space behind the rack so that an individual working behind the rack will have sufficient space (at least 12 to 18 inches). You will also need to secure the rack to the floor so that it does not topple over.

These racks can also include cable management. If you have ever worked with a rack that has more than a few dozen patch cords connected to it with no cable management devices, then you will understand just how messy such a rack can be. Figure 5.11 shows an Ortronics Mighty Mo II wall-mount rack that includes cable management.

FIGURE 5.11:

Ortronics Mighty Mo II
wall-mount rack with cable
management

(Photo courtesy of Ortronics)

Racks are not limited to just patch panels and network connectivity devices. Server computers, for example, can be installed into a rack-mountable chassis. There are many accessories that can be mounted into rack spaces, including utility shelves, monitor shelves, and keyboard shelves. Figure 5.12 shows some of the more common types of shelves available for 19-inch racks. If you have a need for some sort of shelf that is not commercially available, most machine shops are equipped to manufacture what you desire.

FIGURE 5.12:

Shelves available for
19-inch racks

(Photo courtesy of MilesTek)

Full Equipment Cabinets

The most expensive of your rack options, full equipment cabinets, offer the security benefits of locking cabinet doors. Full cabinets can be as simple as the ones shown in Figure 5.13, but they can also become quite elaborate, with Plexiglass doors and self-contained cooling systems. Racks such as the one in Figure 5.13 provide better physical security, cooling, and protection against electromagnetic interference than standard 19-inch rack frames. In some high security environments, this type of rack is required for LAN equipment and servers.

FIGURE 5.13:

Full equipment cabinet

(Photo courtesy of MilesTek)

Cable Management Accessories

If your rack equipment does not include wire management, there are numerous cable management accessories, as shown in Figure 5.14, to suit your organizational requirements. Large wiring closets can quickly make a rat's nest out of your horizontal cable runs and patch cables. Cable hangers on the front of a rack can help arrange bundles of patch cables to keep them neat and orderly. Rear-mounted cable hangers provide strain relief anchors and can help to organize horizontal cables that terminate at the back of patch panels.

FIGURE 5.14:

Cable management acces-
sories from MilesTek

(Photo courtesy of MilesTek)

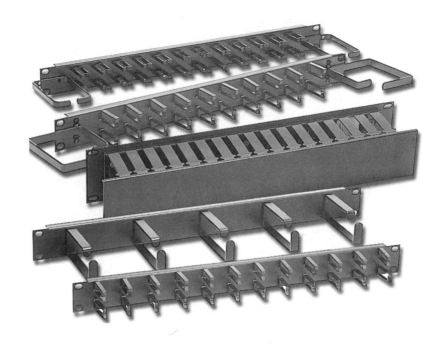

Electrical Grounding

In our discussion on conduit, we stated that regardless of your conduit solution, you will have to make sure that it complies with the TIA/EIA-607 Commercial Building Grounding and Bonding Requirements for Telecommunications standard for electrical grounding. The same holds true for your cable rack implementations. Why is this so important? Well, to put it bluntly, your network can kill you, and in this case, we're not referring to the massive coronary brought on by users' printing challenges!

Don't dismiss This {

For both alternating and direct current systems, electrons flow from a negative to a positive source, with two conductors required to complete a circuit. If a difference in resistance exists between a copper wire path and a grounding path, a voltage potential will develop between your hardware and its earth ground. In the best-case scenario, this voltage potential will form a Galvanic cell, which will simply corrode your equipment. This phenomenon is usually demonstrated in freshman chemistry classes by using a potassium chloride salt bridge to complete the circuit between a zinc anode and a copper cathode. If the voltage potential were to become great enough, simply touching your wiring rack could complete the circuit and discharge enough electricity to kill you or one of your colleagues.

WARNING   One of the authors knows someone who was actually thrown to the ground when he touched an improperly grounded communications rack. Grounding is serious business and should not be undertaken by the layperson. Low voltage does not mean that large shocks cannot be generated.

We recommend working with your electrical contractor and power company to get the best and shortest ground you can afford. One way to achieve this is to deploy separate breaker boxes for each office area. This will shorten the grounding length for each office or group.

Cross-Connect Devices

Fortunately for us, organizations seem to like hiring consultants; however, there are types of consultants most people are usually less than thrilled to see—in particular, space utilization and efficiency experts. Why? Because they make everyone move! *Cross-connect devices* are cabling components you can implement to make impending changes to your network less painful.

66 Punch-Down Blocks

66 punch-down blocks, shown in Figure 5.15, have been used as telephone system cross-connect devices for over 25 years. 66 blocks support 50 pairs of wire. Wires are connected to the terminals of the block using a punch-down tool. When a wire is "punched down" into a terminal, the wire's insulation is pierced and the connection is established to the block. Separate jumpers then connect blocks. When the need arises, jumpers can be reconfigured to establish the appropriate connections.

FIGURE 5.15:

66 punch-down block

(Photo courtesy of The Siemon
Company)

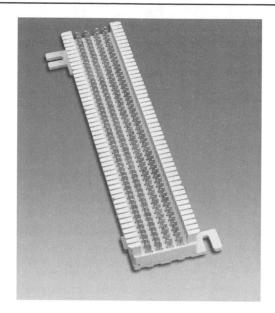

110 and S-210 Punch-Down Blocks

110-blocks (as shown in Figure 5.16) are another flavor of punch-down media;
they are better suited for use with data networks. 110-blocks come in sizes that
support anywhere from 25 to 500 wire pairs. Unlike 66-blocks, 110-blocks are not
interconnected via jumpers, but instead use 24 AWG cross-connect wire. The
Siemon Company produces a connecting block called an S-210 that is capable of
delivering the proposed performance standards for Category 6.

Some installations of data and voice systems require the use of 25-pair connectors. Some network hubs and phone systems use these 25-pair connectors to
interface with their hardware rather than modular-type plugs (such as the RJ-45).
You can purchase 110-style connector blocks that are prewired with 25-pair connector cables, such as the one seen in Figure 5.17.

FIGURE 5.16:

110 punch-down blocks

(Photo courtesy of MilesTek)

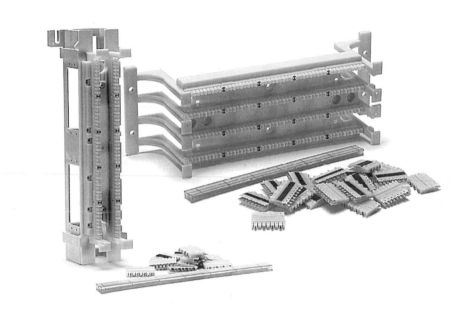

FIGURE 5.17:

The Siemon Company's prewired 110-block with 25-pair connectors

(Photo courtesy of The Siemon Company)

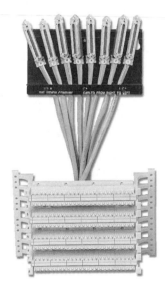

TIP	If you purchase a 110- or 66-style block that is wired to 25-pair connectors, make sure that the equipment is rated to the appropriate Category of cable performance that you intend to use it with. 66-blocks are rarely used for data.

Modular Patch Panels

As an alternative to punch-down blocks, you can also terminate your horizontal cabling directly into RJ-45 patch panels (see Figure 5.18). This approach is becoming increasingly popular because it lends itself to exceptionally easy reconfigurations. To reassign a network client to a new port on the switch, all you have to do is move a patch cable. Another benefit is that when they're installed cleanly, they can make your wiring closet look great!

FIGURE 5.18:

Modular patch panels

(Photo courtesy of MilesTek)

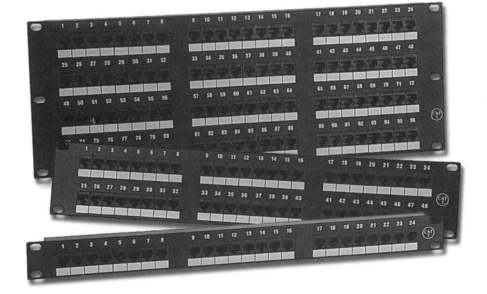

> **TIP**
>
> When ordering any patch panel, make sure that you order one that has the correct wiring pattern (T568A or T568B). The wiring pattern is usually color-coded on the 110-block.

Patch panels normally have 110-block connectors on the back. In some environments, only a few connections are required, so there is no need for a large patch panel. In other environments, it may not be possible to mount a patch panel with a 110-block on the back because of space constraints. In this case, smaller modular jack wall-mount blocks (see Figure 5.19) may be useful. These are available in a variety of sizes and port configurations. You can also get these in either horizontal or backbone configurations.

FIGURE 5.19:

The Siemon Company's S-110 modular jack wall-mount block

(Photo courtesy of The Siemon Company)

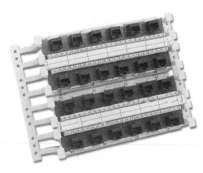

Consolidation Points

Both the TIA/EIA-568-A and ISO/IEC 11801 standards allow for a single transition point or *consolidation point* in horizontal cabling. The consolidation point is usually used to transition between a 25-pair UTP cabling (or separate four-pair UTP cables) that originated in the wiring closet to cable that spreads out to a point where there may be many networked or voice devices, such as with modular furniture. An example of a typical consolidation point (inside a protective cabinet) is shown in Figure 5.20.

FIGURE 5.20:

Consolidation point

(Photo courtesy of The Siemon Company)

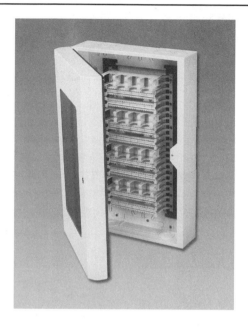

Fiber Optic Connector Panels

If your organization is using optical fiber cabling (either for horizontal or backbone cabling), then you may see *fiber optic connector panels*. These will sometimes look similar to the UTP RJ-45 panels seen earlier in this chapter, but they are commonly separate boxes that contain space for cable slack. A typical 24-port fiber optic panel is pictured in Figure 5.21.

FIGURE 5.21:

Fiber optic connector panel

(Photo courtesy of MilesTek)

Administration Standards

After troubleshooting a network issue and figuring out that it's a problem with the physical layer, have you ever walked to a wiring closet and opened the door to find complete spaghetti? In our consulting practices, we see this all too often. In situations like this, our clients pay two to three times the regular consulting fees because it takes so much time to sort through the mess.

They should have some background →

NOTE   Network administrators should be judged by the neatness of their wiring closets. ↗

To provide a standard methodology for the labeling of cables, pathways, and spaces, the TIA/EIA published the TIA/EIA-606 Administration Standard for the Telecommunications Infrastructure of Commercial Buildings. In addition to guidelines for labeling, the standard also recommends the color-coding scheme shown in Table 5.2.

TABLE 5.2:   Color-Coding Schemes

Sys Include in Adm manual

Color Code	Usage
Black	No termination type assigned
White	1st level backbone (MC/IC or MC/TC terminations)
Red	Reserved for future use
Gray	2nd level backbone (IC/TC terminations)
Yellow	Miscellaneous (auxiliary, security alarms, etc.)
Blue	Horizontal cable terminations
Green	Network connections
Purple	Common equipment (PBX, host LANs, muxes)
Orange	Demarcation point (central office terminations)
Brown	Interbuilding backbone (campus cable terminations)

As well as labeling and color-coding, you should also consider bundling groups of related cables with nylon cable ties. Nylon cable ties come in a variety of sizes for all kinds of applications. When bundling cables, however, be sure not to cinch them too tightly, as you could disturb the natural geometry of the cable. If you ever have to perform maintenance on a group of cables, all you have to do is cut the nylon ties (tie-wraps) and add new ones when you're finished. Nylon tie-wraps are sturdy and very common, but they must be cut to be removed; some companies are now making Velcro tie-wraps.

TIP
Nylon cable ties are inexpensive, and you can never have too many of them.

Whether you implement the TIA/EIA-606 standard or come up with your own methodology, the most import aspect of cable administration is to ensure you have accurate documentation of your cable infrastructure.

Summary

As you've seen, there is a tremendous amount of information we are responsible for as network and cabling professionals. To summarize the key points we've tried to make throughout the chapter, you should always use factory-terminated patch cords to make connections in the work area and between patch panels in the wiring closet. Patch cords are the weakest link within your infrastructure, and patch cords manufactured by a reputable vendor are the only way to ensure consistent performance. You should also insist that the patch cables you purchase have been tested for transmission performance.

When drafting a specification for plenum spaces, insist upon plenum-grade cable with FEP insulators. When evaluating an RFP that doesn't have this specification, point it out to your clients. A simple phone call that points out the differences in plenum cables could be a deciding factor in being awarded a cabling contract.

To protect your fiber investment, you should invest in a fiber protection system. When evaluating the total cost of ownership of such a system, be sure to include installation as well as materials costs. Choose a system that can grow to meet your future fiber requirements as painlessly as possible.

Wiring closets can get hot very quickly. Make sure that your equipment room has adequate ventilation, and consider investing in a separate cooling system.

Power to the room should be provided in its own circuits, and backup power should be provided in the form of uninterruptible power supplies. Neatness is paramount. Label everything in accordance with the TIA/EIA-606 standard, or develop and document your own labeling method. The extra two minutes that labeling takes during installation will save you hours when you have to troubleshoot physical layer issues.

Remember, electricity can kill! Make sure that the equipment in your telecommunications closet is grounded as per the TIA/EIA-607 Commercial Building Grounding and Requirements for Telecommunications standard. Consult Chapter 12, "Cabling System Design and Installation," for more information about grounding.

The wiring equipment discussed in this chapter is commonly found in many cabling installations; larger, more complex installations may have additional components that we did not mention here. The components mentioned in this chapter can be purchased from just about any cabling or telecommunications supplier. Some of the companies that were very helpful in the production of this chapter have much more information online. You can find more information about these companies and their products by visiting them on the Web:

- MilesTek: www.milestek.com
- The Siemon Company: www.siemon.com
- Ortronics: www.ortronics.com   *Include in manual*
- Erico: www.erico.com

chapter 6

Tools of the Trade

- Building a Cabling Tool Kit

- Common Cabling Tools and Their Function

- Cabling Supplies to Have on Hand

- Generic Tools and Supplies That You Should Carry with You

This chapter discusses tools that are essential to proper installation of data and video cabling. It also describes tools, many of which you should already have, that make the overall job of installing cables easier.

Don't start any cabling job without the proper tools. If you're reading this book, it is likely that in some way you're a hands-on individual—either because you're a do-it-yourselfer or you're managing people that are hands-on. The right tools are essential for installing a data cabling system. You might be able to install a data cabling system with nothing but a knife and screwdriver, but you may cost yourself many hours of frustration and diminished quality if you go this route.

If you are a hands-on person, you can probably relate to this story: A number of years ago, Jim was attempting to change the rear shock absorbers on a truck. The nuts holding the shocks were rusted in place and, working in his garage, there was nothing he could do to loosen them. After maybe an hour of frustrating effort, Jim gave up and took the truck to a local service station for help. In literally seconds, the nuts were loose. What made the difference? Tools. The mechanics at the station had access to tools that were missing from Jim's home handyman kit. Using tools like a hydraulic lift and impact wrenches made the job infinitely easier than lying on a garage floor and tugging on a Craftsman Best box-end wrench.

The rather obvious point here is that most jobs have special tools that, at the least, make the job easier and, at the most, may be required to make completion of the job possible at all. Using the appropriate tools also gives you the benefit of doing the job more efficiently, which saves you time and money. Knowing what the right tools are and where to use them is an important part of the job.

The Right Tool and the Right Price

Just as the right tools are important for doing a job well, so is making sure that you have high quality equipment. Suppose you see two punch-down tools advertised in a catalog and one of them is $20 and the other is $60. Ask why one is more expensive than the other is. Compare the features of the two tools; if they seem to be the same, you can usually assume that more expensive tool is designed for professionals.

With all tools there are levels of quality and a range of prices you can choose from. It's trite but true: you get what you pay for, generally speaking, so our advice is to stay away from the really cheap stuff. On the other hand, if you only anticipate light to moderate use, there is no reason to buy top-of-the-line equipment.

Building a Cabling Tool Kit

Throughout this chapter, there are a number of different of tools discussed and photos used to illustrate the various tools being discussed. Don't believe for a minute that we've covered all the models and permutations available! This chapter should serve as an introduction to the types of tools you may require, and it should help you to recognize a particular tool so you can go get the one that best suits you. It is impossible for us to determine your exact tool needs. Keeping your own needs in mind, read through the descriptions that follow and pick and choose those tools that you anticipate using. Then, shop your list.

There are myriad online catalog houses and e-commerce sites where you can browse and buy the tools and parts you need to complete your cabling tool kit. A few of these include:

- IDEAL DataComm at www.idealindustries.com

- MilesTek at www.milestek.com

- Jensen Tools at www.jensentools.com

- The Siemon Company at www.siemon.com

- Radio Shack at www.radioshack.com

If you have to scratch and sniff before buying, visit a local distributor in your area. Check your local phone book for vendors such as Anicom, Anixter, GE Supply, Graybar, and many other distributors that specialize in servicing the voice/data market; many of these vendors have counter sale areas where you can see and handle the merchandise before purchasing.

There is also no way to describe in precise detail how each tool works or all the ways you can apply it to different projects. We'll supply a basic description of each tool's use, but because of the wide variety of manufacturers and models available, you'll have to rely on the manufacturer's instructions on exactly how to use a particular device.

Tools Can Be Expensive

Most people that are not directly involved in the installation of telecommunications cabling systems don't realize how many tools you might actually need to carry or the value of those tools. A do-it-yourselfer can get by with a few hundred dollars' worth of tools, but a professional may need to carry many thousands of dollars' worth, depending on the job that is expected.

A typical cabling team of three or four installers may carry as much as $12,000 in installation gear and tools. If this team carries sophisticated testing equipment such as a fiber optic OTDR, the value of their tools may jump to over $50,000. A fully equipped fiber optic team carrying an OTDR and optical fiber fusion splicer could be responsible for over $100,000 worth of tools. And some people wonder why cabling teams insist on taking their tools home with them each night!

Common Cabling Tools

There are a number of tools that are common to most cabling tool kits. Most of these tools are essential for installing even the most basic of cabling systems. These include wire strippers, wire cutters, cable crimpers, punch-down tools, fish tape, and toning tools.

Wire Strippers

What do you want to strip today? The variety of cable strippers represented in this section is a function of the many different types of cable you can work with, different costs of the cable strippers, and versatility of the tools.

Strippers for UTP and STP cables are used to remove the outer jacket and have to accommodate the fact that the geometry of UTP cables can vary greatly. Unlike coax, which is usually consistently smooth and round, twisted-pair cables can have irregular surfaces due to the jacket shrinking down around the pairs. Additionally, the jacket thickness can differ greatly depending on brand and flame rating. The trick is to aid removal of the jacket without nicking or otherwise damaging the insulation on the conductors underneath.

The wire stripper in Figure 6.1 uses an adjustable blade so that you can fix the depth, matching it to the brand of cable you are working with. Some types use spring tension to help keep the blade at the proper cutting depth.

FIGURE 6.1:

Wire stripper

(Photo courtesy of MilesTek)

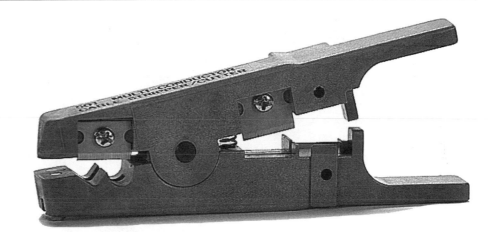

In both cases, the goal is to score (cut) the jacket without penetrating it completely. Then, you flex the cable to break the jacket along the scored line. This ensures that the wire insulation is nick-free since the jacket was never fully cut through. In some models, the tool can also be used to score or slit the jacket lengthwise in the event you need to expose a significant length of conductors.

NOTE When working with UTP or STP cables, you will rarely need to strip the insulation from the conductors themselves. Termination of these cable types on patch panels, cross-connects, and most wall plates employs the use of *insulation displacement connectors* (IDCs) that make contact with the conductor by slicing through the insulation. Should you need to strip the insulation from a twisted-pair cable, keep a pair of common electrician's strippers handy. Just make sure it can handle the finer gauge wires such as 22, 24, and 26 AWG that are commonly used with LAN wiring.

Coaxial Wire Strippers

Coaxial cable strippers are designed with two or three depth settings. These settings correspond to the different layers of material in the cable. Coaxial cables are pretty standardized in terms of central conductor diameter, thickness of the insulating and shielding layers, and thickness of the outer jacket, making this an effective approach.

In the inexpensive (but effective for the do-it-yourself folks) model shown in Figure 6.2, the depth settings are fixed. The wire stripper in Figure 6.2 can be used to strip coaxial cables (RG-59 and RG-6) to prepare them for F-type and twist-on connectors.

FIGURE 6.2:

Inexpensive coaxial wire strippers

(Photo courtesy of MilesTek)

To strip the cable, you insert it in a series of openings that allows the blade to penetrate to different layers of the cable. At every step, you rotate the tool around the cable and then pull the tool toward the end of the cable, removing material down to where the blade has penetrated. The blade is notched at the position used to remove material down to the conductor in order to avoid nicking the conductor itself and thereby providing a point at which the conductor might break.

One problem with the model shown in Figure 6.2 is that you end up working pretty hard to accomplish the task at hand. For its low price, the extra work may be a good tradeoff if stripping coax isn't a day-in, day-out necessity. However, if you are going to be working with coaxial cables on a routine basis, you should consider some heftier equipment. Figure 6.3 shows a model that accomplishes the task in a more mechanically advantageous way (that means it's easier on your hands). In addition, it offers the advantage of adjustable blades so that you can optimize the cutting thickness for the exact brand of cable you're working with.

FIGURE 6.3:

Heavy duty coaxial wire strippers

(Photo courtesy of MilesTek)

Coaxial strippers are commonly marked with settings that assist you in removing the right amount of material at each layer from the end of the cable so it will fit correctly in an F- or BNC-type connector.

Fiber Optic Cable Strippers

Fiber optic cables require very specialized tools. Fortunately, the dimensions of fiber coatings, claddings, and buffers are standardized and manufactured to precise tolerances. This allows tool manufactures to provide tools such as the one shown in Figure 6.4 that will remove material to the exact thickness of a particular layer without damage to the underlying layer. Typically, these look like a conventional multigauge wire stripper with a series of notches to provide the proper depth of penetration.

FIGURE 6.4:

Fiber optic cable stripper

(Photo courtesy of IDEAL DataComm)

Wire Cutters

You can, without feeling very guilty, use a regular set of lineman's pliers to snip through coaxial, UTP, and STP. You can even use them for fiber optic cables, but cutting through the aramid yarns used as strength members can be difficult; you will dull your pliers quickly, not to mention what you may do to your wrist.

KEY TERM　　**Aramid**　*Aramid* is the common name for the material trademarked as Kevlar that's used in bulletproof vests. It is used in optical fiber cable to provide additional strength.

So why would you want a special tool for something as mundane as cutting through the cable? Here's the catch regarding all-purpose pliers: They will mash the cable flat as they cut. All the strippers described above work best if the cable is round. Specialized cutters such as the one shown in Figure 6.5 are designed for coax and twisted-pair cables to preserve the geometry of the cable as they cut. This is accomplished using curved instead of flat blades.

FIGURE 6.5:

FIGURE 6.5:

Typical wire cutters

(Photo courtesy of MilesTek)

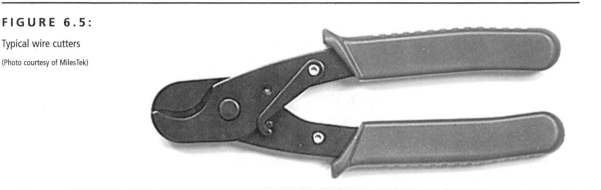

For fiber optic cables, special scissors are available; these scissors are designed to cut through aramid with relative ease. Figure 6.6 shows scissors designed for cutting and trimming the Kevlar strengthening members found in fiber optic cables.

FIGURE 6.6:

IDEAL DataComm's Kevlar scissors

(Photo courtesy of IDEAL DataComm)

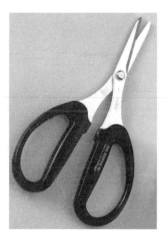

Cable Crimpers

Modular lugs and coaxial connectors are attached to cable ends using crimpers. Crimpers are essentially very specialized pliers. So, why can't you just use a pair of pliers? Crimpers are designed to apply force evenly and properly for the plug or connector being used. Some crimpers use a ratchet mechanism to ensure that a complete crimp cycle has been made. Without this special design, your crimp job will be inconsistent at best, and it may not work at all. In addition, you'll damage connectors and cable ends, resulting in wasted time and materials. Remember that the right tool, even if it's expensive, can save you money!

Twisted-Pair Crimpers

Crimpers for twisted-pair cable must accommodate various sized plugs. The process of crimping involves removing the cable jacket to expose the insulated conductors, inserting the conductors in the modular plug (in the proper order!), and applying pressure to this assembly using the crimper. The contacts for the modular plug (such as the ones shown in Figure 6.7) are actually blades that cut through the insulation and make contact with the conductor. The act of crimping not only establishes this contact, but also pushes the contact blades down into proper position for insertion into a jack. Finally, the crimping die compresses the plug strain relief indentations to hold the connector on the cable.

FIGURE 6.7:

Eight-position modular plug (a.k.a. RJ-45 connector)

(Photo courtesy of The Siemon Company)

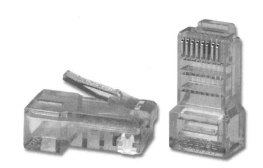

NOTE   Modular plugs for cables with solid conductors (horizontal wiring) are different from plugs for cables with stranded conductors (patch cords). The crimper fits either, but be aware of the difference when you are buying plugs and making your connections.

The crimper shown in Figure 6.8 is designed so that a specific die is inserted, depending on the modular plug being crimped. If you buy a flexible model like this, you will need dies that fit an eight-conductor position (data) (a.k.a. RJ-45) and a six-position type (voice) (a.k.a. RJ-11 or RJ-12) plug at a minimum. If you intend to do any work with telephone handset cords, you should also get a die for four-position plugs.

FIGURE 6.8:

Crimper with multiple dies for RJ-11, RJ-45, and MMJ modular connectors

(Photo courtesy of MilesTek)

Other twisted-pair crimpers are configured for specific plug sizes and don't offer the flexibility of changeable dies. Inexpensive models available at the local home improvement center for less than $15 usually have two positions; these are configured to crimp either eight-, six-, or four-position type plugs. These inexpensive tools often do not have the ratchet mechanism found on professional installation crimpers. Figure 6.9 shows a higher quality crimper tool that has two positions, one for eight-position plugs and one for four-position plugs.

FIGURE 6.9:

IDEAL Ratchet Telemaster crimper tool with crimp cavities for eight- and four-position modular plugs

(Photo courtesy of IDEAL DataComm)

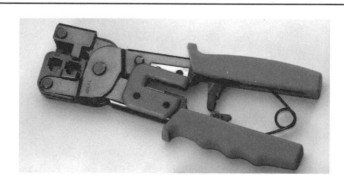

Less expensive crimpers are targeted at the do-it-yourself market—those who are doing a little phone extension work around the house on a weekend or who only crimp a few cables at a time. Better quality units targeted for the intermediate user will usually have one opening for eight-position and one opening for six-position plugs. If you are doing work with data connectors such as the eight-position modular jack (RJ-45), your crimping tool must have a crimp cavity for eight-position plugs.

Coaxial Cable Crimpers

Coaxial cable crimpers also are available with either changeable dies or with fixed-size crimp openings. Models aimed strictly at the residential installer will feature dies or openings suitable for applying F-type connectors to RG-58, RG-59, and RG-6 series coax. For the commercial installer, a unit that will handle dies such as RG-11 and thinnet with BNC-type connectors is also necessary. Figure 6.10 shows IDEAL DataComm's Crimpmaster Crimp Tool, which can be configured with a variety of die sets such as RG-6, RG-9, RG-58, RG-59, RG-62, cable TV F-type connectors, and others.

FIGURE 6.10:

IDEAL Crimpmaster Crimp
Tool frame

(Photo courtesy of IDEAL
DataComm)

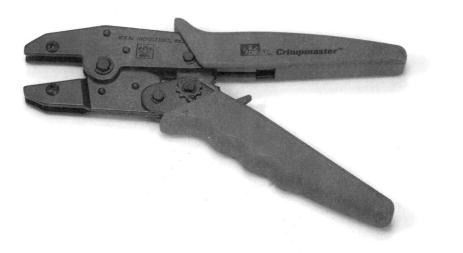

There's a very functional item that is used in conjunction with your crimper to install F-type RG-59 and RG-6 connectors. Figure 6.11 shows an F-plug installation tool. One end is used to ream out space between the outer jacket and the dielectric layer of the coax. On the other end, you thread the F-type connector and use the tool to push the connector down on the cable. This accessory speeds installation of RG-59 connectors and reduces wear and tear on your hands.

FIGURE 6.11:

MilesTek F-plug installation tool

(Photo courtesy of MilesTek)

Punch-Down Tools

Twisted-pair cables are terminated in jacks, cross-connect blocks (66-blocks), or patch panels (110-blocks) that use insulation displacement connectors (IDCs). Essentially, IDCs are little knife blades with a V-shaped gap or slit between them. You force the conductor down into the V and the knife blades cut through the insulation and make contact with the conductor. While you could accomplish this using a small flat-blade screwdriver, doing so very often will guarantee you infamy in the hack hall of fame. It would be sort of like hammering nails with a crescent wrench. The correct device for inserting a conductor in the IDC termination slot is a punch-down tool.

NOTE   You can find more information on 66-blocks and 110-blocks in Chapter 5, "Cabling System Components" and Chapter 7, "Copper Cable Media." Additional information about wall plates can be found in Chapter 8, "Wall Plates."

A punch-down tool is really just a handle with a special "blade" that fits a particular IDC. There are two main types of IDC terminations: the 66-block and the 110-block. 66-block terminals have a long history rooted in voice cross-connects. The 110-block is a newer design, originally associated with AT&T but now generic in usage. In general, 110-type IDCs are used for data and 66-type IDCs are used for voice, but neither is absolutely one or the other.

Different blades are used depending upon whether or not you are going to be terminating on 110-blocks or 66-blocks. Though the blades are very different, most punch-down tools are designed to accept either. In fact, you usually purchase the tool with one and buy the other as an accessory, so that one tool serves two terminals.

Blades are designed with one end being simply for punch down. When you turn the blade end-for-end and apply the other end, it punches down and cuts off excess conductor in one operation. Usually you will use the punch-and-cut end, but for daisy chaining on a cross-connect, you would use the end that just punches down.

TIP

If you are terminating cables in Krone or BIX (by Norcom) equipment, you will need special punch-down blades. These brands use IDC designs that are proprietary.

Punch-down tools are available in their least expensive form as being "nonimpact." Nonimpact tools generally require more effort to make a good termination, but they are well suited for people that only occasionally perform punch-down termination work. Figure 6.12 shows a typical nonimpact punch-down tool.

FIGURE 6.12:

IDEAL DataComm's nonimpact punch-down tool

(Photo courtesy of IDEAL DataComm)

The better quality punch-down tools are "impact" tools that are spring-loaded. When you press down and reach a certain point of resistance, the spring gives way providing positive feedback that the termination is made. Typically, the tool will adjust to "high" and "low" impact settings. Figure 6.13 shows an impact punch-down tool. Notice the dial near the center of the tool; this is the dial that allows the user to adjust the impact setting. The manufacturer of the termination equipment you are using will recommend the proper impact setting.

IDEAL DataComm's impact tool with adjustable impact settings

(Photo courtesy of IDEAL DataComm)

With experience, you can develop a technique and rhythm that lets you punch down patch panels and cross-connects very quickly. However, there is nothing so frustrating as interrupting your sequence rhythm because the blade stayed on the terminal instead of in the handle of the tool. The better punch-down tools have a feature that locks the blade in place, rather than just holding it in with friction. For the occasional user, a friction-held blade is okay, but for the professional, a lock-in feature is a must that will save you time and, consequently, money.

> **TIP**
>
> You should always carry at least one extra blade for each type of termination that you are doing. Once you get the hang of punch-downs, you'll find that the blades don't break often, but they do break occasionally. Extra blades are inexpensive and can be easily ordered from the company you purchased your punch-down tool from.

Some brands of 110-block terminations support the use of special blades that will punch down multiple conductors at once, instead of one at a time.

If you are punching down IDC connectors on modular jacks from The Siemon Company that fit into modular wall plates, a tool from The Siemon Company may be of use to you. Rather than trying to find a surface to hold the modular jack against, you can use the Palm Guard (see Figure 6.14) to hold the modular jack in place while you punch down the wires.

FIGURE 6.14:

Palm Guard

(Photo courtesy of The Siemon Company)

Fish Tapes

A good fish tape is the best friend of the installer who does MACs (moves, adds, changes) or retrofit installations on existing buildings. Essentially, it is a long wire, steel tape, or fiberglass rod that is flexible enough to go around bends and corners but retains enough stiffness so that it can be pushed and worked along a pathway without kinking or buckling.

Like a plumber's snake, a fish tape is used to work blindly through an otherwise inaccessible area. For example, say you needed to run a cable from a ceiling space down inside a joist cavity in a wall to a new wall outlet. From within the ceiling space, you would thread the fish tape down into the joist cavity through a hole in the top plate of the wall. From this point, you would maneuver it in front of any insulation and around any other obstacles such as electrical cables that might also be running in the joist cavity. When the tape became visible through the retrofit outlet opening, you would draw the tape out. Then, you would attach either a pull string or the cable itself and withdraw the fish tape.

Fish tapes are available in various lengths (see Figure 6.15), with 50- and 100-foot lengths being common. They come in spools that allow them to be reeled in and out as necessary and are available virtually anywhere electrical supplies are sold, in addition to those sources mentioned earlier.

FIGURE 6.15:

IDEAL DataComm's fish tape

(Photo courtesy of IDEAL DataComm)

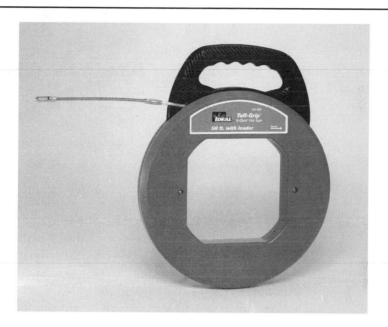

Voltage Meter

There is a right way and a wrong way to determine if an electrical circuit has a live voltage on it. Touching it is the wrong way. A simple voltage meter such as the one pictured in Figure 6.16 is a much better solution, and it won't put your health plan to work. While not absolutely necessary in the average data cabling tool kit, a voltage meter is rather handy.

FIGURE 6.16:

Voltage/continuity tester

(Photo courtesy of IDEAL
DataComm)

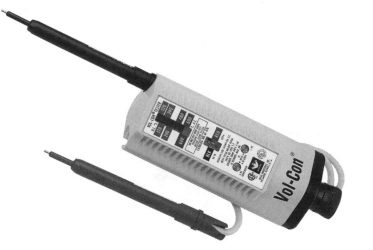

Cable Testing

There are dozens of cable testers available on the market. Some of these sell for less than $100, full-featured ones sell for over $5,000, and high-end fiber optic testers can sell for over $30,000! Chapter 14, "Cable System Testing and Trouble-shooting," discusses cable testing and certification, so we won't steal any thunder from that chapter here. However, there are some basic tools that you should include in your tool kit that you don't need to get a second mortgage on your house to purchase.

Cable testers can be as simple as a cable-toning tool that helps you to identify a specific cable; they can also be continuity testers or the cable testers that cost thousands of dollars.

Cable Toning Tool

A cable toner is a device for determining if the fundamental cable installation has been done properly. It should be noted that we are not discussing the sophisticated type of test set used to certify a particular level of performance, such as a Category 5 link or channel. These are discussed in detail in Chapter 14.

In its simplest form, the toner is a simple continuity tester that is used to confirm that what is connected at one end is electrically continuous all the way to the other end. An electrical signal, or tone, is injected on the circuit being tested and is either received and verified on the other end, or looped back for verification on the sending end. Some tools provide visual feedback (with a meter), while others utilize audio feedback. Testing may require that you have a partner (or a lot of scurrying back and forth on your part) at the far end of the cable to administer the inductive probe or loop-back device. Figure 6.17 shows a tone generator and Figure 6.18 shows the corresponding amplifier probe.

FIGURE 6.17:

Tone generator

(Photo courtesy of IDEAL DataComm)

More sophisticated testers will, in addition to continuity, report length of run and check for shorts and crosses (accidental contact of one conductor with another), reversed pairs, transposed pairs, and split pairs.

FIGURE 6.18:

Amplifier probe

(Photo courtesy of IDEAL
DataComm)

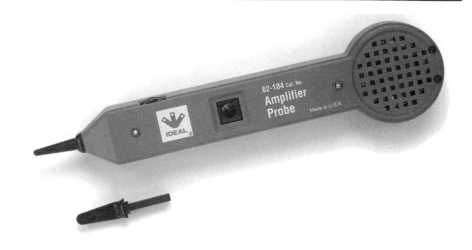

Twisted-Pair Continuity Tester

Many of the common problems of getting cables to work are simple ones. The $5,000 cable testers are nice, but for simple installations they are overkill. A simple continuity tester can help you solve many of the common problems of data and voice twisted-pair cabling, including testing for open circuits and shorts. If the cable installer is not careful during installation, the cable's wire pairs may be reversed, split, or otherwise incorrectly wired.

Figure 6.19 shows a simple continuity tester from IDEAL DataComm; this tester (the LinkMaster Tester) consists of the main testing unit and a remote tester. The remote unit is patched into one side of the cable, and the main unit is patched into the other side. It can quickly and accurately detect common cabling problems such as opens, shorts, reversed pairs, or split pairs. Cable testers such as the one shown in Figure 6.19 are available from many vendors and sell for under $100. Testers such as these can save you many hours of frustration as well as the hundreds or even thousands of dollars that you might spend on a more sophisticated tester.

FIGURE 6.19:

IDEAL's LinkMaster Tester

(Photo courtesy of IDEAL
DataComm)

Coaxial Tester

Though coaxial cable is a little less complicated to install and terminate, problems can still arise during installation. The tester shown in Figure 6.20 is the IDEAL DataComm Mini Coax Tester. This inexpensive, compact tester is designed to test coax cable runs that are terminated with BNC-style connectors. It can test two modes of operation: standard and Hi-Z for long runs. Coaxial cable testers will quickly help you identify opens and shorts.

FIGURE 6.20:

IDEAL's Mini Coax Tester

(Photo courtesy of IDEAL
DataComm)

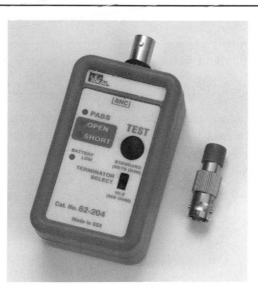

Optical Fiber Testers

Testing optical fiber cable introduces a whole new class of cable testers. Just like copper cable testers, optical fiber testers are specialized devices. Figure 6.21 shows a simple continuity tester that verifies that light is actually being transmitted through the cable.

FIGURE 6.21:

Optical fiber continuity tester

(Photo courtesy of Jensen Tools)

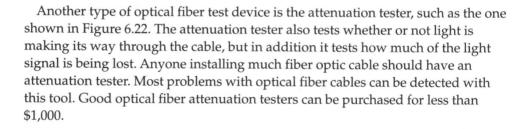

Another type of optical fiber test device is the attenuation tester, such as the one shown in Figure 6.22. The attenuation tester also tests whether or not light is making its way through the cable, but in addition it tests how much of the light signal is being lost. Anyone installing much fiber optic cable should have an attenuation tester. Most problems with optical fiber cables can be detected with this tool. Good optical fiber attenuation testers can be purchased for less than $1,000.

> **NOTE**   An attenuation tester tests how much signal is lost on the cable, whereas a continuity tester only measures whether light is passing through the cable.

Many high-end cable testers, such as those available from Hewlett-Packard, Microtest, and others can test both optical fiber as well as copper (provided you have purchased the correct add-on modules). There are a couple of things that you need to be sure of when you purchase any type of optical fiber tester:

- The tester should include the correct fiber connectors (ST, SC, FDDI, LC, MT-RJ, etc.) for the types of connectors you will be using.

- The tester should support the type of fiber optic cable you need to test (single-mode or multimode).

- The tester should test the bandwidth (for attenuation testers) at which you require the cable to be used (usually 850 or 1300nm).

FIGURE 6.22:

Optical fiber attenuation tester

(Photo courtesy of Jensen Tools)

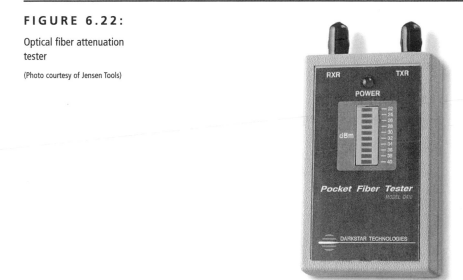

Professional fiber optic cable installers usually carry tools such as an optical time domain reflectometer (OTDR) that performs more advanced tests on optical fiber cable. OTDRs are not for everyone, as they can easily cost in excess of $30,000.

Cabling Supplies and Tools

When you think of cabling supplies, you probably envision boxes of cables, wall plates, modular connectors, and patch panels. True, those are all necessary parts of a cabling installation, but there are other key consumable items you should have in your cabling tool kit that will make your life a little easier.

Some of the consumable items you may carry are fairly generic. A well-equipped cabling technician carries a number of miscellaneous items essential to a cabling install, including the following:

- Electrician's tape—multiple colors are often desirable

- Duct tape

- Plastic cable ties (tie wraps) for permanent bundling and tie-offs

- Hook and loop cable ties for temporarily segregating and bundling cables

- Adhesive labels or specialized cable labeling system

- Sharpies or other type of permanent markers

- Wire nuts or crimp-type wire connectors

An item that most cable installers use all the time is the tie-wrap. Tie-wraps help to make the cable installation neater and more organized. However, most tie-wraps are permanent; you have to cut them to release them. Velcro-type cable wraps (shown in Figure 6.23) give you the ability to quickly wrap a bundle of cable together (or attach it to something else) and then to remove it just as easily. These come in a variety of colors and sizes and can be ordered from most cable equipment and wire management suppliers.

FIGURE 6.23:

Reusable cable wraps

(Photo courtesy of MilesTek)

Cable Pulling Tools

One of the most tedious tasks that a person pulling cables will face is the process of getting the cables through the plenum (the area between the false or drop ceiling tiles and the structural ceiling). This is where most horizontal cabling is installed. One method is to pull out every ceiling tile, pull the cable a few feet, then move your stepladder to the next open ceiling tile and pull the cable a few more feet. Some products that are helpful in the cabling pulling process are telescoping pull tools and pulleys that cable can be threaded through so that more cable can be pulled without exceeding the maximum pull tension.

Figure 6.24 shows the Gopher Pole, which is a telescoping pole that compresses to a minimum length of less than 5 feet and extends to a maximum length of 22 feet. This tool can help when pulling or pushing cable through hard-to-reach places.

Another useful set of items to carry are cable pulleys (shown in Figure 6.25); these pulleys help a single person to do the work of two people when pulling cable. We recommend carrying a set of four pulleys if you are pulling a lot of cable.

FIGURE 6.24:

The Gopher Pole

(Photo courtesy of MilesTek)

FIGURE 6.25:

Cable pulleys

(Photo courtesy of MilesTek)

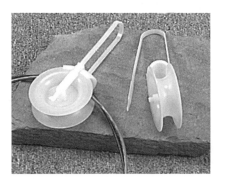

While not specifically a cable pulling tool, equipment to measure distance is especially important. A simple tape measure will suffice for most of us, but devices that can record long distances quickly may also be useful if you measure a lot of distances. While there are sophisticated laser-based tools that measure distances at the click of a button, a more reasonable tool would be something like the rolling measure tool pictured in Figure 6.26. This tool has a measuring wheel that records the distance you traverse while walking.

FIGURE 6.26:

Professional rolling measure tool

(Photo courtesy of MilesTek)

Wire Pulling Lubricant

Wire or cable pulling lubricant is a slippery, viscous liquid goop that you apply to the cable jacket to allow it to slide more easily over surfaces encountered during the cable pull. Wire lubricant (see Figure 6.27) is available in a variety of quantities, from less than a gallon to five-gallon buckets.

The vast majority of cable jackets for premises cables in the U.S. are some form of PVC (yes, even plenum-rated cables use PVC jackets). One characteristic of PVC is that, depending on the specific compound, it has a relatively high coefficient of friction. This means that at the microscopic level, the material is rough, and the rough surface results in drag resistance when the cable jacket passes over another surface. Where two PVC-jacketed cables are in contact, or where PVC conduit is used, the problem is made worse. Imagine two sandpaper blocks rubbing against each other.

FIGURE 6.27:

Wire pulling lubricant

(Photo courtesy of IDEAL DataComm)

In many cases, the use of pulling lubricant is not necessary. However, for long runs through conduit or in crowded cable trays or raceways, you may find that you either cannot complete the pull, or you will exceed the cable's maximum allowable pulling tension unless a lubricant is used.

The lubricant is applied either by continuously pouring it over the jacket near the start of the run, or by wiping it on by hand as the cable is pulled. Where conduit is being used, the lubricant can be poured in the conduit as the cable is pulled.

Lubricant has some drawbacks. Obviously, it can be messy; some types also congeal or harden over time, which makes adjustment or removal of cables difficult because they are effectively glued in place. Lubricant can also create a blockage in conduit and raceways that prevents new cables from being installed in the future.

TIP

Make sure the lubricant you are using is compatible with the insulation and jacket material of which the cables are made (hint: Don't use 10W30). The last thing you need is a call back because the pulling lubricant you used dissolved or otherwise degraded the plastics in the cable, leaving a bunch of bare conductors or fibers.

Cable Marking Supplies

One of our biggest beefs with installed cabling systems (and those yet to be installed) is a profound lack of documentation. If you observe a professional data cable installer in action, you will notice that the cabling system is well documented. Though some professionals will even use color coding on cables, the best start for cable documentation is assigning each cable a number.

The easiest way to number cables is to use a simple numbering system consisting of strips of numbers. These strips are numbered 0 through 9 and come in a variety of colors. Colors include black, white, gray, brown, red, orange, yellow, green, blue, and violet. You can use these strips to create your own numbering system. The cable is labeled at each end (the patch panel and the wall plate), and the cable number is recorded in whatever type of documentation is being used.

The numbered strips are often made of Tyvek, a material invented by DuPont that is well suited for making strong, durable products of high-density polyethylene fibers. Tyvek is nontoxic and chemically inert, so it will not adversely affect cables that it is applied to.

These wire marking labels are available in two flavors: rolls and sheets. The rolls can be used without dispensers. Figure 6.28 shows a 3M dispenser that holds rolls of wire markers; the dispenser also provides a tear-off cutting blade.

FIGURE 6.28:

3M dispenser for rolls of wire marking strips.

(Photo courtesy of MilesTek)

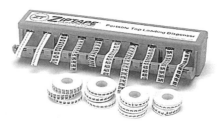

The second way to use wire markers is to use them in sheets. Figure 6.29 shows a booklet of wire marker sheets that allow you to pull off individual numbers. The booklets can be purchased either way.

Booklet of wire marker sheets

(Photo courtesy of IDEAL DataComm)

Wall Plate Marking Supplies

Some wall plate and patch panel systems provide their own documentation tools, but others don't. A well-documented system includes identifying labels on the wall plates. Figure 6.30 shows self-adhesive letters, numbers, and icons that can be used with wall plates and patch panels. Check with the manufacturer of your wall plates and patch panels to see if these are part of the system you are using; if they are not, you should use some labeling system such as these.

FIGURE 6.30:

Letters, numbers, and icons
on self-adhesive strips

(Photo courtesy of MilesTek)

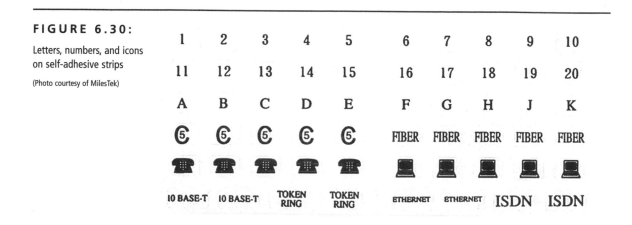

Tools That a Smart Data Cable Technician Carries

Up to this point, all the tools we've described are specific to the wire and cable installation industry. But there are everyday tools that you'll also need in the course of the average install. Even if you don't carry all of these (you'd clank like a knight in armor and your tool belt would hang around your knees if you did), you should at least have them handy in your arsenal of tools:

- Flat blade and #1 and #2 Phillips screwdrivers (power screwdrivers are great time-and-effort savers, but you'll still occasionally need the hand types).

- Hammer.

- Nut drivers.

- Wrenches.

- Flashlight (a no-hands or headband model is especially handy).

- Drill and bits up to 1^1/$_2$-inches.

- A saw that can be used to cut rectangular holes in drywall for electrical boxes.

- A good pocket, electrician's, or utility knife.

- Tape measure.

- Face masks to keep your lungs from getting filled with dust when working in dusty areas.

- A stud finder to locate wooden or steel studs in the walls.

- Simple continuity or multitester.

- A comfortable pair of work gloves.

- Sturdy stepladder, nonconductive recommended.

- Tool belt with appropriate loops and pouches for the tools you use most.

- Two-way radios or walkie-talkies are indispensable for pulling or testing over even moderate distances or between floors. Invest in the hands-free models that have a headset and you'll be glad you did.

- Extra batteries (or recharging stands) for your flashlights, radios, and cable testers.

TIP   Installation Tip: Wall outlet boxes are often placed one hammer length from the floor, especially in residences (this is based on a standard hammer, not the heavier and longer framing hammers). It's a real time saver, but check the boxes installed by the electricians before you use this quick measuring technique for installing the datacom boxes so that they'll all be the same height.

A multipurpose tool is also very handy. One popular choice is a Leatherman model with a coax crimper opening in the jaws of the pliers. It's just the thing for those times when you're up on the ladder looking down at the exact tool you need lying on the floor where you just dropped it.

One of the neatest ideas for carrying tools is something that IDEAL DataComm calls the Bucket Bag (pictured in Figure 6.31). This bag sits over a five-gallon bucket and allows you to easily organize your tools.

FIGURE 6.31:

IDEAL DataComm's
Bucket Bag

(Photo courtesy of IDEAL
DataComm)

A Kit Could Be It

Finally, don't ignore the possibility that a preassembled kit might be just right for you. It may be more economical and less troublesome than buying the individual components. IDEAL DataComm, Jensen Tools, and MilesTek all offer a range of tool kits for the voice and data installer. These are targeted for the professional installer, and they come in a variety of configurations customized to the type of installation you'll do most often. They are especially suitable for the intermediate to expert user. Figure 6.32 shows a tool kit from MilesTek, and Figure 6.33 shows a toolkit from Jensen Tools.

FIGURE 6.32:

MilesTek tool kit

(Photo courtesy of MilesTek)

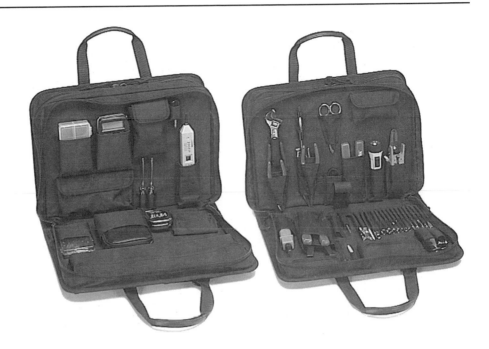

FIGURE 6.33:

Jensen Tools Master Cable
Installer's Kit

(Photo courtesy of Jensen Tools)

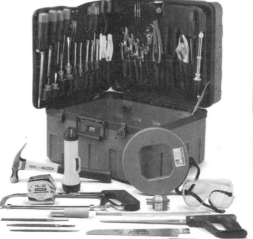

PART **II**

Network Media and Connectors

chapter 7

Copper Cable Media

- Types of Copper Cabling

- Best Practices for Installing UTP Cable

- Copper Cable for Data Applications

- Copper Cable for Voice Applications

Though optical fiber cabling has made some impressive inroads towards becoming the cabling topology of choice for horizontal cable (cable to the desktop), copper-based cabling remains king of the hill. This is, in part, due to the fact that it is inexpensive, well understood, easy to install, and the networking devices required to support copper cabling are inexpensive when compared with their fiber optic counterparts. Cost is almost always the determining factor when deciding whether to install copper or optical fiber cable—unless you have a high-security or high-bandwidth requirement, in which case optical fiber becomes more desirable.

There is a variety of copper cabling types available for telecommunications infrastructures today, but this chapter will focus on the use of Category 5 (and Category 5e) unshielded twisted-pair (UTP) cable. When installing a copper-based cabling infrastructure, one of your principal concerns should be adhering to whichever standard you have decided to use, either the TIA/EIA-568-A Commercial Building Telecommunications Cabling standard or the ISO/IEC 11801 Generic Cabling for Customer Premises standard; in North America, the TIA/EIA-568-A standard is the preferred standard. Both these standards are discussed in more detail in Chapter 2, "Cabling Standards."

Much of the material found in this chapter is repeated in other chapters in the book, but since this book is designed to be a reference, it makes sense to emphasize the individual components of copper cabling where necessary in other chapters.

Types of Copper Cabling

Pick up any larger cabling catalog, and you will find thousands of types of copper cables. However, many of these cables are unsuitable for data and voice communications. Often, cable is manufactured with specific purposes in mind, such as audio, doorbell, remote equipment control, or other low-speed, low-voltage applications. Cable used for data communications must support high-speed and high-bandwidth applications. Even for digital telephones, the cable must be chosen correctly.

There are many types of cable that are used for data and telecommunications. The application that you are using must be taken into consideration when choosing the type of cable you will install. Table 7.1 lists some of the common copper cables that are found today and common applications that run on these cables.

With the UTP cabling types found in Table 7.1, applications that run on lower grade cable will also run on higher grades of cable (for example, digital telephones can be used with Category 3, 4, 5, 5e, or 6 cabling).

TABLE 7.1: Common Types of Copper Cabling and the Applications That Run on These Cables

Cable Type	Common Applications
UTP Category 1	Signaling, door bells, alarm systems
UTP Category 2	Digital phone systems, Apple LocalTalk
UTP Category 3	10Base-T, 4Mbps Token Ring
UTP Category 4	16Mbps Token Ring
UTP Category 5	100Base-TX, 1000Base-T
UTP Category 5e	100Base-TX, 1000Base-T
UTP Category 6*	100Base-TX, 1000Base-T
UTP Category 7*	100Base-TX, 1000Base-T
Backbone UTP cable	Analog and digital voice applications
Shielded twisted-pair (STP)	4Mbps and 16Mbps Token Ring
Screened twisted-pair (ScTP)	100Base-TX, 1000Base-T
Coaxial RG-8	Thick Ethernet (10Base-5), video
Coaxial RG-58	Thin Ethernet (10Base-2)
Coaxial RG-59	Video
Coaxial RG-62	ARCnet, video, IBM 3270

*As of mid-2000, Category 6 and 7 cables are undergoing standardization and are not considered ratified standards.

Major Cable Types Found Today

When you begin to purchase cable for a new installation, the decisions you have to make are mind boggling. What cable will support 100Base-TX? Will this cable support faster applications in the future? Do you choose stranded-conductor cable or solid-conductor cable? Should you use different cable for voice and data?

Do you buy a cable that only supports present standards or one that is designed to support future standards? The list of possible questions goes on and on.

NOTE Solid-conductor cable is used for horizontal cabling. The entire conductor is one single piece of copper. Stranded-conductor cable is used for patch cords and shorter cabling runs; the conductor consists of strands of smaller wire. These smaller strands make the cable more flexible but also cause it to have higher attenuation. Any cable that will be used for horizontal cabling (in the walls) should be solid conductor.

Let's review the different types of cable that we listed in Table 7.1 and expand on the performance characteristics of these cables and some of their possible uses.

The focus of this chapter will be on unshielded twisted-pair (UTP) cabling since that is the most prevalent cable type in use today. When talking about cabling categories and UTP cabling, UTP cables are 100-ohm plus or minus 15 percent, 24 AWG (American Wire Gauge), twisted-pair cables. Horizontal cabling uses unshielded, four-pair cables, but voice applications can use cables with 25, 50, 100, or more pairs bundled together. This horizontal cable UTP consists of a jacket with four pairs of cable such as the one shown in Figure 7.1. In addition, UTP cables may contain a slitting cord or rip cord that makes it easier to strip back the jacket.

FIGURE 7.1:

Common UTP cable

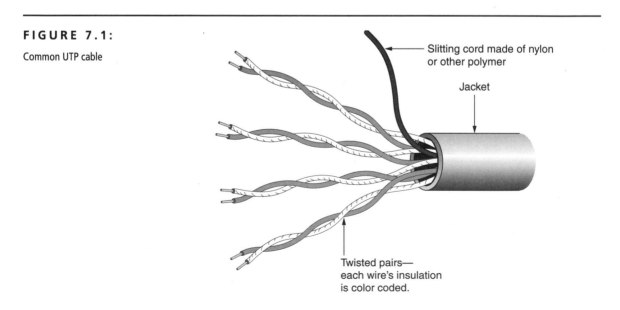

Slitting cord made of nylon or other polymer

Jacket

Twisted pairs—
each wire's insulation
is color coded.

Each of the wires is color-coded to make it easier for the cable installer to identify and correctly terminate the wire.

Color Codes for UTP Cables

The individual wires in a UTP cable are color-coded for ease of identification and termination. A four-pair cable has four tip colors: blue, orange, green, and brown. Each of these is either predominantly that color with a stripe or splash of white, or it is predominantly white with a stripe or splash of the tip color. The tip color is also known as the band color, and the stripe is known as the base color. This becomes more relevant when working with 25-pair or larger cables. A four-pair UTP cable with the base and band colors labeled is shown here.

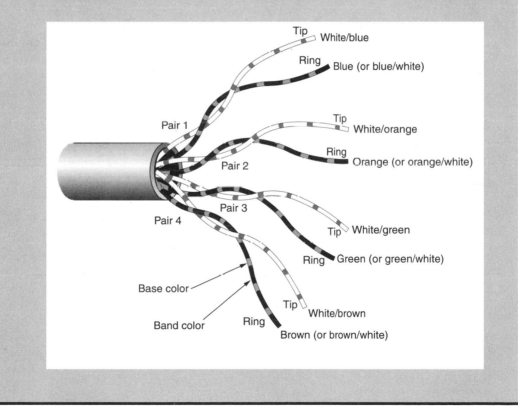

Tip and Ring Colors

The primary color is also known as the tip color and the secondary color is known as the ring color. In a four-pair cable, the cable pairs are coded in a standard color-coding; this color-coding is on the insulation of the individual wires. These colors are

Pair	Tip	Ring
Pair 1	White/blue	Blue (or blue/white)
Pair 2	White/orange	Orange (or orange/white)
Pair 3	White/green	Green (or green/white)
Pair 4	White/brown	Brown (or brown/white)

The color white is the common color in all four-pair cables and is always numbered or inserted into a punch-down block first. For example, in pair number one (the blue pair), the two wires are white/blue and blue. The white (or white/blue) wire has a small blue stripe running down the length of the wire; this wire is the tip. The blue (or blue/white) wire has a small white stripe running down the length of the wire; this wire is the ring. Sometimes, the white wire will just have a smudge of blue every inch or so and the blue wire will be solid. This depends on the cable manufacturer.

Depending on whom you ask, you may get different answers to which wire is considered "primary" and which is considered "secondary." In the United States and much of the world, premises cabling people consider the tip wire to be the primary because that is the wire that is connected to a connecting block first. Others consider the ring wire to be the primary. However, as long as they are wired correctly, it does not matter what you call the tip and ring wires.

The terms *tip* and *ring* are holdovers from when telephone systems were switched by hand using jacks that looked like an stereo RCA jack. The solid color was wired to the ring and the striped color was wired to the tip.

Category 1 UTP Cable

Category 1 cable is UTP cable that is designed to support applications operating at 100KHz or less. Applications operating at less than 100KHz are very low-speed applications such as analog voice, doorbells, alarm systems, RS-232, and RS-422. Category 1 cable is not used very often due to its limited use with data and voice applications and, although it is cheap to install, it will not be possible to use it for anything other than low speed applications in the future.

Category 2 UTP Cable

Category 2 UTP cable is designed to support applications that operate at a frequency rate of less than 4MHz. This cable can be used for low-speed applications such as digital voice, Apple LocalTalk, serial applications, ARCnet, ISDN, some DSL applications, and T-1. Category 2 cable is not used often for anything except digital voice applications because it has limited expansion capabilities. Most telecommunications designers choose a minimum of Category 3 cable for digital voice.

Category 3 UTP Cable

Category 3 UTP cable was the workhorse of the networking industry for a few years after it was approved as a standard. It is designed to support applications requiring bandwidth up to 16MHz. Applications include digital and analog voice, 10Base-T Ethernet, 4Mbps Token Ring, 100Base-T4 Fast Ethernet, 100VG-AnyLAN, ISDN, and DSL applications. Most digital voice applications also use a minimum of Category 3 cabling.

Category 3 cable is usually four-pair twisted-pair cables, but there are backbone (bundled) cables (25-pair, 50-pair, etc.) that are certified for use with Category 3 applications. Those backbone cables are sometimes used with 10Base-T Ethernet applications; they are not recommended.

NOTE   The industry trend is towards installing Category 5 or 5e cabling instead of Category 3 cabling for both voice and data.

Category 4 UTP Cable

Category 4 cable has never quite caught on. It was designed to support applications operating at frequencies up to 20MHz. The price of Category 4 and Category 5 cable is almost identical, so most people choose Category 5 cable since it has the capability of supporting much higher speed applications. The intent of Category 4 cabling was to support Ethernet, 4Mbps Token Ring, and 16Mbps Token Ring, as well as digital voice applications. The next revision of the TIA/EIA-568 standard will remove Category 4 cable as a recommended media.

Category 5/5e UTP Cable

Category 5 cable currently reigns as king in all new installations of UTP cabling for data applications. Category 5 cable was designed to support applications requiring bandwidth up to 100MHz. In addition to applications supported by Category 4 and earlier cables, Category 5 supports 100Base-TX, TP-PMD (FDDI over copper), ATM (155Mbps), and 1000Base-T (Gigabit Ethernet).

In the fall of 1999, the TIA/EIA ratified an addendum to the TIA/EIA-568-A standard to approve additional performance requirements for Category 5e cabling. We recommend installing Category 5e as the minimum Category cable for new UTP installations that will support data and voice applications.

There are manufacturers that make 25-pair backbone (bundled or feeder) cable that support Category 5 installations, but we are a little uncomfortable with using these cables for high-speed applications such as 100Base-TX or 1000Base-T.

NOTE   Category 5 cable will support 1000Base-T provided the installed cabling system passes the performance specifications outlined in TSB-95.

Category 6 UTP Cable

This cable category is currently in development and is not ratified as a standard. Vendors are advertising category 6–level performance, but there is no guarantee that the product will be Category 6–compliant until the standard is ratified. With bandwidth up to 250MHz, this cable category will support any application that Category 5e and lower cables will support. Category 6 cabling is currently about 35 percent more expensive than good quality Category 5e.

NOTE   Watch the case of the "c" in the word *category*. Some vendors advertise "category 6" cable with a lowercase "c." This can be misleading since there is no true Category 6 standard as of mid-2000. The lowercase "c" is your clue that it is not yet standardized, even if the cable meets the current *proposed* Category 6 performance standards.

Category 7 UTP Cable

Category 7 cable specifications are currently in development by the ISO/IEC. It will support applications requiring bandwidth up to 600MHz. The style of connector used with previous cable categories will have to be updated to support Category 7 installations to get the full supported bandwidth.

Shielded Twisted-Pair Cable (IBM Type 1A)

Originally developed by IBM to support applications such as Token Ring and the IBM Systems Network Architecture, shielded twisted-pair (STP) cable can currently support applications requiring bandwidth up to 600MHz. Though there are many types of shielded cable on the market, the Type 1A cable is the most shielded. An IBM Type 1A (STP-A) (shown in Figure 7.2) cable has an outer shield that consists of braided copper; this shield surrounds the 150-ohm, 22 AWG, two-pair conductors. Each conductor is insulated and then each twisted-pair is individually shielded.

FIGURE 7.2:

An STP-A cable and an ScTP cable

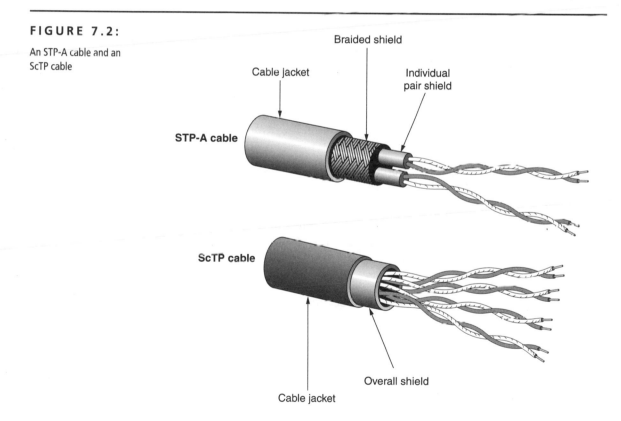

All the shielding in an STP-A cable provides better protection against external sources of EMI than UTP cable does, but the shielding makes the cable thicker and more bulky. Typical applications are 4Mbps and 16Mbps Token Ring and IBM terminal applications (3270 and 5250 terminals). STP cabling is expensive to install, and many people think that it provides only marginally better shielding than UTP. If you are considering STP cabling solely because it provides better shielding and higher potential bandwidth, you should consider using fiber optic cable instead.

There are other types of IBM cabling which are not discussed here. See Chapter 1, "Introduction to Data Cabling," for more detail on the additional IBM cabling types.

> **NOTE**
>
> IBM now recommends Category 5 cabling for Token Ring users.

Backbone (Bundled) UTP Cable

Backbone cable is cable that has more than four pairs. Often called *bundled* or *feeder cable*, backbone usually comes in 25-, 50-, or 100-pair increments, though there are higher pair counts available. Though it is called backbone cabling, this term can be misleading if you are looking at cabling from a data cabling perspective. High pair-count backbone cabling is typically used with voice applications only.

Some vendors sell 25- and 50-pair cable that is certified for use with Category 5 applications, but this many pairs of cable all supporting data in the same sheath makes us nervous. This is because all those individual wire pairs are generating crosstalk that affect all the other pairs; the factor that becomes important in higher pair counts is called *power sum NEXT* (see Chapter 1 for more details on cable performance).

We have also seen applications where someone will mix voice and 10Base-T Ethernet data in the same backbone cable. Sharing the same sheath with two different applications is not recommended either.

> **NOTE**
>
> Many manufacturers make 25-pair and 50-pair cables that are rated to Category 5 level performance, but we recommend using individual four-pair cables when trying to achieve Category 5 performance levels.

Color Codes and Backbone Cables   Color codes for 25-pair cables are a bit more sophisticated than for four-pair cables due to the fact that there are so many additional wire pairs. In the case of 25-pair cables, there is one additional ring color (slate) and there are four additional tip colors (red, black, yellow, and violet). Table 7.2 lists the color coding for a 25-pair cable.

TABLE 7.2:   Color Coding for 25-Pair Cables

Pair Number	Ring Color	Tip Color
1	Blue	White
2	Orange	White
3	Green	White
4	Brown	White
5	Slate	White
6	Blue	Red
7	Orange	Red
8	Green	Red
9	Brown	Red
10	Slate	Red
11	Blue	Black
12	Orange	Black
13	Green	Black
14	Brown	Black
15	Slate	Black
16	Blue	Yellow
17	Orange	Yellow
18	Green	Yellow
19	Brown	Yellow
20	Slate	Yellow
21	Blue	Violet
22	Orange	Violet
23	Green	Violet
24	Brown	Violet
25	Slate	Violet

As with four-pair UTP cable, the tip color is always connected first. For example, when installing terminating 25-pair cable to a 66-block, white/blue would be connected to pin 1, then blue/white would be connected to pin 2, and so forth.

When cable pair counts exceed 25 pairs, the cable is broken up into *binder groups* consisting of 25 pairs of wire. A binder group is marked within the larger bundle with a uniquely colored plastic binder that is wrapped around the 25-pair bundle.

Coaxial Cable

Coaxial cable has been around since local area networking was in its infancy. The original designers of Ethernet picked coaxial cable as their "ether" due to the fact that coaxial cable is well shielded, has high bandwidth capabilities and low attenuation, and is easy to install. Coaxial cables are identified by their "RG" designation. Coaxial cable can have a solid or stranded core and impedance of 50, 75, or 92 ohms. Coaxial such as the one shown in Figure 7.3 is called coaxial cable because it is has one wire that carries the signal surrounded by a layer of insulation and another concentric shield; both the shield and the inner conductor run along the same axis. The outer shield also serves as a ground and should be grounded to be effective.

FIGURE 7.3:

Coaxial cable

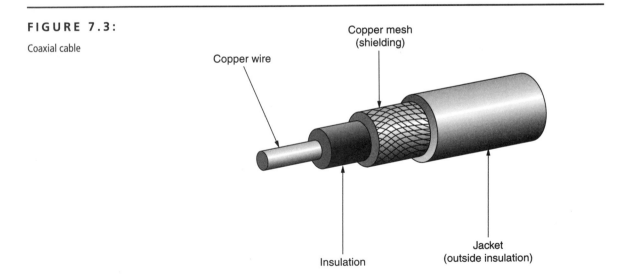

NOTE   Coaxial cable is still widely used for video applications, but it is not recommended for data installations.

There are a number of different types of coaxial cable that are used for data; these are shown in Table 7.3.

TABLE 7.3:   Common Coaxial Cable Types

RG Number	Center Wire Gauge	Impedance	Conductor Core
RG-6/U	18 AWG	75 ohms	Solid
RG-8/U	10 AWG	50 ohms	Solid
RG-58/U	20 AWG	53.5 ohms	Solid
RG-58C/U	20 AWG	50 ohms	Solid
RG-58A/U	20 AWG	50 ohms	Stranded
RG-59/U	20 AWG	75 ohms	Solid
RG-62/U	22 AWG	93 ohms	Solid

NOTE   Sometimes you will see coaxial cable labeled as 802.3 Ethernet Thinnet or 802.3 Ethernet Thicknet. Thin Ethernet cable is RG-58 and is used for 10Base-2 Ethernet, and thick Ethernet cable is RG-8 and is used for 10Base-5 Ethernet.

Hybrid Cable

You may hear the term hybrid cable used. This is not really a special type of cable, but cable that contains two or more different types of cable within a common cable jacket. For example, a common cable that is manufactured now contains four-pair Category 5 UTP cable and two pair of multimode fiber optic cable. The nice thing about these cable types is that you get two different types of media to a single location by pulling only one cable. Manufacturer CommScope builds hybrid cables. For more information, check out CommScope's Web site at www.commscope.com.

Cable Jackets

When choosing cable, one of the most important issues to consider is where the cable will be installed. The major factor here is the type of material that is used for the jacket insulation and the wire insulation. Cable designers have to contend with decisions dealing with the materials that are used in the cable's insulation. There is a fine balance between good dielectric performance (meaning it does not conduct electricity), cost of the materials, and the characteristics of the material when exposed to high temperatures.

The insulation materials used in the cable should not generate excessive smoke or toxic gases when exposed to high temperatures. In addition, the insulation material should ideally have excellent dielectric properties and be plentiful and inexpensive.

Unfortunately, in the real world, these materials are often in short supply and cost more than we want to pay for them. Cheaper insulation can be used but will generate more visible smoke when exposed to high temperatures.

The majority of the horizontal and backbone cable installed today is rated as *plenum* cable. This is cable that can be installed in plenum spaces (such as the space within a building that is designed to circulate air). Cable installed in these spaces must pass certain tests designated by the UL (Underwriters Laboratory) and/or CSA (Canadian Standards Association).

Plenum-rated cable (usually carrying the designation CMP, for communications plenum) can generally be installed in almost any space in a building unless the local building codes specifically prohibit this.

Another type of cable jacket that is common is PVC (polyvinyl chloride). PVC-insulated cable has been found to generate more visible smoke than the UL and the National Electrical Code allows and thus cannot be used in plenum spaces.

NOTE   For a more complete discussion of cable jacket materials, consult Chapter 1.

Picking the Right Patch Cables

Though not really part of a discussion on picking cable types for horizontal cable, the subject of patch cords should be addressed. Patch cables (or patch cords) are the cables that are used to connect 110-type connecting blocks, patch panel ports, or telecommunication outlets (wall plate outlets) to network equipment or telephones.

We have stated this elsewhere in the book, but it deserves repeating: You should purchase factory-made patch cables. Patch cables are a critical part of the link between a network device (such as a PC) and the network equipment (such as a hub). Low quality, poorly made, and damaged patch cables very frequently contribute to network problems. Often the patch cable is considered the weakest link in the structured cabling system. Poorly made patch cables will contribute to attenuation loss and increased crosstalk.

Factory-made patch cables are constructed using exacting and controlled circumstances to assure reliable and consistent transmission performance parameters. These patch cables are tested and guaranteed to perform correctly.

Patch cables are made of stranded-conductor cable to give them additional flexibility. However, stranded cable has up to 20 percent higher attenuation values than solid-conductor cable, so lengths should be kept to a minimum. The TIA/EIA-568-A standard allows for a 6-meter (20 feet) patch cable in the wiring closet and a 3-meter (10 feet) patch cable at the workstation area. In our experience, the 6-meter patch cable is more useful in the workstation location, but your actual mileage may vary. Here are some suggestions to consider when purchasing patch cables:

- Don't make them yourself. Many problems result from bad patch cables.

- Choose the correct category for the performance level you want to achieve.

- Make sure the patch cables you purchase use stranded conductors for increased flexibility.

- Purchase a variety of lengths and make sure you have a few extra of each length

- Consider color-coding your patch cords in the telecommunication closet. An example of this would be

  - Yellow cords for workstations

  - Blue cords for voice

  - Red cords for servers

  - Green cords for hub-to-hub connections

  - Gray for other types of connections

Why Pick Copper Cabling?

Copper cabling has been around and in use since electricity was invented. Despite its antiquity, it is much more popular than optical fiber cabling. And the quality of copper wire has continued to improve. Over the past 100 years, copper manufacturers have developed the refining and drawing processes so that copper is even more high quality.

High-speed technologies such as 155Mbps ATM and Gigabit Ethernet that experts said would never run over copper wire as recently as five years ago are running over copper wiring today.

Manufacturing and termination techniques for copper wiring have greatly reduced crosstalk. Today, 24 AWG copper wire is less susceptible to attenuation than the 24 AWG wire was 20 years ago. This is because the manufacturing processes are continually improved and the purity of the copper is even better than it used to be. AWG (American Wire Gauge) is a measurement that represents the circular area of a wire. The larger the wire gauge, the smaller the actual wire (exactly the opposite of what you would think). A 22 AWG wire is larger than a 24 AWG wire. Table 7.4 shows some common gauges and measurements of wire that are used with telecommunications cabling.

TABLE 7.4:   Common AWG Wire Gauges

AWG Gauge	Diameter (inches)	Diameter (mm)
10	0.1010	2.60
16	0.0508	1.29
18	0.0403	1.02
20	0.0320	0.813
22	0.0253	0.643
24	0.0201	0.511
26	0.0159	0.404
28	0.0126	0.320
30	0.0100	0.254

NOTE   If you have ever handled 10 AWG wire, you can attest to the fact that it is a really thick wire!

Network managers pick copper cabling for a variety of reasons. Copper cable (especially UTP cable) is inexpensive and easy to install, the installation methods are well understood, and the components (patch panels, wall plate outlets, connecting blocks, etc.) are inexpensive. Further, the applications (voice systems, 10Base-T Ethernet, etc.) that use the copper cabling are much more affordable than copper.

NOTE   The main downsides to using copper cable are that copper cable is susceptible to outside interference (EMI), optical fiber provides much greater bandwidth, and the data on copper wire is not as secure as data traveling through an optical fiber.

Table 7.5 lists some of the common technologies that currently use unshielded twisted-pair Ethernet. With the advances in networking technology and twisted-pair cable, it makes you wonder what applications we will see on UTP cables in the future.

TABLE 7.5: Applications That Use Unshielded Twisted-Pair Cables

Application	Data Rate	Encoding Scheme*	Pairs Required
10Base-T Ethernet	10Mbps	Manchester	2
100Base-TX Ethernet	100Mbps	4B5B/NRZI/MLT3	2
100Base-T4 Ethernet	100Mbps	8B6T	4
100Base-T Gigabit Ethernet	1000Mbps	PAM5	4
100Base-VG AnyLAN	100Mbps	5B6B/NRZ	4
4Mbps Token Ring	4Mbps	Manchester	2
16Mbps Token Ring	16Mbps	Manchester	2
ATM-25	25Mbps	NRZ	2
ATM-155	155Mbps	NRZ	2
TP-PMD (FDDI over copper)	100Mbps	MLT-3	2

* Encoding is a technology that allows more than one bit to be passed through a wire during a single cycle (Hertz).

Best Practices for Copper Installation

We used our own installations of copper cabling, as well as the tips and techniques of many others, to create guidelines for you to follow to ensure that your UTP cabling system will support all the applications you intend it to. These guidelines include the following:

- Following standards
- Making sure you do not exceed distance limits
- Good installation techniques

Following Standards

One of the most important things that you can do when planning and deploying a new telecommunications infrastructure is to make sure you are following a standard. In the United States, this standard is the TIA/EIA-568-A Commercial Building Telecommunications Cabling standard. This standard may be purchased from Global Engineering Documents on the Internet at global.ihs.com. We highly recommend that anyone designing a cabling infrastructure own this document.

TIP

Have you purchased or do you plan to purchase the TIA/EIA-568 standard? After mid-2000, check to see if the TIA/EIA-568-B version of the standard is available since this version will be the most up-to-date.

Following the TIA/EIA-568-A standard will ensure that your cabling system is interoperable with any networking or voice applications that has been designed to work with that standard.

The current version of the TIA/EIA-568 standard has components and performance specifications that were developed as many as 10 years ago. Getting the latest innovations incorporated into a standard is difficult because these technologies are often not tested and deployed widely enough for the standards committees to feel comfortable approving them. Some vendors (such as Lucent Technologies SYSTIMAX Structured Connectivity Solutions) install cabling systems that will provide much greater performance than the current standards require and will still remain compatible with existing standards. If a vendor proposes a solution to you that has a vendor-specific performance spin on it, make sure it is backward compatible with the current standards.

Cable Distances

One of the most important things that the TIA/EIA-568-A standard defines is the maximum distance that a horizontal cable should traverse. The maximum distance between the patch panel (or cross-connect, in the case of voice) and the wall plate (the horizontal portion of the cable) *must* not exceed 90 meters (285 feet). Further, the patch cord used in the telecommunications closet (patch panel to hub or cross-connect) cannot exceed 6 meters (20 feet), and the patch cord used on the workstation side must not exceed 3 meters (10 feet).

You may find that higher quality cables will allow you to exceed this distance limit for technologies such as 10Base-T Ethernet or 100VG-AnyLAN. However, there is no guarantee that those horizontal cable runs that exceed 90 meters will work with future technologies designed to work with TIA/EIA-568 standards.

Some tips relating to the installation of copper cabling and distance include:

- Never exceed the 90-meter maximum distance for horizontal cables.

- Don't forget to account for the fact that horizontal cable may be routed up through walls, around corners, and through conduit.

- Account for any additional cable distance that may be required as a result of trays, hooks, and cable management.

- Horizontal cable rarely goes in a straight line from the patch panel to the wall plate. Account for all distances that the cable may have to traverse in the ceiling.

- Leave some slack in the ceiling above the wiring rack in case retermination is required or the patch panel must be moved; cabling professionals call this a *service loop*. Some professional cable installers leave as much as an extra 10 feet in the ceiling bundled together or looped around a hook (as seen in Figure 7.4).

FIGURE 7.4:

Leaving some cable slack in the ceiling

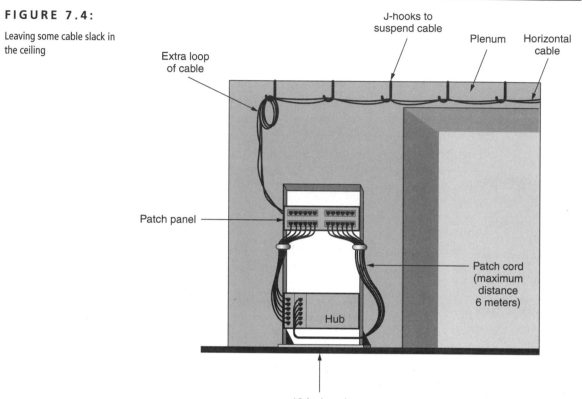

Wiring Patterns

The TIA/EIA-568-A standard recommends one of two wiring patterns for modular jacks and plugs. The wiring patterns are called T568A and T568B, and both of these are recommended as part of the TIA/EIA-568-A standard. There is some misperception that the T568B wiring pattern is part of the forthcoming "B" version of the TIA/EIA-568-A standard, but this is not true.

The only difference between these wiring patterns is that pin assignments for pairs 2 and 3 are reversed. However, these two wiring patterns are constantly causing problems for end users and weekend cable installers. What is the problem? Patch panels and modular wall plate outlets come in either the T568A or

T568B wiring patterns. The actual construction of these devices is exactly the same, but they are color-coded according to either the T568A wiring standard or the T568B wiring standard.

The cable pairs are assigned to specific pin numbers. The pin numbers are numbered from left to right if you are looking into the modular jack or down on the top of the modular plug. Figure 7.5 shows the pin numbers for the eight-position modular jack (RJ-45) and plug.

FIGURE 7.5:

Pin positions for the eight-position modular plug and jack

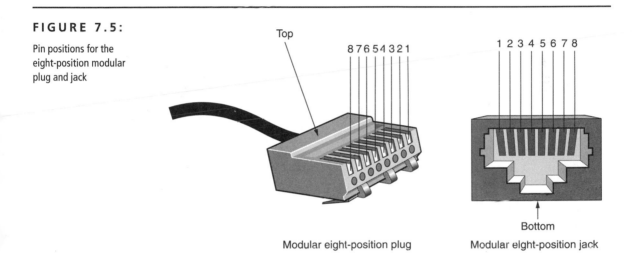

Modular eight-position plug   Modular eight-position jack

Which Wiring Pattern Should You Choose?   The T568A wiring pattern is most prevalent outside of the United States and in U.S. government installations. T568B is more prevalent in private installations in the United States. However, the wiring pattern chosen makes no difference to the applications that are used. The wires are still wired straight through, and electricity does not care what color wire it is running through.

The most important factor is to choose one wiring standard and stick with it. This means when purchasing patch panels, 110-blocks, and wall plates that they should all use the same wiring pattern.

NOTE   More information about the T568A and T568B wiring standards can be found in Chapter 9, "Cable Connectors."

Planning

Planning plays an essential role in any successful implementation of a technology; structured cabling systems are no exception. If you are planning to install a larger structured cabling system (more than a few hundred cable runs), consider hiring a professional consultant to assist you with the planning phases.

NOTE   Chapter 15, "Creating a Request for Proposal (RFP)," has information on planning and preparing a request for proposal for a structured cabling system. Chapter 12, "Cabling System Design and Information," covers the essential design issues you must consider when building a structured cabling system.

Some of the questions you should ask when planning a cabling infrastructure that includes copper cabling include:

- How many cables should be run to each location?
- Should you use cable trays or conduit while the cable is in the plenum?
- Will the voice system use patch panels or will the voice cable be cross-connected via 66-blocks directly to the phone system blocks?
- Is there a danger of cable damage from water, rodents, or chemicals?
- Has proper grounding been taken care of for equipment racks and cable terminations requiring grounding?
- Will you use the same category of cable for voice and data?
- Will new holes be required between floors for backbone cable or through firewalls for horizontal or backbone cable?
- Will any of the cables be exposed to the elements or outdoors?

Cabling @ Work: Critter Damage

Cabling folklore is full of stories of cabling being damaged by termites, rats, and other vermin. This might have been hard for us to believe if we had not seen such damage ourselves. Once such instance of this type of damage occurred because rats were using a metal conduit to run on the cable between walls. Additional cable was installed, which blocked the rats' pathway, so they chewed holes in the cable.

We have heard numerous stories of cable damage as a result of creatures with sharp teeth. Consider any area that cable may be run through and take into consideration what you may need to do to protect the cable.

Cable Management

Good cable management starts with the design of the cabling infrastructure. When installing horizontal cable, consider using cable trays or J-hooks in the ceiling to run the cable. This will prevent the cable from resting on ceiling tiles, power conduits, or air conditioning ducts.

Further, make sure that you plan to purchase and install cable management guides and equipment near patch panels and on racks so that when patch cables are installed, cable management will be available.

Installing Copper Cable

When you start installing copper cabling, a lot can go wrong. Even if you have adequately planned your installation, situations can still arise that will cause you problems either immediately or in the long term. Here are some tips to keep in mind for installing copper cabling:

- Do not untwist the twisted pairs at the cable connector or anywhere along the cable length any more than necessary (less than .5 inches).

- Taps (bridged taps) are not allowed.

- Use connectors, patch panels, and wall plates that are compatible with the cable.

- When tie-wrapping cables, do not over-tighten cable bundles.

- Don't staple the cables too tightly. Use a staple gun and staples (plastic staples, if possible) that are designed to be used with data cables. Do not use a generic staple gun; you will be on the express train to cable damage.

- Never splice a data cable if there is a problem with it at some point through its length; run a new cable instead.

- When terminating, remove as little of the cable's jacket as possible, preferably less than three inches.

- Don't lay data cables directly across ceiling tiles or grids. Use a cable tray, J-hook, horizontal ladder, or other method to support the cables. Avoid any sort of cable suspension device that appears as if it will crush the cables.

- Follow proper grounding procedures for all equipment to reduce the likelihood of electrical shock and reduce the effects of EMI.

- All voice runs should be home-run, not daisy-chained. When wiring jacks for home telephone use, there is the great temptation to daisy-chain cables together from one jack to the next. Each connection causes attenuation and crosstalk, which can degrade the signal even at voice frequencies. Enough noise could occur to drop your modem speed a few Kbps.

- If you have a cable with damaged pairs, replace it. You will be glad you did. Don't use another unused pair from the same cable because other pairs may be damaged to the point where they only cause intermittent problems, which are difficult to solve.

Pulling Cable

If you are just starting out in the cabling business or if you have never been around cable when it is installed, the term "pulling cable" is probably not significant. However, any veteran installer will tell you that "pulling" is exactly what you do. Cable is pulled from boxes or spools, passed up into the ceiling, and then, every few feet, the installers climb into the ceiling and pull the cable along a few more feet. In the case of cable in conduit, the cable is attached to a drawstring and pulled through the conduit. Any way you look at it, though, pulling is involved.

While the cable is pulled, there are a number of things that can happen that will cause irreparable harm to the cable. There are also a number of things you can do to make sure that damage is avoided. Here is a list of copper cabling installation tips:

- Do not exceed the cable's maximum bend radius by making sharp bends. The bend radius for four-pair UTP cables should not exceed 4 times the cable diameter and 10 times the cable diameter for backbone (25-pair and greater cable). Avoid making too many 90-degree bends.

- Do not exceed maximum cable pulling tension (110N or 25 pounds of force for four-pair UTP cable).

- When pulling a bundle of cables, do not tension cables unevenly.

- When building a system that supports both voice and data, run the intended voice lines to a separate patch panel from the data lines.

- Be careful not to twist the cable too tightly; this can damage the conductors and the conductor insulation.

- Avoid sources of heat such as hot water pipes, steam pipes, or warm air ducts.

- Be aware that damage can be caused by all sorts of other evil entities such as drywall screws, wiring box edges, and other sharp objects found in ceilings and walls.

To make the pulling of cable easier, new cable is shipped in reels. Often these reels are in boxes and the cable easily unspools from the boxes as you pull on it. Other times, the cable reels are not in a box and you must use some type of device to allow the reel to turn freely while you pull the cable. In these cases, a device similar to the one pictured in Figure 7.6 may be just the thing. These are often called wire spool trees.

TIP

When troubleshooting any wiring system, disconnect the data or voice application from *both* sides (the phone, PC, hub, and PBX). This goes for home telephone wiring, too!

FIGURE 7.6:

Reel for holding spools
of cable to make cable
pulling easier

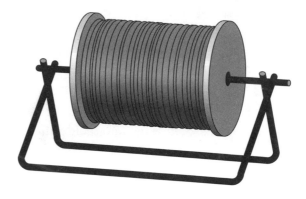

Separating Voice and Data Patch Panels

Some installations of voice and data cabling will terminate the cabling on the same patch panel. While this is not entirely frowned upon by cabling professionals, many will tell you that it is more desirable to have a separate patch panel that is dedicated to voice applications. This is essential if you are using a different category of cable for voice from data (such as if you are using Category 5 cable for data but Category 3 cable for voice).

In the example in Figure 7.7, the wall plate has two eight-position modular outlets (one for voice and one for data). The outlets are labeled V-1 for voice and D-1 for data. In the telecommunications closet, these two cables terminate on different patch panels, but each cable goes to position 1 on the patch panel. This makes the cabling installation much easier to document and to understand. The assumption in Figure 7.7 is that the voice system is terminating to a patch panel rather than a 66-block. The voice system is then patched to another patch panel that has the extensions from the company's PBX, and the data port is patched to a network hub.

FIGURE 7.7:

Using separate patch panels for voice and data

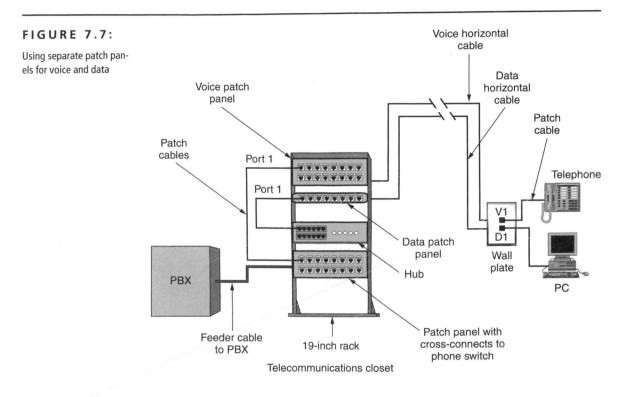

Sheath Sharing

The TIA/EIA-568-A standard does not specifically prohibit sheath sharing. Sheath sharing is when two applications share the same sheath. For example, someone decides that they cannot afford to run two separate cables to a single location and uses different pairs of cable for different applications. Table 7.6 shows the pin arrangement that might be used if a splitter (such as the one described in Chapter 9) were employed. Some installations may split the cable at the wall outlet and patch panel rather than using a splitter.

TABLE 7.6:   Shared Sheath Pin Assignments

Pin number	Usage	T568A Wire Color	T568B Wire Color
Pin 1	Ethernet transmit +	White/green	White/orange
Pin 2	Ethernet transmit −	Green	Orange
Pin 3	Ethernet receive +	White/orange	White/green
Pin 4	Phone inner wire 1	Blue	Blue
Pin 5	Phone inner wire 2	White/blue	White/blue
Pin 6	Ethernet receive −	Orange	Green
Pin 7	Phone inner wire 3	White/brown	White/brown
Pin 8	Phone inner wire 4	Brown	Brown

When two applications share the same cable sheath, performance problems can occur. Two applications (voice and data or data and data) running inside the same sheath may interfere with one another. Applications operating at lower frequencies such as 10Base-T may work perfectly well, but higher frequency applications such as 100Base-TX will operate with unpredictable results.

Since results can be unpredictable, we do not recommend using a single cable for multiple applications simultaneously. Even for home applications where you may want to share voice and data applications (such as Ethernet, DSL, or ISDN), we recommend separate cables. The ringer voltage on a home telephone can disrupt data transmission on adjacent pairs of wire.

Avoiding Electromagnetic Interference

All electrical devices generate electromagnetic fields in the radio frequency (RF) spectrum. These electromagnetic fields produce electromagnetic interference (EMI) and interfere with the operation of other electric devices and the transmission of voice and data. You will notice EMI if you have a cordless or cellular phone and you walk near a microwave oven or other source of high EMI.

Data transmission is especially susceptible to disruption from EMI, so it is essential that cabling installed with the intent of supporting data (or voice) transmissions be separated from EMI sources. Here are some tips that may be helpful when planning pathways for data and voice cabling:

- Data cabling must never be installed in the same conduit with power cables.

- If data cables must cross power cables, they should do so at right angles.

- Power and data cables should never share holes bored through concrete, wood, or steel.

- Telecommunication outlets should be placed at the same height from the floor as power outlets, but they should not share stud space.

- Maintain at least two inches of separation from open electrical cables up to 300 volts.

- Maintain at least six inches of separation from lighting sources or fluorescent light power supplies.

- Maintain at least four inches of separation from antenna leads and ground wires without grounded shields.

- Maintain at least six inches of separation from neon signs and transformers.

- Maintain at least six feet of separation from lighting rods and wires.

- Other sources of EMI include photocopiers, microwave ovens, laser printers, electrical motors, elevator shafts, generators, fans, air conditioners, and heaters.

Cable for Data Applications

In this section of the book, we will discuss using the cable you have run for data applications, and we will give some samples of ways that these applications can be wired. An important part of any telecommunications cabling system that supports data is the 110-block, which is a great place to start.

110-Blocks

The telecommunications industry has been using the 66-style block for many years, and it is considered the mainstay of the industry. 66-blocks are traditionally used only for voice applications; though we have seen them used to cross-connect data circuits, this is not recommended. 110-blocks are newer than 66-blocks and have been designed to overcome some of the problems associated with 66-blocks. 110-blocks were designed to support higher frequency applications, accommodate higher density wiring arrangements, and better separate the input and output wires.

The standard 66-block enabled you to connect 25 pair of wires to it, but the 110-blocks are available in many different configurations supporting not only 25 pairs of wire, but 50, 100, 200, and 300 pairs of wires as well. The 110-block has two primary components: the 110 wiring block on which the wires are placed and the 110-connecting block (shown in Figure 7.8), which is used to terminate the wires. A 110-wiring block will consists of multiple 110-connector blocks; there will be one 110-connector block for each four-pair cable that must be terminated.

FIGURE 7.8:

110-connector block

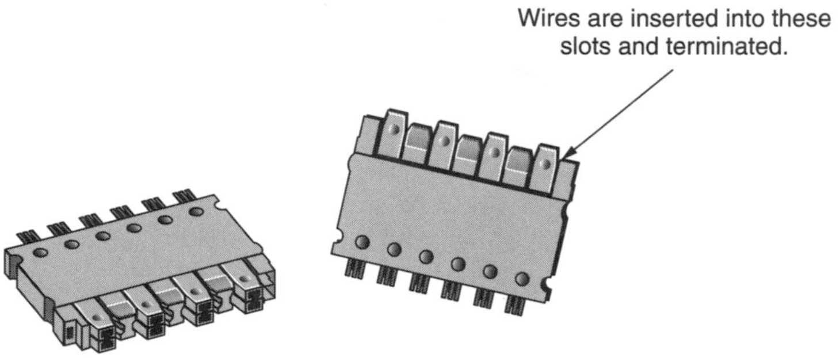

Wires are inserted into these slots and terminated.

The 110-wiring block will consist of a few or many rows of 110-connector blocks. The wires are inserted into the connecting block and terminated by a punch-down tool or vendor-specific tool. These blocks are a type of IDC (insulation displacement connector); as the wires make contact with the metal on the blocks, the insulation is sliced and the metal makes contact with the conductor. Remember, to prevent unnecessary crosstalk, don't untwist the pairs more than .5 inches when terminated onto a 110-connecting block.

110-blocks come in a wide variety of configurations. Some are simply the 110-block that allows the connection of 110-block jumper cables. Figure 7.9 shows a 110-block jumper cable; one side of the cable is connected to the 110-block, and the other side is a modular eight-pin plug (RJ-45).

FIGURE 7.9:

110-block to RJ-45 patch cable

(Photo courtesy of The Siemon Company)

Other 110-blocks have RJ-45 connectors adjacent to the 110-blocks, such as the one shown in Figure 7.10. If the application uses the 50-pin telco connectors such as some Ethernet equipment and many voice applications do, 110-blocks such as the one shown in Figure 7.11 can be purchased that terminate cables to the 110-connecting blocks but then connect to 50-pin telco connectors.

FIGURE 7.10:

110-block with RJ-45 connectors on the front of the block

(Photo courtesy of The Siemon Company)

FIGURE 7.11:

110-block with 50-pin
telco connectors

(Photo courtesy of The Siemon
Company)

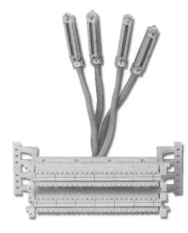

You will also find 110-blocks on the back of patch panels; each 110 connecting
block has a corresponding port on the patch panel. Figure 7.12 shows the 110-block
on the back of a patch panel. The front side of the patch panel shown in Figure 7.13
shows a 96-port patch panel; each port will have a corresponding 110 connecting
block.

FIGURE 7.12:

110-block on the backside
of a patch panel

(Photo courtesy of Computer
Training Academy)

NOTE
The patch panel and 110-block on the back is the most common configuration in modern data telecommunication infrastructures.

FIGURE 7.13:

96-port patch panel

(Photo courtesy of MilesTek)

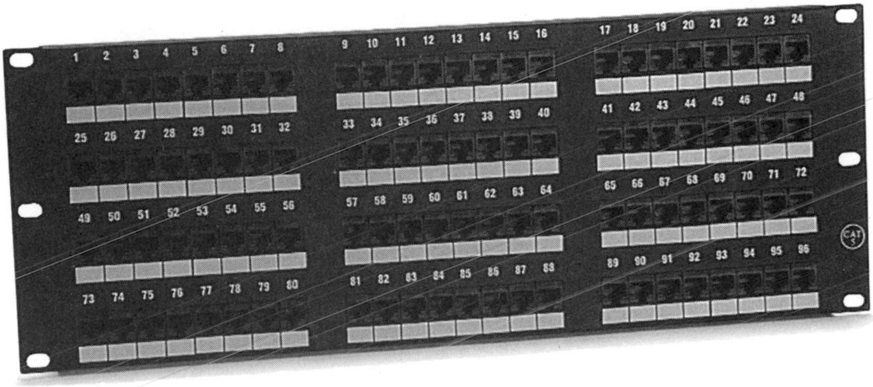

TIP
When purchasing patch panels and 110-blocks, make sure you purchase one that has the correct wiring pattern. Most 110-blocks are color-coded for either the T568A or T568B wiring pattern.

NOTE
110-connecting blocks are almost always designed for solid-conductor wire. Make sure that you are using solid-conductor wire for your horizontal cabling.

Sample Data Installations

As long as you are following the TIA/EIA-568-A standard, most of your communications infrastructure will be pretty similar and will not vary based on whether it is supporting voice or a specific data application. The horizontal cables will all follow the same structure and rules. However, there will be some differences when you start using the cabling for data applications. We will now take a look at a couple of possible scenarios for the usage of a structured cabling system.

The first scenario, shown in Figure 7.14, shows the typical horizontal cabling terminated to a patch panel. The horizontal cable terminates to the 110-block on the back of the patch panel. When a workstation is connected to the network, it is connected to the network hub by means of a RJ-45 patch cable that connects the appropriate port on the patch panel to a port on the hub.

FIGURE 7.14:

Structured cabling system designed for use with data

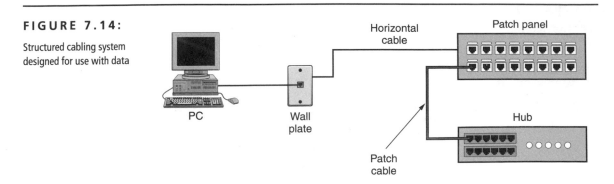

The use of a generic patch panel in Figure 7.14 allows this cabling system to be the most versatile and expandable. Further, the above system can also be used for voice applications if the voice system is also terminated to patch panels.

Another scenario involves the use of 110-blocks with 50-pin telco connectors. These 50-pin telco connectors are used to connect to phone systems or to hubs that are equipped with the appropriate 50-pin telco interface. These are less versatile than the use of a patch panel because each connection must be terminated directly to a connection that connects to a hub.

In past years, we have worked with these types of connections, and network administrators have reported to us that these are more difficult to work with. Further, these 50-pin telco connectors may not be interchangeable with equipment you purchase in the future. Figure 7.15 shows the use of a 110-block connecting to network equipment using a 50-pin telco connector.

FIGURE 7.15:

Structured cabling system terminated into 110-connecting blocks with 50-pin telco connectors

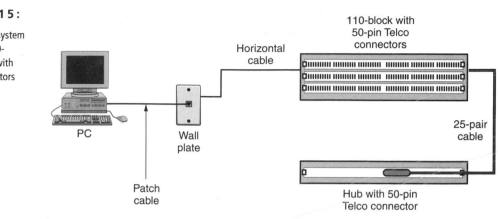

FIGURE 7.15:

110-block with 50-pin Telco connectors

Horizontal cable

PC

Wall plate

Patch cable

25-pair cable

Hub with 50-pin Telco connector

A final scenario that is a combination of the patch panel approach and the 110-block approach is the use of a 110-block and 110-block patch cables (such as the one shown previously in Figure 7.9). This is almost identical to the patch panel approach, except that the patch cables that are used in the telecommunications closet have a 110-block connector on one side and an RJ-45 on the other. This configuration is shown in Figure 7.16.

FIGURE 7.16:

Structured cabling using 110-blocks and 110-block patch cords

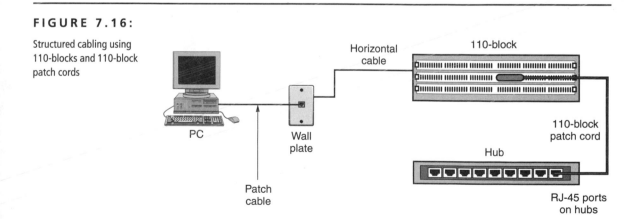

Horizontal cable

110-block

PC

Wall plate

Patch cable

110-block patch cord

Hub

RJ-45 ports on hubs

The previous examples are fairly simple and involve only one wiring closet. Any installation that requires the use of more than one telecommunications closet and also the use of an equipment room will require the service of a data backbone. Figure 7.17 shows an example where data backbone cabling is required. Due to distance limitations on horizontal cable when it is handling data applications, all horizontal cable is terminated to network equipment (hubs) in the telecommunications closet. The hub is then linked to other hubs via the data backbone cable.

FIGURE 7.17:

Structured cabling that includes data backbone cabling

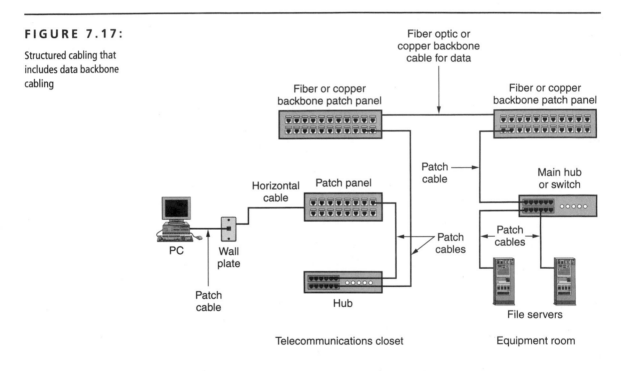

Cable for Voice Applications

Unless you have an extraordinarily expensive phone system, it probably uses copper cabling to connect the desktop telephones to the phone switch or PBX (private branch exchange). Twisted-pair, copper cables have been the backbone of phone systems since the invention of the telephone. The mainstay of copper-based voice systems is the 66-block.

66-Blocks

The 66-block is the most common of the punch-down blocks. It has been used with telephone cabling for many years, and its use continues to be widespread. There are a number of different types of 66-blocks, but the most common is the 66M1-50 pictured in Figure 7.18.

FIGURE 7.18:

66-block

(Photo courtesy of The Siemon Company)

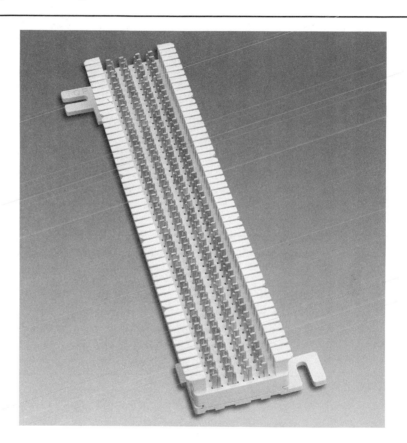

This 66-block has 50 horizontal rows of IDC connectors; each row consists of four prongs called bifurcated contact prongs. A side view of a row of contact prongs is shown in Figure 7.19. They are called *bifurcated contact prongs* because they are split in two pieces. The wire is inserted between one of the clips, then the punch-down (impact) tool applies pressure to insert the wire between the two parts of the clip.

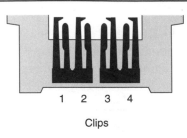

1   2   3   4

Clips

The clips are labeled 1, 2, 3, and 4. The 66-block clips in Figure 7.19 show that the two clips on the left (clips 1 and 2) are electrically connected together, as are the two clips (clips 3 and 4) on the right. However, the two sets of clips are not electrically connected to one another. Wires can be terminated on both sides of the 66-block, and a metal "bridging" clip is inserted between clips 1 and 2 and clips 3 and 4. This bridging clip mechanically joins the two sides together. The advantage to this is that the sides can be disconnected easily if you need to troubleshoot a problem.

NOTE   Some 66-blocks have a 50-pin telco connector on one side of the 66-block.

Figure 7.20 shows a common use of the 66-block; in this diagram, the phone lines from the phone company are connected to one side of the block. The lines into the PBX are connected on the other side. When the company is ready to turn the phone service on, the bridge clips are inserted, which makes the connection.

NOTE   66-blocks are typically designed for solid-conductor cable. Stranded-conductor cables will easily come loose from the IDC style connectors. There are stranded-conductor 66-blocks available, however.

Figure 7.21 shows a 66-block in use for a voice system. In this picture, you can see that part of the 66-block connectors have bridging clips connecting them. This block also has a door that can be closed to protect the front of the block and prevent the bridging clips from being knocked off.

FIGURE 7.20:

66-block separating phone company lines from phone system

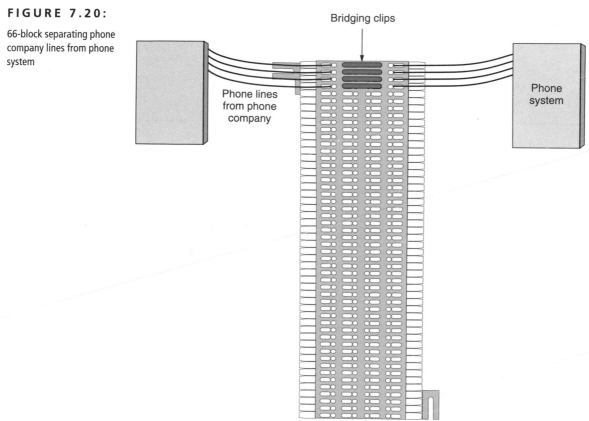

Bridging clips

Phone lines from phone company

Phone system

66-block

FIGURE 7.21:

66-block used in voice applications

(Photo courtesy of Computer Training Center)

25-Pair Wire Assignments

When connecting to a 66-block, the most typical type of cable that is connected to it is the 25-pair cable. The wiring pattern that is used with the 66-block is shown in Figure 7.22. If you look at a 66-block, you will notice notches in the plastic clips on the left and right side. These notches indicate the beginning of the next binder group.

FIGURE 7.22:

66-block wire color/pin assignments for 25-pair cables

Row #	Wire Color
1	White/blue
2	Blue/white
3	White/orange
4	Orange/white
5	White/green
6	Green/white
7	White/brown
8	Brown/white
9	White/slate
10	Blue/white
11	Red/blue
12	Blue/red
13	Red/orange
14	Orange/red
15	Red/green
16	Green/red
17	Red/brown
18	Brown/red
19	Red/slate
20	Slate/red
21	Black/blue
22	Blue/black
23	Black/orange
24	Orange/black
25	Black/green
26	Green/black
27	Black/brown
28	Brown/black
29	Black/slate
30	Slate/black
31	Yellow/blue
32	Blue/yellow
33	Yellow/orange
34	Orange/yellow
35	Yellow/green
36	Green/yellow
37	Yellow/brown
38	Brown/yellow
39	Yellow/slate
40	Slate/yellow
41	Violet/blue
42	Blue/violet
43	Violet/orange
44	Orange/violet
45	Violet/green
46	Green/violet
47	Violet/brown
48	Brown/violet
49	Violet/slate
50	Slate/Violet

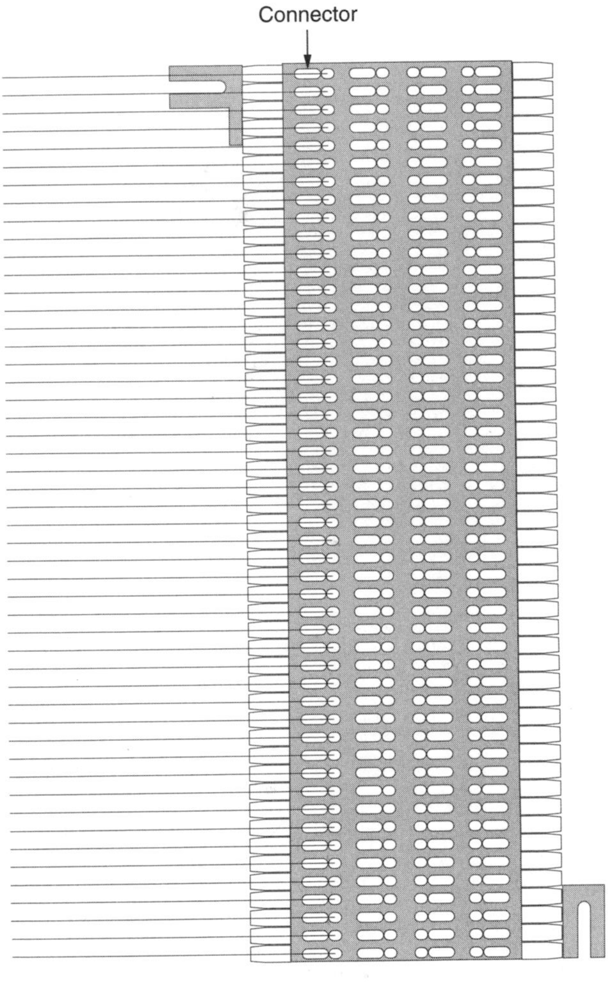

Connector

NOTE   The T568A and T568B wiring patterns do *not* apply to 66-blocks.

If you are using 66-blocks and four-pair UTP cables instead of 25-pair cables, then the wire color/pin assignments are as shown in Figure 7.23.

FIGURE 7.23:

66-block wire color/pin assignments for four-pair cables

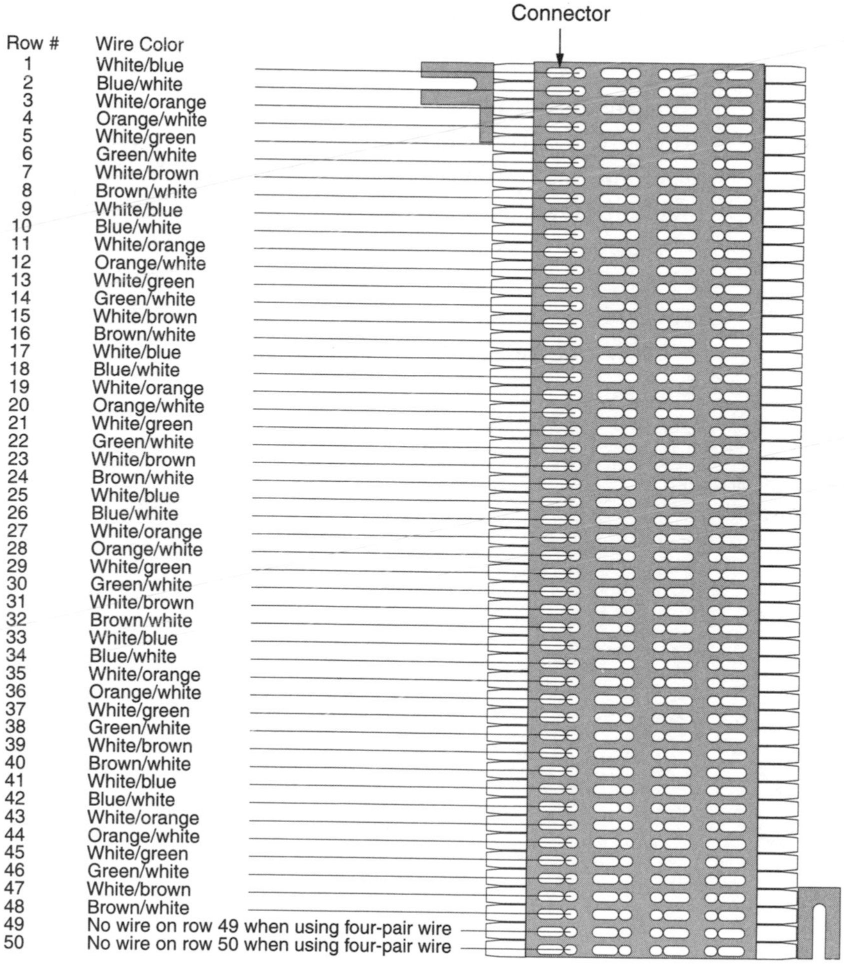

Row #	Wire Color
1	White/blue
2	Blue/white
3	White/orange
4	Orange/white
5	White/green
6	Green/white
7	White/brown
8	Brown/white
9	White/blue
10	Blue/white
11	White/orange
12	Orange/white
13	White/green
14	Green/white
15	White/brown
16	Brown/white
17	White/blue
18	Blue/white
19	White/orange
20	Orange/white
21	White/green
22	Green/white
23	White/brown
24	Brown/white
25	White/blue
26	Blue/white
27	White/orange
28	Orange/white
29	White/green
30	Green/white
31	White/brown
32	Brown/white
33	White/blue
34	Blue/white
35	White/orange
36	Orange/white
37	White/green
38	Green/white
39	White/brown
40	Brown/white
41	White/blue
42	Blue/white
43	White/orange
44	Orange/white
45	White/green
46	Green/white
47	White/brown
48	Brown/white
49	No wire on row 49 when using four-pair wire
50	No wire on row 50 when using four-pair wire

Connector

Sample Voice Installations

In many ways, voice installations are quite similar to data installations. The exception is the type of equipment that each end of the link is being plugged into and, sometimes, the type of patch cables being used. The TIA/EIA-568-A standard requires at least one four-pair, unshielded twisted-pair cable be run to each workstation outlet that is installed. This cable is to be used for voice applications. We recommend using a minimum of Category 3 cable for voice applications; however, if you are purchasing Category 5 or Category 5e cable for data, we advise using the same category of cable for voice.

We now want to show you some sample cabling installations that we have seen installed to support voice and data. Because there are so many possible combinations, we will only be able to show you a few. The first one (shown in Figure 7.24) is common in small- to medium-sized installations. In this example, each horizontal cable designated for voice terminates to a RJ-45 patch panel. A second patch panel has RJ-45 blocks terminated to the extensions on the phone switch or PBX. This makes the process of moving a phone extension from one location to another as simple as moving the patch cable. If this type of flexibility is required, this configuration makes an excellent choice.

FIGURE 7.24:

Voice application using RJ-45 patch panels

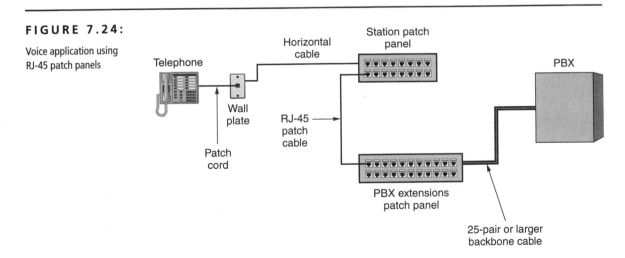

TIP

Any wiring system that terminates horizontal wiring into an RJ-45 type patch panel will be more versatile because any given wall plate port/patch panel port combination can be used for either voice or data. However, cabling professionals generally recommend separate patch panels for voice and data. This prevents interference that might occur as a result of incompatible systems and different frequencies being used on the same patch panels.

The next example illustrates a more complex wiring environment, which includes backbone cabling for the voice applications. This example could employ patch panels in the telecommunications closet or 66-blocks, depending on the flexibility desired. The telecommunications closet is connected to the equipment room via twisted-pair backbone cabling. Figure 7.25 illustrates the use of patch panels, 66-blocks, and backbone cabling.

FIGURE 7.25:

Voice application with a voice backbone, patch panels, and 66-blocks

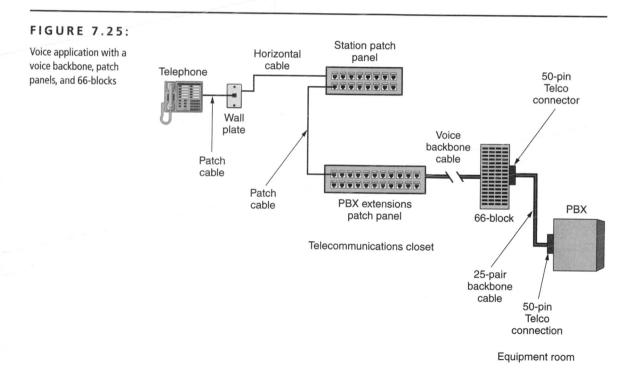

The final example is the most common for voice installations; it uses exclusively 66-blocks. Note that in Figure 7.26 there are two 66-blocks connected by cross-connected cable. Cross-connect cable is simple single-pair, twisted-pair wire that has no jacket. You can purchase cross-connect wire, so don't worry about stripping a bunch of existing cables to get it. The example shown in Figure 7.26 is not as versatile as it would be if you used patch panels because 66-blocks require either reconnecting the cross-connect or reprogramming the PBX.

FIGURE 7.26:

Voice applications using exclusively 66-blocks

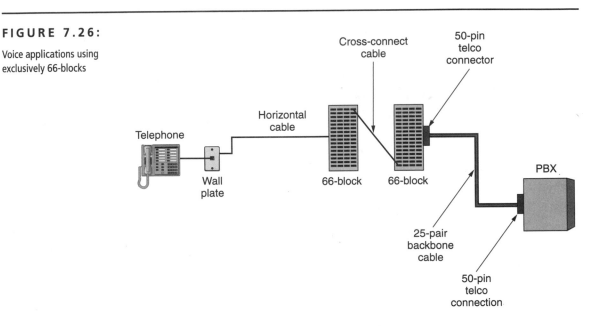

Figure 7.27 shows a 66-block with cross-connect wires connected to it. Though you cannot tell this in black and white, cross-connect wires are often red and white.

The examples of 66-blocks and 110-blocks in this chapter are fairly common, but we could not possibly cover every possible permutation and usage of these types of blocks. We hope we have given you a representative view of some possible configurations.

FIGURE 7.27:

66-block with cross-connect wires

(Photo courtesy of The Siemon Company)

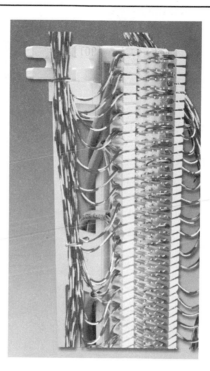

FIGURE 7.27:

66-block with cross-connect wires

(Photo courtesy of The Siemon Company)

Testing

Every cable run must be tested to a minimum level of testing. You can purchase $5000 cable testers that will provide you with many statistics on performance, but the most important test is simply determining that the connection is being made correctly and that the pairs are connected properly.

The $5,000 testers provide you with much more performance data than the simple cable testers and will also certify that each cable run will operate at a specific performance level. Some customers will insist viewing results on the $5,000 cable tester, but the minimum tests you should run will determine continuity and that the wire map is correct. There are a couple of different levels of testing that you can perform. The cable testers that you can use include the following:

- Tone generators and amplifier probes
- Continuity testers

- Wire map testers
- Cable certification testers

Tone Generators and Amplifier Probes

If you have a bundle of cable and you need to locate a single cable within the bundle, using a tone generator and amplifier is the answer. Often, cable installers will pull more than one cable (sometimes dozens) to a single location, but they will not document the ends of the cables. The tone generator is used to send an electrical signal through the cable. On the other side of the cable, the amplifier (a.k.a., an inductive amplifier) is placed near each cable until you hear a sound from the amplifier. This indicates that you have found the cable. Figure 7.28 shows a tone generator and amplifier probe from IDEAL DataComm.

FIGURE 7.28:

Tone generator and amplifier probe

(Photo courtesy of IDEAL DataComm)

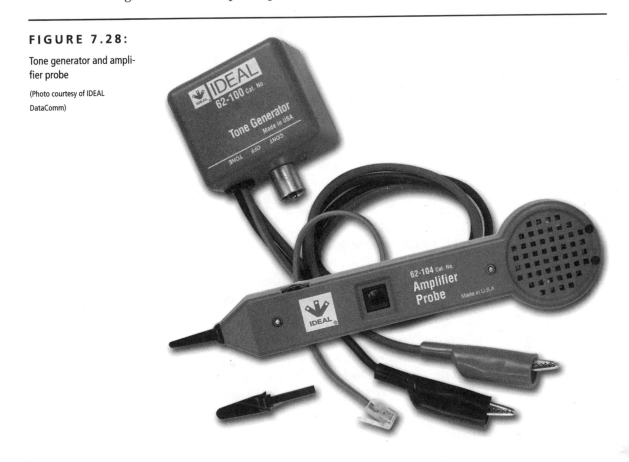

Continuity Testing

The simplest test you can perform on a cable is the continuity test. This test ensures that electrical signals are traveling from the point of origin to the receiving side. Simple continuity testers only guarantee that a signal is being received; they do not test attenuation or crosstalk.

Wire Map

A wire map tester is capable of examining the pairs of wires and indicating whether or not the pairs of wires are connected correctly through the link. These testers will also indicate if the continuity of each wire is good. As long as good installation techniques are used and the correct category of cables, connectors, and patch panels are used, many of the problems with cabling can be solved by a simple wire map tester. Figure 7.30 shows a simple tester from IDEAL DataComm that performs both wire map testing and continuity testing.

FIGURE 7.29:

Simple cable testing tool

(Photo courtesy of IDEAL DataComm)

Cable Certification

If you are a professional cable installer, you may be required to certify that the cabling system you have installed will actually perform at the required levels. These tests are performed by more sophisticated testing tools than a simple continuity tester or wire map tester. These testers have two components, one for each side of the cable link. Tools such as the Microtest PentaScanner or Hewlett Packard WireScope perform many sophisticated tests that the less expensive scanners are not capable of. Cable testing and certification is covered in more detail in Chapter 14, "Cabling System Testing and Troubleshooting."

Common Problems with Copper Cabling

When testing with a sophisticated tester, if the test fails, the tester may provide you with the reason that the test failed. Some of the problems you may encounter include:

- Length problems
- Wire map problems
- NEXT and FEXT (crosstalk) problems
- Attenuation problems

Length Problems

If a cable tester indicates that you have length problems, the most likely cause of this is that the cable you have installed exceeds the maximum length. The cable tester is indicating that the cable run is failing because of this. Length problems may also manifest themselves if there is an open or short in the cable. Another possible problem is that the cable tester's NVP (nominal velocity propagation) setting is configured incorrectly. To correct this, run the tester's NVP diagnostics or setup to make sure that the NVP value is set properly.

Wire Map Problems

When the cable tester indicates that there is a wire map problem, this usually indicates that there are pairs transposed in the wire. This is often a problem when mixing equipment that supports the T568A and T568B wiring patterns; it can also occur if the installer has split the pairs (individual wires are terminated on incorrect pins). This may also indicate an open or short in the cable.

NEXT and FEXT (Crosstalk) Problems

If the cable tester indicates that there are crosstalk problems, this means that the signal in one pair of wires is "bleeding" over onto another pair of wires; when the crosstalk values are strong enough, this can interfere with data transmission. NEXT problems indicate that the cable tester has measured too much crosstalk on the near end of the connection. FEXT problems indicate too much crosstalk on the opposite side of the cable. This is often caused by the pairs of the cable being split too much when they are terminated. Crosstalk problems can also be caused by external interference from EMI sources and cable damage or when components (patch panels and connectors) that are only supported for lower categories of cabling are used.

Attenuation Problems

When the cable tester reports attenuation problems, this indicates that the cable is losing too much signal across its length. This can be a result of the cabling being too long. Also check to make sure the cable is terminated properly. When running horizontal cable, make sure that you are using solid-conductor cable; stranded cable has higher attenuation than solid cable and can contribute to attenuation problems over longer lengths. Other causes of attenuation problems include high temperatures, cable damage, and the wrong category of components (patch panels and connectors) being used.

chapter 8

Wall Plates

- Wall Plate Design and Installation Issues

- Fixed-Design Wall Plates

- Modular Wall Plates

- Biscuit Jacks

In Chapter 5, you learned about the basic components of a structured cabling system. One of the most visible of these components is the wall plate (also called a *workstation* or *station outlet* because it is usually placed near a workstation). As its name suggests, a *wall plate* is a flat plastic or metal plate that usually mounts in or on a wall (although some "wall" plates actually are mounted in floors and ceilings). Wall plates include one or more jacks. A *jack* is the connector in the wall plate that allows a workstation to make a physical and electrical connection to the network cabling system.

Wall plates come in many different styles, types, brands, and yes, even colors (in case you want to color-coordinate your wiring system). In this chapter, you will learn about the different types of wall plates available and their associated installation issues.

WARNING The National Electrical Code dictates how various types of wiring (including power and telecommunications wiring) must be installed, but be aware that NEC compliance varies from state to state. The NEC code requirements given in this chapter should be verified against your local code requirements before you do any kind of structured cable system design or installation.

Wall Plate Design and Installation Issues

When you are planning your cabling system installation, there are a few wall plate installation issues you must be aware of in order to make the most efficient installation. The majority of these installation issues come from compliance with the TIA/EIA-570 (for residential and light commercial installations) and TIA/EIA-568-A (for commercial installations) telecommunications standards. You'll have to make certain choices about how best to conform to these standards based on the type of installation you are doing. These choices will dictate the different steps you'll need to take during the actual installation of the different kinds of wall plates.

The main design and installation issues you must deal with for wall plates are

- Manufacturer system
- Wall plate location
- Wall plate mounting system
- Fixed design or modular plate

In this section, you will learn what each of these installation issues is and how each will affect your cabling system installation.

Manufacturer System

There is no "universal" wall plate. There are hundreds of different wall plates available, each with its own design merits and drawbacks. It would be next to impossible to detail every type of manufacturer and wall plate, so in this chapter we'll just give a few examples of the most popular types. The most important thing to remember about using a particular manufacturer's wall plate system in your structured cabling system is that it is a *system*. Each component in a wall plate system is designed to work together and, generally speaking, can't be used with components from other systems. A *wall plate system* consists of a wall plate and its associated jacks. Usually, you cannot use the jacks made for one wall plate system in the wall plate from another system. When designing your cabling system, you must choose the manufacturer and wall plate system that best suits your needs.

Wall Plate Location

When installing wall plates, you must decide the best location to put them on the wall. Obviously, the wall plate should be fairly near to the workstation, and, in fact, the TIA/EIA-568-A standard says that the maximum length of the workstation to wall plate patch cable can be no longer than three meters (10 feet). This short distance will affect exactly where you place your wall plate in your design. If you already have your office laid out, you will have to locate the wall plates as close as possible to the workstations so that your wiring system will conform to the standard.

Additionally, you want to keep wall plates away from any source of direct heat that could damage the connector or reduce its efficiency. In other words, don't place a wall plate directly above a floor heating register or baseboard heater.

There are a few guidelines for where to put your wall plates on a wall for code compliance and the most trouble-free installation. There are two aspects of the wall plate location you must account for:

- Vertical position

- Horizontal position

Each aspect has its own implications that you must understand before you start designing your own cabling system. Let's examine the vertical placement of the wall plate first.

Vertical Position

When deciding the vertical position of your wall plates, you must take into account either the residential or commercial National Electrical Code (NEC) sections. Which section you go by depends on whether you are performing a residential or commercial installation.

In residential installations, you have some flexibility. You can place a wall plate in almost any vertical position on a wall, but the NEC suggests that you place them so that the top of plate is no more than 18 inches from the subfloor (the same distance as electrical outlets). If the wall plate is servicing a countertop or a wall phone, the top of the plate should be no more than 48 inches from the subfloor. These vertical location requirements are illustrated in Figure 8.1.

NOTE   These heights may be adjusted, if necessary, for elderly or handicapped occupants according to the Americans with Disabilities Act (ADA) guidelines.

FIGURE 8.1:

Wall plate vertical location

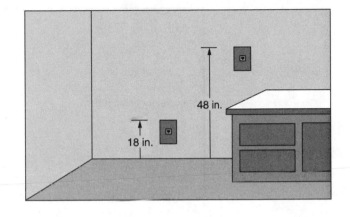

TIP   Remember that these vertical distances may vary from city to city and from residential to commercial electrical codes.

Horizontal Position

The other factor in determining wall plate location is the horizontal position of the wall plate along a wall. Wall plates should be placed so that the work area equipment (computers, phones, etc.) is as close as possible to the wall plate. In fact, the TIA/EIA-568-A standard requires that work area cables should not exceed three meters (10 feet). This means that you will have to know where the furniture is in a room before you can decide where to put the wall plates for the network and phone. Figure 8.2 illustrates this horizontal position requirement.

FIGURE 8.2:

Horizontal wall plate placement

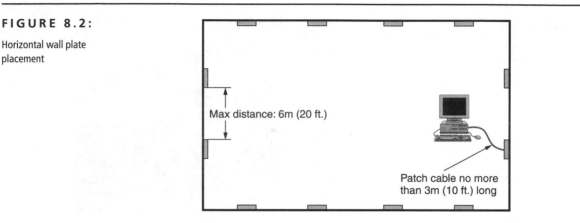

Max distance: 6m (20 ft.)

Patch cable no more than 3m (10 ft.) long

TIP

When placing telecommunications outlets, consider adding more than one per room to accommodate for rearrangement of the furniture. It usually helps to "mirror" the opposing wall outlet layout (i.e., north-south and east-west walls will be mirror images of each other with respect to their outlet layout).

Another horizontal position factor to take into account is the proximity to electrical fixtures. Data communications wall plates and wall boxes cannot be located in the same stud cavity as electrical wall boxes when the electrical wire is not encased in metal conduit. (A *stud cavity* is the space between the two vertical wood or metal studs and the drywall or wallboard attached to these studs.)

This placement rule primarily applies to residential telecommunications wiring as per the TIA/EIA-570 standard. This requirement keeps stray electrical signals from interfering in communications signals. Figure 8.3 illustrates this requirement. Notice that even though the electrical outlets are near to the communications outlets, they are never in the same stud cavity.

FIGURE 8.3:

Placing telecommunications outlets and electrical wall boxes in different wall stud cavities

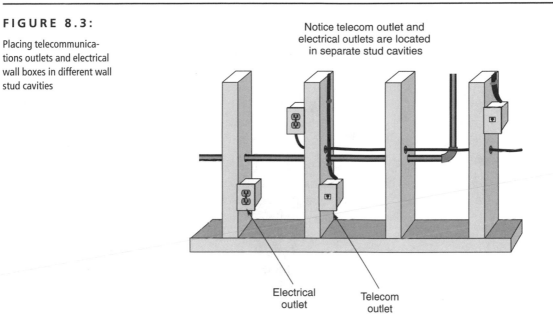

Notice telecom outlet and electrical outlets are located in separate stud cavities

Electrical outlet

Telecom outlet

Wall Plate Mounting System

Another decision you must make regarding your wall plates is how you will mount them to the wall. There are three main systems used to attach wall plates to a wall, each with their own unique applications. The three main systems used are

- Outlet boxes
- Cut-in plates
- Surface mount

The following sections describe each of these mounting systems and their various applications.

Outlet Boxes

The most common wall plate mounting in commercial applications is the outlet box. An *outlet box* is simply a plastic or metal box attached to a stud in a wall cavity. Outlet boxes have screw holes in them that allow a wall plate to be attached. Additionally, they usually have some provision (either nails or screws) that allows them to be attached to a stud. These outlet boxes, as their name suggests, are primarily used for electrical outlets, but they can also be used for telecommunications wiring because the wall plates share the same dimensions and mountings.

Outlet boxes can be either plastic or metal. Plastic boxes are cheaper and are usually found in residential or light commercial installations. Metal boxes are typically found in commercial applications and usually use a conduit of some kind to carry electrical or data cabling. Which you choose depends on the type of installation you are doing. Plastic boxes are fine for simple, residential Category 3 copper installations. However, if you want to install Category 4, 5, 5e, or higher, you must be extremely careful with the wire so that you don't kink or make any sharp bends in the wire. Also, if you run your network cable before the drywall is installed (and in residential wiring with plastic boxes, you almost always have to), it is likely that during the drywall installation the wires could be punctured or stripped.

Metal boxes can have the same problems, but these problems are minimized if the metal boxes are used with conduit. *Conduit* is a plastic or metal pipe that attaches to the box. In commercial installations, a metal box to be used for telecommunications wiring is attached to a stud. Conduit is run from the box to a 45-degree elbow that terminates in the plenum airspace above a dropped ceiling. This installation technique is the most common wiring method in new commercial construction and is illustrated in Figure 8.4. This method allows you to run the telecommunications wire after the wallboard and ceiling have been installed, thus minimizing the chance of damage to the cable.

Common metal box with
conduit commercial
installation

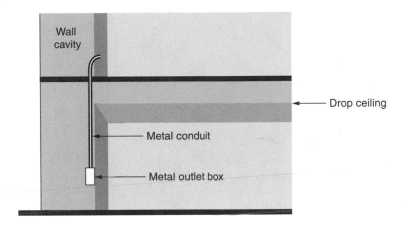

Wall
cavity

← Drop ceiling

— Metal conduit

— Metal outlet box

Cut-In Mounting

Outlet boxes work well as wall plate supports when you are able to get to the studs
during the construction of a building. But what type of wall plate mounting system
do you use once the drywall is in place and you need to put a wall plate on that
wall? The solution to this problem is to use some kind of cut-in mounting hardware. *Cut-in* hardware (also called *remodeling* hardware) is so named because you
cut a hole in the drywall and place some kind of mounting box or plate into this
hole that will support the wall plate. This type of mounting is used when a wall
already is finished and you need to run a cable into a particular stud cavity.

Cut-in mountings fall into two different types: remodel boxes and cover-plate
mounting brackets.

Remodel Boxes   Remodel boxes are simply plastic or metal boxes that mount
to the hole in the drywall using screws or special friction fasteners. The main difference between remodel boxes and regular outlet boxes is that remodel boxes are
slightly smaller and can only be mounted in existing walls. Some examples of
remodel boxes are shown in Figure 8.5.

FIGURE 8.5:

Common examples of
remodel boxes

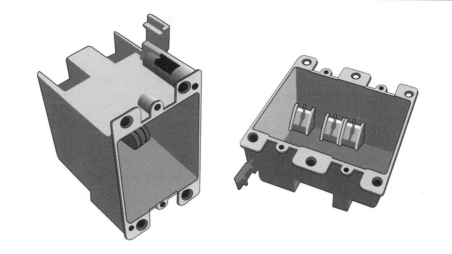

Installing a remodel box so that you can use it for data cabling is simple. Just follow these steps:

1. Determine the location of the new cabling wall plate using the guidelines discussed earlier in this chapter. With a pencil, mark a line indicating the location for the top of the box.

2. Using the hole template provided with the box, trace the outline of the hole to be cut onto the wall with a pencil or marker, keeping the top of the hole aligned with the mark you made in step 1. If no template is provided, use the box as a template by flipping the box over so the face is against the wall and tracing around the box.

3. Using a drywall keyhole saw, cut out a hole, following the lines drawn using the template.

4. Insert the remodel box into the hole you just cut. If the box won't go in easily, trim the sides of the hole with a razor blade or utility knife.

5. Secure the box by either screwing the box to the drywall or by using the friction tabs. To use the friction tabs (if your box has them), just turn the screw attached to the tabs until the tabs are secured against the drywall.

Cover-Plate Mounting Brackets   The other type of cut-in mounting device for data cabling is the *cover-plate mounting bracket*. Also called a *cheater bracket*, this mounting bracket allows you to mount a wall plate directly to the wallboard without installing an outlet box. Figure 8.6 shows some examples of cover-plate mounting brackets before being installed.

FIGURE 8.6:

Cover-plate mounting
bracket examples

These brackets are usually made of steel or aluminum and contain flexible tabs that you push into a precut hole in the drywall. The tabs fold over into the hole and hold the bracket securely to the drywall. Additionally, some brackets allow you to put a screw through both the front of the bracket and the tabs on the back, thus increasing the bracket's hold on the drywall. Figure 8.7 shows a cover-plate mounting bracket installed in a wall ready to accept a wall plate. Once the mounting bracket is installed, the data cable(s) can be pulled through the wall and terminated at the jacks for the wall plate, and the wall plate can be mounted to the bracket.

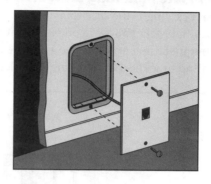

Surface-Mount Outlet Boxes

The final type of wall plate mounting system is the surface-mount outlet box. Surface-mount outlet boxes are used where it is not easy or possible to run the cable inside the wall (in concrete, mortar, or brick walls, for example). Cable is run in a raceway (a round or flat conduit) to an outlet box mounted (either by adhesive or screws) on the outside of the wall. This arrangement is shown in Figure 8.8.

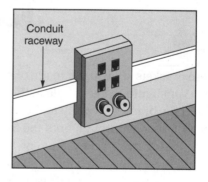

The positive side to surface-mount outlet boxes is their flexibility. They can be placed just about anywhere. The downside is their appearance. Surface-mount installations, even when performed with the utmost care and workmanship, still look cheap and inelegant. But, as mentioned earlier, sometimes they are the only choice.

Fixed-Design or Modular Plate

Another design and installation decision you have to make is whether to use fixed-design wall plates or modular wall plates. *Fixed-design wall plates* (as shown in Figure 8.9) have multiple jacks, but they are molded as part of the wall plate itself. You cannot remove the jack and replace it with a different type of connector.

FIGURE 8.9:

A fixed-design wall plate

Fixed-design plates are usually used in telephone applications rather than LAN wiring applications because, although they are cheap, they have limited flexibility. Fixed-design plates have a couple of advantages and disadvantages (as shown in Table 8.1).

TABLE 8.1: Advantages and Disadvantages of Fixed-Design Wall Plates

Advantages	Disadvantages
Inexpensive	Configuration cannot be changed
Simple to install	Usually not compatible with high-speed networking systems like Gigabit Ethernet

Modular wall plates, on the other hand, use a generic wall plate with multiple jack locations (as shown in Figure 8.10). In a modular wall plate system, this plate is known as a *faceplate* (it's not a wall plate until it has its jacks installed). Jacks for each faceplate are purchased separately from the wall plates and must be the jacks that were designed for the wall plate system.

FIGURE 8.10:

Modular wall plates with
multiple jack locations

Modular wall plates

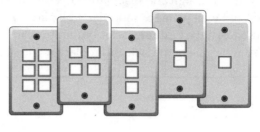

> **TIP**   When using modular wall plates, make sure to use the jacks designed for that wall plate system. Generally speaking, jacks from different wall plate systems are not interchangeable.

You will learn more about these types of wall plates in the next sections.

Fixed-Design Wall Plates

A *fixed-design wall plate* is a wall plate where the port/jack configuration cannot be changed. In this type of wall plate, the jack configuration is determined at the factory, and the jacks are molded as part of the plate assembly.

There are a few issues you must understand before choosing a particular fixed-design wall plate for your cabling installation, including the following:

- Number of sockets
- Types of sockets
- Labeling

In this section, you will learn the details of each issue and how it affects a fixed-design wall plate.

Number of Sockets

Because fixed-design wall plates have their jacks molded into the faceplate assembly, there is a practical limit to how many jacks can fit into a fixed-design faceplate. It is very unusual to find a fixed-design faceplate with more than two jacks (they are usually in an over-under configuration, with one jack above the other). Additionally, most fixed-design wall plates are for UTP copper cable only; there are very few fiber optic fixed-design wall plates available. Figure 8.11 shows some examples of fixed-design wall plates with various numbers of sockets.

FIGURE 8.11:

Fixed-design wall plates with varying numbers of sockets

Types of Sockets

Fixed-design wall plates can accommodate many different types of sockets for different types of data communications media. However, you cannot change a wall plate's configuration once it is in place; instead, you must install a completely new wall plate with a different configuration.

The most common configuration of a fixed-design wall plate is the single RJ-11 or RJ-45 jack (as shown in Figure 8.12), which is most often used for home or office telephone connections. This type of wall plate can be found in your local hardware store or home center.

FIGURE 8.12:

Fixed-design plate with a
single RJ-11 or RJ-45 jack

Other types of fixed-design wall plates can include any combinations of socket connectors, based on market demand and the whims of the manufacturer. Some of the connector combinations commonly found are listed below:

- Single RJ-11
- Single RJ-45
- Single coax (TV cable)
- Single BNC
- Dual RJ-11
- Dual RJ-45
- Single RJ-11, single RJ-45
- Single RJ-11, single coax (TV cable)
- Single RJ-45, single BNC
- Single RJ-11, single

Labeling

Not all wall plate connectors are labeled. Most fixed-design wall plates don't have special reparations for labeling (unlike modular plates). However, that doesn't mean it isn't important to label each connection. On the contrary, it is extremely important to label each connection so that you can tell which connection is which (extremely useful when troubleshooting). Additionally, some jacks, while they look the same, may serve a completely different purpose. For example, RJ-45 jacks can be used for both PBX telephone and Ethernet networking, so it's helpful to label which is which if a fixed-design plate has two RJ-45 jacks.

For these reasons, structured cabling manufacturers have come up with different methods of labeling fixed-design wall plates. The most popular method is using adhesive-backed stickers or labels of some kind. There are alphanumeric labels (e.g., LAN and PHONE) as well as icon labels with pictures of computers for LAN ports and pictures of telephones for telephone ports.

Modular Wall Plates

Modular wall plates are those wall plates that are designed to be modular—that is, they have individual components that can be installed in varying configurations depending on your cabling needs. For example, when you have a cabling design need for a wall plate that can have three RJ-45 jacks in one configuration and one RJ-45 jack and two fiber optic jacks in another configuration, the modular wall plate fills that design need very nicely.

Just like fixed-design wall plates, modular wall plates have their own design and installation issues, including:

- Number of sockets
- Wall plate jack considerations
- Labeling

In this section, you will learn all of the design and installation issues of using modular wall plates.

Number of Sockets

The first decision you must make when using modular wall plates is how many sockets you want for each wall plate. Each socket can hold a different type of jack for a different type of cable media, if necessary. The TIA/EIA-568-A standard recommends, at minimum, two ports for each work area wall plate. These ports can be either side by side or over and under, but they should be in the same wall plate. Additionally, each port must be served by its own cable and at least one of those should be a four-pair, 100-ohm, UTP cable.

The number of sockets a plate can have are based on the size of the plate. Fixed-design wall plates mainly come in one size. Modular plates come in a couple of different sizes. The smallest size for wall plates is single-gang, which measures 4.5 inches high and 2.75 inches wide. The next largest size is called double-gang, which measures 4.5 by 4.5 inches (the same height as single gang plates, but almost twice as wide). There are triple- and quad-gang plates, but they are not used as often as single- and double-gang plates. Figure 8.13 shows the difference between a single- and double-gang wall plate.

FIGURE 8.13:

Single- and double-gang wall plates

Single gang   Double gang

Each manufacturer has different guidelines about how many sockets for jacks fit into each type of wall plate. Most manufacturers, however, agree that six jacks are the most you can fit into a single-gang wall plate.

The TIA/EIA-568-A standard for structured premises wiring recommends a minimum of two ports at each work-area outlet. They can be side by side or over and under, but preferably in the same receptacle. With the advent of new technology and applications, such as videoconferencing and fiber-to-the-desktop, users need more ports and different types of cabling brought to the desktop. Besides using patch panels in the telecommunications closet, you can bring Category 3, Category 5, fiber optic, and coaxial cable to the desktop for voice, data, and video with the newer 6-, 12- and 16-port multimedia outlets.

Wall Plate Jack Considerations

Modular wall plates are the most common type of wall plate in use for data cabling because they meet the various TIA/EIA and NEC standards and codes for quality data communications cabling. For this reason, modular wall plates have the widest variety of jack types available. All the jacks available today differ based on a few parameters. Some of these parameters include the following:

- Wall plate system type
- Cable connection
- Jack orientation
- TIA/EIA–568-A wiring pattern

In this section, you will learn about the differences between the various types of jacks available and the factors that make them different.

Wall Plate System Type

Remember how the type of wall plate you use dictates the type of jacks for that wall plate? Well, the same holds true for jacks. When you pick a certain brand and manufacturer for a jack, you must use the same brand and manufacturer of wall plate.

Cable Connection

Jacks also differ in the way that they connect to the horizontal cable run. Although it seems as if each manufacturer has their own unique method of connecting the individual strands to the pins in a UTP connection, each of these methods works similarly. Each uses insulation displacement connectors (IDCs), which work by using small metal teeth or pins in the connector that are pressed into the individual wires of a UTP cable (or the wires are pressed into the teeth). The teeth puncture the outer insulation of the individual wires and make contact with the conductor inside, thus making a connection. This process (known as *crimping* or *punching down*, depending on the method or tool used) is illustrated in Figure 8.14.

FIGURE 8.14:

Using insulation displacement connectors (IDCs)

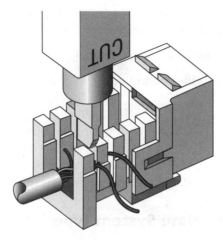

Though they may differ in methods, any connector that uses some piece of metal to puncture through the insulation of a strand of copper cable is an IDC connector.

Jack Orientation

Yes, jack orientation. The individual wall plate systems use many different types of jacks, and some of those systems use jacks with positions other than straight ahead (which is the "standard" configuration). These days, a popular configuration is a jack that's angled approximately 45 degrees down. There are many reasons that this jack became popular. First off, it looks cool. Second, because it's angled, the cable-connect takes up less room (which is nice when a desk is pushed up tight against the wall plate). Finally, the angled connector works well in installations where there is a high dust content because it's harder for dust to rest inside the connector. Figure 8.15 shows an example of an angled connector.

FIGURE 8.15:

An angled RJ-45 connector

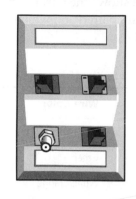

> **NOTE**   Angled connectors are found in many different types of cabling installations, including STP, UTP, and fiber optic.

Wiring Pattern

When connecting copper 10Base-T or 100Base-T RJ-45 jacks, you must wire all jacks and patch points according to either the T568-A or T568-B standard. Figure 8.16 shows both sides of a common snap-in jack with both T568-A and T568-B color-coding. Notice that the wiring schemes are completely different. If your company has a standard wiring pattern and you wire a single jack with the opposing standard, that particular jack will not be able to communicate with the rest of the network.

FIGURE 8.16:

A common snap-in jack showing both T568-A and T568-B wiring schemes

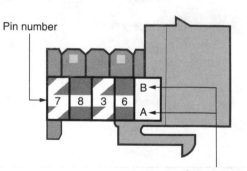

Table 8.2 shows the wiring color scheme for the T568-A standard. Notice how the wires are paired and which color goes to which pin. Table 8.3 shows the same for T568-B.

TABLE 8.2: Wiring Scheme for T568-A

Pin#	Wire Color
1	White/green
2	Green
3	White/orange
4	Blue
5	White/blue
6	Orange
7	White/brown
8	Brown

TABLE 8.3: Wiring Scheme for T568-B

Pin#	Wire Color
1	White/orange
2	Orange
3	White/green
4	Blue
5	White/blue
6	Green
7	White/brown
8	Brown

Labeling

Just like fixed-design wall plates, modular wall plates use labels to differentiate the different jacks in a wall plate by their purpose. In fact, modular wall plates have the widest variety of labels—every modular wall plate manufacturer seems to pride themselves on their varied colors and styles of labeling. However, as with fixed-design plates, the labels are either text (e.g., LAN, Phone), or pictures of their intended use.

Biscuit Jacks

No discussion of wall plates would be complete without a discussion of biscuit jacks. *Biscuit* jacks are surface-mount jacks that look like small biscuits (see Figure 8.17). They were originally used in residential and light commercial installations for telephone applications. In fact, you may have some in your home if it was built before 1975. David's house was built in the 1920s, so when he bought it, the house was lousy with them. When remodeled last summer, he removed all the biscuit jacks and installed wall boxes in all the rooms and ran UTP and coaxial cable to all these boxes and installed modular wall plates, including two RJ-45s and one TV cable jack.

FIGURE 8.17:

An example of a biscuit jack

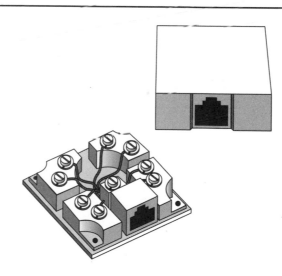

Types of Biscuit Jacks

There are many different types of biscuit jacks, small and large. They differ primarily by size and number of jacks they can support. The smaller of the two sizes measures 2.25 inches wide by 2.5 inches high and, as mentioned previously, is primarily used for residential telephone applications. The smaller size can generally support up to a maximum of two jacks.

The larger sized biscuit jacks are sometimes referred to as simply surface-mount boxes because they don't have the size and shape of the smaller biscuit jacks. These surface-mount boxes are primarily used for data communications applications and come in a variety of sizes. Additionally, these larger biscuit jacks can have any number or type of jacks and are generally modular. Figure 8.18 shows an example of a larger biscuit jack that is commonly used in surface-mount applications.

FIGURE 8.18:

Example of a larger
biscuit jack

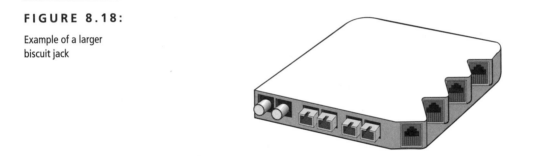

NOTE   Generally speaking, the smaller biscuit jacks are not rated for Category 5 (or any higher categories). They must be specifically designed for a Category 5 application.

Advantages of Biscuit Jacks

There are a few advantages to using biscuit jacks in your structured cabling design. First of all, they are very inexpensive compared to other types of surface-mount wiring systems, which is why many houses that had the old four-pin telephone systems now have biscuit jacks: you could buy 20 of them for around 30 dollars. Even the jacks that support multiple jacks are still fairly inexpensive.

Another advantage of biscuit jacks is their ability to work in situations where standard modular or fixed-design wall plates won't work and other types of surface-mount wiring is too bulky. The best example of this is office cubicles (i.e., modular furniture). A biscuit jack has an adhesive tab on the back that allows it to be mounted anywhere, so you can run a telephone or data cable to a biscuit jack and mount it under the desk where it will be out of the way.

Finally, biscuit jacks are easy to install. The cover is removed with one screw. Inside many of the biscuit jacks there are screw terminals (one per pin in each jack), as shown in Figure 8.19. To install the jack, strip the insulation from each conductor and wrap it clockwise around the terminal, between the washers, and tighten the screw. Repeat this process for each conductor in the cable.

FIGURE 8.19:

Screw terminals inside a biscuit jack

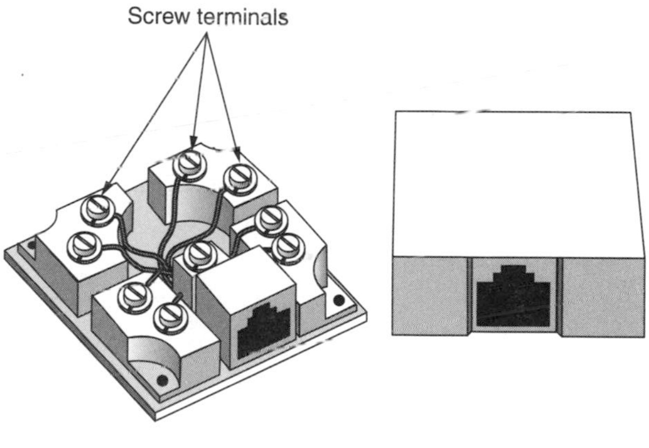

NOTE   Not all biscuit jacks use screw terminals. The more modern data communications jacks use IDC connectors to attach the wire to the jack.

Disadvantages of Biscuit Jacks

The main disadvantage to biscuit jacks is that the older biscuit jacks are not rated for high-speed data communications. Notice that in the biscuit jack shown in Figure 8.19 there are a bunch of screw terminals. When a conductor is wrapped around these terminals, it is exposed to stray electromagnetic interference (EMI) and other interference, which reduces the effective ability of this type of jack to carry data. At most, the older biscuit jacks with the screw terminals can be rated as Category 3 and are not suitable for the 100Mbps communications today's wiring systems must be able to carry.

chapter 9

Connectors

- Twisted-Pair Cable Connectors

- Coaxial Cable Connectors

- Fiber Optic Cable Connectors

Have you ever wired a cable directly into a piece of hardware? Some equipment in years past provided terminals or termination blocks so that cable could be wired directly into a direct component. In modern times, this is considered a bad thing; it is fundamentally against the precepts of a structured cabling system to attach directly to active electronic components either at the workstation or in the equipment closet. On the ends of the cable you install, there has to be something that provides access and transition for attachment to system electronics. Thus, we have connectors.

Cable connectors provide the transition point between the cable and the electrical equipment. Connectors generally have a male component and a female component except in the case of hermaphroditic connectors such as the IBM data connector. Usually jacks and plugs are symmetrically shaped, but sometimes they are *keyed*. This means that they have a unique, asymmetric shape or some system of pins, tabs, and slots that ensure that the plug can be inserted only one way in the jack. This chapter covers many of the connector types you will encounter when working with structured cabling systems.

Twisted-Pair Cable Connectors

Many people in the cabling business use twisted-pair connectors more than any other type of connector. They include the modular "RJ" types of jacks and plugs and the hermaphroditic connector employed by IBM that are used with shielded twisted-pair cabling.

Almost as important as the actual cable connectors is the connector type that is used with patch panels, punch-down blocks, and wall plates; this connector is called an IDC or insulation displacement connector.

Patch Panel Terminations

Most unshielded twisted-pair (UTP), screened twisted-pair (ScTP), and foil twisted pair (FTP) cable installations use patch panels and, consequently, 110-style termination blocks. The 110-block (shown in Figure 9.1) contains rows of specially designed slots in which the cables are terminated using a punch-down tool. Patch panels and 110-blocks are described in more detail in Chapter 5, "Cabling System Components," and Chapter 7, "Copper Cable Media."

S-110-block with wire management

(Photo courtesy of The Siemon Company)

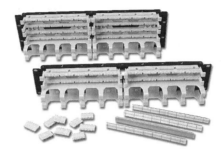

When terminating 66-blocks, 110-blocks, and often, wall plates, both UTP and ScTP connectors use IDC technology to establish contact with the copper conductors. IDC stands for *insulation displacement connector*. What this means is that you don't strip the wire insulation off the conductor as you would with a screw-down connection. Instead, you force the conductor either between facing blades or onto points that pierce the plastic insulation and make contact with the conductor.

Solid versus Stranded Conductor Cables

UTP and ScTP cables have either solid copper conductors or conductors that are made of several tiny strands of copper. Solid conductors are very stable geometrically and, therefore, electrically superior, but they will break if flexed very often. Stranded conductors are very flexible and resistant to bend-fatigue breaks, but their cross-sectional geometry changes as they are moved, and this can contribute to electrical anomalies. Stranded cables also have a higher attenuation (signal loss) than solid-conductor cables.

NOTE   Solid-conductor cables are usually used in backbone and horizontal cabling where, once installed, there won't be much movement. Stranded-conductor cables are used in patch cords, where their flexibility is desirable and their short typical lengths mitigate transmission problems.

The differences in conductors mean a difference in IDC types. You have to be careful when you purchase plugs, wall plates, and patch panels because they won't work interchangeably with solid- and stranded-core cables since the blade designs are different.

WARNING   Using the wrong type of cable/connector combination can be a major source of flaky and intermittent connection errors after your system is up and running.

With a solid-conductor IDC, you are usually forcing the conductor between two blades that form a V-shaped notch. The blades slice through the plastic and into the copper conductor, gripping it and holding it in place. This makes a very reliable electrical contact. If you force a stranded conductor into this same opening, contact may still be made. But, because one of the features of a stranded design is that the individual copper filaments can move (this provides the flexibility), they will sort of mush into an elongated shape in the V. Electrical contact may still be made, but the grip on the conductor is not secure and often becomes loose over time.

The blade design of IDC connectors that are designed for stranded-core conductors is such that forcing a solid-core conductor onto the IDC connector can break the conductor or miss contact entirely. Broken conductors can be especially problematic because the two halves of the break can be close enough together that contact is made when the temperature is warm, but the conductor may contract enough to cause an open condition when cold.

Some manufacturers of plugs advertise that their IDC connectors are universal and may be used with either solid or stranded conductors. Try them if you like, but if you have problems, switch to a plug specifically for the type of cable you are using.

Jacks and termination blocks are almost exclusively solid-conductor devices. You should never punch down on a 66, 110, or modular jack with stranded conductors.

Modular Jacks and Plugs

Twisted-pair cables are most commonly available as UTP, but recent developments in screened twisted pair cables (ScTP) are making ScTP more common. In an ScTP cable, the individual twisted pairs are not twisted, but all the pairs collectively have a thin shield around the shield of foil around them. Both UTP and ScTP cables use modular jacks and plugs. Modular jacks been commonplace in the home for telephone wiring for decades.

Modular connectors come in four-, six-, and eight-position configurations. This number of positions defines the width of the connector. However, many times only some of the positions have metal contacts installed. Make sure that the connectors you purchase are properly populated with contacts for your application.

Commercial grade jacks are made to snap into modular cutouts in faceplates. (More information is available on modular wall plates in Chapter 8, "Wall Plates.") This gives you the flexibility of using the faceplate for voice, data, coax, and fiber connections, or combinations thereof. Figure 9.2 shows a modular plug; Figure 9.3 shows the modular jack used for UTP. Figure 9.4 shows a modular jack for ScTP cables; note the metal shield around the jack. This shield is designed to help reduce EMI emissions and to help reduce interference from outside sources.

FIGURE 9.2:

Eight-position modular plug for UTP cable

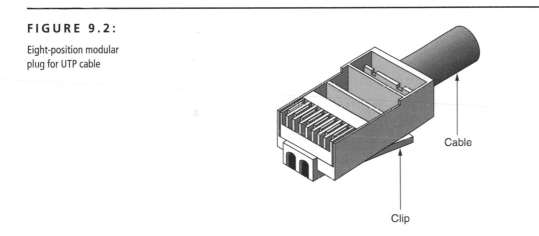

Cable

Clip

> **NOTE** The quality of plugs and jacks varies widely. Make sure that you are using plugs and jacks that are rated to the category of cabling you are purchasing.

FIGURE 9.3:

Eight-position modular jack for UTP cable

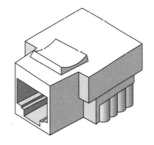

FIGURE 9.4:

Eight-position modular jack
for ScTP cable

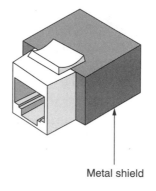

Metal shield

Though the correct name is *modular jack*, they are commonly referred to as RJ-type connectors (e.g., RJ-45). The RJ (registered jack) prefix is one of the most commonly (and incorrectly) used prefixes in the computer industry; nearly everyone, including cabling companies, is guilty of referring to an eight-position modular jack (sometimes called an 8P8C) as an RJ-45. Bell Telephone originated the RJ prefix and the Universal Service Ordering Code (USOC) to indicate to telephone technicians what type of service was to be installed and the wiring pattern of the jack. Since the breakup of AT&T and the divestiture of the Regional Bell Operating Companies, "Registration" has lost most of its meaning. However, the FCC has codified a number of RJ-type connectors and detailed the designations and pinout configurations in FCC Part 68, Subpart F, Section 68.502. Table 9.1 shows some of the common modular jack configurations.

TABLE 9.1:   Common Modular Jack Designations and Their Configuration

Designation	Positions	Contacts	Used For	Wiring Pattern
RJ-11	6	2	Single-line telephones	USOC
RJ-14	6	4	Single- or dual-line telephones	USOC
RJ-22	4	4	Phone cord handsets	USOC
RJ-25	6	6	Single-, dual-, or triple-line telephones	USOC
RJ-45	8	8	Data (10Base-T, 100Base-TX, etc.)	T568A or T568B
RJ-48	8	4	1.544Mbps (T1) connections	System dependent
RJ-61	8	8	Single through quad line telephones	USOC

The standard six- and eight-position modular jacks are not the only ones that you may find in use. Digital Equipment Corporation designed their own six-position modular jack called the MMJ (modified modular jack). The MMJ moved the clip portion of the jack to the right to reduce the likelihood that phone equipment would accidentally be connected to a data jack. The MMJ and DEC's wiring scheme for it are shown in Figure 9.5. While the MMJ is not as common as standard six-position modular connectors (a.k.a. RJ-11), the displaced clip connector on the MMJ, when combined with the use of plugs called the MMP (modified modular plug), certainly helps reduce accidental connections by phone or non-DEC equipment.

FIGURE 9.5:

The DEC MMJ jack and wiring scheme

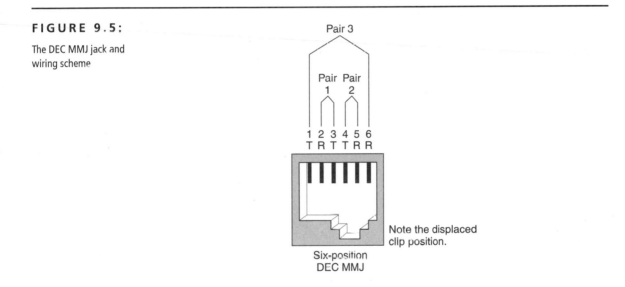

Another connector type that may occasionally be lumped in the eight-position modular jack architecture is actually called the eight-position *keyed* modular jack (see Figure 9.6). This jack has a key slot on the right side of the connector. The keyed slot serves the same purpose as the DEC MMJ when used with keyed plugs; it prevents the accidental connection of equipment that should be not be connected to a particular jack.

The eight-position keyed modular jack

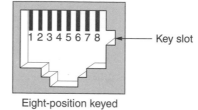

Any wiring pattern can be used.

1 2 3 4 5 6 7 8

Key slot

Eight-position keyed

Can a Six-Position Plug Be Used with an Eight-Position Modular Jack?

The answer is maybe. A couple of things need to be considered. The first is how many of the pairs of wires the application requires. If the application requires all eight pairs, or if it requires the use of pins 1 and 8 on the modular jack, then it will not work.

Further, repeated inserting and extracting of a six-position modular plug into an eight-position modular jack may eventually damage pins 1 and 8.

Wiring Schemes

The wiring scheme that you choose indicates in what order the color-coded wires will be connected to the jacks. These schemes are an important part of standardization of a cabling system. Almost all UTP cabling uses the same color-coded wiring schemes for cables; the color-coding scheme uses a solid color cable, and it has a partner that is white with a stripe the same color as its partner. The orange pair, for example, is often called "orange and white/orange." Table 9.2 shows the color-coding and wires pair numbers for each color code.

TABLE 9.2: Wire Color Codes and Pair Numbers

Pair Number	Color Code
Pair 1	White/blue and blue
Pair 2	White/orange and orange
Pair 3	White/green and green
Pair 4	White/brown and brown

NOTE When working with a standardized, structured cabling system, the only wiring patterns you will need to worry about are the T568A and T568B patterns specified in the TIA/EIA-568-A standard. The TIA/EIA-570 standard for home wiring recommends the T568A wiring pattern standard.

Determining the Pin Numbers

Which one is pin or position number 1? When you start terminating wall plates or modular jacks, you will need to know this.

Wall plate jacks usually have a printed circuit board that identifies exactly which IDC connector you should place each wire into. However, to identify the pins on a jack, hold the jack so that you are facing the side that the modular plug connects to. Make sure that the clip position is facing down. Pin 1 will be on the left-most side and pin 8 will be on the right-most side.

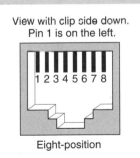

View with clip side down.
Pin 1 is on the left.

1 2 3 4 5 6 7 8

Eight-position

Continued on next page

For modular jacks, hold the jack so that the portion that connects to a wall plate or network equipment is facing away from you. The clip should be facing down and you should be looking down at the connector. Pin 1 is the left-most pin and thus pin 8 will be the right-most pin.

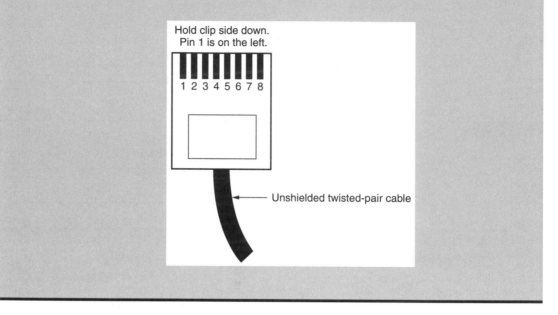

Hold clip side down.
Pin 1 is on the left.

1 2 3 4 5 6 7 8

— Unshielded twisted-pair cable

USOC Wiring Scheme   The Bell Telephone Universal Service Order Code (USOC) wiring scheme is simple and easy to terminate in up to an eight-position connector; this wiring scheme is shown in Figure 9.7. The first pair is always terminated on the center two positions. Pair 2 is split and terminated on each side of pair 1. Pair 3 is split and terminated on each side of pair 2. Pair 4 continues the pattern; it is split and terminated on either side of pair 3. This pattern is always the same regardless of the number of contacts you are populating. You start in the center and work your way to the outside, stopping when you reach the maximum number of contacts in the connector.

Tip and Ring Colors

When looking at wiring schemes for modular plugs and jacks, you may see the letters "T" and "R" used, as in Figure 9.7. The "T" is used to identify the *tip* or *primary* color. The "R" is used to identify the *ring* or *secondary* color. In a four-pair cable, the cable pairs are

Continued on next page

coded in a standard color-coding, which is on the insulation of the individual wires. In a four-pair cable, the tip is the wire that is predominantly white, and the ring identifies the wire that is a predominantly solid color.

The terms *ring* and *tip* are holdovers from when telephone systems were switched by hand using jacks that looked like a stereo RCA jack. The primary color (solid) was wired to the ring, and the secondary color was wired to the tip.

FIGURE 9.7:

Universal Service Order Code (USOC) wiring scheme

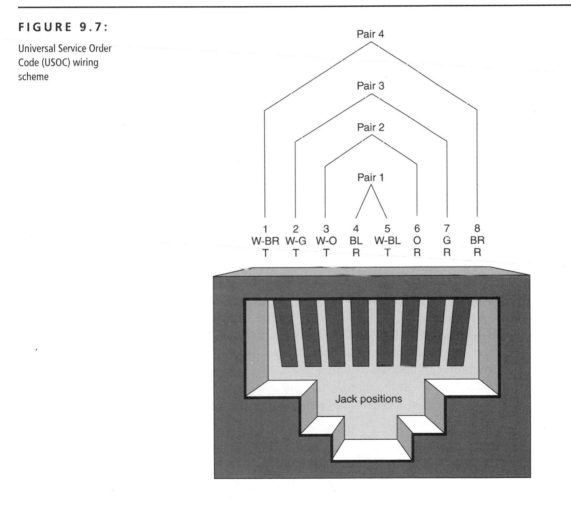

WARNING   Do not use the USOC wiring scheme for systems that will support data transmission.

If you look at the wire colors and the associated pin assignments, the pin assignments for USOC will look like this:

Pin	Wire Color
1	White/brown
2	White/green

Pin	Wire Color
3	White/orange
4	Blue
5	White/blue
6	Orange
7	Green
8	Brown

USOC is used for analog and digital voice systems but should *never* be used for data installations. Splitting the pairs can cause a number of transmission problems when used at frequencies greater than those employed by voice systems. These problems include excessive crosstalk, impedance mismatches, and unacceptable signal delay differential.

TIA/EIA-568-A Wiring Schemes T568A and T568B   ANSI/TIA/EIA-568-A is the United States standard that defines proper techniques for the installation of communications infrastructure. It does not sanction the use of the USOC scheme. Instead, two wiring schemes are specified, both of which are suitable for either voice or high-speed LAN operation. These are designated as T568A and T568B wiring schemes.

NOTE   In the United States, the T568B wiring pattern is the most commonly used wiring pattern; however, unless a waiver is granted, the U.S. government requires all government cabling installations to use the T568A wiring pattern. In much of the rest of the world, the T568A pattern is preferred.

Both T568A and T568B are universal in that all LAN systems and most voice systems can utilize either wiring sequence without system errors. After all, the electrical signal really doesn't care if it is running on pair 2 or pair 3, as long as there is a wire connected to the pin it needs to use. The TIA/EIA standard specifies eight-position, eight-contact jacks and plugs, and four-pair cables, fully terminated, to facilitate this universality.

The T568B wiring configuration is the most commonly used scheme, especially for commercial installations; it is shown in Figure 9.8. The TIA/EIA adopted the T568B wiring scheme from the AT&T 258A wiring scheme. The 568A scheme (shown in Figure 9.9) is well suited to upgrades and new installations in residences because the wire termination pattern for pairs 1 and 2 are the same as for USOC.

FIGURE 9.8:

T568B wiring pattern

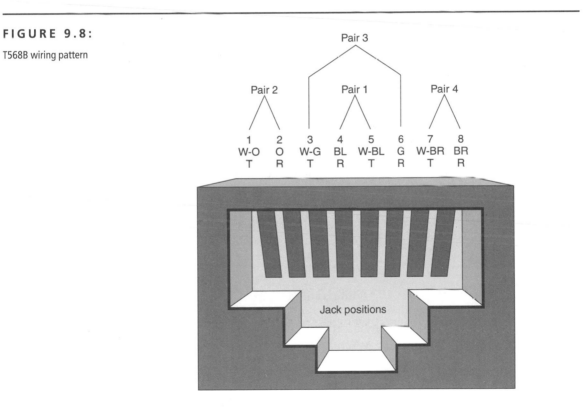

FIGURE 9.9:

T568A wiring pattern

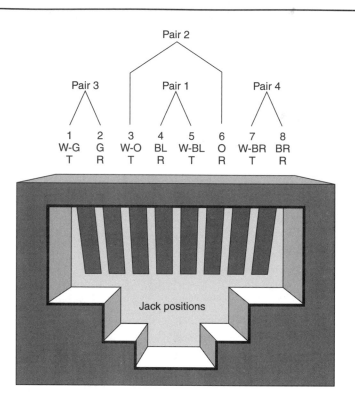

The wire colors and the associated pin assignments for the T568B wiring scheme will look like this:

Pin	Wire Color
1	White/orange
2	Orange
3	White/green
4	Blue
5	White/blue
6	Green
7	White/brown
8	Brown

Looking at the wire colors and associated pin assignments, the pin assignments for the T568B wiring schemes are identical except that wire pairs 2 and 3 are reversed. The pattern looks like this:

Pin	Wire Color
1	White/green
2	Green
3	White/orange
4	Blue
5	White/blue
6	Orange
7	White/brown
8	Brown

Note that when you buy eight-position modular jacks, you must specify whether you want a T568A or T568B scheme. The reason for this is that the jacks often have IDC connections on the back where you punch the pairs down in sequence from 1 to 4. The jacks have an internal PC board that takes care of all the pair splitting and proper alignment of the cable conductors with the pins in the jack.

TIP   Whichever scheme you use, T568A or T568B, you must also use that scheme for your patch panels and follow it in any cross-connect blocks you install. Consistency is the key to a successful installation.

Be aware that modular jacks pretty much look alike even though their performance may differ dramatically. Be sure you also specify the performance level (e.g., Category 3, Category 5, Category 5e, etc.) when you purchase your jacks.

When working with ScTP wiring, the drain wire makes contact with the cable shield along its entire length; this provides a ground path for EMI energy that is collected by the foil shield. When terminating ScTP, the drain wire within the cable is connected to a metal shield on the jack. This must be done at both ends of the cable. If left floating or if connected only on one end, instead of providing a barrier to EMI, the cable shield becomes a very effective antenna for both emitting and receiving stray signals.

In a cable installation that utilizes ScTP, the plugs, patch cords, and patch panels must be shielded as well.

Tips for Terminating UTP Connectors

- Do not untwist UTP more than ½-inch when connecting to jacks and plugs.

- Always use connectors, wall plates, and patch panels that are compatible with the grade of cable that is being used.

- Terminate all four pairs, even if the application requires only two of the pairs.

- Remember that the T568A wiring scheme is compatible with USOC wiring schemes that use pairs 1 and 2.

- When terminating ScTP cables, always terminate the drain wire on both ends of the connection.

Other Wiring Schemes   There are other wiring schemes that you may come across depending upon the demands of the networking or voice application that is to be used. UTP Token Ring requires that pairs 1 and 2 be wired to the inside four pins, as shown in Figure 9.10. The T568A, T568B and USOC wiring schemes can be used. You can also use a six-position modular jack rather than an eight-position modular jack, but we recommend against that since your cabling system would not follow the TIA/EIA-568-A standards.

The ANSI X3T9.5 TP-PMD standard uses the two outer pairs of the eight-position modular jack; this wiring scheme is used with FDDI over copper. This wiring scheme (shown in Figure 9.11) is compatible with both the T568A and T568B wiring patterns.

FIGURE 9.10:

Token Ring wiring scheme

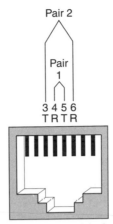

Eight-position modular jack
wired only for Token Ring
(pairs 1 and 2)

FIGURE 9.11:

ANSI X3T9.5-PMD wiring
scheme

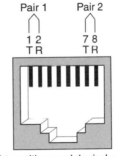

Eight-position modular jack wired
for TP-PMD (ANSI X379.5)

If you are wiring a six-position modular jack (RJ-11) for home use, there are a few things that are not covered by the TIA/EIA-568-A standard. First, the typical home telephone cable uses a separate color-coding scheme. The wiring pattern used is the USOC wiring pattern, but the colors are different. The wiring pattern and colors for a typical home cable and RJ-11 are as follows:

Pin Number	Pair Number	Wire Color
1	Pair 3	Orange
2	Pair 2	Yellow
3	Pair 1	Green
4	Pair 1	Red
5	Pair 2	Black
6	Pair 3	Blue

Pins 3 and 4 carry the telephone line. Pair 3 is rarely used in home wiring for RJ-11 jacks. Splitters are available to split pins 2 and 5 into a separate jack for use with a separate phone line.

Pins Used by Specific Applications

Common networking applications require the use of specific pins in the modular connectors. The most common of these is 10Base-T and 100Base-TX. Table 9.3 shows the pin assignments and what each pin is used for.

TABLE 9.3: 10Base-T and 100Base-TX Pin Assignments

Pin	Usage
1	Transmit +
2	Transmit –
3	Receive +
4	Not used
5	Not used
6	Receive –
7	Not used
8	Not used

Using a Single Horizontal Cable Run for Two 10Base-T Connections

Let's face it, there will be times when you just do not run enough cable to a certain room. You need an extra workstation in an area and you don't have enough connections. Knowing that you have a perfectly good four-pair UTP cable in the wall and only two of those pairs are in use makes your mood even worse. Modular Y-adapters can come to your rescue.

Several companies make Y-adapters that function as a splitter. They take the four pairs of wire that are wired to the jack and split them off into two separate connections. The Siemon Company makes a variety of modular Y-adapters (see Figure 9.12) for splitting 10Base-T, Token Ring, and voice applications. This splitter will split the four-pair cable up so that it will support two separate applications, provided that each application requires only two of the pairs. You must specify the type of splitter you need (voice, 10Base-T, Token Ring, etc.). Don't forget, for each horizontal cable run you will be splitting, you will need two of these adapters, one for the patch panel side and one for the wall plate.

FIGURE 9.12:

Modular Y-adapter for splitting a single four-pair cable into a cable that will support two separate applications

(Photo courtesy of The Siemon Company)

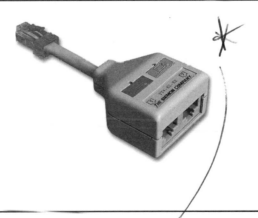

TIP

Many cabling professionals are reluctant to use Y-adapters due to the fact that the high-speed applications such as 10Base-T Ethernet and Token Ring may interfere with one another if they are operating inside of the same sheath. Do not use these for applications such as 100Base-TX.

Crossover Cables

One of the most asked frequently questions on wiring newsgroups and bulletin boards is "How do I make a crossover cable?" Computers that are equipped with 10Base-T or 100Base-TX network adapters can be connected "back-to-back;" this means that they do not require a hub to be networked together. This is really handy in a small office or home office. Crossover cables are also used to link together two hubs if the hubs do not have an uplink or crossover port built-in.

In order to make a crossover cable, you will need a crimping tool, a couple of eight-position modular plugs (a.k.a. RJ-45 plugs), and the desired length of cable. Cut and crimp one side of the cable as you would normally, following whichever wiring pattern you desire. When you crimp the other side, what you are essentially doing is connecting the transmit wire to the receive pin.

If you are using the T568A wiring standard, the wire color and pin assignments will follow the ones shown in Table 9.4.

TABLE 9.4:   Crossover Cable Using T568A Pin/Color Assignments

Side One Pins	Wire Colors	Side Two Pins
1 (Transmit +)	White/green	3 (Receive +)
2 (Transmit –)	Green	6 (Receive –)
3 (Receive +)	White/orange	1 (Transmit +)
6 (Receive –)	Orange	2 (Receive –)

Shielded Twisted-Pair Connectors

In the U.S., the most common connectors for cables that have individually shielded pairs in addition to an overall shield are based on a pre-1990 proprietary cabling system specified by IBM. Designed originally to support Token Ring applications using a two-pair cable (shielded twisted-pair, or STP), the connector is *hermaphroditic.* In other words, the plug looks just like the jack, but in mirror image. Each side of the connection has a connector and a receptacle to accommodate it. Two hermaphroditic connectors are shown in Figure 9.13. This connector is known by a number of other names, including the STP connector, the IBM data connector, and the universal data connector.

FIGURE 9.13:

Hermaphroditic data connectors

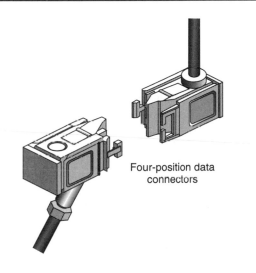

Four-position data connectors

The original Token Ring had a maximum throughput of 4Mbps (and later 16Mbps) and was designed to run over STP cabling. When using 16Mbps Token Ring, it used a 16MHz spectrum to achieve this throughput. Cables and connectors rated to 20MHz were required to allow the system to operate reliably, and the original STP hermaphroditic connectors were limited to a 20MHz bandwidth. There have been enhancements to these connectors that increase the bandwidth limit to 300MHz. These higher-rated connectors (and connectors) are designated as STP-A.

STP connectors are the Jeeps of the connector world. They are large, rugged, and versatile. Both the cable and connector are enormous compared to four-pair UTP and RJ-type modular plugs. They also have to be assembled and have more pieces than an Erector set. Cabling contractors used to love the STP connectors because of the premium they could charge based on the labor required to assemble and terminate them.

Darwinian theory prevailed, however, and now the STP and STP-A connectors are all but extinct—they've been crowded out by the smaller, less expensive, and easier-to-use modular jack and plug.

Coaxial Cable Connectors

Unless you have operated a 10Base-2 or 10Base-5 Ethernet network, you are probably familiar only with the coaxial connectors you have in your home for use with televisions and video equipment. There are actually a number of different types of coaxial connectors.

F-Series Coaxial Connectors

The type of coax connector you are most familiar with is probably the one you have in your home for use with video equipment. These are referred to as F-series connectors (shown in Figure 9.14). The F-connector consists of a ferrule that fits over the outer jacket of the cable and is crimped in place. The center conductor is allowed to project from the connector and forms the business end of the plug. A threaded collar on the plug screws down on the jack, forming a solid connection. F-connectors are used primarily in residential installations for RG-58, RG-59, and RG-6 coaxial cables to provide CATV, security camera, and other video service.

FIGURE 9.14:

The F-type coaxial cable connector

There are two types of F-connectors commonly available, one-piece and two-piece designs. In the two-piece design, the ferrule that fits over the cable jacket is a separate sleeve that you slide on before you insert the collar portion on the cable. Experience has shown us that that the single-piece design is superior. Fewer parts usually means less fumbling, and the final crimped connection is both more aesthetically pleasing and more durable. However, this is largely a function of the design and brand of the two-piece product. Some two-piece designs are very well received by the CATV industry.

A cheaper F-type connector available at some retail outlets attaches to the cable by screwing the outer ferrule onto the jacket instead of crimping it in place. These are very unreliable and pull off easily. Their use in residences is not recommended, and they should never be used in commercial installations.

N-Series Coaxial Connectors

The N-connector is very similar to the F-connector, with the addition of a pin that fits over the center conductor; the N-connector is shown in Figure 9.15. This pin forms a rigid member suitable for insertion in the jack and must be used if the center conductor is stranded instead of solid. The assembly is attached to the cable by crimping it in place. A screw-on collar ensures a reliable connection with the jack. The N-type connector is used with RG-8, RJ-11U, and thicknet cables for data and video backbone applications.

FIGURE 9.15:

The N-type coaxial connector

The BNC Connector

When coaxial cable is used to distribute data in commercial environments, the BNC connector is often used. BNC stands for Bayonet Niell-Concelman, which describes both the method of securing the connection and its inventors; you may occasionally hear this connector referred to as the British Naval Connector. Used with RG -6, RG-58A/U thinnet, RG-59, and RG-62 coax, the BNC utilizes a center pin, as in the N-connector, to accommodate the stranded center conductors usually found in data coax.

The BNC connector (shown in Figure 9.16) can come as a crimp-on or a design that screws onto the coax jacket. As with the F-connector, the screw-on type is not considered reliable and should not be used. The rigid pin that goes over the center conductor may require crimping or soldering in place. The rest of the connector assembly is applied much like an F-connector, using a crimping die made specifically for a BNC connector.

FIGURE 9.16:

The BNC coaxial connector

Connector

To secure a connection to the jack, the BNC has a rotating collar with slots cut into it. These slots fit over combination guide and locking pins on the jack. Lining up the slots with the pins, you push as you turn the collar in the direction of the slots. The slots are shaped so that the plug is drawn into the jack, and locking notches at the end of the slot ensure positive contact with the jack. This method allows quick connection and disconnection while providing a secure match of plug and jack.

Be aware that you must buy BNC connectors that match the impedance of the coaxial cable to which they are applied. Most commonly, they are available in 75-ohm and 50-ohm types, with 93-ohm as a less-used option.

TIP

With all coaxial connectors, be sure to consider the dimensions of the cable you will be using. Coaxial cables come in a variety of diameters that are a function of their transmission properties, "series" rating, and number of shields and jackets. Buy connectors that fit your cable.

Fiber Optic Cable Connectors

If you have been working with twisted-pair copper, you are in for a bit of a surprise when you start trying to figure out which fiber optic connectors you need to use. There's a regular rogue's gallery of them. This is likely the result of competing proprietary systems in the early days of fiber deployment.

This section of the chapter focus on the different types of fiber connectors and discusses how they are installed onto fiber optic cable.

Fiber Optic Connector Types

Fiber optic connectors use bayonet, screw-on, or snap 'n' lock methods to attach to the jacks; a newer connector called the MT-RJ uses a connector that is remarkably similar to the eight-position modular connectors (a.k.a. RJ-45) that copper folks have been using for years.

To transmit data, two fibers are required. One strand of fiber is used to send and the other to receive. Fiber optic connectors fall into one of two categories based on how the fiber is terminated:

- Simplex connectors terminate only a single fiber in the connector assembly.

- Duplex connectors terminate two fibers in the connector assembly.

The disadvantage of simplex connectors is that you have to keep careful track of polarity. In other words, you must always make sure that the plug on the "send" fiber is always connected to the "send" jack and that the "receive" plug is always connected to the "receive" jack. The real issue is, for example, when normal working folk need to move furniture around and disconnect from the jack in their work area and then get their connectors mixed up. Experience has shown us that they are not always color-coded or labeled properly. Getting these reversed means, at the least, that link of the network won't work.

Duplex plugs and jacks take care of this issue. Once terminated, color-coding and keying ensures that the plug will be inserted only one way in the jack and will always achieve correct polarity.

Table 9.5 lists some common fiber optic connectors. These connectors can be used for either single-mode or multimode fibers, but make sure you order the correct model connector depending on the type of cable you are using.

TABLE 9.5: Fiber Optic Connectors

Designation	Connection Method	Configuration	Figure
SC	Snap-in	Simplex	Figure 9.17
Duplex SC	Snap-in	Duplex	Figure 9.18
ST	Bayonet	Simplex	Figure 9.19
Duplex ST	Snap-in	Duplex	Figure 9.20
FDDI (MIC)	Snap-in	Duplex	Figure 9.21
FC	Screw-on	Simplex	Figure 9.22

FIGURE 9.17:

SC fiber optic connector

FIGURE 9.18:

Duplex SC fiber optic
connector

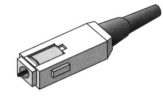

FIGURE 9.19:

ST connector

FIGURE 9.20:

Duplex ST fiber optic
connector

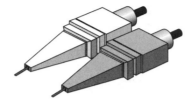

FIGURE 9.21:

FDDI fiber optic connector

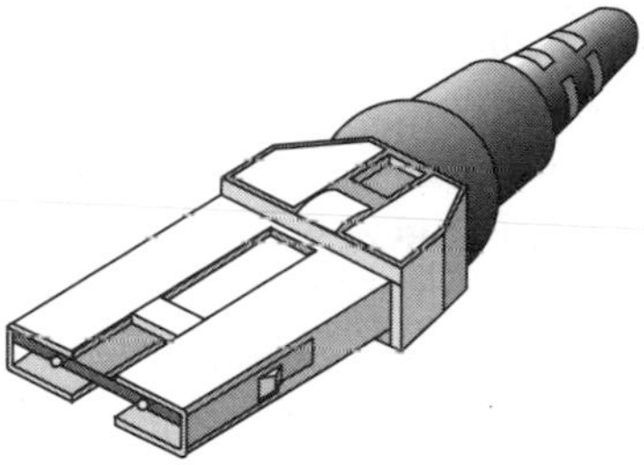

FIGURE 9.22:

FC fiber optic connector

Of the four layers of a tight-buffered fiber (the core, cladding, coating, and buffer), only the core where the light is actually transmitted differs in diameter. In their infinite wisdom and foresight, the lesser gods who originally created fiber cables made the cladding, coating, and buffer diameters identical, allowing universal use of stripping tools and connectors.

Of the connectors in Table 9.5, the ST is most widely deployed and is recognized by the ANSI/TIA/EIA-568-A standard, but the duplex SC is specified in the standard as the connector to be used. Migration options for making the transition from ST to SC are also specified in the standard. Other specifications, including those for ATM, FDDI, and broadband ISDN, now also specify the duplex SC.

This wide acceptance in system specifications and standards (acceptance in one begets acceptance in others), along with ease of use and positive assurance that polarity will be maintained, are all contributors to the duplex SC being the current connector of choice.

The SFF Issue

As this book is being written, so-called "connector wars" are being waged. The issue is the development of a small form factor (SFF) connector and jack system for fiber optic cables. Currently, the connectors shown in Table 9.5 all take up more physical space than their RJ-45 counterparts on the copper side. This makes multimedia receptacle faceplates a little crowded and means that you get fewer terminations in closets and equipment rooms than you can get with copper in the same space. The goal is to create an optical fiber connector with the same cross-sectional footprint as an RJ-45 style connector. For manufacturers, the Holy Grail of this quest is to have their design win out in the marketplace and become the de facto SFF connector of choice.

SFF connectors were withheld from being included in recent revisions to the TIA standard because the standards committees felt that none of the SFF connector designs were mature enough to include. This is because different manufacturers were proposing different designs, all of which were new to the market. None of the designs had achieved widespread acceptance, so there was no clear de facto standard. ANSI frowns on, if not outrightly prohibits, adoption of single-manufacturer proprietary designs as standards because such action awards competitive advantage.

However, as this is being written, the situation is changing, and SFF fiber optic connectors are being promoted and supported by equipment vendors. Three of these are the LC, the VF-45, and the MT-RJ. The MT-RJ currently may have a slight popularity edge, but there is no overwhelming (or underwhelming) decision from the market at this time. The LC connector (the connector on the lower part of Figure 9.23) is also widely used and is regarded by many optical fiber professionals as the superior connector. SFF has been taken up as a subject of consideration in TIA working group TR-48.8.1, and small form factor connectors may soon be included along with the duplex SC as the recommended or recommended alternative connector for use in fiber optic installations.

FIGURE 9.23:

Duplex SC (top), simplex ST (middle), and LC (bottom) connectors

(Photo courtesy of The Siemon Company)

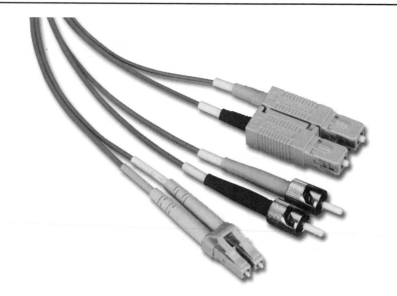

Installing Fiber Optic Connectors

With twisted-pair and coax cables, connectors are joined to the cable and conductors using some form of crimping or punch-down, applying mechanical force to force the components into place. With fiber optic cables, there are a variety of methods of joining the fiber with its connector. Each manufacturer of connectors, regardless of type, specifies the method to be used, the materials that are acceptable, and sometimes, specialized tools required to complete the connection.

With fiber connectors, when the fiber connector is inserted into the receptacle, the fiber optic core in the plug is placed in end-to-end contact with the fiber in the jack. Two issues are of vital importance:

- The fiber optic cores must be properly aligned. The end-to-end contact must be perfectly flush with no change in the longitudinal axis. In other words, they can't meet at an angle.

- The surfaces must be free of defects such as scratches, pits, protrusions, and cracks.

To address the first critical issue, fiber connector systems must incorporate a method that both aligns and fixes the fiber in its proper position. The alignment is usually accomplished by inserting the fiber in a built-in sleeve or ferrule. Some technique—either gluing or crimping—is then applied to hold it in place. There are three types of adhesives used to gluing the fiber into position:

Heat-cured After the material is injected and the fiber is inserted into the connector assembly, it is placed in a small oven to react with the adhesive and harden it. This is time consuming—heat-cured adhesives require as much as 20 minutes of hardening. Multiple connectors can be done at one time, but the time required to cure the adhesive still increases labor time and the oven is, of course, extra baggage to pack to the job site.

UV-cured Rather than hardening the material in an oven, an ultraviolet light source is used. You may have had something similar done at your dentist the last time you had a tooth filled. Only about a minute of exposure to the UV light is required to cure the adhesive, making this a more time-effective process.

Anaerobic-cured This method relies on the chemical reaction of two elements of an epoxy to set up and harden. A resin material is injected in the ferrule. Then a hardener catalyst is applied to the fiber. When the fiber is inserted in the ferrule, the hardener reacts with the resin to cure the material. No extra equipment is required beyond the basic materials and tools. Hardening can take place as quickly as 15 seconds.

Crimp-style connector systems for fiber optic cable are always manufacturer-specific regarding the tools and materials required. Follow the manufacturer's instructions carefully. With crimp connectors, the fiber is inserted into the connector and the assembly is then placed in a crimping tool that holds the fiber and connector in proper position. The tool is then used to apply a very specific amount of pressure in a very controlled range of motion to crimp the connector to the buffer layer of the fiber.

To address the second critical issue, part of the connecting process usually involves a polishing step. With the fiber firmly established in the connector, the end of the fiber is rough-trimmed. A series of abrasive materials is then used to finely polish the end of the fiber.

There are connector systems available that do not require the polishing step. These rely on a clean, straight "cleave" (a guillotine-type method of cutting the fiber in two) and positive mechanical force to hold the ends of the fibers together in such a way that a polished surface is not as critical. Such connectors are used primarily, if not exclusively, with multimode fibers because of the larger core diameter of multimode fiber optic cable.

Fiber Optic Media

- How Fiber Optic Transmissions Works

- Advantages and Disadvantages of Fiber Optic Cabling

- Types of Fiber Optic Cables

- Fiber Installation Issues

*F*iber optic media (or *fiber*, for short) are any network transmission media that use glass fiber to transmit network data in the form of light pulses. Data is encoded within these pulses of light using either a laser diode or light emitting diode (LED).

Within the last five years, fiber optic media has become an increasingly popular type of network transmission media. Let's begin this chapter with a brief look at how fiber optic transmissions work.

How Fiber Optic Transmissions Work

Fiber optic technology is more complex in its operation than standard copper media. The source of this complexity is the fact that fiber optic transmissions are light pulses instead of voltage transitions. Fiber optic transmissions encode the ones and zeros of a network transmission into ons and offs of some kind of light source. This light source is usually either a laser or some kind of light emitting diode (LED). The light from the light source is flashed on and off in the pattern of the data being encoded.

These light pulses travel from source to destination almost instantaneously within a glass (or sometimes plastic) conductor. This conductor (or *core*, as it is known) is surrounded by a coating known as the *cladding*. Cladding a glass fiber allows the light signal to bounce around inside the fiber (as shown in Figure 10.1) because the cladding has a lower refractive index than the core, and it acts like a mirror, reflecting the light signal back into the core. The cladding makes it possible for the signal to travel in angles other than a straight line from sender to recipient—it's kind of like shining a flashlight onto one mirror and reflecting the light onto another, then another, and so on. The light bounces around inside the fiber until the light signal gets to its intended destination.

Cable Connector
and Tool
Identification
Guide

This *Cable Connector and Tool Identification Guide* will allow you to view connectors and tools in living color. Many items in the data-communications industry are color-coded; for example, orange is used to designate fiber optic cable. Some of the products shown in the following pages are:

- ▲ Connectors
- ▲ Cables
- ▲ Mount box
- ▲ Wall plates
- ▲ Jacks
- ▲ Face plates
- ▲ Cable strippers
- ▲ Connectorizing kits

- ▲ Fiber optic test scope
- ▲ Cable tester
- ▲ Punch-down block
- ▲ Fiber patch panel
- ▲ Telephone installation
- ▲ Fiber optic breakout box
- ▲ Wiring closet
- ▲ Tractor-mounted unspooler

FIBER OPTIC PATCH CABLE
with MT-RJ connectors

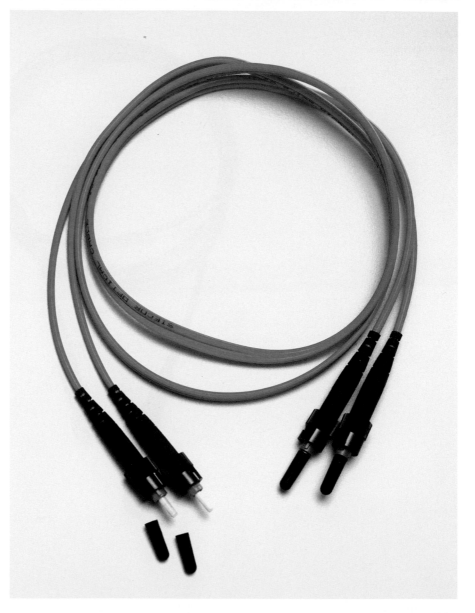

A SIX-FIBER MULTIMODE FIBER OPTIC CABLE

Notice Kevlar fibers (yellow) at top.

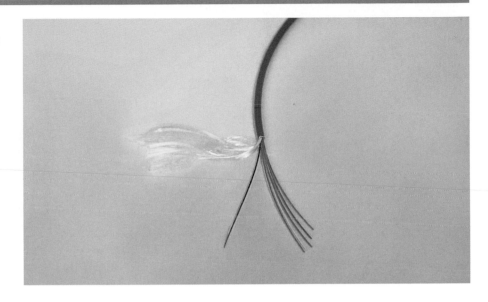

A 25-PAIR UTP CABLE

This cable is often used for telephone applications.

TYPE 1 TOKEN RING CABLE
Notice the shielding and unique connector.

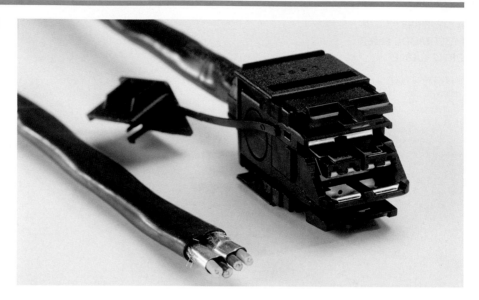

ARMORED FIBER OPTIC CABLE

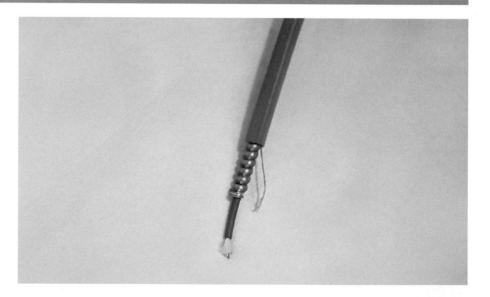

TWIN-AXIAL CABLE

SILVER SATIN CABLE
with an RJ-45 connector

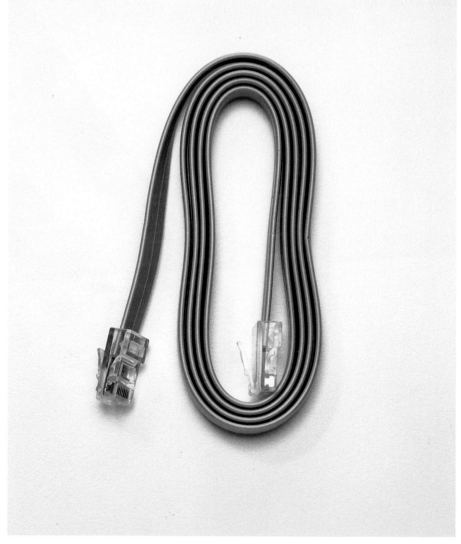

**TWIN-AXIAL CABLE
TO RJ-11 BALUN**

**COLOR CODE FOR
BOTH 568A AND
568B WIRING
SCHEMES**

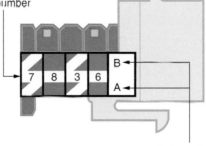

Pin number

7 8 3 6

B

A

Color code for
T568A and B wiring

**3M HOTMELT™
ST FIBER OPTIC
CONNECTOR**

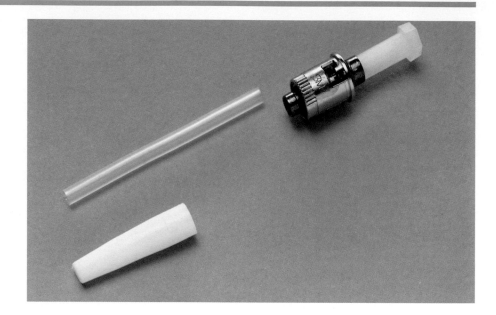

**RACEWAY AND
SURFACE MOUNT
BOX**

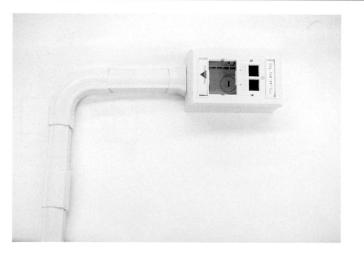

RJ-45 CRIMP-ON CONNECTOR

(Photo courtesy of The Siemon Company)

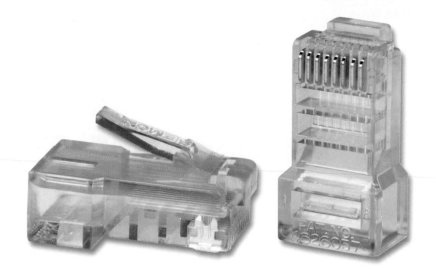

CABLE WITH BOTH 110 AND RJ-45 ENDS

(Photo courtesy of The Siemon Company)

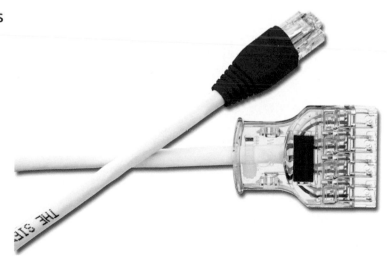

MODULAR WALL PLATE

with RJ-45, coaxial video, RCA, S-Video, and fiber optic connectors

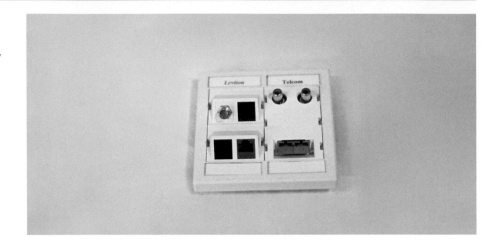

SURFACE-MOUNT, MODULAR MULTIMEDIA BOX

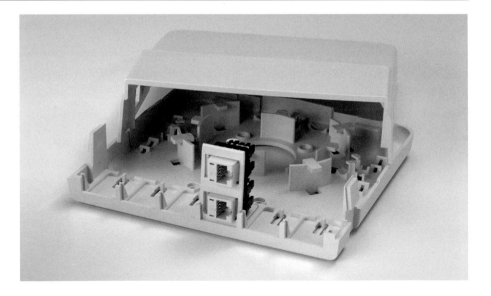

**EXAMPLE OF A
SURFACE-MOUNT
BISCUIT JACK**

**FIXED-DESIGN,
DUPLEX, RJ-45 WALL
PLATE THAT USES
110 PUNCH-DOWNS**

FIXED DESIGN WALL PLATES

From left: Token Ring, RJ-11, and dual cable TV (coax).

MODULAR FURNITURE WITH FOUR ANGLED JACKS

(one with a dust cover)

MODULAR
FURNITURE
FACEPLATES

both low profile (foreground)
and normal (background)

WALL PLATES

From left: Modular 3
position with three RJ-45
jacks, modular with six
RJ-45 jacks, and fixed
design with single
RJ-45 jack.

MORE EXAMPLES OF WALL PLATES

From left to right: A 6-port wall plate filled with various types of multimedia jacks; a 4-port metal wall plate; a 4-port wall plate filled with RJ-45 jacks; a 6-port wall plate filled with various types of RJ-45 jacks.

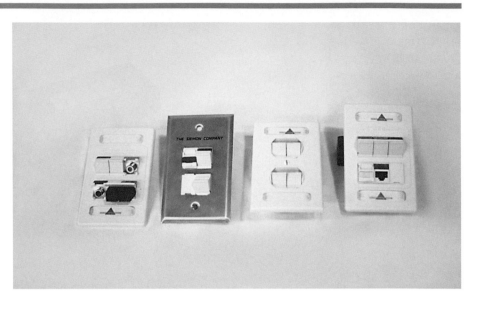

6A FIBER OPTIC WALL PLATE SURROUND ADD-ON

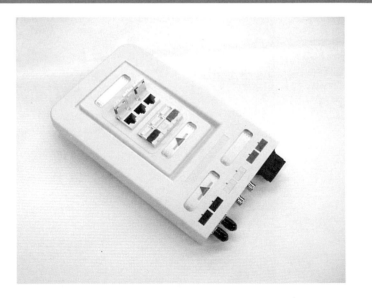

**HEAVILY SHIELDED
110-TO-RJ-45
PUNCH-DOWN
BLOCK**

**SIX-GANG,
MODULAR
FURNITURE WALL
PLATE WITH ANGLED
JACKS**

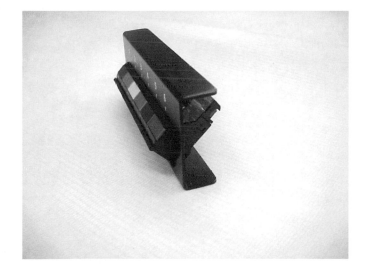

**DUAL SC
CONNECTOR FIBER
PATCH PANEL**

**TELEPHONE WALL
PLATE WITH
MODULAR JACK**

**66-BLOCK WITH A
50-PAIR CABLE
CONNECTOR**

SIDE VIEW OF A 110 PUNCH-DOWN BLOCK

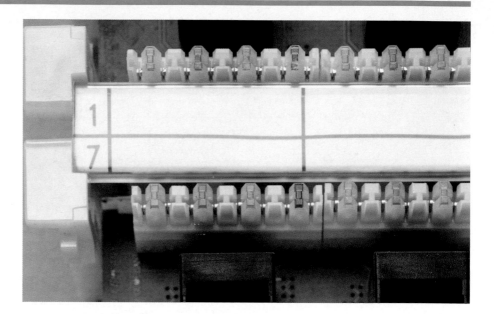

SIDE VIEW OF A 210 PUNCH-DOWN BLOCK

Note pairs are separated from each other.

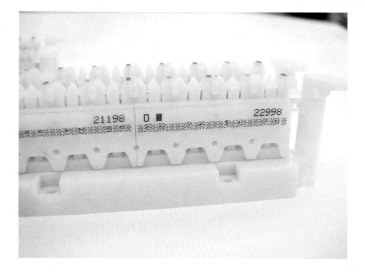

**CABLE
MANAGEMENT
D-RINGS**

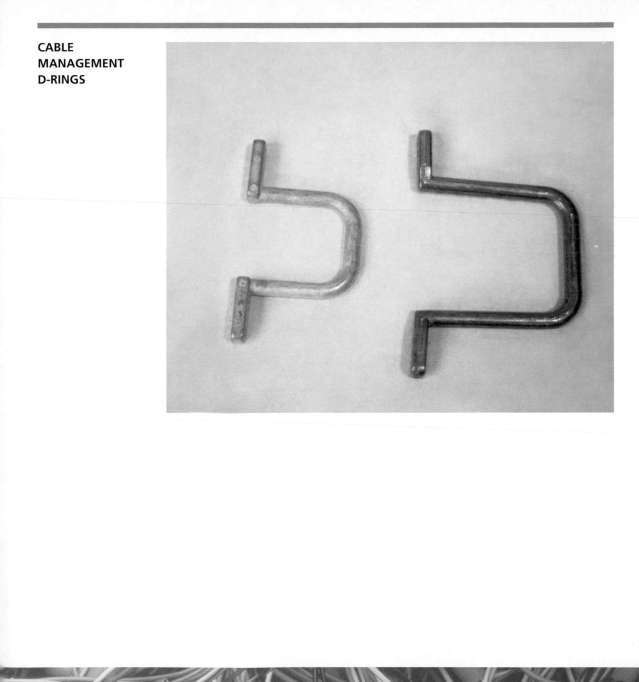

**ANOTHER EXAMPLE
OF A 110-TO-RJ-45
PUNCH-DOWN**

(Photo courtesy of The
Siemon Company)

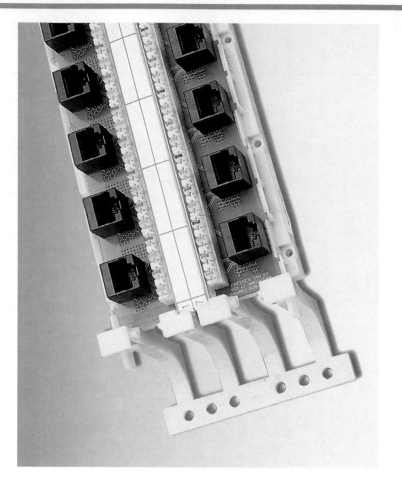

SAMPLE TELEPHONE INSTALLATION

Notice the 66- blocks, biscuit jacks, PBX, cable management rings, and 50-pair cable connections.

(Photo courtesy of Computer Training Academy)

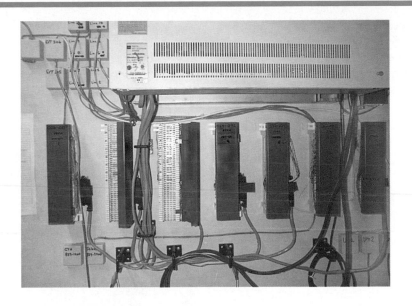

FIBER OPTIC BREAKOUT BOX

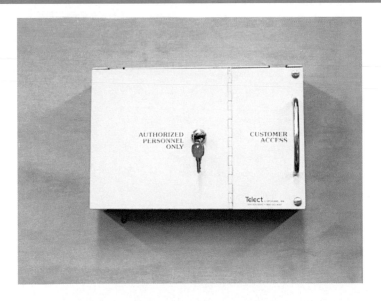

EXAMPLE OF A WIRING CLOSET WITH RACK-MOUNTED PATCH PANELS

(Photo courtesy of Computer Training Academy)

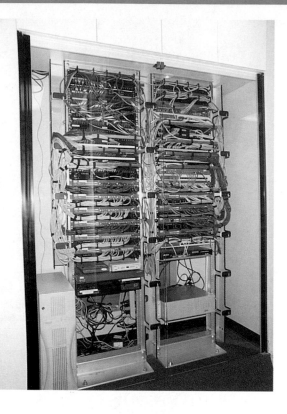

RACK WITH COLOR-CODED PATCH CORDS

(Photo courtesy of The Siemon Company)

50-PAIR UTP TELEPHONE CABLES TERMINATED TO THE BACK OF A 110-TO-RJ-45 RACK-MOUNT PATCH PANEL

(Photo courtesy of Computer Training Academy)

**THE BACK OF A
110-TO-RJ-45
RACK-MOUNTED
PATCH PANEL**

(Photo courtesy of
Computer Training
Academy)

**MODULAR JACK
PUNCH-DOWN AID
("PUCK")**

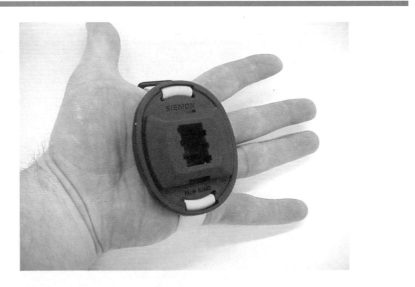

ANGLED PICK PROBE

SIMPLE CABLE
JACKET STRIPPER

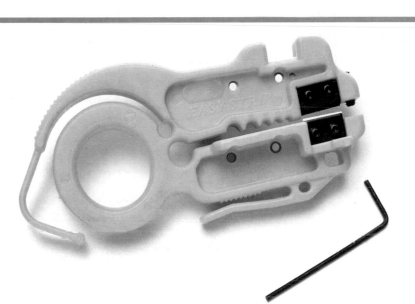

**CABLE STRIPPER
WITH BOTH UTP
AND COAX DIES**

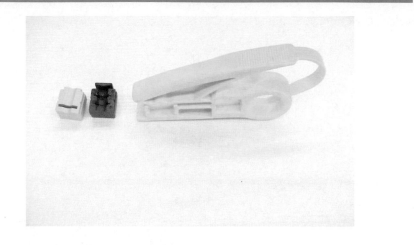

**FIBER OPTIC TEST
SCOPE**

**SIMPLE CABLE
TESTER**

**FIBER OPTIC
CONNECTORIZING
KIT**

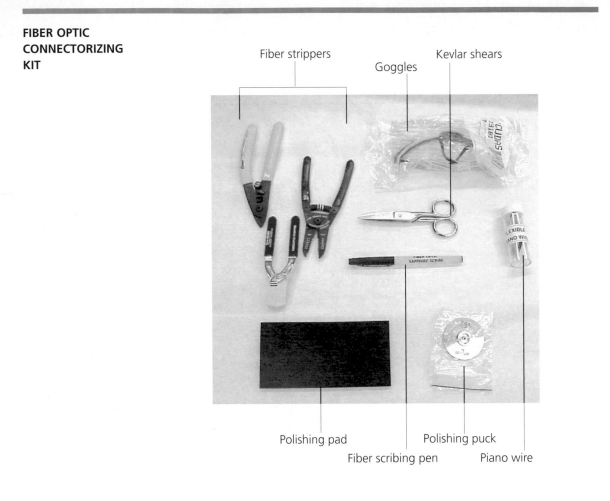

Fiber strippers

Goggles

Kevlar shears

Polishing pad

Fiber scribing pen

Polishing puck

Piano wire

3M HOTMELT CONNECTORIZING KIT

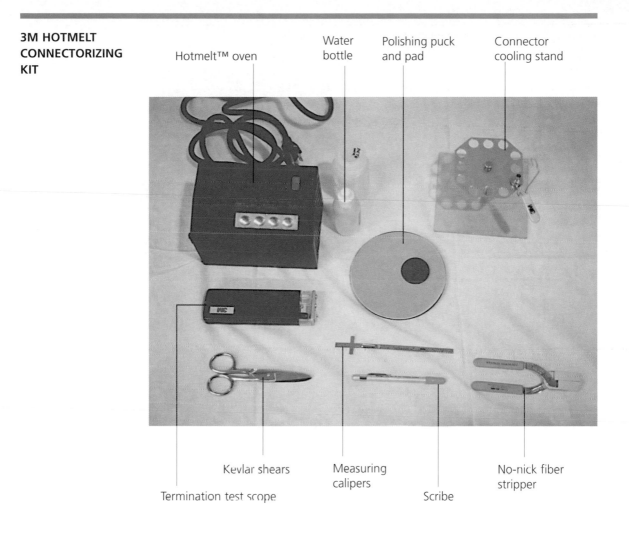

Hotmelt™ oven

Water bottle

Polishing puck and pad

Connector cooling stand

Kevlar shears

Measuring calipers

Scribe

No-nick fiber stripper

Termination test scope

TRACTOR-MOUNTED UNSPOOLER

for optical raceway used for outdoor installations

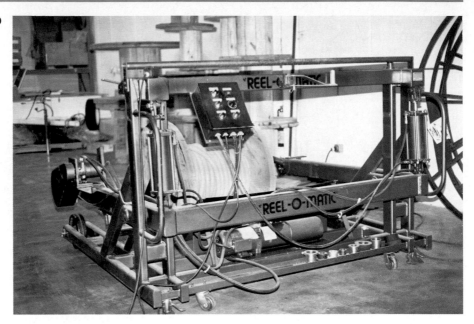

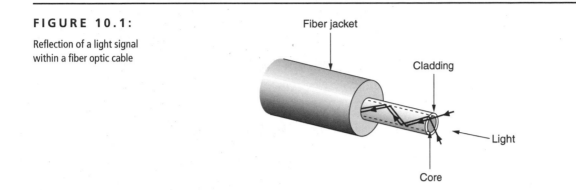

When the light pulses reach the destination, a sensor picks up the presence or absence of the light signal and transforms those ons and offs back into electrical signals that represent 1s and 0s.

It is important to note that the more the light signal bounces, the more possibility there is for signal loss (also known as *attenuation*). Additionally, for every fiber optic connector between signal source and destination, there is a possibility for signal loss. Thus, the connectors must be installed perfectly at each connection.

Most kinds of LAN/WAN fiber transmission systems use two fibers: one fiber for transmitting and one for reception. This system is used because light only travels in one direction for fiber systems—the direction of transmission. It would be difficult (and expensive) to transform a fiber optic transmitter into a dual-mode transmitter/receiver (one that could receive and transmit within the same connector).

Advantages of Fiber Optic Cabling

The main reason fiber optic cabling is currently enjoying popularity as a network cabling medium is because of its advantages over other types of cabling systems. Some of these advantages include the following:

- Immunity to electromagnetic interference (EMI)

- Higher data rates

- Longer maximum distances
- Better security

Let's begin our discussion of the advantages of fiber optic cabling with a discussion of fiber's immunity to electromagnetic interference (EMI).

Immunity to Electromagnetic Interference (EMI)

All copper cable network media share one common problem: they are susceptible to electromagnetic interference (EMI). EMI is a type of interference to proper data transmission that occurs due to stray electromagnetism. All electrical cables generate a magnetic field around their central axis. If you pass a metal conductor through a magnetic field, an electrical current is generated in that conductor. Similarly, if you pass an electrical field through a conductor, a magnetic field is formed around the axis of the conductor.

You may be asking yourself, "Okay, but what does that have to do with fiber optics?" Well, when you place two copper cables next to each other, this principle will cause signals from one cable to be induced into the other in a phenomenon known as *crosstalk* (often abbreviated as *xtalk* or *xt*). The longer a particular copper cable run goes, the more chance there is for crosstalk.

WARNING Never place copper cables next to AC current-carrying wires or power supplies. These devices produce very large magnetic fields and thus will introduce large amounts of crosstalk into any copper cable placed next to them. For data cables, this will almost certainly cause data transmissions on that particular cable to fail completely.

Fiber optic cabling is immune to crosstalk because fiber uses light signals in a glass fiber to transmit data rather than electrical signals. Because of this, it cannot produce a magnetic field, and thus it is immune to EMI. Fiber optic cables can be run in areas considered to be "hostile" to regular copper cabling (e.g., elevator shafts, near transformers, in tight bundles with other electrical cables) because of their immunity to EMI.

Higher Possible Data Rates

Because light is immune to interference and travels almost instantaneously to its destination, much higher data rates are possible with fiber optic cabling technologies than they are with traditional copper systems. Data rates in the gigabit per second (Gbps) range and higher are possible.

Longer Maximum Distances

Typical copper data transmission media are subject to distance limitations of maximum segment lengths no longer than one kilometer. Because they don't suffer from the EMI problems of traditional copper cabling and because they don't use electrical signals that can degrade substantially over long distances, fiber optic cables can span distances greater than three kilometers.

Better Security

As you know, *eavesdropping* is the practice of listening in on other people's conversations without the knowledge of the participants. Copper cable transmission media are susceptible to eavesdropping through the use of "taps." A *tap* (short for wiretap) is any device that punctures through the outer jacket of a copper cable and touches the inner conductor. The tap intercepts signals sent on a LAN and sends them to another (unwanted) location. Electromagnetic (EM) taps are similar devices, but rather than puncturing the cable, they use the tendency of the cable to produce magnetic fields similar to the pattern of electrical signals to provide the signal for the tap. If you'll remember, simply placing a conductor next to a copper conductor with an electrical signal in it will produce a duplicate (albeit a lower-power version) of the same signal. The EM tap then simply amplifies that signal and sends it on to the unwanted person who initiated the tap.

Because fiber optic cabling uses light instead of electrical signals, it is immune to most types of eavesdropping. Traditional taps won't work because any intrusion on the cable will cause the light to be blocked and the connection simply won't function. EM taps won't work because there is no magnetic field generated. Because of its immunity to traditional eavesdropping tactics, fiber optic cabling is used in networks that must remain secure, such as government and research networks.

Disadvantages of Fiber Optic Cabling

With all of its advantages, many people are using fiber optic cabling on their networks. However, fiber optic cabling does have a couple of major disadvantages, including the following:

- Higher cost
- Difficult to install

Let's examine these drawbacks to fiber optic cabling, starting with its higher cost.

Higher Cost

The first disadvantage of fiber optic as a transmission medium is its higher cost per foot (thus a higher total cost). The prices for cables are typically given in cents per foot. Traditional unshielded twisted pair (UTP) copper cabling for a data network costs in the range of $0.03 to $0.05 per linear foot. At the time of the writing of this book, costs for fiber optic cable are between $0.20 and $1.50 per foot, depending on the number of fibers. Even though these prices are coming down, fiber is still used primarily only for backbone links. However, as more people begin to use fiber optic for cabling their networks, the price will go down, and fiber to the desktop will become affordable for more and more organizations.

Difficult to Install

The other main disadvantage to fiber optic cabling is that it's more difficult to install. Copper cable ends simply need a mechanical connection to make an electrical connection, and those connections don't have to be perfect. Most often, the connectors for copper cables are crimped on (as discussed in Chapter 8, "Wall Plates").

Fiber optic cables are much trickier to make connections for. This is mainly because of the nature of the glass or plastic core of the fiber cable. When you cut or "cleave" (in fiber optic terms) the inner core, the end of the core consists of many very small shards of glass that diffuse the light signal. This will prevent the entire light signal from hitting the receiver correctly. The end of the core must be polished with a special polishing tool in order to make the end of the core perfectly flat so that the light will shine through correctly. Figure 10.2 illustrates the difference between a polished and a nonpolished fiber optic cable core end. This polishing step adds extra complexity to the installation of cable ends. The extra complexity translates to a longer, and thus more expensive, cabling plant installation.

FIGURE 10.2:

The difference between a freshly cut and a polished end

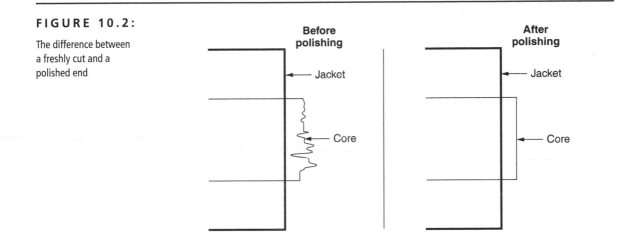

Types of Fiber Optic Cables

Now that you've learned about the basics of fiber optic cabling systems, including how they work and their advantages and disadvantages, it's time to learn the details of the individual cables. Some of the topics you'll learn about in this section include the following:

- Composition of a fiber optic cable
- Designations of fiber optic cables

Let's start with a discussion of the composition of a fiber optic cable.

Composition of a Fiber Optic Cable

A typical fiber optic cable (if there is such a thing) consists of several components, including the following:

- Optical fiber

- Buffer
- Strength members
- Outer jacket

Each of these components has a specific function within the cable to help ensure the data gets transmitted reliably. Figure 10.3 shows a cutaway diagram of a typical fiber optic cable. Note the individual components and their relationship to each other.

FIGURE 10.3:

Cutaway diagram of a typical fiber optic cable

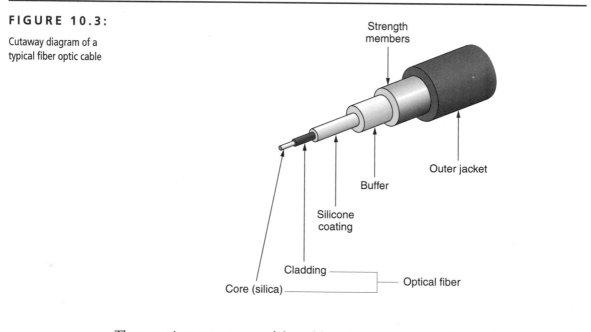

Strength members

Outer jacket

Buffer

Silicone coating

Cladding

Core (silica)

Optical fiber

The most important part of the cable is the core, so let's discuss that first.

Optical Fiber

An *optical fiber* (also called an *optical waveguide*) is the central part of a fiber optic cable. It consists of three main parts: the core, its cladding, and often, a protective coating. These three parts are usually manufactured together because of their close relationship.

A fiber optic cable's *core*, which is usually anywhere from two to several hundred microns thick (a *micron* is a millionth of a meter, usually designated by the symbol µ), is the central part of the fiber optic cable that actually carries the light signal. To put that size in perspective, a human hair is around 75 microns.

The fiber core is usually made of some type of plastic or glass. As a matter of fact, there are several types of materials that make up the core of a typical optical fiber. Each material differs in its chemical makeup and cost as well as its index of refraction. The *index of refraction* is a number for a particular material that indicates how much light will bend when passing through that material. It also indicates how fast light will travel through a particular material. The cladding for the core has a lower index of refraction than the core itself. Therefore, light from the core that hits the "wall" between the core and cladding will be reflected back into the core.

A fiber optic cable's *cladding* is the coating around the central core that performs two functions. First, it is the first, albeit the smallest, layer of protection around the glass or plastic core. Second, as mentioned earlier, it provides a surrounding surface for the light inside the core to reflect off of. This is because the cladding has a lower index of refraction than the core. Cladding is usually fairly thin (around 25 microns), except in the case of single-mode glass core fibers.

The *protective coating* around the optical fiber at the center of a fiber optic cable protects the fiber core and cladding from damage. It does not participate in the transmission of light at all. It is simply a protective measure. It protects the cladding from abrasion damage and adds additional strength to the core.

Some of the types of optical cable, listed from highest quality to lowest, include the following:

- Single-mode glass
- Graded-index glass
- Step-index glass
- Plastic-clad silica (PCS)
- Plastic

In this section, you'll learn about each of these types and how they differ from each other.

Single-Mode Glass   A *single-mode glass fiber core* is a core, made of silica glass, where the core is very narrow (usually less than 10 microns). Conversely, to keep the cable size manageable, the cladding for a single-mode glass core is usually

10 times the size of the core (around 125 microns). It is called single mode because only one light path is possible. This single path reduces the light loss (attenuation) in the signal. Single-mode fibers are expensive, but because of the lack of attenuation (less than 2dB per kilometer),very high speeds are possible. In some cases, speeds of up to 50Gbps are possible. Figure 10.4 shows an example of a single-mode glass fiber core.

FIGURE 10.4:

An example of a single-mode glass fiber core

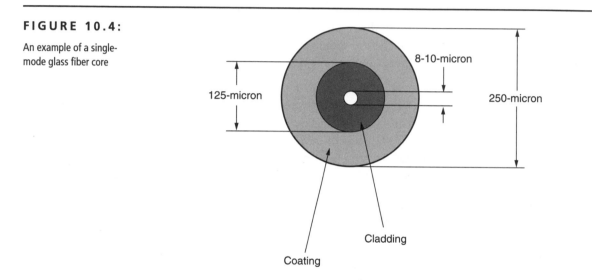

Graded-Index Glass   A graded-index glass fiber core is a core fiber made of silica glass, where the index of refraction changes gradually from the center outward to the cladding. The center of the cable has the highest index of refraction; thus the signals travel slowest in the center of the cable. If the signals travel outside the center of the core, the lower index of refraction will bend them back towards the center, but they will travel faster. This allows light signals to travel in the exact center of a larger diameter cable. The larger the diameter of the core, the greater the cost, but the equipment (i.e., connection) costs will be lower.

Figure 10.5 shows an example of graded-index glass core. Notice that the core is bigger than the single-mode core and that there is a smooth transition from the center of the core out.

FIGURE 10.5:

A graded-index glass
fiber core

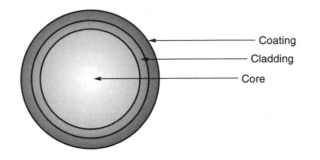

FIGURE 10.5:

A graded-index glass
fiber core

Step-Index Glass   A *step-index glass core* is a glass fiber core similar to a single-mode glass but with a much larger core diameter (usually around 62.5 microns, although it can vary largely in size between 50 and 125 microns). It gets its name from the large step in the change of index of refraction from the glass core to the cladding. In fact, a step-index glass core has a uniform index of refraction. Because the signal bounces around inside the core, it is less controllable and thus suffers from larger attenuation values and, effectively, lower bandwidths. However, equipment for cables with this type of core is cheaper than other types of cable, so step-index glass cores are found in many cables.

Figure 10.6 shows an example of a step-index glass core optical fiber. Notice the larger diameter glass core.

FIGURE 10.6:

A step-index glass core
optical fiber

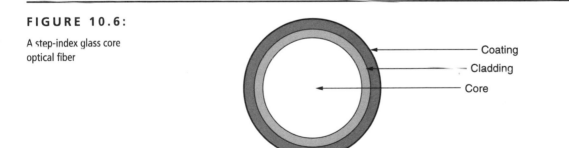

Plastic-Clad Silica (PCS)   A *plastic-clad silica (PCS) fiber core* is a fiber core made out of glass clad with a plastic coating around the central glass core, hence the name. PCS optical fibers are usually very large (200 microns or larger) and thus have limited bandwidth availability. However, the PCS core optical cables are relatively cheap when compared to their glass-clad counterparts.

Plastic   Plastic optical fibers consist of a plastic core of anywhere from 50 microns up to any size surrounded by a plastic cladding of a different index of refraction. Generally speaking, these are the lowest quality optical fibers and are seldom of sufficient quality to transmit light over long distances. Plastic optical cables are used for very short distance data transmissions, but they are more often used for decoration.

Buffer

In addition to the optical fiber, the *buffer* is the component of a fiber optic cable that provides the most protection of the optical fibers inside the cable. The buffer does just what its name implies: it acts as a buffer, or cushion, between the optical fiber and the outer jacket of the fiber optic cable.

Optical fiber buffers are categorized as either tight or loose. *Tight buffers* are optical fiber protection where there is a protective coating (usually a 900-micron thermoplastic covering) over each optical fiber in the cable. Tight buffers on the fibers within a fiber optic cable make the entire cable more durable, easier to handle, and easier to terminate (put connectors on). Figure 10.7 shows an example of tight buffering.

FIGURE 10.7:

A fiber optic cable using tight buffering

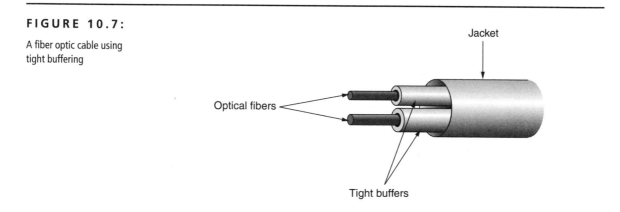

A *loose buffer*, on the other hand, is a type of buffer where all optical fibers in the cable are encased in one plastic tube (often called a *loose tube*). The tube is then filled with a protective substance to provide cushioning, strength, and protection from the elements. The protective substance is usually a water-blocking gel.

Figure 10.8 shows an example of a loose-buffered fiber optic cable. Notice that the cable shown uses water-blocking gel.

FIGURE 10.8:

A fiber optic cable using loose buffering with water-blocking gel

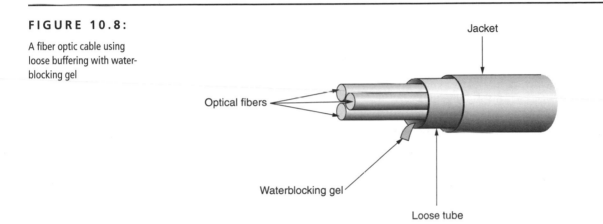

Strength Members

Some cables require additional support to prevent breakage of the delicate optical fibers within the cable. That's where the strength member part of some fiber optic cables comes in. The *strength member* of a fiber optic cable is the part of the fiber optic cable that provides additional tensile strength through the use of an additional strand or fibers of material.

The most common strength member is *aramid yarn*, a popular type of which is the product known as Kevlar™, the same material found in bulletproof vests. Larger fiber optic cables sometimes use a strand of either fiberglass or steel wire as strength members. Fiber optic cables can use strength members around the perimeter of a bundle of optical fibers within a single cable, or the strength member can be located in the center of the cable with the individual optical fibers clustered around it.

> **TIP**
>
> Kevlar is extremely durable, so cables that use this type of buffering require a special cutting tool to cut them, called Kevlar scissors. They cannot be cut with ordinary cutting tools.

Cable Jacket

The *cable jacket* of a fiber optic cable is the outer coating of the cable that protects all the inner optical fibers from damage. It is usually made of a durable rubberized or plastic material and comes in various colors.

There are two main categories of fiber optic cable jackets: PVC and plenum-rated. *Polyvinyl chloride (PVC)* is a plastic that is cheap to manufacture and is a durable coating for cables; thus, it is a very popular coating for many types of LAN cables, including fiber optic cables. Unfortunately, the main drawback to PVC-coated cables is that when they burn, the PVC coating turns to two toxic chemicals, hydrochloric acid and the toxic gas dioxin. Both substances are particularly nasty.

For this reason, the National Electrical Code (NEC) specifies that when installing cables in common air spaces (known as plenums), that the cable should have a *plenum-rated* jacket. Plenum-rated cable jackets will not turn into toxic gas when burned, so they are safe to use in plenum airways.

Exterior Protection of Fiber Optic Cables

If you ever need to install fiber optic cabling outdoors, you will need to keep some things in mind. First of all, the cable you install should be rated for an exterior installation. An exterior rating means that the cable was specifically designed for outdoor use. It will have features such as UV protection, superior crush and abrasion protection, protection against the extremes of temperature, and an extremely durable strength member. If you use standard indoor cable in an outdoor installation, the cables could get damaged and not function properly. Make sure to look for a cable rated for an outdoor installation when performing outdoor installations.

Designations of Fiber Optic Cables

In addition to the composition of the optical fibers, fiber optic cables have different designations of types and ratings of cables. When buying fiber optic cables, you will have to decide which fiber ratings you want for each type of cable you need. Some of these ratings include the following:

- Single-mode or multimode

- Useable wavelengths

- Core/cladding sizes

- Number of optical fibers

- LAN/WAN application

Let's begin this discussion of fiber optic cable ratings with the difference between single-mode and multimode optical fibers.

Single-Mode or Multimode

All fiber optic cables are designated as either single-mode or multimode. They differ mainly by the number of *modes*, or signals they can carry. *Single-mode* optical fibers (sometimes called *monomode* fibers), as the name suggests, can carry only one optical signal at a time. Generally speaking, these cables use the single-mode optical fibers and are very small, which keeps attenuation of the light signal to a minimum. Additionally, because of their simplicity, single-mode cables can transmit data over great distances and at very high rates. Many LAN backbones use single-mode fiber optic cables because of their high bandwidth and distance capabilities.

As you may have guessed, *multimode* fiber optic cables can transmit more than one signal at a time. This is because their optical fiber cores are larger in diameter. Many signals can travel over a multimode fiber cable, but there is a finite amount of bandwidth available. Each additional signal that is placed on a multimode fiber decreases the bandwidth available to each fiber. This is mainly because the signal is less concentrated within the optical fiber core.

Also, multimode cables suffer from a unique problem known as modal dispersion. *Modal dispersion* is a situation that causes transmission delays in multimode fibers. Here's how this situation occurs. The angle through which an optical fiber can accept incoming signals is known as the *acceptance angle* and is measured relative to the axis of the optical fiber (or the *acceptance cone* when measured around the axis). The different modes (signals) enter the multimode fiber at different angles. The different angles mean that the different signals will bounce differently inside the fiber and arrive at different times (as shown in Figure 10.9). The more severe the difference between the entrance angles, the greater the arrival delay between the modes. In Figure 10.9, mode A will exit the fiber first because it has fewer "bounces" inside the core than mode B. Mode A has fewer bounces because its entrance angle is less severe (i.e., it's of a *lower order*) than that of mode B. The difference between the time mode A and mode B exit is the modal dispersion. Modal dispersion gets larger as the difference between the entrance angles increases.

FIGURE 10.9:

Illustration of modal dispersion

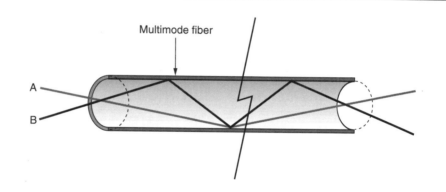

Multimode fiber

A

B

Useable Wavelengths

Another of the many types of fiber optic designations is the wavelength of light used to transmit data. The *wavelength* of a particular light source is the length between wave peaks in a typical light wave from that light source (as shown in Figure 10.10). This length is measured in *nanometers* (billionths of a meter). You can think of the wavelength of light as its color. Different wavelengths produce different colors. For example, when a laser produces a green light, it is producing light in the 500 nanometer (nm) range.

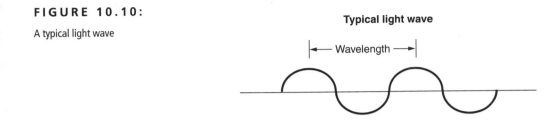

Fiber optic cables are optimized for use with a specific wavelength of light. Typically, optical fibers use wavelengths between 800 and 1500nm, depending on the light source. For a reference, visible light (the light that you can see) has wavelengths in the range between 400 and 700nm. Most fiber optic light sources operate in the infrared range (between 700 and 1100nm). Infrared light is light that you can't see and is a very effective fiber optic light source.

> **NOTE** Most traditional light sources can only operate within the visible wavelength spectrum. Additionally, they can only operate over a range of wavelengths, not one specific wavelength. The only light source that can transmit light at a specific wavelength is a *laser* (light amplification by stimulated emission of radiation) device. Many fiber optic devices use lasers to provide light at a particular wavelength.

Core/Cladding Size

In addition to other methods of designating fiber optic cables, the individual fiber optic cables within a cable are most often rated with a ratio of core to cladding size. The *core/cladding size* (also known as the optical fiber size) is the size of both the core and the cladding of a single optical fiber within the cable. This size is shown as two numbers, expressed as a ratio. The first number is the diameter of the optical fiber core, given in microns (µ). The second number is the outer diameter of the cladding for that optical fiber, also given in microns. For example, a picture with a 10-micron core with a 50-micron cladding would be designated as 10/50.

There are three major core/cladding sizes in use today:

- 8/125

- 62.5/125

- 100/140

Let's take a brief look at each of these sizes and what each one looks like as well as its major use(s).

NOTE   Sometimes, you will see a third number in this ratio (e.g., 8/125/250). The third number is the outside diameter of the protective coating around the individual optical fibers.

8/125   An 8/125 optical fiber is one where the core fiber has a diameter of 8 microns and the surrounding cladding is 125 microns in diameter (as shown in Figure 10.11). These fibers are almost always designated as single-mode fibers because the core size is only approximately 10 times larger than the wavelength of the light it's carrying, and thus there isn't much room in the fiber for the light to bounce around. Essentially, the light is traveling in a straight line through the fiber.

FIGURE 10.11:

An 8/125 optical fiber

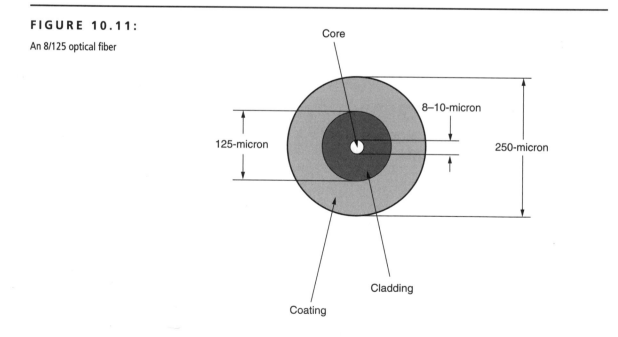

As discussed earlier, 8/125 optical fibers are used for high-speed applications like backbone fiber topologies such as FDDI, ATM, and Gigabit Ethernet.

62.5/125   Of all the fiber cable designations, the most common is 62.5/125. This is because optical fibers with this designation are large enough to be multimode fibers (i.e., support more than one signal within the fiber core). A standard multimode fiber optic cable (the most common kind of fiber optic cable), uses an optical fiber with a 62.5-micron core with 125-micron cladding (as shown in Figure 10.12).

FIGURE 10.12:

A sample 62.5/125 optical fiber

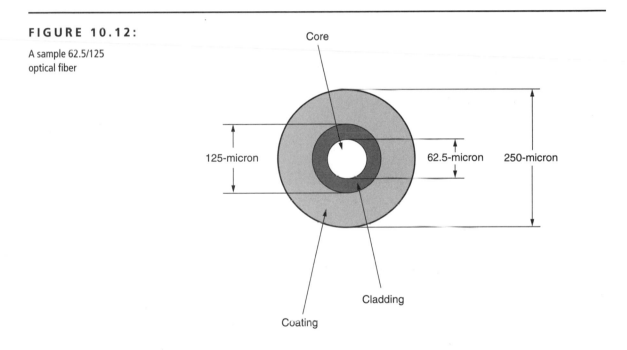

62.5/125 optical fibers are used mainly in LAN/WAN applications as a kind of "general use" fiber (if there really is such a thing).

100/140   An optical fiber with the 100/140 designation is not found in the mainstream. As you would expect, a 100/140 designation for an optical fiber means that that fiber has a 100-micron diameter core with a 140-micron diameter cladding (as shown in Figure 10.13).

This is a rather odd combination, as you can see. However, because of its rather odd sizing and, therefore, very specialized application, you might be able to guess the vendor who primarily uses this combination. Not sure? It's the designer of such proprietary technologies as Token Ring and Micro channel: International Business Machines, or IBM. IBM uses a 100/140 optical fiber in the cables for their fiber optic implementation of Token Ring.

FIGURE 10.13:

A 100/140 optical fiber

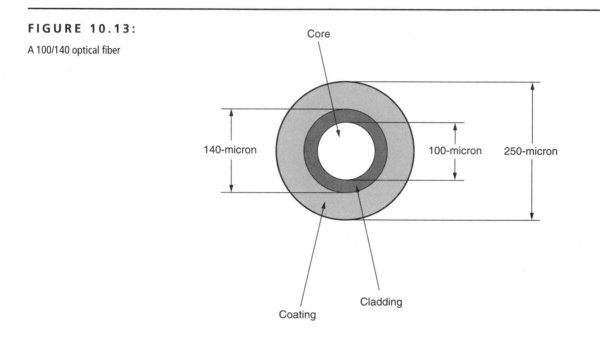

Number of Optical Fibers

Yet another difference between fiber optic cables is the number of individual optical fibers within them. The number of fibers in each cable differs depending on the intended use of the cable and can increase the cable's size, cost, and capacity.

Fiber optic cables can be divided into three categories based on the number of optical fibers:

- Simplex cables
- Duplex cables
- Multifiber cables

A *simplex fiber optic cable* is a type of fiber optic cable that has only one optical fiber inside the cable jacket. An example of a simplex cable was shown earlier in this chapter in Figure 10.3. Since simplex cables only have one fiber inside them, there is usually a larger buffer and a thicker jacket to make the cable easier to handle.

Duplex cables, in contrast, have two optical fibers inside of a single jacket (as shown in Figure 10.14). The most popular use for duplex fiber optic cables is as a fiber optic LAN backbone cable. Duplex cables are perfect for this because all LAN connections need a transmission fiber and a reception fiber. Duplex cables have both inside a single cable, and running a single cable is of course easier than running two.

FIGURE 10.14:

A sample duplex fiber optic cable

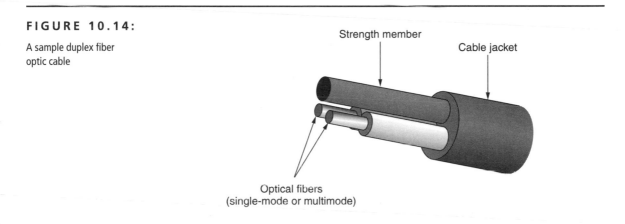

Strength member

Cable jacket

Optical fibers
(single-mode or multimode)

TIP

There is one type of fiber optic cable that is called a duplex cable but technically is not one. This cable is known as *zipcord*. Zipcord is really two simplex cables bonded together into a single flat optical fiber cable. It's called a duplex because there are two optical fibers, but it's not really duplex, because the fibers aren't covered by a common jacket. Zipcord is used primarily as a duplex patch cable. It is used instead of true duplex cable because it is cheap to make and to use. Figure 10.15 shows an example of a zipcord fiber optic cable.

FIGURE 10.15:

A sample zipcord cable

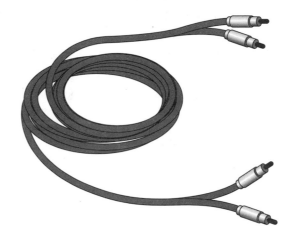

Finally, there are fiber optical cables that contain more than two optical fibers in one jacket. These cables are known as *multifiber* cables. There are multifiber cables with anywhere from three to several hundred optical fibers in them. More often than not, however, the number of fibers in a multifiber cable will be a multiple of two because, as discussed earlier, LAN applications need to have a send and a receive optical fiber for each connection.

LAN/WAN Application

Different fiber cable types are used for different applications within the LAN/WAN environment. Table 10.1 summarizes this section by showing the relationship between the fiber network type and the wavelength and fiber size for both single-mode and multimode fiber optic cables.

TABLE 10.1: Network Type Fiber Applications

Network Type	Single Mode Wavelength–Size	Multimode Wavelength–Size
Ethernet	1300nm – 8/125-micron	850nm – 62.5/125-micron
Fast Ethernet	1300nm – 8/125-micron	1300nm – 62.5/125-micron
Token Ring	Proprietary – 8/125-micron	Proprietary – 62.5/125-micron
ATM 155Mbps	1300nm – 8/125-micron	1300nm – 62.5/125-micron
FDDI	1300nm – 8/125-micron	1300nm – 62.5/125-micron

Fiber Installation Issues

Now that we've discussed details about the fiber optic cable itself, we must cover some of the issues involved with actually installing it into a LAN or WAN. These issues include, but are not limited to the following:

- Components of a typical fiber installation
- Fiber optic performance factors

Let's examine some of these fiber optic installation issues, starting with the components of a typical fiber optic installation.

NOTE   The actual process of installing fiber optic cable will be covered in Part III, "Cabling Design and Installation."

Components of a Typical Installation

Just like copper-based cabling systems, fiber optic cabling systems have a few specialized components that are used only on fiber optic cabling systems. Some of these components include the following:

- Fiber optic cable
- Fiber optic enclosures
- Fiber optic connectors

Fiber Optic Cable

Although it seems like we've already discussed fiber optic cable to death, it has to be mentioned in this section because choosing the right fiber optic cable for your installation is critical. If you don't, your fiber installation is doomed from the start. A few things to remember:

Match the rating of the fiber you are installing to the equipment you are installing.   It may seem a bit obvious, but if you are installing fiber for a hub and workstations with single-mode connections, it is not a good idea to use multimode fiber, and vice versa.

Use fiber optic cable appropriate for the locale.   Don't use outdoor cable in an interior application. That would be overkill. Similarly, don't use interior cable outside. The interior cable doesn't have the protection features that the exterior cable has.

Unterminated fiber is dangerous.   Fiber can be dangerous in two ways: You can get glass slivers in your hands from touching the end of a glass fiber. Also, laser light is dangerous to unprotected eyes. Many fiber optic transmitters use laser light that can damage the cornea of the eyeball when looked at. Bottom line: protect the end of an unterminated fiber cable.

Fiber Optic Enclosures

Because laser light is dangerous, the ends of every fiber optic cable must be encased in some kind of enclosure. The enclosure not only protects the fiber from damage, but also protects humans from exposure to dangerous laser light (as discussed earlier). There are two main types of fiber enclosures: wall plates and patch panels. You learned about wall plates in Chapter 8, so let's discuss patch panels here.

When most people think about a fiber enclosure, a fiber patch panel is what comes to mind. A *fiber patch panel* allows connections between different devices to be made and broken at the will of the network administrator. Basically, a bunch of fiber optic cables will terminate in a patch panel. Then, short fiber optic *patch cables* are used to make connections between the various cables. Figure 10.16 shows an example of a fiber optic patch panel. Note that there are dust caps on all the fiber optic ports. This is to prevent dust from getting into the connector and preventing a proper connection.

In addition to the standard fiber patch panels, a fiber optic installation may have one or more fiber distribution panels. A *fiber distribution panel* is just like a patch panel, in that many cables interconnect in this box. However, in a distribution panel (see Figure 10.17), the connections are more permanent. Distribution panels usually have a lock and key to prevent end users from getting in the panel and making unauthorized changes. Generally speaking, a patch panel is found wherever fiber optic equipment (i.e., hubs, switches, and routers) is found. Distribution panels are found wherever multifiber cables are split out into individual cables.

FIGURE 10.16:

An example of a fiber optic patch panel

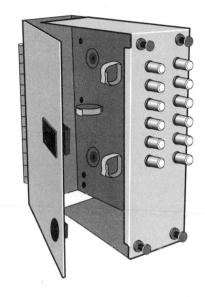

FIGURE 10.17:

A sample fiber optic distribution panel

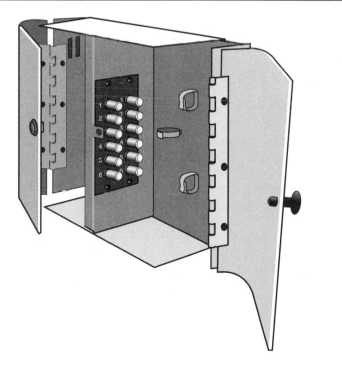

Fiber Optic Connectors

Fiber optic connectors are unique in that they must make both an optical and a mechanical connection. Connectors for copper cables, like the RJ-45 connector used on UTP, make an electrical connection between the two cables involved. However, the pins inside the connector only need to be touching to make a sufficient electrical connection. Fiber optic connectors, on the other hand, must have the fiber internally aligned almost perfectly in order to make a connection. The fiber optic connectors use various methods to accomplish this.

Some of the types of optical connectors currently in use include the following:

- Subscriber connector (SC)
- 568SC (Duplex SC)
- Straight-tip (ST)
- Duplex ST
- Biconic
- FDDI (MIC)
- FC
- Enterprise system connection (ESCON)
- SMA

In this subsection, we will briefly examine each connector type, starting with the SC connector. Note that each connector differs primarily in the way the connection is made, the maximum number of connections (called *mating cycles*), and the size of the connector.

NOTE Fiber optic connector installation (called connectorizing) is covered in more detail in Chapter 13, "Cable Connector Installation."

Subscriber Connector (SC)

The *subscriber connector (SC)* (also sometimes known as a *square connector*) is a type of fiber optic connector, as shown in Figure 10.18. As you can see, SC connectors are latched connectors. This makes it impossible for the connector to be pulled out without releasing the connector's latch, usually by pressing some kind of button or release.

A sample SC connector

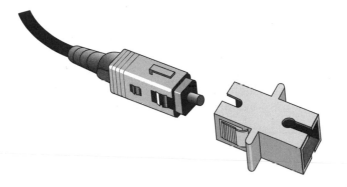

SC connectors work with either single- or multimode optical fibers and will last for around 1000 matings. They are currently seeing increased use but they still aren't as popular as ST connectors for LAN connections are.

568SC (Duplex SC)   *568SC connectors* (also known as *duplex SC* connectors) are basically a pair of SC connectors in a single plastic enclosure. Figure 10.19 shows a 568SC connector. Compare the connector shown in Figure 10.19 with the one in Figure 10.18 and notice the similarities.

FIGURE 10.19:

A sample 568SC connector

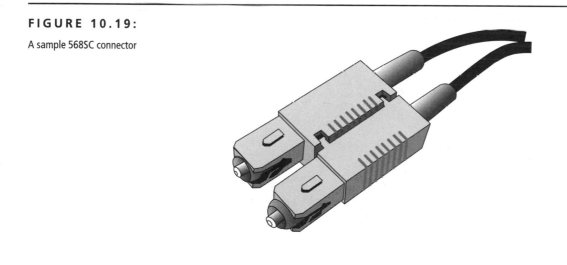

Because the SC and Duplex SC connectors are basically the same, they share the same characteristics, including maximum matings and support for single- and multimode optical fibers.

Straight Tip (ST)   The straight tip (ST) fiber optic connector, developed by AT&T, is probably the most widely used fiber optic connector. It uses a BNC attachment mechanism, similar to the thinnet Ethernet connection mechanism, which makes connections and disconnections fairly easy. The ease of use of the ST is one of the attributes that makes this connector so popular. Figure 10.20 shows some examples of ST connectors. Notice the BNC attachment mechanism.

FIGURE 10.20:

Some examples of ST connectors

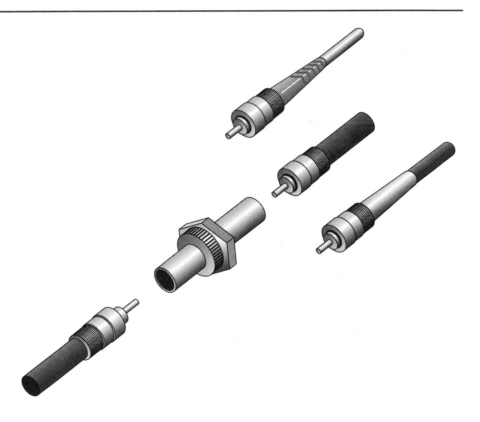

Because it is so widely available, adapters to other fiber connector types are available for this connector type. Additionally, this connector type has a maximum mating cycle of around 1000 matings.

NOTE   Some ST connectors use a plastic end; these will only survive around 250 mating cycles.

Duplex ST   Like the duplex SC connector, the *duplex ST* connector is simply a pairing up of the single connector version of its namesake (in this case, the ST connector). It shares the same details of its singular version.

Biconic   The biconic connector was developed by AT&T; it has fallen out of favor with fiber installers. It uses a screw-together connection system, as you can see in Figure 10.21. Biconic connectors are available for both single- and multi-mode optical fibers.

FIGURE 10.21:

A biconic fiber optic connector

FDDI (MIC)   Since the fiber-distributed data interface (FDDI) has become popular as a LAN type, the *media interface connector* (MIC) for FDDI is a popular connector choice for terminating fiber and is the main choice for use with FDDI. Figure 10.22 shows an example of an FDDI (MIC) connector. Notice that it is keyed (the red tab on top of the connector). This prevents the connector from being installed incorrectly.

FIGURE 10.22:

An FDDI (MIC) connector

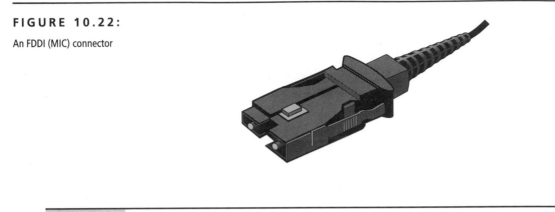

> **NOTE**   FDDI connectors work ONLY with multimode fiber.

FC   The FC connector was one of the first of the smaller connectors used. The FC fiber optic connector has a keyed all-metal connector with a screw-on fastening system. Along with its derivative, the D4 connector, it is quickly becoming one of the more popular small-size connectors. Figure 10.23 shows an example of an FC connector. Note the all-metal construction that makes it a durable connector despite its small size.

FIGURE 10.23:

An FC fiber optic connector

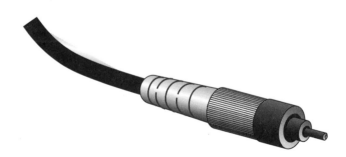

The D4 connector is a variant of the FC connector that is often confused with the FC connector. The D4 connector is basically the same as the FC, but there is a "hood" over the end of the connector to prevent damage to the fiber (as shown in Figure 10.24). Compare the D4 connector in Figure 10.24 to the FC connector in Figure 10.23.

FIGURE 10.24:

A D4 fiber optic connector

Enterprise System Connection (ESCON)   The Enterprise System Connection (ESCON) connector is much like the FDDI (MIC) fiber optic connector, except that the ESCON connector has a retractable cover and lower max mating cycle (only 500 matings). Figure 10.25 shows an example of an ESCON connector. Note the similarities between the ESCON connector shown here and the FDDI (MIC) connector shown earlier in Figure 10.22.

FIGURE 10.25:

An ESCON connector

SMA   The SMA connector, developed by AMP Corporation, was designed to be a low-cost multimode fiber connector. As you can see in Figure 10.26, it's a fairly simple connector. Because it is simple and made of plastic, it is only rated for a maximum of 200 mating cycles. However, it is rated for military use. That, along with its low cost, makes it a very popular connector type.

FIGURE 10.26:

An SMA fiber optic connector

NOTE SMA connectors are currently available for both single- and multimode optical fibers.

Fiber Optic Performance Factors

During the course of a normal fiber installation, there are a few factors that you must be aware of. If not acknowledged, these factors can cause a serious degradation in performance.

Some of the factors that can negatively affect performance include the following:

- Attenuation
- Acceptance angle
- Numerical aperture (NA)
- Light source type

Attenuation

The biggest factor in any fiber optic cabling installation is attenuation. *Attenuation* is the loss or decrease in power of a data-carrying signal (in this case, the light signal). It is measured in decibels (dB or dB/km for a particular cable run). In real world terms, a 3dB attenuation loss in a fiber connection is equal to about a 50 percent loss of signal. Figure 10.27 graphs attenuation in decibels versus percent signal loss. Notice that the relationship is exponential.

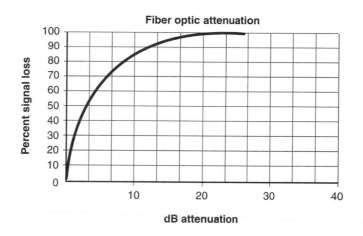

FIGURE 10.27:

Relationship of attenuation
to percent signal loss of a
fiber optic transmission

The more attenuation that exists in a fiber optic cable from transmitter to receiver, the shorter the maximum distance between them. Attenuation negatively affects transmission speeds and distances of all cabling systems, but fiber optic transmissions are particularly sensitive to attenuation.

There are many different problems that can cause attenuation of a light signal in an optical fiber. Some of those problems include the following:

- Excessive gap between fibers in a connections

- Improperly installed connectors

- Impurities in the fiber itself

- Excessive bending of the cable

- Excessive stretching of the cable

These problems will be covered in Chapter 14, "Cabling System Testing and Troubleshooting." For now, just realize that these problems cause attenuation, an undesirable effect.

Acceptance Angle

Another factor that affects the performance of a fiber optic cabling system is the acceptance angle of the optical fiber core. The acceptance angle (as shown in Figure 10.28) is the angle over which a particular (multimode) fiber can accept light as an input to that fiber.

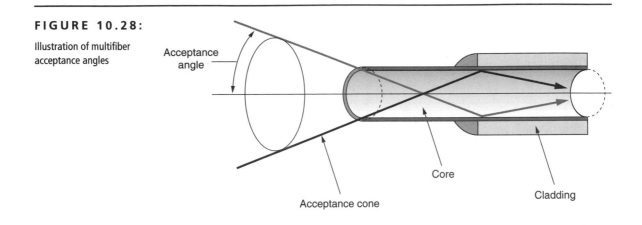

The greater the acceptance angle difference between two or more signals in a multimode fiber, the greater the effect of modal dispersion (discussed earlier in this chapter; see the section "Single-Mode or Multimode"). The modal dispersion effect also has a negative effect on the total performance of a particular cable segment.

Numerical Aperture (NA)

One of the most misunderstood performance factors of fiber optic cable is the numerical aperture (NA). Most people ignore this value when choosing their fiber optic cable. However, it is a very important performance factor, especially when splicing two optical cables. The *numerical aperture (NA)* is a number that reflects the ability of a particular optical fiber to accept light. The number is the result of a mathematical equation involving the acceptance angle.

The value of the NA is a decimal value between the numbers of 0 and 1. A value for NA of 0 indicates that the fiber gathers no light. A value of 1 for NA indicates that the fiber will accept all light it's exposed to. The lower the NA, the less light that gets accepted into the fiber, and thus the less distance the signal can travel. However, a lower NA also means there is more possible bandwidth available. Conversely, a higher NA means that the signal can travel farther, but there is lower bandwidth for that signal. Figure 10.29 illustrates the difference between high and low NA values.

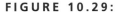

FIGURE 10.29:

The difference between
high and low NA values

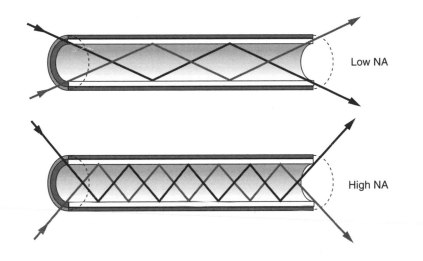

Low NA

High NA

Chromatic Dispersion

The last fiber optic performance factor is a factor known as chromatic dispersion, which limits the bandwidth of certain single-mode optical fibers. *Chromatic dispersion* is when the various wavelengths of light spread out as they travel through an optical fiber. This happens because different wavelengths of light travel different speeds through the same media. As they bounce around through the fiber, the different wavelengths will reflect off the sides of the fibers at different angles (as shown in Figure 10.30). The different wavelengths of light will spread farther and farther apart until the different wavelengths arrive at the destination at completely different times.

FIGURE 10.30:

Single-mode optical fiber
chromatic dispersion

Single-mode optical fiber

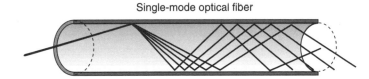

Unbounded (Wireless) Media

- Infrared

- Radio Frequency (RF)

- Microwave

Unbounded (wireless) LAN media are becoming extremely popular in modular office spaces. *Unbounded media* is a type of network media where the network signals are not bound by any type of fiber or cable. These media are also called wireless technologies because they don't use any kind of wire or cable for a network cable.

You may ask, "Why talk about wireless technologies in a book about cabling?" The answer is that today's networks aren't comprised of a single technology or wiring scheme. Today's networks are known as *heterogeneous* networks. That is to say, they are made up of many different technologies and cabling systems, all from different vendors. Wireless technologies are just one way of solving a particular cabling need in a heterogeneous cabling system. Wireless networks can carry data where traditional cabled networks cannot.

In this chapter, you will get a brief introduction to some of the wireless technologies found on both LANs and WANs and how they are used in these applications. Let's start this discussion with a look at infrared transmissions.

NOTE   This chapter is only meant to give you an introduction to wireless networks. For more information, go to your favorite Internet search engine and type in "wireless networking."

Infrared Transmissions

Everyone who has a television with a remote control has performed an infrared transmission. *Infrared (IR) transmissions* are signal transmissions that use infrared radiation as their transmission medium. Infrared radiation is part of the electromagnetic spectrum. It has a wavelength shorter than visible light (actually, it's shorter than the red wavelength in the visible spectrum) with more energy. Infrared is a very popular method of wireless networking. As such, let's examine some of the details of infrared transmissions:

- How infrared transmissions work

- Advantages of using infrared transmissions in LANs and WANs

- Disadvantages of infrared transmissions

- Examples of infrared networking equipment

How Infrared Transmissions Work

Infrared transmissions are very simple. All infrared connections work similar to LAN transmissions, except that there is no cable to contain the signal. The infrared transmissions travel through the air instead of inside of a copper or fiber cable. These transmissions are comprised of infrared radiation that is modulated in order to encode the LAN data within the infrared transmission.

A device known as a laser diode usually produces the infrared radiation. A *laser diode* is a small electronic device that can produce single wavelengths or frequencies of light or radiation. In the case of infrared transmissions, the laser diode creates infrared radiation. A laser diode differs from a regular laser in that the laser diode is much simpler, smaller, and lower powered, and thus the signals can only travel over shorter distances (usually less than 500 feet).

All devices that are going to communicate via infrared need both an infrared transmitter and an infrared receiver. The infrared transmitter is the component that creates the infrared signal (as discussed in the last paragraph). The receiver is often a device known as a photodiode. A *photodiode* is a device that is sensitive to a particular wavelength of light or radiation and will convert the infrared signals back into the digital signals that a computer will understand.

In some cases, the infrared transmitter and receiver are built into a single device known as an infrared transceiver. An *infrared transceiver* is the device that can both transmit and receive infrared signals. Infrared transceivers are used primarily in short-distance infrared communications. For communications that must travel over longer distances (e.g., infrared WAN communications must travel over several kilometers), a separate infrared transmitter and receiver are contained in a single housing. The transmitter is usually a higher-powered infrared laser. In order to function correctly, the lasers in both devices (sender and receiver) must be aligned with the receivers on the opposite device (as shown in Figure 11.1).

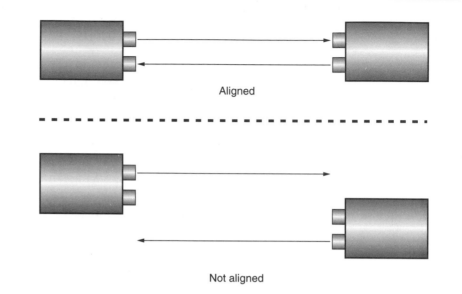

Aligned

Not aligned

There are two types of infrared transmissions: point-to-point and broadcast. Each has its own unique elements. Let's take a brief look at each.

Point-to-Point

The most common type of infrared transmission is the point-to-point transmission. *Point-to-point* infrared transmissions are those infrared transmissions that use tightly focused beams of infrared radiation to send information or control information over a distance (i.e., from one "point" directly to another). The aforementioned infrared remote control for your television is one example of a point-to-point infrared transmission.

LANs and WANs can use point-to-point infrared transmissions to transmit information over short or long distances. Point-to-point infrared transmissions are used in LAN applications for connecting buildings together over short distances.

Using point-to-point infrared media reduces attenuation and makes eavesdropping difficult. Typical point-to-point infrared computer equipment is similar to that used for consumer products with remote controls, except with much higher power. Careful alignment of the transmitter and receiver is required, as mentioned earlier. Figure 11.2 shows how a network might use point-to-point infrared transmission. Note that the two buildings are connected via a direct line-of-sight with infrared transmission and that the buildings are about 1000 feet apart.

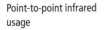
FIGURE 11.2:

Point-to-point infrared usage

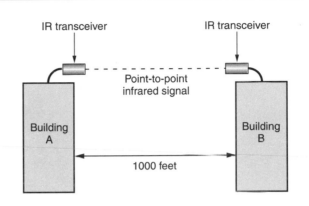

Point-to-point infrared systems have the following characteristics:

Frequency range   Infrared light usually uses the lowest range of light frequencies, between 100GHz and 1,000 Terahertz (THz).

Cost   The cost depends on the kind of equipment used. Long-distance systems, which typically use high-power lasers, can be very expensive. Equipment that is mass-produced for the consumer market and can be adapted for network use is generally inexpensive.

Installation   Infrared point-to-point requires precise alignment. Take extra care if high-powered lasers are used, because they can damage or burn eyes.

Capacity   Data rates vary between 100Kbps to 16Mbps (at one kilometer).

Attenuation   The amount of attenuation depends on the quality of emitted light and its purity, as well as general atmospheric conditions and signal obstructions.

EMI   Infrared transmission can be affected by intense light. Tightly focused beams are fairly immune to eavesdropping because tampering usually becomes evident by the disruption in the signal. Furthermore, the area in which the signal may be picked up is very limited.

Broadcast

Broadcast infrared systems spread the signal to cover a wider area and allow reception of the signal by several receivers. One of the major advantages is mobility; the workstations or other devices can be moved more easily than with point-to-point infrared media. Figure 11.3 shows how a broadcast infrared system might be used.

FIGURE 11.3:

An implementation of broadcast infrared media

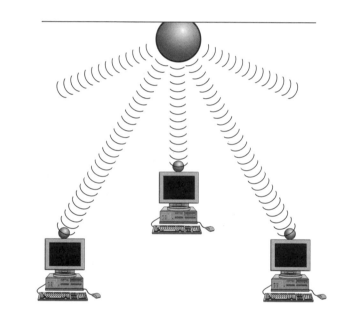

Because broadcast infrared signals (also known as *diffuse infrared*) are not as focused as point-to-point, this type of system cannot offer the same throughput. Broadcast infrared is typically limited to less than 1Mbps, making it too slow for most network needs.

Broadcast infrared systems have the following characteristics:

Frequency range   Infrared systems usually use the lowest range of light frequencies, between 100GHz to 1,000THz.

Cost   The cost of infrared equipment depends on the quality of light required. Typical equipment used for infrared systems is quite inexpensive. High-power laser equipment is much more expensive.

Installation Installation is fairly simple. When devices have clear paths and strong signals, they can be placed anywhere the signal can reach, making reconfiguration easy. One concern should be the control of strong light sources that might affect infrared transmission.

Capacity Although data rates are less than 1Mbps, it is theoretically possible to reach much higher throughput.

Attenuation Broadcast infrared, like point-to-point, is affected by the quality of the emitted light and its purity and by atmospheric conditions. Because devices can be moved easily, however, obstructions are generally not of great concern.

EMI Intense light can dilute infrared transmissions. Because broadcast infrared transmissions cover a wide area, they are more easily intercepted for eavesdropping.

Advantages of Infrared

As a medium for LAN transmissions, infrared transmissions are a pretty good choice. They have many advantages that make them a logical choice for many LAN/WAN applications. These advantages include the following:

Relatively inexpensive Infrared equipment (especially the short-distance broadcast equipment) is relatively inexpensive when compared to other wireless methods like microwave or radio frequency (RF) methods. Because of its low cost, many laptop and portable computing devices contain an infrared transceiver on them that allows these devices to connect to each other and transfer files. Additionally, as a WAN transmission method, you pay for the equipment once; there are no recurring line charges.

High bandwidths Point-to-point infrared transmissions support fairly high (around 1.544Mbps) bandwidths. They are often used as WAN links because of their speed and efficiency.

No FCC license required If a wireless transmission is available for the general (i.e., United States) public to listen to, it is usually governed by the Federal Communications Commission (FCC). The FCC licenses certain frequency bands for use for radio and satellite transmission. Because infrared transmissions are short range and their frequencies fall outside the FCC bands, you don't need to apply for an FCC-licensed frequency (a long and costly process) to use them.

NOTE   More information on the FCC can be found at their Web site: `www.fcc.gov`.

Ease of installation   Installation of most infrared devices is very simple. Connect the transceiver to the network (or host machine) and point it at the device you want to communicate with. Broadcast infrared devices don't even need to be pointed at their host devices. Long distance infrared devices may need a bit more alignment, but the idea is the same.

High security on point-to-point connections   Because point-to-point infrared connections are line-of-sight and any attempt to intercept a point-to-point infrared connection will block the signal, point-to-point infrared connections are very secure. The signal can't be intercepted without the knowledge of the sending equipment.

Portability   Short-range infrared transceivers and equipment are usually small and have lower power requirements. Thus, these devices are great choices for portable, flexible networks. Broadcast infrared systems are often set up in offices where the cubicles are rearranged often. This does NOT mean that the computers can be in motion while connected. As discussed later in this section, infrared requires a constant line-of-sight. If you should walk behind an object and obstruct the line-of-sight between the two devices that are communicating, the connection will be interrupted.

Disadvantages of Infrared

Just as with any other network technology, infrared has its disadvantages. Some of these include the following:

Line-of-sight needed for focused transmissions   Infrared transmissions are line-of-sight transmissions. That is, there must be an unobstructed path between sender and receiver (i.e., you can "see" from source to destination with no obstructions in between). Infrared transmissions are similar to regular light transmissions in that the signals don't "bend" around corners without help, nor can the transmissions go through walls. Some transmissions are able to bounce off surfaces, but each "bounce" takes away from the total signal strength (usually halving the effective strength for each bounce).

NOTE There are some products that achieve non-line-of-sight infrared transmissions by bouncing the signal off of walls or ceilings. You should know that for every "bounce," the signal can degrade as much as 50 percent. For that reason, we have stated here that focused infrared is primarily a line-of-sight technology.

Weather attenuation   Because infrared transmissions travel through the air, any change in the air can cause degradation of the signal over a distance. Humidity, temperature, and ambient light can all negatively affect signal strength in low-power infrared transmissions. In outdoor, higher power infrared transmissions, fog, rain, and snow can all reduce the effectiveness of an infrared transmission.

Examples of Infrared Transmissions

As mentioned earlier, you have used infrared transmissions to change the channel on your television. There are other applications of infrared transmissions in the PC world. Some of these examples include the following:

- IrDA ports
- Infrared laser devices

Let's briefly examine these two examples of infrared technology.

IrDA Ports

More than likely, you've seen an IrDA port. IrDA ports are the small, dark windows on the backs of laptops and handheld PCs that allow two devices to communicate via infrared. IrDA is actually an abbreviation for the standards body that came up with the standard method of short-range infrared communications, the Infrared Data Association. Based out of Walnut Creek, California, and founded in 1993, it is a membership organization that is dedicated to developing standards for wireless, infrared transmission systems between computers. With IrDA ports, a laptop or PDA can exchange data with a desktop computer or use a printer without a cable connection.

Computing products with IrDA ports began to appear in 1995, and the LaserJet 5P was one of the first printers with a built-in IrDA port. You could print to the LaserJet 5P from any laptop or handheld device (as long as you had the correct driver installed) by simply pointing the IrDA port on the laptop or handheld at the IrDA port on the 5P. This technology became known as *point and print*. Figure 11.4 shows an example of an IrDA port on a handheld PC. Notice how small it is compared to the size of the PC.

FIGURE 11.4:

An example of an IrDA port

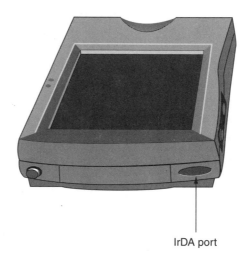

IrDA port

NOTE   For more information about the IrDA, its membership, and the IrDA port, see their Web site at www.irda.org.

Infrared Laser Devices

Longer distance communications via infrared transmissions are possible, but they require the use of a special class of devices, known as infrared laser devices. These devices have a transmitting laser, which operates in the infrared range (a wavelength of between 750 to 2500nm and a frequency of around 1THz), and an infrared receiver to receive the signal. As discussed earlier in this chapter, these devices are usually used to connect multiple buildings within a campus or to connect multiple sites within a city. One such example of this category of infrared devices is the TerraLink system from AstroTerra (as shown in Figure 11.5). This system provides data rates between 10 and 155Mbps and distances of up to 3.75 km (2.33 miles) between sender and receiver.

FIGURE 11.5:

TerraLink infrared laser device

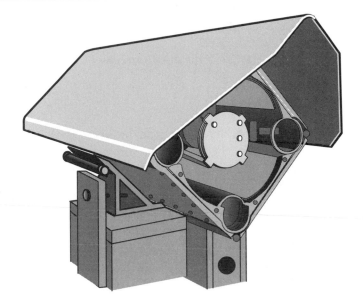

NOTE   You can find out more information about the TerraLink system on AstroTerra's
Web site at www.astroterra.com.

Radio Frequency (RF) Systems

Radio frequency (RF) transmission systems are those network transmissions that use radio waves to transmit data. In late 1999, RF transmission systems saw a sharp increase in use. Many companies are installing RF access points in their networks to solve certain mobility issues. The relatively low cost and ease of installation of RF systems play a part in their popularity.

In this section, we will cover RF systems and their application to LAN and WAN uses. Some of these topics include the following:

- How RF systems work

- Advantages of using RF systems in LANs and WANs

- Disadvantages of using RF systems

- Examples of RF systems

Let's start with the details of how RF systems work.

How RF Works

Radio waves have frequencies between 10 kilohertz (KHz) and 1 gigahertz (GHz). The range of the electromagnetic spectrum between 10KHz and 1GHz is called *radio frequency* (RF). RF systems use the radio waves in this frequency band to transmit data.

Most radio frequencies are regulated; some are not. To use a regulated frequency, you must receive a license from the regulatory body over that area (in the United States, the FCC). Getting a license can take a long time and can be costly; it also makes it more difficult to move equipment. However, licensing guarantees that, within a set area, you will have clear radio transmission.

The advantage of unregulated frequencies is that there are few restrictions placed on them. One regulation, however, does limit the usefulness of unregulated frequencies: unregulated frequency equipment must operate at less than one watt. The point of this regulation is to limit the range of influence a device can have, thereby limiting interference with other signals. In terms of networks, this makes unregulated radio communication bandwidths of limited use.

WARNING   Because unregulated frequencies are available for use by others in your area, you cannot be guaranteed a clear communications channel.

In the United States, the following frequencies are available for unregulated use:

- 902 to 928MHz

- 2.4GHz (also internationally)

- 5.72 to 5.85GHz

Radio waves can be broadcast either omnidirectionally or directionally. Various kinds of antennas can be used to broadcast radio signals. Typical antennas include the following:

- Omnidirectional towers
- Half-wave dipole
- Random-length wire
- Beam (such as the Yagi)

Figure 11.6 shows these common types of radio frequency antennas.

FIGURE 11.6:

Typical radio frequency antennas

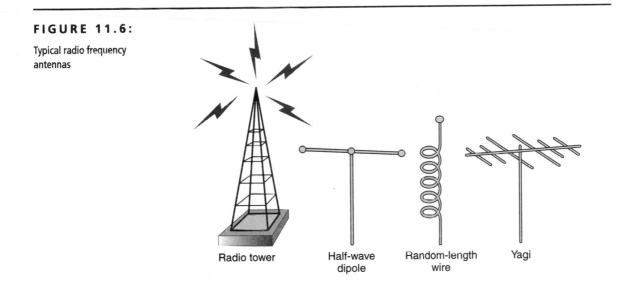

Radio tower   Half-wave dipole   Random-length wire   Yagi

The power of the RF signal is determined by the antenna and transceiver. Each range has characteristics that affect its use in computer networks. For computer network applications, radio waves are classified in three categories:

- Low-power, single-frequency
- High-power, single-frequency
- Spread-spectrum

Table 11.1 summarizes the characteristics of the three types of radio wave media that are described in the following sections.

TABLE 11.1: Radio Wave Media

Factor	Low-Power,	High-Power, Single-Frequency	Spread-Spectrum Single-Frequency
Frequency range	All radio frequencies (typically low GHz range)	All radio frequencies (typically low GHz range)	All radio frequencies (typically 902 to 928MHz in U.S; 2.4 also used)
Cost	Moderate for wireless	Higher than low-power, single-frequency	Moderate
Installation	Simple	High	Moderate
Capacity	From below 1 to 10Mbps	From below 1 to 10Mbps	2 to 6Mbps
Attenuation	High (25 meters)	Low	High
EMI	Poor	Poor	Fair

Low-Power, Single-Frequency

As the name implies, single-frequency transceivers operate at only one frequency. Typical low-power devices are limited in range to around 20 to 30 meters. Although low-frequency radio waves can penetrate some materials, the low power limits them to the shorter, open environments.

Low-power, single-frequency transceivers have the following characteristics:

Frequency range   Low-power, single-frequency products can use any radio frequency, but higher gigahertz ranges provide better throughput (data rates).

Cost   Most systems are moderately priced compared with other wireless systems.

Installation   Most systems are easy to install if the antenna and equipment are preconfigured. Some systems may require expert advice or installation. Some troubleshooting may be involved to avoid other signals.

Capacity   Data rates range from 1 to 10Mbps.

Attenuation   Attenuation is determined by the radio frequency and power of the signal. Low-power, single-frequency transmissions use low power and consequently suffer from attenuation.

EMI   Resistance to EMI is low, especially in the lower bandwidths where electric motors and numerous devices produce noise. Susceptibility to eavesdropping is high, but with the limited transmission range, eavesdropping is generally limited to within the building where the LAN is located.

High-Power, Single-Frequency

High-power, single-frequency transmissions are similar to low-power, single-frequency transmissions but can cover larger distances. They can be used in long-distance outdoor environments. Transmissions can be line-of-sight or can extend beyond the horizon as a result of being bounced off the earth's atmosphere. High-power, single-frequency can be ideal for mobile networking, providing transmission for land-based or marine-based vehicles as well as aircraft. Transmission rates are similar to low-power rates but at much longer distances.

High-power, single-frequency transceivers have the following characteristics:

Frequency range   As with low-power transmissions, high-power can use any radio frequency, but networks favor higher gigahertz ranges for better throughput (data rates).

Cost   Radio transceivers are relatively inexpensive, but other equipment (antennas, repeaters, and so on) can make high-power, single-frequency radio moderately to very expensive.

Installation   Installations are complex. Skilled technicians must be used to install and maintain high-power equipment. The radio operators must be licensed by the FCC, and their equipment must be maintained in accordance with FCC regulations. Equipment that is improperly installed or tuned can cause low data-transmission rates, signal loss, and even interference with local radio.

Capacity   Bandwidth is typically between 1 and 10Mbps.

Attenuation   High-power rates improve the signal's resistance to attenuation, and repeaters can be used to extend signal range. Attenuation rates are fairly low.

EMI   Much like low-power, single-frequency transmission, vulnerability to EMI is high. Vulnerability to eavesdropping is also high. Because the signal is broadcast over a large area, it is more likely that signals can be intercepted.

Spread-Spectrum

Spread-spectrum transmissions use the same frequencies as other radio frequency transmissions, but they use several frequencies simultaneously rather than just one. Two modulation schemes can be used to accomplish this, direct frequency modulation and frequency hopping.

Direct frequency modulation is the most common modulation scheme. It works by breaking the original data into parts (called *chips*), which are then transmitted on separate frequencies. To confuse eavesdroppers, spurious signals can also be transmitted. The transmission is coordinated with the intended receiver, who is aware of which frequencies are valid. The receiver can then isolate the chips and reassemble the data while ignoring the decoy information. Figure 11.7 illustrates how direct frequency modulation works.

FIGURE 11.7:

Direct frequency
modulation

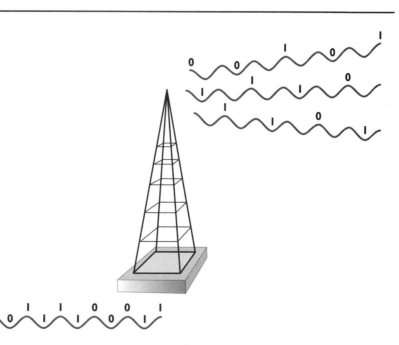

The signal can be intercepted, but it is difficult to watch the right frequencies, gather the chips, know which chips are valid data, and find the right message. This makes eavesdropping difficult.

Current 900MHz direct-sequence systems support data rates of 2 to 6Mbps. Higher frequencies offer the possibility of higher data rates.

Frequency hopping rapidly switches among several predetermined frequencies. In order for this system to work, the transmitter and receiver must be in nearly perfect synchronization. Bandwidth can be increased by simultaneously transmitting on several frequencies. Figure 11.8 shows how frequency hopping works.

FIGURE 11.8:

Frequency hopping

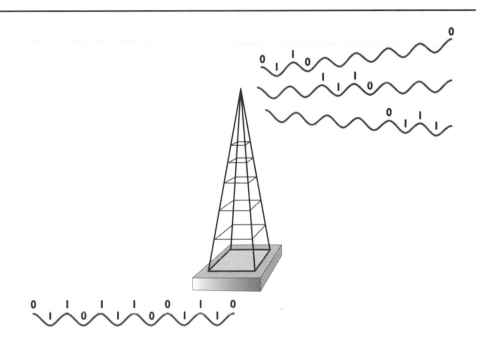

Spread-spectrum transceivers have the following characteristics:

Frequency range   Spread-spectrum generally operates in the unlicensed frequency ranges. In the United States, devices using the 902 to 928MHz range are most common, but 2.4GHz devices are also becoming available.

Cost   Although costs depend on what kind of equipment you choose, they are typically fairly inexpensive when compared with other wireless media.

Installation   Depending on the type of equipment you have in your system, installation can range from simple to fairly complex.

Capacity   The most common systems, the 900MHz systems, support data rates of 2 to 6Mbps, but newer systems operating in gigahertz produce higher data rates.

Attenuation   Attenuation depends on the frequency and power of the signal. Because spread-spectrum transmission systems operate at low power, which produces a weaker signal, they usually have high attenuation.

EMI   Immunity to EMI is low, but because spread-spectrum uses different frequencies, interference would need to be across multiple frequencies to destroy the signal. Vulnerability to eavesdropping is low.

Advantages of RF

As mentioned earlier, RF systems are widely used in LANs today because of many factors. Some of those factors include:

No line-of-sight needed   Radio waves can penetrate walls and other solid obstacles, so a direct line-of-sight is not required between sender and receiver.

Low cost   Radio transmitters have been around since the early twentieth century. After 100 years, high quality radio transmitters have become extremely cheap to manufacture.

Flexible   Some RF LAN systems allow laptop computers with wireless PC card NICs to roam around the room while remaining connected to the host LAN.

Disadvantages of RF

As with the other types of wireless networks, RF networks are not without their disadvantages. Some of these disadvantages include:

Susceptible to jamming and eavesdropping   Because RF signals are broadcast in all directions, it is very easy for someone to intercept and interpret a LAN transmission without the permission of the sender or receiver. Those RF systems that use spread-spectrum encoding are less susceptible to this problem.

Susceptible to RF interference   All mechanical devices with electric motors produce stray RF signals. The larger the motor, the stronger the RF signals it generates. These stray RF signals can interfere with the proper operation of an RF transmission-based LAN. When this happens, the stray signals are known as *RF noise*.

Limited range   RF systems don't have the range of satellite networks (although they can travel longer distances than infrared networks). Because of their limited range, RF systems are normally used for short-range network applications (e.g., from a PC to a hub).

Examples of RF

RF systems are being used all over corporate America. The RF networking hardware that is available today makes it easy for people to connect wirelessly to their corporate network as well as to the Internet.

The most popular example of an RF network today is what is known as an *ad hoc RF network*. These networks are created when two or more entities with RF transceivers that support ad hoc networking are brought within range of each other. The two entities send out radio waves to each other and both recognize that there is another RF device close by that they can communicate with. These ad hoc networks allow people with laptops or handheld devices to create their own networks on-the-fly and transfer data. Figure 11.9 shows an example of an ad hoc network between three notebooks. These three notebooks all have the some RF devices that support ad hoc and have been configured to talk to each other.

FIGURE 11.9:

An example of an ad hoc
RF network

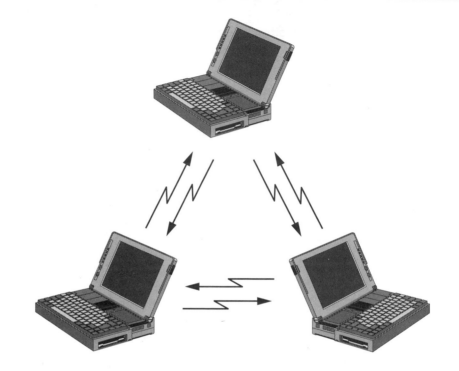

The other example of an RF network is a multipoint RF network. This type of RF network has many stations, each with an RF transmitter and receiver, that communicate with a central device known as a wireless bridge. A *wireless bridge* (known as an RF access point in RF systems) is a device that provides a transparent connection to the host LAN via an Ethernet or Token Ring connection and uses some wireless method (e.g., infrared, RF, or microwave) to connect to the individual nodes. This type of network is mainly used for two applications: office "cubicle farms" and metropolitan-area wireless Internet access. Each of these applications requires that the wireless bridge be installed at some central point and that the stations that are going to access the network be within the operating range of the bridge device. Figure 11.10 shows an example of this type of network. Note that the workstations at the top of the figure can communicate wirelessly to the server and printer connected to the same network as the bridge device.

FIGURE 11.10:

An example of an RF multi-point network

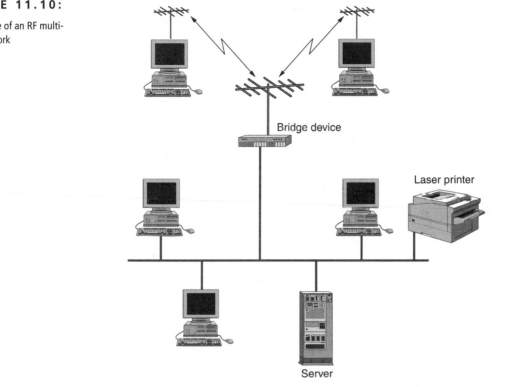

There are many different brands, makes, and models of RF LAN equipment. This used to be a source of difficulty with LAN installers. In its infancy, every company used different frequencies, different encoding schemes, different antennas, and different wireless protocols. The marketplace was screaming for a standard to be proposed. For this reason, the IEEE 802.11 standard was developed. Standard 802.11 specifies various protocols for wireless networking. It does, in fact, specify that either infrared or RF can be used for the wireless network, but most RF systems are the only ones advertising IEEE 802.11–compliance.

Table 11.2 shows some examples of the available RF wireless networking products available at the time of the writing of this book. This table shows which RF technology each product uses as well as its primary application.

TABLE 11.2:   Available RF Wireless Networking Product Examples

Product	RF Technology	Application	Speed
Breezecom BreezNET	Spread spectrum	Multipoint and ad hoc	1 to 3Mbps
Lucent WaveLAN	Spread spectrum	Multipoint	1 to 11Mbps
Apple AirPort	Spread spectrum	Multipoint	11Mbps

Microwave Communications

You've seen them: the satellite dishes on the tops of buildings in larger cities. These dishes are most often used for microwave communications. Microwave communications use very powerful, focused beams of energy to send communications over very long distances.

In this section, we will cover the details of microwave communications as they apply to LAN and WAN communications, including the following:

- How microwave communications work

- Advantages of microwave communications

- Disadvantages of microwave communications

- Examples of microwave technology

How Microwave Communications Works

Microwave communications make use of the lower gigahertz frequencies of the electromagnetic spectrum. These frequencies, which are higher than radio frequencies, produce better throughput and performance than other types of wireless communications. There are two types of microwave data communication systems, terrestrial and satellite.

Table 11.3 shows a brief comparison of the terrestrial microwave and satellite microwave transmission systems.

TABLE 11.3:   Terrestrial Microwave and Satellite Microwave

Factor	Terrestrial Microwave	Satellite Microwave
Frequency range	Low gigahertz (typically between 4 to 6 or 21 to 23GHz)	Low gigahertz (typically 11 to 14)
Cost	Moderate to high	High
Installation	Moderately difficult	Difficult
Capacity	1 to 100Mbps	1 to 100Mbps
Attenuation	Depends on conditions (affected by atmospheric conditions)	Depends on conditions (affected by atmospheric conditions)
EMI resistance	Poor	Poor

Terrestrial

Terrestrial microwave systems typically use directional parabolic antennas to send and receive signals in the lower gigahertz frequency range. The signals are highly focused, and the physical path must be line-of-sight. Relay towers are used to extend signals. Terrestrial microwave systems are typically used when the cost of cabling is cost-prohibitive.

TIP   Because they do not use cable, microwave links are often used to connect separate buildings where cabling would be too expensive, difficult to install, or prohibited. For example, if two buildings are separated by a public road, you may not be able to get permission to install cable over or under the road. Microwave links would be a good choice in this type of situation.

Because terrestrial microwave equipment often uses licensed frequencies, additional costs and time constraints may be imposed by licensing commissions or government agencies (the FCC in the United States).

Figure 11.11 shows a microwave system connecting separate buildings. Smaller terrestrial microwave systems can be used within a building as well. Microwave LANs operate at low power, using small transmitters that communicate with omnidirectional hubs. Hubs can then be connected to form an entire network.

FIGURE 11.11:

Terrestrial microwave connecting two buildings

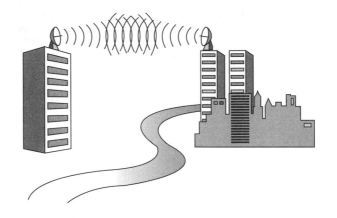

Terrestrial microwave systems have the following characteristics:

Frequency range   Most terrestrial microwave systems produce signals in the low gigahertz range, usually at 4 to 6GHz and 21 to 23GHz.

Cost   Short-distance systems can be relatively inexpensive, and they are effective in the range of hundreds of meters. Long-distance systems can be very expensive. Terrestrial systems may be leased from providers to reduce startup costs, although the cost of the lease over a long term may prove more expensive than purchasing a system.

Installation   Line-of-sight requirements for microwave systems can make installation difficult. Antennas must be carefully aligned. A licensed technician may be required. Also, because the transmission must be line-of-sight, suitable transceiver sites can be a problem. If your organization does not have a clear line-of-sight between two antennas, you must either purchase or lease a site.

Capacity   Capacity varies depending on the frequency used, but typical data rates are from 1 to 100Mbps.

Attenuation   Attenuation is affected by frequency, signal strength, antenna size, and atmospheric conditions. Normally, over short distances, attenuation is not significant, but rain and fog can negatively affect higher frequency microwaves.

EMI   Microwave signals are vulnerable to EMI, jamming, and eavesdropping (although microwave transmissions are often encrypted to reduce eavesdropping). Microwave systems are also affected by atmospheric conditions.

Satellite

Satellite microwave systems transmit signals between directional parabolic antennas. Like terrestrial microwave systems, they use low gigahertz frequencies and must be in line-of-sight. The main difference with satellite systems is that one antenna is on a satellite in geosynchronous orbit about 50,000 kilometers (22,300 miles) above the earth. Because of this, satellite microwave systems can reach the most remote places on earth and communicate with mobile devices.

Here's how it usually works. A LAN sends a signal through cable media to an antenna (commonly known as a *satellite dish*), which beams the signal to the satellite in orbit above the earth. The orbiting antenna then transmits the signal to another location on the earth or, if the destination is on the opposite side of the earth, to another satellite, which then transmits to a location on earth.

Figure 11.12 shows a transmission being beamed from a satellite dish on earth to an orbiting satellite and then back to earth.

FIGURE 11.12:

Satellite microwave transmission

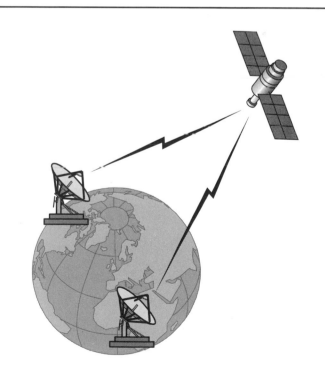

Because the signal must be transmitted 50,000 kilometers to the satellite and 50,000 kilometers back to earth, satellite microwave transmissions take about as long to cover a few kilometers as they do to span continents. This causes delays between the transmission of a satellite microwave signal and its reception. These delays are called *propagation delays*. Propagation delays range from .5 to 5 seconds.

Satellite microwave systems have the following characteristics:

Frequency range   Satellite links operate in the low gigahertz range, typically between 11 and 14GHz.

Cost   The cost of building and launching a satellite is extremely expensive—as high as several hundred million dollars or more. Companies such as AT&T, Hughes Network Systems, and Scientific-Atlanta lease services, making them affordable for a slightly larger number of organizations. Although satellite communications are expensive, the cost of cable to cover the same distance may be even more expensive.

Installation   Satellite microwave installation for orbiting satellites is extremely technical and difficult and certainly should be left to professionals in that field. The earth-based systems may require difficult, exact adjustments. Commercial providers can help with installation.

Capacity   Capacity depends on the frequency used. Typical data rates are 1 to 10Mbps.

Attenuation   Attenuation depends on frequency, power, antenna size, and atmospheric conditions. Higher frequency microwaves are more affected by rain and fog.

EMI   Microwave systems are vulnerable to EMI, jamming, and eavesdropping (although the transmissions are often encrypted to reduce eavesdropping). Microwave systems are also affected by atmospheric conditions.

Advantages of Microwave Communications

Microwave communications have limited use in LAN communications. However, because of their great power, they have many advantages in WAN applications. Some of these advantages include:

Very high bandwidth   Of all the wireless technologies, microwave systems have the highest bandwidth because of the high power of the transmission systems. Speeds of 100Mbps and greater are possible.

Transmissions travel over long distances   As already mentioned, their higher power makes it possible for microwave transmissions to travel over very long distances. Transmissions can travel over distances of several miles (or several thousand miles, in the case of satellite systems).

Signals can be point-to-point or broadcast   As with other types of wireless communications, the signals can be focused tightly for point-to-point communications, or they can be diffused and sent to multiple locations via broadcast communications. This allows for the maximum flexibility for the most applications.

Disadvantages of Microwave Communications

Microwave communications are not an option for most users because of their many disadvantages. Specifically, there are a few disadvantages that make microwave communications viable for only a few groups of people. Some of these disadvantages include the following:

Equipment is expensive   Microwave transmission and reception equipment is the most expensive of all the types of wireless transmission equipment discussed in this chapter. A single microwave transmitter/receiver combo can cost upwards of $5,000 in the U.S. (and two transmitters are required for communications to take place). There are cheaper microwave systems available, but their distance and features are more limited.

Line-of-sight required   In order for microwave communications to take place, there must be a line-of-sight between sender and receiver. Generally speaking, the signal can't be bounced off any objects.

Atmospheric attenuation   As with other wireless technologies (such as infrared laser), atmospheric conditions (e.g., fog, rain, snow) can negatively affect microwave transmissions. For example, a thunderstorm between sender and receiver can prevent reliable communication between the two. Additionally, the higher the microwave frequency, the more susceptible to attenuation the communication will be.

Propagation delay   This is primarily a disadvantage of satellite microwave. When sending between two terrestrial stations using a satellite as a relay station, it can take almost a full second to send from the first terrestrial station through the satellite to the second station.

Safety   Because the microwave beam is very high-powered, it can pose a danger to any human or animal that comes between transmitter and receiver. Imagine putting your hand in a microwave on low power. It may not kill you, but it will certainly not be good for you.

Examples of Microwave Communications

Microwave equipment differs from infrared and RF equipment because it is more specialized and is usually only used for WAN connections. The high power and specialization makes it a poor choice for a LAN media (you wouldn't want to put a microwave dish on top of every PC in an office!). Microwave systems are very specialized and, therefore, instead of listing a few of the common microwave products, Table 11.4 lists a few microwave product companies and their Web site addresses so you can examine their product offerings for yourself.

TABLE 11.4:   Microwave Product Companies and Web Sites

Company	Web Site
Adaptive Broadband	www.adaptivebroadband.com
BelStar	www.belstar.net/
M/A-COM	www.macom.com
Southwest Microwave	www.telspec.com/swmicro.htm

Cabling Design and Installation

chapter 12

Cabling System Design and Installation

- Elements of a Successful Cabling Installation System

- Cabling Topologies

- Cabling Plant Uses

- Choice of Media

- Telecommunications Closets

- Cabling Management

- Data and Cabling Security

- Cabling Installation Procedures

The previous chapters in this book were designed to teach you the basics of telecommunications cabling procedures. You learned about the various components of a typical telecommunications installation and their functions.

It is good to know these things, but it is more important to understand how to put these items together into a cohesive cabling system design. That is, after all, why you bought this book, is it not? Each of the components of a cabling system can fit together in many different ways. Additionally, you must design the cabling system so that each component of that system meets or exceeds the goals of the cabling project.

In this chapter, you will learn to apply the knowledge you learned in the previous chapters to designing and installing a structured cabling system.

Elements of a Successful Cabling Installation

Before you can understand how to design and install a cabling system, you must know what aspects affect the successful installation of a cabling system. Some of these include the following:

- Using proper design
- Using quality materials
- Practicing good workmanship

Each of these aspects can drastically change the layout and design of the cabling system as well as the performance of the network that uses it.

Proper Design

A proper cabling system design is paramount to a well-functioning cabling infrastructure. As with any other major project, the key to a successful cabling installation is that four-letter word: P-L-A-N. A proper cabling system design is simply a plan for installing the cable runs and their associated devices.

So what is a "proper" design? A proper cabling system design will take into account four primary criteria:

- Desired standards and performance characteristics
- Flexibility
- Longevity
- Ease of administration

Failure to take these criteria into account can cause usability problems and poor network performance. Let's take a brief look at each of these factors, starting with meeting the desired standards.

Desired Standards and Performance Characteristics

Of the proper cabling design criteria listed, this is the most critical. As discussed earlier in Chapter 1, "Introduction to Data Cabling," standards ensure that products from many different vendors can communicate. When you design your cabling layout, you should decide on standards for all aspects of your cabling installation so that the various products used will interconnect. Additionally, you should choose products for your design that will meet desired performance characteristics. For example, if you will be deploying a broadcast video system over your LAN in addition to the everyday file and print traffic, it is important that the cabling system be designed with a higher-capacity network in mind (e.g., Fast Ethernet or fiber optic).

Flexibility

No network is a stagnant entity. Networks are constantly changing. As new technologies are introduced, companies will adopt them at different rates. When designing a cabling system, you should keep flexibility of the design in mind. Flexibility in cabling design means you should plan for MACs (moves, adds, and changes) so that if your network changes, your cabling design will be able to accommodate these changes. In a properly designed cabling system, a new device or technology will be able to connect to any point within the cabling system.

One aspect of flexibility that many people overlook is the number of cabling outlets or "drops" in a particular room. Many companies take a minimalist approach, that is, they put only the number of drops in each room that is currently necessary. This type of design is fine for the time being, but what happens when an additional device or devices are needed? It is usually easier to have an extra drop or two (or five) installed while all of the others are being installed than it is to return later to install a single drop.

As with any other planning and design concept, it is more efficient to spend extra time planning than it is to spend extra time and expense coming back later and reinstalling.

Longevity

Let's face it, cabling is hard work. You must climb above ceilings and, on occasion, snake through crawlspaces to properly run the cables. Therefore, when designing a cabling system, you want to make sure that the design will stand the test of time and last for a number of years without having to be replaced. A great case in point: Many companies are currently removing their coaxial cable-based networks in favor of the newer, cheaper, more reliable UTP cabling. Others are removing their UTP cabling in favor of fiber optic cabling's higher bandwidth. Now, wouldn't it make more sense for those companies that currently have coaxial cable to directly upgrade to fiber optic cable (or at least a high-quality Category 6e copper UTP cabling system), rather than having to "rip and replace" again in a few years? Definitely. If you have to upgrade your cabling system or are currently designing your system, it is usually best to upgrade to the most current technology.

Ease of Administration

The final element of a proper cabling design is ease of administration. This means that a network administrator should be able to access the cabling system and make additions and changes, if necessary. Some of these changes might include the following:

- Removing a station from the network

- Replacing hubs, routers, and other telecommunications equipment

- Installing new cables

- Repairing existing wires

There are many elements that make cabling system administration easier, the biggest of which is documentation (discussed later in this chapter). Another element is neatness. A rat's nest of cables is difficult to administrate because it is difficult to tell which cable goes where.

Quality Materials

Another element of a successful cabling installation is the use of quality materials. The quality of the materials used in a cabling installation will directly affect the transmission efficiency of a network. Many times, a vendor will sell many different cabling product lines, each with a different price point. The old adage that you get what you pay for really does apply to cabling supplies.

All the components that make up a cabling plant can be purchased in both high and low quality product lines. For example, you can buy RJ-45 connectors from one vendor that are $0.03 apiece but only rated at Category 3 (i.e., they won't work for 100Mbps networks). Another vendor's RJ-45 connectors may cost twice as much but be rated for Category 6 (155Mbps over copper and above).

That doesn't always mean that low price means low quality. There are vendors who make low price, high-quality cabling supplies. Without playing favorites to a particular vendor, let's just say that it doesn't hurt to shop around when buying your cabling supplies. Check the Internet sites of many different cabling vendors to compare prices.

In addition to price, you should check how the product is assembled. Quality materials are sturdy and well constructed. Low quality materials will not be durable and may actually break while you are handling them.

Good Workmanship

There is a saying that any job worth doing is worth doing correctly. When installing cabling, this saying is especially true because shoddy workmanship can cause data transmission quality problems and thus lower the network's effective throughput. If you try to rush a cabling job to meet a deadline, you will usually end up doing some or all of the job over again. For example, when punching down the individual wires in a UTP installation, excessive untwisting of the individual wires can cause excessive near-end crosstalk (NEXT), thus lowering the effective data-carrying capacity of that connection. The connection must be removed and reterminated to correct the problem.

The same holds true for fiber optic cable connections. If you rush any part of the connector installation, the effective optical transmission capacity of that connection will probably be reduced. A reduced capacity means that you may not be able to use that connection at all because the light is being refracted too far outside of the fiber and too much extraneous light gets into the connection, which causes it to fail.

Cabling Topologies

Now that you understand some of the basics of cabling design philosophy, you need to understand physical topologies. A *topology* is basically a map of a network. The *physical topology* of a network describes the layout of the cables and workstations and the location of all network components. Choosing the layout of how computers will be connected in a company's network is critical. It is one of the first choices you will make during the design of the cabling system, and it is an important one because it tells you how the cables are to be run during the installation. Making a wrong decision regarding physical topology and media is costly and disruptive because it means changing an entire installation once it is in place. The typical organization changes the physical layout and physical media of a network only once every 5 to 10 years, so it is important to choose a configuration that you can live with and that allows for growth.

Throughout this book, we've discussed the different types of cabling media and connectors. In this section, we'll look at how to connect the devices in a network using the four most common topologies:

- Bus

- Ring

- Star

- Mesh

For each topology, we will go over how the cables are laid out and the advantages and disadvantages of each topology.

Bus Topology

In a bus topology, all computers are attached to a single cable; this is the simplest way to create a physical network. Originally, computers were attached to the cable with wiretaps. This did not prove practical, so drop cables are now used to attach computers to the main cable. Figure 12.1 shows an example of a bus network. Notice how the cable runs from computer to computer with several bends and twists.

FIGURE 12.1:

An example of a physical bus topology

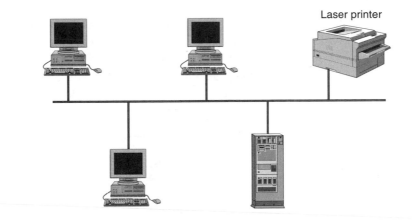

Laser printer

You can see the simplicity of a bus topology. However, what happens if the wire breaks or is disconnected? Neither side can communicate with the other, and signal bounce occurs on both sides, the result being that the entire network is down. For this reason, bus topologies are considered to have very little fault tolerance.

NOTE   Sometimes, because a cable is inside a wall, you cannot physically see a break. To determine if a break has occurred, you can use a tool known as a *time domain reflectometer*, or *TDR (also called a cable tester)*. This device sends out a signal and measures how much time it takes to return. Programmed with the specifications of the cable being tested, it determines where the fault lies with a high degree of accuracy. We'll discuss cable testers in Chapter 14, "Cabling System Testing and Troubleshooting."

There are pros and cons to a bus topology. A bus topology has the following advantages:

- Simple to install
- Relatively inexpensive
- Uses less cable than other topologies

On the other hand, a bus topology has the following disadvantages:

- Difficult to move and change
- Little fault tolerance (a single fault can bring down the entire network)
- Difficult to troubleshoot

The Star Topology

Unlike a bus topology, a star topology connects each computer to a central point with a separate cable. The central point is a device known as a *hub*. Although this setup uses more cable than a bus, a star topology is much more fault tolerant than a bus topology because if a failure occurs along one of the cables connecting to the hub, only that portion of the network is affected, not the entire network. Figure 12.2 shows a typical star topology.

FIGURE 12.2:

A typical star topology with a hub

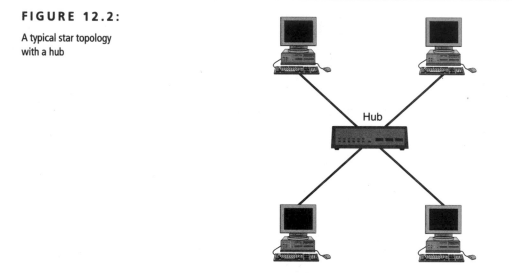

The design of a star topology resembles an old wagon wheel with the wooden spokes extending from the center point. The center point of a wagon wheel is also known as a hub and, like the wagon wheel, the network's most vulnerable point is the hub. If it goes awry, the whole system collapses. Fortunately, hub failures are uncommon.

Just as with the bus topology, the star topology has advantages and disadvantages. The increasing popularity of the star topology is mainly due to the large number of advantages, which include the following:

- It can be reconfigured quickly.

- A single cable failure won't bring down the entire network.

- It is relatively easy to troubleshoot.

The disadvantages of a star topology include the following:

- Total installation cost can be higher because of the larger number of cables.
- It has a single point of failure, the hub.

The Ring Topology

In the ring topology, each computer is connected directly to two other computers in the network. Data moves down a one-way path from one computer to another, as shown in Figure 12.3. The good news about laying cable out in a ring is that the cable design is simple. The bad news is that, as with bus topology, any break, such as adding or removing a computer, disrupts the entire network. For this reason, the physical ring topology is seldom used.

FIGURE 12.3:

A typical ring topology

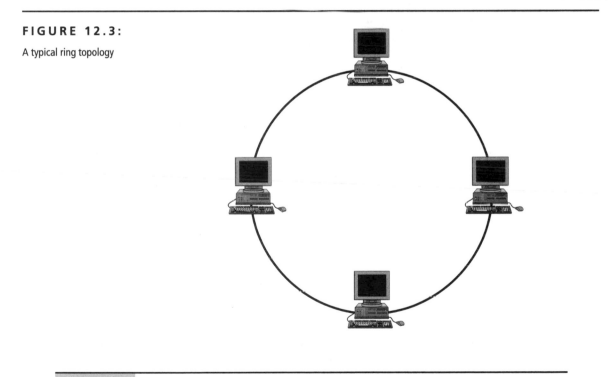

| NOTE | Although its name suggests a relationship, Token Ring does not use a physical ring topology; it uses a physical star, logical ring topology. |

There are a few pros to a ring topology, but there many more cons, which why it is seldom used. On the pro side, the ring topology is relatively easy to troubleshoot. A station will know when a cable fault has occurred because it will stop receiving data from its upstream neighbor.

On the con side, a ring topology is

- Expensive because multiple cables are needed for each workstation.

- Difficult to reconfigure.

- Not fault tolerant. A single cable fault can bring down the entire network.

The Mesh Topology

In a mesh topology (as shown in Figure 12.4), a path exists from each station to every other station in the network. While not usually seen in LANs, a variation on this type of topology, the hybrid mesh, is used on the Internet and other WANs in a limited fashion. *Hybrid mesh* topology networks can have multiple connections between some locations, but this is done for redundancy. Also, there is not a true mesh because there is not a connection between each and every node; there are just a few, for backup purposes. Notice how complex connections become with four connections, however.

FIGURE 12.4:

A typical mesh topology

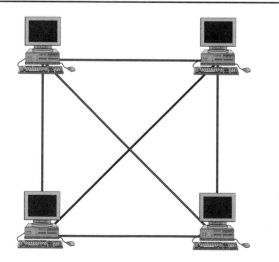

As you can see in Figure 12.4, a mesh topology can become quite complex as wiring and connections increase exponentially. For every n stations, you will have $n(n-1)/2$ connections. For example, in a network of four computers, you will have $4(4-1)/2$ connections, or six connections. If your network grows to only 10 computers, you will have 45 connections to manage! Given this impossible overhead, only small systems can be connected this way. The advantage to all the work this topology requires is a more fail-safe or fault-tolerant network, at least as far as cabling is concerned. On the con side, the mesh topology is expensive and, as you have seen, quickly becomes too complex. Today, the mesh topology is rarely used, and then only in a WAN environment because it is fault-tolerant. Computers or network devices can switch between these multiple, redundant connections if the need arises.

Backbones and Segments

With complex networks, there must be a way of intelligently identifying which part of the network you are discussing. For this reason, networks are commonly broken into backbones and segments. Figure 12.5 shows a sample network and identifies the backbones and segments. You can refer to this figure as necessary as we discuss backbones and segments.

FIGURE 12.5:

Backbones and segments on a sample network

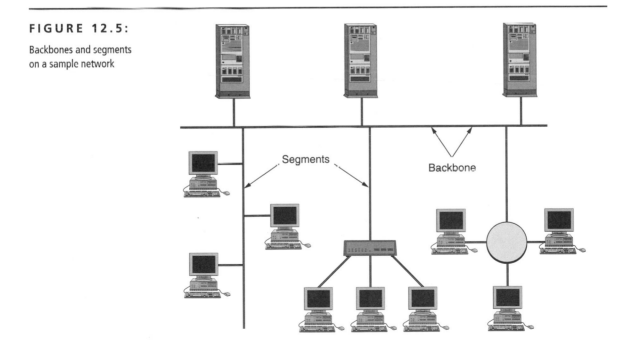

Understanding the Backbone

The *backbone* is the part of the network to which all segments and servers connect. A backbone provides the structure for a network and is considered the main part of any network. It usually uses a high-speed communications technology of some kind (such as FDDI [Fiber Distributed Data Interface] or 100Mb Ethernet). All servers and all network segments typically connect directly to the backbone so that any segment is only one segment away from any server on that backbone. Having all segments close to the servers makes the network efficient. Notice in Figure 12.5 that the three servers and three segments all connect to the backbone.

Understanding Segments

Segment is a general term for any short section of the network that is not part of the backbone. Just as servers connect to the backbone, workstations connect to segments. Segments are connected to the backbone to allow the workstations on them access to the rest of the network. Figure 12.5 shows three segments.

Selecting the Right Topology

It is clear that each topology has its advantages and drawbacks. The process of selecting a topology can be much like buying a pair of shoes: it's a matter of finding something that fits, feels right, and is within your budget. Instead of asking questions such as what your shoe size is, however, you need to ask how much fault tolerance is necessary and how often you'll need to reconfigure the network. A bus topology is usually the most efficient choice if you're creating a simple network for a handful of computers in a single room because it is simple and easy to install. Larger environments are usually wired in a star topology because MACs to the network are accomplished more efficiently with a physical star.

On the other hand, if *uptime* is your primary definition of fault resistant (that is, 99 percent uptime, or less than eight hours total downtime per year), you should seriously consider a mesh layout. However, while you are thinking about how fault tolerant a mesh network is, let the word *maintenance* enter your thoughts. Remember, you will have $n(n-1)/2$ connections to maintain, and this can quickly become a nightmare and exceed your maintenance budget.

Generally speaking, balance the following considerations when choosing a physical topology for your network:

- Cost

- Ease of installation
- Ease of maintenance
- Cable fault tolerance

Cabling Plant Uses

Another consideration to take into account when designing and installing a structured cabling system is the intended use of the various cables in the system. A few years ago, "structured cabling system" usually meant a company's data network cabling. Today, cabling systems are used to carry various kinds of information, including the following:

- Data
- Telephone
- Television
- Fire detection and security

When designing and installing your cabling system, you must keep in mind what kind of information is going to be traveling on this network and what kinds of cables are required to carry that information.

Since this entire book is mainly about data cabling, we'll assume you know that cables can be run for data. So, let's start this discussion with a discussion of telephone wiring.

Telephone

The oldest (and probably most common) use for a cabling system is to carry telephone signals. In the old days, pairs of copper wires were strung throughout a building to carry the phone signal from a central telephone closet to the individual telephone handsets. In the telephone closet, the individual wires were brought together and mechanically and electrically connected to all the incoming telephone lines so that the entire building was connected to the outside world. Surprisingly, the basic layout for a telephone cabling system has changed very little. The major difference today is that telephone systems have become digital, so most require a device known as a *private branch exchange* (PBX). A PBX is a special device that connects all the individual telephones together so the telephone calls can go out over one high-speed line (called a *trunk line*), rather than multiple individual lines. Figure 12.6 shows how a current telephone network is arranged.

FIGURE 12.6:

An example of a telephone network

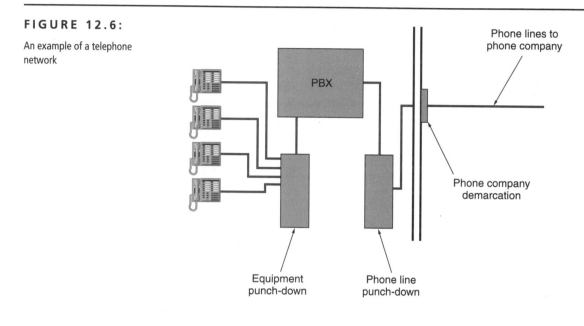

Generally speaking, today's telephone networks are run along the same cabling paths as the data cabling for a company. Additionally, telephone systems use the same UTP cable that many networks use for carrying data. They will usually share the same wiring closets with the data and television cabling. The wires from telephone connections can be terminated almost identically to data cabling.

Television

With the increase in the use of on-demand video technology, it is now commonplace to run television cable alongside data and television cabling. In businesses where local cable access is possible, television cable will be run into the building and distributed to many areas in the building to provide cable access. You may be wondering what cable TV has to do with business. The answer is plenty. News, stock updates, technology access, public access programs, and most importantly,

Internet connections can all be delivered through television cable. Additionally, television cable is used for security cameras in buildings.

Like telephone cable, television cables can share the wiring pathways with their data counterparts. Television cable typically uses coaxial cable (usually RG-6/U cable) along with screw-on, 75-ohm coaxial connectors. The cables to the various outlets are run back to a central point where they are connected to a distribution device. This device is usually an unpowered splitter, but it can also be a powered, complex device known as a television distribution frame. Figure 12.7 shows how a typical television cabling system might look. Notice the similarities between Figures 12.7 and 12.6. The topology is basically the same.

FIGURE 12.7:

A typical television cable installation

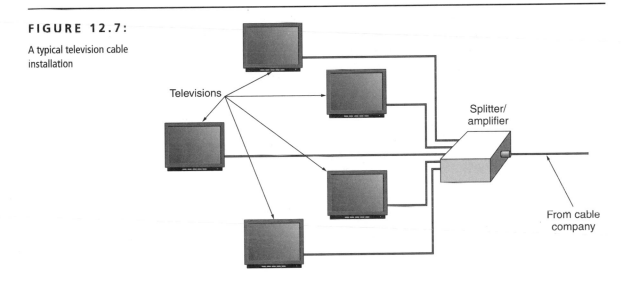

Fire Detection and Security Cabling

One category of cabling that often gets overlooked is the cabling for fire detection and security devices. Examples of these devices include glass breakage sensors, smoke alarms, motion sensors, and door opening sensors. These devices usually run on DC current anywhere from +12 to +24 volts. Cables must be run from each of these devices back to the central security controller. These cables can be (and usually are) UTP cables. Because they usually carry power, these cables should be run separately from, or at least perpendicular to, copper cables that are carrying data.

Choice of Media

A very important consideration when designing a cabling system for your company is which media to use. Different media have different specifications that make them better suited for a particular type of installation. For example, for a simple, low-cost installation, some types of copper media might be a better choice because of its ease of installation and low cost. In previous chapters, you learned about the different types of cabling media that are available and their different communication aspects, so we won't reiterate them here. However, to make your design and installation decisions easier, Table 12.1 summarizes each type.

TABLE 12.1: Summary of Cabling Media Types

Media	Advantages	Disadvantages
Copper	• Cheap • Widely available • Mature standards • Easy to install	• Susceptible to EMI and eavesdropping • Only covers short (<1Km) distances without additional devices
Fiber	• High data rates possible • Immune to EMI and eavesdropping	• Moderately expensive • Difficult to install
Wireless	• Few distance limitations • Relatively easy to install	• Atmospheric attenuation • More expensive than cabled media • Some wireless frequencies require an FCC license

Telecommunications Closets

Telecommunications closets (also called *cabling closets*) are the closets within a building where all telecommunications wiring terminates. These closets are the start and endpoints of all telecommunications cabling within a single floor of a building; there is usually one closet on each floor of a building, and it is usually in a central location. Cables are generally run from these closets to the individual stations or to other telecommunications closets. Figure 12.8 shows an example of how telecommunications closets are placed in an average building.

FIGURE 12.8:

Placement of telecommunications closets

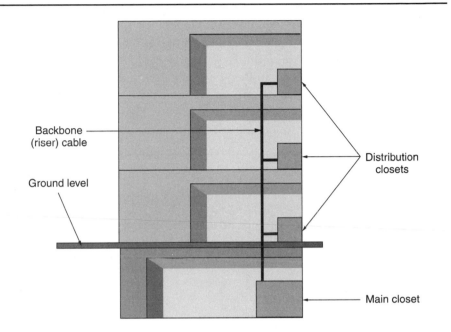

In this section, you will learn what components can be found inside a telecommunications closet and some of the considerations to take into account when bringing cables and devices into a telecommunications closet, including the following:

- LAN wiring
- Telephone wiring
- Power requirements
- HVAC considerations

Each of these will have an impact on the design, ease of installation, and operation of your cabling system. Therefore, they must be taken into consideration when designing the system.

LAN Wiring

The first item that will draw your attention inside a telecommunications closet is the large bundle of cables coming into the closet. This bundle contains the cables that run from the closet to the individual stations. Additionally, this bundle may contain cables that run from this closet to other closets in the building. The bundle of cables is usually bound together with straps of some kind and leads the LAN cables to a cabling device known as a patch panel. This device connects the individual wires within a particular cable to network ports on the front of the panel. These ports can then be connected to the network equipment (hubs, switches, routers, and so on). Additionally, two ports can be connected together using a small cable known as a *patch cable*. Figure 12.9 shows an example of the hardware typically found in a telecommunications closet.

FIGURE 12.9:

Telecommunications closet hardware examples

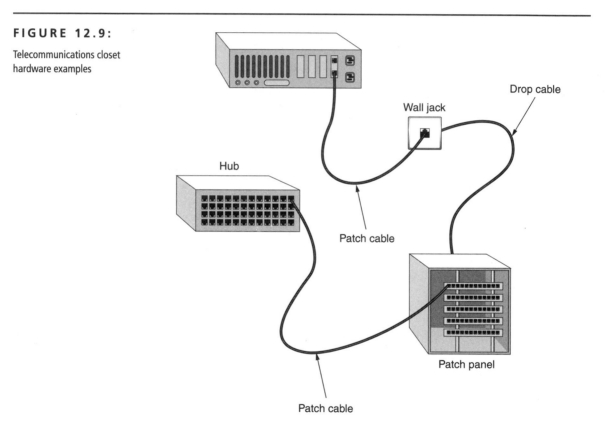

Patch panels come in many different shapes and sizes (as shown in Figure 12.10). Some are mounted on a wall and are known as *surface-mount patch panels* (also called p*unch-down blocks*). Others are mounted in a rack and are called *rack-mount patch panels*. Each type has its own benefits. Surface-mount panels are cheaper and easier to work with, but they can't hold as many cables and ports. Rack-mount panels are more flexible, but they are more expensive. Surface-mount patch panels make good choices for smaller (less than 50 drops) cabling installations. Rack-mount patch panels make better choices for larger installations. Patch panels are the main products used in LAN installation today because they are extremely cost-effective.

FIGURE 12.10:

Patch panel examples

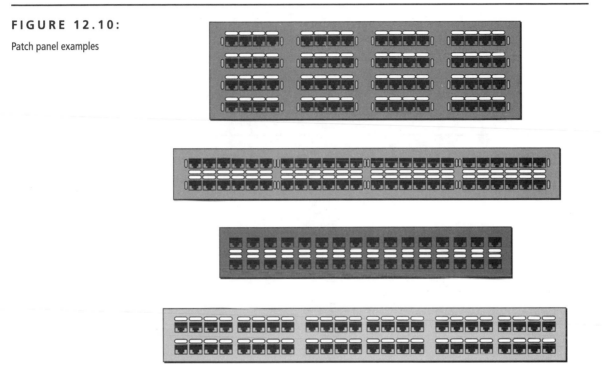

Telephone Wiring

In addition to the LAN wiring components found in the telecommunications closet, you will usually also find all of the wiring for the telephone system. This is because the two are interrelated. In most companies, you will find both a computer and a telephone on every desk. There are even software programs available that can connect the two technologies and allow you to receive all of your voice-mails as e-mails. These programs integrate with your current e-mail system to provide integrated messaging services (a technology known as *telephony*).

The telephone cables from the individual telephones will come into the tele-communications closet in approximately the same location. They will then be terminated in some kind of patch panel. More often than not, the individual wires will be punched down in what is known as a 66-block. A *66-block* is a type of punch-down block that uses small "fingers" of metal to connect different UTP wires together. The wires on one side of the 66-block are from the individual wires in the individual cables for the telephone system.

The wires on the other side of the block usually come from the telephone PBX. The PBX controls all the incoming and outgoing calls as well as which pair of wires is for which telephone extension. The PBX has connectors on the back that allow 25 telephone pairs to be connected to a single 66-block at a time using a single 50-pin connector (as shown in Figure 12.11).

FIGURE 12.11:

Connecting a PBX to a 66-block

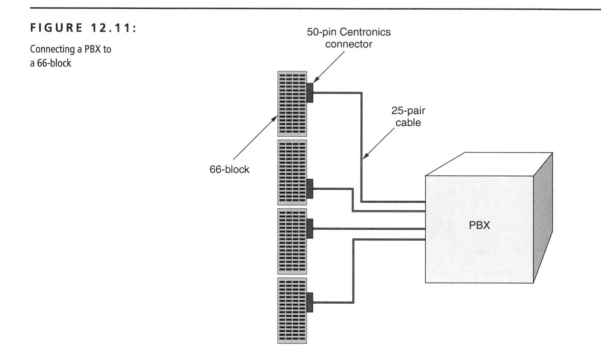

Many of these 66-blocks are placed on a large piece of plywood fastened to the wall (as shown in Figure 12.12). Typically, there are a large number of 66-blocks on this piece of plywood—as many as are required to support the number of cables for the telephone system.

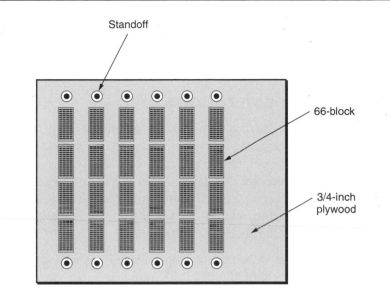

Multiple 66-blocks in a wiring closet

Power Requirements

With all of these devices in the wiring closet, it stands to reason that you are going to need some power receptacles in the closet. Telecommunications closets have some unique power requirements. First of all, each of the many small electronic devices will need power, and a single duplex outlet will not have enough outlets for all these devices. Additionally, these devices should all be on an electrical circuit that is dedicated to that wiring closet and is separate from the rest of the building. This circuit should have its own isolated ground. An *isolated ground* in commercial wiring is where a ground wire for the particular isolated outlet is run in the same conduit as the electrical supply connectors. This ground is called isolated because it is not tied into the grounding of the conduit at all. The wire runs from the receptacle back to the point where the grounds and neutrals are tied together in the circuit panel. You can identify isolated ground outlets in a commercial building because they are orange with a small green triangle on them.

NOTE   Most, if not all, residential outlets have an isolated ground because conduit is not used and these outlets have to have a ground wire in the cable.

As to the number of outlets needed for a telecommunications closet, usually a few strategically placed duplex receptacles (space for four plugs) will suffice. If any more are needed, rack-mount power strips can be (and often are) used. Just make sure you don't exceed the amperage rating of the power strip.

HVAC Considerations

In case you haven't heard it before, the abbreviation *HVAC* stands for heating, ventilation, and air conditioning and is usually used to refer to the various climate-control machinery installed in a building to keep rooms at a constant temperature and humidity. Computer and networking equipment generates a lot of heat. Place enough equipment in a telecommunications closet without ventilation, and the temperature will quickly rise to dangerous levels. High temperatures are the downfall of electronic components.

For this reason, telecommunications closets should be sufficiently ventilated. At the very least, there should be some kind of fan to exchange the air in the closet. Some telecommunications closets aren't closets at all but are, in fact, pretty good-sized rooms with their own HVAC controls.

Cabling Management

Another aspect of a good cabling design and installation is cabling management. *Cabling management* is the process of guiding the cable to its intended destination without damaging it or its data-carrying capabilities. There are many different cabling products available to protect cable, make it look good, and help find the cables faster. They fall into three categories:

- Physical protection
- Electrical protection
- Fire protection

In this section, we will look at the various devices used to provide each level of protection and the concepts and procedures that go along with them.

Physical Protection

Cables are fragile things that are easily cut and broken. When performing a proper cabling design and installation, cables should be protected. There are many items that are currently used to protect cables from damage, including the following:

- Conduit
- Cable trays
- Standoffs
- D-rings

Let's take a brief look at each of these items and the different ways they are used to protect cables from damage in a cabling system.

Conduit

The simplest form of cable protection is the use of a metal or plastic conduit to protect the cable as it travels through walls and ceilings. Conduit is really nothing more than a thin-walled plastic or metal pipe. Conduit is used in many commercial installations to contain electrical wires. When electricians run conduit for electrical installation in a new building, they can also run additional conduit for network wiring. Conduit is put in place and the individual cables are run inside the conduit.

The main advantage to conduit is that it is the simplest and most robust protection for a network cable. Also, if you use plastic conduit, it can be a relatively cheap solution (metal conduit is more expensive).

Cable Trays

When running cable, the cable must be supported every approximately 6 to 12 inches when hanging horizontally. Supporting the cable prevents it from sagging and putting stress on the conductors inside. For this reason, special devices are installed in ceilings known as *cable trays* (also sometimes called *ladder racks*, because of their appearance). The horizontal cables from the telecommunications closets that run to the individual telecommunications outlets are usually placed into this tray to support them as they run horizontally. Figure 12.13 shows an example of a cable tray. This type of cable support system hangs from the ceiling and can support hundreds of individual cables.

Standoffs

When terminating UTP wires for telephone applications in a telecommunications closet, you will often see telephone wires run from a 100-pair cable to the 66-punch-down-block. To be neat, the individual conductors are run around the outside of the board that the punch-down blocks are mounted to (as shown in Figure 12.14). To prevent damage to the individual conductors, they are bent around devices known as standoffs. These objects are usually made of plastic and are screwed to the mounting board every foot or so (also shown in Figure 12.14).

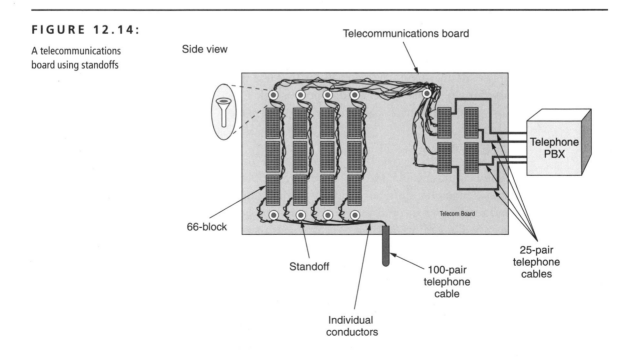

D-Rings

For LAN installations that use racks to hold patch panels, you need some method of keeping the cables together and organized as they come out of the cable trays or ladder racks and enter the telecommunications closet to be terminated. On many racks, special metal rings called *D-rings* (named after their shape) are used to keep the individual cables in bundles and keep them close to the rack (as shown in Figure 12.15).

FIGURE 12.15:

D-rings in a cabling closet for a cabling rack

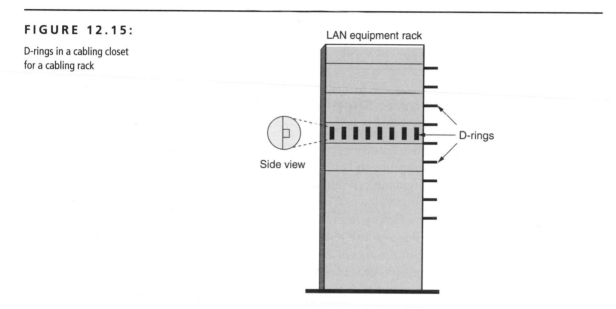

In addition to managing cable for a cabling rack, D-rings are also used on punch-down boards on the wall to manage cables, much in the same way standoffs are. Instead of standoffs, D-rings are put in place to support the individual cables, and the cables are run to the individual punch-down blocks on the wall. This setup is similar to the one shown earlier in Figure 12.14.

Electrical Protection (Spike Protection)

In addition to physical protection, you must take electrical protection into account when designing and installing your cabling system. Electricity powers the network, switches, hubs, PCs, and computer servers. Variations in power can cause problems ranging from having to reboot after a short loss of service to damaged equipment and data. Fortunately, a number of products are available to help protect sensitive systems from the dangers of lightning strikes, dirty (uneven) power, and accidental power cable disconnection, including surge protectors, standby power supplies, uninterruptible power supplies, and line conditioners.

NOTE
Power output from battery-powered inverters isn't exactly perfect. Normal power output alternates polarity 60 times a second (60Hz). When graphed, this output looks like a sine wave. Output from inverters is stepped to approximate this sine wave output, but it really never duplicates it. Today's inverter technology can come extremely close, but the differences between inverter and true AC power can cause damage to computer power supplies over the long run.

Standby Power Supply (SPS)

A standby power supply (SPS) contains a battery, a switchover circuit, and an inverter (a device that converts the DC voltage from the battery into the AC voltage that the computer and peripherals need). The outlets on the SPS are connected to the switching circuit, which is in turn connected to the incoming AC power (called line voltage). The switching circuit monitors the line voltage. When it drops below a factory preset threshold, the switching circuit switches from line voltage to the battery and inverter. The battery and inverter power the outlets (and, thus, the computers or devices plugged into them) until the switching circuit detects line voltage is present again at the correct levels. The switching circuit then switches the outlets back to line voltage.

Uninterruptible Power Supply (UPS)

A UPS is another type of battery backup often found on computers and network devices today. It is similar to an SPS in that it has outlets, a battery, and an inverter. The similarities end there, however. A UPS uses an entirely different method to provide continuous AC voltage to the equipment it supports.

In a UPS, the equipment is always running off the inverter and battery. A UPS contains a charging/monitoring circuit that charges the battery constantly. It also monitors the AC line voltage. When a power failure occurs, the charger stops charging the battery, but the equipment never senses any change in power. The monitoring part of the circuit senses the change and emits a beep to tell the user the power has failed.

Fire Protection

All buildings and their contents are subject to destruction and damage if a fire occurs. The cabling in a building is no exception. There are a few cabling design concerns you must keep in mind to prevent fire, smoke, or heat from damaging your cabling system, the premises on which they are installed, or any occupants.

The primary concern should be for human safety. Remember that some types of cable (specifically, PVC-jacketed cable) give off a toxic gas, dioxin, when burned. Therefore, you should never install PVC-jacketed cable in a plenum airway (as discussed earlier in Chapter 1). Instead, you should make sure to install only plenum-rated cables in plenum air spaces. It may cost a few cents more per linear foot, but the cost is worth it for health and safety.

Another concern is the puncturing of fire barriers. In most residential and commercial buildings, there are walls built specifically to stop the spread of a fire within a building. Whenever there is an opening in a floor or ceiling that could possibly serve as a conduit for fire to travel through, it is walled over with fire-rated drywall to make a firewall that will prevent the spread of fire (or at least slow it down). In commercial buildings, cinder block walls are often erected as firewalls between rooms.

Because firewalls prevent the spread of fire, it is important not to compromise the protection they offer by punching holes in them for network cables. If you need to run a network cable through a firewall, first try to see if there is another possible route that won't compromise the integrity of the firewall. If there isn't, you must use an approved firewall penetration device (see Figure 12.16). These devices have gaskets that form a tight seal over each cable that passes through the firewall. These gaskets are made of materials that are *intumescent*, that is, they expand several times their normal size when exposed to very high heat (fire temperatures). During a fire, the intumescent materials in these gaskets expand to seal the hole in the firewall. That way, the gases and heat from a fire won't pass through the firewall.

FIGURE 12.16:

An example of a firewall penetration device

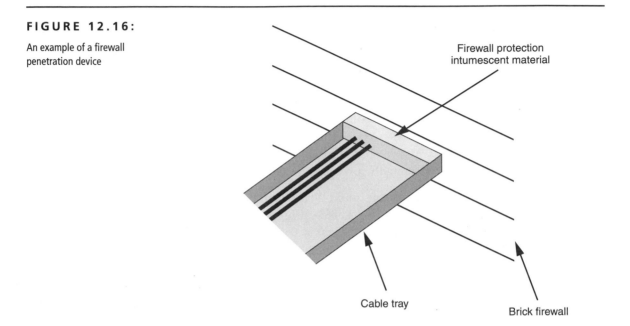

Firewall protection intumescent material

Cable tray

Brick firewall

Data and Cabling Security

Your network cables carry all the data that crosses your network. If the data your cables carry is sensitive and should not be viewed by just anyone, you may need to take extra steps when designing and installing your cabling system to ensure that the data stays where it belongs: inside the cables. The level of protection you employ depends on how sensitive the data is and how much of a problem could be caused by someone stealing the data. Cabling security measures can range from the simple to the absurdly complex.

There are a few ways to prevent data from being intercepted by anyone other than the intended recipient. These methods include the following:

- EM (electromagnetic) transmission regulation
- Tapping prevention

EM (Electromagnetic) Transmission Regulation

As mentioned in earlier chapters, every current-carrying conductor produces a magnetic field. You should know that the pattern of the magnetic field matches the pattern of the signals being transmitted. Based on this concept, there are devices that can be placed around a cable to intercept these magnetic signals and turn them back into an electrical signals that can be sent to another (unwanted) location. This process is known as *EM (electromagnetic) signal interception*.

This kind of signal interception can be minimized by using shielded cables or by encasing all cabling runs in a grounded metal conduit from source to destination. These shielding methods reduce the amount of stray EM signals.

Tapping Prevention

The process of installing listening devices to intercept LAN EM signals is known as *tapping*. Tapping is done by anyone who has something to gain by intercepting those LAN signals. These people will place an interception device (known as a *tap*) around the cable so that it can intercept the EM signals. Some tapping devices will actually puncture the outer jacket of a cable and touch the metal inner conductor of the cable, allowing it to intercept all signals sent through that cable.

To prevent taps, the best course of action is to install the cables in metal conduit or to use armored cable, where practical. When the metal conduit is grounded, this will provide protection from both types of taps. When not practical, physical security can make tapping much more difficult. If the person trying to tap your communications can't get to your cables, they can't tap them. This means you must install cables in secure locations and restrict access to them by locking the cabling closets. Remember: if you don't have physical security, you don't have network security.

Cabling Installation Process

Now that we've covered some of the factors to take into account when designing a cabling system, it's time to discuss the process of actually installing an entire cabling system, from start to finish. A cabling installation is a five-step process:

1. Design the cabling system.

2.   Schedule the installation.

3.   Install the cables.

4.   Terminate the cables.

5.   Test the installation.

Design the Cabling System

We've already covered this part of the installation in detail in this chapter. However, it's important enough to reiterate: Following proper cabling design procedures will ensure the success of your cabling system installation. Before you pull a single cable, you should have a detailed plan of how the installation will proceed. You should also know the scope of the project (how many cable runs need to be made, what connections need to made and where, how long this project will take, and so on). Finally, you should have the design plan available to all people involved with the installation of the cable. That list of people includes the cabling installer, the electrical inspector, the building inspector, the customer (even if you are the customer), and so on. Be sure to include anyone who needs to refer to the way the cabling is being installed. At the very least, this information should contain a blueprint of how the cables will be installed.

Schedule the Installation

In addition to having a proper cabling design, you should also know approximately how long the installation will take and pick the best time to do it. For example, the best time for a new cabling installation is while the building studs are still exposed and electrical boxes can be easily installed. From a planning standpoint, this is approximately the same time in new construction where the electrical cabling is installed. In fact, because of the obvious connection between electrical and telecommunications wiring, many electrical contractors are now learning how to do low voltage (data) wiring so they can contract the wiring for both the electrical system and the telecommunications systems.

For installations that happen after construction, you should schedule them so they have the least impact on the existing network or existing building infrastructure and the building's occupants.

Install the Cabling

Once you have a design and a proper schedule, you can proceed with the actual installation of the cables for the cabling system. This is probably the most repetitious part of the entire cabling system installation, during which you install cable from the telecommunications closet(s) to the locations of the individual devices in the network. These are some of the items you must understand for the installation of the cable:

- Cabling tools
- Pulling cable
- Cabling system documentation
- Copper-specific cabling installation issues
- Fiber-specific cabling installation issues

Let's start this discussion with a brief discussion of the tools you will need in order to do this.

Cabling Tools

"The right tool for the right job." How many times have you heard that phrase? Just like any other industry, cable installation has its own tools, some of which are not so obvious, including the following:

- Pen and paper
- Hand tools
- Cable spool racks
- Fish tape
- Fish cord
- Cable pulling lubricant
- Two-way radio
- Labeling materials
- Tennis ball

Let's go over how each of these tools is used in the process of installing the cables for a cabling system.

NOTE   Tools are covered in more detail in Chapter 6, "Tools of the Trade."

Pen and Paper   Not every cabling installer may think of these as tools, but they are. It is a good idea to have a pen and paper handy when installing the individual cables so that you can make notes about how particular cables are routed and installed. You should also note any problems that occur during installation. Finally, during the testing phase (discussed later), you can record test data in the notebook.

These notes are invaluable when it's time to troubleshoot an installation. You'll know exactly where particular wires run and how they were installed. This information can save you hours of troubleshooting, especially when you have to trace a particular cable.

Hand Tools   It's fairly obvious that a variety of hand tools are needed during a cabling installation. During the course of the installation, you will need to remove various screws, assemble various types of screws, hit things, cut things, and perform various types of construction and destruction tasks. Some examples of the hand tools you should make sure to include in your tool kit are (but are not limited to) the following:

- Screwdrivers (Phillips, slotted, and Torx drivers)
- Hammer
- Cable cutters
- Wire strippers
- Punch-down tool
- Drywall saw

Cable Spool Racks   It is usually inefficient to pull one cable at a time during installation. Typically, more than one cable will be going from the cabling closet (usually the source of a cable run) to a workstation outlet. For this reason, a cable installer will tape several cables together and pull them as one bundle. This approach will allow all the cables to be pulled in a shorter period of time than if each cable were pulled separately.

The tool used to assist in pulling multiple cables is the *cable spool rack* (see Figure 12.17). As you can see, the spools of cable are mounted on the rack. These racks can hold multiple spools to facilitate the pulling of multiple cables simultaneously.

FIGURE 12.17:

Cable spool rack

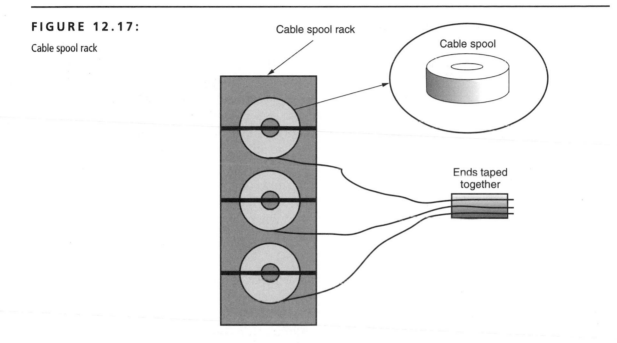

Fish Tape   Many times, you will have to run cable into narrow conduits or narrow crawl spaces. Cables are flexible, much like rope. Just as you really can't push rope into a small space or push it up a vertical conduit, when you try to stuff a cable into a narrow space, it simply bunches up inside the conduit. You need a way of pulling the cable through that narrow space or providing some rigid backbone: fish tape. A *fish tape* is really nothing more than a roll of $1/4$-inch wide spring steel with a hook on the end. A bunch of cables can be hooked and pulled through a small area, or the cables can be taped to the fish tape and "pushed" through the conduit or wall cavity.

Fish Cord   Another way to pull cables through small spaces is through the use of nylon fish cord. *Fish cord* (also called a *pull string*) is simply a cord made of nylon fibers that is strong enough to pull several cables through a conduit or wall cavity. The fish cord is either put in place before all the cables are pulled, or it is run at the same time as the cables. If the fish cord is run at the same time, it can be used to pull additional cables through the same conduit as already installed cables.

Cable Pulling Lubricant   It is important not to put too much stress on network cables as they are being pulled. If too much stress is put on the cable, the conductors could lose their transmission efficiency. At the worst, they could break. To prevent stress on the cable during the pulling of a cable through a conduit, a chemical lubricant known as *cable pulling lubricant* is applied. This lubricant reduces the friction between the cable being pulled and its surroundings and is specially formulated so as not to plug up the conduit or dissolve the jackets of the other cables. It should be used any time cable needs to be pulled in tight quarters.

Labeling Materials   With the hundreds of cables that need to be pulled in large cabling installations, it makes a great deal of sense to label both ends of each cable while it's being pulled. That way, when it's time to terminate each individual cable, you will know which cable goes where, and you can document that fact on your cabling map.

For this purpose, you will need some labeling materials. The most common cable-labeling materials are the sticky numbers sold by Panduit and other companies (check with your cabling supplier to see what they recommend). You should pick a numbering standard, stick with it, and record all the numbered cables and their uses in your cabling documentation. A good system is to start with 1 for the first cable and go up from there without duplicating numbers. You could also use combinations of letters and numbers. To label the cables, stick a number on each of the cables you are pulling and stick another of the same number on the box or spool of cable that the cable is coming out of. That way, when you are finished pulling the cable, both ends will be numbered. You can cut the cable and stick the number from the cable spool onto the cut end of the cable. Voila! Both ends are numbered. Don't forget to record the number of each cable and where it's going on your notepad.

Two-Way Radio   This cabling tool isn't used as often as some of the others listed here, but it comes in handy when two people are pulling cable as a team.

Two-way radios allow two people who are cabling within a building to communicate with each other without having to shout down a hallway or use cell phones. This is especially true if the radios have hands-free headset microphones. Many two-way radios have maximum operating ranges of greater than several kilometers; this makes them effective for cabling even very large factories and buildings.

Tennis Ball   You may be saying, "Okay. I know why these other tools are listed here, but a tennis ball?" Think of this situation. You've got to run several cables through a plenum airspace above a suspended ceiling. Let's say the cable run is 75 meters (around 225 feet) long. The conventional way to run this cable is to remove the ceiling tiles that run underneath the cable path, climb a ladder, and run the cable as far as you can reach (or throw). Then move the ladder, pull the cable a few feet farther, and repeat until you reach the end. An easier way to do it is to tie a pull string to a tennis ball (using duct tape, nails, screws, or whatever) and throw the tennis ball from source to destination. The other end of the pull string can be tied to the bundle of cables so that it can be pulled from source to destination without going up and down ladders too many times.

TIP
You may think using a tennis ball is a makeshift tool, but cabling installers have been making their own tools for as long as there have been installers. You may find that a tool you make yourself works better that any tool you can buy.

Pulling Cable

The process of running the individual network cables from the telecommunications closet to an outlet is known as *pulling cable*. This is because you actually pull the cables through the ceiling and walls. The cable will unspool from its container as you pull. Once the cable has been pulled from one location to another, you can cut the cables, label them (on both ends, of course), and start another pull.

There are several considerations to keep in mind when pulling cable to ensure the proper operation of the network. These considerations include the following:

- Tensile strength
- Bend radius
- Protecting the cable while pulling

Tensile Strength   Contrary to popular opinion, network cables are fragile. They can be damaged in any number of ways, especially during the pulling process. The most important consideration to remember when pulling cable is the tensile strength of the cable you are pulling. A cable's *tensile strength* is a measure of how strong a cable is along its axis. The higher the tensile strength, the more resistant the cable is to stretching, and thus, breaking. A cable's tensile strength is normally given in pounds per square inch (psi). The higher the value, the more tensile strength a particular cable has and the harder you can pull on it before causing damage to the cable.

> **TIP**
>
> When pulling cable, don't exert a pull force on the cable greater than the tensile strength of the cable. If you do, you will cause damage to the cable and its internal conductors. If a conductor break occurs, you may not know it until you terminate and test the cable. If it breaks, you will have to replace the whole cable.

Bend Radius   Most cables are designed to flex, and it's this flexibility that makes them easy to use and install. Unfortunately, just because they can flex doesn't mean that they should be bent as far as possible around corners and other obstacles. Both copper and fiber optic cables have a value known as the *maximum bend radius* of that cable. TIA/EIA-568-A specifies that copper cables should be bent no tighter than four times their diameter. For example, if a cable has $1/4$-inch radius, it should be bent no tighter than two inches. That is, a $1/4$-inch radius equals a $1/2$-inch diameter. Four times $1/2$ of an inch is two inches, so that means you can bend this cable no more than two inches. Figure 12.18 illustrates how bend radius is measured.

> **TIP**
>
> There are some devices you can purchase from cabling products vendors to aid in the pulling of cable so that the maximum bend radius is not exceeded. These devices are basically plastic or metal corners with large bend radii to help guide a cable around a corner.

FIGURE 12.18:

Bend radius for cable
installation

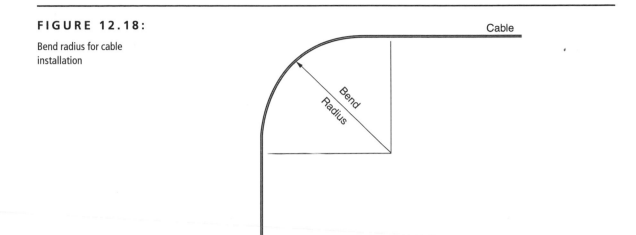

Protection While Pulling   In addition to being careful not to exceed either the tensile strength or bend radius of a particular cable when pulling it, you should also be careful not to pull the cable over or near anything that could damage it. For example, never pull cables over sharp, metal corners as these could cut into the outside jacket of the cable and, possibly, the interior conductors.

There are many things that could damage the cable during its installation. Just use common sense. If you would damage your finger (or any other body part) by running it across the surface you want to pull the cable across, chances are that it's not a good idea to run a cable over it either.

Cabling System Documentation

The most often overlooked item during cable installation is the documentation of the new cabling system. Cabling system documentation includes information about what components make up a cabling system, how it is put together, and where to find individual cables. This information is compiled in a set of documents that can be referred to by the network administrator or cabling installer any time moves, adds, or changes need to be made to the cabling system.

The most useful piece of cabling system documentation is the cabling map. Just as its name implies, a *cabling map* indicates where every cable starts and ends. It also indicates approximately where each cable runs. Additionally, a cabling map can indicate things like the location of workstations, segments, hubs, routers, closets, and other cabling devices.

To make an efficient cabling map, you need to have unique numbers for *all* parts of your cabling system. For example, a single cable run from a cabling closet to wall plate should have the same number on the patch panel port, patch cable, wall cable, and wall plate. This way, you can refer to a specific run of cable at any point in the system, and you can put numbers on the cabling map to refer to each individual cable run.

The bottom line is that every cable should have an alphanumeric designation that translates to both a number on the wall plate and a number on a patch panel. This will make your job much easier when you're tracing a cable.

Cable Termination

Now that you've learned about installing the actual cable, you need to know what to do with both ends of the cable. *Terminating* the cables involves installing some kind of connector on each end (either a connector or a termination block) so that the cabling system can be accessed by the devices that are going to use it. This is the part of cabling system installation that requires the most painstaking attention to detail, because the quality of the termination greatly affects the quality of the signal being transmitted. Sloppy termination will yield an installation that won't support higher-speed technologies.

There are many different termination methods; however, they can really be classified as one of two methods: connectorizing or patch panel termination. *Connectorizing* (putting some kind of connector directly on the end of the cable in the wall) is covered in detail in Chapter 13, "Cable Connector Installation," so let's briefly discuss patch panel termination.

There are many different types of patch panels, some for copper, some for fiber. Copper cable patch panels for UTP all have a few similar characteristics, for the most part. First off, most UTP LAN patch panels (as shown in Figure 12.19) have UTP ports on the front and punch-down blades (see Figure 12.20) in the back. During termination, the individual conductors in the UTP cable are pressed between the metal blades to make both the mechanical and electrical connection between the cable and the connector on the front of the patch panel. This type of patch panel is known as a *110-punch-down-block* (or 110-block, for short).

FIGURE 12.19:

A sample patch panel

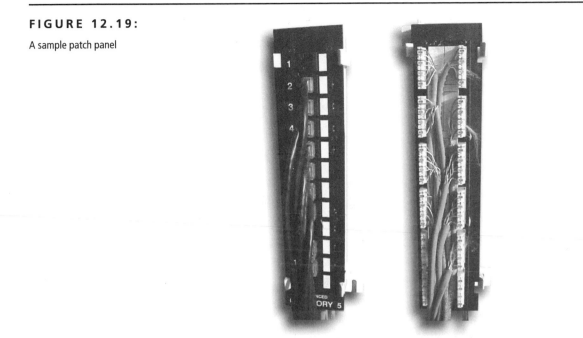

FIGURE 12.20:

Punch-down blade on a
110-block

The procedure for connecting an individual cable is as follows:

1. Route the cable to the back of the punch-down block.

2. Strip off about $1/2$–$3/4$ inches of the cabling jacket. (Be careful not to strip off too much as that can cause interference problems.)

3. Untwist each pair of UTP conductors and push each conductor onto its slot between the color-coded "finger," as shown here.

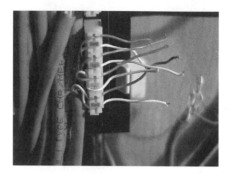

WARNING   Make sure that no more than ½ inch of each twisted conductor pair is untwisted when terminated.

4. Using a 110-punch-down tool, push the conductor into the 110-block so that the metal fingers of the 110-block cut into the center of each conductor, thus making the connection, as shown here.

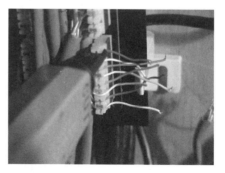

5. Repeat steps 3 and 4 for each conductor.

The above process works only for UTP cables. Fiber optic cables use different termination methods. For the most part, fiber optic cables do use patch panels, but you can't punch down a fiber optic cable because of the delicate nature of the optical fibers. Instead, the individual fiber optic cables are simply connectorized and connected to a special "pass-through" patch panel (as shown in Figure 12.21).

FIGURE 12.21:

A fiber optic patch panel

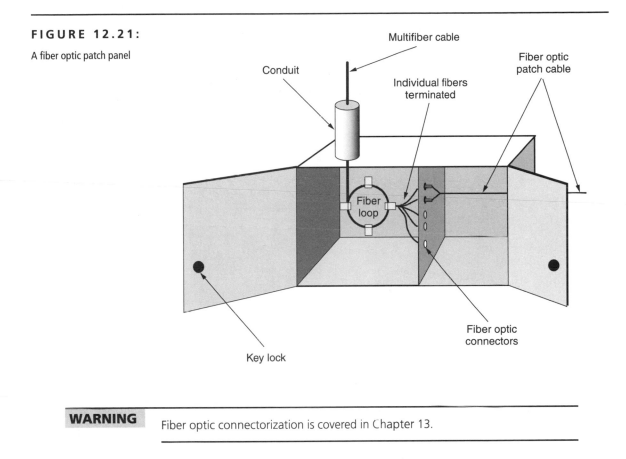

WARNING   Fiber optic connectorization is covered in Chapter 13.

Test the Installation

Once you have a cable or cables installed and terminated, you must test the connection. This is the last step in a cabling installation. Each connection must be tested for proper operation, category rating, and possible connection problems. If the connection has problems, it must either be reterminated or, in the worst case scenario, the entire cable must be repulled.

The method of testing individual cables is done most effectively and quickly with a LAN cable tester (as shown in Figure 12.22). This cable tester usually consists of two parts: the tester itself and a signal injector. The tester is a very complex electronic device that measures not only the presence of a signal, but the quality and characteristics of the signal. Cable testers are available for both copper and fiber optic cables.

FIGURE 12.22:

A LAN cable tester

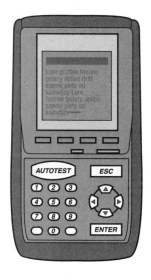

NOTE   Testing tools and procedures are covered in more detail in Chapter 14.

You should test the entire cabling installation before installing any other hardware (hubs, PCs, etc.). That way, you avoid having to troubleshoot cabling-related problems later (or at least you minimize later possible problems).

chapter 13

Cable Connector Installation

- Installing Twisted-Pair Cable Connectors

- Installing Coaxial Cable Connectors

- Installing Fiber Optic Cable Connectors

Throughout this book, you have learned about the installation of cables and the patching process. In today's cabling installation, the cables you install into the walls and ceilings are usually terminated at either punch-down blocks or patch panels and wall outlets. In some cases (as with patch cables, for example), you may need to put a connector on the end of a piece of cable. This process of installing connectors onto a cable is known as connectorization and is an important skill for the cabling installer to know.

For this reason, this chapter will cover the basics of cable connector installation and teach you how to install the connectors for each type of cable.

Twisted-Pair Cable Connector Installation

For LAN installations, there is no cable type that is currently more ubiquitous than twisted-pair copper cabling. Twisted-pair cabling comes in two types—shielded and unshielded. The unshielded type (unshielded twisted-pair, or UTP) is usually used in LAN installations, although some LAN technologies, like Token Ring, require shielded twisted-pair (STP) cable. But, since UTP is almost always used in Ethernet installations, we'll assume we're talking about UTP in our discussion of twisted-pair connectorizing, unless we state otherwise.

Because of their popularity, we will discuss the connectorization of the various types of copper twisted-pair cables first. The main method that is used to put connectors on twisted-pair cables (both UTP and STP) is known as *crimping*. In crimping, you use a tool called a *crimper* to push the metal contacts inside the connector onto the individual conductors in the cable, thus making the connection.

In this section, you will learn the types of connectors used when connectorizing twisted-pair copper cables as well as the procedures used to install them.

NOTE	This topic of this chapter is *not* cable termination (which we discussed in Chapter 12, "Cabling System Design and Installation"). Connectorization is normally done for patch and drop cables, whereas termination is done for the horizontal cables from the patch panel in the wiring closet to the wall plate at the workstation.

Types of Connectors

There are two main types of connectors used for connectorizing twisted-pair cable in data communications installations: the RJ-11 and RJ-45 connectors. Figure 13.1 shows an example of both an RJ-11 and RJ-45 connector for twisted-pair cables. Notice that these connectors are basically the same, except the RJ-45 has more conductors and thus, is slightly larger.

FIGURE 13.1:

RJ-11 and RJ-45 connectors

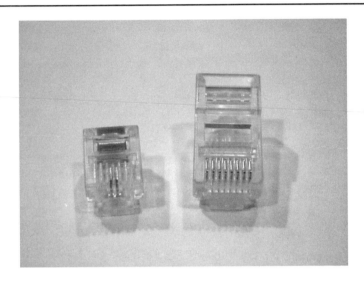

RJ-11 connectors, because of their small form factor and simplicity, are primarily used in telephone applications. RJ-45 connectors, on the other hand, because of the number of conductors they support (eight total), are used primarily in LAN applications. It should be noted, however, that because RJ-11 and RJ-45 support the same shape, many cabling installers will install RJ-45 jacks for telephone applications because these jacks support both RJ-11 and RJ-45 connectors.

Both types of conductors are made of plastic with metal "fingers" inside them (as you can see in Figure 13.1). These fingers are pushed down into the individual conductors in a twisted-pair cable during the crimping process. Once these fingers are crimped and make contact with the conductors in the twisted-pair cable, they are the contact point between the conductors and the pins inside the RJ-11 or RJ-45 jack.

In addition to the different RJ connectors, there are different versions of each connector for stranded-conductor or solid-conductor twisted-pair cables. Stranded-conductor twisted-pair cables are those where the individual conductors in the cable are made up of many tiny hairlike strands of copper twisted together into a single conductor. These conductors have more surface area to make contact with, but they are more difficult to crimp. Because of their difficulty to connectorize, they are usually used as patch cables.

On the other hand, most UTP cable that is installed in the walls and ceilings between patch panels and wall plates is solid-conductor cable. Although they are not normally used as patch cables, solid-conductor cables are easiest to connectorize. For this reason, many people make their own patch cords out of solid-conductor UTP.

Conductor Arrangement

When making UTP cables with crimped ends, you can make many different types of cables. The different types are determined by the order in which their color-coded wires are arranged. Inside a normal UTP cable with RJ-45 ends, there are four pairs of conductors (eight total). Each pair is color-coded blue, orange, green, and brown. Each wire will either be the solid color or a white wire with a stripe of its pair's solid color (e.g., the orange and the white/orange pair).

These wires can be organized in many different ways. Table 13.1 illustrates some of these ways.

TABLE 13.1:   Color-Coding Order for Various Standards

Wiring Standard	Pin #	Color Order
568A	1	White/green
	2	Green
	3	White/orange
	4	Blue
	5	White/blue
	6	Orange
	7	White/brown
	8	Brown

Continued on next page

TABLE 13.1 CONTINUED: Color-Coding Order for Various Standards

Wiring Standard	Pin #	Color Order
568B	1	White/orange
	2	Orange
	3	White/green
	4	Blue
	5	White/blue
	6	Green
	7	White/brown
	8	Brown
Crossover	1	White/green
	2	Green
	3	White/orange
	4	Blue
	5	White/blue
	6	Orange
	7	White/brown
	8	Brown
10Base-T only	1	White/blue
	2	Blue
	3	White/orange
	6	Orange
Generic USOC	1	White/brown
	2	White/green
	3	White/orange
	4	Blue
	5	White/blue
	6	Orange
	7	Green
	8	Brown

When connectorizing cables, make sure you understand which standard your cabling system uses and stick to it.

Connector Crimping Procedures

Now that you know about the different kinds of twisted-pair connectors, you need to know how to install them. The procedure is pretty straightforward. The only difficult part is knowing what "hiccups" you might run into when installing these connectors.

Prerequisites

Before you can install connectors on twisted-pair cables, you must do a few things. As with any project, the first thing you must do is to gather all the items you will need to install the connector. These items include the following:

- Cable

- Connectors

- Stripping and crimping tools

We've already discussed the cable and connectors earlier in this chapter, so let's take a brief look at the tools you are going to need to install the RJ-series of connectors on a twisted-pair cable.

The first tool you're going to need is a cable jacket stripper. This tool (as shown in Figure 13.2) will only cut through the outer jacket of the cable, not through the conductors inside. There are many different kinds of cable strippers, but the most common are the small, plastic ones (as shown in Figure 13.2) that easily fit into a shirt pocket. They are cheap to produce and purchase.

FIGURE 13.2:

Common twisted-pair
cable stripper

> **NOTE**   These strippers don't work well (if at all) on flat cables, like silver satin. But then, technically, those cables aren't twisted-pair cables.

Another tool you're going to need when installing connectors on UTP or STP cable is a cable connector crimper. There are many different styles of crimpers that can crimp connectors on UTP or STP cables. Figure 13.3 shows an example of a crimper that can crimp both RJ-11 and RJ-45 connectors. Notice the two holes for the different connectors and the cutting bar.

FIGURE 13.3:

A crimper for RJ-11 and RJ-45 connectors

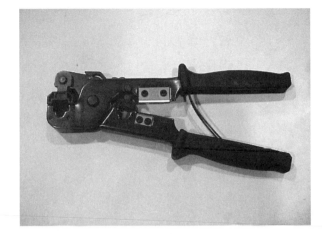

The last tool you're going to use when installing connectors is a cable tester. This device tests not only for a continuous signal from the source connector to the destination, but it also tests the quality of that connection. We won't devote much space to it in this chapter, as it will be covered in Chapter 14, "Cabling System Testing and Troubleshooting."

In addition to all these tools, you must have a supply of the connectors you are going to install as well as the cable you're going to install them on.

Installing the Connector

Now that you have all the tools and supplies you are going to need, it's time to go over the steps for installing the connectors. Pay particular attention to the order of these steps, and make sure to follow them exactly.

WARNING   Each manufacturer may vary from these steps slightly. Make sure you check with the manufacturer's instructions before installing any connector.

---

1. Measure the cable you want to put ends on and trim it to the proper length using your cable cutters (as shown here). Cut the cable about 3 inches longer than the final patch cable length. If you want a 10-foot patch cable, cut the cable to 10 feet, 3 inches.

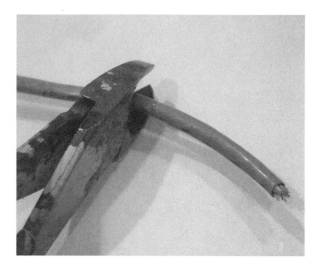

2. Using your cable stripper, strip about 1.5 inches of the jacket from the end of the cable. To do this, insert the cable into the stripper so that the cutter bar in the stripper is 1.5 inches from the end of the cable (as shown in the graphic). Then, rotate the stripper around the cable twice. This will cut through the jacket. Remove the stripper from the cable and pull the trimmed jacket from the cable, exposing the inner conductors (as shown in the second graphic).

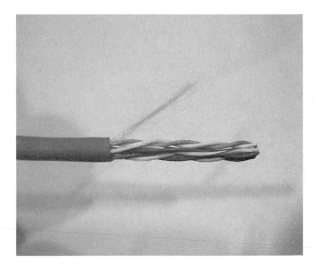

3.   Untwist all in the inner conductor pairs and spread them apart so that you can see each individual conductor, as shown here.

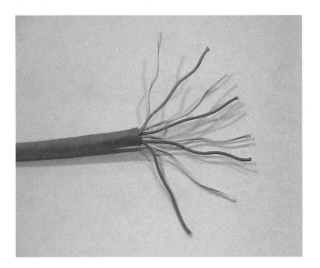

4.   Line up the individual conductors so that the color code matches the standard for the color-coding standard you are using (see Table 13.1, shown previously). The alignment in the graphic shown here is for 568B, with #1 at the top.

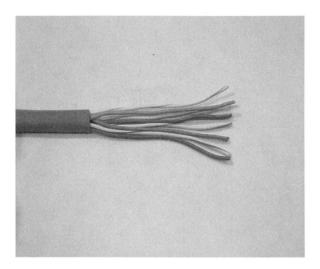

5. Trim the conductors so that the ends are even with each other, making sure that the jacket of the cable will be inside the connector (as shown here). The total length of exposed connectors after trimming should be no longer than $1/2$" to $5/8$" (as shown in the second graphic).

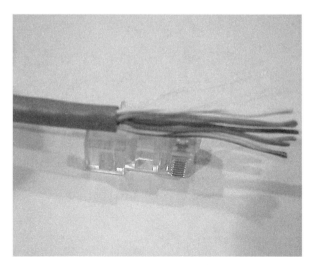

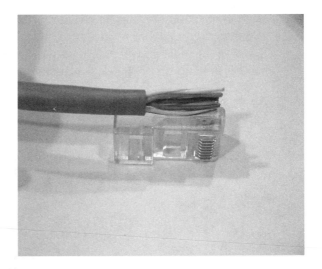

6. Insert the conductors in the connector, ensuring that all conductors line up properly with the pins as they were aligned in the last step. If they don't line up, pull them out and line them up. Do this carefully, as it's the last step before crimping on the connector.

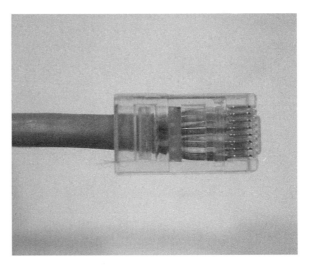

7. Carefully insert the connector and cable into the crimping tool (as shown in the following graphic). Squeeze the handle firmly as far as it will go and hold it with pressure for three seconds. As you will see in the second graphic, the

crimping tool has two dies that will press into the connector and push the pins in the connector into the conductors inside the connector. There is also a die in the crimping tool that will push a plastic divider into the cable jacket of the cable to hold it securely inside the connector.

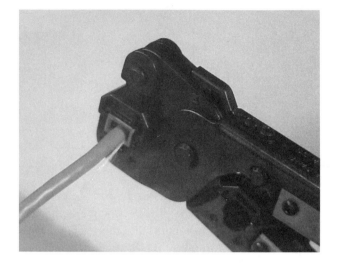

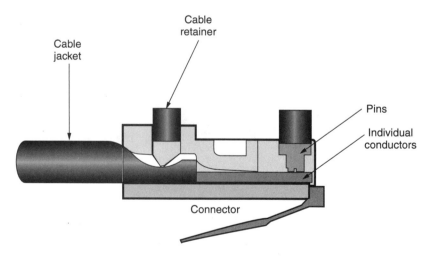

8. Now that you've crimped the connector, remove it from the crimping tool and examine it (as shown here). Check to ensure all conductors are making

contact and that all pins have been crimped into their respective conductors. If some of the pins did not crimp all the way into their respective conductors, reinsert the connector into the crimping tool and recrimp it. If the connector doesn't crimp properly, cut off the connector and redo it.

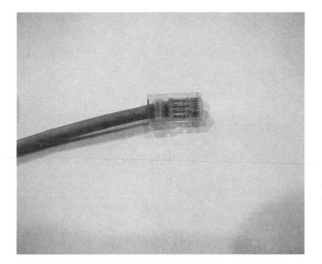

9. To finish the patch cable, put a connector on the other end of the cable and follow these steps again, starting with step 2.

Testing

Now that you have got connectors on both ends of a cable, you should ensure that the connectorization was done correctly by testing the cable with a cable tester. Put the injector on one end of the cable and put the tester on the other end. Once you have the tester hooked up, you can test the cable for continuity (no breaks in the conductors), near-end crosstalk (NEXT), and Category rating (all quality-of-transmission issues). The specific procedures for testing a cable vary depending on the cable tester being used. However, usually you tell the tester what type of cable you are testing, hook up the cable being tested, then press a button labeled something like "Begin Test." If the cable does not work or meet the testing requirements, reconnectorize the cable.

NOTE   Cable testers are covered in more detail in Chapter 14.

Coaxial Cable Connector Installation

Although it is used less than either twisted-pair or fiber optic cables, coaxial cable is still used in some installations because of its simplicity and very low cost. It is often seen in small office installations and for easy connections between hubs in larger installations.

In this section, you will learn the topics relating to connectorizing coaxial cable, including:

- Types of connectors
- Connector crimping procedures

After reading this section, you should be able to install a connector on a coaxial cable.

Types of Connectors

As discussed in Chapter 9, "Cable Connectors," there are many types of coaxial cable, including RG-6, RG-58, and RG-62. However, LAN applications primarily use RG-62 and RG-58–designated coaxial cables. RG-62 is used primarily for ARCNet networks and RG-58 is used primarily for Ethernet. RG-6 is used primarily in video and television cable installations. The process for connectorizing RG-6, RG-58, and RG-62 is basically the same, except that different connectors are used for different applications, either LAN or video. You can identify which type of cable by examining the writing on the side of the actual cable. The different types of cable will be labeled with their RG designation.

For LAN applications, the BNC connector (shown in Figure 13.4) is used with RG-58 or RG-62 coaxial cable. The male BNC connectors are easily identified by their knurled grip and quarter-turn locking slot. Video applications, on the other hand, use what is commonly known as a *coax cable TV connector* or *F connector* (as shown in Figure 13.5) and RG-6 cable.

FIGURE 13.4:

Male and female BNC
connectors

Male

Female

FIGURE 13.5:

A coax cable TV F connector

In addition to their physical appearance, coax connectors differ based on their installation method. There are basically two types: *crimp-on* and *screw-on* (also known as a *threaded*) connectors. The crimp-on connectors require that you strip the cable, insert the cable into the connector, and then crimp the connector onto the jacket of the cable to secure it. Most BNC connectors used for LAN applications use this installation method. Screw-on connectors, on the other hand, have threads inside the connector that allow the connector to be screwed on to the jacket of the coaxial cable. These threads cut into the jacket and keep the connector from coming loose. Coaxial cable TV connectors for video applications primarily use this installation method.

Connector Crimping Procedures

Now that you understand the basic connector types, you can proceed to installing the coaxial connectors. The basic procedural outline is similar to installing twisted-pair connectors. There are three topics you need to understand:

- Connectorization prerequisites
- Installing the connector
- Testing the connection

Prerequisites

Before installing the connector, you must complete a few prerequisites. First of all, you must have the right type of cable and connectors for the application of the cable you are making. For example, if you are making an Ethernet connection cable, you must have both RG-58 coaxial cable and BNC connectors available. Similarly, if you are making an ARCNet cable, you need to have RG-62 coaxial cable and BNC connectors.

In addition to having the right cable and connectors available, you must have the right tools available. The four main tools you need are cable cutters, a cable stripper, a crimper for the type of connectors you are installing, and a cable tester. These tools were discussed in the last section and also in more detail in Chapter 6, "Tools of the Trade."

Installing the Connector

Now that you have got all the tools and supplies you are going to need, it's time to go over the steps for installing the connectors. The connector you are going to learn how to install here is the most common crimp-on style that comes in three pieces: the center pin, the crimp sleeve, and the connector housing. Pay particular attention to the order of these steps, and make sure to follow them exactly.

WARNING   Each manufacturer may vary from these steps slightly. Make sure you check with the manufacturer's instructions before installing any connector.

---

1. Measure the cable you want to put ends on and trim it to the proper length using your cable cutters. Cut the cable to exactly the length you want the cable to be.

2. Put the crimp-on sleeve on the cable jacket on the end of the cable you are going to connectorize.

3. Using your cable stripper, strip about $5/8''$ of the jacket from the end of the cable. To do this, insert the cable into the stripper so that the cutter bar in the stripper is one inch from the end of the cable (as shown in the graphic). Then, rotate the stripper around the cable twice. This will cut through the jacket. Remove the stripper from the cable and pull the trimmed jacket from the cable, exposing the braided shield and inner conductors.

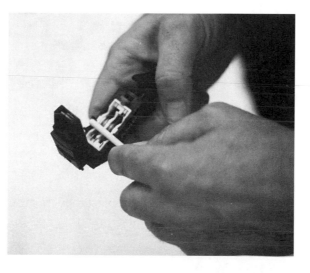

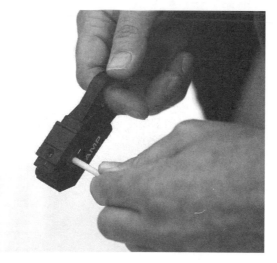

4. Trim the braided shielding so that there is $^7/_{32}$" of braid showing, as shown in the following graphic.

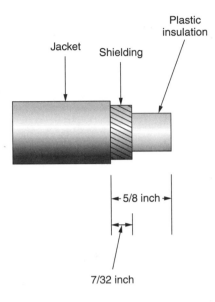

5. Strip the inner protective plastic shield around the center conductor so that there is $^7/_{16}$" of plastic showing (thus $^3/_{16}$" of conductor is showing), as shown in the next graphic.

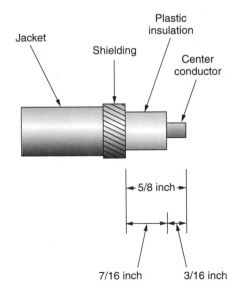

6. Insert the center conductor into the center pin of the connector, as shown. Crimp the pin twice with the ratcheting crimper. After crimping (shown in the second graphic), you shouldn't be able to twist the pin around the center conductor.

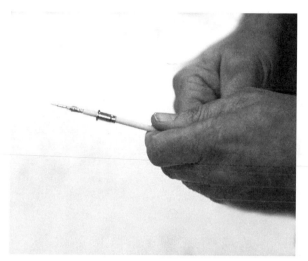

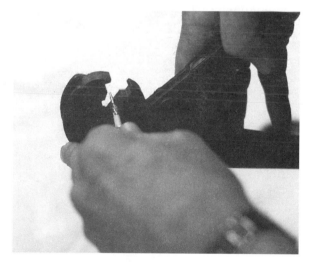

7.   Push the connector onto the end of the cable. The barrel of the connector should slide under the shielding. Push the connector until the center pin clicks into the connector, as shown in the following graphic.

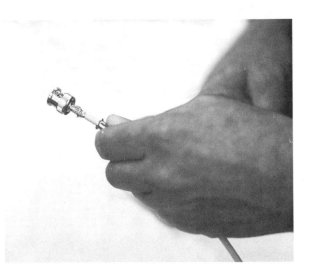

8.   Slide the crimp on sleeve up the cable so that it pushes the braided shielding around the barrel of the connector. Crimp the barrel twice, once at the connector side and again at the jacket side, as shown in the following two graphics.

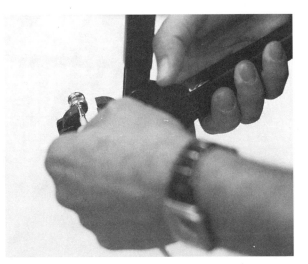

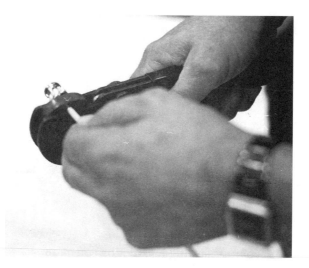

9. Now that you've crimped the connector, remove it from the crimping tool and examine it. Check to see that the connector is securely attached to the end of the cable—you should not be able to move it. If the connector doesn't crimp properly, cut off the connector and redo it.

10. To finish the patch cable, put a connector on the other end of the cable and follow these steps again, starting with step 2.

Testing

Now that you have got connectors on both ends of a cable, you should ensure that the connectorization was done correctly by testing the cable with a cable tester. Once you have the tester hooked up, you can test the cable to ensure that the cable is connectorized properly and that there are no breaks in the cable. The specific procedures for testing a cable vary depending on the cable tester being used. However, usually you simply tell the tester what type of cable you are testing, hook up the cable being tested, and press a button labeled something like "Begin Test." If the cable does not work or meet the testing requirements, reconnectorize the cable.

NOTE   Cable testing procedures are covered in more detail in Chapter 14.

Fiber Optic Cable Connector Installation

In the early days of fiber optic connections, connectorizing a single fiber optic cable could take up to a half-hour. These days, an experienced cable installer can put a connector on a fiber optic connector in less than five minutes.

Fiber optics are seeing increased use in LANs, and fiber optic connections to the desktop will soon be ubiquitous. For this reason, it is important that we discuss installing connectors on fiber optic cables. Some of the concepts you need to understand are

- Connector types
- Connectorizing methods
- Connectorizing installation procedures

Connector Types

As discussed in Chapter 10, "Fiber Optic Media," there are a number of different connector types for the different fiber optic cables. Each connector type differs based on its form factor and the type(s) of fiber optic cables it supports. Some of the most common fiber optic connector types include the following:

- SC
- ST
- Biconic
- FDDI
- FC
- ESCON
- SMA

Each of these types of connectors is discussed in detail in Chapter 10.

Connectorizing Methods

Almost as numerous as the different types of connectors are the different methods of attaching them to the optical fiber. Optical fibers are made of glass and, unlike copper connections, a mechanical connection isn't enough. The light has to come out of the end of the fiber evenly with minimal loss of signal. The optical fiber has to be aligned precisely to the optical port on the device the fiber optical cable is connected to. Simply stripping the cable and placing the optical fiber inside a connector isn't enough; the connection has to be precise.

To get the best possible connection, many connectorization methods have been developed. The most common ways of attaching connectors include the following:

- Epoxy connectors
- Epoxyless connectors

Each of these methods has been developed by the manufacturer of a particular connector. When one manufacturer sees that people are using a certain connectorizing system, they will implement their own version of that connectorizing system.

Epoxy Connectors

The epoxy system uses a special two-part glue known as an epoxy. The optical fibers are trimmed and the epoxy is applied. Then the fiber is inserted into the connector. Some epoxy systems don't use a tube of adhesive but have the adhesive preloaded into the connector. In this case, the adhesive is not activated until it's acted on by some outside action. For example, 3M's HotMelt system uses a thermosetting adhesive, which means that it uses a high temperature to activate the adhesive and cause it to set. Other types of adhesive are activated by UV light.

Once the fiber is in the connector and the adhesive has been activated, the assembly is either placed aside to air dry, or the connector is inserted into a curing oven to speed the drying process.

The majority of fiber optic connectors being installed are using some type of epoxy method, mainly because of its simplicity and ease of installation while retaining quality.

Epoxyless Connectors

The main disadvantage to epoxy-based termination is the time and extra equipment needed to terminate a single connector. It may take up to 15 minutes per connector to terminate them. For this reason, many companies have developed connectors that don't need any kind of adhesive to hold them together. This category of fiber optic connector is known as *epoxyless connectors*.

Generally speaking, epoxyless connectors don't use glue of any kind to hold the fiber in place. Instead, they use some kind of friction method, like crimping, to hold the fiber in place in the connector. The fiber is inserted in the connector, and some kind of restraint keeps the optical fiber in place and lined up with the receiving connector. The 3M Cimplok™ connector system is one example of an epoxyless connector.

Connector Installation Procedures

Now that you've learned about the different types of connectors and the different types of connectorization methods, it is time to learn how to actually put the connectors on a fiber optic cable. To do this, we'll need to make the assumption that most fiber optic terminations have similar operations. In this section, you are going to learn how to connectorize a single multimode fiber optic cable with an ST connector (the most popular type). The procedures for installing different connectors differ only slightly. Where necessary, we'll point out where other connectorizing methods differ.

Prerequisites

As with the other types of connectorization, the first step is to gather all the tools and items you are going to need. You are going to need some specialized fiber optic tools, including epoxy syringes, curing oven, cable jacket stripper, fiber stripper, fiber polishing tool (including fiber polishing puck and abrasive pad), Kevlar™ scissors, and a fiber optic loss tester. In addition to these tools, you will need a few consumable items, like cable, connectors, alcohol and wipes (for cleaning the fiber), epoxy (self-curing or thermosetting, depending on the application), and polishing cloths. You can usually buy kits that contain all of these items.

Before you start terminating the fiber, gather all these tools together and have them available. Additionally, if your fiber termination system uses an oven or UV-curing device, plug it in so that it will be ready for use by the time you need it. If possible, make sure you have adequate space to terminate the fiber, along with an adequate light source.

| **TIP** | If you can, work on a black surface. It makes the fiber easier to see while terminating it. It is hard to see optical fiber on a white space. |

| **WARNING** | BE EXTREMELY CAREFUL WHEN DEALING WITH BARE FIBER! Most optical fibers in fiber optic cables are made of glass. Small shards of glass with many sharp ends are produced when cutting or cleaving optical fibers. Always wear safety glasses to protect your eyes from flying shards of glass. Properly dispose of any cut fiber scraps. |

Finally, before you start, make sure you are familiar with the connector system you are using. If possible, have the directions from the fiber connector's manufacturer available while doing the termination.

Installing the Connector

Now that you have take care of the prerequisites, you are ready to start installing the actual connector. There are many complex steps to this process. Unlike terminating copper, terminating fiber is a very tricky operation. You must take your time and perform the following steps correctly:

1. Cut and strip the cable.
2. Trim the aramid yarn.
3. Strip optical fiber buffer.
4. Prepare the epoxy.
5. Epoxy the connector.
6. Insert the fiber in the connector.
7. Dry the epoxy.
8. Scribe and remove extra fiber.
9. Polish the tip.
10. Perform a visual inspection .
11. Finish up.

We have included several figures that show how to perform each operation.

Cut and Strip the Cable   The first step when connectorizing fiber optic cables is to cut and strip the cable. Cutting the fiber is fairly simple: simply cut through the jacket and strength members using the fiber shears included in the fiber optic termination kit. Optical fiber cannot be cut with regular cutters, mainly because many fiber optic cables contain aramid yarn strength members, which are next to impossible to cut with regular cutters. Trim the cable exactly to the length that you want.

Once you have the cable cut to length, you can continue the connectorizing process by stripping one end of the cable. This must be done in two steps. You must first strip the outer jacket of the fiber optic cable, thus exposing the buffered fiber and the aramid yarn strength members. Then, you can carefully strip the buffer from the optical fiber, exposing the optical fiber so you can insert it in the connector.

TIP

> If you are stripping a relatively short cable (less than 25 feet) without connectors on either end, tie a knot in the end of the cable opposite of the end you are trying to strip. That way, you can't pull the strength members out of the cable while you strip it.

To strip the buffer, use the stripping guide diagram on the package that the connector came in (an example of a diagram like this is shown in Figure 13.6). This guide will show how much of each component to strip off of the cable and will show actual measurements of how much of each part of the cable should be stripped, or it will have an "actual size" drawing of the stripped cable.

TIP

> Before you get out the strippers, there is one operation you should do to make the installation go smoothly. Open the fiber optic connector package and remove the strain relief boot and crimp sleeve. Place these items on the cable *before* you strip it and slide them down, out of the way. That way, you don't have to try and push them over an optical fiber and aramid yarn.

FIGURE 13.6:

Strip guide for a
fiber optic cable

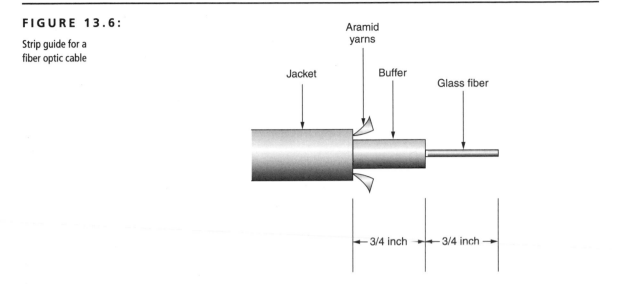

FIGURE 13.7:

Using a cable jacket
stripper

The first part of the cable you need to strip off is the cable jacket itself. To do this, use the cable jacket stripper (as shown in Figure 13.7). Set the jacket stripper to the size recommended by the manufacturer (3mm fiber in this case) and squeeze the handle. The stripper will bite through the outer jacket only. Release the handle and remove the stripper. You should then be able to pull off the outer jacket as shown in Figure 13.8.

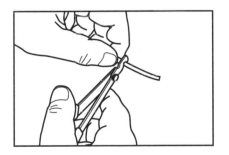

FIGURE 13.8:

Pulling off the outer jacket
of a fiber optic cable

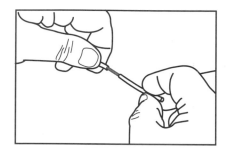

WARNING Never strip a fiber optic cable as you would a copper cable (i.e., by twisting the stripper and pulling the stripper off with the end of the jacket). This can damage the cable.

Trim the Aramid Yarn Once you have removed the outer jacket, you must trim the aramid yarn (also called by the DuPont trademark *Kevlar*) to the length that is specified by the manufacturer of the connector system you are using. As already mentioned, this must be done using special aramid yarn scissors. To cut the yarn, grab the bundle of fibers together and loop them around your finger (as shown in Figure 13.9). Cut the fibers with the special scissors so that about 1/4″ (more or less, depending on the connector) of yarn fiber is showing.

FIGURE 13.9:

Cutting the aramid yarn of
a fiber optic cable

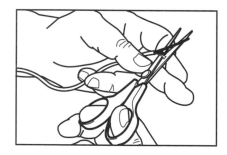

TIP   If you have trouble loosening the aramid yarn fibers from the inside of the cable, try blowing on them or shaking the cable to shake them free.

Strip Optical Fiber Buffer   Now that you've got the jacket and aramid yarn cut and stripped properly, you can strip the buffer from around the optical fiber. This step must be performed with *extreme* care. At this point, the fiber is exposed and can be damaged or broken. If this happens, you must cut off the ends you just stripped and start over.

This step is done with a different stripping tool than the stripper used to strip the cable jacket in the first step of this process. There are two types of fiber buffer strippers: the Miller tool and the No-Nik stripper. Most first-time installers like the Miller tool, but most professionals prefer the No-Nik tool. Many fiber connectorization tool kits contain both types of strippers. For our purposes, we will show pictures of the Miller tool.

To remove the buffer, position the stripper at a 45-degree angle to the fiber (as shown in Figure 13.10) to prevent the stripper from bending, and possibly breaking, the optical fiber while stripping. Position the stripper to only remove about 1/8" to 1/4" of buffer. Slowly but firmly squeeze the stripper to cut through the buffer. Make sure you have cut through the entire buffer. Then, using the stripper, pull the buffer from the fiber slowly and steadily, making sure to pull straight along the fiber and not bend it. You will have to exert some pressure, as the buffer will not come off easily. Repeat this process to remove additional 1/8" to 1/4" "bites" of buffer until sufficient buffer has been removed from the fiber and between 1/2" to 1" (depending on the type of connector being used) of fiber is exposed.

FIGURE 13.10:

Stripping buffer from the optical fiber with the Miller tool

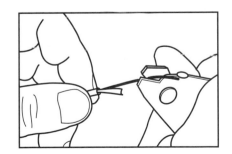

FIGURE 13.11:

The optical fiber after stripping the buffer from the fiber

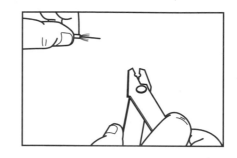

> **TIP**
>
> It's better to have too much fiber exposed than not enough because you will trim off excess fiber in a later step.

Prepare the Epoxy Now that the fiber optic cable and optical fiber have been stripped and the cable is ready, set it aside and get the epoxy ready to use (assuming, of course, your connector system uses epoxy). Epoxy is a two-part chemical glue that will not work unless both parts are mixed. The epoxy usually comes in packets with a syringe (see Figure 13.12) so that you can inject the epoxy into the connector.

FIGURE 13.12:

An epoxy packet with a syringe

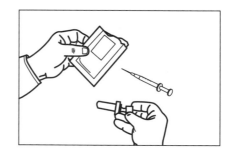

To start preparing the epoxy for use, open the envelope or bag that contains the plastic epoxy envelope and the syringe. Remove the divider from the envelope and mix the epoxy by kneading it with your fingers or running the flat side of a pencil over the envelope (as shown in Figure 13.13). The epoxy is mixed when it is a uniform color and consistency. It should take a couple of minutes to fully mix the epoxy, especially if you are using your fingers.

NOTE
Once the two chemicals that make up the epoxy are mixed, it will remain workable for only a short time (usually anywhere from 15 minutes to a half hour). If you are terminating several cables, you should have them all prepared before mixing the epoxy to make the best use of the time you have.

FIGURE 13.13:

Mixing the epoxy

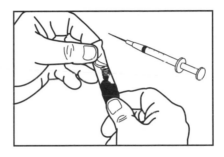

Once the epoxy is fully mixed, you can then open the epoxy envelope and pour the epoxy into a syringe for use. Take the new syringe out of its wrapper and remove the plunger. Hold the epoxy envelope gently (don't put a large amount of pressure on the envelope) and cut one corner so a very small opening ($1/16$" to $1/8$") is formed (see Figure 13.14).

WARNING
Don't use the aramid yarn scissors to cut the epoxy envelope! Epoxy is very sticky and will ruin the scissors (and they aren't cheap scissors). Find a pair of cheap scissors and put these in your fiber termination kit.

FIGURE 13.14:

Opening the epoxy envelope

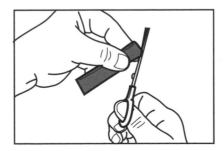

Hold the envelope in one hand and the empty syringe body in the other. Slowly pour the epoxy into the syringe, while being careful not to get epoxy on your hands or on the outside of the syringe (see Figure 13.15). Once the syringe is almost full (leave a $1/8"$ gap at the top), stop pouring and set the epoxy envelope aside (preferably on a wipe or towel, in case the epoxy spills), or throw it away if it's empty.

FIGURE 13.15:

Pouring epoxy into the syringe

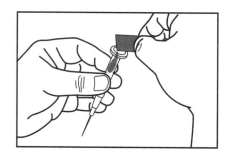

Once you're done pouring, gently place the plunger into the end of the syringe, but *don't* push it down. Just seat it in the end of the syringe to hold it in place. Invert the syringe so that the needle is at the top. Tap the side of the syringe while holding the syringe in this position. This will cause the epoxy to sink to the bottom and the air bubbles to rise the top. Grab a wipe from your termination kit and hold it above and around the needle (as shown in Figure 13.16). Slowly squeeze the air bubbles out of the syringe until the only thing left in the syringe is epoxy.

FIGURE 13.16:

Removing air from the syringe

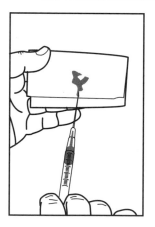

Once all the air is out of the syringe, stop pushing on the plunger. When no more epoxy comes out, pull very slightly on the plunger so there is a tiny bubble at the tip of the needle. Put the cap on the needle (if there is one) and set the syringe aside, out of the way.

Epoxy the Connector   Once you have the epoxy ready, it's time to put the connector on the fiber. Remove the rest of the components from the connector package (you already have the strain relief on the cable, remember?) and lay them out in front of you. Remove the dust cap from the end of the connector and the cap from the syringe. Push the plunger on the syringe lightly to expel the small air bubble in the needle. Insert the needle into the connector body on the cable side (the side that faces the cable, not the side that faces the equipment the connector connects to).

To epoxy the connector, squeeze the plunger and expel epoxy into the inside of the connector. Continue to squeeze until a very small bead of epoxy appears at the ferrule inside the connector (as shown in Figure 13.17). The size of this bead is important, as too large of a bead means you will have spend a lot of time polishing off the extra epoxy. On the other hand, too small of a bead may not support the optical fiber inside the connector.

TIP   The proper size bead of epoxy to expel into the connector is approximately half the diameter of the inside of the ferrule.

FIGURE 13.17:

Putting epoxy inside the connector

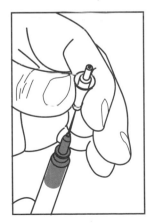

Once the bead appears at the ferrule, pull the needle halfway out of the connector and continue to squeeze the plunger. Keep squeezing until the connector is filled with epoxy and the epoxy starts to come out of the backside of the connector (see Figure 13.18). Remove the needle completely from the connector and pull back slightly on the plunger to prevent the epoxy from dripping out of the needle. At this point, you can set the connector aside and clean the needle off with a wipe.

FIGURE 13.18:

Finish epoxying the connector

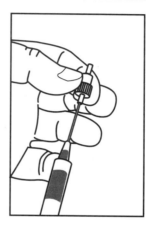

Insert the Fiber into the Connector   Once the needle is clean and the connector contains epoxy, set the syringe aside and prepare the fiber for insertion. The fiber must be clean and free of all dirt and oil to ensure the best possible adhesion to the epoxy. Most fiber termination kits come with special wipes soaked in alcohol, known as Alco wipes. Hold one of these wipes in one hand, between your thumb and forefinger, and run the fiber between them (see Figure 13.19). This will take off any dirt or fingerprints that may remain on the fiber.

FIGURE 13.19:

Cleaning the fiber

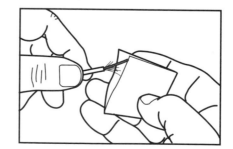

Pick up the connector in one hand and carefully slide the fiber into the epoxy-filled center. While pushing the fiber in, rotate the connector back and forth. This will accomplish two goals: it will spread the epoxy evenly around the outside of the optical fiber, and it will help to center the fiber in the connector. Don't worry if some epoxy leaks out onto the aramid yarn—that will actually help to secure the cable to the connector.

FIGURE 13.20:

Inserting the fiber into the connector

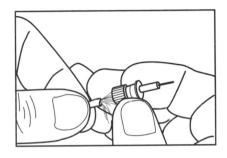

To secure the cable permanently to the connector, slide the crimp sleeve up from around the cable and over the aramid fibers so that it sits against the connector (see Figure 13.21). You must now use the crimpers that come with your fiber optic termination kit and crimp this sleeve in two places: once at the connector and once at the fiber. The crimper has two holes for crimping, a larger and a smaller hole. Crimp the sleeve at the connector end using the larger hole, and crimp the sleeve at the cable jacket end using the smaller hole (as shown in Figure 13.22).

FIGURE 13.21:

Putting on the crimping sleeve

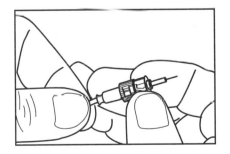

Crimping the sleeve

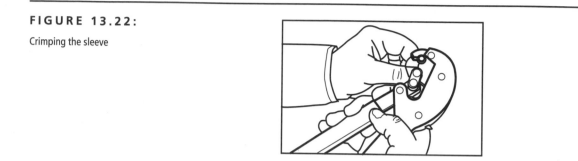

TIP   While crimping, make sure to hold the connector against the jacket so that a tight connection is made.

When you have finished crimping the sleeve, slide the strain relief boot up from the cable up over the crimp sleeve (see Figure 13.23). The connector is now secure to the cable. However, there should be a short piece of fiber protruding from the connector. Be careful not to break off this piece of fiber. It will be scribed and polished off correctly in the next step.

WARNING   If you do break this piece of protruding fiber, you will have to cut off the connector and start over.

FIGURE 13.23:

Installing the strain relief boot

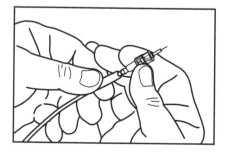

Dry the Epoxy   You must set the connector aside for the dry. Most epoxies take anywhere from 12–24 hours to set completely by themselves. However, you can speed up this process either by using a curing oven (shown in Figure 13.24) or a UV setting device (depending on the type of epoxy used). To dry the epoxy using one of these devices, carefully (so that you don't break the fiber) insert the connector into the slots or holes provided in the oven. Let the connector sit in the oven as long as the manufacturer requires (usually somewhere between 5 and 15 minutes). Then, remove the connector and place it on a cooling rack.

TIP   While the connectors are curing in the oven, you can connectorize more fibers. Remember, you only have a short time before the epoxy is no longer usable

FIGURE 13.24:

Drying the epoxy using an oven

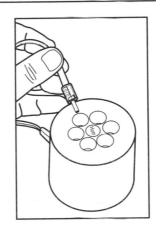

Scribe and Remove Extra Fiber   After the connector has sufficiently cooled and the epoxy has dried in the connector, you are ready to cut of the excess fiber. This is done with a special tool known as a *scribe*. It's impossible to get any kind of cutting tool close enough to the connector to cut off the remaining fiber and glass is difficult to cut, so instead, you cut this glass fiber by scratching one side of it and breaking off the fiber.

To do this, hold the connector firmly in one hand and use the scribe to scratch the protruding fiber just above where it sticks out from the bead of epoxy on the connector ferrule (as shown in Figure 13.25). Use a *very* light touch when doing this. Remember, the glass is very small, and it doesn't take much to break it.

FIGURE 13.25:

Scribing the protruding fiber

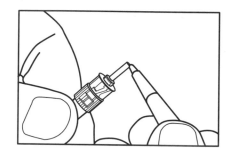

To remove the fiber, grab the protruding piece of fiber and sharply pull up and away from the connector (see Figure 13.26). The glass should break cleanly (there is still a rough edge, although you may not be able to see it). Dispose of the fiber remnant properly in a specially designed fiber optic trash bag.

FIGURE 13.26:

Removing the fiber

Polish the Tip   Now that you have cut the fiber, the end will look similar to the one shown at the left side of Figure 13.27. To make a proper connection, you must polish the end to a perfectly flat surface. This is done with varying grits of polishing films (basically the same idea as sandpaper, only much, much finer). The idea is to use the polishing cloth to remove a little bit of the protruding fiber at a time until the fiber is perfectly flat and level.

FIGURE 13.27:

Fiber before and after polishing

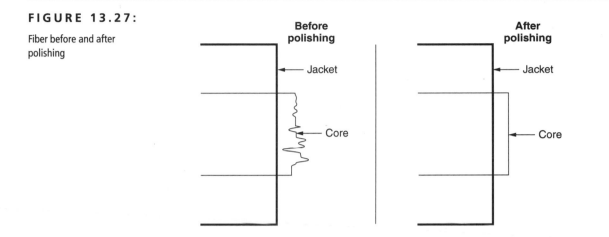

The first step in polishing the fiber is the coarse polishing. This is done to remove the burrs and sharp ends of the fiber after you've broken off the fiber. To do this, grab a sheet of 12-micron film and hold it as shown in Figure 13.28. Bring the connector into contact with the polishing film and move the connector in a figure-eight motion. Polish the connector for around 15 seconds, or until you hear a change in the sound made as the fiber scrapes along the polishing cloth. This process is known as "air polishing" because you aren't using a backing for the polishing film.

WARNING   This step will take some practice. Do not over-polish the fiber! If you do, the fiber will not transmit light correctly and will have to be cut off and reterminated.

FIGURE 13.28:

"Air polishing" the fiber after scribing

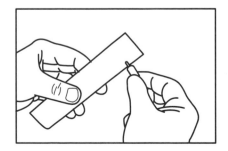

When you are done, there should be a small amount of epoxy left, and the glass will not be completely smooth (as seen in Figure 13.29). Don't worry, this will be taken care of in the next part of the polishing procedure. Before proceeding, clean the end of the fiber with an Alco pad to remove any loose glass shards or epoxy bits that might scratch the fiber during the next polishing step.

FIGURE 13.29:

Results of air polishing

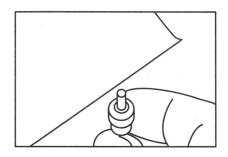

Hold the polishing puck in one hand and insert the connector into the puck (as shown in Figure 13.30). Then, very gently place the puck with the connector in it on some 3-micron polishing film that should go on the polishing pad. Move the puck in a figure-eight motion four or five times (see Figure 13.31). Stop polishing when the connector fiber doesn't scrape along the polishing cloth and feels somewhat slick.

FIGURE 13.30:

Insert the connector into the polishing puck

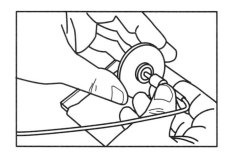

FIGURE 13.31:

Polishing the tip of the fiber

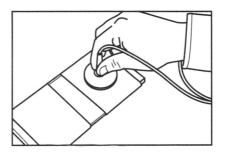

FIGURE 13.31:

Polishing the tip of the fiber

WARNING Don't over-polish the conductor. Over-polishing will cause the glass fiber end to be undercut and cause light loss at the optic connection.

Once you've finished polishing the connector on the 3-micron film, remove it and clean it with an Alco wipe to remove any debris before polishing again. Once clean, gently place the puck on some 0.3-micron film and give it five or six quick figure eights with little or no pressure to fine-polish the fiber. When you've finished this, remove the connector from the polishing puck and wipe it with an Alco pad. You're done. It's time to test the connector to see how you did.

Inspect the Connector   Now that you have installed the connector, you should check it with a fiber optic microscope for any flaws that might cause problems. A fiber optic microscope allows you to look very closely at the end of the fiber you just terminated (usually magnifying the tip 100 times or more). Different microscopes work slightly differently, but the basic procedure is still the same.

To test the connector you just terminated, insert it into the fiber microscope (as shown in Figure 13.32). Look into the eyepiece and focus the microscope using the thumbwheel or slider so that you can see the tip of the fiber. Under 100-times magnification, the fiber should look like the image shown in Figure 13.33. What you see in this image is the light center (the core) and the darker ring around it (the cladding). Any cracks or imperfections will show up as very dark blotches. If you see any cracks or imperfections in the cladding, it's no problem because the cladding doesn't carry a signal. However, if there are cracks in the core, try first repolishing the fiber on the 0.3-micron polishing film to see if that takes care of it. If the crack still appears, you may have to cut the connector off and reterminate the connector.

FIGURE 13.32:

Insert the fiber into the fiber microscope

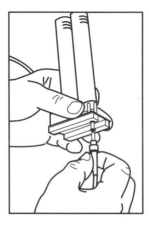

FIGURE 13.33:

Sample fiber tip image in a fiber optic microscope

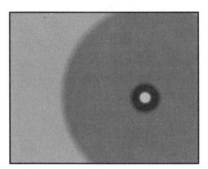

Finish Up   If this connector passes the test, you can use various other cable testing tools to check the quality of the connection. At this point, you can also terminate the other end of the cable you are making. Then you can use a standard fiber cable tester or optical time domain reflectometer (OTDR) to test the cable that you have made. You will learn more about optical fiber testing in Chapter 14.

Cable System Testing and Troubleshooting

- Installation Testing

- Cable Plant Certification

- Cable Testing Tools

- Troubleshooting Cabling Problems

Testing a cable installation is an essential part of both installing and maintaining a data network. This chapter will examine the cable testing procedures that you should integrate into the installation process and that you are likely to need afterwards in order to troubleshoot network communication problems. We will also examine the standards up to which you should hold your cable installation and the tools you will need to ensure that the cable runs are functioning properly.

Installation Testing

As you've learned in earlier chapters, installing the cable plant for a data network incorporates a large number of variables. Not only must you select the appropriate cable and other hardware for your applications and your environment, but you must also install the cable so that environmental factors have as little effect on the performance of the network as possible. Part of the installation process should include an individual test of each cable run to eliminate the cables as a possible cause of any problems that might occur later when you are connecting the computers to the network and trying to get them to communicate. Even if you are not going to be installing or testing the cabling yourself, you should be familiar with the tests that the installers perform and the results that they receive.

Incorporating a cable test into the installation process performs several functions, including the following:

Connections Have the connectors been attached to the cable properly? Have the wires been connected to the correct pins at both ends?

Cable performance Is the cable itself free from defects that can affect performance?

Environment Has the cable been properly routed around possible sources of interference, such as light fixtures and electrical equipment?

Certification Does the entire end-to-end cable run, including connectors, wall plates, and other hardware, conform to the desired standard?

The following sections examine the tests that you can perform on copper and fiber optic cables, the principles involved, and the tools needed to perform the tests. However, this does not necessarily mean that you must perform every one of these tests on every cable installation. To determine which tests you need to perform and what results you should expect, see the section "Creating a Testing Regimen," later in this chapter.

Copper Cable Tests

Most of the copper cable installed today is twisted-pair of one form or another, and the number of individual wire connections involved makes the installation and testing process more complicated, particularly in light of the various standards available for the connector pinouts. The following sections list the tests for copper cables and how they work.

> **NOTE** For more information on the equipment used to perform these tests, see the section "Cable Testing Tools," later in this chapter. For more information on correcting the problems detected by these tests, see the section "Troubleshooting Cable Problems," also later in this chapter.

Wire Mapping

Wire mapping is the most basic and obvious test for any copper cable installation, particularly those that use twisted-pair cable. Because the coaxial cable used in data networks has only two conductors that are easily distinguishable, there is usually no need for a wire mapping test, unless you are pulling several cables at once, in which case you want to make sure that each cable is connected to the proper terminus. To test the continuity of a coaxial cable, you can use a digital multimeter (DMM), an inexpensive, dedicated coaxial tester; or a multifunction tester that supports coaxial cable.

For twisted-pair cables, however, you must test each cable run to make sure that the individual wires within the cable are connected properly, as shown in Figure 14.1. As mentioned earlier in this book, you can select either the T568-A or T568-B pinouts for a twisted-pair installation. Because all of the pairs are wired straight through and the difference between the two standards is minimal, there is no functional difference between them. However, in the interest of consistency, you should select one pinout standard and stick to it throughout your entire installation, including patch cables. This way you can perform end-to-end tests as needed without being confused by mixed wire pair colors. That doesn't mean you shouldn't follow some kind of wiring color-code mapping, however. It is important that you follow a standard throughout your entire network so that you—and others—can always tell what color is for what.

FIGURE 14.1:

A properly connected four-pair cable, using the T568-A pinout

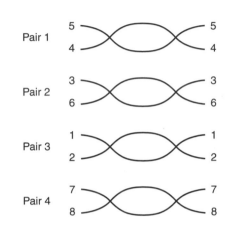

A perfunctory wire mapping test can be performed visually by simply checking the pinouts at both ends of the cable. However, there are problems that can occur that are not visible to the naked eye. A proper wire mapping tester can detect any of the following faults, as illustrated in Figure 14.2.

Open pair   An open occurs when one or more of the wires in a cable are not connected to any pin at either end.

Shorted pair   A short occurs when the conductors of a wire pair are connected at any location in the cable.

Short between pairs   A short between pairs occurs when the conductors of two wires in different pairs are connected at any location in the cable.

Reversed pair   A reversed pair (sometimes called a tip/ring reversal) occurs when the two wires in a single pair are connected to the opposite pins of the same color.

Crossed pairs   Crossed (or transposed) pairs occur when both wires of one color pair are connected to the pins of a different color pair at the opposite end.

Split pairs   Split pairs occur when one wire on each of two pairs is reversed at both ends of the run. This is technically not a wire-mapping fault because all of the wires are connected to their equivalent pins at both ends. Because this type of fault essentially requires that the same mistake be made at both ends of the connection, accidental occurrence of split pairs is relatively rare. The more likely reason is the use of the USOC connector pinouts, which are suitable for voice traffic but not data.

FIGURE 14.2:

Common wire mapping faults

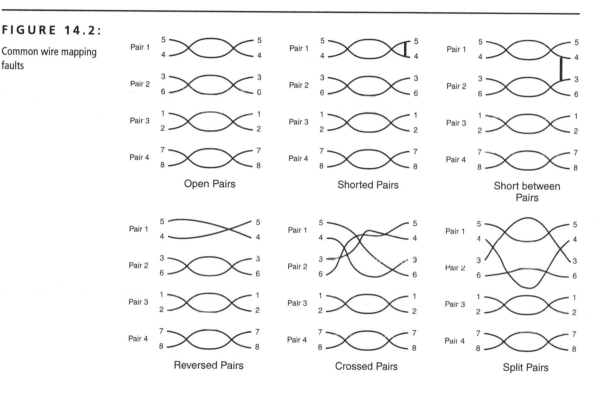

Open Pairs   Shorted Pairs   Short between Pairs

Reversed Pairs   Crossed Pairs   Split Pairs

NOTE   The examples shown in Figures 14.1 and 14.2 use the T568-A pinout standard. If you are using the T568-B pinout, pairs 2 and 3 should be reversed.

Wire mapping faults are usually caused by improper installation practices, although some problems like opens and shorts can result from faulty or damaged cable. The process of testing a connection's wire mapping is fairly straightforward and requires a tester with a remote unit that you attach at one end of the connection and a main unit for the other end. Wire map testing is usually included in multifunction cable testers, but you can also purchase dedicated wire map testers that are far less expensive.

To test the wire mapping, the tester's main unit simply transmits a signal over each wire and detects which pin at the remote unit receives the signal. The problem of split pairs is the only one that is not immediately detectable using this method. This means that two wires in different pairs are transposed at both ends of the connection. Because each pin is connected to the correct pin at the other end of the connection, the wire map may appear to be correct and the connection may appear to function properly when it is first put into service. However, the transposition causes two different signals to run over the wires in a single twisted pair. This can result in an excess of near-end crosstalk that will cause the performance of the cable to degrade at high speeds. Although the occurrence of split pairs is relatively unlikely compared to the other possible wire mapping faults, the ability to detect split pairs is a feature that you may want to check for when evaluating cable testing products.

Cable Length

All LAN technologies are based on standards that dictate the physical layer specifications for the network, including the type of cable you can use and the maximum length of a cable segment. Cable length should be an important consideration from the very beginning of the network planning process. You must locate the components of your network so that the cables connecting them do not exceed the specified maximums.

You may, therefore, question why it is necessary to test the length of your cable connections if you have a plan that already accounts for their length. You may also deduce (correctly) that the maximum cable length specifications are based, at least in part, on the need to avoid the signal degradation that can be caused by attenuation and crosstalk. If you are going to perform separate tests for these factors, why test the cable lengths, too?

There are several reasons. One is that if your network doesn't come close to exceeding the specifications for the protocol you plan to use, you may be able to double-check your cable lengths and omit other tests like those for crosstalk and attenuation. Another reason is that a cable length test can also detect opens, shorts, and cable breaks in a connection. A third reason is that a length test measures the actual length of the wires inside the cable. Because the cable's wire pairs are twisted inside the casing, the actual length of the wires is longer than the length of the cable.

Time Domain Reflectometry   The length of a cable is typically tested in one of two ways: either by time domain reflectometry or by measuring the cable's total resistance. A *time domain reflectometer (TDR)* works much like radar, by transmitting a signal on a cable with the opposite end left open and measuring the amount of time that it takes for the signal's reflection to return to the transmitter, as shown in Figure 14.3. When you have this elapsed time measurement, called the *nominal velocity of propagation (NVP)*, and you know the speed at which electrons move through the cable, you can determine the length of the cable.

FIGURE 14.3:

Time domain reflectometry measures the time needed for a pulse to travel to the end of a cable and back.

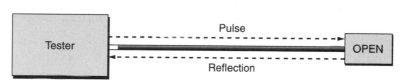

The NVP for a particular cable is usually provided by its manufacturer along with other specifications, measured as a percentage of the speed of light. Some manufacturers provide the NVP as a percentage, such as 72 percent, while others express it as a decimal value multiplied by the speed of light (c), such as 0.72c. Many cable testers compute the length internally, based on the results of the TDR test and an NVP value that is either preprogrammed or that you specify for the cable you're testing.

When testing cable length, it's critically important that your tester use the correct NVP value. The NVP values for various cables can range from 60 percent (0.6c) to 90 percent (0.9c), which creates a margin of error for the cable length results of up to 30 percent if the tester is using the wrong value. Time domain reflectometry has other potential sources of inaccuracy as well. The NVP can vary as much as 4 to 6 percent between the different wire pairs in the same cable, and the pulse generated by the TDR can be distorted from a square wave to one that is roughly sawtooth-shaped, causing a variance in the measured time delay of several nanoseconds, which converts to several feet of cable length.

Because of these possible sources of error, you should be careful when planning and constructing your network not to use cable lengths that closely approach or exceed the maximum recommended in your protocol specification.

Locating Cable Faults   Time domain reflectometry has other applications in cable testing as well, such as the detection and location of cable breaks, shorts, and terminators. The reflection of the test pulse back to the transmitter is caused by a change in impedance on the cable. On a properly functioning cable, the open circuit at the opposite end produces the only change in impedance, but if an open or short exists at some point midway in the cable run, it too will cause a reflection back to the transmitter. The size of the pulse reflected back is in direct proportion to the magnitude of the change in impedance, so a severe open or short will cause a larger reflection than a relatively minor fault, such as a kink, a frayed cable, or a loose connection. If there is no reflection at all, this indicates that the cable has been terminated at the opposite end, which causes the pulse signal to be nullified before it can reflect back.

Cable testers use TDR to locate breaks and faults in cable by distinguishing between these various types of reflections. For example, an open located at 25 feet in a cable run that should be at least 100 feet long indicates that a fault in the cable exists and specifies its approximate location (see Figure 14.4). The problem may be caused by a cable that has been entirely severed or by faulty or damaged wires inside the cable sheath. Sometimes you can't tell that a cable is faulty by examining it from the outside. This is why a test of each cable run during the installation process is so important.

FIGURE 14.4:

TDRs are also used to locate breaks and other faults in a cable.

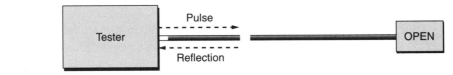

Resistance Measuring   The second method for determining the length of a cable is to measure its total resistance (also called the *loop resistance*) using a digital multimeter (DMM). All cables have a resistance rating, expressed in ohms per meter (or sometimes ohms per 100 meters or ohms per foot). If you know the resistance rating for the cable per unit of length, you can take the cable's total resistance and divide it by the rating to determine the cable's length. In the same way, if you already know the length of the cable from a TDR test, you can use the rating to determine the cable's total resistance.

Impedance

Impedance is the resistance of a cable at a particular frequency and, as you learned earlier, it is variations in impedance that causes the signal reflections that a TDR uses to measure the length of a cable. These reflections are useful in a testing environment, but when the network is in operation, you want to avoid them. Signal reflections can be caused by different factors, including variations in the cable manufacture itself. The statistic that measures the uniformity of the cable's impedance is called its *structural return loss (SRL)*, which is measured in decibels (dB), with higher values indicating a better cable. The SRL is a characteristic of the cable itself and is not usually affected by the installation. SRL values in different cable lots can vary, however, which is why it is a good idea to use cable from the same lot for an installation.

Even when the SRL of a particular cable is acceptable, it is still possible for an installation of that cable to suffer from variations in impedance that cause signal reflections. When you construct a network to conform to a particular cabling specification, such as Category 5 UTP, to maintain a consistent level of impedance throughout the entire length of the cable run you have to use connectors and other hardware that have the same rating as the cable.

If, for example, during a twisted-pair installation, you fail to maintain the twist of the wire pairs up to a point no more than 13mm from each connection, you run the risk of varying the impedance to the point at which a reflection occurs (as well as causing additional crosstalk). The cumulative amount of reflection caused by variations in impedance on a cable run is called its *return loss*, which, like the impedance itself, is measured in ohms. If the return loss is too large, signal transmission errors can occur at high transmission speeds.

Most high-end, multifunction cable testers can measure a cable's impedance and return loss. However, both of these characteristics vary significantly with frequency, so when you perform these tests, you should be sure to use a tester that supports the frequency the network will use. If you plan an eventual upgrade to a faster network protocol, such as from Fast Ethernet to Gigabit Ethernet, you should test at both frequencies.

Attenuation

You learned in Chapter 1, "Introduction to Data Cabling," that one of the major hindrances to high-speed data transfer is attenuation, the weakening of a signal as it travels along a cable. Attenuation is caused by the cable's impedance, and like the impedance itself, it is dependent on the frequency of the signals the cable is carrying. Attenuation is one of the most important specifications for high-speed networks; if it is too high, the signals can degrade prematurely and data can be lost. This is especially true if your network uses cable lengths that approach the maximum permitted by your networking protocol.

Testing the attenuation of a cable run requires a unit at both ends of the connection, one to transmit a calibrated signal and another to receive the signal and calculate how much it has degraded during the trip. Attenuation is measured in decibels (dB), and most good quality cable testers include the secondary module needed to perform the test.

TIP   Attenuation is not always a characteristic inherent to the cable itself. The installation can conceivably have an effect on a cable run's attenuation, especially in the case of coaxial cables that are kinked or otherwise damaged.

Near-End Crosstalk (NEXT)

Along with attenuation, *near-end crosstalk (NEXT)* is one of the major impediments to successfully installing and running a high-speed data network on twisted-pair cabling. Whenever one pair of wires in a cable is carrying data, it produces an electromagnetic field that can cause interference on the other pairs, and increasing the transmission speed only enhances the effect. Twisting the wire pairs causes the opposing fields to cancel each other out. The whole concept of twisting each pair of wires within the cable sheath at a different rate is intended to reduce this interference and minimize NEXT. Because of this, controlling NEXT on your network is contingent on the quality of the installation, even more so than attenuation or any of the other characteristics discussed thus far. If you do not maintain the twist of each wire pair up to within 13mm of every cable termination, you run the risk of increasing NEXT to levels that can inhibit data communications. Increased levels of NEXT can also result from the use of inferior quality components, such as connectors, punch-down blocks, or patch cords and from split pairs, as described in the section "Wire Mapping," earlier in this chapter. The faster you intend to run your network, the more important is to keep NEXT within acceptable levels.

Testing for NEXT is a relatively simple process. After terminating the far end of the cable run to prevent any reflections from interfering with the test, a signal is transmitted over one pair, and the magnitude of the crosstalk signal is measured on the other pairs (in decibels). For a complete assessment, you must test each wire pair against each of the three other pairs, for a total of six tests, and you must perform the six tests from both ends of the cable.

The term *crosstalk* is derived from telephony applications in which a user in the midst of a call can hear another call faintly in the background. In effect, the talk from one call has crossed over into another, and the same thing can happen on a LAN. Crosstalk is most commonly generated near the connection at one end of a cable, and NEXT refers to crosstalk generated at the connection nearest to the node transmitting a signal. The strong signal being transmitted by a node crosses over into the pair of wires through which that same node receives incoming traffic (see Figure 14.5). Because the incoming signal arriving at the node is relatively weak (due to attenuation), and the crosstalk signal is also relatively weak, the two signals arriving over the same wire pair can be confused by the node, causing data loss. It is not so much the existence of crosstalk that inhibits network communications that causes problems; it is when the magnitude of the crosstalk is similar to that of the signal that belongs on the wire pair that problems occur. As a result, a low NEXT rating is a high number (40dB or above at 100MHz, for example), because the magnitude of the crosstalk is much higher than that of the regular signal. A high NEXT rating is a low number (below 30dB at 100MHz, for example), which indicates that the magnitude of the crosstalk is closer to that of the signal.

FIGURE 14.5:

Near-end crosstalk

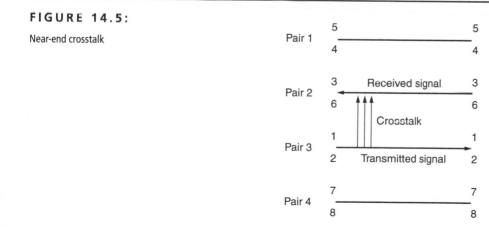

Power Sum NEXT

Power sum NEXT (sometimes called *PS-NEXT*) is not really a separate test, but rather a calculation based on the results of a complete NEXT test. Traditional networking protocols like Ethernet and Token Ring use only two of the four wire pairs in a twisted-pair cable, but some of the higher speed technologies, such as 100Base-T4 Ethernet, ATM, and Gigabit Ethernet, use all four pairs. Because these technologies transmit over multiple pairs at once, it is possible for crosstalk to originate from several sources, as shown in Figure 14.6. PS-NEXT is a measurement of the cumulative effect of crosstalk on each wire pair when the other three pairs are transmitting data simultaneously. Each pair is calculated separately, yielding four results.

FIGURE 14.6:

Some high-speed protocols can generate excessive crosstalk by transmitting over two wire pairs at once.

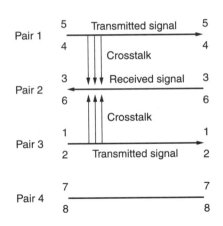

Attenuation to Crosstalk Ratio (ACR)

NEXT occurs at the point where the transmitted signal on the outgoing wire pair is strongest and the received signal on the incoming pair is weakest. This is because the received signal has been attenuated during its trip along the cable. The amount of signal degradation on the incoming pair is proportional to the cable's length, because more cable means more attenuation. As mentioned earlier, it is the comparison between the magnitude of the received signal and the crosstalk from the other pair that determines whether or not the incoming data will be corrupted.

The *attenuation to crosstalk ratio (ACR)* is the difference between the attenuation for the cable run and the amount of crosstalk it exhibits, both of which are measured in decibels. The ACR is one of the best measurements of a cable run's quality. If, for example, the attenuation for a particular cable run is 15dB and its crosstalk is 35dB, the ACR for that run is 20dB. The higher the ACR, the better, because this means that the magnitudes of the signal strength and the crosstalk are sufficiently different for the two signals not to be confused by the receiving system. Because crosstalk varies at either end of the cable run, you must run an ACR test at both ends. The worst of the ACR measurements is the rating for the cable run. You can also compare the PS-NEXT rating with the attenuation to determine the cable's *power sum ACR*.

> **NOTE**
>
> It is important to remember that ACR is measured in decibels, which is based on a logarithmic scale. For example, an ACR rating of 20dB means that the crosstalk is ten times stronger than the attenuation, while a 6dB rating means that the crosstalk is only two times stronger.

Far-End Crosstalk (FEXT)

Far-end crosstalk (FEXT) occurs when a signal crosses over to another wire pair as it approaches the far end of the cable, opposite the system that transmitted it. FEXT is a far less serious problem than NEXT, and by itself is a relatively useless measurement because the amount of crosstalk at the far end is dependent on the length of the cable and the amount of attenuation it provides. To equalize the FEXT measurement for the amount of attenuation present, you simply subtract the attenuation value from the FEXT value to achieve what is called the *equal level FEXT (ELFEXT)*. This is the equivalent of the ACR for the far end of the cable. There is also a *power sum ELFEXT (PS-ELFNEXT)* test, which is a combined measurement for all of the wire pairs in the cable, and a *worst pair-to-pair ELFEXT* test. In most cases, these measurements are not vital to an installation test, but some emerging technologies, such as Gigabit Ethernet, call for them, and some of the newer testers on the market are capable of performing them.

Propagation Delay and Delay Skew

The length of time required for a signal to travel from one end of a cable run to the other, usually measured in nanoseconds (ns), is called its *propagation delay*. Because of the different twist rates used, the lengths of the wire pairs in a cable can vary, and because of differences in insulation, so can their NVP values. As a result, the propagation delay for each wire pair can be slightly different. When your network is running a protocol that uses only one pair of wires to transmit data, such as standard Ethernet, 100Base-TX Ethernet, and Token Ring, these variations are not a problem. However, protocols that transmit over multiple pairs simultaneously, such as 100Base-T4 and Gigabit Ethernet, can lose data when signals arrive over the different pairs too far apart. To quantify this variation, some testers can measure a cable run's *delay skew*, which is the difference between the lowest and the highest propagation delay for the wire pairs within a cable. Delay skew is a characteristic that is not usually affected by the installation, so testing it is usually not mandatory, but it is something you should check when purchasing cable for a network that will run one of the high-speed protocols that uses multiple pairs.

Noise

Most cable tests attempt to detect and quantify problems that result from the effects of the installation on the cable's own characteristics. However, there are also environmental factors that can affect the functionality of the cable installation, and you should be sure to test each cable run for noise that emanates from outside sources. Outside noise is usually generated either by *electromagnetic interference (EMI)*, which is low-frequency, high-amplitude noise generated by AC power lines, electric motors, and fluorescent lights, or *radio frequency interference (RFI)*, which is high-frequency, low-amplitude noise created by radio and television sets and cellular phones. Once again, this type of noise is usually not a problem on lower-speed networks, but it can be on protocols that run the network at 100MHz or more.

Testing for outside noise is a matter of shutting off or detaching all devices on the LAN and testing the cable for electrical activity. One of the most important elements of this kind of test is to perform it when all of the equipment at the site is operating as it normally does during work hours. For example, performing a noise test on an office network during the weekend, when most of the lights, copiers, coffee machines, air conditioning units, and other equipment is shut down will not give you an accurate reading.

Fiber Optic Tests

Just as installing fiber optic cable is completely different from a copper cable installation, the testing processes also differ greatly. Much of the copper cable testing revolves around the various types of interference that can affect the performance of a network. Fiber optic cable is completely immune from interference caused by crosstalk, EMI, and RFI, however, so tests for these are not needed. What you do need for a fiber optic installation is to ensure that the signals arrive at their destinations with sufficient strength to be read and that the installation process has not degraded that strength.

Because of its superior signal carrying capabilities, fiber optic cable installations can include various types of cable runs. The typical LAN arrangement consists of single-fiber links that connect a patch panel in a wiring closet or data center to wall plates or other individual equipment sites over relatively short distances, with patch cables at both ends to connect to a backbone network and to computers or other devices. Because of the limited number of connections they use, testing these types of links is fairly straightforward. However, fiber optic can also support extremely long cable runs that require splices every two to four kilometers, which introduces a greater potential for connection problems.

To completely test a fiber optic installation, you should perform your battery of tests three times. The first series of tests should be on the spooled cable before the installation to ensure that no damage occurred during shipping. The installation costs for fiber optic cable are high—often higher than the cost of the cable and other hardware—so it's worthwhile to test the cable before investing in its installation. Because excessive signal loss is caused mostly by the connections, simply testing the continuity of the cable at this stage is usually sufficient.

The second series of tests should be performed on each separate cable segment as you install it, to ensure that the cable is not damaged during the installation and that each individual connector is installed correctly. By testing at this stage, you can localize problems immediately, rather than trying to track them down after the entire installation is completed. Finally, you should test the entire end-to-end connection, including all patch cables and other hardware, to ensure that cumulative loss is within certified parameters.

For fiber optic LAN installations, only two tests are generally required: optical power and signal loss. The following sections examine these tests and how you perform them. There are other types of tests used on long distance fiber optic links and in troubleshooting that are much more complex and require more elaborate equipment. For more information on these, see the section "Cable Testing Tools," later in this chapter.

Optical Power

The most fundamental test of any fiber optic cable plant is the optical power test, as defined in the EIA's FOTP-95 standard, which determines the strength of the signal passing through a cable run and is the basis for a loss measurement (attenuation) test. The testing process involves connecting a fiber optic power meter to one end of the cable and a light source to the other. The power meter uses a solid state detector to measure the average optical power emanating from the end of the cable, measured in decibels. For data networks using multimode cable, you should perform optical power tests at 850 and 1,300nm wavelengths; many testers run their tests at both settings automatically. Single-mode cables require a 1,300nm test and sometimes 1,550nm, as well. The 1,550nm test determines whether the cable will support wavelength division multiplexing and can detect losses due to microbending that are not apparent at 1,300nm.

WARNING   Some people also claim that you can use an optical time domain reflectometer (OTDR) to test optical power and cable plant loss but, generally speaking, these people are either mistaken or trying to sell you an OTDR. The combination of a fiber optic power meter and light source is the industry standard solution for measuring optical power and signal loss. These tools are also, by far, the more inexpensive solution.

Loss (Attenuation)

Loss testing, along with optical power, are the two most important tests for any fiber optic cable installation. Loss is the term commonly used in the fiber optic world for attenuation; it is the weakening of the signal as it travels through the cable. The fiber optic cable itself is much more resistant to attenuation than any copper cable, which is why fiber cable segments can usually be much longer than copper ones. However, even if your network does not have extremely long fiber cable runs, there can be a significant amount of loss, not because of the cable itself, but because of the connections created during the installation. Loss testing verifies that the cables and connectors were installed correctly.

Measuring the loss on a cable run is similar in practice to measuring its optical power, except that you use a calibrated light source to generate the signal and a fiber optic power meter to measure how much of that signal actually makes it to the other end of the cable run. The combination of the light source and the power meter into one unit is called an *optical loss test set (OLTS)*. Because of the different applications that use fiber optic cable, you should be sure to use test equipment that is designed for your particular type of network. For example, a light source might use either a laser or an LED to create the signal, and the wavelengths it uses may vary as well. For a fiber optic LAN, you should choose a product that uses an LED light source at wavelengths that are the same as the ones your network equipment will use. This will ensure that your tests generate the most accurate possible results.

The testing procedure begins with connecting the light source to one end of a *reference test cable* (also called the *launch cable*) and the power meter to the other end. The reference test cable functions as a baseline against which you measure the loss on your installed cable runs and should use the same type of cable as your network. After measuring the power of the light source over the reference test cable, you disconnect the power meter, connect the reference cable to the end of the cable you want to test, and connect the power meter to the other end. Some testers include a variety of adapters to accommodate various connector types. By taking another power reading and comparing it to the first one, you can calculate the loss for the cable run. As with the optical power test, you should use both 850 and 1,300nm wavelengths for multimode fiber tests; you should also test the cable from the other direction in the same way. When you have the results, compare them to the *optical link budget (OLB)*, which is the maximum amount of signal loss permitted for your network and your application.

WARNING   Be sure to protect your reference test cables from dirt and damage. A faulty reference cable can produce false readings of high loss in your tests.

This type of test effectively measures the loss in the cable itself and in the connector to which the reference test cable is attached. The connection to the power meter itself at the other end introduces virtually no additional signal loss. To test the connectors at both ends of the cable run, you can add a second reference test cable to the far end, which is called a *receive cable*, and connect the power meter to it. This is known as a *double-ended loss test*. The type of test you perform depends on the type of cable run you are testing and the standard you're using as the model for your network.

The standard single-ended loss test is described in the FOTP-171 standard, which was developed by the EIA in the 1980s and intended for testing patch cables. The double-ended loss test for multimode cables is defined in the OFSTP-14 standard and is used to test an installed cable run. Another standard, the OFSTP-7, defines testing standards for single-mode cables. The document describes two testing methods: the double-ended source/meter test from OFSTP-14 and an OTDR test, but when the results differ (and they usually will), the source/meter test is designated as the definitive authority.

WARNING   Some older manuals recommend that you calibrate your power meter using both launch and receive cables, connected by a splice bushing, when you are going to perform double-ended loss tests. This practice introduces additional attenuation into your baseline and can obscure the fact that one of your reference test cables is dirty or damaged. Always establish your testing baseline using a launch cable only.

Depending on the capabilities of your equipment, the loss testing process might be substantially easier. Some power meters have a *zero loss reference* capability, meaning that you can set the meter to read 0dB while measuring the reference test cable. Then, when you test the installed cable run, the meter displays only the loss in decibels; no calculation is necessary.

Cable Plant Certification

So far in this chapter, you've learned about the types of tests you can perform on a cable installation, but not about which tests you should perform for a particular type of network—or the results that you should expect from these tests. The tests you perform and the results you receive enable you to certify your cable installation as complying with a specific standard of performance. Many of the high-quality cable testers on the market perform their various tests automatically and provide you with a list of pass/fail results, but it is important to know not only what is being tested, but what results the tester is programmed to evaluate as passes and failures.

Changing standards and new technologies can affect the performance levels that you should expect and require from your network, and a tester that is only a year or two old may yield results that ostensibly pass muster, but which are actually insufficient for the network protocol you plan to run. Always check to see what standards a tester is using to evaluate your cable's performance. In some testers, the results that determine whether a cable passes or fails a test can be calibrated with whatever values you wish, while others are preprogrammed and cannot easily be changed. Obviously, the former is preferable, as it enables you to upgrade the tester to support changing standards.

The certification that you expect your network to achieve should be based not only on today's requirements, but also on your expectation of future requirements. Professional consultants have been recommending that clients install Category 5 cable for many years, long before most of these clients even considered upgrading to Fast Ethernet or another technology that requires Category 5. This was because the additional investment for a Category 5 installation was then minimal compared to the cost of completely recabling the network later on.

For the same reason, it may be a good idea for the cabling you install today to conform to the requirements for technologies you're not yet considering using. A few years ago, Fast Ethernet was a new and untried technology, yet now it is commonplace. It makes sense to assume that Gigabit Ethernet will be just as common a few years from now. Installing Category 5e or 6 cable now and certifying it to conform to the highest standards currently available may not benefit you today, but in future years, you may be proud of your foresight.

Creating a Testing Regimen

The level of performance that you require from a cable installation should specify which tests you have to perform during the installation process and what test results are acceptable. For example, a UTP installation intended only for voice telephone traffic requires nothing more than a wire mapping test to ensure that the appropriate connections have been made. Other factors will probably not affect the performance of the network sufficiently to warrant testing them. A data network, on the other hand, requires additional testing, and as you increase the speed at which data will travel over the network and the wire pairs used, the need for more extensive testing increases as well. Table 14.1 lists the most common data link layer protocols used on copper cable networks and the tests you should perform on a new cable installation for each one.

TABLE 14.1: Cable Tests Required for Copper-Based Networking Protocols

Network Type	Tests Required
Voice telephone	Wire mapping
10Base-T Ethernet	Wire mapping, length, attenuation, NEXT
100Base-TX	Wire mapping, length, attenuation, NEXT, propagation delay, delay skew
100Base-T4	Wire mapping, length, attenuation, NEXT, propagation delay
100VG-AnyLAN	Wire mapping, length, attenuation, NEXT, delay skew
Token Ring	Wire mapping, length, attenuation, NEXT
TP-PMD FDDI	Wire mapping, length, attenuation, NEXT
155Mbps ATM	Wire mapping, length, attenuation, NEXT
Gigabit Ethernet	Wire mapping, length, attenuation, NEXT, propagation delay, delay skew, PS-NEXT, ELFNEXT, PS-ELFNEXT, return loss

For fiber optic cable installations, optical power and loss testing is sufficient for all multimode fiber LANs. For single-mode networks with long cable runs, OTDR testing is also recommended, as described in the section "Optical Time Domain Reflectometers" later in this chapter.

Copper Cable Certification

While the TIA/EIA-568-A standard includes performance requirements for horizontal and backbone cabling, it provides no guidelines for the testing of Category 5 cable installations. As a result, the TIA/EIA PN-3287 Link Performance task group was formed, which in October 1995 published a document called "TIA/EIA Telecommunications Systems Bulletin 67: Transmission Performance Specifications for Field Testing of Unshielded Twisted-Pair Cabling Systems" or, more simply, TSB-67.

The TSB-67 document defines two types of horizontal links for the purposes of testing. The *basic link* (also called the *permanent link* by other standards) refers to the permanently installed cable connection that typically runs from a wall plate at the equipment site to a patch panel in a wiring closet or data center. The *channel link* refers to the complete end-to-end cable run including the basic link and the patch cables used to connect the equipment to the wall plate and the patch panel jack to the hub or other device.

Annex A to TSB-67 also defines two levels of cable performance requirements: Level I and Level II, the latter of which is more stringent. There are two levels to take into account the differences in hardware required to test basic links and channel links. When testing a channel, you nearly always have to use an RJ-45 jack on the tester to connect to the cable run, introducing (temporarily) a source of additional crosstalk that you don't want to include in the final results of the test. Level I calls for lower performance standards to compensate for the presence of the additional connector. When testing a basic link, however, the tester can use an interface built into the unit that adds very little additional crosstalk, and the higher performance levels required by Level II provide an accurate test. If you plan to purchase an automated cable tester to certify your installation, look for one that is compliant with the TSB-67 standard, and be sure to find out which levels of performance the unit supports.

TSB-67 defines performance levels for only four tests: wire mapping, cable length, attenuation, and NEXT. However, more advanced networking protocols have appeared since TSB-67 was published, such as Gigabit Ethernet, which require specific performance levels for other tests, such as return loss and ELFEXT. In addition, standards are also in the process of being established for new categories of UTP cable, including Category 5e (enhanced) and Category 6.

As a result of these new advances, several addenda to the TIA/EIA-568-A have been published that take the additional cable requirements into account. These documents include "TIA/EIA-568-A-1 Propagation Delay and Delay Skew Specifications for 100-ohm Four-Pair Cable," "TIA 568-A-2 Correction and Additions to TIA/EIA-568-A," and "TIA/EIA-568-A-5 Additional Transmission Performance Specifications for Four-Pair 100-ohm Enhanced Category 5 Cabling," among others. These documents define performance requirements for the following tests, in addition to the basic four defined in TSB-67:

- Power sum NEXT (PS-NEXT)
- Return loss
- Worst pair-to-pair ELFEXT
- Power sum ELFEXT (PS-ELFEXT)
- Propagation delay
- Delay skew

Tables 14.2 and 14.3 summarize the performance levels required for copper cable testing, broken down by cable category and frequency, for basic link and channel link testing, respectively.

TABLE 14.2: TIA Basic Link Testing Performance Standards

	Category 3	Category 5	Category 5e	Category 6
Wire mapping	All pins properly connected	All pins properly connected	All pins properly connected	All pins properly connected
Length (in meters, including tester cords)	<94	<94	<94	<94
Attenuation (dB)				
@ 1MHz	3.2	2.1	2.1	2.1
@ 10MHz	10.0	6.3	6.3	6.2
@ 100MHz	N/A	21.6	21.6	20.7
@ 200MHz	N/A	N/A	N/A	30.4
NEXT (dB)				
@ 1MHz	40.1	60.0	64	73.5
@ 10MHz	24.3	45.5	49	57.8
@ 100MHz	N/A	29.3	32.3	41.9
@ 200MHz	N/A	N/A	N/A	36.9
PS-NEXT (dB)				
@ 1MHz	N/A	N/A	60	71.2
@ 10MHz			45.5	55.5
@ 100MHz			29.3	39.3
@ 200MHz			N/A	34.3
ELFNEXT (dB)				
@ 1MHz	N/A	57	61	65.2
@ 10MHz		37	41	45.2
@ 100MHz		17	21	25.2
@ 200MHz		N/A	N/A	19.2
PS-ELFNEXT (dB)				
@ 1MHz	N/A	54.4	58	62.2
@ 10MHz		34.4	38	42.2
@ 100MHz		14.4	18	22.2
@ 200MHz		N/A	N/A	16.2
Return loss (dB)	N/A	8	10	12
Propagation delay	N/A	<548ns	<548ns	<548ns
Delay skew	N/A	<45ns	<45ns	<45ns

TABLE 14.3:   TIA Channel Link Testing Performance Standards

	Category 3	Category 5	Category 5e	Category 6
Wire mapping	All pins properly connected	All pins properly connected	All pins properly connected	All pins properly connected
Length (in meters, including tester cords)	<100	<100	<100	<100
Attenuation (dB)				
@ 1MHz	4.2	2.5	2.1	2.2
@ 10MHz	11.5	7.0	6.3	6.4
@ 100MHz	N/A	24.0	24.0	21.6
@ 200MHz	N/A	N/A	N/A	31.8
NEXT (dB)				
@ 1MHz	39.1	60.3	63.0	72.7
@ 10MHz	22.7	44.0	47.0	56.6
@ 100MHz	N/A	27.1	30.1	39.9
@ 200MHz	N/A	N/A	N/A	34.8
PS-NEXT (dB)				
@ 1MHz	N/A	N/A	60.0	71.2
@ 10MHz			44.0	54.0
@ 100MHz			27.1	37.1
@ 200MHz			N/A	31.9
ELFNEXT (dB)				
@ 1MHz	N/A	57	59	63.2
@ 10MHz		37	39	43.2
@ 100MHz		17	17.4	23.2
@ 200MHz		N/A	N/A	17.2
PS-ELFNEXT (dB)				
@ 1MHz	N/A	54.4	56	60.2
@ 10MHz		34.4	36	40.2
@ 100MHz		14.4	14.4	20.2
@ 200MHz		N/A	N/A	14.2
Return loss (dB)	N/A	8	10	12
Propagation delay	N/A	<548ns	<548ns	<548ns
Delay skew	N/A	<45ns	<45ns	<45ns

> **NOTE**   Some of the figures included in Tables 14.2 and 14.3 are derived from standards still in various stages of development. The actual values in the final published standards may vary slightly.

Fiber Optic Certification

After testing the signal loss generated by a fiber optic cable run, you compare the results to the optical loss budget (OLB) for the cable to determine if the installation is within performance parameters. The OLB is a calculation based on the number of connectors and splices in a cable run and the length of the cable. The basic formula for computing the OLB is as follows:

```
OLB = cable loss + connector loss + splice loss
```

Essentially, you are adding together the amount of acceptable loss for the length of the cable and for the number of splices and connectors. You do this by multiplying the actual cable length and the number of splices and connectors by predefined coefficients. These coefficients vary according to the type of fiber cable you're using, the wavelength of the network, the standard you adhere to, and the sources you consult. The values you opt to use for the coefficients determine how stringent your tests will be. Lower coefficients result in a lower OLB, meaning that you will tolerate a smaller amount of attenuation on your network.

For the connectors, coefficients range from 0.5 to a maximum of 0.75. For the splices, coefficients are 0.2 or 0.3. For the cable length coefficient, use the values listed in Table 14.4.

TABLE 14.4:   Cable Coefficients for Optical Link Budget Calculations

	850nm	1,300nm	1,550nm
Multimode fiber	3 to 3.75dB/km	1 to 1.5dB/km	N/A
Single-mode fiber	N/A	0.4dB/km	0.3dB/km

Using these coefficient values, you construct an OLB formula like the following, which provides for the most stringent possible test standard on a multimode cable run at 850nm:

```
OLB = (number of connectors*0.5) + (number of splices*0.2) + (cable
length*3.0 dB/km)
```

Third-Party Certification

Testing your cable installation for compliance to a specific standard is a great way to ensure that the cable plant will support the networking protocol you plan to run. If you have installed the cabling yourself, testing is needed to check your work, and if you have the cable installed by a third party, testing ensures that the job was done correctly. Hand-held testers can perform a comprehensive battery of tests and provide results in a simple pass/fail format, but these results depend on what standards the device is configured to use.

In most cases, it isn't difficult to modify the parameters of the tests performed by these devices (either accidentally or deliberately) so that they produce false positive results. Improper use of these devices can also introduce inaccuracies into the testing process. As a general rule, it isn't a good idea to have the same people check the work that they performed. This is not necessarily an accusation of duplicity. It's simply a fact of human nature that intimate familiarity with something can make it difficult to recognize faults in it.

For these reasons, you may want to consider engaging a third-party testing and certification company to test your network after the cable installation is completed and certify its compliance with published standards. If your own people are installing the cable, then this is a good way to test their work thoroughly without having to purchase expensive testing equipment. If your cable is being installed by an outside contractor, adding a clause into the contract that states that final acceptance of the work is contingent on the results of an independent test is a good way of ensuring that you get a quality job, even if you accept the lowest bid you're offered. What contractor would be willing to risk having to reinstall an entire network?

Cable Testing Tools

The best method for addressing a faulty cable installation is to avoid the problems in the first place by purchasing high quality components and installing them carefully. But no matter how careful you are, problems are bound to arise. This section covers the tools that you can use to test cables both at the time of their installation and afterwards, when you're troubleshooting cable problems. Cable testing tools can range from simple, inexpensive, mechanical devices to elaborate, electronic testers that automatically supply you with a litany of test results in an easy-to-read pass/fail format.

The following sections list the types of tools that are available for both copper and fiber optic cable testing. This is not to say that you need all of the tools listed here. In fact, some of the following sections attempt to steer you away from certain types of tools. In some cases, there are both high-tech and low-tech devices available that perform roughly the same function, and you can choose which you prefer according to the requirements of your network, your operational budget, or your temperament. Some of the tools are extremely complicated and require extensive training to use effectively, while others are usable by anyone who can read.

You should select the types of tools you need based on the descriptions of cable tests given earlier in this chapter, the test results required by the standards you're using to certify your network, and the capabilities of the people that will be doing the actual work—not to mention the amount of money you want to spend.

Wire Map Testers

A wire map tester is a device that transmits signals through each wire in a copper twisted-pair cable to determine if it is connected to the correct pin at the other end. Wire mapping is the most basic test for twisted-pair cables because the eight separate wire connections involved in each cable run are a common source of installation errors. Wire map testers detect transposed wires, opens (broken or unconnected wires), and shorts (wires or pins improperly connected to each other)—all problems that can render a cable run inoperable.

Wire map testing is nearly always included in multifunction cable testers, but in some cases it may not be worth the expense to spend thousands of dollars on a comprehensive device. Dedicated wire map testers are relatively inexpensive (from $200 to $300) and enable you to test your installation for the most common faults that occur during installations and afterwards. If you are installing voice-grade cable, for example, a simple wire mapping test may be all that's needed. There are also slightly more expensive (under $500) devices that do wire map testing in addition to other basic functions, such as TDR length testing.

A wire map tester consists of a remote unit that you attach to the far end of a connection and the battery-operated, hand-held main unit that displays the results. Typically, the tester displays various codes to describe the type of faults it finds. In some cases, you can purchase a tester with multiple remote units that are numbered, so that one person can test several connections without constantly traveling back and forth from one end of the connections to the other to move the remote unit.

> **WARNING** The one wiring fault that is not detectable by a dedicated wire map tester is split pairs, because even though the pinouts are incorrect, the cable is still wired straight through. To detect split pairs, you must use a device that tests the cable for the near-end crosstalk that split pairs cause.

Continuity Testers

A continuity tester is an even simpler and less expensive device than a wire map tester. It is designed to check a copper cable connection for basic installation problems, such as opens, shorts, and crossed pairs. At $50 to $200, these devices usually cannot detect more complicated twisted-pair wiring faults such as split pairs, but they are sufficient for basic cable testing, especially for coaxial cables, which have only two conductors that are not easily confused by the installer. Like a wire map tester, a continuity tester consists of two separate units that you connect to each end of the cable to be tested. In many cases, the two units can snap together for storage and easy testing of patch cables.

Tone Generators

The simplest type of copper cable tester is also a two-piece unit and is called a tone generator and probe, also sometimes called a "fox and hound" wire tracer. This type of device consists of a unit that you connect to a cable with a standard jack or to an individual wire with alligator clips, which transmits a signal over the cable or wire. The other unit is a penlike probe that emits an audible tone when touched to the other end of the cable or wire or even to its insulating sheath.

This type of device is most often used to locate a specific connection in a punch-down block. For example, some installers prefer to run all of the cables for a network to the central punch-down block without labeling them and then to use a tone generator to identify which block is connected to which wall plate and label the punch-down block accordingly. You can also use the device to identify a particular cable at any point between the two ends. Since the probe can detect the cable containing the tone signal through its sheath, you can locate one specific cable out of a bundle in a ceiling conduit or other type of raceway by connecting the tone generator to one end and touching the probe to each cable in the bundle until you hear the tone.

In addition, by testing the continuity of individual wires using alligator clips, you can use a tone generator and probe to locate opens, shorts, and miswires. An open wire will produce no tone at the other end, a short will produce a tone on two or more wires at the other end, and an improperly connected wire will produce a tone on the wrong pin at the other end.

This process is extremely time-consuming, however, and it's nearly as prone to errors as the cable installation itself. You either have to continually travel from one end of the cable to the other to move the tone generator unit, or use a partner to test each connection, keeping in close contact using radios or some other means of communication in order to avoid confusion. When you consider the time and effort involved, you will probably find that investing in a wire map tester is a more practical solution.

Time Domain Reflectometers (TDR)

As described earlier in the section "Cable Length," a time domain reflectometer (TDR) is the primary tool used to determine the length of a copper cable and to locate the impedance variations that are caused by opens, shorts, damaged cables, and interference with other systems. There are two basic types of TDRs available: those that display their results as a waveform on an LCD or CRT screen, and those that use a numeric readout to indicate the distance to a source of impedance. The latter type of TDR provides less detail but is easy to use and relatively inexpensive. Many of the automated copper cable testers on the market have a TDR integrated into the unit. Waveform TDRs are not often used for field testing these days, because they are much more expensive than the numeric type and require a great deal more expertise to use effectively.

You can use a TDR to test any kind of cable that uses metallic conductors, including the coaxial and twisted-pair cables used to construct LANs. A high quality TDR can detect a large variety of cable faults, including open conductors; shorted conductors; loose connectors; sheath faults; water damage; crimped, cut, or smashed cables; and many other conditions. In addition, the TDR can measure the length of the cable and the distance to any of these faults. Many people also use the TDR as an inventory management tool to ensure that a reel contains the length of cable advertised and to determine if a partially used reel contains enough cable for a particular job.

NOTE   There is also a special kind of TDR used to test fiber optic cables called an optical time domain reflectometer (OTDR). For more information, see the section "Optical Time Domain Reflectometers (OTDRs)" later in this chapter.

Fault Detection

When a TDR transmits its signal pulse onto a cable, any extraordinary impedance that the signal encounters causes it to reflect back to the unit, where it can be detected by a receiver. The amount of impedance determines the magnitude of the reflected signal. The TDR registers the magnitude of the reflection and uses it to determine the source of the impedance. The TDR also measures the elapsed time between the transmission of the signal and the receipt of the reflection and, using the NVP that you supply for the cable, determines the location of the impedance. For example, on an unterminated cable with no faults, the only source of impedance is the end of the cable, which registers as an open, enabling the TDR to measure the overall length of the cable.

When there are faults in the cable, they return reflections of different magnitudes. A complete open caused by a broken cable prevents the signal from traveling any farther down the cable, so it appears as the last reflection. However, less serious faults enable the signal to continue on down the cable, possibly generating additional reflections. A waveform TDR displays the original test signal on an oscilloscopelike screen, as well as the individual reflections. An experienced operator can analyze the waveforms and determine what types of faults caused the reflections and where they are located.

Automated TDRs analyze the reflections internally and use a numerical display to show the results. Some of these devices are dedicated TDR units that can perform comprehensive cable fault tests at a substantially lower price than a waveform TDR and are far easier to use. The unit displays the distance to the first fault located on the cable and may also display whether the reflection indicates a high impedance change (denoting an open) or a low impedance change (denoting a short). Some of these units even offer the ability to connect to a standard oscilloscope in order to display waveform results, if desired.

Blind Spots

Some TDRs enable you to select from a range of pulse widths. The *pulse width* specifies the amount of energy the unit transmits as its test pulse. The larger the pulse width, the longer the signal travels on the cable, enabling the TDR to detect faults at greater distances. However, signals with larger pulse widths also take longer to transmit, and the TDR is all but incapable of detecting a fault during the time that it is transmitting. For example, since the signal pulse travels at approximately 3ns per meter, a 20ns pulse means that the beginning of the pulse will be about 6.6 meters from the transmitter when the end of the pulse leaves the unit. This time interval during which the pulse transmission tales place is known as a *blind spot*, and it can be a significant problem, because faults often occur in the patch cables, wall plates, and other connectors near to the end of the cable run.

When you have a TDR with a variable pulse width control, you should always begin your tests with the lowest setting so that you can detect faults that occur close to the near end of the cable. If no faults are detected, you can increase the setting to test for faults at greater distances. Larger pulse widths can also aid in detecting small faults that are relatively close. If a cable fault is very subtle and you use a low pulse width setting, the attenuation of the cable may prevent the small reflection from being detected by the receiver. Larger pulse widths may produce a reflection that is more easily detected.

If your TDR uses a fixed-pulse width, you may want to connect an extra jumper cable between the unit and the cable run to be tested. This jumper cable should be at least as long as the blind spot and should use cable of the same impedance as the cable to be tested. It should also have high-quality connections to both the tester and the cable run. If you choose to do this, however, be sure to subtract the length of the jumper cable from all distances given in the test results.

Integrated TDRs

Many of the combination cable testers on the market include TDR technology, primarily for determining the cable length, but they may not include the ability to detect subtle cable faults like the dedicated units. Obviously, a severed cable is always detectable by the display of a shorter length than expected, but other faults may not appear. Some units are not even designed to display the cable length by default, but instead simply present a pass/fail result based on a selected network type. If, for example, you configure the unit to test a 10Base-T cable, any length under 100 meters may receive a pass rating. For the experienced installer, a unit that can easily display the raw data in which the pass/fail results are based is preferable.

Another concern when selecting a TDR is its ability to test all four of the wire pairs in a twisted-pair cable. Some devices use time domain reflectometry only to determine the length of the cable and are not intended for use as fault locators. As a result, they might not test all of the wire pairs, making it seem as though the cable is intact for its entire length when, in fact, there could be opens or shorts on one or more pairs.

Fiber Optic Power Meters

A fiber optic power meter is a device that measures the intensity of the signal being transmitted over a fiber optic cable. The meter is similar in principle to a multimeter that measures electric current, except that it works with light instead of electricity. The meter uses a solid state detector to measure the signal intensity and incorporates signal conditioning circuitry and a digital display. There are different meters for different fiber optic cables and applications. Meters for use on short wavelength systems, up to 850nm, use a silicon detector, while long wavelength systems need a meter with a germanium or InGaAs detector that can support 850 to 1,550nm. In many cases, optical power meters are marketed in models intended for specific applications, such as CATV (cable television), telephone systems, and LANs.

Other, more expensive units can measure both long and short wavelength signals. Given that the cost of fiber optic test equipment can be quite high, you should generally try to find products specifically suited for your network and application, so that you're not paying for features you'll never use. Low-end power meters that provide the basic features for a specific network type run from $300 to $500. Higher-end devices can run from $500 to over $1,000.

A good optical power meter enables you to display results in various units of measure and signal resolutions, can be calibrated to different wavelengths, and measures power in the range of at least 0dBm to –50dBm. Some meters intended for special applications can measure signals as high as +20dBm to –70dBm. An optical power meter registers the average optical power over time, not the peak power, so it is sensitive to a signal source with a pulsed output. If you know the pulse cycle of the signal source, you can compute the peak power from the average power reading.

A fiber optic power meter that has been properly calibrated to NIST (the United States' National Institute of Standards and Technology) standards typically has a +/–5 percent margin for error, due primarily to variances introduced by the connection to the cable being tested, low-level noise generated by the detector, and the meter's signal conditioning circuitry. These variances are typical for all optical power meters, regardless of their cost and sophistication.

The ability to connect the power meter to the cables you want to test is obviously important. Most units use modular adapters that enable you to connect to any of the dozens of connector styles used in the fiber optic industry, although ST and SC connectors are most commonly used on LANs. The adapters may or may not be included with the unit, however, and reference test cables usually are not, so be sure to get all of the accessories you need to perform your tests.

Fiber Optic Test Sources

In order to measure the strength of an optical signal, there must be a signal source at the other end of the cable. While you can use a fiber optic power meter to measure the signal generated by your actual network equipment, accurately measuring the signal loss of a cable requires a consistent signal generated by a fiber optic test source. Companion to the power meter in a fiber optic tool kit, the test source is also designed for use with a particular type of network. Sources typically use LEDs (for multimode fiber) or lasers (for single-mode fiber) to generate a signal at a specific wavelength, and you should choose a unit that simulates the type of signals used by your network equipment.

Like power meters, test sources must be able to connect to the cable being tested. Some sources use modular adapters like those on power meters, but others, especially laser sources, use a fixed connector that requires you to supply a hybrid jumper cable that connects the light source to the test cable.

Like optical power meters, light sources are available in a wide range of models. LED sources can range from $300 to $1,500, while laser sources can run to well over $2,000. Beware, however, of extremely inexpensive (under $100) light sources, because there are some that are intended only for identifying a particular cable in a bundle using visible light. These devices are not suitable for testing signal loss in combination with a power meter.

Optical Loss Test Sets and Test Kits

In most cases, you need both an optical power meter and a test source in order to properly install and troubleshoot a fiber optic network, and you can usually save a good deal of money and effort by purchasing the two together. This practice ensures that you purchase units that both support the wavelengths and power levels you need and that are calibrated for use together. You can purchase the devices together in two ways: as a single combination unit called an optical loss test set (OLTS), or as separate units in a fiber optic test kit.

An OLTS is generally not recommended for field testing, because it is a single unit. While useful in a lab or for testing patch cables, two separate devices would be needed to test a permanently installed link because you have to connect the light source to one end of the cable and the power meter to the other. However, for fiber optic contractors involved in large installations, it may be practical to give workers their own OLTS set so that they can work with a partner and easily test each cable run in both directions.

Fiber optic test kits are the preferable alternative for most fiber optic technicians because they include a power meter and light source that are designed to work together, usually at a price that is lower than the cost of two separate products. Many test kits also include an assortment of accessories needed to test a particular type of network, such as adapters for various types of connectors, reference test cables, and a carrying case. Prices for test kits can range from $500 to $600 for basic functionality, to as much as $5,000 for a comprehensive kit that can test virtually every type of fiber optic cable.

TIP Communications can be a vital element of any cable installation in which two or more people are working together, especially when the two ends of the permanent cable runs can be a long distance apart, as on a fiber optic network. Some test sets address this problem by incorporating voice communication devices into the power meter and light source, using the tested cable to carry the signals.

Optical Time Domain Reflectometers (OTDRs)

An optical time domain reflectometer (OTDR) is the fiber optic equivalent of the TDR that is used to test copper cables. The OTDR transmits a calibrated signal pulse over the cable to be tested and monitors the signal that returns back to the unit. Instead of measuring signal reflections caused by electrical impedance as a TDR does, however, the OTDR measures the signal returned by backscatter, a phenomenon that affects all fiber optic cables. *Backscatter* is caused by photons bouncing off of the inside walls of the cable in every direction, as shown in Figure 14.7. The backscattered signal returned to the OTDR is much weaker than the original pulse due to the attenuation of the outgoing pulse, the relatively small amount of signal that is scattered (called the *backscatter coefficient* of the cable), and the attenuation of the scattered signal on its way back to the source.

FIGURE 14.7:

OTDRs detect the scattered photons that return to the transmitter on a fiber optic cable.

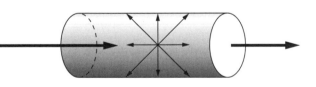

As with a TDR, the condition of the cable causes variances in the amount of backscatter returned to the OTDR, which is displayed on an LCD or CRT screen as a waveform. By interpreting the signal returned, it's possible to identify cable faults of specific types and other conditions. An OTDR can locate splices and connectors and measure their performance; identify stress problems caused by improper cable installation; and locate cable breaks, manufacturing faults, and other weaknesses. Knowing the speed of the pulse as it travels down the cable, the OTDR can also use the elapsed time between the pulse's transmission and reception to pinpoint the location of specific conditions on the cable.

The two primary tasks that OTDRs should *not* be used for are measuring a cable's signal loss and locating faults on LANs. Measuring loss is the job of the power meter and light source, which are designed to simulate the actual conditions of the network. Using an OTDR, it is possible to compute a cable's length based on the backscatter returned to the unit, but the results are almost certain to be far less accurate. The only possible advantage to using an OTDR for this purpose is that you can test the cable from one end, while the traditional method requires that the light source be connected to one end and the power meter to the other.

OTDRs also have limited distance resolution capabilities, making them quite difficult to use effectively in a LAN environment where the cables are only a few hundred feet long. OTDRs are used primarily on long distance connections, such as those used by telephone and cable television networks. As a result, you might find people who are experts at fiber optic LAN applications that have never seen or used an OTDR. There are other possible reasons why they may not have used an OTDR as well. One is that, as with TDRs, interpreting the waveforms generated by an OTDR takes a good deal of training and experience. Another reason is their jaw-dropping price. Full-featured OTDR units can cost anywhere from $17,000 to $30,000. There are also smaller units (sometimes called mini-OTDRs) with fewer features that can run from $7,000 to $15,000.

Fiber Optic Inspection Microscopes

Splicing and attaching connectors to fiber optic cables are tasks that require great precision, and the best way to inspect cleaved fiber ends and polished connection ferrules is with a microscope. Fiber optic inspection microscopes are designed to hold cables and connectors in precisely the correct position for examination, enabling you to detect dirty, scratched, or cracked connectors and ensure that cables are cleaved properly in preparation for splicing. Good microscopes typically provide approximately 100 power magnification (although products range from 30 to 800 power), have a built-in light source (not a fiber optic light source, but a source of illumination for the object under the scope), and are able to support various types of connectors using additional stages, which may or may not be included. A cost of $100 to $200 is typical.

Visual Fault Locators

The light that carries signals over fiber optic cable is invisible to the naked eye, making it difficult to ensure that installers have made the proper connections without a formal test. A visual fault locator (sometimes called a cable tracer) is a quick and dirty way to test the continuity of a fiber cable connection by sending visible light over a fiber optic cable. A typical fault locator is essentially a flashlight that applies its LED or incandescent light source to one end of a cable, which is visible from the other end. This enables you to locate a specific cable out of a bundle and ensure that a connection has been established.

More powerful units that use laser light sources can actually disclose points of high loss in the cable visually, such as breaks, kinks, and bad splices, as long as the cable sheath is not completely opaque. For example, the yellow or orange-colored sheaths commonly used on single-mode and multimode cables (respectively) usually admit enough of the light energy lost by major cable faults to make them detectable from outside. In a world of complex and costly testing tools, fault locators are one of the simplest and most inexpensive items in a fiber optic toolkit, usually costing well under $100. Their utility is limited when compared to some of the other tools described here, but they are a convenient means of finding a particular cable and locating major installation faults.

Multifunction Cable Scanners

The most heavily marketed cable testing tools available today are the multifunction cable scanners, sometimes called certification tools. These are devices that are available for both copper and fiber optic networks and perform a series of tests on a cable run, compare the results against either preprogrammed standards or parameters that you supply, and display the outcome as a series of pass or fail ratings. Most of these units perform the basic tests called for by the most commonly used standards, such as wire mapping, length, attenuation, and NEXT for copper cables, and optical power and signal loss for fiber optic. Many of the copper cable scanners also go beyond the basics to perform a comprehensive battery of tests, including propagation delay, delay skew, PS-NEXT, ELFNEXT, PS-ELFNEXT, and return loss.

The primary advantage of this type of device is that anyone can use it. You simply connect the unit to a cable, press a button, and read off the results after a few seconds. Many units can store the results of many individual tests in memory, download them to a PC, or output them directly to a printer. This primary advantage, however, is also the primary disadvantage of this type of device. The implication behind these products is that you don't really have to understand the tests being performed, the results of those tests, or the cabling standards used to evaluate them. The interface insulates you from the raw data, and you are supposed to trust the manufacturer implicitly and believe that a series of pass ratings means that your cables are installed correctly and functioning properly.

The fundamental problem with this process, however, is that the standards used to assess the test results gathered by the device are not necessarily reliable. Some units claim to certify Category 6 and Category 7 cables, for example, when standards for these cables have not yet been ratified. One must even question the validity of the testers that claim to certify Category 5e cables, since this standard was ratified only recently. When evaluating products like these, it's important to choose units that are upgradable or manually configurable so that you can keep up with the constantly evolving standards.

This configurability can lead to another problem, however. In many cases, it isn't difficult to modify the testing parameters of these units to make it easier for a cable to pass muster. For example, simply changing the NVP for a copper cable can make a faulty cable pass the unit's tests. An unscrupulous contractor can conceivably perform a shoddy installation using inferior cable and use his own carefully prepared tester to show the client a list of perfect "pass" test results.

As another example, some of the more elaborate (and more expensive) fiber optic cable testers attempt to simplify the testing process by supplying main and remote units that both contain an integrated light source and semiconductor detector and by testing at the 850nm and 1,300nm wavelengths simultaneously. This type of device enables you to test the cable in both directions and at both wavelengths simply by connecting the two units to either end of a cable run; there is no need to use reference test cables to swap the units to test the run from each direction or to run a separate test for each wavelength.

However, these devices, apart from costing several times as much as a standard power meter/light source combination ($4,000 or more, in some cases), do not compare the test results to a baseline established with that equipment. Instead, they compare them to preprogrammed standards, which, when it comes to fiber optic cables, can be defined as somewhat loose. The result is a device that is designed primarily for use by people who really don't understand what they are testing and who will trust the device's pass or fail judgment without question, even when the standards used to gauge the test results are loose enough to permit faulty installations to receive a pass rating.

This is not to say that these multifunction devices are completely useless. In fact, they can be an extremely efficient means of testing and troubleshooting your network. The important thing is to understand what they are testing and to either examine the raw data gathered by the unit or verify that the standards used to formulate the pass/fail results are valid. The prices of these products can be shocking, however. Both copper and fiber optic units can easily run to several thousand dollars, with top-of-the-line models exceeding $5,000.

Troubleshooting Cabling Problems

Cabling problems account for a substantial number of network support calls; some authorities say as many as 40 to 50 percent. Whether or not this is so, there are bound to be occasions in any network administrator's career when network communication problems can be attributed to no other cause than the network cabling. The type of cable your network uses and how it is installed will have a big effect on the frequency and severity of cabling problems.

For example, a coaxial thin Ethernet network allowed to run wild on floors and behind furniture is far more likely to experience problems than a 10Base-T network installed inside the walls and ceilings. This is true not only because the coaxial cables are exposed and more liable to be damaged, but also because the bus topology is more sensitive to faults and the BNC connectors are more easily loosened. This goes to show that you can take steps towards minimizing the potential for cable problems by selecting the right products and installing them properly.

Establishing a Baseline

Many cable problems manifest themselves similarly to software problems, so it can often be difficult to determine when a problem is actually caused by the cable. The first step in simplifying the process of isolating the source of network problems is to make sure that all of your cables are functioning properly at the outset. You do this by testing all of your cable runs as you install them, as described earlier in this chapter, and documenting your network installation.

If you use a multifunction cable tester, you can usually store the results of your tests in some way by retaining them in the tester's memory, copying them to a

PC, or printing them out. By doing this, you establish a performance baseline against which you can compare future test results. For example, by recording the lengths of all your cable runs at the time of the installation, you can tell if a cable break has occurred later by retesting and seeing if the length results are different than before. In the same way, you can compare the levels of crosstalk, outside noise, and other characteristics that may have changed since the cable was installed. Even if your tester does not have these data storage features, you should manually record the results for future reference.

Another good idea is to create and maintain a map of all your cable runs on a floor plan of your site. Sometimes cable problems can be the result of outside factors, such as interference from electrical equipment in the building. A problem that affects multiple cable runs might be traced to a particular location where new equipment was installed or existing equipment modified. When you install your cables inside walls and ceilings (and especially when outside contractors do it for you), it can be difficult to pinpoint the routes that individual cables take. A map serves as a permanent record of your installation, both for yourself and any future people working on the network.

Locating the Problem

Troubleshooting your network's cable plant uses many of the same common sense skills as any other troubleshooting task. You try to isolate the cause of the problem by asking questions like the following:

- Has the cable has ever worked properly?
- When did the malfunctions start?
- Do the malfunctions occur at specific times?
- What has changed since the cable functioned properly?

Once you've gathered all the information you can, the general troubleshooting process consists of steps like the following:

1. Split the system into its logical elements.
2. Locate the element that is most likely the cause of the problem.
3. Test the element or install a substitute to verify it as the cause of the problem.

4.   If the suspected element is not the cause, move on to the next likely element.

5.   After locating the cause of the problem, repair or replace it.

Thus, you might begin troubleshooting by determining for sure that the cable run is the source of the problem. You can do this by connecting different devices to both ends of the cable to see if the problem continues to occur. Once you verify that the cable is at fault, you can logically break it down into its component elements. For example, a typical cable run might consist of two patch cables (one at each end), a wall plate, a punch-down block, and the permanently installed cable itself.

In this type of installation, the easiest thing to do is test the patch cables, either by replacing them or testing them with a cable scanner. Replacing components can be a good troubleshooting method, as long as you know that the replacements are good. If, for example, you purchase a box of 100 cheap patch cables that are labeled Category 5 when they actually use Category 3 cable, replacing one with another won't do any good.

The most accurate method is to test the individual components with a cable scanner. If the patch cables pass, then proceed to test the permanent link. If you don't have a scanner available, you can examine the connectors at either end of the cable run and even reconnect or replace them to verify that they were installed correctly. However, there's little you can do if the problem is inside a wall or in some other inaccessible place. If you do have a scanner, the results of the tests should provide you with the information you need to proceed.

Resolving Specific Problems

Cable testers, no matter how elaborate, can't tell you what to do to resolve the problems they disclose. The following sections examine some of the courses of action you can take to address the most common cabling problems.

Wire Map Faults

Wire map faults are the result of an improper installation. When the wires within a twisted-pair cable are attached to the wrong pins, the cable is no longer wired straight through. If the pairs used to carry network data are involved, then signals won't reach their destination. In most cases, this fault occurs on a permanent link, although it is possible for a patch cable to be miswired.

The possible causes of wire map faults are simple errors made during the installation or the use of different pinouts at each end of the cable. If the installer working at one end is using the T568-A pinouts and the other end is connected using T568-B, then faults will occur. Whatever the cause, however, the remedy is to rewire the connectors on one or both ends so that each pin at one end is connected to its equivalent pin at the other end.

Excessive Length

Cable lengths should be carefully planned before the network is installed and tested immediately after the installation to make sure that the cables are not longer than the recommended maximum for the network protocol you plan to use. Problems like late collisions on an Ethernet network or excessive retransmissions due to attenuated signals can be caused by cable runs that are too long. Don't be overly concerned, however, if the maximum allowable length for a cable segment is 100 meters and you have a run that is 101 meters long. Most protocols have some leeway built into them that permit a little excess.

TIP   It's possible for a cable tester to generate length readings that are incorrect if the tester is improperly calibrated. If the cable length seems wrong, check to make sure that the nominal velocity of propagation (NVP) setting for the cable is correct.

To address the problem, you can start by using shorter patch cables, if possible. In some cases, you may find that an installer has left extra cable coiled in a ceiling or wall space that can be removed, and the end can be reconnected to the wall plate or punch-down block. Sometimes a more efficient cable route can enable you to rewire the run using less cable. If, however, you find that the problem is caused by bad planning in the first place and the wall plate is literally too far away from the punch-down block, there are several actions you can take.

The first and easiest action is to test the attenuation and NEXT on the cable run to see if they exceed the requirements for the protocol. These characteristics are often the primary reasons for these maximum length specifications. If you have installed cable that is of a higher quality than is required, you may be able to get away with the additional length. The other alternative is to use a repeater to amplify the signal at some point along the run. Standalone repeaters for coaxial cables and mini-hubs for twisted-pair cables can provide the additional boost needed to avoid signal degradation caused by attenuation and crosstalk on an excessively long cable.

Opens and Shorts

Opens and shorts can be caused by improper installation, or they can occur later if a cable is damaged or severed. If the cable's length is correct but one or more wires is open or shorted, then it is likely that a connector is faulty or has come loose and needs repairing or replacing. If all of the wires in a cable are reported as open in the same place, or if the length of all the wires is suddenly shorter than it should be, it's possible that the cable has been accidentally cut at some point by nearby equipment or by someone working in the area. Cables that are damaged but not completely severed may show up with drastically different lengths for the wire pairs or as shorts at some interim point.

Cable scanners usually display the distance to the open or short so that you can more easily locate and repair it. For cables installed in walls and ceilings, this is one occasion when the cable map you (hopefully) created during the installation can come in handy. If you don't know the cable's route, you can use a tone generator and probe to trace the cable to the point of the break.

In some cases, you may be able to rejoin the ends of severed wires, but for high-speed networks with tight tolerances, completely replacing the permanent cable run is preferable. Splices or couplers in the middle of a run can generate additional attenuation, NEXT, and other problems. Broken or damaged patch cables should be discarded.

Excessive Attenuation

There are several different reasons a cable run can exhibit excessive attenuation, most of which are attributable to improper installation practices. The most obvious cause is excessive length. The longer the cable, the more the signals attenuate. Address this problem as you would any other excessive length condition.

Another possible cause is that the cable used in the run is not suitable for the rate at which data will be transmitted. If, for example, you try to run a 100Base-TX network using Category 3 cable, one of the reasons it will fail is that the inferior cable causes the signals to attenuate too much. In this case, there is no other alternative than to replace the cable with the proper grade. Inferior or untwisted patch cables are a frequent cause of this type of problem. These are easily replaced, but if your permanent links are inferior, the only alternatives are to replace them or use another protocol. In the example just given, you could conceivably switch to 100Base-T4, which uses all four pairs of Category 3 cable, instead of using 100Base-TX, which requires two pairs of Category 5. This would require different network interface cards, but the relatively minor inconvenience and expense may be preferable to completely reinstalling the cable plant.

Excessive attenuation can also be caused by other components that are of an inferior grade, such as connectors or punch-down blocks. Fortunately, these are generally easier to replace than the entire cable.

Excessive NEXT

Near-end crosstalk is a major problem that can have many different causes, including the following:

Inferior cable   The cables are not of the grade required for a protocol can produce excessive crosstalk levels. The only solution is to replace the cable with the appropriate grade.

Inferior components   All of the components of a cable run should be rated at the same grade, including all connectors. Using Category 3 connectors on a Category 5 network can introduce excessive crosstalk and other problems. Replace inferior components with those of the correct grade.

Improper patch cables   Replace inappropriate cables with twisted-pair patch cables that are rated the same as your permanent links. Silver satin patch cables used for telephone systems may appear at first to work with data connections, but the wire pairs in these cables are not twisted, and the main reason for twisting them is to minimize crosstalk.

Split pairs   Incorrect pinouts that cause data-carrying wires to be twisted together result in additional crosstalk, even when both ends are wired in the same way. Split pairs can be the result of mistakes during the installation or the use of the USOC pinouts. The solution is to reattach the connectors at both ends using either the T568-A or T568-B pinouts.

Couplers   Using couplers to join short lengths of cable generates more NEXT than using a single cable segment of the appropriate length. Use one 12-foot patch cable (for example) instead of two 6-foot cables joined with a coupler. When repairing broken permanent links, pull a new length of cable rather than using couplers to join the broken ends together.

Twisting   The individual wire pairs of every Category 5 cable must be twisted up to a point no further than 13mm from any connector. If the wires are too loosely twisted, reattach the connectors, making sure that all of the wire pairs are twisted tightly.

Sharing cables   Many network protocols use only two of the four wire pairs in a standard twisted-pair cable, and this leads some people to believe that they can utilize the other two pairs for voice traffic or some other application. This is not the case, however, because having other signals running over the same cable can cause additional NEXT. The problem may be difficult to diagnose in these cases, because the crosstalk only occurs when the other application is using the other wire pairs, such as when the user is talking on the phone. If this condition occurs, you must install new cabling for one application or the other so that they no longer share a cable.

Excessive Noise

The potential for noise generated by outside sources should be considered during the planning phase of a network installation. Cables should be routed away from AC power lines, light fixtures, electric motors, and other sources of EMI and RFI. Sometimes outside noise sources can be difficult to detect. You may, for example, test your cables immediately after you install them and detect no excess noise from outside sources and then find that the performance of your network is severely degraded by noise during later testing. It is entirely possible that a new source of interference has been introduced into the environment, but you also have to consider the possibility that your original tests were not valid.

If you installed and tested the cable plant during nights and weekends, your tests for outside noise may have generated all pass ratings because some of the possible sources of noise were not operating during that time. Lights that are turned off and machinery that isn't operating don't generate interference, but when they're turned on Monday morning, you may find that the noise levels are excessive. Always test your cable runs in the actual environmental conditions in which they'll be used.

If excessive noise levels appear after an installation has been performed because of an unpredicted or new source, the only solutions are to either move the cables and the source of the noise away from each other, or to replace your UTP cables with shielded twisted-pair (STP) or fiber optic cable.

Summary

Testing and troubleshooting are vital elements of installing and maintaining network cables. You should consider purchasing the correct testing tools and learning how to use them as part of the expense of installing a network. In this chapter, you've learned about the tests you can perform on different cable types, the tools you need to perform them, the results you should expect, and the actions you should take to remedy the problems that testing may disclose.

Creating a Request for Proposal (RFP)

All journeys begin with a single step. In the case of a telecommunications infrastructure and/or hardware project that is not being performed in-house, that first step is the creation of the *Request for Proposal (RFP)*. The RFP is essential to the success of your telecommunications infrastructure project.

Anyone who rushes into a project without a clear view of what they need to accomplish is foolish. A vendor who accepts a job without a clear definition of the work that is to be performed is also a fool. The RFP is essential for setting the pace of a project that is going to involve both a client and an outside vendor. You may choose to write your own RFP, or you may choose to hand the entire cabling design project and RFP generation over to a specialized consulting company. Another option is to work with the consulting company and do a lot of the groundwork for them before they start the project. Any of these three choices still requires that you have a good knowledge of the process of generating an RFP.

As mentioned, there are consulting companies that will perform the steps documented in this chapter. These companies are experts in their field and can save you time and money. However, for installations that are smaller than a few hundred locations, you may not need a consulting company to prepare an RFP. Regardless of what you choose to do, understanding the process and the content of the RFP is still important.

What Is a Request for Proposal?

The Request for Proposal (RFP) is essential for defining what you want designed and built for the physical layer of your voice and data networks. An improperly constructed physical layer will contribute to poor reliability and poor performance. When defining your requirements for your physical infrastructure, you must carefully document what it is that you are expecting for the physical infrastructure project.

NOTE   The RFP is your letter to Santa Claus defining exactly what you want and when it is to be delivered.

The RFP is a document that sets the tone for the entire cabling infrastructure project; the RFP documents your own requirements as well as your expectations of prospective vendors. A well thought out and well-written RFP goes a very long way towards ensuring the success of the project. On the other hand, a poorly thought out and badly written RFP can make your project a potential nightmare.

NOTE   Not all cabling projects require an RFP. Though certainly medium- and large-scale projects will require an RFP, smaller projects (a few dozen cabling runs) on which you're working with a trusted vendor do not require an extensive RFP.

The best way to think of an RFP is as a combination of a guidebook, map, and rulebook. An RFP is a document that clearly articulates the project, goals, expectations, and terms of engagement between the parties. In addition, for it to serve your best interests, it must be designed to be fair to all parties involved in the project.

Having been on both sides of the fence on this issue, we have seen the influence that the RFP has on both parties and upon the overall success of an effort. One of the mistakes that we have seen made is that the "buyer" and the "vendor" often see the RFP as a tool with which to take advantage of the other party. This is most unfortunate because it sets the stage for an adversarial relationship right from the beginning.

WARNING   The RFP is a tool for ensuring a successful relationship with your vendor and the successful completion of your cabling project. Unfortunately, some see it as a tool for taking advantage of the other party. We do *not* recommend using an RFP in this way!

The best way to prevent such a scenario from occurring is by making sure that the RFP is used as a tool to clearly describe the scope of the project, the buyer's requirements and expectations of the vendor, and the responsibilities of all parties involved. Since it is to be used as a "rule book," it must be designed to promote fairness, and will thereby establish the tone or the "spirit" of the upcoming working relationship.

To create such a document, there is a lot of preplanning that must take place on many levels. This planning often involves many people to ensure that many of the issues associated with the effort are identified, defined, addressed, and properly articulated in the RFP document.

It is important to remember that although the project involves the installation of technology, the actual act of conducting that business involves many departments of the organization outside of the technology group. This could include management, finance, facility management, and legal departments as well as the departments that are getting the new network. Before we get into some of the nuts and bolts aspects of creating the RFP, let's talk about what the goal of the project should be.

What Do We Want in Life?

The goal of every physical layer of the RFP should be the creation of an infrastructure that satisfies the needs of the organization today while being flexible enough to handle the emerging technologies of tomorrow. Everyone wants a system that they do not have to upgrade every time they need to install a faster piece of hardware or advanced application. In addition, no one wants to have to spend megabucks on their infrastructure, upgrading it every $1^{1}/_{2}$ years to keep pace with industry advancements.

The goal of every physical layer RFP should also be to create an infrastructure that appears to be invisible. Wouldn't it be nice if an IT cabling infrastructure could be as invisible as electrical wiring? Think about your electrical wiring for just a second; when was the last time you had to upgrade your electrical wiring because you upgraded your LAN hardware? Or when did you have to add additional breakers to your electrical panel because you wanted to plug in another lamp or another PC (or Macintosh)? And did you have to put in new electrical wiring when you upgraded from 10Base-T to 100Base-TX?

Well, the good news is that with the proper planning and design, your communication infrastructure can become virtually invisible. Within the past five years, there have been many advancements and improvements within the infrastructure segment of the telecommunication and information industries. There have been so many, in fact, that it is now possible, with the proper background and understanding, to plan, design, and install a communications infrastructure cabling system that is both stable and flexible enough to become almost invisible to its users. It is also now possible to create customized cabling configurations that can and should become standard throughout every type of office in every site within your organization.

Perhaps the best part is that the installed system will not limit the types of data communications hardware purchased or the pool of infrastructure contractors from which you can invite to bid on the installation. It can also be flexible enough to satisfy everyone's needs. Sounds like a pipe dream, doesn't it? Well, it isn't. A well-designed, well-engineered, and well-installed infrastructure becomes the "enabler" for the rest of your applications and future technology requirements.

Developing a Request for Proposal

The actual process of developing the RFP involves quite a bit of work, depending on the size of the project and the size of your organization. The first part of the development process involves analyzing exactly what your current and future needs are. Along with this, you must determine any restrictions and constraints that may be placed upon the system you are installing.

Once you know what your needs are and the factors that will constrain you, the next phase is to design the system and determine the components you will need. Once you have the system design and components necessary, you can proceed with putting together the RFP document.

The Needs Analysis

The first and most important step in creating an RFP is to do a needs analysis. This is actually the first step within the first step. There will be many people involved in this phase of planning, and you must be thorough. One of the reasons this step is important is because you can use this opportunity to establish "buy-in" from others in your organization.

For the sake of this discussion, we must assume that the infrastructure project being planned is at least of medium-sized scope. As one who is in charge of such things, your task may be to handle a simple 20-network node expansion. Then again, perhaps you have been given the task of overseeing and implementing an organization-wide infrastructure installation or upgrade involving hundreds of users located in multiple sites. In either scenario, the same basic approaches should be taken.

The objective of the needs analysis is to define the specific project. The needs analysis should involve anyone who will be affected by the installation of this system. Depending on the size of your organization, some of the people you will want to solicit advice from include:

- Those who are responsible for any type of information technology that will be affected by your project

- The people in facilities and/or facilities management

- The electrician or electrical contractor

- Managers who can help you gain a better understanding of the long-term goals of the organization as they relate to information technology and facilities

Getting Input from Key Players

It is important to get input from upper management and the strategic planners within your organization so you can understand the types of technology-dependent services, applications, and efficiencies that they may require or need to have deployed in order to realize the company's goals.

It is through these meetings that the entire scope of the project, the intent, deadlines, payment terms, bonding, and insurance issues will be defined by those who are responsible for these issues. These meetings serve as the raw chunk of clay from which you will begin to sculpt your RFP.

All these meetings and solicitation of input may sound a bit like overkill, but we can assure you, they are not. You may be saying to yourself, "Why would I want to make my life even more miserable than it already is by inviting all of these people's opinions into my project?" You may be surprised, but by doing so you will, in fact, be making your life much easier. Plus, you will save yourself a great deal of time, money, and aggravation in the not-too-distant future. Trust us on this one: A little bit of self-induced insanity today will save you from stark raving madness tomorrow.

All of these people from whom you have solicited opinions are going to have an opinion anyway. Furthermore, it is safe to assume that these opinions will be communicated to you about two hours after it is too late to do anything reasonable about them. In addition, think of all the new friends you will make (just what you were looking for, we're sure)! Most of these people are just dying to tell you what to do and how to do it. By asking them for their opinion up-front, you are taking away their right to give you another one later. "Speak now or forever hold your peace" strictly applies here.

NOTE   One IT director we know held "town hall" meetings with her company's managers when she began planning the infrastructure for their new location. The meetings often demonstrated how quickly the managers rushed to protect their own fiefdoms, but the combination of all the managers discussing the infrastructure needs also generated new ideas and requirements that she had not previously thought of.

Most important, though, is that scheduling meetings with these folks will help you understand the organization's overall needs from a variety of vantage points. The information you procure and the understanding you receive will help you to get through the overall process. For instance, perhaps the facilities folks have information that, once conveyed to you and the wiring contractors, will lower the project cost and/or eliminate change orders and cost overruns. Or perhaps the in-house electrician or telephone department is planning to do an installation in the same buildings during the same time frame, which would allow you to combine efforts and create efficiencies that would save time, money, and work. And finally, getting feedback from upper management about their long-range plans could prevent you from being hit with a new imaging application rollout that will require "only" one more CAT-5 circuit to be installed to every outlet location you just paid to have cabled two months ago!

You'd be surprised at some of details that we have unearthed from employers and clients during the initial cabling system planning meetings. Some of these details would have caused time, money, and effort to be wasted if they had not been revealed, including:

- An entire wing of a building was to be renovated three months after the new cable was to have been installed.

- Major expansion was planned in six months, and an area that currently had only a few workstation locations would be accommodating several dozen additional sales people.

- A departmental restructuring was taking place, and an entire group of people was going to be moved to a new location.

- The local building codes did not allow any data, voice, or electrical cabling in the plenum unless it was in conduit.

- Telecommunications infrastructure designs had to be approved by a registered, professional engineer. (This was required by the state in which the customer was located.)

- A new phone switch and voicemail system was being purchased and would also have to be cabled shortly after the data cabling project. Management mistakenly viewed this as a separate project.

- In a law firm, all the attorneys were going to be given a notebook computer in addition to their desktop computers. These notebook computers would require network access while the attorneys were in their offices. This meant that each attorney's office would require two network connections.

- A new photocopier tracking system was to be installed that would require cabling to tracking computer located in the computer room. In addition, these new photocopiers were going to function as network devices and would require their own 10Base-T connections.

- Management wanted all offices of managers and senior project personnel, as well as conference rooms, to have cable TV hookups.

In each of these cases, we thought we had a pretty good idea of what the company was planning to do prior to the initial meetings. The additional information was helpful (and sometimes vital) to the successful installation of the new cabling installation.

The Bonus: Getting Buy-In   As we've said, when you start getting input from key players, you are going to gather a lot more pertinent information. In addition to this advantage, you get another bonus. This type of wisely inclusive communication will get you "buy-in" on your project. In other words, if you speak to the people involved and show them respect by bringing them into the loop, you will find that many of them will buy in to your project, meaning that they will feel a part of what is going on and (we hope) won't fight against it.

We must issue a warning here, however! Be very careful not to let their input control your project. You are the boss of the project and must remain the boss of the project. If you let others control that which you are responsible for, you have a recipe for disaster. Make certain that they know that you are not creating a democratic process. They must know that although you seek their input and council, you are not creating a democracy. No one gets a "vote" in Cableland. They need to know that they are witnessing what could be called at best a benevolent dictatorship, and you are the dictator. If you let others control your cabling and something blows up, all that buy-in we just talked about will be immediately replaced by "sell out"! The responsibility will still be yours.

NOTE   Responsibility for a project and the authority to make the final decision on a project need to go hand-in-hand.

Any time a manager creates or participates in a scenario in which the one responsible for a project cannot, or will not, take authority over the project, be prepared to witness a potential disaster. Likewise if the one who has authority over the project is not held responsible for the outcome of the project. For any project to have a chance of succeeding, these two components must be welded together. We encourage you seek the input of others when working on a project, but make sure that you do not relinquish too much control.

Cabling @ Work: Questions to Ask When Gathering Information

You have the key players in a room and you have outlined what your cabling project will entail. They may look at you with a "So what am I doing here?" look on their faces. What are some of the key questions that you may want to ask them? Here is a list of our favorites:

- How long is the company planning to occupy the space we are cabling?

- Are there new technologies that will be implemented in the near or long term? These may include voice, data, video, giving employees network-attached PDAs, notebook computers, remote controlled devices, security systems, new photocopier technology, etc.

- Are there new voice and data applications that require fiber optic cabling? What type of fiber optic cable do these applications require?

- What electrical code requirements and building requirements will influence the data communications cabling?

- Are the telecommunications closets properly grounded?

Continued on next page

- Are there installation time requirements? Will the areas that need to be worked in be accessible only during certain hours? Are they accessible on weekends and at night? Will the installation personnel have to work around existing office furniture and/or employees?

- Are there building security requirements for contract personnel working in the areas in question? Are there places that contractors must be escorted?

- Does the contractor have to be unionized? Are there areas of the installation that will be affected by union rules, such as the loading dock and elevators?

- Are there plans to move to faster networking technologies, such as 100Base-TX, 155Mbps ATM, 622Mbps ATM, or Gigabit Ethernet?

- How many work area outlets should be installed? (You may have your own opinions on this, but it is a good idea to hear others' thoughts on the matter.)

- If they are not already, should the voice and data cabling infrastructures be combined?

- What insurance should the contractor carry? Should they be bonded? Licensed? Certified?

- Are there deadlines within the company that construction or rewiring will affect?

- Are there areas of the building that are not part of your leased space that the contractor will have to access (e.g., entrance facilities and telecommunication closets)?

- Will the company be providing parking and working space (e.g., storage space, office, telephone, fax, etc.) for the contractor and their employees?

- If the organization spans multiple floors of a single building, is there space available in the risers (conduits between floors) to accommodate additional cables? If not, who will have to give approval for new risers to be drilled?

- If the organization spans multiple buildings, how will the cable (usually fiber) be connected between buildings?

These are all questions that you would want to know the answers to if you were writing an RFP or if you were a contractor responding to an RFP. Some of these questions may be answered by your new-found friends, while others may have to be answered by you.

Designing the Project for the RFP

Once you have completed the needs analysis of your project, you should be prepared to enter into the design phase of the project. While a lot of the design may be left up to the contractor whom you choose to install your system, many of the design-related questions should be answered in the RFP. This may seem a bit intimidating to the uninitiated, but we assure you that if you break down and divide the project down into small "bit-sized" pieces, you will conquer the task. Even the largest and most intimidating projects become manageable when broken into small tasks.

Components of a Cabling Infrastructure

The first step in "dividing" the project is to identify the four major subsystems of a cabling infrastructure. These are the telecommunications closets, the backbone cabling, the horizontal cabling, and the work area components. These and other subsystems are described by the TIA/EIA-568-A standard and are discussed in more detail in Chapter 2, "Cabling Standards." Within each of these categories are several components.

NOTE   When designing cabling systems, you should conform to a known standard. In the United States, the standard you should use is the TIA/EIA-568-A Commercial Building Telecommunications Cabling Standard. (In mid-2000, this standard is expected to be updated with TIA/EIA-568-B.) In Europe and other parts of the world, the ISO/IEC 11801 Generic Cabling for Customer Premises standard is the one to use. Most other countries in the world have adopted one of these standards as their own, but they may call it something different.

Backbone Cabling   The backbone (a.k.a. vertical, trunking, or riser cabling) cabling connects the telecommunication closets (TC) with the equipment room; the equipment room is where the central phone and data equipment is located. While the TIA/EIA-568 standard allows for an intermediate telecommunications closet, we don't recommend these for data applications. Telecommunications closets should be connected to the equipment room via backbone cabling in hub-and-spoke manner.

Many RFPs will leave the determination of the number of cables and pairs up to the company that responds to the RFP; the responding company will figure out the number of pairs and feeder cables based on requirements you supply for voice and data applications. Other RFP authors will specify exactly how many cables and multipair cables must be used. The decision is up to you, but if you have little experience specifying backbone capacity, you may want to leave the decision to a professional. Some decisions that you may have to make with respect to backbone cable include:

- The number of multipair copper cables that must be used for voice applications.

- How many pairs of fiber optic cable must be used between closets for data and voice applications.

- Whether single-mode or multimode fiber optic cable will be used. Most data applications use multimode fiber, though some newer voice and applications use single-mode fiber.

- Whether there will be any four-pair UTP cable (Category 5, 5e, or 6) installed as backbone cabling.

WARNING   Backbone sizing can be tricky. If you are not careful, you will calculate the backbone capacity you need incorrectly. If you are not sure of the exact capacity you require, leave it to the contractor to specify the right amount.

Telecommunications Closets   Still more decisions must be made about the telecommunications closet. Some of these decisions will be yours to make, while others will be made by someone else in your organization. Here are some points about telecommunications closets that you may need to think about:

- If the telecommunications closet is to house electrical equipment, the room should be environmentally conditioned (temperature and humidity need to be maintained at acceptable levels).

- Appropriate grounding for racks and equipment has to exist. This is often the responsibility of the electrician. Don't ignore good grounding rules. Consult TIA/EIA-607 and the NEC for more information. If the closets are not grounded properly, you need to know who will be responsible for installing grounding.

- Sufficient space and lighting need to be provided so that all necessary equipment can be installed and people can be in the closet working on it.

- Backup power or uninterruptible power supplies (UPSs) should be installed in the telecommunications closets.

- Proper access should be given to information technology personnel. However, the closets should be secure to prevent unwanted tampering or data theft.

The typical telecommunications closet is going to include components such as the following:

- Punch-down blocks (66-blocks) for voice. There are punch-down blocks that can be used to cross-connect data circuits, but they are generally not recommended.

- Wall space, if you are going to use punch-down blocks such as 66-blocks (they are usually mounted on plywood, which is then mounted to the wall).

- Patch panels for copper and fiber circuits. It is a good practice to separate the patch panels that are used for data applications from the patch panels that are used for voice applications.

- Racks, cabinets, and enclosures for patch panels, telecommunication gear, UPSs, LAN hubs, etc. Shelves for the racks and cabinets are often forgotten on RFPs and in the initial design. Don't forget extra mounting hardware for the racks, cabinets, and enclosures.

- Wire management equipment used on the walls and on the racks. These are also often forgotten during the initial design phase. Good wire management practice means that the telecommunications closets will be cleaner and easier to troubleshoot.

- Patch cables for the copper and fiber optic patch panels and hubs. These are the most commonly forgotten components on RFPs. Make sure that the patch cables match the category of cable that you are using. TIA/EIA-568-A allows for patch cables up to six meters (20 feet) in the telecommunications closet; however, if you don't need cables this long, you should use only the length necessary. You may want to order varying lengths of patch cables to keep things neat and untangled.

Horizontal Cabling   The horizontal cabling is also sometimes called the distribution cabling. This is the cabling that runs from the telecommunications closet to the work area. The horizontal cabling is one of the components that is most often planned incorrectly. Cabling contractors know this and will often bid extremely low on the overall cost of a job so that they can get the follow-on work of adds, moves, and changes. This is because running single runs of horizontal cable is far more costly than installing many runs of cable at one time. To save yourself future unnecessary costs, make sure that you plan for a sufficient amount of horizontal cable.

Some of the components you will have to think about when planning your horizontal cable include:

- How much cable should run between each work area and a telecommunications closet? TIA/EIA-568-A recommends either a minimum of one UTP and one fiber cable or two UTP cables. In an all-UTP environment, we recommend running four UTP cables to each work area.

- What category of UTP cable should be run? Most telephone applications today will use Category 3 cabling; 10Base-T Ethernet will also run on Category 3 cable. Faster Ethernet and other twisted-pair technologies require at least Category 4 (which is almost never used today) or Category 5 cabling. 100Base-TX requires Category 5 cabling.

- If using fiber optic cable, what type of fiber cable should you use and how many pairs should you run to each work area? Typically, two pairs of multi-mode fiber optic cable are used for horizontal cable, but this will depend on the applications that are in use and the number of data connections that are to be installed at each location. Care should be taken to ensure that no applications require single-mode fiber optic cable.

- Per TIA/EIA-568-A, the maximum distance that horizontal cable can extend (not including patch cables and cross-connects) is 90 meters (285 feet).

- Should you use some type of "shared sheath" cabling for horizontal cabling? For example, since 10Base-T only uses two pairs of a four-pair cable, some network managers decide to use the other two pairs for an additional 10Base-T connection or a telephone connection. We *highly discourage* the use of a shared sheath for data applications.

Work Area   The final major area is the work area; this area includes the wall plates, user patch cables, and user equipment. The work area can also include adapters such as baluns that modify the cable impedance. A lot of the design issues relating to the work area will revolve around the choice of wall plates. Here are some components to think about relating to the work area:

- What type of wall plates you will use. The wall plate must have sufficient information outlets to accommodate the number of horizontal cables you are using. There are many varieties of modular wall plates on the market that will accommodate fiber, copper, video, audio, and coaxial modules in the same plates. See Chapter 8, "Wall Plates," for more information.

- For UTP cabling, the connecting hardware must also match the category of UTP cable you are using.

- For fiber optic cable, the wall plate connecting hardware and connector types must match the cable type you are using and the requirements for the station cables (station patch cables) and fiber optic connector types.

- Don't forget to estimate the number of patch cables you will need, and include this in the RFP. TIA/EIA-568-A specifies a maximum length for patch cables of three meters (10 feet). UTP patch cables should be stranded copper cable and should match the category of cable being used throughout the installation.

- Though not as common now as they were a few years ago, impedance-changing devices such as baluns might be necessary. Make sure that you have specified these in your cabling RFP if they are not being provided elsewhere.

How Much Is Enough?

Now that the categories and their components have been identified, the next order of business is to determine how much of these items will be needed in your system. This is when you will begin to realize the benefits of the needs analysis that you performed. The size and components of your infrastructure are always based upon the immediate needs of your organization coupled with a factoring in of "realistic" future needs.

Wall Plates and Information Outlets   When designing a cabling infrastructure, always start from the desktop and work backward. For instance, an accurate count of the number of people and their physical locations will determine the minimum number of information outlets that will be needed and where they will be installed.

KEY TERMS **Wall Plates and Information Outlets** Depending on the design of the wall plate, a single *wall plate* can accommodate multiple *information outlets*. An information outlet can accommodate voice or data applications.

Some IT and cabling professionals will automatically double this minimum number in order to give themselves room to grow. Our experience with information outlets is that, once you have your cabling system in place, you never seem to have enough. With wall plates in particular, there never seems to be one close to where you want to put phones and data equipment. Here are some ideas that may help you to plan information outlets:

- Don't forget locations such as network printer locations and photocopier locations.

- In some larger offices, it may be helpful to install two wall plates at each location, one on one wall and one on the opposite wall. This keeps the station patch cable lengths to a minimum and also helps keep cable clutter to a minimum, since cables do not have to cross the entire length of a large office.

- Special use rooms, such as conference rooms and war rooms, should be cabled with at least one wall plate identical to a typical workstation area.

- Training rooms should have at least four more information outlets than you anticipate needing.

- Use extreme caution when cabling to locations outside of your organization's office space, such as a shared building conference room; it may allow outsiders to access your data and voice systems. While this seems unlikely, we have seen it happen.

Backbone and Horizontal Cabling The amount of information outlets required and their wall plate locations will be used to determine the sizing of your horizontal cables (fiber strands and copper pairs) as well as the amount and placement of your main distribution frame (MDF) and any required intermediate distribution frames (IDFs). The applications to be run and accessed at the desktop determine the types of cables to be installed and the amount of circuits needed at each wall plate location.

Some RFPs merely provide the numbers of wall plates and information outlets per wall plate and leave the rest of the calculations up to the cabling contractor.

Other RFPs don't even get this detailed and expect the contractor to gather this information during their walk-through. Our preference is to have this information readily available to the contractor prior to the walk-through and site survey. The less ambiguous you are and the more you put into writing, the easier your job and your contractor's job will be. Information about wall plates and information outlets has to be gathered and documented by someone; you are the person who has to live with the results. Always remain open minded to contractor's suggestions for additional locations, though.

Cabling @ Work: Putting Data Cables in Places You Would Never Imagine

A few years ago during a hotel's remodeling project, the hotel wired only the minimum locations required to install their new local area network. Later that year during a phone system upgrade, the hotel had to rewire each room.

Shortly after that, this hotel decided to offer in-room fax machines and additional telephones on additional lines. Each room had to have additional cabling installed. Now the hotel is again succumbing to the pressures of the traveling businessperson and is installing 10Base-T Internet connections. At the same time, they are wiring their restaurants and retail locations for Category 5e cabling because their new cash register system uses 10Base-T network connections.

Though no precise figures have been calculated to see exactly how much they would have saved by doing the entire job at one time, estimates indicate that the 400-room hotel could have saved as much $80,000 by performing all the cabling infrastructure work at the same time.

Rules for Designing Your Infrastructure

As you gather information and start planning the specifics of your cabling infrastructure, keep in mind some of our rules and experiences. Some of these are from our own experiences, and others have been contributed to us by cabling and information technology professionals.

- Think "flexibility" and design accordingly. You will always find more uses and have more requirements of your infrastructure than you are seeing today. Technology changes and organizations change; be prepared.

- Create organizational standards and stick to them. Define the different outlet types that exist in your facility. For instance, those in the accounting department may have a need for fewer circuits than those in operations, and operations may need a different configuration than those in sales. Once you determine the various types of configurations required, standardize them and commit to installing the same configuration throughout the department. On the other hand, you may decide that it makes sense to give *everyone* the same configuration. Some companies shift employees and departments around frequently; this is something you should think about based on how your organization works. Whether you give everyone the same standard is up to you, but whatever you do, standardize one level or another and stick to it. There is no reason why each of your facilities cannot have an identical infrastructure "footprint" that appears the same regardless of the location of the site, whether it's the closet you are in or the outlet at which you are looking. Complying with this step will make troubleshooting, ordering of parts, and adds, moves, and changes much less confusing.

- Use modular wall plates. Buy a wall plate that has more "openings" than circuits installed at the location. If you are installing two cables, buy wall plates that have three or four ports. The cost difference is minimal, and you will preserve your investment in the event extra cables are installed or activated.

- Never install any UTP cable that is not at least Category 5–rated. For data applications, Category 3 is dead. You should even strongly consider installing an enhanced cable such as Category 5e, if your budget will allow. There are three things in life that never change: death, taxes, and the need for more bandwidth.

- Always try to install one more cable at each location than is going to be immediately used. If your budget is tight, you may choose not to terminate or test the circuit or not to add the necessary patch panel ports, but do try to install the extra "pipe." Invariably, organizations find a use for that extra circuit. That cable will also enable you to quickly respond to any late special connectivity needs with minimal cost and disruption.

- Use wire management above and below each patch panel. A neat patch panel begets a neat patch field. A messy patch field begets trouble.

- Make sure your connectors, patch cables, patch panels, and wall jacks are rated the same as your cable. Category 5 for Category 5. Category 5e for Category 5e. The same should hold true for installation practices.

- If you venture into the world of Category 6 or Category 7 cabling systems, remember that these cabling systems are not standardized as of this writing. Further, vendor claims about the performance of these cables may be true only if you use all components from the same vendor.

- Label the circuits at the wall plate and at the patch panel. While some people feel it is important to label the cable itself, do so only if it does not increase the cost of the cabling installation.

- Never under-install fiber strands. *Never, ever, ever* install only two strands of fiber optic cable between telecommunication closets and the equipment room! Install only four strands if you have no money at all. You must try to install a minimum of six or eight strands. There is so much convergence occurring in the low voltage industries wherein alarm systems, HVAC systems, and CCTV systems are all using digital information and running on fiber backbones. The installation of additional fiber beyond your current data needs could make you a hero the next time there is an alarm system or HVAC system upgrade going on. You can also rent the use of your fiber to the other department that needs to ride on it. Remember *Field of Dreams*: Build it and they will come.

- Include a few strands (two or four pairs) of single-mode fiber with your multimode fiber backbone. Even if you do not see the need for it today, put it in. To save money, you may choose not to terminate or test it, but it should be part of your backbone. Video applications and multimode's inability to handle some of the emerging higher bandwidth and faster-moving data applications makes this a very smart bet.

- Oversize your voice/copper backbone by a minimum of 10 to 25 percent if you can afford it. A safe way to size your voice copper trunk is to determine the maximum number of telephone stations you anticipate you will need in your facility. Determine the number of voice locations that will be fed from each closet and then size your voice backbone to reflect 2.5 pairs per station fed. For example, in the case of a closet that will feed a maximum of 100 telephone stations, you should install a 250-pair cable.

- Test and document all copper distribution. If you are installing Category 5 cable and components, insist upon 100 percent Category 5–compliance on all copper distribution circuits. All conductors of all circuits must pass. More sophisticated UTP cable testers provide printed test results; you should obtain and keep the test results from each location. Some testing software packages will allow you to keep these in a database. Tests should be reviewed prior to acceptance of the work. Note, though, that if you ask for Category 5 cable testing for each circuit, it may increase the cost of the overall installation.

- Test and document all fiber backbone cable. Bidirectional attenuation testing using a power meter is sufficient for LAN applications. (*Bidirectional* refers to the act of testing each strand by shooting the fiber from the MDF to the IDF and then reversing the act and shooting the fiber from the IDF to the MDF.) Testing should be done at both 850nm and 1300nm on multimode fiber. Much has been made of the need to use an OTDR (optical time domain reflectometer) to test fiber; however, this is overkill. The key factor in the functionality of the fiber backbone is attenuation. The use of an OTDR increases the cost of testing significantly while providing nonessential additional information.

- Document the infrastructure on floor plans. Once this is done, maintain the documentation and keep it current. Accurate documentation is an invaluable troubleshooting and planning tool. Show the outlet location and use a legend to identify the outlet types. Differentiate between these:

  - Data only, voice only, and voice/data locations

  - The circuit numbers for each circuit at that location

  - All MDF and IDF locations

  - Backbone cable routings

Although there is more to the process of designing a telecommunications infrastructure system, the information in this section provides some basic guidelines that should help to remove some of the mystery from the process.

Writing the RFP

If you have been successful at gathering information and asking the right questions, you are ready to start writing your RFP. While there is no e*xact* guideline for writing an RFP, this section provides a list of suggested guidelines to follow when writing an RFP and some implementation suggestions. (We have also included a sample RFP at the end of this chapter.) By following these steps, you will be able to avoid many mistakes that could become very costly during the course of the project and/or the relationship.

After all, regardless of how much ink is used to contractually try to tie someone up, it is the spirit of the agreement under which everyone operates that really works to make a project successful.

Including the Right Content in the RFP

Are you putting the right specifications into the RFP? Will it accurately specify what you want? These are questions you need to ask yourself as you start writing the RFP. Tasks that you should start during the preplanning phase include:

- Educate yourself about the components of the system to be specified and some of the options available to you.

- Evaluate specific desired features and functionality of the proposed system, required peripherals, interfaces, and expectations for life cycle and warranty period.

- Solicit departmental/organizational input for desired features, requirements, and financial considerations.

- Determine the most cost-efficient solution for one-year, three-year, and even perhaps five-year projections.

- Evaluate unique applications/transmission requirements, departmental or operational requirements/restraints, wireless, voice messaging, fiber, etc.

- Analyze perceived versus actual needs/requirements of features and functionality, future applications, system upgradability, etc.

- Discuss language that is geared toward defining contractor qualifications. Strongly consider requirements that call for vendors to be certified by the infrastructure component manufacturer whose products they are proposing to install. The same holds true for hardware bids. It is important that any vendor selling hardware be an authorized reseller hardware component manufacturer. Call for proof of each certification and authorization as part of the initial bid submittal.

- Prepare a draft outline of selected requirements and acceptable timelines (that is subject to minor changes by mutual agreement).

- Prepare a detailed RFP, including scope of work, testing acceptance, proposed payment schedules, liquidated damages, restoration, licensing, permits fees, milestone dates, etc.

- Define project milestones and completion dates. Milestones include bid conference dates, walk-through dates, dates to submit clarifications, final bid due, acceptance dates, project start dates, installation milestones, etc.

- Call for all pricing to be in an itemized format, listing components to be installed, quantities to be installed, and unit and extended prices.

- Request that costs to add or delete circuits—on a per circuit basis—be included in the response to the RFP.

- Include detailed language addressing the "intent" of the bid. Such language should articulate that the intent is to have a system installed that contains all of the components necessary to create a fully functional system. Language should be included that calls for the contractors to address any omissions in the bid that would prohibit the system from being fully functional at time of contract completion.

- Ask for references from similar jobs.

- Make sure to allow for adequate time for detailed site survey/estimating.

- Upon receipt of bids, narrow field to three finalists and

  - Correlate information and prioritize or rank three remaining bids on cost versus performance. Don't get hung up on costs. If a bid seems too good to be true, there may be a reason. Examine the vendor's qualifications and the materials they are specifying.

  - Schedule meetings and/or additional surveys for best-and-final bids from remaining vendors.

  - Specify that the RFP is the intellectual property of the client and should not be distributed. Though this won't stop an unscrupulous vendor from passing around information about your infrastructure, you have instructed them not to. One consulting company we know of actually assigns each vendor's copy of the RFP a separate number that appears on the footer of each page.

What Makes a Good RFP?

What makes a good RFP? Does it have a lot of pages (did you do in a few trees printing it)? Can you take advantage of the contractor? These are *not* good benchmarks for determining if your RFP will help to create a good working relationship between yourself and the company that you contract. Here are a few questions you may want to ask yourself about the RFP you are generating:

- Is it fair?

- Does it work to ensure that only competent bidders will meet the contractor qualifications?

- Is it nondiscriminatory?

- Does it communicate the objectives and the wishes of the client clearly and accurately?

- Does it provide protection to both the client and the service provider?

- Does it provide opportunities for dialog between the parties (e.g., mandatory site walk-throughs, regular progress meetings, etc.)?

- Does it clearly state all deadlines?

- Does it define payment terms?

- Does it define the relationship of the parties?

- Does it address change order procedures?

Distributing the RFP and Managing the Vendor Selection Process

Once the RFP has been written, you may think you are home free. However, the next step is just as important as the creation of the RFP itself: you are now ready to distribute the RFP to prospective vendors and begin the vendor selection process.

Distributing RFPs to Prospective Vendors

If you worked with an infrastructure consultant on your RFP, they may already have a list of contractors and vendors that you can use to fulfill your vendor needs. Many of these vendors may have already been tried and tested by your consultant. However, if you have developed your own RFP, your next step will be to find prospective vendors to whom you can distribute your RFP to solicit bids.

How do you go about finding the right people to send your RFP to? We suggest the following ways:

- Ask IT professionals from companies similar to yours for a list of vendors they have used for cabling.

- If you are a member of a users group or any type of professional organization, ask for vendor suggestions at your next group meeting.

- If you work with a systems integration company, ask your contact at that company if they have one or more vendor recommendations. Chances are good that they have worked with vendors in the past that can respond to your RFP.

- Consult your phone system (PBX) vendor. Many phone system companies have a division that does cabling.

- If you have a contact at the telephone company, consult them for suggestions.

As you distribute RFPs to potential vendors, be prepared to start scheduling vendor meetings and site inspections. For a cabling installation that involves approximately 500 to 2000 nodes, you can expect to spend at least one full day in meetings and on-site inspections for each vendor to whom you submit the cabling RFP.

Vendor Selection

When reviewing the proposals you get, you may be tempted to simply pick the lowest cost proposal. However, we recommend that you select a vendor based upon criteria that include, but are not limited to the following:

- Balance between cost and performance

- Engineering design and innovative solutions

- Proven expertise in projects of similar scope, size, and complexity

- Quality craftsmanship

- Conformance with all appropriate codes, ordinances, articles, and regulations

Check references. Ask not only about the quality of work, but about the quality of a relationship the reference had with the specific vendor and whether the vendor completed all tasks on time.

Insist on a detailed warranty of a system's life cycle. Consider the ability to perform and any other requirements deemed necessary to execute the intent of contract.

Present a detailed description of work to be performed, payment agreements, and compliance with items contained in the RFP. Include this in the contract.

Identify key project personnel from both sides of the agreement, including the staff associated with accountability/responsibility for making decisions.

NOTE   Once you have selected a vendor, make sure to promptly send letters or place phone calls to the vendors that you have rejected. We agree that it is hard to tell someone they have not been accepted, but it is worse if they hear about it through the grapevine or if they have to call you to find out.

Project Administration

You have accepted the RFP and are now ready for the next phase of your installation challenge, the project administration phase. This phase is no less critical than the others are. Here are some tips we have found to be helpful during an infrastructure deployment:

- Schedule regular progress meetings. Progress reports should be submitted and compared to project milestones. Accountability should be assigned, with scheduled follow-up and resolution dates.

- Make sure that the contractor supervises 100 percent of the quality inspections of work performed. Cable certification reports should be maintained and then submitted at progress meetings.

- Make sure that the contractor maintains and provides as-built documentation. The progress of this documentation should be inspected at the regular progress meetings. The as-built documentation may include: outlet locations, circuit numbers, telecommunication closet locations, backbone and distribution routing. Particular care should be taken to make sure this documentation is done properly, as it tends to slip through the cracks.

Cutover

If you are installing cabling in a new building or location that you do not yet occupy, you do not have to worry about cutover from an existing system. As long as the new cabling system is properly designed, it is relatively easy to move to the new system as you move into the new location.

However, if you are supervising the installation of a new cabling infrastructure that is in an existing facility, you are going to have take into consideration interoperability and the task of switching over to a new system. In a small system (less than 200 horizontal runs), this may occur very quickly, but in medium to large systems, cutover can take days or weeks.

- Cutover preparation should begin 5 to 15 days prior to the scheduled date, unless otherwise mutually agreed upon.

- Cutover personnel and backups should be designated and scheduled well in advance.

- Cutover personnel should have access to all records, diagrams, drawings, or other documentation prepared during the course of the project.

- Acceptance should begin at the completion of the cutover and could continue for a period of 5 to 10 working days prior to signing. The warranty should begin immediately upon signing of acceptance.

- Acceptance criteria should include 100 percent of all circuits installed. All circuits should pass specified performance tests and be duly documented and recorded in the project history file and cable management systems.

By following the guidelines appropriate to your particular situation, you can greatly reduce the chances of any aspect of your project spiraling out of control.

The final part of this chapter provides a sample of an RFP that has been successfully used in several projects in which we have been involved. Although we caution anyone from adopting an existing RFP without first doing a thorough analysis of their own specific needs, the following document can serve as a guide to help you to get started.

Request for Proposal Technology Network Infrastructure (A Sample RFP)

The following sample RFP may help you generate your own RFP. It is suitable for small installations (fewer than 500 circuits). For larger installations, consider working with an infrastructure consultant. The sample RFP below was used for a school. Remember, this document will probably not fit anyone's needs exactly.

General

The general section of this RFP includes contractor's requirements and defines the purpose of the RFP, the work that the RFP covers, and the RFP intent.

Contractor's Requirements

(a)   The successful contractor must be a certified installer on infrastructure components being provided and show proof thereof.

(b)   The contractor must be an authorized reseller of the networking and infrastructure components quoted and show proof thereof.

(c)   Work will be supervised by a registered communications distribution designer (RCDD) during all phases of the installation. An RCDD must be on-site and available to technicians and installers any time work is being performed.

Purpose of This RFP

(a)   The purpose of the "Technology Network Infrastructure RFP" is to provide a functional specification for a comprehensive technology network system, including required network cabling and components and required network devices. The purpose of this is also to provide adequate details and criteria for the design of this technology network system to provide the school building(s) with a complete, integrated networking infrastructure.

(b)   The contractor shall provide cables, network equipment, and components necessary to construct an integrated Local Area Networking infrastructure.

(c)   The contractor shall be responsible for the installation of the technology network systems as defined in the "Specification Section."

This document provides specifications to be used to design the installation of a networking infrastructure and associated equipment for the item(s) referenced above. The contractor shall furnish all labor, materials, tools, equipment, and reasonable incidental services necessary to complete an acceptable installation of:

- The horizontal and riser data communications cabling plant. This is to include, but is not necessarily limited to faceplates, modular jacks, connectors, data patch panels, equipment racks, cable, and fiber optics.

- Furnishing and installation of the active equipment as defined in the specifications to include networking hardware components.

Work Included

Work shall include all components for both a horizontal and riser data cable plant from workstation outlet termination to wire closet terminations. All cable plant components such as outlets wiring termination blocks, racks, patch cables, intelligent hub equipment, etc. will be furnished, installed, and tested by this contractor. The data cable plant is designed to support a 100Mbps Ethernet computer network. The data cabling plant and components shall carry a manufacturer-supported 10-year performance warranty for data rates up to 100Mbps. The bidder must provide such manufacturer guarantee for the above requirements as part of the bid submission.

The scope of work includes all activities needed to complete the wiring described in this document and the drawings that will be made available during the mandatory walk-through.

Any and all overtime or off-hours work required to complete the scope of work within the time frame specified is to be included in the contractor's bid. No additional overtime will be paid.

The awarded contractor must instruct the owner's representative in all the necessary procedures for satisfactory operation and maintenance of the plant relating to the work described in their specifications and provide complete maintenance manuals for all systems, components, and equipment specified. Maintenance manuals shall include complete wiring diagrams, parts lists, etc., to enable the owner's representative to perform any and all servicing, maintenance, troubleshooting, inspection, testing, etc., as may be necessary and/or requested.

The contractor shall respond to trouble calls within twenty-four (24) hours after receipt of such a call considered not in need of critical service. Critical service calls must be responded to, on-site, within four hours of receipt of a trouble call. Bidder must acknowledge their agreement to this requirement as part of the RFP response.

All basic electronic equipment shall be listed by Underwriters Laboratories, Inc. The contractor shall have supplied similar apparatus to comparable installations rendering satisfactory service for at least three years where applicable.

The installation shall be in accordance with the requirements of the National Electrical Code, state and local ordinances, and regulations of any other governing body having jurisdiction.

The cable system design is to be based on the TIA/EIA-568-A Commercial Building Telecommunications Cabling Standard and Bulletins TSB-36 and TSB-40. No deviation from the standards and recommendations is permitted unless authorized in writing.

Intent

This network cable system design will provide the connectivity of multiple microcomputers, printers, and/or terminals through a Local Area Network environment. Each designated network interface outlet will have a capacity to support the available protocols, asynchronous, 10 and 100Mbps Ethernet, 4 and 16Mbps Token Ring, FDDI, etc., through the network cabling and topology specified. The school may select one or any combination of the above-mentioned media and access protocol methods; therefore, the design and installation shall have the versatility required to allow such combinations.

It is the intent of this document to describe the functional requirements of the computer network and components that comprise the "Technology Network System." Bid responses must include all of the above, materials, appliances, and services of every kind necessary to properly execute the work and to cover the terms and conditions of payment thereof and to establish minimum acceptable requirements for equipment design and construction and contract performance to assure fulfillment of the educational purpose.

Cable Plant

The following section covers the installation of horizontal cabling, backbone cabling, cable pathways, fire code compliance, wire identification, and distribution frames.

Horizontal Cable

The following requirements apply for horizontal cabling:

(a) Each classroom shall have two quad outlet wall plates installed. Each of the four information outlets shall be terminated with 8-pin modular jacks (RJ-45). The wall plates will be placed on opposite walls. There are a total of 37 classrooms.

(b) The computer skills classroom shall have 15 quad outlet wall plates installed. Each will have four information outlets terminated using 8-pin modular jacks. Each wall plate will be located to correspond to a computer desk housing two computers. These locations will be marked on the blueprints supplied during the walk through.

(c) Each administration office shall have one quad outlet wall plate with four information outlets, each terminated using 8-pin modular jacks. There are 23 such office locations.

(d) Common administrative areas shall have one quad outlet wall plate with four information outlets terminated with 8-pin modular jacks. There are 17 such common administrative areas.

(e) The school library shall have quad outlet plates placed in each of the librarian work areas, the periodical desk, and the circulation desk. The student research area shall have two quad outlet plates. There are a total of eight work areas that require quad outlets. The exact locations of where these are to be installed will be specified on the blueprints supplied during the walk-through.

(f) The school computer lab shall have 20 quad outlet wall plates installed. The locations of these will be specified on the blueprints to be supplied during the walk-through.

(g) Horizontal cable shall never be open, but rather will run through walls or be installed in the raceway if the cable cannot be installed in walls.

(h) The contractor is responsible for pulling, terminating, and testing all circuits being installed.

(i) The horizontal cable for the data network shall be twisted-pair wire specified as Category 5 by the TIA/EIA-568-A standard and UL-certified. If required by fire codes, cable shall have fire retardant and smoke producing requirements of the National Electrical Code (NEC), Section 800-3(d) and Section 800-3(b), according to UL.

(j) Testing for the distribution components will comply with TIA/EIA-568-A Category 5 specifications and will certify 100 percent functionality of all conductors. All circuits must be tested and found to be in compliance with TSB-95. All testing results will be provided to customer in a hard copy and electronic Excel format.

(k) The data cable specifications are intended to describe the minimum standard for use in the "Technology Network System." The use of higher-grade data cabling is recommended if such can be provided in a cost-effective manner.

(l) Each cable shall be assigned a unique cable number.

(m) In the telecommunications closet, the contractor shall install four separate color-coded patch panels. Each wall plate's information outlet shall use a different patch panel, and the wall plate information outlets will be documented using the patch panel's color code and the patch panel number.

(n) Wire management shall be employed in all telecommunications closets and the equipment room.

Data Backbone Cabling

The following specifications apply to the data backbone cabling:

(a) TIA/EIA-568-A–compliant 62.5/125-micron multimode fiber optic cable network is to be the backbone between the equipment room (the MDF) and any telecommunications (wiring) closets.

(b) All telecommunications closets shall have six pairs of multimode fiber optic cable between the telecommunications closet and the equipment room.

(c) All fiber must be FDDI- and 100Base-FX–compatible.

(d) All fibers are to be terminated using SC-type connectors.

(e) All fiber is to be installed in an innerduct from rack to rack. A 15-foot coil of fiber is to be safely and securely coiled at each rack. The contractor will be responsible for any drilling or core holes and sleeving necessitated by national, state, and/or local codes.

(f) The fiber optic patch panels are to be configured to the amount of strands terminated at each location. Fiber optic panels shall be metallic, are to have a lockable slack storage drawer that can pull out, and shall occupy one rack position.

(g) Testing of fibers will be done using a power meter. The tests will be conducted at 850nm and 1300nm, bidirectionally. All test results will be provided to the customer in hard copy format.

Fire Code Compliance

All cabling installed in the riser and horizontal distribution shall meet or exceed all local fire codes.

Wiring Pathways

The following are related to the installation of cable in plenum and other cable pathways:

(a) Cable pathway design should follow the TIA/EIA-569 (Commercial Buildings Standards for Telecommunications Pathways and Spaces) standard.

(b) The methods used to run cable through walls, ceilings, and floor shall be subject to all state and local safety code and fire regulations. The contractor assumes all responsibility for ensuring that these regulations are observed.

(c)   Cables shall be routed behind walls wherever possible. Surface mount raceway shall be used where necessary.

(d)   New cables shall be independently supported using horizontal ladders or other wire suspension techniques. Cables shall not be allowed to lie on ceiling tiles or attached to electrical conduits.

(e)   System layout shall restrict excessive cable lengths; therefore, routing of cables shall be in a manner as not to exceed 90 meters from device plate to patch panel located in MDF/IDF distribution rack in the assigned wiring closet. Each cable shall be a home run directly from main distribution frame (MDF) or intermediate distribution frame (IDF) to the wall plate.

(f)   Cables shall be terminated at the rear of the patch panel within the MDF or IDF and at the wall plates only. There shall be no splicing of any of the cables installed. Intermediate cross-connects and transition points are not allowed.

(g)   The following are the minimum distances that Category 5 UTP shall be run from common sources of EMI.

EMI Source	Minimum Cable Separation
Fluorescent lighting	12 inches
Neon lighting	12 inches
Power cable 2 KVA or less	5 inches
Unshielded power cable over 2 KVA	39 inches
Transformers and motors	39 inches

Wiring Identification

All cables, wall jacks, and patch panel ports shall be properly tagged in a manner to be determined at a later date. Each cable end must be identified within six inches from the termination point.

Telecommunications Closets

The following are related to the installation of the telecommunications (wiring) closets:

(a)   The wiring closets to be used as the originating points for network cables that home run to the room outlets are referred to as wire closets or telecommunications closets.

They may also be referred to as main distribution frames (MDF) and intermediate distribution frames (IDF). All racks and their exact locations will be confirmed during the mandatory walk-through; their locations are specified on the blueprints that will be provided during the initial walk-through.

(b)   Rack layout should provide enough space to accommodate the cabling, equipment racks, patch panels, and network control equipment, as required. Additionally, the locations should provide for convenient access by operational personnel.

(c)   All racks are to be configured as shown on the attached diagram, with all the fiber optic cables at the top of the rack, the distribution below the fiber, and the hardware components mounted below the distribution patch panels.

(d)   All racks, panels, and enclosures for mounting equipment shall meet 19-inch EIA mounting width specifications. Each equipment rack should include two 19-inch rack shelves that can support the weight of a 50-pound uninterruptible power supply.

(e)   Equipment racks shall be properly grounded to nearest building ground and must be properly attached to the floor and supporting wall by means of horizontal rack bracket mount. All equipment racks must have a six-outlet 20-amp power strip installed inside with surge protection.

MDF/IDF Cable Management

The following relates to cable management for the main distribution frame (MDF) and intermediate distribution frame (IDF) in the equipment room and telecommunications closets.

(a)   The contractor is required to install cable management on all racks installed. Cable management is to consist of horizontal management between each panel and vertical management on the sides of the rack.

(b)   All cable management is to be of the "base and cover" style. Cable management is to be provided for the front of the rack only.

As-Built Diagrams

Contractor will provide As-Built documentation within 15 days of completion of the project. These prints will include outlet locations, outlet numbers, MDF/IDF locations, trunk cable routing, and legends for all symbols.

Network Hardware Specifications

The networking hardware should be provided, installed, and serviced through a certified reseller/integrator or direct from the manufacturer.

Bidding Process

All work is to be completed based on the dates from the attached schedule. Dates on the attached schedule include walk-through dates, bid submission dates, and expected project start and completion dates. Questions and comments are welcomed; prospective contractors are encouraged to submit these questions in writing.

Bid Submittals

The following are related to submittal of bids:

(a) All bids are to be submitted in triplicate.

(b) Each bid is to list all labor, material, and hardware costs in an itemized fashion. The detail is to include itemized unit pricing, cost per unit, and extended prices for each of the material and hardware components as well as the specific labor functions.

(c) To be included in the pricing format is to be a cost per outlet to add or delete outlet locations. This cost is not to include any changes in hardware or patch panel quantities.

(d) There is also to be a scope of work provided that details all of the functions that will be provided by the contractor for the project.

(e) Quote optional Category 5 patch cables and station cables on a per unit cost basis. List pricing for 3-foot, 5-foot, 7-foot, 9-foot, and 14-foot patch cables.

(f) Quote optional network cutover assistance on a per-hour basis per technician.

Miscellaneous

All data found in this RFP and associated documents is considered to be confidential information. Further, data gathered as a result of meetings and walk-through visits is considered to be confidential information. This confidential information shall not be distributed outside of organizations directly related to the contractor without expressed, written approval.

Further, all data submitted by prospected contractors will be treated as confidential and proprietary; it will not be shared outside of the vendor evaluation committee.

chapter 16

Cabling @ Work:
Experience from the Field

- Hints and Guidelines for Cabling Installations

- Cabling Case Studies

Throughout the research phase for this book, cabling installers related to us their experiences, hints, tips, and stories from the field. There is no substitute for advice and stories from people that have been in the trenches themselves. Though some of the topics mentioned in this chapter are also mentioned elsewhere in the book, we felt it was important to reiterate them and present them to you from the perspective of the people working in the trenches.

Much of this chapter is targeted towards the professional cable installer, but anyone installing cabling will find some helpful information here. First, we'll give you some guidelines about the business of cable installation, and then we'll guide you through a handful of case studies drawn from our experience in the industry.

Hints and Guidelines

There are a handful of things you'll learn after a few years in the cabling business—skills and approaches to problems that aren't specifically related to cabling technology but that, when you embrace them, will mark your work as professional. These things will help you whether you are planning to become a professional cable installer or you're simply evaluating the work of others. They are as follows:

- Know what you're doing.
- Plan the job.
- Have the right equipment.
- Test and document.
- Train your crew.
- Work safely.
- Make it pretty.
- Look good yourself.
- Plan for contingencies.
- Match your work to the job.
- Waste not, want not.

Know What You Are Doing

Purchasing (and reading!) this book is a step in the right direction. You need to know more than just how to install cable, however—in order to design and implement a good cable plant for yourself or for a customer, you also need to know how networks are used and how they grow.

Understand current technology   You need to understand which technologies are appropriate for a given situation in a network. Copper (Category 5 or greater) is the king of desktop cabling, for example, while optical fiber cabling has become the rule for campus backbones. Wireless works great in mobile environments but over long distances introduces licensing issues. Read this book for information on cabled technologies, and check other networking magazines and books for details on competing technologies.

Understand the standards that apply to your work   The TIA/EIA publishes the TIA/EIA-568-A standard and the ISO/IEC publishes the ISO/IEC 11801 standard. Both of these are discussed in Chapter 2, "Cabling Standards." Professionals will be intimately familiar with one or the other of these standards (in the United States, it will be the TIA/EIA-568-A standard).

Know the limitations of the technology you are using   Don't try to run Category 5 twisted-pair cable for 500 meters, for example. Point-to-point lasers don't cope well with snow. Single-mode fiber can carry a signal farther than multimode fiber. You can pull only so many twisted-pair cables through a conduit. Outside plant cable is not the same as inside plant cable, which can be divided into plenum and nonplenum (you do know the difference, don't you? Your fire marshal and building inspector certainly do). This book tells you what you need to know about current network cable technology.

Keep an eye on new developments   Keep an eye out for changes in technology. Which advancements in networking will make your cabling setup obsolete and which advancements will enhance it? We know people who were putting in 10Base-2 and 10Base-5 coaxial cable for networking in 1995, cable that was used for a year or two and then never used again because all local area networking moved to Category 5 twisted-pair cable. One of the interesting developments occurring as this book is being written is high-density fiber-optic connectors that allow the simultaneous connection of several fibers at once, much like the way RJ-45 jacks connect four pairs of cable at the same time. We suggest you subscribe to the cabling industry's trade magazines to keep abreast of the field; information about these magazines can be found in Appendix B, "Cabling Resources."

Understand the business of cabling   Even if you are just installing a network for your own company's use, you should strive to perform a professional job. After all, you are the customer in that instance, and you want to be pleased with the results. You should know how to plan the job, acquire materials, assemble a team, train and supervise the crew, oversee the actual installation, test, document, and "sign off" or close the job. Read the rest of this chapter for some hints on the business of cabling. There are numerous industry periodicals that can keep you up-to-date on the latest in cabling business and technology. See Appendix B for more information.

Understand the business of business   If you are installing networks for others, you need to need to know how to run a business (or you need to hire people that will do it for you). You need to know all about attracting work, bidding, developing and negotiating contracts, hiring, scheduling, billing, accounting, and so on. For more detailed information on the business of business, check out your local college or university's business school.

Plan the Installation

Every well-executed job was at one point merely a well-planned job with realistic appraisals of the time, equipment, materials, and labor required. The following steps will help you develop that realistic plan:

Get the complete specification   Obtain in writing, with detailed and accurate blueprints, exactly what sort of network the customer wants. Often it is up to you to plan the cable paths, but the customer usually has a good idea of where the network drops should be located and where the patch panels should be placed. Don't forget to confirm that the blueprints are accurate and up-to-date.

Perform a job walk   Go to the site and walk through the job. Peer up into ceilings and look at conduits. Examine any walls that you'll have to penetrate. Make sure that there's room for your own racks and patch panels in the wiring closet. Some areas are much easier to network than others—an office building that uses ceiling tiles and is still under construction, for example, is much easier to wire than an old brick building with plastered ceilings or an aircraft carrier with watertight bulkheads and convoluted cable paths.

Clarify inconsistencies and ambiguities   If you don't see a way to get a cable from one location to another, point it out. Ask why the front desk doesn't have a drop planned—doesn't the receptionist have a computer? Will there be one placed there in the future? Questions you ask at this stage can save you from change orders later.

Calculate the lengths of network runs   With an accurate blueprint, you can do this away from the site. Otherwise you'll have to break out the measuring wheel and walk the path of the cables. You will have to use the measuring wheel for any outside cable runs (from one building to another, for example).

Plan for service loops and waste   The last bit of cable you pull from the spool is always too short. Runs often have to go around unexpected obstacles. When you pull a group of cables to the same general area, some will need more length to get to their actual destination than others—but you'll still have to pull the same amount of cable in the bundle for all the runs in an area and trim each cable to fit. You should trim the cable a little too long and push the extra back up into the wall or ceiling so that, if necessary, the jack location can be moved later without requiring the whole run to be pulled through again. All of this adds up to 10 to 30 percent more cable than a naïve plan would indicate.

Evaluate your manpower and skill level   How many feet of cable can your installers pull in an hour? Do you have enough teams to pull groups of cable in different directions—and do you have supervisors for the teams? How many faceplates can each installer punch down in an hour? After you've gained some experience, you will be able to look at a job and know how long it will take your team. In the meantime, calculate it out.

Have the Right Equipment

The right tools indicate your commitment to doing the job right. There are varying qualities of cable installation tools that are discussed in Chapter 6, "Tools of the Trade." Some of these tools are designed for the do-it-yourselfer while others are designed for professionals that install cable every day. When you set out to install a cable plant, get the right tools for the job. The following is a list of equipment that all experienced cable installers should carry:

Punch-down tools   Don't use the little plastic tabs that come with the network faceplates to punch down the pairs onto them. You'll wear out your thumbs and your customer's patience that way. Get each cable installer a good metal spring-loaded punch tool to work with.

Screwdrivers   You have to fasten the faceplates to their receptacles with something. A good screwdriver with a selection of tips fits the bill nicely.

Snips   Cable installers are constantly cutting and stripping cable. A good pair of snips (these are *not* your mother's sewing scissors) will stand up to the abuse of cutting through copper cable all day long and still remain sharp enough to score the jacket of a Category 5 cable without nicking the pairs twined within.

Twine and fish tape   Sometimes it can be difficult to feed a huge bundle of cables behind walls, through rafters, or down a conduit. Twine (sometimes pushed along with some fish tape) will often travel the path more easily, and you can then tie the twine to the cables and pull the cables through.

Electrical tape   After you tie the twine to the cable, but before you pull it through, you can tape the twine and cables together. Taper the whole assembly to pass corners and smaller diameter holes more easily.

Measuring wheel   This is used to make sure that you've got enough cable for that really long run.

Cable tester   You need this so that you can make sure that what you've installed actually works.

Patch panel lights   These will help you match up a drop location to a patch panel location for labeling, testing, and documentation.

Test and Document

Many cable installers view testing and documentation as a convenience to the customer and an annoyance to be avoided. We view the lack of testing and documentation as a threat to everyone's sanity.

We can't count the number of times a customer has come to one of us and said, "This cable that you installed is bad. None of us can get any work done, and it is all your fault." If you kept the test documents (and you should *always* keep a copy of them for your own records), you can point to them and say, "But it passed with flying colors then, and you signed here. Of course, we stand by our work and we'll come out and fix it if it's broken, but you just might want to check your network adapter settings [or jumper cable or network hub] before someone drives all the way out there…"

NOTE   Don't discount the fact that damage can occur to a cable, jack, or patch panel connection after the cabling system is installed.

Another common problem professional cable installers report is being called in to fix cabling problems left by another installer who didn't bother to test their work. Honest mistakes can be made in any cabling installation; these mistakes include the following:

- Copper cables were routed past RF-noisy power lines.

- Cables had their jackets scraped off when pulled through narrow places or around corners.

- Installed cables, jacks, and/or patch panels were labeled incorrectly.

- Fiber optics were bent in too tight a radius.

- Category 5 copper cables had their wires punched down in the wrong order.

- Cable was installed that exceeds the maximum length specified by the standards.

Testing your cable plant after you install it will pinpoint any of these problems. We are amazed that some installers simply assume that they've made no mistakes. Nobody's perfect—but you don't have to remind your customers of that.

Train Your Crew

You can get any group of enthusiastic guys together and pull cable through a ceiling. Punching down the little colored strands of wire at the end of the cable into the faceplate is a different matter—show them how to do it first, give them some cable scraps, and have them punch down both ends. Then test those short cables.

Until your crew gets a feel for punching down the cables correctly, you'll find crossed wires, marginal connections, and strands cut too short and too long. It takes practice to do it right, but the time you spend training your crew will be well worth the number of problems you won't have to fix on the job site.

Terminating fiber optic cable requires a different order of training altogether. Unless your installers have spent hours cutting, stripping, polishing, and terminating fiber optic cable and then examining what they've done wrong in a microscope, they'll never get it done right. Have your installers make all their mistakes on your own property rather than your customers'.

Work Safely

Train your crew in safety as well as proper cabling methodology. In most areas of the U.S., the cabling business is booming and you need every able-bodied and trained installer you can get your hands on. Also, taking some basic steps to reduce the likelihood of accidents and your liability in the case of an accident will help you sleep better at night.

Make sure that the safety lectures you give are themselves done safely, too. For example, once we had a contract to install fiber optic cable in military hospitals. This was a retrofit situation, so we did not have precut holes in the drop locations; we had to cut the holes ourselves. A supervisor was showing how to properly wield a drill with a hole-saw bit installed and said, "And never chock the bit with your hand, like this—,"whereupon he grabbed the hole-saw bit with one hand and touched the trigger of the drill with the other to tighten the bit. Naturally, the drill whined, the bit spun, and blood dripped on the floor from the new gouge in the supervisor's hand. Fortunately, he did not drill a new hole through his hand, and this occurred at the job site (in a wing of the hospital), so a nurse took him away and bandaged his hand. He returned shortly thereafter and resumed his safety lecture. "And in the case of an on-the-job accident," he continued after looking at his watch, "you can take 15 minutes off." He was kidding, of course, but his unintentional example made an impression on the crew.

Network installers do a lot of work in ceilings, tight places, new construction areas, dusty areas, and around all sorts of construction equipment. Make sure your employees know proper safety methods for handling ladders, wearing safety helmets, using dust masks, and so on.

Make It Pretty

The cable we install looks good. We are proud of our work, and so is the customer when we're done. Our network closets look like something important happens there—huge bundles of cable swoop out of conduits and separate into neatly dressed branches that flow across to their requisite rack locations. There are two reasons we don't leave tangled, messy wiring closets behind: 1) the customer appreciates a wiring closet that looks orderly, and 2) an orderly wiring closet is easier to diagnose and fix network problems in. There is no jiggling and pulling of cables to figure out which direction a bad line is running—when you look at it you know just by where it is. This saves a tremendous amount of time, both for us and for the customer, long after we're gone.

You can feel a real sense of pride when cabling systems you have installed are printed up in magazines. In one case, a cabling company was installing a fiber-to-the desk network for a local biotech company. This was when fiber was new and expensive (as opposed to fiber network equipment now, which is simply expensive), and the supervisor was nervous about its installation and anxious to test it to make sure it all worked properly. Once the far ends of the cables had all been terminated, he terminated the fiber patch panels (which involves a lot of cutting, polishing, gluing, and so forth and isn't something you just redo without a lot of expense). Unfortunately, he neglected to dress the cables first. Now, you can't untangle a knot once you've glued the ends together, which is essentially what he'd done. Fortunately, he'd left enough cable for a service loop (see the section "Plan for Contingencies"), and he used the extra length to push his new and permanent knot up into the ceiling where it couldn't be seen. With a junction box around the knot (look—cables go in, cables come out—never mind what's inside!) the plant was neat and ready for the photographers.

Look Good Yourself

For professional cabling installation crews, appearance is important. It is important that you and your installation crew look appropriate for the job you are performing. The customer forms an impression about you and your company by how you walk, talk, and dress. The customer is reassured and happy when he sees professionals behaving in a professional manner; he is dismayed and apprehensive when he sees yokels yokeling. Even if you are installing cable for your own company, the way you and your crew carry yourself will carry over into the work you do. Of course, this doesn't mean you and your installers should be running around in three-piece suits pulling cables through walls, but neither should you look like you've been dragged out of the nearest alley.

Every cabling company we have worked with has had a dress code of jeans and a T-shirt for their installers, and the company provides the T-shirts (with a company logo on the back, of course.) The T-shirts identify the work crew on the site and provide free off-site advertisement as well (if the logo is not too terribly designed and the installers aren't embarrassed to wear them at home!).

Plan for Contingencies

No job ever goes exactly as planned. If you have only enough time, materials, and manpower for the job as planned, you will inevitably come up short. Make sure to keep the following possibilites in mind as you plan:

Service loops   If you've read this far, you've already seen one reason for leaving service loops in installed cable (a service loop is an extra length of cable coiled up and left in the ceiling or wall). Another reason to leave service loops comes from a basic rule of cable—you can always cut it shorter, but you can't cut it longer. Inevitably, racks need to be moved, desks are reoriented, partitions are shifted—often even before you're done with the job. If the cable is a bit longer than you originally needed, you can just pull it over to the new location and reterminate rather than pulling a whole new cable to the new location. Also, if you determine while you're testing the plant (you *are* testing, aren't you?) that the cable has been punched down incorrectly, you will need an extra couple of inches to punch it down correctly. The service loop provides those inches.

Additional drops   Customers are always forgetting locations that they need network connectivity in ("Oh, you mean the printer requires a LAN connection too?"), so you should be prepared with additional cable, faceplates, and jacks for the inevitable change order. You can charge for the extra time and material required to install the extra drops, of course. Some companies bid low and expect to make their profit on exorbitant change-order costs, but we prefer to plan ahead and pleasantly surprise the customer with reasonable change order prices. Jim estimates that at least 75 percent of all cabling installations he has worked on required additional drops within the first month after installation.

Extra time required   What do you do when the installers punch down your entire network using Token Ring faceplates instead of Ethernet faceplates? (This actually happened to someone we know once, and although Ethernet and Token Ring use the same jack form factor, they connect different pins to the cable and the faceplates are not interchangeable. However, if the four-pair cable and either the T568A or T568B wiring patterns were used, the jack would support either type of connection.) What you do is tear out all the incorrect faceplates and reterminate your network. This takes time, and if you haven't budgeted extra time for mix-ups like this, you risk serious disruption of your (and your customer's) schedule.

Manpower shortages   People get sick. They drill holes in their hands with drills. Competitors steal your best employees. The customer wants all four phases rolled out at once instead of week-by-week as you'd originally planned. Either you need to budget extra time for shortages in manpower or you need the ability to bring more installers on the job. Customers are always delighted when you beat your schedule, so it pays to pad the time budget a little bit (as long as you don't pad it so much you lose the bid).

Equipment and material shortages   When you plan a network installation, the amount of cable you allow for is always an estimate. Short of pulling lots of string from one location to another, there is no way of determining beforehand exactly how much cable an installation will require because the actual cable paths deviate from the planned ones due to interposed air ducts, inconvenient patch panels, already-full conduits, and so on. Typically, the amount of cable actually used exceeds the planned amount by 10 to 30 percent. Professionals are pretty good at estimating cable usage and will subconsciously add the "fudge factor" to their own calculations so that they are seldom more than 10 percent off (to the installers' chagrin—see the section "Waste Not, Want Not"), but cable isn't the only thing you can run short of. Depending on the job, you may need inner-duct tubing, racks, panels, faceplates, jacks, jumpers, rack screws, raceways, zip ties, string, T-shirts, and Coca-Cola. It helps to have some spares on hand for when material is shipped to the wrong site, is held up in manufacturing, mysteriously disappears, gets used up too quickly, or gets stripped, scraped, burnt, painted, flooded, or stepped on. It pays especially to be sure of the arrival of any specialized equipment or peculiar material—for one job in particular, we were held up waiting for a manufacturer to actually *manufacture* the fiber optic cable we needed.

Match Your Work to the Job

No two potential networks have exactly the same requirements. At first glance, two network jobs may appear to be identical—each may specify the same type of cable and indicate the same number of network drops to be installed in the same office environment with the same number of rack locations and so on. However, one job may take twice as long to execute as the other job. When a customer relaxes a constraint on how you install cable, or if there are special considerations for a particular job, you should take advantage of the specific circumstances of that job.

When we install network cable, we find that some of our customers care about the order in which drop locations show up on the wiring closet patch panels. Other customers do not care, so long as the patch panels are clearly labeled. This simple distinction has a huge impact on how long it takes to physically install the network cables. One typical customer of ours (who, refreshingly, had a complete and comprehensive requirement for us to work from) specified the rack layout and cable arrangement all the way down to which location on each patch panel should correspond to which faceplate location in the building.

In order to get the right cable to the right location to satisfy this requirement, we had to start in the wiring closet, physically label one of each cable, pull them in groups to the general location of their destinations, and then cut and label the other ends. There were 40 or 50 cable drops in each general area, so we had to sort out the cables and pull them to their ultimate destinations from the general location that all the cables were originally pulled to. (We were lucky that none of the cable numbering had been rubbed off during the cable pulling!) We then cut them to the correct length and punched them down at the drop end.

At the wiring closet end of the cables the network technician also had the unwelcome job of sorting all those cables and punching them into the rack in correct order. All that writing and searching and sorting takes a lot of time because you must not pull the wrong cable to the wrong location.

The other job we ran at the same time went far more quickly because the network administrator didn't care which patch panel location went to which drop location—he was just going to plug them into a hub anyway. We just pulled cable from the closets to the drop locations, trimmed them, and terminated them in the wall sockets. The network technician in the wiring closet simply punched that end of the cables down one by one, regardless of where the other end of the cable went.

Of course, we then had to determine which cable went where for testing purposes (*always* test, document, and label your work). However, we have some nifty jacks that we plug into the patch panels that light up when a technician sticks a probe in the drop end of the cable. The technician calls out over the radio where that drop is, the patch panel technician writes down the patch panel location, they remove the LEDs and insert the test modules, and they move on to the next location. (If you are looking for these handy little gadgets, you can find them on the Internet at www.idealindustries.com.)

A job done this second way can take half the time (and therefore can be performed at a lower cost) of one done the hard way—but, of course, it should only be done this way if the customer doesn't mind that the drop locations show up in random order in the patch panels.

Waste Not, Want Not

One cabling company owner found a good method for solving the pernicious problem of cleaning up after a job. As the crew installs the cable, a good 10 to 30 percent of the cable ends up around the job site as trash. About half of the waste piles up next to the wiring closets, while the rest lies scattered throughout the drop locations. He observed that all those cable ends contained quite a bit of high quality copper. His concern was not to pull every last dime out of the cable, however—his priority was to make sure that the client had the best possible experience working with his company so that the client would pass on recommendations to others in their industry.

He instituted a policy that all the leftover copper the installation technicians could scavenge from the cable belonged to the technicians, and proceeds from the recycling of it would go toward a company party. All they had to do was gather it up, bag it, and place it in the back of his truck—one of the supervisors took it to the recycling plant for processing. The technicians are meticulous about cleaning up now—even the inch or two of a cable trimmed to be the right length is picked up and stuck in the back pocket of a technician to go toward the fund. Of course, they have strict instructions not to pick up any of the other contractors' cable.

Customers are amazed at how clean this cabling company owner's job sites are when he gives the customer a final walk-through. He now has an excellent reputation in the industry that sprung from the way he handles this and other details of his business. And, finally, his employees enjoy working for him, have a reason to clean up their work, and have really cool parties.

Case Studies

To give you a better idea of what it is like to install network cable, here are a handful of case studies that, while the names have been changed to protect the innocent, are drawn from the experiences of real cabling installers and contractors out there in the field.

A Small Job

Recently, a medical Web site development company we'll call Quasicom decided to replace all the cables that were strewn through their hallways with a real network. They contacted a cabling contractor to whom they had been referred by someone who said that they would not have to worry about the quality of the work when it was completed. Quasicom asked the contractor to come take a look at their problem and give them a quote for installing the network.

This contractor likes to take a hands-on approach so he came down himself to perform the job walk. He talked with Quasicom's IS (Information Services) staff to determine their needs and got a written document from them that detailed where they wanted the network locations and where the rack was to go. With such a small network, the contractor didn't have much calculation to do, so he presented Quasicom with an offer that they accepted.

Two days later, after a contract was signed and exchanged, the contractor dispatched a team of two installers to the job site. Neither installer was a supervisor, but the senior member of the crew had enough experience to see that the job was done right. The company owner himself met the crew at the job site and handed them the plans, showing them where to put the rack and to run the cables and the wiring standard to use when punching down the faceplates. He then left them to do the work (he had another job walk-through to do for a much larger customer).

Quasicom's premises were of typical modern office construction—a removable tile drop ceiling provided an easy way to run the cables from one location to another, and it is not hard to drop the network cables down behind the drywall once you know how. The crew expected no difficulties in installing the cable.

The two installers started by setting up several boxes of spooled cable in the location where the rack was to be (in this case, it was not in a wiring closet but in their server room where all their Web hosts were hooked up to the Internet). The plan indicated that the biggest run they had was of eight cables to the eight drops in the front office area, so they set up all eight boxes of cable. Quasicom's IS staff wanted the patch panel terminations of the wire to be in room number order, so the installers marked the ends of the cable and the boxes they came in with indelible black marker.

The crew then pulled out the requisite number of feet of cable (normally they would measure it, but in this case they just pulled it down the hall to its approximate drop point and made allowance for going up into the wall and down behind the drywall and added some service loop extra). They then used their snips to cut the cable off and marked the other end according to which box it came from.

They did the same thing with four boxes of cable for the quad run back to the back offices. That left two locations, each with a double jack faceplate, which did not share a run with any other locations. They picked the two boxes that looked like they had just enough cable left in them to pull those runs from, and they drew those cable runs out as well.

Now it was time to put the cable up in the ceiling. The crew started by removing a few ceiling tiles so that they had access to the ceiling space. Then they tied the bundle of eight cables to the free end of a ball of twine and tossed the twine through the ceiling to a reasonably central area for all of the front office drops. They used the twine to pull the cables through and down to that point. They performed the same operation for the other bundles of cables.

At this point, they had all the cables almost where they needed to be—just 20 feet shy of their goal. They removed the ceiling tiles directly above the drop locations to determine that there would be no inconvenient obstacles (such as power conduits) and then used drywall saws to cut holes in the wall for the faceplates. For each location, one member of the installation team then found the corresponding cable and fed it across the ceiling to the other installer. That installer dropped it down the wall for the first installer to pull out of the hole.

Now all the cable was in place and merely needed to be terminated. While pulling cable is a team process, terminating it is a solitary one. One member of the team began installing the boxes for the faceplates, stripping and punching down the faceplates (leaving enough cable length pushed up in the wall for a service loop), and screwing the faceplates into the box on the wall. The other team member went back to the server room to set up the rack and dress the cable for punching down on the rack.

This contractor always has his best installers perform the important job of punching down the racks. There is a small margin for error when you terminate cable on a rack because there are so many cables all feeding into the same space-constrained location. If you make a mistake punching the cable down, you have to draw more cable out of your service loop (you *do* have one, don't you?) in order to reterminate. This messes up the pretty swooping lines of cable you've already tie-strapped to the rack and to the raceways. You can't terminate first and dress the cable later because then you'll end up with an ugly knot of cable in the ceiling. That afternoon, the cabling contractor came back with his test equipment, and he and his crew verified that all of the drop locations passed a full Category 5 scan. They used a label gun to identify all of the drops and their corresponding rack locations and then had Quasicom's IS manager accompany them in a final walk-through. They provided Quasicom's manager with the documentation (the same plans he'd given them along with a printout of the test results), got his signature on an acceptance document, and it was all over but for the billing.

Job Summary: Quasicom

Type of network: Interior Category 5

Number of drops: 16

Number of wiring closets: 1

Total cable length: 800 feet

Crew required: 2

Duration: 6 hours

A Large Job

The job walk-through that our contractor friend left to perform was for a defense contractor we'll call TechnoStuff who had a new building under construction. For this job, our contractor was a subcontractor for another firm that had bid for all of the premises wiring for the new location. The Category 5 cable plant was to provide network access to a maze of cubicles and a handful of offices on two floors of the building. All but two of the wiring closets were on the first floor.

Wiring cubicles is different from wiring offices because you have no walls to come down inside of. Also, interior design consultants have the alarming tendency to move cubicles around. This means that instead of coming down the walls to faceplate locations, the runs to cubicle locations come up from locations in the floor. Sometimes the cables are terminated there (using *very* tough receptacles in the floor), and sometimes the customer wants the cables drawn up from the floor and along raceways in the cubicle walls to faceplates in the cubicles. In TechnoStuff's case, they wanted it terminated in the cubicles.

Our contractor walked the site and examined the network plan. He talked with the foreman about construction schedules and when his crew would have access to the area (because he wanted to get in after the framing was done but before the drywall went up) and who would be putting in the conduit and boxes and so on. He emphasized that the conduit had to have string left in it (it's a pain to get cable through it otherwise). He also asked if he had to drill his own holes in the floor (typically the answer to this question is yes).

The next week, the contractor took his crew out and showed the supervisors what had to be done. At that point, they had the left wing of the first floor of TechnoStuff available to them, along with all of the wiring closets. An office furniture contractor was busy setting up the cubicles in the right wing. Our contractor assigned one crew to set up the racks and pull the fiber optic backbone from the periphery wiring closets to the central one. He directed the other two crews to pull the cable for that wing from the closets to the cubicle locations. He then left the supervisors in charge because he had a meeting with TechnoStuff regarding materials delivery timetables and the pay schedule.

The supervisors took over. As soon as they had cable to the cubicle locations, one team began terminating the cable while the other continued pulling cable. TechnoStuff had no preference about which patch panel location ended in what cubicle, so the teams simply grabbed the next available cable in the area where they all came up out of the floor to terminate for each location. The cables were pulled in bundles of 25 (when the bunches get any thicker they grow unwieldy).

The contractor had evaluated the timetable and his available manpower correctly. The crew had just finished punching down the cable in the left wing when the right wing cubicles were all set up (the cable pullers had drawn their cables into the space and let the cubicles be set up around them). The first team had finished pulling and terminating the fiber optic backbone and began terminating the Category 5 patch panels for the first floor.

The contractor came back at the end of the week to deal with some miscommunication about who was to provide the wall plates for the offices and found to his disgust that the answer was he. The drywall had already gone up, and his crew would have to punch holes in it and dangle the cable down behind it instead of putting the cable in when the walls were open and easy to work with. In addition, TechnoStuff had decided at the last minute that they really did need network connections in their conference rooms, so extra cable had to be pulled to those locations as well. The contractor gave his supervisors the revised plans and additional instructions. He left to go make sure that the additional cable and supplies would arrive in time.

With so much work in the open basement pulling cable from one place to another along the ceiling, one of the installers decided to "walk" his ladder from one hole to another while he was still on the ladder instead of getting down and carrying it. Naturally, he overbalanced and fell, spraining his ankle. The supervisor sent him to get it checked out and the cable-pulling crew was down one member. He replaced him by pulling an installer off the punch-down crew, which was getting ahead of the cable pullers anyway.

At the end of two weeks, all of the cables were in place and terminated, and it was time to test and document. The contracting company discovered where each cable actually ended up by putting indicator lights in the patch panels and having an installer walk from location to location with a radio and a tool that would light up the indicator for that location when he plugged it in the faceplate. When the patch panel location was found, they swapped the locator for the tester and measured the performance of that cable.

After all of the cables had been tested, labeled, and documented (and a handful of mistakes fixed) the supervisor took TechnoStuff's representative on a final walk-through and had him sign off to accept the job.

Job Summary: TechnoStuff

Type of network: Interior Category 5 with fiber optic backbone

Number of drops: 500 (x 4 jacks per location)

Number of wiring closets: 6

Total cable length: 300,000 feet

Crew required: 12

Duration: 2 weeks

A Peculiar Job

One interesting job another contractor did a number of years ago required a great deal of ingenuity and adaptive thinking. A marine research institute had contracted with a local shipbuilding firm to construct from scratch a vessel designed for deep-sea exploration that we'll call (naturally) Cool Marine Institute Research Vessel—or CMIRV, for short. CMIRV wanted a ship designed for science, not just a fishing boat crudely adapted with generators, probes, computers, and insufficient living space for a bunch of scientists. The shipbuilding firm took the job but found themselves at sea when it came to putting in a wholly fiber optic network with over 200 drops in a boat that was itself just 140 feet long.

The cabling contracting company had put networks in ships before (for the U.S. Navy) and felt comfortable putting in a bid for this job. They were awarded the job. The customer then asked the contractor if they could put in a telephone system, an alarm system, and a video system while they were at it! Of course, the contractor said yes.

The contracting company learned quickly that putting systems into a vessel under construction is a far different matter than retrofitting 10- and 20-year-old ships with a new network. First of all, they could not perform a job walk-through when they bid on or accepted the job because the boat hadn't even been built yet. Second, the pace for installing cable and equipment is slow but strict—you have to be prepared to run a cable when the path is accessible, and there could be no drilling holes in bulkheads later. Also, CMIRV's main contractor required that the cabling contractor maintain a presence on the job site whether or not there was anything to do in order to resolve conflicts and ambiguities about cable and device placement, access requirements, and so on.

What the cabling contractor did was to place a reliable and steady employee at the job site and have him put in a portion of the network whenever it was possible for him to do so. They occasionally sent out additional crew when, for example, it was time to terminate a bunch of fiber optic cable that had been pulled, to install and calibrate the cameras for the video system, or to hook up and program the telephone system.

Job Summary: Cool Marine Institute Research Vessel

Type of network: Interior fiber optic

Number of drops: 200

Number of wiring closets: 1

Total cable length: 10,000 feet

Crew required: 1+

Duration: 1 year

An Inside Job

Don't think that good contractors and installers have always done cabling the right way. For many of us, our introduction to the art of network cabling installation came while performing a job completely unrelated to cabling. One person we know got her introduction to cabling while working for a university, managing the computer department for one of the colleges, which we'll call Budget Nets College. It was finally time for Budget Nets to upgrade the campus network from ARCnet to Ethernet, and they had raised enough funds to do it internally rather than going through the traditional university appropriations channels. (There was quite a bit of fuss about Budget Nets going outside of the usual channels to do it, but after they got their LAN upgraded, the University's main Information Services group was more attentive to the other individual colleges' needs—probably because they were afraid their jobs would become obsolete!)

Since Budget Nets had gone their own way to upgrade their network instead of waiting in queue for the university's dedicated networking crews to come in and do it for them, they had to find someone else to pull the cable. It turned out that the campus physical plant department was happy to do that for them—all Budget Nets had to do was provide a requirement. The physical plant department would make a proposal and, if Budget Nets agreed to the cost, the plant would pull the cable.

The physical plant's electrical workers knew everything there is to know about pulling wires through walls. They were even aware of the problems of RF interference and cable length issues. They were not, however, experts in all the different kinds of jacks and jumpers that computer networking uses. Before Budget Nets knew it, the entire first floor of their building was wired with Token Ring instead of Ethernet faceplates.

Being a new administrator, our friend did not know what to do about the situation. The proper course of action would have been to call the electrical workers back in, make them take out the wrong faceplates, and have them put in the right ones. But meanwhile, the faculty and staff of her school needed to get back to work.

Now, both Ethernet and Token Ring when used over twisted-pair cabling use two pairs of the cable—one pair to receive and another pair to transmit. Unfortunately, Ethernet and Token Ring do not use the same pairs so you cannot use Token Ring faceplates in an Ethernet network. Unless, of course, you make custom cables that switch the pairs being used. That is what she did.

NOTE

If the network had been wired to the TIA/EIA-568-A recommended wiring pattern (T568A or T568B), then this situation would not have occurred. If you only wire the pin positions you need, the cabling infrastructure will only support applications that use those particular pins.

Although this plan worked as a necessary quick fix for our administrator, we do not suggest you take this course of action in a similar situation, because it confuses people terribly when they find out that one cable will work in their outlet but another almost identical one will not. Eventually, she had to pull all those faceplates out and replace them. Those custom cables still show up on occasion and cause problems.

Job Summary: Budget Nets College

Type of network: Interior Category 5

Number of drops: 160

Number of wiring closets: 2

Total cable length: 32,000 feet

Crew required: 4

Duration: 1 week

Summary

The problem with network cabling is that it looks so easy to do. Just run a line from point A and point B and terminate it, right? Unfortunately, there is more to professionally installing a cable plant that will serve for years without problems than that. You have to know what you're doing, you have to carefully plan the job, you have to take care when you execute your plan in order to do it right, and you have to test the cable plant afterwards.

Dictionary of Cabling and Telecommunications Terms and Concepts

1Base-5   StarLAN network with a 1Mbps data transfer rate. Developed by AT&T, this network has not been common since the late 1980s.

2B+D   Shortcut for describing basic ISDN service (2B+D = two bearer channels and one data channel, which indicates two 64Kbps channels and one 16Kbps channel used for link management).

4B/5B   Signal encoding method used in 100Base-TX/FX Fast Ethernet and FDDI standards. Four-bit binary values are encoded into five-bit symbols.

8B/10B   Signal encoding method used by the 1000Base-X Gigabit Ethernet standards.

8B6T   Signal encoding method used in 100Base-T4 Fast Ethernet standard.

10Base-2   Ethernet (10Mbps) based on Manchester signal encoding over thin coaxial cable. Commonly called *thinnet* or *cheapernet*. This implementation of Ethernet uses a 10Mbps signaling rate, baseband signaling, and coaxial cable with a maximum segment length of 185 meters.

10Base-5   Ethernet (10Mbps) based on Manchester signal encoding over thick coaxial cable. Also called *thicknet*. This was the original Ethernet medium.

10Base-F   Ethernet (10Mbps) based on Manchester signal encoding over fiber optic cable.

10Base-T   Ethernet (10Mbps) based on Manchester signal encoding over Category 3 or better twisted-pair cable. This IEEE standard defines the requirement for sending information at 10Mbps on unshielded twisted-pair cabling and defines various aspects of running Ethernet on this cabling.

10Broad-36   Ethernet (10Mbps) on broadband cable. Not very common.

50-pin connector   Commonly referred to as a *telco*, *CHAMP*, or *blue ribbon connector*. Commonly found on telephone switches, 66-blocks, 110-blocks, and 10Base-T Ethernet hubs and used as an alternate twisted-pair segment connection method. The 50-pin connector connects to 25-pair cables, which are frequently used in telephone wiring systems and typically meet Category 3. Some manufacturers also make Category 5–rated cables and connectors.

66-type connecting block   Connecting block used by voice-grade telephone installations to terminate twisted pairs. Not recommended for LAN use.

100Base-FX   Fast Ethernet (100Mbps) based on 4B/5B signal encoding over fiber optic cable.

100Base-T2   Fast Ethernet (100Mbps) based on PAM5 signal encoding and using two pairs of Category 3 or better unshielded twisted-pair cable. This implementation of Ethernet is not very common.

100Base-T4   Fast Ethernet (100Mbps) based on 8B6T signal encoding and using four pairs of Category 3 or better unshielded twisted-pair cable. This implementation of Ethernet is not very common.

100Base-TX   Fast Ethernet (100Mbps) based on 4B/5B signal encoding and using two pairs of Category 5 or better unshielded twisted-pair cable.

100Base-X   Defines any 100Mbps Fast Ethernet system based on 4B/5B signal encoding, including 100Base-TX and 100Base-FX. IEEE 802.3 shorthand term for entire 100Mbps Fast Ethernet system.

110-block   A connecting block that is designed to accommodate higher densities of connectors and to support higher frequency applications. 110-blocks are found on patch panels and cross-connect blocks for data applications. See Chapter 7 for more information.

1000Base-CX   Gigabit Ethernet (1000Mbps) based on 8B/10B signaling over copper cable; used over short distances.

1000Base-LX   Gigabit Ethernet (1000Mbps) based on 8B/10B signaling using long wavelength laser transmitters over fiber optic cable. Designed to be used over long distances.

1000Base-SX   Gigabit Ethernet (1000Mbps) based on 8B/10B signaling using short wavelength laser transmitters over fiber optic cable. Designed for optical fiber that is used as horizontal cabling.

1000Base-T   Gigabit Ethernet (1000Mbps) based on PAM5 signal encoding over unshielded twisted-pair cable (Category 5 or better) that has passed all performance tests specified by TSB-95.

1000Base-X   Any 1000Mbps Gigabit Ethernet based on 8B/10B signaling. These technologies includes 1000Base-T, 1000Base-CX, 1000Base-LX, and 1000Base-SX.

A

abrasion mark   A flaw on an optical surface usually caused by an improperly polished termination end.

absorption The loss of power (signal) in an optical fiber resulting from conversion of optical power into heat and caused principally by impurities, such as transition metals and hydroxyl ions, and by exposure to nuclear radiation. Expressed in dB/km (decibels per kilometer). Absorption and scattering are the main causes of attenuation (loss of signal) of an optical waveguide.

abstract syntax notation (ASN) 1
Used to describe the language interface standards for interconnection of operating systems, network elements, workstations, and alarm functions.

AC See *alternating current*.

acceptance angle With respect to optical fiber cable, the angle over which light entering the fiber core will be guided along the core rather than reflected off of the surface or lost through the cladding. Often expressed as the half angle of the cone and measured from the axis. Generally measured as numerical aperture (NA); it is equal to the arcsine. See also *numerical aperture*.

acceptance cone The cross section of an optical fiber is circular; the light waves accepted by the core are expressed as a cone. The larger the acceptance cone, the larger the numerical aperture (NA); this means that the fiber is able to accept and propagate more light.

acceptance pattern The amount of power transmitted represented as a curve over a range of launch angles. The actual fiber angle can be characterized as geometry of core terminations to find the optimal angle of entry.

access coupler An optical device to insert or withdraw a signal from a fiber from between two ends. Many couplers require connectors on either end, and for many applications they must be APC (angled physical contact) connectors. The most popular access coupler is made by the fused biconic taper process, wherein two fibers are heated to the softening point and stretched so that the mode fields are brought into intimate contact, thus allowing a controlled portion of light to move from one core to the other.

access method Rules by which a network peripheral accesses the network medium to transmit data on the network. All network technologies use some type of access method; common approaches include carrier sense multiple access/collision detection (CSMD/CD), token passing, and demand priority.

ACK See *acknowledgment*.

acknowledgment (ACK) A message confirming that a data packet was received.

ACR See *attenuation crosstalk ratio*.

active branching device   Converts an optical input into two or more optical outputs without gain or regeneration.

active coupler   A device similar to a repeater that includes a receiver and one or more transmitters. The idea is to regenerate the input signal and then send them on. These are used in optical fiber networks.

active laser medium   Lasers are defined by their medium; laser mediums such as gas, (CO_2, helium, neon) crystal (ruby) semiconductors, and liquids are used. Almost all lasers create coherent light on the basis of a medium being activated electronically. The stimulation can be electronic or even more vigorous, such as exciting molecular transitions from higher to lower energy states, which results in the emissions of coherent light.

active monitor   In Token Ring networks, the active monitor is a process that prevents data frames from roaming the ring unchecked. If a Token Ring frame passes the active monitor too many times, it is removed from the ring. The active monitor also ensures that a token is always circulating the ring.

active splicing   A process performed with an alignment device, using the light in the core of one fiber to measure the transmittance to the other. Ensures optimal alignment before splicing is completed. The active splicing device allows fusion splicing to perform much better with respect to insertion losses when compared to most connectors and splicing methods. A splicing technician skilled at the use of an active splicing device can reliably splice with an upper limit of .03dB.

A/D   Analog to digital.

AD or ADC   See *analog-to-digital converter*.

adapter   With respect to optical fiber, a passive device used to join two connectors and fiber cores together. The adapter is defined by connector type, such as SC, FC, ST, LC, MT-RJ, FDDI, etc. Hybrid adapters can be used to join dissimilar connectors together, such as SC to FC. The adapter's key element is a "split sleeve," preferably made from zirconia and having a specific resistance force to insertion and withdrawal of a ferrule. This resistance, typically between 4 and 7 grams, ensures axial alignment of the cores.

address   An identifier that uniquely identifies nodes on a network.

adjustable attenuator   An attenuator in which the level of attenuation is varied with an internal adjustment. Also known as variable attenuator.

administration   With respect to structured cabling, the functions needed in the wire center to accurately maintain records and identification of circuit related records. The TIA/EIA-606 Administration Standard for Telecommunications Infrastructure of Commercial Buildings defines standards for this purpose.

ADSL   See *Asymmetric Digital Subscriber Line*.

Advanced Intelligent Network (AIN)
Developed by Bell Communications Research, a telephone network architecture that separates the service logic from the switching equipment. This allows the rapid deployment of new services with major equipment upgrades.

aerial cable   Telecommunications cable installed on aerial supporting structures such as poles, towers, sides of buildings, and other structures.

AGC   Automatic gain control.

AI   Amplitude imbalance.

alternating current (AC)   An electric current that cyclically reverses the direction of flow. Frequency is the rate at which a full cycle occurs in one second.

AM   See *amplitude modulation*.

American Standard Code for Information Interchange (ASCII)   A means of encoding information.

American Wire Gauge (AWG)   Standard measuring gauge for nonferrous conductors (i.e., noniron and nonsteel). Gauge is a measure of the diameter of the conductor (the thickness of the cable). The higher the AWG number, the smaller the diameter of the wire. See Chapter 1 for more information.

ampere   A unit of measure of electrical current.

amplifier   Any device that intensifies a signal without distorting the shape of the wave.

amplitude   The maximum value of a varying signal.

amplitude modulation (AM)   A method of signal transmission technique in which the amplitude of the carrier is varied in accordance with the signal. With respect to optical fiber cabling, the modulation is done by varying the amplitude of a light wave, common in analog/RF applications.

analog   A continuously variable signal. A mercury thermometer, which gives a variable range of temperature readings and sound waves, is an example of an analog instrument. Analog signals are measured in hertz (Hz). Analog is the opposite of *digital*.

analog signal   An electrical signal that varies continuously without having discrete values (as opposed to a digital signal).

analog-to-digital converter   A device used to convert analog signals to digital signals.

angle of incidence   With respect to fiber optics, the angle formed between a beam of light striking a surface and the normal angle to that surface.

angle of reflection   With respect to fiber optics, the angle formed between the normal and a reflected beam. The angle of reflection equals the angle of incidence.

angle of refraction   With respect to fiber optics, the angle formed between the normal and a refracted beam.

angled end   An optical fiber whose end is polished with purpose to an angle to reduce reflectance.

angled physical contact (APC) connector   A single-mode optical fiber connector whose angled end-face helps to ensure low mated reflectance and low unmated reflectance.

angular misalignment   The loss of optical power caused by deviation from optimum alignment of fiber-to-fiber or fiber-to-waveguide. Loss at a connector due to fiber angles being misaligned. Also known as angular misalignment loss.

ANSI   American National Standards Institute.

antireflection (AR)   Coating used on optical fiber cable to reduce light reflection.

APC connector   See *angled physical contact (APC) connector*.

APL   See *average picture level*.

AppleTalk   Apple Computer's networking protocol and networking scheme, integrated into most Apple system software, that allows Apple computing systems to participate in peer-to-peer computer networks and to access the services of AppleTalk servers. AppleTalk operates over Ethernet (EtherTalk), Token Ring (TokenTalk), and FDDI (FDDITalk) networks. See also *LocalTalk*.

application   (1) A program running on a computer. (2) A system, the transmission method of which is supported by telecommunications cabling, such as 10Base-T Ethernet, 622Mbps ATM, digital voice, etc.

AR   See *antireflection*.

aramid   See *aramid strength member*.

aramid strength member   The generic name for Kevlar. A yarn used in fiber optic cable that provides additional tensile strength, resistance to bending, and support to the fiber bundle. It is not used for data transmission.

aramid yarn   See *aramid strength member*.

ARCnet (Attached Resource Computer network)   Developed by Datapoint, a relatively low speed form of LAN data link technology (2.5Mbps, in which all systems are attached to a common coaxial cable or an active or passive hub). ARCnet uses a token-bus form of medium access control; only the system that has the token can transmit.

armoring   Provides additional protection for cables. Usually consists of plastic coated steel and may be corrugated for flexibility to provide protection against severe outdoor environments.

ARP table   A table used by the ARP protocol on TCP/IP-based network nodes that contains known TCP/IP addresses and their associated MAC (media access control) addresses. The table is cached in memory so that ARP lookups do not have to be performed for frequently accessed TCP/IP and MAC addresses. See also *address resolution protocol*.

ASCII   See *American Standard Code for Information Interchange*.

ASTM   American Society for Testing and Materials.

Asymmetric Digital Subscriber Line (ADSL)   One of the most exciting developments in telephone technology over the past few years, also sometimes called *Universal ADSL* or *G.Lite*. ADSL makes it possible to use ordinary phone lines to transmit up to 1.5Mbps. An ADSL modem replaces your regular modem and you subscribe to the ADSL service from your local phone service provider. ADSL is also called *splitterless DSL* because it does not require the installation of a splitter to separate voice and data signals.

asynchronous   Transmission where sending and receiving devices are not synchronized (without a clock signal). Data must carry signals to indicate data division.

asynchronous transfer mode (ATM)
Not to be confused with automated teller machines, asynchronous transfer mode is a relatively new connection-oriented networking technology that uses a form of very fast packet switching in which data is carried in fixed length units. These fixed length units are called *cells*; each cell is 53 bytes in length, with 5 bytes used as a header in each cell. Since the cell size does not change, they can be switched very quickly. ATM networks can transfer data at extremely high speeds. ATM employs mechanisms that can be used to set up virtual circuits between users, in which a pair of users appear to have a dedicated circuit between them. ATM is defined in specifications from the ITU and ATM Forum. For more information, see the ATM Forum's Web site at www.atmforum.org.

ATM   See *asynchronous transfer mode*.

attachment unit interface (AUI) port
A 15-pin connector found on older network interface cards (NIC). This port allowed connecting the NIC to different media types by using an external transceiver. The cable that connected to this port was known as a transceiver cable or a drop cable.

attenuation   A general term indicating a decrease in power (loss of signal) from one point to another. This loss can be a loss of electrical signal or light strength. In optical fibers, it is measured in decibels per kilometer (dB/km) at a specified wavelength. The loss is measured as a ratio of input power to output power. Attenuation is caused by poor quality connections, defects in the cable, and loss due to heat. The lower the attenuation value, the better. Opposite of *gain*. See Chapter 1 for additional information on attenuation and the use of decibels.

attenuation to crosstalk ratio (ACR)
A copper cabling measurement, the difference between attenuation and crosstalk (NEXT), measured in dB, at a given frequency. A quality factor for cabling to assure that the signal sent down a twisted pair is stronger at the receiving end of the cable than any interference imposed on the same pair by crosstalk from other pairs. ACR measurements are not used with optical fiber cabling since crosstalk is not an issue. See Chapter 1 for more information.

attenuation-limited operation   In a fiber optic link, the condition when operation is limited by the power of the received signal (rather than by bandwidth or distortion).

attenuator   A passive device that intentionally reduces the optical signal by inducing loss.

audio   Used to describe the range of frequencies within range of human hearing; approximately 20 to 20,000Hz.

AUI   See *attachment unit interface port.*

auxiliary AC power   Typically an AC 110V supply of power to equipment area for operation of some equipment such as computer equipment but primarily used for appliance outlets for portable test equipment.

avalanche photodiode (APD)   With respect to optical fiber equipment, a photodiode that is designed to take advantage of avalanche multiplication of photocurrent. As the reverse-bias voltage approaches the breakdown voltage, hole-electron pairs created by absorbed photons acquire sufficient energy to create additional hole-electron pairs when they collide with ions; thus a multiplication or signal gain is achieved.

average picture level (APL)   A video parameter.

average power   The energy per pulse, measured in joules, times the pulse repetition rate, measured in hertz (Hz). This product is expressed as watts.

average wavelength (I)   The average of the two wavelengths for which the peak optical power has dropped to half.

AWG   See *American Wire Gauge.*

axial ray   A light ray that travels along the axis of an optical fiber.

B

back reflection   See *backscatter.*

backbone   A cable connection between telecommunications or wiring closets, floor distribution terminals, entrance facilities, and equipment rooms either within or between buildings. This cable can service voice communications or data communications. In star topology data networks, the backbone cable interconnects hubs and similar devices, as opposed to cables running between hub and station. In a bus topology data network, the bus cable. Also called *vertical cable* or *trunk cable.*

backbone subsystem   The main feeder cable running from the cable entrance point to the distribution frame near the equipment area.

backbone wiring   The physical/electrical interconnections between telecommunications closets and equipment rooms. See *backbone.*

backscatter   Usually a very small portion of an overall optical signal, occurs when a portion of scattered light returns to the input end of the fiber; the scattering of light in the direction opposite to its original propagation. Light that propagates back towards the transmitter. Also known as *back reflection* or *backscattering*.

balance   An indication of signal voltage equality and phase polarity on a conductor pair. Perfect balance occurs when the signals across a twisted-pair cable are equal in magnitude and opposite in phase with respect to ground.

balanced cable   A twisted-pair cable that has two identical conductors that carry voltages of opposite polarities and equal magnitude with respect to ground. The conductors are twisted to maintain balance over a distance.

balanced coupler   A coupler whose output has balanced splits, for example, one by two is 50/50, or one by four is 25/25/25/25.

balanced line   See *balanced cable*.

balanced signal transmission   Two voltages, commonly referred to as *tip and ring*, equal and opposite in phase with respect to each other across the conductors of a twisted-pair cable. Balanced signal transmission occurs when you dedicate one wire to transmitting and one to receiving.

balun   A device that is generally used to connect balanced twisted-pair cabling with unbalanced coaxial cabling. The balun is an impedance-matching transformer that converts the impedance of one interface to the impedance of another interface. Balun is short for balanced/unbalanced.

bandpass   A range of wavelengths over which a component will meet specifications.

bandwidth   Used to measure the information-carrying capacity of a cable (fiber or copper). A range of frequencies between the highest and the lowest frequencies of a transmission channel (path for information transmission). Identifies the amount of data that can be sent through a given channel. Measured in hertz (Hz); higher bandwidth numbers mean higher data capacity. With copper cable, using higher frequencies than the recommended bandwidth causes excessive signal loss (attenuation) and crosstalk. With fiber optic cable, using high frequencies causes modal dispersion, which distorts the signal and makes it unreadable.

bandwidth-limited operation   Systems can be limited by power output or bandwidth; bandwidth-limited operation is the prevailing condition when the system bandwidth, rather than the amplitude of the signal, limits performance. The condition is reached when modal dispersion distorts the shape of the waveform beyond specified limits.

barrier layer   A layer of glass deposited on the optical core to prevent diffusion of impurities into the core.

baseband   A method of communication in which the entire bandwidth of the transmission medium is used to transmit a single digital signal. The signal is driven directly onto the transmission medium without modulation of any kind. Baseband uses the entire bandwidth of the carrier, whereas broadband only uses part of the bandwidth. Baseband is simpler, cheaper, and less sophisticated than broadband.

basic rate interface (BRI)   As defined by ISDN, consists of two 64Kbps B-channels used for data and one 16Kbps D-channel. Thus, a basic rate user can have up to 128Kbps service.

battery distribution fuse bay (BDFB)   An intermediate cabling interface that serves as a distribution point for converting from power feeder cables to distribution cables that, in turn, are distributed to transmission equipment.

baud   The number of changes in signal level transitions per second. Commonly confused with bits per second, the baud rate does not necessarily transmit an equal number of bits/sec. In some encoding schemes, baud will equal bits per second, but in others it will not. For example, a signal with four voltage levels may be used to transfer two bits of information for every baud.

B-channel   See *bearer channel*.

beacon   A special frame in Token Ring systems indicating a serious problem with the ring such as a break. Any station on the ring can detect a problem and begin beaconing.

beamsplitter   An optical device, such as a partially reflecting mirror, that splits a beam of light into two or more beams. Used in fiber optics for directional couplers.

beamwidth   The distance between two diametrically opposed points at which the irradiance is a specified fraction of the beam's peak irradiance; most often applied to beams that are circular in cross section.

bearer channel (B-channel) On an ISDN network, carries the data. Each bearer channel typically has a bandwidth of 64Kbps.

bel Named for Alexander Graham Bell, this unit represents the logarithm of the ratio of two levels. See Chapter 1 for an explanation of *bel* and *decibels*.

bend loss A form of increased attenuation in a fiber where light is escaping from bent fiber. Bend loss is caused by bending a fiber around a restrictive curvature (a macrobend) or from minute distortions in the fiber (microbend). The attenuation may be permanent if fractures caused by the bend continue to affect transmission of the light signal.

bend radius (minimum) The smallest bend a cable can withstand before the transmission is affected. UTP copper cabling usually has a bend radius that is four times the diameter of the cable; optical fiber is usually 10 times the diameter of the cable. Bending a cable any more than this can cause transmission problems or cable damage. Also referred to as *cable bend radius*.

BER See *bit error rate*.

BERT See *bit error rate tester*.

biconic connector Optical connector with a conical shape for highly repeatable optical connections. The biconic connector was developed by AT&T but is not commonly used.

BICSI See *Building Industry Consulting Service International*.

bidirectional couplers Couplers that operate in both directions and function in the same way in both directions.

binder A tape or thread used to hold assembled cable components in place.

binder group A group of 25 pairs of wires in a cable with 50 pairs or more; the binder group has a strip of colored plastic around it to differentiate it from other binder groups in the cable.

BISDN See *broadband ISDN*.

bistable optics Optical devices with two stable transmission states.

bit A binary digit, the smallest element of information in binary system. A 1 or 0 of binary data.

bit error rate (BER)   In digital applications, a measure of data integrity. It is the ratio of bits received in error to bits sent. The ratio of incorrectly transmitted bits to correctly transmitted bits. BERs of one error per billion bits sent are typical.

bit error rate tester (BERT)   A device that tests the bit error rate across a circuit. One common device that does is this is called a T-BERT because it is designed to test T-1 and leased line error rates.

bit stream   A continuous transfer of bits over some medium.

bit stuffing   A method of breaking up continuous strings of 1 bits by inserting a 0 bit. The 0 bit is removed at the receiver.

bit time   The length of time required to transmit one bit of information.

bits per second (bps)   The number of energy pulses (bits) passing a given point in a transmission medium in one second.

BL   Blue. Refers to blue cable pair color in UTP twisted-pair cabling.

black body   A body or material that, in equilibrium, will absorb 100 percent of the energy incident upon it, meaning it will not reflect the energy in the same form. It will radiate nearly 100 percent of this energy, usually as heat and/or IR (infrared).

blown fiber   A method for installing fiber in which fibers are blown through a conduit or tube using air.

BNC   Bayonet-Neill-Concelman (Neill and Concelman were the inventors), sometimes called British Naval Connector. A coaxial connector that uses a "bayonet"-style turn and lock mating method. Used with RG-58 or smaller coaxial cable. Used with 10Base-2 Ethernet thin coaxial cable.

BNO   Broadband network operator.

bonding   (1) The method of permanently joining metallic parts to form an electrical contact that will ensure electrical continuity and the capacity to safely conduct any current likely to be imposed on it. (2) Grounding bars and straps used to bond equipment to the building ground. (3) Combining more than one ISDN B-channel using ISDN hardware.

bounded medium   A network medium that is used at the physical layer where the signal travels over a cable of some kind, as opposed to an unbounded medium such as wireless networking.

BPON   Broadband passive optical network.

bps   See *bits per second*.

BR   Brown. Refers to brown cable pair color in UTP twisted-pair cabling.

braid   A group of textile or metallic filaments interwoven to form a tubular flexible structure that may be applied over one or more wires or flattened to form a strap. Designed to give a cable more flexibility or to provide shielding from EMI or grounding.

break-out cable   Multifiber cables where each fiber has additional protection by using additional jackets and strength elements such as aramid yarn.

break-out kit   Used to build up the outer diameter of fiber cable when connectors are being installed.

BRI   see *basic rate interface*.

bridge   A network device, operating at the data link layer of the OSI model, that logically separates a single network into segments but lets the two segments appear to be one network to higher layer protocols.

bridged tap   Multiple appearances of the same cable pair at several distribution points. Bridged taps are allowed in coaxial cable but not in optical fiber or twisted-pair cables. Also known as *parallel connections*.

broadband   A transmission facility, typically referring to copper, that has the ability to handle a wide range of frequencies simultaneously. Broadband transmission medium has a bandwidth sufficient to carry multiple voice, video, or data channels simultaneously. Each channel occupies (is modulated to) a different frequency bandwidth on the transmission medium and is demodulated to its original frequency at the receiving end. Channels are separated by "guard bands" (empty spaces) to ensure that each channel will not interfere with its neighboring channels. This technique is used to provide many CATV channels on one coaxial cable.

broadband ISDN   New ISDN technology that can expand the capabilities of ISDN. Emerging because digital systems such as ISDN will not be able to completely replace analog-based systems in the foreseeable future.

broadcast Sending data simultaneously to more than one receiving device at a time.

B-router A device that combines the functionality of a bridge and a router but can't be distinctly classified as either. Most routers on the market incorporate features of bridges into their feature set. Also called a *hybrid router*.

buffer (buffer coating) A protective coating applied to a fiber optic cable. This layer of material, usually thermoplastic or acrylic polymer, is applied in addition to the optical fiber coating, which provides protection from stress and handling. Fabrication techniques include tight or loose tube buffering as well as multiple buffer layers. In tight buffer constructions, the thermoplastic is extruded directly over the coated fiber. In loose buffer constructions, the coated fiber "floats" within a buffer tube that is usually filled with a nonhygroscopic gel. See Chapters 1 and 10 for more information.

buffer tube Used to provide protection and isolation for optical fiber cable. Usually hard plastic tubes, with an inside diameter several times that of a fiber, which holds one or more fibers.

buffered fiber See *buffer*.

buffering See *buffer*.

building cable In-building plant cable, as opposed to outside plant (OSP) cable. Building cable typically will not protect the transmission media from moisture or other environmental factors found in the outside plant, and it is constructed from nonflammable grade materials.

building distributor (BD) An ISO/IEC 11801 term that describes a location where the building backbone cable terminates and where connections to the campus backbone cable may be made.

building entrance The location in a building where a trunk cable between buildings is typically terminated and fiber is distributed through the building. Also the location where services enter the building from the phone company and antennas.

Building Industry Consulting Service International (BICSI) A nonprofit association concerned with promoting correct methods for all aspects of the installation of communications wiring. More information can be found on their Web site at www.bicsi.org.

bundle (fiber) A group of individual fibers packaged or manufactured together within a single jacket or tube. Also a group of buffered fibers distinguished from another group in the same cable core.

bundled cable   An assembly of two or more cables continuously bound together to form a single unit prior to installation.

bus topology   In general, a physical layout of network devices in which all devices must share a common medium to transfer data.

butyl rubber   A synthetic rubber with good electrical insulating properties.

bypass   The ability of a station to isolate itself optically from a network while maintaining the continuity of the cable plant.

byte   A group of eight bits.

(

c   The symbol for the speed of light in a vacuum.

C   The symbol for both capacitance and Celsius.

cable   (1) Copper: A group of insulated conductors enclosed within a common jacket. (2) Fiber: One or more optical fibers enclosed within a protective covering and material to provide strength.

cable access fireproofing   Procedure and materials required to apply firestopping to openings where cables pass between floors or walls.

cable assembly   With respect to optical fiber cables, cable that has connectors installed on one or both ends. If connectors are attached to only one end of the cable, it is known as a *pigtail*. If its connectors are attached to both ends, it is known as a *jumper*. General use of these cable assemblies includes the interconnection of multimode and single-mode fiber optical cable systems and optical electronic equipment.

cable bend radius   See *bend radius*.

cable duct   A single pipe, tube, or conduit that holds cabling.

cable entrance conduits   Typically, holes in the wire center foundation where cable conduits enter into the cable entrance facility (CEF).

cable entrance facility (CEF)   Primary entrance point for cables into a building, typically where conduits from the street end. The CEF usually has a framing structure (such as 19-inch racks or plywood on the wall) for the organization of splices, cables, cross-connects, and network equipment.

cable management system   A total cable pathway system from point-to-point within the wire center designed so that cable placement will be clear and growth will be easy to accomplish.

cable modem   Connects to your CATV connection (usually with coaxial cable) and provides you with a 10Base-T connection for your computer. All of the cable modems attached to a cable TV company line communicate with a cable modem termination system (CMTS) at the local CATV office. Cable modems can receive and send signals only to and from the CMTS and not to other cable modems on the line. Some services have the upstream signals returned by telephone rather than cable, in which case the cable modem is known as a *telco-return* cable modem; these require the use of a phone line. The theoretical data rate of a CATV line is up to 27Mbps on the download path and about 2.5Mbps of bandwidth for upload. The overall speed of the Internet and the fact that the cable provider may not have a line faster than a T-1 (1.544Mbps) to the Internet restricts the actual amount throughput. However, even at the lower end of the possible data rates, the throughput is many times faster than traditional modem connections to the Internet.

cable plant   Consists of all the copper and optical elements including patch panels, patch cables, fiber connectors, splices, etc., between a transmitter and a receiver.

cable rearrangement facility (CRF) A splice cabinet that can be used in place of a splice closure, especially in the vertical splice arrangement.

cable sheath   A covering over the conductor assembly that may include one or more metallic members, strength members, or jackets.

cable TV   See *community antenna television*.

campus   The buildings and grounds of a complex, such as a university, college, industrial park, or military establishment.

campus backbone   Cabling between buildings that share data and telecommunications facilities.

campus distributor (CD)   The ISO/IEC 11801 term for the main cross-connect; this is the distributor from which the campus backbone cable emanates.

CAN   Cable area network.

capacitance   The ability of a dielectric material between conductors to store electricity when a difference of potential exists between the conductors. The unit of measurement is the *farad*, which is the capacitance value that will store a charge of a one coulomb when a one-volt potential difference exists between the conductors. In AC, one farad is the capacitance value, which will permit one ampere of current when the voltage across the capacitor changes at a rate of one volt per second.

carrier   An electrical signal of a set frequency that can be modulated in order to carry data.

carrier detect (CD)   Equipment or a circuit that detects the presence of a carrier signal on a digital or analog network.

carrier sense   With Ethernet, a method of detecting the presence of signal activity on a common channel.

carrier sense multiple access/collision avoidance (CSMA/CA)   A network media access method that sends a request to send (RTS) packet and waits to receive a clear to send (CTS) packet before sending. Once the CTS is received, the sender sends the packet of information. This method is in contrast to CSMA/CD, which merely checks to see if any is currently using the media.

carrier sense multiple access/collision detect (CSMA/CD)   A network media access method employed by Ethernet. CSMA/CD network stations listen for traffic before transmitting. If two stations transmit simultaneously, a collision is detected and both stations wait a brief (and random) amount of time before attempting to transmit again.

Category 1   Also called *Cat 1*. Unshielded twisted pair used for transmission of audio frequencies up to 100KHz. Used as speaker wire, doorbell wire, alarm cable, etc. Category 1 cable is not suitable for networking applications or digital voice applications. See Chapters 1 or 7 for more information.

Category 2   Also called *Cat 2*. Unshielded twisted pair used for transmission at frequencies up to 4MHz. Used in analog and digital telephone applications. Category 2 cable is not suitable for networking applications. See Chapters 1 or 7 for more information.

Category 3   Also called *Cat 3*. Unshielded twisted pair with 100-ohm impedance and electrical characteristics supporting transmission at frequencies up to 16MHz. Used for 10Base-T Ethernet and digital voice applications. Defined by the TIA/EIA-568-A specification. See Chapters 1 or 7 for more information.

Category 4   Also called *Cat 4*. Unshielded twisted pair with 100-ohm impedance and electrical characteristics supporting transmission at frequencies up to 20MHz. Not commonly used. Defined by the TIA/EIA-568-A specification. See Chapters 1 or 7 for more information.

Category 5   Also called *Cat 5*. Unshielded twisted pair with 100-ohm impedance and electrical characteristics supporting transmission at frequencies up to 100MHz. This is currently the most common cable installed. Defined by the TIA/EIA-568-A specification. See Chapters 1 or 7 for more information.

Category 5e   Also called *Cat 5e* or *Enhanced Cat 5*. A new standard that will specify transmission performance that exceeds Cat 5. Cat 5e has improved specifications for NEXT, PS-ELFEXT, and attenuation. Like Category 5, it consists of unshielded twisted pair with 100-ohm impedance and electrical characteristics supporting transmission at frequencies up to 100MHz. See Chapters 1 or 7 for more information.

Category 6   Also called *Cat 6*. A proposed standard that aims to support transmission at frequencies up to 250MHz over 100-ohm twisted pair. See Chapters 1 or 7 for more information.

Category 7   Also called *Cat 7*. A proposed ISO/IEC standard that aims to support transmission at frequencies up to 600MHz over 100-ohm twisted pair. See Chapters 1 or 7 for more information.

CATV   See *community antenna television*.

CBX   Computerized branch exchange.

CCD   Change coupled devices.

CCIR   Consultative Committee on Radio.

CCIT   See *International Telephone and Telegraph Consultative Committee*.

CCTV   Closed-circuit television.

CD   See *carrier detect*.

CDDI   See *Copper Distributed Data Interface*.

CDMA   See *code division multiple access*.

CEF   See *cable entrance facility*.

center wavelength (laser)   The nominal value central operating wavelength defined by a peak mode measurement where the effective optical power resides.

center wavelength (LED)   The average of two wavelengths measured at the half amplitude points of the power spectrum.

central member   The center component of a cable, which serves as an antibuckling element to resist temperature-induced stresses. Sometimes serves as a strength element. The central member is composed of steel, fiberglass, or glass-reinforced plastic.

central office (CO)   The telephone company building where subscriber's lines are joined to telephone company switching equipment that serves to interconnect those lines. Also known as an exchange center or head end. Some places call this a public exchange.

central office ground bus   A ground bar that is connected into the central office ground system to provide for multiple connections on a particular floor.

CEPT   See *Conference of European Postal and Telecommunications Administrations.*

CEV   See *controlled environmental vault.*

channel   The end-to-end transmission or communications path at which application specific equipment is connected. Through multiplexing several channels, voice channels can be transmitted over an optical channel.

channel bank   Equipment that combines a number of voice channels into a digital signal; in the case of a T-1 channel bank, it converts 24 separate voice channels into a single digital signal.

channel insertion loss   With respect to fiber optic links, the static loss of a link between a transmitter and receiver. It includes the loss of the fiber, connectors, and splices.

channel service unit/digital service unit (CSU/DSU)   A hardware device that is similar to a modem that connects routers' or bridges' WAN interfaces (V.35, RS-232, etc.) to wide area network connections (Fractional-T1, T-1, Frame Relay, etc.). The device converts the data from the router or bridge to frames that can be used by the WAN. Some routers will have the CSU/DSU built directly into the router hardware, while other arrangements require a separate unit.

characteristic impedance   The impedance that an infinitely long transmission line would have at its input terminal. If a transmission line is terminated in its characteristic impedance, it will appear (electrically) to be infinitely long, thus minimizing signal reflections from the end of the line.

cheapernet   A nickname for thin Ethernet (thinnet) or 10Base-2 Ethernet systems.

chromatic dispersion The spreading of a light pulse caused by the difference in refractive indices at different wavelengths. Different wavelengths travel along an optical medium at different speeds. Wavelengths reach the end of the medium at different times, causing the light pulse to spread. This chromatic dispersion is expressed in picoseconds per kilometer per nanometer (of bandwidth). It is the sum of material and waveguide dispersions.

churn Cabling slang for the connection, disconnection, and rearrangement activity of cross-connections of a frame. Office environments where network equipment and phones are frequently moved will experience a high churn rate.

CIR See *committed information rate*.

circuit A communications path between two pieces of associated equipment.

cladding The layer of material (usually glass) that surrounds the core of an optical fiber. The cladding has a lower index of refraction that causes the transmitted light to travel down the core. The interface between the core and the cladding creates the mode field diameter, wherein the light is actually held reflectively captive within the core.

cladding mode A mode of light that propagates through and is confined to the cladding.

Class A (1) ISO/IEC 11801 designation for twisted-pair cabling rated to 100KHz. Used in voice and low frequency applications. Comparable to Category 1 cabling; not suitable for networking applications. (2) IP addresses that have a range of numbers from 1 through 127 in the first octet.

Class B (1) ISO/IEC 11801 designation for twisted-pair cabling rated to 1MHz. Used in medium bit-rate applications. Comparable to Category 2 cabling; not suitable for networking applications. (2) IP addresses that have a range of numbers from 128 through 191 in the first octet.

Class C (1) ISO/IEC 11801 designation for twisted-pair cabling rated to 16MHz. Used in high bit-rate applications. Corresponds to TIA/EIA Category 3 cabling. (2) IP addresses that have a range of numbers from 192 through 223 in the first octet.

Class D (1) ISO/IEC 11801 designation for twisted-pair cabling rated to 100MHz. Used in very high bit-rate applications. Corresponds to TIA/EIA Category 5 cabling. (2) IP addresses used for multicast applications that have a range of numbers from 224 through 239 in the first octet.

Class E   (1) ISO/IEC proposal for twisted-pair cabling rated to 250MHz. Corresponds to the proposed TIA/EIA Category 6 cabling standard. (2) IP addresses used for experimental purposes that have a range of numbers from 240 through 255 in the first octet.

cleave   The process of separating an unbuffered optical fiber by a controlled fracture of the glass for the purpose of obtaining a fiber end that is flat, smooth, and perpendicular to the fiber axis. This is done prior to splicing or terminating the fiber.

closet   An enclosed space for housing telecommunications and networking equipment, cable terminations, and cross-connect cabling. It contains the horizontal cross-connect where the backbone cable cross-connects with the horizontal cable. Called a *telecommunications closet* by the TIA/EIA standards; sometimes referred to as a *wiring closet*.

cm   Centimeter. Approximately 0.4 inches.

CO   See *central office*.

coating   A material surrounding the cladding of a fiber and put on a fiber during the drawing process to protect it from the environment. Do not confuse the coating with the buffer.

coaxial cable   Also called *coax*. Coaxial cable was invented in 1929 and was in common use by the phone company by the 1940s. Today it is commonly used for cable TV and by older Ethernet; twisted-pair cabling has become the desirable way to install Ethernet networks. It is called coaxial because it has a single conductor surrounded by insulation and then a layer of shielding. The outer shielding serves a ground and to reduce the effects of EMI. Can be used at high bandwidths over long distances.

code division multiple access (CDMA)
In time division multiplexing (TDM), one pulse at a time is taken from several signals and combined into a single bit stream.

coherence   In light forms, characterized as a consistent, fixed relationship between points on the wave. In each case, there is an area perpendicular to the direction of the light's propagation in which the light may be highly coherent.

coherence length or time   The distance time over which a light form may be considered coherent. Influenced by a number of factors, including medium, interfaces, launch condition, etc. Time, all things being equal, is calculated by the coherence length divided by the phase velocity of light in the medium.

coherent communications   Where the light from a laser oscillator is mixed with the received signal, and the difference frequency is detected and amplified.

coherent light   Light in which all parameters are predictable and correlated at any point in time or space, particularly over an area in a lane perpendicular to the direction of propagation or over time at a particular point in space.

collision   The network error condition that occurs when electrical signals from two or more devices sharing a common data transfer medium crash into one another. This commonly happens on Ethernet-type systems.

committed information rate (CIR)   A commitment from your service provider stating the minimum bandwidth you will get on a frame relay network.

common mode transmission   A transmission scheme where voltages appear equal in magnitude and phase across a conductor pair with respect to ground. May also be referred to as *longitudinal mode*.

communication panel   A piece of auxiliary communication equipment that provides various voice communication circuits that are used in system maintenance operations. The panel may provide access to an order wire, which provides maintenance communications between the central office and any repeater location along a span.

community antenna television (CATV)   More commonly known as *cable TV*, a broadband transmission facility that generally uses a 75-ohm coaxial cable to carry numerous frequency-divided TV channels simultaneously. CATV is now carrying high-speed Internet service in many parts of the world.

compliance   A wiring device that meets all characteristics of a standard is said to be in compliance with that standard. For example, a data jack that meets all of the physical, electrical, and transmission standards for TIA/EIA-568 Category 5 is compliant with that standard.

concatenation   The process of joining several fibers together end to end.

concatenation gamma   The coefficient used to scale bandwidth when several fibers are joined together.

concentrator   A multiport repeater or hub.

conductivity The ability of a material to allow the flow of electrical current; the reciprocal of resistivity. Measured in "mhos" (the word *ohm* spelled backward).

conductor A material or substance (usually copper wire) that offers low resistance (opposition) to the flow of electrical current.

conduit A rigid or flexible metallic or nonmetallic raceway of circular cross section in which cables are housed for protection and to prevent burning cable from spreading flames or smoke in the event of a fire.

Conference of European Postal and Telecommunications Administrations (CEPT) A set of standards adopted by European and other countries, particularly defining interface standards for digital signals.

connecting block A basic component of a distribution frame. Also called a *terminal* block, a *punch-down* block, a *quick-connect* block, and a *cross-connect* block, a connecting block is a plastic block containing metal wiring terminals to establish connections from one group of wires to another. Usually each wire can be connected to several other wires in a bus or common arrangement. There are several types of connecting blocks: 66 clip, BIX, Krone, 110, etc. A connecting block has insulation displacement connections (IDCs), which means

you don't have to remove insulation from around the wire conductor before you punch it down or terminate it.

connectionless protocol A transport protocol that does not create a virtual connection between sending and receiving stations.

connection-oriented protocol A transport protocol that uses acknowledgments and responses to establish a virtual connection between sending and receiving stations.

connector With respect to fiber optics, a device attached to the end of a fiber optic cable, receiver, or light source that joins it with another device or fiber. A connector is a mechanical device used to align and join two fibers together to provide a means for attaching and decoupling it to a transmitter, receiver, or another fiber. Commonly used connectors include the FC, ST, LC, MT-RJ, FDDI, Biconic, and SMA connectors.

connector-induced optical fiber loss With respect to fiber optics, the part of connector insertion loss due to impurities or structural changes to the optical fiber caused by the termination within the connector.

connector plug With respect to fiber optics, a device used to terminate an optical fiber.

connector receptacle   With respect to fiber optics, the fixed or stationary half of a connection that is mounted on a patch panel or bulkhead.

connector variation   With respect to fiber optics, the maximum value in decibels of the difference in insertion loss between mating optical connectors (e.g., with remating, temperature cycling, etc.). Also known as *optical connector variation*.

consolidation point (CP)   A location defined by the TIA/EIA-568-A standard for interconnection between horizontal cables that extends from building pathways and horizontal cables that extend into work area pathways. Often an entry point into modular furniture for voice and data cables. The ISO/IEC 11801 defines this as a *transition point (TP)*.

consumables kit   Resupply material for splicing or terminating fiber optics.

continuity   An uninterrupted pathway for electrical signals.

controlled environmental vault (CEV)   A cable termination point in a belowground vault whose humidity and temperature are controlled.

Copper Distributed Data Interface (CDDI)   A version of FDDI that uses copper wire media instead of fiber optic cable and operates at 100Mbps. See also *twisted-pair physical media dependent (TP-PMD)*.

core   The central region of an optical fiber through which light is transmitted. Common core sizes are 8.3 microns, 50 microns, and 62.5 microns. The core is surrounded by a cladding that has a higher refractive index that keeps the light inside the core.

core eccentricity   A measure of the displacement of the center of the core relative to the cladding center.

counter-rotating   An arrangement whereby two signal paths, one in each direction, exist in a ring topology.

coupler   With respect to optical fiber, a passive, multiport device that connects three or more fiber ends, dividing the input between several outputs or combining several inputs into one output.

coupling   The transfer of energy between two or more cables or components of a circuit. With respect to copper wire coupling, see also *crosstalk*.

coupling efficiency The efficiency of optical power transfer between two components.

coupling loss The power loss suffered when coupling light from one optical device to another.

coupling ratio/loss The ratio/loss of optical power from one output port to the total output power, expressed as a percent. This percentage represents the percentage of light transferred to a receiving output port with respect to the total power of all output ports.

CPC Customer premises communication.

CPE Customer premises equipment.

CRC See *cyclic redundancy check*.

critical angle The smallest angle of incidence at which total internal reflection occurs. At lower angles, the light is refracted through the cladding and lost. Due to the fact that the angle of reflection equals the angle of incidence, total internal reflection assures that the wave will be propagated down the length of the fiber.

cross-connect A facility enabling the termination of cables as well as their interconnection or cross-connection with other cabling or equipment. Also known as a *punch-down* or *distributor*. In a copper-based system, jumper wires or patch cables are used to make connections. In a fiber optic system, fiber optic jumper cables are used.

cross-connection A connection scheme between cabling runs, subsystems, and equipment using patch cords or jumpers that attach to connecting hardware at each end.

crossover A conductor that connects to a different pin number at each end. See also *crossover cable*.

crossover cable A twisted-pair patch cable wired in such a way as to route the transmit signals from one piece of equipment to the receive signals of another piece of equipment, and vice versa. Crossover cables are often used with 10Base-T Ethernet cards to connect two Ethernet cards together "back-to-back" or to connect two hubs together if the hubs do not have crossover or uplink ports. See Chapter 9 for more information on Ethernet crossover cables.

crosstalk   The coupling or transfer of unwanted signals from one pair within a cable to another pair. Crosstalk can be measured at the same (near) end or far end with respect to the signal source. Crosstalk is considered noise or interference and is expressed in decibels. Chapter 1 has an in-depth discussion of crosstalk.

crush impact   A test is typically conducted using a press that is fitted with compression plates of a specified cross sectional area. The test sample is placed between the press plates and a specified force is applied to the test specimen. Cable performance is evaluated while the cable is under compression and/or after removal of load depending on the test standard specifications.

CSA   Canadian Standards Association.

CSMA/CA   See *carrier sense multiple access/collision avoidance.*

CSMA/CD   See *carrier sense multiple access/ collision detect.*

CSU   Channel service unit. See *channel service unit/digital service unit.*

CSU/DSU   See *channel service unit/digital service unit.*

current   The flow of electrons in a conductor. See also *alternating current* and *direct current.*

curvature loss   The macro-bending loss of signal in an optical fiber.

customer premises   The buildings, offices, and other structures under the control of an end-user or customer.

cutback   A technique or method for measuring the optical attenuation or bandwidth in a fiber by measuring first from the end and then from a shorter length and comparing the difference. Usually one is at the full length of the fiber optic cable and the other is within a few meters of the input.

cutoff wavelength   For a single-mode fiber, the wavelength above which the operation switches from multimode to single-mode propagation. This is the longest wavelength at which a single-mode fiber can transmit two modes. At shorter wavelengths the fiber fails to function as a single-mode fiber.

cut-through resistance   A material's ability to withstand mechanical pressure (such as a cutting blade or physical pressure) without damage.

cycles per second   The count of oscillations in a wave. Once cycle per second equals a hertz.

cyclic redundancy check (CRC) An error-checking technique used to ensure the accuracy of transmitting digital code over a communications channel before and after the data is transmitted. Transmitted messages are divided into predetermined lengths that are divided by a fixed divisor. The result of this calculation is appended on to the message and sent with it. At the receiving end, the computer performs this calculation again. If the value that arrived with the data does not match the value the receiver calculated, an error has occurred during transmission.

D

D/A Digital to analog.

DAC See *dual attachment concentrator*.

daisy chain In telecommunications, a wiring method where each telephone jack in a building is wired in series from the previous jack. Daisy chaining is *not* the preferred wiring method, since a break in the wiring would disable all jacks "downstream" from the break. Attenuation and crosstalk are also higher in a daisy-chained cable. See also *home run cable*.

dark current The external current that, under specified biasing conditions, flows in a photo detector when there is no incident radiation.

dark fiber An unused fiber; a fiber carrying no light. Common when extra fiber capacity is installed.

DAS See *dual attachment station*.

data communication equipment (DCE) With respect to data transmission, the RS-232 interface that is used by a modem to communicate with a computer.

data connector See *IBM data connector*.

data-grade A term used for twisted-pair cable that is used in networks to carry data signals. Data-grade media has a higher frequency rating than voice-grade media used in telephone wiring does. Data-grade cable is considered Category 3 or higher cable.

data packet The smallest unit of data sent over a network. A packet includes a header, addressing information, and the data itself.

data rate   The maximum number of bits of information that can be transmitted per second, as in a data transmission link. Typically expressed as megabits per second (Mbps) for LANs, but often expressed as kilobits per second (Kbps) in WANs. The data rate may or may not be equal to the baud rate.

data terminal equipment (DTE)   (1) The interface that a computer uses to communicate with a modem or other serial device. This port is often called the computer's RS-232 port or the serial port. (2) Any piece of equipment at which a communications path begins or ends.

datagram   A unit of data smaller than a packet.

dB   See *decibel*.

DB-9   Standard 9-pin connector used with Token Ring and serial connections.

DB-15   Standard 15-pin connector used with Ethernet transceiver cables.

DB-25   Standard 25-pin connector used with serial and parallel ports.

dBm   Decibels below 1mW.

DC   See *direct current*.

DC loop resistance   The total DC resistance of a cable.

DC resistance   See *resistance*.

DCE   See *data communication equipment*.

D-channel   Delta channel. On ISDN networks, the channel that carries control and signaling formation at 16Kbps for BRI ISDN services or 64Kbps for PRI ISDN services.

D-connector   See *subminiature D-connector*.

decibel (dB)   A measurement of gain or loss in optical or electrical power. A unit of measure of signal strength, usually the relation between a transmitted signal and a standard signal source. Expressed as the logarithmic ratio of the strength of a received signal to the strength of the originally transmitted signal. For example, every 3dB equals 50 percent of signal strength, so therefore a 6dB loss equals a loss of 75 percent of total signal strength. See Chapter 1 for more information.

degenerate waveguides   A set of waveguides having the same propagation constant for all specified frequencies.

delay skew   The difference in propagation delay between the fastest and slowest pair in a cable or cabling system. See Chapter 1 for more information on delay skew.

delta   In fiber optics, equal to the difference between the indices of refraction of the core and the cladding divided by the index of the core.

delta channel   See *D-channel*.

demand priority   A network access method used by Hewlett Packard's 100VG-AnyLAN. The hub arbitrates requests for network access received from stations and assigns access based on priority and traffic loads.

demarc   See *demarcation point*.

demarcation point   A point where the operational control or ownership changes, such as the point of interconnection between telephone company facilities and a user's building or residence.

demultiplex   The process of separating channels that were previously joined using a multiplexer.

detector   (1) A transducer that provides an electrical output signal in response to an incident optical signal. The current is dependent on the amount of light received and the type of device. (2) An optoelectric transducer used in fiber optics to convert optical power to electrical current. In fiber optics, the detector is usually a photodiode.

detector noise limited operations   Occur when the detector is unable to make an intelligent decision on the presence or absence of a pulse due to the losses that render the amplitude of the pulse too small to be detected.

DGM   Data-grade media. See also *data-grade*.

diameter mismatch loss   The loss of power that occurs when one fiber transmits to another and the transmitting fiber has a diameter greater than the receiving fiber. It can occur at any type of coupling where the fiber/coupling sizes are mismatched: fiber-to-fiber, fiber-to-device, fiber-to-detector, or source-to-fiber. Fiber optic cables and connectors should closely match the size of fiber required by the equipment.

dichromatic filter   Selectively transmits or reflects light according to selected wavelengths. Also referred to as *dichromatic mirror*.

dichromatic mirror   See *dichromatic filter*.

dielectric   Material that does not conduct electricity; such as nonmetallic materials that are used for cable insulation and jackets. Optical fiber cables are made of dielectric material.

dielectric constant The property of a dielectric material that determines the amount of electrostatic energy that can be stored by the material when a given voltage is applied to it. The ratio of the capacitance of a capacitor using the dielectric to the capacitance of an identical capacitor using a vacuum as a dielectric. Also called *permittivity*.

dielectric loss The power dissipated in a dielectric material as the result of the friction produced by molecular motion when an alternating electric field is applied.

dielectric nonmetallic Refers to materials used within a fiber optic cable.

differential mode attenuation A variation in attenuation in and among modes carried in an optical fiber.

differential mode transmission A transmission scheme where voltages appear equal in magnitude and opposite in phase across a twisted-pair cable with respect to ground. Differential mode transmission may also be referred to as *balanced mode*. Twisted-pair cable used for Category 1 and above is considered differential mode transmission media or balanced mode cable.

diffraction The deviation of a wavefront from the path predicted by geometric optics when a wavefront is restricted by an edge or an opening of an object. Diffraction is most significant when the aperture is equal to the order of the wavelength.

diffraction grating An array of fine, parallel, equally spaced reflecting or transmitting lines that mutually enhance the effects of defraction to concentrate the diffracted light in a few directions determined by the spacing of the lines and by the wavelength of the light.

digital Refers to transmission, processing, and storage of data by representing the data in two states: on or off. On is represented by the number 1 and off by the number 0. Data transmitted or stored with digital technology is expressed as a string of 0s and 1s.

digital loop carrier A carrier system used for pair gain in loop applications.

digital signal (DS) Transmission rates and coding schemes in the time-division multiplex hierarchy. In North American digital hierarchy, a DS-1 operates at 1.544Mbps per second, a DS-1C at 3.152Mbps, and a DS-3 at 44.736Mbps. The term DS-0 generally applies to the 64Kbps component of a DS-1 signal that represents the equivalent of a voice channel. A DS-1 circuit consists of 24 individual DS-0 circuits. Digital signal rates are documented by industry standards organizations such as the American National Standards Institute (ANSI), the Conference of European Postal and Telecommunications Administrations (CEPT), and the International Telephone Union (ITU).

digital signal cross-connect (DSX) A centralized termination, interconnection, and test point for digital equipment at a particular digital signal bit rate. DSXs are identified by the transmission rate of the signals terminated on them. The DSX-1 is for DS-1 signals; the DSX-3 is for DS-3 signals. These capabilities enable a DSX frame to provide several operational functions, including equipment interconnection, test access, and patching. All equipment terminated on a DSX must conform to the industry standards for the DS transmission rate.

digital subscriber line (DSL) A relatively new technology for delivering high bandwidth to homes and business using standard telephone lines. Though many experts believed that standard copper phone cabling would never be able to support high data rates, local phone companies are deploying equipment that is capable of supporting up to theoretical rates of 8.4Mbps. Typical throughput downstream (from the provider to the customer) are rates from 256Kbps to 1.544Mbps. DSL lines are capable of supporting voice and data simultaneously. There are many types, including HDSL (high bit-rate DSL) and VDSL (very high bit-rate DSL).

DIL Dual in-line.

diode A device that allows a current to move in only one direction. Some examples of diodes are light emitting diodes (LEDs), laser diodes, and photodiodes.

direct current (DC) An electric current that flows in one direction and does not reverse direction, unlike alternating current (AC). Direct current also means a current whose polarity never changes.

direct inside wire (DIW) Twisted-pair wire used inside a building, usually two- or four-pair AWG 26.

dispersion A general term for the phenomena that cause a broadening or spreading of light as it propagates through an optical fiber. There are three major types of dispersion: modal, material, and waveguide. Modal dispersion is caused by differential optical path lengths in a multimode fiber. Material dispersion is caused by a differential delay of various wavelengths of light in a waveguide material. Waveguide dispersion is caused by light traveling in both the core and cladding materials in single-mode fibers. Dispersion is one of the limits on bandwidth on fiber optic cables. It is also called *pulse spreading* because dispersion causes a broadening of the input pulses along the length of the fiber.

dispersion flattened fiber   A single-mode optical fiber that has a low chromatic dispersion throughout the range between 1300nm and 1600nm.

dispersion limited operation   Describes cases where the dispersion of a pulse rather than loss of amplitude limits the distance an optical signal can be carried in the fiber. If this is the case, the receiving system may not be able to receive the signal.

dispersion shifted fiber   A single-mode fiber that has zero dispersion wavelength at 1550nm. Dispersion shifted fibers are made so that optimum attenuation and bandwidth are at 1550nm.

dispersion unshifted fiber   A single-mode optical fiber cable that has zero dispersion wavelength at 1300nm. Often called *conventional* or *unshifted fiber*.

distortion   Any undesired change in a waveform or signal.

distortion-limited operation   In fiber optic cable, synonymous with bandwidth limited operation.

distribution subsystem   A basic element of a structured distribution system. The distribution subsystem is useful for terminating and distributing cables to equipment. Typical functions include electrical protection, interconnection, gauge-size conversion, and cross-connection or interconnection. Other subsystems include the cable entrance facility, backbone or riser, distribution frame, and equipment cabling. Also called *distribution frame subsystem*.

distributor   See *cross-connect*.

DIW   See *direct inside wire*.

DLC   Digital loop carrier.

DNP   See *dry nonpolish connector*.

DoD Networking Model   The Department of Defense's four-layer conceptual model describing how communications should take place between computer systems. The four layers are process/application, host-to-host, Internet, and network access.

drain wire   An uninsulated wire in contact with a shielded cable's shield throughout its length. It is used for terminating the shield. If a drain wire is present, it should be terminated.

dry nonpolish connector (DNP)
Optical fiber connector used for POF (plastic optical fiber).

DS   See *digital signal*.

DS-1   See *T-1*.

DS-3   See *T-3*.

DSL   See *digital subscriber line*.

DSU   See *channel service unit/digital service unit*.

DSX   See *digital signal cross-connect*.

DSX bay   A supporting structure called a frame and all the DSX apparatus mounted on it.

DSX complexes   One or more DSX lineups that are interlinked with tie circuits to provide the DSX functions.

DSX lineup   One or more contiguous DSX bays that are equipped with the necessary jumper pathways to provide the ability to perform all required DSX functions.

DTE   See *data terminal equipment*.

DTMF   See *dual tone multifrequency* or *tone dial*.

D-type connector   A type of network connector that connects computer peripherals. It contains rows of pins or sockets shaped in a sideways D. Common connectors are the DB-9 and DB-25.

DU connector   A fiber optic connector developed by the Nippon Electric Group in Japan.

dual attachment concentrator (DAC)
An FDDI concentrator that offers two attachments to the FDDI network that are capable of accommodating a dual (counter-rotating) ring.

dual attachment station (DAS)   A term used with FDDI networks to denote a station that attaches to both the primary and secondary rings; this makes it capable of serving the dual (counter-rotating) ring. A dual attachment station has two separate FDDI connectors.

dual ring   A pair of counter-rotating logical rings.

dual tone multifrequency (DTMF)   The signal that a touch tone phone generates when you press a key on it. Each key generates two separate tones, one in a high frequency group of tones and one from a low frequency group of tones.

dual window fiber   An optical fiber cable manufactured to be used at two different wavelengths. Single-mode fiber cable that is usable at 1300nm and 1550nm is dual window fiber. Multimode fiber cable is optimized for 850nm and 1300nm operations and is also dual window fiber.

duct   (1) A single enclosed raceway for wires or cable. (2) An enclosure in which air is moved.

duplex   With respect to data communications, a circuit used to transmit signals simultaneously in both directions.

duplex cable   A two-fiber cable suitable for duplex transmission. Usually two fiber strands surrounded by a common jacket.

duplex transmission   Data transmission in both directions, either one direction at a time (*half duplex*) or both directions simultaneously (*full duplex*).

duty cycle   With respect to a digital transmission, the ratio of high levels to low levels.

E

E-1   The European version of T-1 data circuits. Runs at 2.048Mbps.

E-3   The European version of T-3 data circuits. Runs at 34.368Mbps.

earth   A term for zero reference ground (not to mention the planet most of us live on).

ECMA   See *European Computer Manufacturer's Association*.

EIA   See *Electronic Industries Association*.

electromagnetic compatibility (EMC)
The ability of a system to minimize radiated emissions and maximize immunity from external noise sources.

electromagnetic field   The combined electric and magnetic field caused by electron motion in conductors.

electromagnetic interference (EMI)
Electrical noise generated in copper conductors when electromagnetic fields induce currents. Copper cables, motors, machinery, and other equipment that uses electricity may generate EMI. Copper-based network cabling and equipment are susceptible to EMI and also emit EMI, which results in degradation of the signal. Fiber optic cables are desirable in environments that have high EMI because they are not susceptible to the effects of EMI.

Electronic Industries Association (EIA)
An association of manufacturers and users that establishes standards and publishes test methodologies. The EIA (with the TIA and ANSI) helped to publish the TIA/EIA-568-A cabling standard.

electrostatic coupling   The transfer of energy by means of a varying electrostatic field. Also referred to as *capacitive coupling*.

electrostatic discharge (ESD)   A problem that exists when two items with dissimilar static electrical charges are brought together. The static electrical charges jump to the item with fewer electrical charges, which causes ESD; ESD can damage electrical and computer components.

ELFEXT   See *equal level far-end crosstalk*.

EMD   Equilibrium mode distribution.

EMI   See *electromagnetic interference*.

emitter   A source of optical power.

encoding   A method of combining timing and data information into a synchronized stream of signals. Encoding is accomplished by representing digital 1s and 0s through combining high and low signal voltage or light states.

end finish   The quality of a fiber's end surface.

end separation   The distance between the ends of two joined fibers. The end separation is important because the degree of separation causes an extrinsic loss, depending on the configuration of the connection.

end–to-end loss   The optical signal loss experienced between the transmitter and the detector due to fiber quality, splices, connectors, and bends.

energy density   Expressed in joules per square meter. Sometimes called *irradiance*.

entrance facility (EF)   A room within a building where antenna, public, and private network service cables can enter the building and be consolidated. Should be located as close as possible to the entrance point. Entrance facilities are often used to house electrical protection equipment and connecting hardware for the transition between outdoor and indoor cable. Also called *entrance room*.

entrance point   The location where telecommunications enter a building through an exterior wall, a concrete floor slab, a rigid metal conduit, or an intermediate metal conduit.

entrance room   See *entrance facility*.

E/O   Electronic to optical.

EPR   See *ethylene-propylene copolymer rubber*.

equal level far-end crosstalk (ELFEXT)
Crosstalk that is measured at the opposite end from which the disturbing signal is transmitted and normalized by the attenuation of the cable.

equipment cable   Cable or cable assembly used to connect telecommunications equipment to horizontal or backbone cabling systems in the telecommunications closet and equipment room. Equipment cables are considered to be outside the scope of cabling standards.

equipment cabling subsystem   Part of the cabling structure, typically between the distribution frame and the equipment.

equipment room (ER)   A centralized space for telecommunications equipment that serves the occupants of the building or multiple buildings in a campus environment. Usually considered distinct from a telecommunications closet because it is considered to serve a building or campus; the telecommunications closet serves only a single floor. The equipment room is also considered distinct because of the nature of complexity of the equipment that is contained in it.

error detection   The checking of a signal for line-code violations, such as bipolar violations.

error rate   The frequency of errors detected in a data service line, usually expressed as a decimal.

ESD   See *electrostatic discharge*.

Ethernet   A local area network (LAN) architecture developed by Xerox that is defined in the IEEE 802.3 standard. Ethernet nodes access the network using the carrier sense multiple access/collision detect (CSMA/CD) access method.

ethylene-propylene copolymer rubber (EPR)   A material with good insulating properties.

European Computer Manufacturer's Association (ECMA)   A European trade organization that issues its own standards and is a member of the ISO.

excess loss   (1) In a fiber optic coupler, the optical loss from that portion of light that does not emerge from the nominally operational pods of the device. (2) The ratio of the total output power of a passive component with respect to the input power.

exchange center A local telephone exchange building where switching systems are located. Also called *exchange office* or *central office*.

extrinsic loss In a fiber interconnection, the portion of loss that is not intrinsic to the fiber but is related to imperfect joining, which may be caused by the connector or splice. These are losses caused by defects and imperfections that cause the loss to exceed the theoretical minimum loss that is intrinsic (called *intrinsic loss*).

F

f Frequency.

fan-out cable A multifiber cable that is designed for easy connectorization. These cables are sometimes sold with installed connectors or as part of a splice pigtail, with one end carrying many connectors and the other installed in a splice cabinet or panel ready for splicing or patching.

fan-out kit Used to build up the outer diameter of fiber cable for connectorization.

farad A unit of capacitance that stores one coulomb of electrical charge when one volt of electrical pressure is applied.

faraday effect A phenomenon that causes some materials to rotate the polarization of light in the presence of a magnetic field.

far-end crosstalk (FEXT) Crosstalk that is measured on the wires that are not being used for transmission at the opposite end from the source (the transmitter) of energy on the active line. FEXT is not typically measured in cabling; near-end crosstalk (NEXT) is the predominant crosstalk measurement. See Chapter 1 for more information on various types of crosstalk.

fast Ethernet Ethernet standard supporting 100Mbps operation.

FC connector A threaded optical fiber connector that was developed by Nippon Telephone and Telegraph in Japan. The FC connector is good for single-mode or multimode fiber and applications requiring low back reflection. The FC is a screw type and is prone to vibration loosening.

FCC Federal Communications Commission.

FCS See *frame check sequence*.

FDDI See *fiber distributed data interface*.

FDM See *frequency division multiplexing*.

FDMA Frequency division multiplex access.

feeder cable   A voice backbone cable that runs from the equipment room cross-connect to the telecommunications cross-connect. A feeder cable may also be the cable running from a central office to a remote terminal, hub, head end, or node.

FEP   See *fluorinated ethylene propylene*.

FER   Forward error correction.

ferrule   A small alignment tube attached to the end of the fiber and used in connectors. These are made of stainless steel, aluminum, or zirconia. The ferrule is used to confine and align the stripped end of a fiber.

fiber   A single, separate optical transmission element characterized by core and cladding. The fiber is the dielectric material that guides light or waveguides.

fiber building cable   A nonflammable cable containing one or multiple fibers.

fiber channel   A fiber optic connection that is used for server-to-storage system connections.

fiber curl   Occurs when there is misalignment in a mass or ribbon splicing joint. The fiber or fibers curl away from the joint to take up the slack or stress caused by misalignment of fiber lengths at the joint.

fiber distributed data interface (FDDI)   ANSI standard X3.166-1990, Fiber Distributed Data Interface (FDDI)—Token Ring Physical Layer Medium Dependent (PMD). This standard details the requirements for all attachment devices concerning the 100Mbps fiber optic network interface. It uses a counter-rotating ring topology. FDDI is typically known as a backbone LAN because it is used for joining file servers together and for joining other LANs together.

fiber distribution frame (FDF)   A cross-connect or interconnect system using fiber optic jumpers and cables. See also *horizontal distribution frome*.

fiber illumination kit   Used to visually inspect continuity in fiber systems and to inspect fiber connector end-face for cleanliness and light quality.

fiber-in-the-loop (FITL)   Indicates deployment of fiber optic feeder and distribution facilities.

fiber loss   The attenuation of light in an optical fiber transmission.

fiber optic attenuator   An active component that is installed in a fiber optic transmission system that is designed to reduce the power in the optical signal. It is used to limit the optical power received by the photodetector to within the limits of the optical receiver.

fiber optic cable   Cable containing one or more optical fibers.

fiber optic communication system
Involves the transfer of modulated or unmodulated optical energy (light) through optical fiber media.

fiber optic interrepeater link (FOIRL)
An Ethernet fiber optic connection method intended for connection of repeaters.

fiber optic pigtail   Used to splice outside plant cable to the backside of a fiber optic patch panel.

fiber optic test procedures (FOTP)
Test procedures outlined in the EIA-RS-455 standards.

fiber optic transmission   A communications scheme whereby electrical data is converted to light energy and transmitted through optical fibers.

fiber optic transmission system (FOTS)
A set of transmission equipment and facilities used for optical communications.

fiber optic waveguide   A long thin strand of transparent material (glass or plastic), which can convey electromagnetic energy in the optical waveform longitudinally by means of internal reflection.

fiber optics   The optical technology in which communication signals in the form of modulated light beams are transmitted over a glass or plastic fiber transmission medium. Fiber optics offers high bandwidth and protection from electromagnetic interference and radioactivity; it also has small space needs.

fiber protection system (FPS)   A system of ducts and supports that includes guides and transition pieces that are used for organizing and protecting fiber building cables and individual fiber interconnection cables. The fiber protection system is used to protect installed fiber optic cabling as well as to ensure fiber minimum bend radius criteria.

fiber test equipment   Diagnostic equipment used for the testing, maintenance, restoration, and inspection of fiber systems. This equipment includes optical attenuation meters and optical time domain reflectometers (OTDRs).

fibre The British spelling of fiber.

fillers Nonconducting components cabled with insulated conductors or optical fibers to impart flexibility, tensile strength, roundness, or a combination of all three.

FIR Finite impulse response.

firestop Material, device, or collection of parts installed in a cable pathway (such as a conduit or riser) at a fire-rated wall or floor to prevent passage of flame, smoke, or gases through the rated barrier.

firestopping material Nonflammable material specifically designed to block cable holes and ducts, thereby limiting the propagation of a fire. See also *firestop*.

FITL See *fiber-in-the-loop*.

flex life The ability of a cable to bend many times before breaking.

floating A floating circuit is one that has no ground connection.

floor distributor (FD) The ISO/IEC 11801 term for horizontal cross-connect. The floor distributor is used to connect between the horizontal cable and other cabling subsystems or equipment.

fluorinated ethylene propylene (FEP) A thermoplastic with excellent dielectric properties that is often used as insulation in fire-rated cables. FEP has good electrical insulating properties and chemical and heat resistance. FEP is the most common material used for wire insulation in Category 5 and better cables.

FM See *frequency modulation*.

FOIRL See *fiber optic interrepeater link*.

FOTP See *fiber optic test procedures*.

FOTS Fiber optic transmission system.

FOX Fiber optic extension.

FOXI Fiber optic transparent synchronous transmitter-receiver interface.

frame check sequence (FCS) The error detection field.

frame relay A wide area networking (WAN) technology that allows switched digital channels (such as 1.5 Mbps) to be offered to customers upon demand.

frequency The number of cycles per second at which a waveform alternates. Frequency is expressed in hertz (Hz); one hertz equals one cycle per second.

frequency division multiplexing (FDM)
A technique for combining many signals onto a single circuit by dividing the available transmission bandwidth by frequency into narrower bands; each band is used for a separate communication channel. FDM can be used with any and all of the sources created by wavelength division multiplexing (WDM).

frequency modulation (FM) A method of adding information to a sine wave signal in which its frequency is varied to impose information on it. Information is sent by varying the frequency of an optical or electrical carrier. Other methods include *amplitude modulation (AM)* and *phase modulation (PM)*.

frequency response The range of frequencies over which a device operates as expected.

Fresnel diffraction pattern The near-field diffraction pattern.

Fresnel loss The loss at a joint due to a portion of the light being reflected.

Fresnel reflection The reflection of light from an optical discontinuity; it occurs at the air/glass interfaces at entrance and exit ends of an optical fiber.

Fresnel reflection method A method for measuring the index profile of an optical fiber by measuring reflectance as a function of position on the end-face.

FTF Fiber trunk feeder.

FTM Fiber telecommunications module.

FTMB Fiber to major business.

FTP (1) Foil twisted-pair cable. See also *screened twisted-pair (ScTP) cable*. (2) Abbreviation for *file transfer protocol*.

FTTB Fiber to the business.

FTTC Fiber to the curb.

FTTD Fiber to the desk.

FTTH Fiber to the home.

FTTS Fiber to the school.

full duplex transmission Data transmission over a circuit capable of transmitting in both directions simultaneously.

fundamental mode The lowest order mode of a waveguide.

fusion splicing   A splicing method accomplished by the application of localized heat sufficient to fuse or melt the ends of the optical fiber, forming continuous single strand of fiber. As the glass is heated it becomes softer, and it is possible to use the glass's "liquid" properties to bond glass surfaces permanently.

FUT   Fiber under test.

G

G   Green. Used when referring to color-coding of cables.

gamma   The coefficient used to scale bandwidth with fiber length.

gap loss   The loss that results when two axially aligned fibers are separated by an air gap. This loss is often most significant in reflectance. The light must launch from one medium to another (glass to air to glass) through the waveguide capabilities of the fiber.

Gbps   Gigabits per second.

GHz   See *gigahertz*.

gigahertz (GHz)   A billion hertz or cycles per second.

GIPOF   Graded index plastic optical fiber.

GOSIP   Government open system interconnect protocol.

graded index fiber   An optical fiber cable design in which the index of refraction of the core is lower toward the outside of the core and progressively increases toward the center of the core, thereby reducing modal dispersion of the signal. Light rays are refracted within the core rather than reflected as they are in step index fibers. Graded index fibers were developed to lessen the modal dispersion effects found in multimode fibers with the intent of increasing bandwidth.

ground   A common point of zero potential such as a metal chassis or ground rod that grounds a building to the earth. The TIA/EIA-607 Commercial Building Grounding and Bonding Requirements for Telecommunications standard is the standard that should be followed for grounding requirements for telecommunications. Grounding should never be undertaken without consulting with a professional licensed electrician.

ground loop   A condition where an unintended connection to ground is made through an interfering electrical conductor that causes electromagnetic interference. See also *ground loop noise*.

ground loop noise Electromagnetic interference that is created when equipment is grounded at ground points having different potentials, thereby creating an unintended current path. Equipment should always be grounded to a single ground point.

ground window A single point used to isolate the sensitive electronics associated with the electronic switching system.

guided ray A ray that is completely confined to the fiber core.

H

half duplex transmission Data transmission over a circuit capable of transmitting in either direction. Transmission can be bidirectional but not simultaneously.

halogen One of the following elements: chlorine, fluorine, bromine, or iodine.

hard-clad silica fiber An optical fiber with a hard plastic cladding surrounding a step index silica core.

hardware address A data link layer address assigned to every network interface card at the media access control (MAC) sublayer. The address is in the format xx:xx:xx:xx:xx:xx; each xx is a two-digit hexadecimal number. Also called the *physical address*; see also *MAC address*.

hardware loopback Connects the transmission pins directly to the receiving pins, allowing diagnostic software to test whether a network interface card can successfully transmit and receive.

HC See *horizontal cross-connect*.

HDSL High bit-rate digital subscriber line. See *digital subscriber line*.

head end (1) The central facility where signals are combined and distributed in a cable television system or a public telephone system. See *central office*. (2) That position in the ring where the signals are captured, often by microwave or by from the backbone, and entered into the system.

header The section of a packet (usually the first part of the packet) where the source and destination addresses reside.

headroom   The number of decibels by which a system exceeds the minimum defined requirements. The minimum defined requirements are defined by the amount by which a cable's attenuation to crosstalk ratio (ACR) exceeds 10dB. The TIA/EIA-568-A standard states that a minimum of 10dB of ACR is required for an unshielded twisted pair to be certified as Category 5. The benefit of more headroom is that it reduces the bit-error rate (BER) and provides a performance safety net to help ensure that current and future high-speed applications will run at peak accuracy, efficiency, and throughput. Also called *overhead* or *margin*.

Hertz (Hz)   A measurement of frequency as defined as cycles per second.

HF   High frequency.

hicap service   A high capacity communications circuit service such as a private line T-1 or T-3.

home run cable   A cable run that connects a user outlet directly with the telecommunications or wiring closet. This cable has no intermediate splices, bridges, taps, or other connections. Every cable radiates out from the central equipment or wiring closet. This configuration is also known as star topology. This is the opposite of a daisy-chained cable that may have taps or splices along its length. Home run cable is the recommended installation method for horizontal cabling in a structured cabling system.

hop   One pass through a router.

horizontal cabling   The cabling between and including the telecommunications outlet and the horizontal cross-connect. Horizontal cabling is considered the permanent portion of a link; may also be called *horizontal wiring*.

horizontal cross-connect (HC)   A cross-connect of horizontal cabling (cable that runs to the work area outlets) to other cabling, such as voice backbone cable and LAN equipment.

horizontal distribution frame   A physical structure, usually constructed of steel and lying on the floor, which contains the components that provide interconnection between inter- and intrabuilding cabling. There are many names for this; see also *fiber distribution frame*.

HRC   Hybrid ring control.

hub   A physical layer hardware device that contains multiple independent but connected modules of network and internetworking equipment. Hubs that repeat the signals that are sent to them are called *active hubs*. Hubs that do not repeat the signal and merely split the signal sent to them are called *passive hubs*. In some cases, hub may also refer to a repeater, bridge, switch, or any combination of these.

HVAC   Heating, ventilation, and air conditioning.

hybrid cable   A cable that contains fiber, coaxial, and/or twisted-pair conductors bundled in a common jacket. May also refer to a fiber optic cable that has strands of both single-mode and multimode optical fiber.

hybrid connector   A connector containing both fiber and electrical connectivity.

hydrogen loss   Optical signal loss (attenuation) resulting from hydrogen found in the optical fiber. Hydrogen in glass absorbs light and turns it into heat and thus attenuates the light. For this reason, glass manufacturers serving the fiber optic industry must keep water and hydrogen out of the glass and deliver it to guaranteed specifications in this regard. In addition, they must protect the glass with a cladding that will preclude the absorption of water and hydrogen into the glass.

hypalon   A DuPont trade name for a synthetic rubber (chlorosulfonated polyethylene) that is used as insulating and jacketing material for cabling.

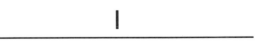

I   Symbol used to designate current.

IBM data connector   Used to connect IBM Token Ring stations using Type 1 shielded twisted-pair 150-ohm cable. This connector has both male and female components, so every IBM data connector can connect to any other IBM data connector

IC   See *intermediate cross-connect*.

ICEA   Insulated Cable Engineers Association.

ICS IBM cabling system.

IDC See *insulation displacement connector*.

IDF See *intermediate distribution frame*.

IDP Integrated detector/preamplifier.

IEC International Electrotechnical Commission.

IEEE 802.1 LAN/MAN Management
The IEEE standard that specifies network management, internetworking, and other issues that are common across networking technologies.

IEEE 802.2 Logical Link Control   The
IEEE standard that provides specifications for the operation of the logical link control (LLC) sublayer of the OSI data link layer. The LLC sublayer provides an interface between the MAC sublayer and the network layer.

IEEE 802.3 CSMA/CD Networking   The
IEEE standard that specifies a network that uses a logical bus topology, baseband signaling, and a CSMA/CD network access method. This is the standard that defines Ethernet networks. See also *carrier sense multiple access/collision detect*.

IEEE 802.4 Token Bus   The IEEE standard
that specifies a physical and logical bus topology that uses coaxial or fiber optic cable and the token passing media access method.

IEEE 802.5 Token Ring   The IEEE stan-
dard that specifies a logical ring, physical star, and token passing media access method based on IBM's Token Ring.

EEE 802.6 Distributed Queue Dual Bus (DQDB) Metropolitan Area Network
The IEEE standard that provides a definition and criteria for a Metropolitan Area Network (MAN), also known as a Distributed Queue Dual Bus (DQDB).

IEEE 802.7 Broadband Local Area Networks   The IEEE standard for developing
local area networks (LANs) using broadband cabling technology.

IEEE 802.8 Fiber Optic LANs and MANs
The IEEE standard that contains guidelines for the use of fiber optics on networks, including FDDI and Ethernet over fiber optic cable.

IEEE 802.9 Integrated Services (IS) LAN Interface   The IEEE standard that contains
guidelines for the integration of voice and data over the same cable.

IEEE 802.10 LAN/MAN Security   The IEEE standard that provides a series of guidelines dealing with various aspects of network security.

IEEE 802.11 Wireless LAN   The IEEE standard that provides standards for implementing wireless technologies such as infrared and spread-spectrum radio.

IEEE 802.12 Demand Priority Access Method   The IEEE standard that defines the concepts of a demand priority network such as HP's 100VG-AnyLAN network architecture.

IF   Intermediate frequency.

ILD   See *injection laser diode*.

impact test   Used to determine a cable's susceptibility to damage when subjected to short duration crushing forces. Rate of impact, the shape of the striking device, and the force of the impact all are used to define the impact test procedures.

impedance   The total opposition (resistance and reactance) a circuit offers to the flow of alternating current. It is measured in ohms and designated by the symbol Z.

impedance match   A condition where the impedance of a particular cable or component is the same as the impedance of the circuit, cable, or device to which it is connected.

impedance matching transformer   A transformer designed to match the impedance of one circuit to another.

incident angle   The angle between the subject light wave and a plane perpendicular to the subject optical surface.

index matching gel   A fluid with a refractive index close to glass that reduces refractive index discontinuities that can cause reflective loss.

index matching material   A material in liquid, paste, gel, film, or cement form whose refractive index is nearly equal to the core index; it is used to reduce Fresnel reflections from a fiber end-face. Liquid forms of this are also called *index matching gel*.

index of refraction   The ratio of light velocity in a vacuum to its velocity in a given transmission medium. This is usually abbreviated *n*.

index profile   The curve of the refractive index over the cross section of an optical waveguide.

infrared   The infrared spectrum consists of wavelengths that are longer than 700nm but shorter than 1mm. Humans cannot see infrared radiation, but we feel it as heat. The commonly used wavelengths for transmission through optical fibers are in the infrared at wavelengths between 1100nm and 1600nm.

injection laser   Another name for a semiconductor or laser diode.

injection laser diode (ILD)   A laser diode in which the lasing takes place within the actual semiconductor junction and the light is emitted from the edge of the diode.

insertion loss   A critical measurement for optical fiber connections, insertion loss measures the attenuation of a device by determining the output of a system before and after the device is inserted into the system. Loss in an optical fiber can be due to absorption, dispersion, scattering, microbending, diffusion, and the methods of coupling the fiber to the power. Usually measured in dB per incident; for example a coupler, connector, splice, or fiber is measured in dB per km. Most commonly used to describe the power lost at the entrance to a waveguide (an optical fiber is a waveguide) due to axial misalignment, lateral displacement, or reflection that is most applicable to connectors.

inside plant (IP)   Cables that are the portion of the cable network that is inside buildings, where cable lengths are usually shorter than 100 meters. This is the opposite of outside the plant (OP or OTP) cables.

Institute of Electrical and Electronic Engineers (IEEE)   A publishing and standards making body responsible for many standards used in LANs, including the 802 series of standards.

insulation   A material with good dielectric properties that is used to separate close electrical components, such as cable conductors and circuit components. (Good dielectric properties mean that the material is nonconductive to the flow of electrical current.)

insulation displacement connection (IDC)   A type of wire termination in which the wire is punched down into a metal holder that cuts into the insulation wire and makes contact with the conductor, thus causing the electrical connection to be made. These connectors are found on 66-blocks, 110-blocks, and telecommunications outlets.

integrated optical circuit   An optical circuit that is used for coupling between optoelectronic devices and providing signal processing functions. It is composed of both active and passive components.

integrated optics   Optical devices that perform two or more functions and are integrated on a single substrate; analogous to integrated electronic circuits.

integrated optoelectronics   Similar in concept to *integrated optics* except that one of the integrated devices on the semiconductor chip is optical and the other electronic.

Integrated Services Digital Network (ISDN)   A telecommunications standard that is used to digitally send voice, data, and video signals over the same lines. This is a network in which a single digital bit stream can carry a great variety of services. For the Internet it serves much better than analog systems on POTS (plain old telephone service), which is limited to 53Kbps. See also *basic rate interface* and *primary rate interface*.

intelligent hub   A hub that performs bridging, routing, or switching functions. Intelligent hubs are found in collapsed backbone environments.

intelligent network (iN)   A network that is capable of carrying overhead signaling information and services.

intensity   The square of the electric field amplitude of a light wave. Intensity is proportional to irradiance and may be used in place of that term if relative values are considered.

interbuilding backbone   A telecommunications cable that is part of the campus subsystem that connects one building to another.

interconnect   A circuit administration point, other than a cross-connect or an information outlet, that provides capability for routing and rerouting circuits. It does not use patch cords or jumper wires and is typically a jack-and-plug device that is used in smaller distribution arrangements or connects circuits in large cables to those in smaller cables.

interconnect cabinet   Cabinets containing connector panels, patch panels, connectors, and patch cords to interface from inside the plant to outside the plant. The interconnect cabinet is used as an access point for testing and rearranging routs and connections.

interconnection   A connection scheme that provides direct access to the cabling infrastructure and the capability to make cabling system changes using patch cords.

interference   (1) Fiber optic: the interaction of two or more beams of coherent or partially coherent light. (2) Electromagnetic: interaction that produces undesirable signals that interfere with the normal operation of electronic equipment or electronic transmission.

intermediate cross-connect (ICC)   A cross-connect between first level and second level backbone cabling. This secondary cross-connect in the backbone cabling is used to mechanically terminate and administer backbone cabling between the main cross-connect and horizontal cross-connect (station cables).

intermediate distribution frame (IDF)   A metal rack (or frame) designed to connect cables that is located in an equipment room or telecommunications (wiring) closet. Consists of components that provide the connection between interbuilding cabling and the intrabuilding cabling, for instance between the equipment room (where the MDFs are located) and the telecommunications closets (where the IDFs are located). There's usually a permanent, large cable running between the MDF and IDF. Changes to the wiring are usually performed at the IDF and sometimes at the MDF.

International Organization for Standardization (ISO)   The standards organization that developed the OSI model. This model provides a guideline for how communications occur between computers. See www.iso.ch for more information.

International Telecommunications Union (ITU)   The branch of the United Nations that develops communications standards.

International Telephone and Telegraph Consultative Committee (CCiTT)   International standards committee that develops standards for interface and signal formats.

Internet Architecture Board (IAB)   The committee that oversees management of the Internet, which is made up of several subcommittees including the Internet Engineering Task Force (IETF), the Internet Assigned Numbers Authority (IANA), and the Internet Research Task Force (IRTF). See www.iab.org for more information.

Internet Engineering Task Force (IETF)   An international organization that works under the Internet Architecture Board to establish standards and protocols relating to the Internet. See www.ietf.org for more information.

Internet Research Task Force (IRTF)   An international organization that works under the Internet Architecture Board to research new Internet technologies. See www.irtf.org for more information.

interoffice trunks (IOF)   Copper and fiber trunks.

intrabuilding backbone   Telecommunications cables that are part of the building subsystem that connect one telecommunications closet to another or a telecommunications closet to the equipment room.

intrinsic joint loss   The theoretical minimum loss that a given joint or device will have as a function of its nature. Intrinsic joint loss may also be used to describe the given theoretical minimum loss that a splice joint, coupler, or splitter may achieve.

intrinsic loss splice   The optical signal loss arising from differences in the fibers being spliced.

intrinsic performance factor (IPF)   Performance specification whereby total optical channel performance is specified, rather than performance of individual components.

I/O   Input and output.

IOC   See *integrated optical circuit*.

IOF   See *interoffice trunks*.

ion exchange techniques   A method for making and doping glass by ion exchange.

IPF   See *intrinsic performance factor*.

IR   See *infrared*.

irradiance   The power density at a surface through which radiation passes at the radiating surface of a light source or at the cross section of an optical waveguide. The normal unit is watts per centimeters squared.

ISDN   See *Integrated Services Digital Network*.

ISDN terminal adapter   The device used on ISDN networks to connect a local network or single machine to an ISDN network. The ISDN terminal adapter provides line power and translates data from the LAN or individual computer for transmission on the ISDN line.

ISO   See *International Organization for Standardization*.

isochronous   Signals that are dependent on some uniform timing or carry their own timing information imbedded as part of the signal.

isolated ground   A separate ground conductor that is insulated from the equipment or building ground.

isolation   The ability of a circuit or component to reject interference.

ITU   See *International Telecommunications Union*.

J

jabber   A term used with Ethernet to describe the act of continuously sending data. When a station is jabbering, its network adapter circuitry or logic has failed, and it has locked up a network channel with its nonstop transmission.

jack   A receptacle used in conjunction with a plug to make electrical contact between communication circuits. A variety of jacks and their associated plugs are used to connect hardware applications, including cross-connects, interconnects, information outlets, and equipment connections. Jacks are also used to connect cords or lines to telephone systems. A jack is the female component of a plug/jack connector system and may be standard, modified, or keyed.

jacket   The outer protective covering of a cable, usually made of some type of plastic or polymer.

jitter   A slight movement of a transmission signal in time or phase that can introduce errors and loss of synchronization. The longer the cable, the more jitter will be encountered. Other causes of jitter include cables with high attenuation and signals at high frequencies. Also called *phase jitter*, *timing distortion*, or *intersymbol interference*.

joint   Any joining or mating of a fiber by splicing (by fusion splicing or physical contact of fibers) or connecting.

jumper   (1) A manually placed wire, cable, or fiber connection between two terminations, usually on some form of distributing frame. The connection may be single or multiconductor. A jumper is also called a *cross-connection*. (2) A small connector (cap or plug) that connects pins. This creates a circuit that indicates a setting to a device.

jumper wire   An assembly of twisted pairs without connectors on either end used to join telecommunications links at a cross-connect.

junction laser   A semiconductor diode laser.

K

Kevlar   A strong, synthetic material developed and trademarked by DuPont; the preferred strength element in cable. Also used as a material in body armor and parts for military equipment. Also known by the generic name aramid; see also *aramid yarn*.

keying   A mechanical feature of a connector system that guarantees correct orientation of a connection. The key prevents the connection to a jack or an optical fiber adapter of the same type that was intended for another purpose.

kHz   KiloHertz; 1000 Hertz.

kilometer   One thousand meters; 3281 feet. The kilometer is a unit of measurement for fiber optics.

KPSI   A unit of tensile strength expressed in thousands of pounds per square inch.

L

L   Symbol used to designate inductance.

LAN   See *local area network*.

LAN adapter   See *network interface card*.

large core fiber   Usually a fiber with a core of 200 microns or more. This type of fiber is not common in structured cabling systems.

laser   Acronym for *light amplification by stimulated emission radiation*. The laser produces a coherent source of light with a narrow beam and a narrow spectral bandwidth (about 2cm). Lasers in fiber optics are usually solid state semiconductor types.

laser diode (LD)   A semiconductor diode that emits coherent light above a threshold current. Laser diodes are usually used in higher speed applications (622Mbps to 10Gbps) such as ATM, 1000Base-LX, and SONET. The mode is usually ellipse shaped and therefore requires a lens to make the light symmetrical with the mode of the fiber, which is usually round.

lasing threshold   The lowest excitation level at which a laser's output is dominated by stimulated emission rather than spontaneous emission.

LATA   Local access and transport area.

lateral displacement loss   The loss of signal power that results from lateral displacement from optimum alignment between two fibers or between a fiber and an active device.

launch angle   The angle between the propagation direction of the incident light and the optical axis of an optical waveguide.

launch cable   Used to connect fiber optic test equipment to the fiber system.

launch fiber   An optical fiber used to couple and condition light from an optical source into another optical fiber. Launch fibers are most often used in test systems to improve the precision of measurements. Also referred to as *launching fiber*.

launching fiber   See *launch fiber*.

lay   The axial distance required for one cabled conductor or conductor strand to complete one revolution around the axis around which it is cabled.

lay direction   The direction of the progressing spiral twist of twisted-pair wires while looking along the axis of the cable away from the observer. The lay direction can be either left or right.

Layer 2 switch   A switching hub that operates at the data link layer and builds a table of the MAC addresses of all the connected stations.

Layer 3 switch   A switch functioning at the network layer that performs the multiport, virtual LAN, data pipelining functions of a standard Layer 2 switch and can also perform routing functions between virtual LANs.

lbf   Abbreviation for pounds force.

leakage   An undesirable passage of current over the surface of or through a connector.

leaky modes   In the boundary region between the guided modes of an optical waveguide, light waves are not capable of propagation so they are called leaky modes; they are not guided but are capable of limited propagation with increased attenuation. Leaky modes may be a possible source of error in the measurement of fiber loss, but the effect of leaky modes can be reduced by mode strippers.

leased line   A private telephone line (usually a digital line) rented for the exclusive use of a leasing customer without interchange switching arrangements.

LED   See *light emitting diode*.

LF   Low frequency.

light   The electromagnetic radiation visible to the human eye between 400nm and 700nm. The term is also applied to electromagnetic radiation with properties similar to visible light; this includes the invisible near-infrared radiation in most fiber optic communication systems.

light emitting diode (LED)   A semiconductor device used in a transmitter to convert information from electric to optical form. The LED typically has a large spectral width; LED devices are usually used on low-speed applications (100–256Mbps) such as 100Base-F and FDDI.

light waves   Electromagnetic waves in the region of optical frequencies. The term *light* was originally restricted to light that is visible to the human eye with wavelengths between 400nm and 700nm. Referring to light waves that are in the adjacent spectral regions to visible light (infrared from 700nm to about 2000nm) as *light* emphasizes the physical and technical characteristics they have in common with visible light.

lightguide cable   An optical fiber, multiple fiber, or fiber bundle that includes a cable jacket and strength members and is fabricated to meet optical, mechanical, and environmental specifications.

line build-out (LBO)   An attenuator inserted into the signal path to ensure that the received power level is within the manufacturer's specification.

line conditioner   A device used to protect against power surges and spikes. Line conditioners use several electronic methods to clean all power coming into the line conditioner so that clean, steady power is put out by the line conditioner.

link   An end-to-end transmission path provided by the cabling infrastructure. Cabling links include all cables and connecting hardware that compose the horizontal or backbone subsystems. Equipment and work area cables are not included as part of a link.

link light   A small light emitting diode (LED) that is found on both the NIC and the hub and is usually green and labeled "Link." A link light indicates that the NIC and the hub are making a data link layer connection.

listed   Equipment included on a list published by an organization, acceptable to the authority having jurisdiction, that maintains periodic inspection of production of listed equipment, and whose listing states either that the equipment or material meets appropriate standards, or that it has been tested and found suitable for use in a specified manner. In the United States, electrical and data communications equipment is typically listed with Underwriters Laboratories (UL).

LLDPE   Linear low density polyethylene jacketing.

lobe An arm of a Token Ring that extends from a multistation access unit (MSAU) to a workstation adapter.

local area network (LAN) A network connecting multiple nodes within a defined area, usually within a building. The linking can be done by cable that carries optical fiber or copper. These are usually high bandwidth (4Mbps or greater) and connect many nodes within a few thousand meters. LANs can, however, operate at lower data rates (less than 1Mbps) and connect nodes over only a few meters.

local exchange carrier (LEC) The local regulated provider of public switched telecommunications services. The LEC is regulated by the local Public Utilities Commission.

local loop The loop or circuit between receivers (and, in two-way systems, receivers and senders), who are normally the customers or subscribers to the systems products, and the terminating equipment at the central office.

LocalTalk A low-speed form of LAN data link technology developed by Apple Computer. It was designed to transport Apple's AppleTalk networking scheme; it uses a carrier sense multiple access/collision avoidance (CSMA/CA) form of medium access control. Supports transmission at 230Kbps.

logical network addressing The addressing scheme used by protocols at the OSI network layer.

logical ring topology A network topology in which all network signals travel from one station to another, being read and forwarded by each station. A Token Ring network is an example of a logical ring topology.

logical topology Describes the way the information flows. The types of logical topologies are the same as the physical topologies, except that the information flow specifies the type of topology.

long wavelength Light whose wavelength is greater than 1000nm (longer than one micron).

longitudinal conversion loss (LCL) A measurement (in decibels) of the differential voltage induced on a conductor pair as a result of subjecting that pair to longitudinal voltage. This is considered to be a measurement of circuit balance.

longitudinal conversion transfer loss (LCTL)   Measures cable balance by the comparison of the signal appearing across the pair to the signal between ground and the pair, where the applied signal is at the opposite end of the cable from the location at which the across-pair signal is measured. LCTL is also called *far-end unbalance attenuation*.

longitudinal modes   Oscillation modes of a laser along the length of its cavity. Each longitudinal mode contains only a very narrow range of wavelengths; a laser emitting a single longitudinal mode has a very narrow bandwidth. The oscillation of light along the length of the laser's cavity are normally such that two times the length of the cavity will equal an integral number of wavelengths. Longitudinal modes are distinct from transverse modes.

loop   (1) A complete electrical circuit. (2) The pair of wires that winds its way from the central office to the telephone set or system at the customer's office, home, or factory.

loopback   A type of diagnostic test in which a transmitted signal is returned to the sending device after passing through a data communications link or network. This test allows the comparison of a returned signal with the transmitted signal to determine if the signal is making its way through the communications link and how much signal it is losing upon its return.

loose tube   A protective tube loosely surrounding a cabled optical fiber, often filled with gel used as a protective coating. Fiber optic cables designed using the loose tube type of cable design are encased in buffer tubes and offer excellent fiber protection and segregation. Fibers are usually buffered to 250 microns.

loss   The attenuation of optical or electrical signal, normally measured in decibels. With respect to fiber optic cables, there are two key measurements of loss, insertion loss and return loss; both of these are measured in decibels. The higher the decibel number, the more loss there is. Some copper-based and optical fiber–based materials are lossy and absorb electromagnetic radiation in one form and emit it in another; for example, heat. Some optical fiber materials are reflective and return electromagnetic radiation in the same form as it is received, usually with little or no power loss. Still others are transparent or translucent, meaning they are "window" materials; loss is the portion of energy applied to a system that is dissipated and performs no useful work. See also *attenuation*.

loss budget   A calculation and allowance for total attenuation in a system that is required in order to ensure that the detectors and receivers can make intelligent decisions about the pulses they receive.

lossy   Describes a connection having poor efficiency with respect to loss of signal.

M

mA   Milliampere (one thousandth of an ampere).

MAC   (1) See *media access control*. (2) Abbreviation for *moves, adds, and changes*.

macrobending   Macroscopic axial deviations (visible bends) of a fiber from a straight line, in contrast to microbending.

macrobending loss   Optical power loss due to large bends in the fiber.

main cross-connect   A cross-connect for first level backbone cables, entrance cables, and equipment cables. The main cross-connect is at the top level of the premises cabling tree.

main distribution frame (MDF)   A wiring arrangement that connects the telephone lines coming from outside on one side and the internal lines on the other. The MDF may be a central connection point for data communications equipment in addition to voice communications. An MDF may also carry protective devices or function as a central testing point.

MAN   See *metropolitan area network*.

Manchester coding   A method of encoding a LAN in which each bit time that represents a data bit has a transition in the middle of the bit time. Manchester coding is used with 10Mbps Ethernet (10Base-2, 10Base-5, 10Base-F, and 10Base-T) and Token Ring LANs.

margin   The allowance for attenuation in addition to that explicitly accounted for in system design.

mass splicing   The concurrent and simultaneous splicing of multiple fibers at one time. Currently mass splicing is done on ribbon cable, and the standard seems to be ribbon cable with 12 fibers. Special splice protectors are made for this purpose, as well as special equipment for splicing.

material dispersion   A pulse dispersion that results from each wavelength traveling at a speed different from other wavelengths through an optical fiber. See also *chromatic dispersion*.

MBE   Molecular beam epitaxy.

Mbps (megabits per second)   A data rate of one million bits per second.

MC   See *main cross-connect*.

MCVD   Modified chemical vapor deposition.

MDF   See *main distribution frame*.

MDI   See *media dependent interface*.

MDPE   Medium density polyethylene jacketing.

MDU   Multiple dwelling unit.

meantIme between failures (MTBF)   A measurement of how reliable a hardware component is. Usually measured in thousands of hours.

mechanical splice   With respect to fiber optic cables, a splice in which fibers are joined mechanically (e.g., glued, crimped, or otherwise held in place) but not fused together using heat. Mechanical splice is the opposite of a fusion splice in which the two fiber ends are butted and then joined by permanently bonding the glass end-faces through the softening of the glass, which is fused together.

media   Wire, cable, or conductors used for transmission of signals.

media access   The process of vying for transmission time on the network media.

media access control (MAC)   A sublayer of the OSI data link layer (Layer 2) that controls the way multiple devices use the same media channel. It controls which devices can transmit and when they can transmit. For most network architectures, each device has a unique address that is sometimes referred to as the MAC address. See also *media access control (MAC) address*.

media access control (MAC) address

Network adapter cards such as Ethernet, Token Ring, and FDDI cards are assigned addresses when MAC addresses are built. A MAC address is six bytes long. No two cards have the same hardware address. The IEEE helps to achieve this by assigning three-byte prefixes to manufacturers so that no two manufacturers have the same first three bytes in their MAC address. The MAC address is also called the *hardware address*.

medium attachment unit (MAU)

When referring to Ethernet LANs, the transceiver in Ethernet networks.

media filter
An impedance-matching device used to change the impedance of the cable to the expected impedance of the connected device. For example, media filters can be used in Token Ring networks to transform the 100-ohm impedance of UTP cabling to the 150-ohm impedance of media interface connections.

media interface connector (MIC connector)
A pair of fiber optic connectors that links the fiber media to the FDDI network card or concentrator. The MIC consists of both the MIC plug termination of an optical cable and the MIC receptacle that is joined with the FDDI node.

medium dependent interface (MDI)

Used with Ethernet systems; it is the connector used to make the mechanical and electrical interface between a transceiver and a media segment. An 8-pin RJ-45 connector is the MDI for the 10Base-T, 100Base-TX, 100Base-T2, 100Base-T4, and 1000Base-T media systems.

medium independent interface (MII)

Used with 100Mbps Ethernet systems to attach MAC-level hardware to a variety of physical media systems. Similar to the AUI interface used with 10Mbps Ethernet systems. The MII is a 40-pin connection to outboard transceivers or PHY devices.

mega
Prefix meaning one million.

megahertz (Mhz)
A unit of frequency that is equal to one million hertz.

meridian plane
Any plane that includes or contains the optical axis.

meridianal ray
A light ray that passes through the axis of an optical fiber.

metropolitan area network (MAN)
A network that encompasses an entire city or metropolitan area.

MFD
See *mode field diameter*.

MHz See *megahertz*.

MIC connector See *media interface connector*.

micro Prefix meaning one millionth.

microbending Minute but severe bends in fiber cable that involve axial displacements of a few micrometers and spatial wavelengths of a few millimeters. Microbends cause loss of light and consequently increase the attenuation of the fiber. Most microbending can be avoided by selecting proper buffer materials and proper cabling, handling, and installation techniques.

microbending loss The optical power loss due to microscopic bends in the fiber.

microfarad One millionth of a farad. Abbreviated μF and, less commonly, *μfd*, *mf*, or *mfd*.

micrometer Also referred to as a *micron*; one millionth of a meter, often abbreviated as um or with the symbol μ. A micrometer is equal to 10^{-6} meters. Fiber optics can only be understood in these dimensions; optical wavelengths are measured in nanometers. Fiber that carries these optical wavelengths is measured in microns.

micron (μ) See *micrometer*.

midsplit broadband A broadcast network configuration in which the cable is divided into two channels, each using a different range of frequencies. One channel is used to transmit signals and the other is used to receive.

MII See *medium independent interface*.

milli Prefix meaning one thousandth.

misalignment loss The loss of optical power resulting from angular misalignment, lateral displacement, or end separation.

mixing segment An Ethernet term that is used in IEEE 802.3 standards to describe a segment that may have more than two MDI connections.

MLM Multilongitudinal mode.

MMF See *multimode fiber*.

MMJ See *modified modular jack*.

modal bandwidth The bandwidth-limiting characteristic of multimode fiber systems caused by the variable arrival times of various modes.

modal dispersion The spreading that arises from differences in the times that different modes take to travel through multimode fibers.

modal noise   The disturbance in multi-mode fibers fed by laser diodes. This occurs when fibers contain elements with mode-dependent attenuation, such as imperfect splices; the better the coherence of the laser light, the more severe the modal noise is.

mode   A single electromagnetic wave traveling in an optical fiber or in a light path through a fiber. Light has modes in optical fiber cable. In a single-mode fiber, only one mode (the fundamental mode) can propagate through the fiber. Multimode fiber has several hundred modes that differ in field pattern and propagation velocity. The upper limit to the number of modes is determined by the core diameter and the numerical aperture of the waveguide.

mode field diameter (MFD)   The diameter of optical energy in a single-mode fiber optic cable. Since the mode field diameter is greater than the core diameter, mode field diameter replaces the core diameter as a practical parameter.

mode filter   A device that can select, attenuate, or reject a specific mode. Mode filters are used to remove high-order modes from a fiber and thereby simulate EMD.

mode mixing   The numerous modes of a multimode fiber differ in their propagation velocities. As long as they propagate independently of each other, the fiber bandwidth varies inversely with the fiber length due to multimode distortion. As a result of irregularities in the geometry of the optical fiber cable and of the index profile, a gradual energy exchange occurs between modes with differing velocities. Due to this mode mixing, the bandwidth of long multimode fibers is greater than the value obtained by linear extrapolation from measurements on short fibers.

mode scrambler   A device composed of one or more optical fibers in which strong mode coupling occurs. Mode scramblers are frequently used to provide a mode distribution that is independent of source characteristics.

mode stripper   A device that removes high-order modes in a multimode fiber to give standard measurement conditions.

modem   A device that implements modulator-demodulator functions to convert between digital data and analog signals.

modified modular jack (MMJ)   A six-wire modular jack used by the DEC wiring system. The MMJ has a locking tab that is shifted to the right-hand side.

modular   Equipment is said to be modular when it is made of plug-in units that can be added together to make the system larger, improve the capabilities, or expand its size. Faceplates made for use with structured cabling systems are often modular and permit the use of multiple types of telecommunications outlets or modular jacks such as RJ-45, coaxial, audio, fiber, etc.

modular jack   A female telecommunications interface connector. Modular jacks are typically mounted in a fixed location and may have four, six, or eight contact positions; though most typical standards-based cabling systems will have an eight-position jack. Not all positions need be equipped with contacts. The modular jack may be keyed or unkeyed so as to permit only certain types of plugs to be inserted into the jack.

modulation   (1) Coding of information onto the carrier frequency. This includes amplitude, frequency, or phase modulation techniques. (2) When light is emitted by a medium, it is coherent, meaning that it is in a fixed phase relationship within fixed points of the light wave. This light is used because it is a continuous, or sinusoidal, wave (a white or blank form) upon which a signal can be superimposed by modulation of that form. The modulation is a variation imposed upon this white form, a variation of amplitude, frequency, or phase of the light. There are two basic forms of this modulation, one by an analog form, another by a digital signal. This signal is created in the form of the "intelligence" and superimposed upon the light wave. It is then recovered by a photodetector and converted into electrical energy.

monitor level signal   A digital signal that is 20dB below the standard DS-1 or DS-3 signal level.

monochromatic   Light consisting of a single wavelength. In practice, radiation is never perfectly monochromatic but at best displays a narrow band of wavelengths.

Motion Pictures Experts Group (MPEG) A standards group operating under the ISO that develops standards for digital video and audio compression.

MOVPE   Metal organic vapor phase epitaxy.

MPEG   See *Motion Pictures Experts Group.*

MRN   See *multiple reflection noise.*

MSAU   See *multistation access unit.*

MTBF   See *meantime between failures.*

MT-RJ connector   A proposed duplex fiber optic connector standard from AMP/Siecor that looks similar to the RJ-45-type connector.

multifiber jumpers   Used to interconnect fiber optic patch panels from point to point.

multimedia   (1) An application that communicates to more than one of the human sensory receptors such as audio and video components. (2) Applications that communicate information by more than one means or cabling media.

multimode   Transmission of multiple modes of light. See also *mode*.

multimode distortion   The signal distortion in an optical waveguide resulting from the superposition of modes with differing delays.

multimode fiber   Optical fiber cable whose core is between 8 and 200 microns with a refractive index that is graded or stepped; multimode fiber supports the propagation of multiple modes (several beams of light). It allows the use of inexpensive LED light sources, and connector alignment and coupling is less critical than with single-mode fiber. Distances of transmission and transmission bandwidth are less than with single-mode fiber due to dispersion. The TIA/EIA-568-A standard recommends the use of 62.5/125-micron multimode fiber for horizontal cabling.

multimode laser   A laser that produces emissions in two or more longitudinal modes.

multiple reflection noise (MRN)   The noise at the receiver caused by the interface of delayed signals from two or more reflection points in an optical fiber span.

multiplex   The combination of two or more signals to be transmitted along a single communications channel.

multiplexer   A device that combines two or more discrete signals into a single output. There are many types of multiplexing; including time division multiplexing and wavelength division multiplexing.

multistation access unit (MAU or MSAU)   Used in Token Ring LANs, a wiring concentrator that allows terminals, PCs, printers, and other devices to be connected in a star-based configuration to Token Ring LANs. MAU hardware can be either active or passive and is not considered to be part of the cabling infrastructure.

multiuser telecommunications outlet assembly (MuTOA)   A connector that has several telecommunications/outlet connectors in it. These are often used in a single area that will have several computers and telephones.

mutual capacitance   The capacitance between two conductors when all other conductors are connected together.

MUX   See *multiplexer*.

Mylar   The DuPont trademark for polyethylene terephtalete (polyester) film.

MZI   Mach Zehnder Interferometer.

N

NA   See *numerical aperture*.

nanometer   A unit of measurement equal to one billionth of a meter; abbreviated *nm*.

nanosecond   One billionth of a second; abbreviated *ns*.

National Electrical Code (NEC)   An electrical wiring code that specifies safety standards for cooper and fiber optic cable. See Chapter 4 for more information.

National Security Agency (NSA)   The U.S. government agency responsible for protecting U.S. communications and producing foreign intelligence information. It was established by presidential directive in 1952 as a separately organized agency within the Department of Defense.

N-connector   A coaxial cable connector used for Ethernet 10Base-5 thick coaxial segments.

NDFA   Neodymium doped fiber amplifier.

near-end crosstalk (NEXT)   Crosstalk between two twisted pairs measured at the "near" end of the cable. Near is defined as the end of the cable where the original transmission originated. NEXT is the best measurement of interest for crosstalk specifications. See Chapter 1 for more information.

near-field radiation pattern   The distribution of the irradiance over an emitting surface (over the cross section of an optical waveguide).

near infrared   The part of the infrared spectrum near the visible spectrum, typically 700nm to 1500nm or 2000nm; it is not rigidly defined.

NEC   See *National Electrical Code*.

NEMA   National Electrical Manufacturers Association.

NEP (noise equivalent power)   The radiant power that provides a noise to signal ratio of one at the output of a given detector within defined parameters for modulation, frequency, wavelength, and a given effective noise bandwidth.

network   Ties things together. Computer networks connect all types of computers and computer-related peripherals—terminals, printers, modems, door entry sensors, temperature monitors, etc. The networks we're most familiar with are long distance ones, such as phone or train networks. Local area networks (LANs) connect computer equipment within a building or campus.

network interface card (NIC)   A circuit board installed in a computing device that is used to attach the device to a network. An NIC performs the hardware functions that are required to provide a computing device physical communications capabilities with a network.

network media   The physical cables that link computers in a network; also known as physical media.

NEXT   See *near-end crosstalk*.

NFPA   National Fire Protection Association. See Chapter 4 for more information.

nibble   One-half byte.

NIC   See *network interface card*.

NIC diagnostics   Software utilities that verify that the NIC is functioning correctly and that test every aspect of NIC operation, including connectivity to other nodes on the network.

Nippon Telephone and Telegraph (NTT)   The Japanese equivalent of AT&T.

NIR   Near-end crosstalk-to-insertion loss ratio.

node   End point of a network connection. Nodes include any device connected to a network such as file servers, printers, or workstations.

noise   In a cable or circuit, any extraneous signal that interferes with the desired signal normally present in or passing through the system.

noise equivalent power (NEP)   The optical input power to a detector needed to generate an electrical signal equal to the inherent electrical noise.

Nomex   A DuPont trademark for a temperature resistant, flame retardant nylon.

nominal velocity of propagation (NVP)
The speed that a signal propagates through a cable expressed as a decimal fraction of the speed of light in a vacuum. Typical copper cables have an NVP value of between 0.6 and 0.9 percent.

non-return to zero (NRZ)   A digital code in which the signal level is low for a 0 bit and high for a 1 bit and which does not return to 0 between successive 1 bits.

normal angle   The angle that is perpendicular to a surface.

NRZ   See *non-return to zero*.

NRZI   Non-return to zero inverted.

NT-1   An ISDN device that converts a two-wire ISDN U interface to a four-wire S/T interface.

NTSC   National Television Standards Code.

NTT   See *Nippon Telephone and Telegraph*.

numerical aperture (NA)   The light gathering ability of a fiber, defining the maximum angle to the fiber axis at which light will be accepted and propagated through the fiber.

NVOD   Near video on demand.

NVP   See *nominal velocity of propagation*.

O

O   Orange, when used in conjunction with color-coding for twisted-pair cabling.

OC-1   Optical carrier level one, equal to 51.84Mbps. This is a SONET channel, whose format measures 90 bytes and is composed of the transport overhead and the synchronous payload envelope.

OC-2   SONET channel of 622.08Mbps.

OC-48   SONET channel of 2.4Gbps.

OC-192   SONET channel of 13Gbps, currently the highest level now available.

octet   Eight bits (also called a *byte*).

ODC   See *optical directional coupler*.

O/E   Optical to electronic.

OEIC   Optoelectronic-integrated chip.

OEM   Original equipment manufacturer.

OFDM   Orthogonal frequency division multiplexing.

off-hook   The handset's state of being lifted from its cradle. The term originated from when the early handsets were actually suspended from a metal hook on the phone. With modern telephones, when the handset is removed from its hook or cradle, it completes the electrical loop, thus signaling the central office to provide dial tone. Opposite of *on-hook*.

office principle ground point (OPGP)
The principle ground point/bus that is directly connected to the office ground array or water pipe.

OFSTP   Optical fiber standard test procedure.

ohm   A unit of electrical resistance. The value of resistance through which a potential of one volt will maintain a current of one ampere.

OIU   Optical interface unit.

OLTS   Optical loss test set.

on-hook   The telephone handset's state of resting in its cradle. The phone is not connected to any particular line. Only the bell is active—i.e., it will ring if a call comes in. Opposite of *off-hook*.

ONU   Optical network unit.

open circuit   A break in a cable.

open fault   A break in the continuity of a circuit. This means that the circuit is not complete or the cable/fiber is broken. This condition is also called *unmated, open,* or *unterminated.*

open systems interconnect (OSI)   A model defined by the ISO to categorize the process of communication between computers in terms of seven layers. See also *International Organization for Standardization.*

operations, administration, maintenance, and provisioning (OAM&P)   A common industry term given to the functions performed in support of the telecommunications network.

OPM   Open power meter.

optical amplifier   Increases the power of an optical signal without converting any of the signals from optical to electrical energy and then back to optical so that the amplification processes the optical signal wholly within optical amplification equipemnt. The two most common optical amplifiers are semiconductor laser amplifiers and those made from doped fiber, such as the EDFA (erbium doped fiber amplifier), which amplifies with a laser pump diode and a section of erbium doped fiber.

optical attenuator   Reduces the intensity of light waves, usually so that the power is within the capacity of the detector. There are three basic forms of attenuators: fixed optical attenuators, stepwise variable optical attenuators, and continuous variable optical attenuators. Attenuation is normally achieved either by a doped fiber or an offset or core misalignment. See also *attenuator*.

optical bandpass   The range of optical wavelengths that can be transmitted through a component.

optical cable entrance facility (OCEF)
An area providing space for splicing fibers connecting equipment to outside plant.

optical carrier *n*   Optical signal standards. The *n* indicates the level where the respective data rate is exactly *n* times the first level OC-1. OC-1 has a data rate of 51.84Mbps. OC-3 is three times that rate, or 155.52Mbps, etc. Associated with SONET.

optical detector   A transducer that generates an electronic signal when excited by an optical power source.

optical directional coupler (ODC)   A directional coupler used to combine or separate optical power.

optical fiber cable   An assembly consisting of one or more optical fibers. These optical fibers are thin glass or plastic filaments used for the transmission of information via light signals. This is the signal carrying part of a fiber optic cable. See also *single-mode fiber* and *multimode fiber*.

optical fiber duplex adapter   A mechanical media termination device designed to align and join two duplex connectors.

optical fiber duplex connector   A mechanical media termination device designed to transfer optical power between two pairs of optical fibers.

optical isolator   A component used to block out reflected and other unwanted light.

optical loss test set   An optical power meter and a light source calibrated for use together to detect and measure loss of signal on an optical cable.

optical polarization   A term used to describe the orientation in space of time varying field vector of an optical signal.

optical receiver   An optoelectronic circuit that converts an incoming signal to an electronic signal. The optical receiver will include a transducer in the form of a detector, which might be a photodiode or other device. When irradiated by an optical power device, it will be able to translate the optical signal into an electronic signal.

optical reference plane   Defines the optical boundary between the MIC (media interface connector) plug and the MIC receptacle.

optical repeater   An optoelectronic device, which could include an amplifier, that receives a signal and amplifies it, especially in the case of analog signals. In the case of a digital signal, the optical repeater reshapes or retimes the signal and then retransmits it.

optical return loss (ORL)   The ratio (expressed in decibels) of optical power reflected by a component or an assembly to the optical power incident on a component port when that component or assembly is introduced into a link or system.

optical spectrum   Starts with red, then orange, yellow, green, blue, indigo, and finally violet. Each color represents a wavelength or frequency of electromagnetic energy; the spectrum is between 400nm and 700nm. 400nm is the ultraviolet portion of the spectrum and 700nm is the infrared portion of the spectrum. Lasers are often used to create light of very precise and pure color.

optical time domain reflectometer (OTDR)   A device and method for characterizing a fiber wherein an optical pulse is transmitted through the fiber, and the resulting backscatter and reflections to the input are measured as a function of time. Useful in estimating attenuation coefficient as a function of distance and identifying defects and other localized losses.

optical transmitter   An optoelectronic circuit that converts an electronic signal into an optical signal.

optical waveguide   Any structure that can guide light; the optical waveguide is a dielectric waveguide with a core consisting of optically transparent material of low attenuation (usually silica glass) and with cladding consisting of optically transparent material of lower refractive index than that of the core. It is used for the transmission of signals with light waves and is frequently referred to as *fiber*.

optoelectronic   Pertains to a device that responds to optical power, emits or modifies optical radiation, or utilizes optical radiation for its internal operation. Any device that functions as an electrical-to-optical or optical-to-electrical transducer.

OSI   Open systems interconnection.

OTDR   See *optical time domain reflectometer*.

outlet   See *telecommunications outlet*.

outlet box   A metallic or nonmetallic box mounted within a wall, floor, or ceiling used to hold outlet, connector, or transition devices.

output   The useful signal or power delivered by a circuit or device.

outside plant (OSP) cables   Typically used outside of the wire center but also may be routed into the CEF. Since OSP cables are more flammable than plenum-grade cables, the distance of penetration into the building must be limited.

oversampling   A method of synchronous bit synchronization. The receiver samples the signal at a much faster rate than the data rate. This permits the use of an encoding method that does not add clocking transitions.

over-voltage threshold   The level of over-voltage that will trip the circuit breaker in a surge protector.

P

P region   The area in a semiconductor that is doped to have an abundance of electron acceptors in which vacancies in the valence electron level are the dominant current carriers.

PABX   See *private branch exchange*.

packet   Bits grouped serially in a defined format containing a command or data message sent over a network. The packet is the basic division of data sent over a network.

packet switching   The process of breaking messages into packets. Each packet is then routed optimally across the network. Packet sequence numbers are used at the destination node to reassemble packets.

packing fraction   The fraction of the surface area of a fiber optic bundle that is fiber core.

PAD   Packet assembler/dissembler.

PAM5x5   The signal-encoding technique used in the Ethernet 100Base-T2 and 1000Base-T media systems.

panel   See *patch panel*.

Part 68 requirements   Specifications established by the FCC as the minimum acceptable protection that communications equipment must provide to the telephone network.

PAS   See *profile alignment system*.

passive branching device   A device that divides an optical input into two or more optical outputs.

passive coupler   Divides light without generating new light.

patch cable   Any flexible piece of cable that connects one network device to the main cable run or to a patch panel that in turn connects to the main cable run; also called *patch cord*. Used for interconnecting circuits on a patch panel or cross-connect. Patch cables are short distance, usually have connectors preinstalled on both ends, are used to connect equipment, and are generally between three and six meters long.

patch panel   A connecting hardware that typically provides means to connect horizontal or backbone cables to an arrangement of fixed connectors that may be accessed using patch cords or equipment cords to form cross-connections or interconnections. Patch panels may connect either copper or optical fiber cables.

patching   A means of connecting circuits via cords and connectors that can be easily disconnected and reconnected at another point. May be accomplished by using modular patch cords connected between jack fields or by patch cord assemblies that plug onto connecting blocks.

pathway   A facility (e.g., conduit, cable tray, raceway, ducting, or plenum) for the placement and protection of telecommunications cables.

PBS   Polarizing beam splitter.

PBX   See *private branch exchange.*

PCC   Premises communication cable (a CSA cable designation).

PCM   Pulse code modulation.

PCS fiber   See *plastic-clad silica fiber.*

PDN   Public data network.

PE   See *polyethylene.*

peak   The maximum instantaneous value of a varying current or voltage.

peak wavelength   The wavelength at which the optical power of a source is at a maximum.

pedestal   A device, usually mounted on the floor, which is used to house voice/data jacks or power outlets at the point of use. Also commonly referred to as a *monument, tombstone, above-floor fitting,* or *doghouse.*

periodicity   Uniformly spaced variations in the insulation diameter of a transmission cable that result in reflections of a signal.

permanent virtual circuit (PVC)   Technology used by frame relay that allows virtual data communications (circuits) to be set up between the sender and receiver over a packet-switched network.

permittivity   See *dielectric constant.*

phase   An angular relationship between waves or the position of a wave in its oscillation cycle.

phase modulation (PM)   One of three basic methods of adding information to a sine wave signal in which its phase is varied to impose information on it. See also *amplitude* and *frequency modulation.*

phase shift   A change in the phase relationship between two alternating quantities.

photo-bleaching   A reduction in added loss that occurs when a fiber is exposed to light. Ionizing radiation causes added loss. This loss can be reduced by transmitting light through the fiber during normal operation or by exposing the fiber to sunlight.

photocurrent   The current that flows through a photosensitive device, such as a photodiode, as the result of exposure to radiant power (light).

photodetector   An optoelectronic transducer, such as a pin photodiode or avalanche photodiode, that acts a light detector.

photodiode   A diode designed to produce photocurrent by absorbing light. Photodiodes are used for the detection of optical power and for the conversion of optical power into electrical power.

photon   A quantum of electromagnetic energy.

photonic   A term coined to describe devices using photons, analogous to *electronic*, describing devices working with electrons.

PHY   Physical layer device.

physical bus topology   A network that uses one network cable that runs from one end of the network to the other. Workstations connect at various points along this cable. These networks are easy to run cable for, but they are typically not as reliable as a star topology. 10Base-2 Ethernet is a good example of a network architecture that uses a physical bus topology.

physical mesh topology   A network configuration that specifies a link between each and every device in the network. A physical mesh topology requires a lot of cabling and is very difficult to reconfigure.

physical ring topology   A network topology that is set up in a circular fashion. Data travels around the ring in one direction, and each device on the ring acts as a repeater to keep the signal strong as it travels. Each device incorporates a receiver for the incoming signal and a transmitter to send the data on to the next device in the ring. The network is dependent on the ability of the signal to travel around the ring. Cabling a physical ring topology is difficult because of the amount of cable that must be run. FDDI is an example of a network that can be wired to use a physical ring topology.

physical star topology   A network in which a cable runs from each network device to a central device called a hub. The hub allows all devices to communicate as if they were directly connected. The network may electrically follow another type of topology such as bus or ring topology, but the wiring is still a star topology.

physical topology   The physical layout of a network, such as bus, star, ring, or mesh.

PIC   Photo-optic integrated circuit.

pico   Prefix meaning one millionth of one millionth.

picofarad   One millionth of one millionth of a farad. Abbreviated *pf*.

picosecond (PS)   One trillionth of a second.

pigtail   (1) A short length of fiber with a permanently attached device, usually a connector, on one end. (2) A fiber optic cable assembly consisting of a connector and an unterminated fiber at the other end. Normally found in applications wherein a splice is convenient for terminating a device with a connector. Also used when the loss characteristics of the connector must be known precisely. For instance, a splice of .03dB might be reliably predicted and controlled, but the variability of most commercially available terminations is unacceptable so a precharacterized cable assembly is cut into a pigtail and attached to the device through splicing.

PIN device   Positive intrinsic negative device.

plain old telephone service (POTS)
The basic service that supplies standard single line telephones, telephone lines, and access to the public switched network; it only receives and places calls and has no added features like call waiting or call forwarding.

planar waveguide   A waveguide fabricated in a flat material such as a thin film.

plastic-clad silica (PCS) fiber   A step index multimode fiber that has a silica core and is surrounded by a lower index plastic cladding.

plastic fiber   Optical fiber having a plastic core and plastic cladding rather than using glass.

plasticizer   A chemical added to plastics to make them softer and more flexible.

plenum   The air handling space between the walls, under structural floors, and above drop ceilings used to circulate and otherwise handle air in a building. A space is considered a plenum only if it is used for air handling. Plenum-grade cable can be run through these spaces if local building codes permit it.

plenum cable   Cable whose flammability and smoke characteristics allow it to be routed in plenum spaces without being enclosed in a conduit.

plug   The male component of a plug/jack connector system. In premises cabling, a plug provides the means for a user to connect communications equipment to the communications outlet.

PMD   Physical media dependent.

POF   Plastic optical fiber.

POFDI Plastic optical fiber distributed interface.

point-to-point transmission Carrying a signal between two endpoints without branching to other points.

polarity Identifies which side of an electrical circuit is positive and which is negative.

polarization (1) Alignment of the electric and magnetic fields that make up an electromagnetic wave. Normally refers to the electric field. If all light waves have the same alignment, the light is polarized. (2) The direction of the electric field in the light wave.

polarization maintaining fiber Optical fiber that maintains the polarization of light that enters it.

polarization stability The variation in insertion loss as the polarization state of the input light is varied.

polling A media access control method that uses a central device called a controller, which polls each device in turn and asks if it has data to transmit. 100VG-AnyLAN hubs poll nodes to see if they have data to transmit.

POLSK Polarization shift keying.

polybutadene A type of synthetic rubber often blended with other synthetic rubbers to improve their dielectric properties.

polyethylene (PE) A thermoplastic material with excellent electrical properties used to make cable jacketing.

polymer A substance made of repeating chemical units or molecules. The term is often used as a synonym for plastic, rubber, or elastomer.

polypropylene A thermoplastic material that is similar to polyethylene but is somewhat stiffer and has a higher softening point (temperature).

polyurethane (PUR) A broad class of polymers that are noted for good abrasion and solvent resistance. Not as common as PVC (polyvinyl chloride).

polyvinyl chloride (PVC) A general purpose thermoplastic used for wire and cable insulation and plastics. PVC is known for high flexibility and has good dielectric properties. Often used in nonplenum wire insulation and cable jackets. A modified version of the material may be found in jacketing of some plenum rated cables.

PON Passive optical network.

POTS See *plain old telephone service*.

potting The process of sealing by filling with a substance to exclude moisture.

power brownout Occurs when power drops below normal levels for several seconds or longer.

power distribution system The system of cables, connectors, and distribution frames required to efficiently deliver power from the power plant to the network elements.

power level The difference between the total power delivered to a circuit, cable, or device and the power delivered by that device to a load.

power overage Occurs when too much power is coming into a piece of equipment. See also *power spike* and *power surge*.

power ratio The ratio of power appearing at the load to the input power. Expressed in decibels.

power sag Occurs when the power level drops below normal and rises to normal in less than one second.

power spike Occurs when the power level rises above normal and drops back to normal for less than a second. See also *power overage* and *power surge*.

power sum A test method for cables with multiple pairs of wire whereby the mathematical sum of pair-to-pair crosstalk from a reference wire pair is measured while all other wire pairs are carrying signals. Power sum tests are necessary on cables that will be carrying bidirectional signals on more than two pairs. Most commonly measured on four-pair cables.

power surge Occurs when the power level rises above normal and stays there for longer than a second or two. See also *power overage* and *power spike*.

power underage Occurs when the power level drops below the standard level. Opposite of *power overage*.

prefusing Fusing the end of a fiber optic cable with a low current to clean the end; it precedes fusion splicing.

premises A telecommunications term for the space occupied by a customer or an authorized/joint user in a building on continuous or contiguous property that is not separated by a public road or highway.

premises wiring system The entire wiring system on a user's premises, especially the supporting wiring that connects the communications outlets to the network interface jack.

prewiring Wiring that is installed before walls and ceilings are enclosed. Prewiring is often easier than waiting until the walls are built to install wire.

PRI See *primary rate interface*.

primary coating The plastic coating applied directly to the cladding surface of the fiber during manufacture to preserve the integrity of the cladding surface.

primary rate interface (PRI) As defined by the ISDN standard, consists of 23 B-channels (64Kbps each) and one 64Kpbs D-channel (delta channel) in the United States, or 30 B-channels and one D-channel in Europe.

private branch exchange (PBX)
A private telephone switching system usually serving an organization, such as a business, located on the customer's premises. It switches calls both inside a building and outside to the telephone network, and it can sometimes provide access to a computer from a data terminal. Now used interchangeably with *PABX (private automatic branch exchange)*.

profile alignment system (PAS) A fiber splicing technique for using nonelectro-optical linked access technology for aligning fibers for splicing.

propagation delay The amount of time that passes between when a signal is transmitted and when it is received at the opposite end of a copper or optical fiber cable.

protector A device that limits damaging voltages on metallic conductors by protecting them against surges and transients.

protocol A set of predefined, agreed upon rules and message formats for exchanging information among devices on a network.

protocol analyzer A software and hardware troubleshooting tool used to decode protocol information to try to determine the source of a network problem and to establish baselines.

PS See *picosecond*.

PS-ELFEXT Power sum equal level far-end crosstalk.

PS-NEXT Power sum near-end crosstalk.

PSTN See *public switched network*.

public data network   A network established and operated for the specific purpose of providing data transmission services to the public. See also *public switched network*.

public switched network   A network provided by a common carrier that provides circuit switching between public users, such as the public telephone network, telex, Sprint's TELENET, or MCI's Execunet.

public switched telephone network (PSTN)   The basic phone service provided by the phone company. See also *plain old telephone service*.

pull strength   The pulling force that can be applied to a cable without damaging a cable or affecting the specified characteristics of the cable. Also called *pull tension*.

pull tension   See *pull strength*.

pulse   A current or voltage that changes abruptly from one value to another and back to the original value in a finite length of time.

pulse code modulation (PCM)   The most common method of representing an analog signal, such as speech, by sampling at a regular rate and converting each sample to an equivalent digital code.

pulse dispersion   The dispersion of pulses as they travel along an optical fiber.

pulse spreading   The dispersion of an optical signal with time as it propagates through an optical fiber.

punch-down   A method for securing copper wire to a quick clip in which the insulated wire is placed in the terminal groove and pushed down with a special tool. As the wire is seated, the terminal displaces the wire insulation to make an electrical connection. The punch-down operation may also trim the wire as it terminates. Punch-downs are performed on telecommunications outlets, 66-blocks, and 110-blocks. Also called *cut down*.

PUR   See *polyurethane*.

PVC   See *polyvinyl chloride* and *permanent virtual circuit*.

PVDF   Polyvinylidene fluoride.

Q

QAM   See *quadtrature amplitude modulation*.

QoS   See *quality of service*.

QPSK   Quadrature phase shift key.

quadtrature amplitude modulation (QAM) The modulation of two separate signals onto carriers at a single frequency and kept separate by having the two signals 90 degrees out of phase.

quality of service (QoS) Data prioritization at the network layer of the OSI model. QoS results in guaranteed throughput rates.

quartet signaling The encoding method used by 100VG-AnyLAN, in which the 100Mbps signal is divided into four 25Mbps channels and then transmitted over different pairs of a cable. Category 3 cable transmits one channel on each of four pairs.

quick clip An electrical contact used to provide an insulation displacement connection (IDC) to telecommunications cables.

R

R Symbol for *resistance*.

raceway Any channel designated for holding wires or cables. Raceways may be metallic or nonmetallic and may totally or partially enclose the wiring (e.g., conduit, cable trough, cellular floor, electrical metallic tubing, sleeves, slots, under-floor raceways, surface raceways, lighting fixture raceways, wireways, busways, auxiliary gutters, and ventilated flexible cableways). See also *pathway*.

radial refractive index profile The refractive index measured in a fiber as a function of the distance from the axial core or center.

radian flux The time rate in watts of flow of radiant energy.

radiation (rad) hardened Used to describe material that is not sensitive to the effects of nuclear radiation; such material is usually used for military applications.

radio frequency (RF) The frequencies in the electromagnetic spectrum that are used for radio communications.

radio frequency interference (RFI) The interference on copper cabling systems caused by radio frequencies.

Raleigh scattering   A loss due to scattering of the light wave due to the atomic and molecular structure of the wave guide (optical fiber), which is dependent upon the material and the distance considered. The Raleigh scattering is named after the English physicist who used it to explain the apparent blueness of the sky.

ray   A geometric representation of a light path through an optical medium; a line normal to the wave front indicating the direction of radiant energy flow.

RBOC (Regional Bell Operating Company)   Seven RBOCs (pronounced "R-bocks") exist, each of which owns two or more Bell Operating Companies (BOCs). The RBOCs were the result of the AT&T/Bell System divestiture in 1984.

RCDD   See *Registered Communications Distribution Designer.*

reactance   A measure of the combined effects of capacitance and inductance on an alternating current. The amount of such opposition varies with the frequency of the current. The reactance of a capacitor decreases with an increase in frequency. The opposite occurs with an inductance.

receiver   A device whose purpose is to capture transmitted signal energy and convert that energy for useful functions. In fiber optic systems, an electronic component that converts light energy to electrical energy.

receiver sensitivity   The optical power required by a receiver for low error signal transmission. In the case of digital signal transmission, the mean optical power is usually quoted in watts or dBm (decibels referred to 1 milliwatt).

reflectance   Light that is reflected back along the path of transmission from the coupling region, the connector, or a terminated fiber.

reflection   (1) A return of electromagnetic energy that occurs at an impedance mismatch in a transmission line, such as a LAN cable. See also *return loss.* (2) In fiber optics, the abrupt change in direction of a light beam at an interface between two dissimilar media so that the light beam returns into the media from which it originated. Reflection causes several spectral problems including high optical distortion and enhanced intensity noise.

refraction   The bending of a beam of light at an interface between two dissimilar media (such as the core and cladding of an optical fiber cable) or a medium whose refractive index is a continuous function of position (graded index medium).

refractive index   The ratio of the speed of light in a vacuum to the speed of light in a given material; it is abbreviated *n*. See also *index of refraction*.

refractive index gradient   The change in refractive index with respect to the distance from the axis of an optical fiber.

regenerative repeater   A repeater designed for digital operations that both amplifies and reshapes the signal.

regenerator   A receiver-transmitter pair that detects a weak signal, cleans it up, then sends the regenerated signal through another length of fiber.

Registered Communications Distribution Designer (RCDD)   A professional title, the rating of which is granted by BICSI (the Building Industry Consulting Service International). RCDDs have demonstrated a superior level of knowledge of the telecommunications wiring industry and associated disciplines.

registered jack (RJ)   Telephone and data jacks/applications that are registered with the FCC. Numbers such as RJ-11 and RJ-45 are widely misused in the telecommunications industry—the *RJ* abbreviation was used to identify a type of service and wiring pattern to be installed, not a specific jack type. A much more precise way to identify a jack is to specify the number of positions (width of opening) and number of conductors. Examples include the eight-position, eight-conductor jack and the six-position, four-conductor jack.

REM   Remote electronic maintenance.

repeater   (1) A device that receives, amplifies (and sometimes reshapes), and retransmits a signal. It is used to boost signal levels and extend the distance over which a signal can be transmitted. It can physically extend the distance of a LAN or connect two LAN segments. (2) In an optical system, an optoelectronic device or module that receives an optical signal, converts it to electrical form, amplifies or reconstructs it, and retransmits it in optical form.

rerouting   Changing the route or spans that the system traverses.

resistance   In DC (direct current) circuits, the opposition a material offers to current flow, measured in ohms. In AC (alternating current) circuits, resistance is the real component of impedance and may be higher than the value measured at DC.

responsivity   The ratio of a detector's output to input, usually measured in units of amperes per watt (or microamperes per microwatt).

retermination   The process of moving cable terminations from one location to another, usually by Y-splicing old cables.

retractile cord   A cord with a specially treated insulation or jacket that causes it to retract like a spring. Retractile cords are commonly used between a telephone and a telephone handset.

return loss   The ratio of reflected power to inserted power. Return loss is a measure of the signal reflections occurring along a channel or basic link and is related to various electrical mismatches along the cabling. This ratio, expressed in decibels, describes the ratio of optical power reflected by a component, for instance a connector, to the optical power introduced to that component.

return to zero   A digital coding scheme where the signal level is low for a 0 bit and high for a 1 bit during the first half of a bit interval; in either case, the bit returns to zero (0) for the second half of the interval.

reversed pair   A wiring error in twisted-pair cabling where the conductors of a pair are reversed between connector pins at each end of a cable. A cabling tester can detect a reversed pair.

RF   See *radio frequency*.

RFI   See *radio frequency interference*.

RFITL   Rural fiber in the loop.

RFP   Request for Proposal.

RFQ   Request for Quote or Quotation.

RG-58   The type designation for the coaxial cable used in thin Ethernet (10Base-2). It has a 50-ohm impedance rating and uses BNC connectors.

RG-62   The type designation for the coaxial cable used in ARCNet networks. It has a 93-ohm impedance and uses BNC connectors

RG/U   Radio grade/universal. RG is the common military designation for coaxial cable.

ribbon   Up to 12 fibers clad in a single optical fiber cable.

ribbon cable   A cable in which many fibers are embedded in a plastic material in parallel, forming a flat, ribbonlike structure.

ring   (1) A polarity designation of one wire of a pair indicating that the wire is that of the secondary color of a five-pair cable (which is not commonly used anymore) group (e.g., the blue wire of the blue/white pair). (2) A wiring contact to which the ring wire is attached. (3) The negative wiring polarity (see also *tip*). (4) Two or more stations in which data is passed sequentially between active stations, each in turn examining or copying the information before finally returning it to the source. See also *ring network*.

ring architecture   A network scheme in which a transmission line forms a complete ring. If the ring is broken, signals can still be sent among the terminals.

ring conductor   A telephony term used to describe one of the two conductors that is in a cable pair used to provide telephone service. This term was originally coined from its position as the second (ring) conductor of a tip-ring-sleeve switchboard plug. See also *ring*.

ring network   A network topology in which terminals are connected in a point-to-point serial fashion in an unbroken circular configuration. Many logical ring topologies such as Token Ring are wired as a star for greater reliability.

riser   (1) A cable typically used in vertical cabling runs between floors. Fire-code rating for indoor cable that is certified to pass through the vertical shaft from floor to floor. (2) A space for indoor cables that allow cables to pass between floors, normally a vertical shaft or space.

riser cable   A type of cable used in vertical building shafts, such as telecommunications and utility shafts. Riser cable typically has more mechanical strength than general use cable and has an intermediate fire protection rating.

RJ   See *registered jack*.

RJ-45   A USOC code identifying an eight-pin modular plug or jack used with unshielded twisted-pair cable. Officially, a RJ-45 connector is a telephone connector designed for voice-grade circuits only. RJ-45-type connectors with better signal handling characteristics are called eight-pin connectors in most standards documents, though most people continue to use the RJ-45 name for all eight-pin connectors.

RJ-connector   A modular connection mechanism that allows for as many as eight copper wires (four pairs). Commonly found in phone (RJ-11) or 10Base-T (RJ-45) connections.

RMS   Root mean square.

rolling   Usually a telephone company term for reassigning part of a circuit from one piece of digital equipment to another with minimum effect on the digital transmission. Patching and rolling are used in a variety of operations, including retermination and rerouting.

rope strand   A conductor composed of groups of twisted strands.

router   A device that connects two networks and allows packets to be transmitted and received between them. A router may also determine the best path for data packets from source to destination. Routers usually operate on Layer 3 (the network layer) of the OSI model.

routing   A function of the network layer that involves moving data throughout a network. Data passes through several network segments using routers that can select the path the data takes.

RS-232C   The EIA's registered standard that defines the interface that computers use to talk to modems and other serial devices such as printers or plotters.

RSU   Remote service unit.

Rx   Receive.

RZ   See *return to zero*.

S

SAS   See *single attachment station*.

SC connector   An optical fiber connector made from molded plastic using push-pull mechanics for joining to a fiber adapter. The SC connector has a 2.5mm ferrule push-pull latching mechanism and can be snapped together to form duplex and multifiber connectors. SC connectors are the preferred fiber optic cable for premises cabling and are recommended by the TIA/EIA-568-A standard for structured cabling. Used with Ethernet 100Base-FX and 1000Base-LX/SX fiber optic media systems.

scanner   A cable-testing device that uses TDR methods to detect cable transmission anomalies and error conditions.

scattering   A property of glass that causes light to deflect from the fiber and contributes to losses.

SCM   Subcarrier multiplex.

screen   See *shield*.

screened twisted-pair (ScTP) cable   A balanced four-pair UTP with a single foil or braided screen surrounding all four pairs in order to minimize EMI radiation or susceptibility. Screened twisted-pair is also sometimes called *foil twisted-pair (FTP)*. ScTP is a shielded version of Category 3, 4, and 5 UTP cables; they are less susceptible to electromagnetic interference than UTP cables but are more susceptible than STP cables.

ScTP   See *screened twisted-pair cable*.

segment   A portion of a network that uses the same length of cable (electrically contiguous). Also the portion of a network that shares a common hub or set of interconnected hubs.

Selfoc Lens   A trade name used by the Nippon Sheet Glass Company for a graded index fiber lens. A segment of graded index fiber made to serve as a lens.

semiconductor   In wire industry terminology, a material possessing electrical conductivity that falls somewhere between that of conductors and insulators. Usually made by adding carbon particles to an insulator. This is not necessarily the same as semiconductor materials such as silicon, germanium, etc.

semiconductor laser   A laser in which the injection of current into a semiconductor diode produces light by recombination of holes and electrons at the junction between p- and n-doped regions. Also called a *semiconductor diode laser*.

sensitivity   For a fiber optic receiver, the minimum optical power required to achieve a specified level of performance, such as BER.

separator   Pertaining to wire and cable, a layer of insulating material such as textile, paper, Mylar, etc., which is placed between a conductor and its dielectric, between a cable jacket and the components it covers, or between various components of a multiple conductor cable. It can be utilized to improve stripping qualities or flexibility, or it can offer additional mechanical or electrical protection to the components it separates.

series wiring   See *daisy chain*.

service loop   A loop or slack left in a cable when the cable is installed and terminated. This loop allows future trimming of the cable or movement of equipment if necessary.

service profile identification (SPID)   The ISDN telephone number issued by the phone company that identifies the ISDN terminal equipment attached to an ISDN line.

SFF connector   See *small form factor connector*.

sheath   An outer protective layer of a fiber optic or copper cable that includes the cable jacket, strength members, and shielding.

shield   A metallic foil or multiwire screen mesh that is used to prevent electromagnetic fields from penetrating or exiting a transmission cable. Also referred to as a *screen*.

shield coverage   The physical area of a cable that is actually covered by shielding material, often expressed as a percentage.

shield effectiveness   The relative ability of a shield to screen out undesirable interference. Frequently confused with the term *shield coverage*.

shielded twisted pair (STP)   A type of twisted-pair cable in which the pairs are enclosed in an outer braided shield, although individual pairs may also be shielded. STP most often refers to the 150-ohm IBM Type 1, 2, 6, 8, and 9 cables used with Token Ring networks. Unlike UTP cabling, the pairs in STP cable have an individual shield, and the individual shielded cables are wrapped in an overall shield. The primary advantages of STP cable are that it has less attenuation at higher frequencies and is less susceptible to electromagnetic interference. STP cable is becoming less popular as UTP cable capabilities become better and as optical fiber becomes more affordable.

short wavelength   In reference to light, a wavelength shorter than 1000nm.

SI units   The standard international system of metric units.

signal   The information conveyed through a communication system.

signal encoding   The process whereby a protocol at the physical layer receives information from the upper layers and translates all the data into signals that can be transmitted on a transmission medium.

signaling   The process of transmitting data across the medium. Two types of signaling are digital and analog.

signal-to-noise ratio (SNR or S/N)
The ratio of received signal level to received noise level, expressed in decibels and abbreviated *SNR* or *S/N*. A higher SNR ratio indicates better channel performance. The relationship between the usable intended signal and extraneously present noise present. If the SNR limit is exceeded, the signal transmitted will be unusable.

silica glass   Glass made mostly of silicon dioxide used in conventional optical glass that is used commonly in optical fiber cables.

Silicone   A General Electric trademark for a material made from silicone and oxygen. Can be in thermosetting elastomer or liquid form. The thermosetting elastomer form is noted for high heat resistance.

silver satin cable   The silver-gray voice-grade patch cable used to connect a telephone to a wall jacket such as is used by home telephones. Silver satin cables are unsuitable for use in LAN applications because they do not have twisted pairs, and this results in high levels of crosstalk.

simplex cable   A term sometimes used to describe a single-fiber cable.

simplex transmission   Data transmission over a circuit capable of transmitting in only one direction.

single attachment station (SAS)
With FDDI networks, denotes a station that attaches to only one of two rings in a dual ring environment.

single-ended line   An unbalanced circuit or transmission line, such as a coaxial cable (see also *balanced line* and *unbalanced line*).

single-frequency laser   A laser that emits a range of wavelengths small enough to be considered a single frequency.

single-mode fiber (SMF)   Optical fiber cable with a small core, usually between two and nine microns, which can support only one wavelength. It requires a laser source for the input because the acceptance cone is so small. The small core radius approaches the wavelength of the source. Single-mode optical fiber cable is typically used for backbones and to transmit data over long distances.

single polarization fibers   Optical fibers capable of carrying light in only one polarization.

sinusoidal   A signal that varies over time in proportion to the sine of an angle. Alternating current (AC) is sinusoidal.

skew ray   A light ray that does not intersect the fiber axis and generally enters the fiber at a very high angle.

skin effect   The tendency of alternating current to travel on the surface of a conductor as the frequency increases.

SLA   Semiconductor laser amplifier.

SLED   Surface emitting light emitting diode.

SLM   Single longitudinal mode.

SMA connector   See *surface mount assembly connector*.

small form factor (SFF) connector
A type of optical fiber connector that provides support for two strands of optical fiber in a connector enclosure that is similar to an RJ-45. There is currently no standard for SFF connectors; types include the LC and the MT-RJ connectors.

SMDS   Switched multimegabit data service.

SMF   See *single-mode fiber*.

SMOLTS   Single-mode optical lost test set.

SMSR   Side-mode suppression ratio.

S/N   See *signal-to-noise ratio*.

sneak current   A low level current that is of insufficient strength to trigger electrical surge protectors and thus may be able to pass between these protectors undetected. The sneak current may result from contact between communications lines and AC power circuits or from power induction. This current can cause equipment damage unless secondary protection is used.

SNR   See *signal-to-noise ratio*.

solid state laser   A laser whose active medium is a glass or crystal.

soliton   A device used in fiber optic communications in combination with optical amplifiers to help carry a signal longer distances.

SONET   See *Synchronous Optical Network*.

source   In fiber optics, the device that converts the electrical information carrying a signal to an optical signal for transmission over an optical fiber. A fiber optic source may be a light emitting diode or laser diode.

source address The address of the station that sent a packet, usually found in the source area of a packet header. In the case of LAN technologies such as Ethernet and Token Ring, the source address is the MAC (media access control) address of the sending host.

spectral bandwidth (1) The difference between wavelengths at which the radiant intensity of illumination is half its peak intensity. (2) Radiance per unit wavelength interval.

spectral width A measure of the extent of a spectrum. For a source, the width of wavelengths contained in the output at one half of the wavelength of peak power. Typical spectral widths are between 20nm and 60nm for an LED and between 2nm and 5nm for a laser diode.

spectrum Frequencies that exist in a continuous range and have a common characteristic. A spectrum may be inclusive of many spectrums; the electromagnetic radiation spectrum includes the light spectrum, the radio spectrum, and the infrared spectrum.

speed of light (c) In a vacuum, light travels 299,800,000 meters per second. This is used as a reference for calculating the index of refraction.

SPID See *service profile identification*.

splice (1) A permanent joint between two optical waveguides. (2) Means for joining two fiber ends.

splice closure A container used to organize and protect splice trays.

splice tray A container used to organize and protect spliced fibers.

splicing The permanent joining of fiber ends to identical or similar fibers without the use of a connector. See also *fusion splicing* and *mechanical splice*.

split pair A wiring error in twisted-pair cabling where one of a pair's wires is interchanged with one of another pair's wires. Split pair conditions may be determined with simple cable testing tools (simple continuity tests will not reveal the error because the correct pin-to-pin continuity exists between ends). The error may result in impedance mismatch, excessive crosstalk, susceptibility to interference, and signal radiation.

splitting loss See *coupling ratio/loss*.

splitting ratio The ratio of power emerging from two output ports of a coupler.

spontaneous emission   Occurs when there are too many electrons in the conduction band of a semiconductor. These electrons drop spontaneously into vacant locations in the valence band, a photon being emitted for each electron. The emitted light is incoherent.

ScTP   See *screened twisted-pair cable*.

S/T interface   The four-wire interface of an ISDN terminal adapter. The S/T interface is a reference point in ISDN.

ST connector   A fiber optic connector with a bayonet housing; it was developed by AT&T but is not in favor as much as SC or FC connectors. It is used with older Ethernet 10Base-FL and FIORL links.

stabilized light source   An LED or laser diode that emits light with a controlled and constant spectral width, central wavelength, and peak power with respect to time and temperature.

standards   Mutually agreed upon principles of protocol or procedure. Standards are set by committees working under various trade and international organizations.

star coupler   A fiber optic coupler in which power at any input port is distributed to all output ports.

star network   A network in which all stations are connected through a single point such as a hub in an ArcNet network.

star topology   (1) A method of cabling each telecommunications outlet/connector directly to a cross-connect in a horizontal cabling subsystem. (2) A method of cabling each cross-connect to the main cross-connect in a backbone cabling subsystem. (3) A topology in which each outlet/connector is wired directly to the hub or distribution device.

star wiring   See *home run*.

static charge   An electrical charge that is bound to an object.

station   A unique, addressable device on a network.

stay cord   A component of a cable, usually of high tensile strength, used to anchor the cable ends at their points of termination and keep any pull on the cable from being transferred to the electrical conductors.

step index fiber   An optical fiber cable, usually multimode, having a uniform refractive index within the core; at the core/cladding interface there is a sharp decrease in refractive index. The light is reflected down the path of the fiber rather than refracted as in graded index fibers. Step index multimode fibers generally have lower bandwidths than graded index multimode fibers.

step index single-mode fiber   A fiber with a small core that is capable of carrying light in only one mode. Sometimes referred to as *single-mode optical fiber cable*.

step insulated   A process of applying insulation to a cable in two layers. Typically used in shielded networking cables so that the outer layer of insulation can be removed and the remaining conductor and insulation can be terminated in a connector.

stimulated emission   Occurs when the photons in a semiconductor stimulate available excess charge carriers to the emission of photons. The emitted light is identical in wavelength and phase with the incident coherent light.

stitching   The process of terminating multiconductor cables on a punch-down block such as a 66-block or 110-block.

STP   See *shielded twisted pair*.

STP-A   Refers to the enhanced IBM Cabling System specifications with the Type A suffix. The enhanced Type 1A, 2A, 6A, and 9A cable specifications were designed to support operation of 100Mbps FDDI signals over copper. See *Type 1A*, *Type 2A*, *Type 6A*, or *Type 9A*.

strength member   The part of a fiber optic cable composed of Kevlar aramid yarn, steel strands, or fiberglass filaments that increases the tensile strength of the cable.

structural return loss (SRL)   A measurement of the impedance uniformity of a cable. It measures energy reflected due to structural variations in the cable. The higher the SRL number, the better the performance; this means more uniformity and lower reflections.

structured cabling   Telecommunications cabling that is organized into a hierarchy of wiring termination and interconnection structures. The concept of structured wiring is used in the common standards from the TIA and EIA. See Chapter 1 for more information on structured cabling and Chapter 2 for more information on structured cabling standards.

submarine cable   A cable designed to be laid underwater.

subminiature D-connector   The subminiature D-connector is a family of multipin data connectors available in 9-, 15-, 25- and 37-pin configurations. Sometimes referred to as DB9, DB15, DB25, and DB37 connectors respectively.

subnetwork   A network that is part of another network. The connection is made through a gateway, bridge, or router.

supertrunk   A cable that carries several video channels between the facilities of a cable television company.

surface emitting diode   A light emitting diode (LED) that emits light from its flat surface rather than its side. These are simple and inexpensive and provide emission spread over a wide range.

surface mount assembly (SMA) connector   An optical fiber cable connector that is a threaded type connector. The SMA 905 version is a straight ferrule design, whereas the SMA 906 is a stepped ferrule design.

surge   A rapid rise in current or voltage, usually followed by a fall back to a normal level. Also referred to as a *transient*.

surge protector   A device that contains a special electronic circuit that monitors the incoming voltage level and then trips a circuit breaker when an over-voltage reaches a certain level, called the *over-voltage threshold*.

surge suppression   The process by which transient voltage surges are prevented from reaching sensitive electronic equipment. See also *surge protector*.

switched network   A network that routes signals to their destinations by switching circuits. Two different packets of information may not take the same route to get to the same destination in a switched network.

synchronous   Transmission in which the data and bits are transmitted at a fixed rate with the transmitter and receiver being synchronized.

Synchronous Optical Network (SONET)
The underlying architecture in most systems, which uses cells of fixed length. Until recently it was thought that ATM and SONET would be in conflict, but new developments show that ATM will be superimposed upon the embedded SONET architecture. Issues of survivability have or are in the process of being solved.

T

T-1   A standard for digital transmission in North America. A digital transmission link with a capacity of 1.544Mbps (1,544,000 bits per second), T-1 lines are used for connecting networks across remote distances. Bridges and routers are used to connect LANs over T-1 networks. Also referred to as *DS-1* (data services).

T-3   A 44.736Mbps multichannel digital transmission system for voice or data provided by long distance carriers. T-3C operates at 90Mbps. Also referred to as *DS-3* (data services).

tap   (1) A device for extracting a portion of the optical fiber. (2) On Ethernet 10Base-5 thick coaxial cable, a method of connecting a transceiver to the cable by drilling a hole in the cable, inserting a contact to the center conductor, and clamping the transceiver onto the cable at the tap. These taps are referred to as *vampire taps*.

tap loss   In a fiber optic coupler, the ratio of power at the tap port to the power at the input port. This represents the loss of signal as a result of tapping.

tapered fiber   An optical fiber whose transverse dimensions vary monotonically with length.

TC   See *telecommunications closet*.

T-carrier   A carrier or provider that is operating at one of the standard levels in the North American digital hierarchy, such as T-1 (1.544Mbps) or T-3 (44.736Mbps).

T-coupler   A coupler having three ports.

TDM   See *time division multiplexing*.

TDR   See *time domain reflectometry*.

Teflon   DuPont Company trademark for flourocarbon resins. See also *fluorinated ethylene propylene* and *tetrafluoroethylene*.

telco   An abbreviation for *telephone company*.

telecommunications   Any transmission, emission, or reception of signs, signals, writings, images, sounds, or information of any nature by cable, radio, visual, optical, or other electromagnetic systems.

telecommunications closet (TC)   An enclosed space for housing telecommunications equipment, cable terminations, and cross-connect cabling used to serve work areas located on the same floor. The telecommunications closet is the typical location of the horizontal cross-connect and is considered distinct from an equipment room because it is considered to be a floor serving (as opposed to building or campus serving) facility. Also known as a *wiring closet*.

telecommunications equipment room
See *equipment room*.

Telecommunications Industry Association (TIA)   The standards body that helped to author the TIA/EIA-568-A Commercial Building Telecommunications Cabling standard in conjunction with EIA and which continues to update this standard along with standards for pathways spaces, grounding, bonding, administration, field testing, and other aspects of the telecommunications industry. See Chapter 2 for more information.

telecommunications infrastructure   A collection of telecommunications components that together provide the basic support for the distribution of all information within a building or campus. This excludes equipment such as PCs, hubs, switches, routers, phones, PBXs, and other devices attached to the telecommunications infrastructure.

telecommunications outlet   A fixed connecting device where the horizontal cable terminates that provides the interface to the work area cabling. Typically found on the floor or in the wall. Sometimes referred to as a *telecommunications outlet/connector* or a *wall plate*.

Telecommunications Systems Bulletin (TSB)   A document released by the TIA to provide guidance or recommendations for a specific TIA standard.

terminal   (1) A point at which information may enter or leave a communications network. (2) A device by means of which wires may be connected to each other.

terminal adapters   ISDN customer premise equipment that is used to connect non-ISDN equipment (computers and phones) to an ISDN interface.

terminate   To connect a wire conductor to something, typically a piece of patch panel, cross-connect, or telecommunications outlet.

terminator   A device used on coaxial cable networks that prevents a signal from bouncing off the end of the network cable, which would cause interference with other signals. Its function is to absorb signals on the line, thereby keeping them from bouncing back and being received again by the network or colliding with other signals.

tetrafluoroethylene (TFE)   A thermoplastic material with good electrical insulating properties and chemical and heat resistance.

TFE   See *tetrafluoroethylene*.

theoretical cutoff wavelength   The shortest wavelength at which a single light mode can be propagated in a single-mode fiber. Below the cutoff several modes will propagate; in this case, the fiber is no longer single-mode but multimode.

thermal rating   The temperature range in which a material will perform its function without undue degradation such as signal loss.

thermoplastic   A material that will soften, flow, or distort appreciably when subjected to sufficient heat and pressure. Examples are polyvinyl chloride and polyethylene, which are commonly used in telecommunications cable jackets.

thicknet   Denotes a coaxial cable type (RG-8) that is commonly used with Ethernet (10Base-5) backbones. Originally, thicknet cabling was the only cabling type used with Ethernet, but it is now being replaced as backbone cabling by optical fiber cabling. Thicknet cable has an impedance of 50 ohms and is commonly about 0.4 inches in diameter.

thinnet   Denotes a coaxial cable type (RG-58) that is commonly used with Ethernet (10Base-2) local area networks. This coaxial cable has an impedance of 50 ohms and is 0.2 inches in diameter. It is also called *cheapernet* due to the fact that it was cheaper to purchase and install than the bulkier (and larger) thicknet Ethernet cabling. The maximum distance for a thinnet segment is 180 meters.

TIA   See *Telecommunications Industry Association*.

tight buffer   A type of optical fiber cable construction where each glass fiber is buffered tightly by a protective thermoplastic coating to a diameter of 900 microns. High tensile strength rating is achieved, providing durability and ease of handling and connectorization.

time division multiple access (TDMA)   A method used to divide individual channels in broadband communications into separate time slots, allowing more data to be carried at the same time.

time division multiplexing (TDM)
Digital multiplexing that takes one pulse at a time from separate signals and combines them in a single stream of bits.

time domain reflectometry A technique for measuring cable lengths by timing the period between a test pulse and the reflection of the pulse from an impedance discontinuity on the cable. The returned waveform reveals undesired cable conditions, including shorts, opens, and transmission anomalies due to excessive bends or crushing. The length to any anomaly, including the unterminated cable end or cable break, may be computed from the relative time of the wave return and nominal velocity of propagation of the pulse through the cable. For optical fiber cables, see also *optical time domain reflectometry*.

tinsel A type of electrical conductor composed of a number of tiny threads, each having a fine, flat ribbon of copper or other metal closely spiraled about it. Used for small size cables requiring limpness and extra-long flex life.

tip (1) A polarity designation of one wire of a pair indicating that the wire is that of the primary (common) color of a five-pair cable (which is not commonly used anymore) group (e.g., the white/blue wire of the blue pair). (2) A wiring contact to which the tip wire is connected. (3) The positive wiring polarity. See also *ring*.

tip conductor A telephony term used to describe the conductor of a pair that is grounded at the central office when the line is idle. This term was originally coined from its position as the first (tip) conductor of a tip-ring-sleeve switchboard plug. See also *tip*.

TNC A threaded connector used to terminate coaxial cables. TNC is an acronym for Threaded Neill-Concelman (Neill and Concelman invented the connector).

token passing A media access method in which a token (data packet) is passed around the ring in an orderly fashion from one device to the next. A station can transmit only when it has the token. The token continues around the network until the original sender receives the token again. If the host has more data to send, the process repeats. If not, the original sender modifies the token to indicate that the token is free for anyone else to use.

Token Ring   A ring topology for a local area network (LAN) in which a supervisory frame, or token, must be received by an attached terminal or workstation before that terminal or workstation can start transmitting. The workstation with the token then transmits and uses the entire bandwidth of whatever communications media the token ring network is using. The most common wiring scheme is called a star-wired ring. Only one data packet can be passed along the ring at a time. If the data packet goes around the ring without being claimed, it eventually makes its way back to the sender. The IEEE standard for Token Ring is 802.5.

tone dial   A push-button telephone dial that makes a different sound (in fact, a combination of two tones) for each number pushed. The technically correct name for tone dial is *dual tone multifrequency* (DTMF) since there are two tones generated for each button pressed.

tone generator   A small electronic device used to test network cables for breaks and other problems that sends an electronic signal down one set of UTP wires. Used with a tone locator or probe.

tone locator   A testing device or probe used to test network cables for breaks and other problems; designed to sense the signal sent by the tone generator and emit a tone when the signal is detected in a particular set of wires.

topology   The geometric physical or electrical configuration describing a local communication network, as in network topology; the shape or arrangement of a system. The most common topologies are bus, ring, and star.

total internal reflection   The reflection of light back into a material after reaching an interface with a material of a lower refractive index at an angle at or above the critical angle. Total internal reflection occurs at the core/cladding interface within an optical fiber cable.

TP   See *transition point*.

TPON   Telephone passive optical network.

TP-PMD   See *twisted pair–physical media dependent*.

tracer   The contrasting color-coding stripe along an insulated conductor of a wire pair.

transceiver   The set of electronics that sends and receives signals on the Ethernet media system. Transceivers may be small outboard devices or they may be built into an Ethernet port. Transceiver is a combination of the words transmitter and receiver.

transducer   A device for converting energy from one form to another, such as optical energy to electrical energy.

transfer impedance   For a specified cable length, relates to a current on one surface of a shield to the voltage drop generated by this current on the opposite surface of the shield. The transfer impedance is used to determine shield effectiveness against both ingress and egress of interfering signals. Shields with lower transfer impedance are more effective than shields with higher transfer impedance.

transient   A high-voltage burst of electrical current. If the transient is powerful enough, it can damage data transmission equipment and devices that are connected to the transmission equipment.

transition point (TP)   ISO/IEC 11801 term that defines a location in the horizontal cabling subsystem where flat under-carpet cabling connects to round cabling or where cable is distributed to modular furniture. The TIA/EIA-568-A equivalent of this term is *consolidation point*.

transmission line   An arrangement of two or more conductors or an optical waveguide used to transfer a signal from one location to another.

transmission loss   The total signal loss encountered in transmission through a system.

transmission media   Anything such as wire, coaxial cable, fiber optics, air, or vacuum that is used to carry a signal.

transmitter   With respect to optical fiber cabling, a device that changes electrical signals to optical signals using a laser and associated electronic equipment such as modulators. Among various types of light transmitters are light emitting diodes (LEDs), which are used in lower speed (100 to 256Mbps) applications such as FDDI, and laser diodes, which are used in higher speed applications (622Mbps to 10Gbps) such as ATM and SONET.

transverse modes   In the case of optical fiber cable, light modes across the width of the waveguide.

tree coupler   A passive fiber optic component in which power from one input is distributed to more than two output fibers.

tree topology   A LAN topology similar to linear bus topology, except that tree networks can contain branches with multiple nodes.

triaxial cable   Coaxial cable with an additional outer copper braid insulated from signal carrying conductors. It has a core conductor and two concentric conductive shields. Also called *triax*.

triboelectric noise   Electromagnetic noise generated in a shielded cable due to variations in capacitance between the shield and conductor as the cable is flexed.

trunk   (1) A phone carrier facility such as phone lines between two switches. (2) A telephone communication path or channel between two points, one of them usually being a telephone company facility.

trunk cable   The main cable used in thicknet Ethernet (10Base-5) implementations.

trunk line   A transmission line running between telephone switching offices.

TSB   See *Telecommunications Systems Bulletin*.

T-series connections   A type of digital connection leased from the telephone company or other communications provider. Each T-series connection is rated with a number based on speed. T-1 and T-3 are the most popular. The phone company refers to these as DS-1 and DS-3 circuits, respectively.

TSI   Time slot interchanger.

turn-key agreement   A contractual arrangement in which one party designs and installs a system and "turns over the keys" to another party who will operate the system. A system may also be called a turn-key system if the system is self-contained or simple enough that all the customer has to do is "turn the key."

turnoff time   See *fall time*.

twinaxial cable   A type of communications cable consisting of two center conductors surrounded by an insulating spacer, which is in turn surrounded by a tubular outer conductor (usually a braid, foil, or both). The entire assembly is then covered with an insulating and protective outer layer. Twinaxial is often thought of as dual coaxial cable. Twinaxial cable was commonly used with Wang VS terminals, IBM 5250 terminals on System/3x, and AS/400 minicomputers. Also called *twinax*.

twin lead   A transmission line used for television receiving antennas having two parallel conductors separated by insulating material. Line impedance is determined by the diameter and spacing of the conductors and the insulating material. The conductors are usually 300 ohms.

twisted pair　Two insulated copper wires twisted around each other to reduce induction (thus interference) from one wire to the other. The twists, or lays, are varied in length to reduce the potential for signal interference between pairs. Several sets of twisted-pair wires may be enclosed in a single cable. In cables greater than 25 pairs, the twisted pairs are grouped and bound together in groups of 25 pairs. Twisted pair comes in two varieties: shielded twisted pair (STP) and unshielded twisted pair (UTP). A third variety of twisted-pair cabling, screened twisted-pair (ScTP) cabling, is also becoming popular.

twisted-pair–physical media dependent (TP-PMD)　Technology developed by the ANSI X3T9.5 working group that allows 100Mbps transmission over twisted-pair cable. Also called *CDDI* or *copper distributed data interface.*

Tx　Transmit.

Type 1　150-ohm shielded twisted-pair (STP) cabling conforming to the IBM Cabling System specifications. Two twisted pairs of 22 AWG solid conductors for data communications are enclosed in a braided shield covered with a sheath. Type 1 cable has been tested for operation up to 16MHz. Available in plenum, nonplenum, riser, and outdoor versions.

Type 1A　An enhanced version of IBM Type 1 cable rated for transmission speeds up to 300Mhz. Meets electrical specifications for 150-ohm STP-A cable as documented in the TIA/EIA-568-A standard.

Type 2　150-ohm shielded twisted-pair (STP) cabling conforming to the IBM Cabling System specifications. Type 2 cable is popular with those who insist on following the IBM Cabling System because there are two twisted pairs of 22 AWG solid conductors for data communications that are enclosed in a braided shield. In addition to the shielded pairs, there are four pairs of 22 AWG solid conductors for telephones that are included in the cable jacket but outside the braided shield. Tested for transmission speeds up to 16MHz. Available in plenum and nonplenum versions.

Type 2A　An enhanced version of IBM Type 2 cable rated for transmission speeds up to 300Mhz. Meets electrical specifications for 150-ohm STP-A cable as documented in the TIA/EIA-568-A standard.

Type 3　100-ohm unshielded twisted-pair (UTP) cabling similar to TIA/EIA Category 3 cabling. 22 AWG or 24 AWG conductors with a minimum of two twists per linear foot. Typically four twisted pairs enclosed within cable jacket.

Type 5 100/140-micron optical fiber cable conforming to the IBM Cabling System specifications. Type 5 cable has two optical fibers that are surrounded by strength members and a polyurethane jacket. There is also an IBM Type 5J that is a 50/125-micron version defined for use in Japan.

Type 6 150-ohm shielded twisted-pair (STP) cabling that conforms to the IBM Cabling System specifications. Two twisted pairs of 26 AWG stranded conductors for data communications. Flexible for use in making patch cables. Tested for operation up to 16MHz. Available in nonplenum version only.

Type 6A An enhanced version of IBM Type 6 cable rated for transmission speeds up to 300Mhz. Meets electrical specifications for 150-ohm STP-A cable as documented in the TIA/EIA-568-A standard.

Type 8 150-ohm under-carpet cable conforming to the IBM Cabling System specifications. Two individually shielded parallel pairs of 26 AWG solid conductors for data communications. The cable includes "ramped wings" to make it less visible when installed under carpeting. Tested for transmission speeds up to 16MHz. Type 8 cable is not very commonly used.

Type 9 150-ohm shielded twisted-pair (STP) cabling that conforms to the IBM Cabling System specifications. A plenum-rated cable with two twisted pairs of 26 AWG solid or stranded conductors for data communications enclosed in a braided shield covered with a sheath. Tested for transmission speeds up to 16MHz.

Type 9A An enhanced version of IBM Type 9 cable rated for transmission speeds up to 300MHz. Meets electrical specifications for 150-ohm STP-A cable documented in the TIA/EIA-568-A standard.

U

UL See *Underwriters Laboratories, Inc.*

ultraviolet The electromagnetic waves invisible to the human eye with wavelengths between 10nm and 400nm.

unbalanced line A transmission line in which voltages on the two conductors are unequal with respect to ground; one of the conductors is generally connected to a ground point. An example of an unbalanced line is a coaxial cable. This is the opposite of a balanced line or balanced cable.

underground cable Cable that is designed to be placed beneath the surface of the ground in ducts or conduit. Underground cable is not necessarily intended for direct burial in the ground.

Underwriters Laboratories, Inc. (UL)
A privately owned company that tests to make sure that products meet safety standards. UL also administers a program for the certification of Category-rated cable with respect to flame ratings. See Chapter 4 for more information on Underwriters Laboratories.

uniformity The maximum insertion loss difference between ports of a coupler.

uninterruptible power supply (UPS)
A natural line conditioner that uses a battery and power inverter to run the computer equipment that plugs into it. The battery charger continuously charges the battery. The battery charger is the only thing that runs off line voltage. During a power problem, the battery charger stops operating, and the equipment continues to run off of the battery.

Universal Service Order Code (USOC)
Developed by AT&T/the Bell System, the Universal Service Order Code (pronounced "U-sock") identifies a particular service, device, or connector wiring pattern. Often used to refer to an old cable color-coding scheme that was current when USOC codes

were in use. USOC is not used in wiring LAN connections and is not supported by current standards due to the fact that high crosstalk is exhibited at higher frequencies. See Chapter 9 for more information.

unmated Optical fiber connectors in a system whose end-faces are not in contact with another connector, resulting in a fiber that is launching light from the surface of the glass into air. Also called *unterminated* or *open*.

unshielded twisted pair (UTP)
Unshielded twisted-pair (UTP) cable consists of multiple pairs of copper wire where each wire pair is twisted around one another between two or more times per foot (higher grade UTP cable can have more than 20 twists per foot). The twists serve to cancel out electromagnetic interference that the transmission of electrical signal through the pairs generates. An overall jacket made of some type of plastic then surrounds the individual twisted pairs. The most common UTP cables used in business environments are the four-pair, 50-ohm UTP cables. Twisted-pair cabling includes no shielding. UTP most often refers to the 100-ohm Categories 3, 4, and 5 cables specified in the TIA/EIA 568-A standard.

UPS See *uninterruptible power supply.*

USOC See *Universal Service Order Code.*

UTP   See *unshielded twisted pair*.

V

V   Symbol for *volt*.

VA   See *volt ampere*.

vampire tap   See *tap*.

VCSE   Vertical cavity emitting surface.

VCTV   Viewer-controlled TV.

velocity of propagation   The transmission speed of electrical energy in a length of cable compared to speed in free space. Usually expressed as a percentage. Test devices use velocity of propagation to measure a signal's transit time and thereby calculate the cable's length. See also *nominal velocity of propagation (NVP)*.

vertical equalizer   A part of the telephone company's central office grounding system that equalizes the electrical potential from one floor to the next.

vertical trough   A jumper pathway that is provided between adjacent bays or modules in a frame, which allows jumpers to run vertically on the frame from one panel location to another or between a panel and the upper or lower express trough.

very high frequency (VHF)   Frequency band extending from 30MHz to 300MHz.

very low frequency (VLF)   Frequency band extending from 10KHz to 30KHz.

VGM   Voice-grade media. See *voice-grade*.

VHDSL   Very high digital subscriber line.

VHF   See *very high frequency*.

video   A signal which contains visual information, such as a picture in a television system.

videoconferencing   The act of conducting conferences via a video telecommunications system, local area network, or wide area network.

videophone   A telephonelike device that provides a picture as well as sound.

visible light   Electromagnetic radiation visible to the human eye at wavelengths between 400nm and 700nm.

VLF See *very low frequency*.

VOD Video on demand.

voice circuit A telephone company circuit capable of carrying one telephone conversation. The voice circuit is the standard unit in which telecommunications capacity is counted. The U.S. analog equivalent is 4KHz. The digital equivalent is 56Kbps in the U.S. and 64Kbps in Europe. In the U.S., the Federal Communications Commission restricts the maximum data rate on a voice circuit to 53Kbps.

voice-grade A term used for twisted-pair cable used in telephone systems to carry voice signals. Usually Category 3 or lower cable, though voice signals can be carried on cables that are higher than Category 3.

volt A unit of expression for electrical potential or potential difference. Abbreviated by *V*.

voltage drop The voltage developed across a component by the current flow through the resistance of the component.

volt ampere (VA) A designation of power in terms of voltage and current.

VSB Vestigial sideband.

W

W (1) Symbol for *watt* or *wattage*. (2) Abbreviation for *white* when used in conjunction with twisted-pair cable color codes; may also be "Wh."

WAN See *wide area network*.

watt A unit of electrical power.

waveform A graphical representation of the amplitude of a signal over time.

waveguide A structure that guides electromagnetic waves along their length. The core fiber in an optical fiber cable is an optical waveguide.

waveguide couplers A connection in which light is transferred between planar waveguides.

waveguide dispersion That part of the chromatic dispersion resulting from the different speeds at which light travels in the core and cladding of a single-mode fiber. For the most part, this deals with the fiber as a waveguide structure.

waveguide scattering   The variations caused by subtle differences in the geometry and fiber index profile of an optical fiber.

wavelength   With respect to optical fiber communications, the distance an electromagnetic wave travels in the time it takes to oscillate through a complete cycle. This distance is the distance between successive peaks or nodes of a wave; wavelengths of light are measured in nanometers or micrometers.

wavelength division multiplexers   A multiplexing transmission technique in which separate optical channels that are distinguished by their wavelength are multiplexed onto a single optical fiber for transmission.

wavelength division multiplexing (WDM)   Multiplexing technique whereby signals are multiplexed by transmitting them at different wavelengths through the same optical fiber cable. See also *frequency division multiplexing*.

wavelength isolation   A wave division multiplexer's isolation of a light signal from the unwanted optical channels in the desired optical channel.

wavelength variance   The variation in an optical parameter caused by a change in the operating wavelength.

webbed conductors   A manufacturing process that binds the conductor insulation of the wire pairs of an unshielded twisted-pair cable.

WIC   Wavelength independent coupler.

wide area network (WAN)   A network that crosses local, regional, and international boundaries. Some types of WAN technology such as a leased-line, ATM, or frame relay connect local area networks (LANs) together to form WANs.

wire center   (1) Another name for a wiring or telecommunications closet. (2) A telephone company building where all local telephone cables converge for service by telephone switching systems. Also called *central office* or *exchange center*.

wire cross-connect   A piece of equipment or location at which twisted-pair cabling is terminated to permit reconnection, testing, and rearrangement. Cross-connects are usually located in equipment rooms and telecommunications closets and are used to connect horizontal cable to backbone cable. Wire cross-connects typically use a 66- or 110- block. These blocks use jumpers to connect the horizontal portion of the block to the backbone portion of the block.

wire fault   A break in a segment or cable that causes an error. A wire fault might also be caused by a break in the cable's shield.

wiring closet   See *telecommunications closet*.

work area   The area where horizontal cabling is connected to the work area equipment by means of a telecommunications outlet. A telecommunications outlet serves a station or desk. See also *work area telecommunications outlet*.

work area cable   A cable used to connect equipment to the telecommunications outlet in the user work area. Sometimes called a *patch cable* or *patch cord*, work area cables are considered to be outside the scope of structured cabling standards.

work area telecommunications outlet Sometimes called a *wall plate*, a connecting device located in a work or user area where the horizontal cabling is terminated. A work area telecommunications outlet provides connectivity for work area patch cables, which in turn connect to end-user equipment such as computers or telephones. The telecommunications outlet can be recessed in the wall, mounted on the wall or floorboard, or recessed in the floor or a floor monument.

workgroup   A collection of workstations and servers on a LAN that are designated to communicate and exchange data with one another.

workstation   A computer connected to a network at which users interact with software stored on the network. Also called a *PC (personal computer)*, *network node*, or *host*.

X

X   (1) Symbol for reactance. (2) Symbol often used on wiring diagrams to represent a cross-connect.

***x*DSL**   A generic description for the different DSL technologies such as ADSL, HDSL, RADSL. See also *digital subscriber line*.

XTC   An optical fiber connector developed by OFTI; not in general use.

Y

Y-coupler   In fiber optics, a variation on the T-coupler, where input light is split between two channels that branch out like a "Y" from the input

Y-splice   Used to bridge a circuit or connection to another location. The Y-splice is a direct tap of a pair of wires onto another pair of wires.

Z

Z   Symbol for impedance.

zero dispersion slope   In single-mode fiber, the chromatic dispersion slope at the fiber's zero dispersion wavelength.

zero dispersion wavelength   In single-mode fiber, the wavelength where waveguide dispersion cancels out material dispersion and total chromatic dispersion is zero. This arises when waveguide dispersion cancels out material dispersion.

Cabling Resources

This appendix contains information about vendor resources, Internet sites, books, publications, and other tools that may be useful when learning more about cabling. These resources are generally listed in order of our favorites and the ones that we find most useful.

Informational Internet Resources

The Internet is a wonderful thing, both because it enables speedy communication and because there is so much valuable information out there. Without the Internet, projects such as this book would be much lengthier, but luckily there are a lot of dedicated individuals out there providing Web sites that are chock-full of standards information, FAQs, tutorials, and more. These people put a tremendous amount of work into their sites. With that said, we should also issue a few words of caution: Just because it is on the Internet does not mean it is true. We found the sites listed here to be reliable and trustworthy sources of information.

wiring.com

Our favorite cabling site on the Internet is www.wiring.com. From here you can link to information on network, electrical, home, cable TV, and alarm wiring. Janice Boothe, RCCD, maintains this Web site, which has technical information, links to white papers, product reviews, current cabling news, and common pinouts. Best of all, there is a cabling Q&A where you can post questions, read other people's questions, and even offer your own answers to others' queries. This site should be bookmarked in every cable professional's Web browser.

Engineering Notebook for Communication Cables

David Barnett, RCDD, has 18 years of experience in the engineering and marketing of communication cables and wires. As a hobby, he maintains the Engineering Notebook for Communication Cables site at home1.gte.net/res025bi/index.htm. The site is geared toward wiring for the home and the SOHO (small office, home office), but even professional cable installers will find useful information here. This site has a lot of great information on color-coding, NEC flame ratings, cabling categories, codes, and residential wiring basics. (David's insight, knowledge, and critical eye were also indispensable in the development of this book.)

comp.dcom.cabling

If you have newsreader software (such as Outlook Express), point your news-reader to the USENET newsgroup comp.dcom.cabling. This interactive forum has a plethora of information. You can post your own questions, respond to others' questions, or just read the existing postings and learn from them. This particular forum has a number of dedicated and knowledgeable individuals who monitor it and try to assist everyone who posts queries.

The Cabling News Group FAQ

If you begin to frequent the comp.dcom.cabling newsgroup, you will see references to "the FAQ," the group's list of frequently asked questions. Before posting to this newsgroup, it is considered good forum etiquette to read the FAQ to make sure your question has not been previously asked. The FAQ can be found on the Internet at netman.cit.buffalo.edu/FAQs/cabling.faq.

whatis

whatis is one of our favorite reference sites on the Internet; their URL is www.whatis .com. It contains over 2,000 commonly used computer and telecommunications terms and seems to grow every day. Also included at this reference site is the word of the day, information for the beginner, concepts, and book recommendations.

CableDesign.com

We discovered www.cable-design.com during the research phase of this book and have found it to be a valuable source for information, current news, references, documents, and more.

TIA Online

The Telecommunication Industry Association's Web site is found at www.tiaonline .org. This Web site is the place to go for updated information on the TIA committee meetings, current proposals and standards, and current events; it also includes a tremendous glossary and more.

TechFest

Everything you ever wanted to know about networking? Well, pretty close. There is a huge amount of information on LANs, WANs, cabling, protocols, switching, networking standards, ATM, and more at www.techfest.com/networking/.

TechEncyclopedia

CMP's TechWeb sponsors the TechEncyclopedia. This thorough listing of over 13,000 computer- and technology-related terms can be found at www.techweb .com/encyclopedia.

Residential Cable System

Thinking about wiring your home or SOHO (small office, home office) for the future? Here is the first place on the Web that you should stop. Design tips, FAQs, installation tips, products, and more can be found on this useful and relevant Web site at www.residentialcabling.com.

Global Technologies, Inc.

Global Technologies has a great technical information section to their Web site (www.globaltec.com/tech.htm) that includes pinout diagrams, standards information, networking basics, organization information, wiring diagrams, and more.

The Telecommunications Corner

The Telecommunications Corner is a great technical reference site. It contains information about telecommunications history, networking, switching, modulation, and data transmission. Find it on the Web at telecom.tbi.net/index.html.

Cabletesting.Com

This is a great site to visit to learn more about cable testing, the progress of the standards committees, and more. Microtest (www.microtest.com) sponsors the site; they are one of the leading manufacturers of cable testing and certification tools. The cable testing site can be found at www.cabletesting.com.

National Electrical Code Internet Connection

This site is operated by Mike Holt (better known among electrical and data cabling professionals as Mr. Code). Mike Holt is *the* expert on the National Electrical Code. He gives excellent seminars around the world. Visit his site for more information on the National Electrical Code, some really interesting stories from people in the field, his free e-mail newsletter, and more. Mr. Holt has also written a number of books on how to interpret and work with the National Electrical Code; professional electricians and data communications designers should own his book on the 1999 NEC. The site can be found at `www.mikeholt.com`.

Charles Spurgeon's Ethernet Web Site

This is the first place on the Internet we go for information on Ethernet, Fast Ethernet, and Gigabit Ethernet. This site can be found at `www.ots.utexas.edu/ethernet/ethernet.html`. There is great information here about various Ethernet technologies, help for planning cabling for Ethernet, information about Ethernet analyzing software, FAQs, technical papers, a history of Ethernet, and troubleshooting information. On the home page is a neat drawing of Ethernet that was done by Bob Metcalfe, the original designer of Ethernet.

Federal Standard 1037C: Glossary of Telecommunications Terms

Federal Standard 1037C is one of the most thorough Internet sites you can use for finding technology-related terms. This site is sponsored by the U.S. National Communications System Technology and Standards Division and can be found at `ntia.its.bldrdoc.gov/fs-1037`.

Cable Topics

Concise with useful information and links related to cabling, this site serves as a great starter for people looking for an overview of cabling. It can be found at `www.geekboy.net/services/tech/cable/cable.html`.

Twisted-Pair Ethernet

This site has a great overview for cabling an Ethernet network; much of the information on this site also applies to 100Base-T networks. This site can be found at `www.wown.com/j_helmig/thisted.htm`.

Networking Hardware Course Notes

While researching material for this book, we stumbled across this neat assemblage of notes for a networking course at Del Mar College. It includes good information on network architectures, cabling, and data transfers. The site can be found at www.delmar.edu/Courses/ITNW2313.

Directory for WAN, LAN, and ATM Protocols

Though not specifically related to cabling, we found a great site for learning more about WAN, LAN, and ATM protocols. The site includes protocol references and physical network interfaces; of particular interest were pinouts for different WAN interface technologies. This site can be found at protocols.com/protoc.htm.

Webopedia: Online Computer Dictionary for Internet Terms and Technical Support

Another great site for finding technology-related terms is Webopedia. This online dictionary has a thorough computer dictionary, technology-related news, and a listing of the top terms. It can be found at Webopedia.internet.com.

Books, Publications, and Videos

There are a number of books and videos that you may wish to own as part of your professional library. In addition, two publications that we highly recommend are listed in this section.

Cabling Business Magazine

Cabling Business Magazine is a monthly magazine that covers copper and fiber optic cabling for voice, data, and imaging. They have monthly features written by some of the leaders in the industry, a stock market watch, how-to columns, and more. *Cabling Business Magazine* also offers seminars and classes on a variety of telecommunications topics. For more information on the magazine or information on a free subscription to qualified subscribers, check them out on the Web at www.cablingbusiness.com.

Cabling Installation and Maintenance

Cabling Installation and Maintenance is a monthly magazine published by Pennwell. This magazine has monthly columns including Q&A, Standards Watch, and more. Their Web site is www.cable-install.com; it has links to contractors, a buyers' guide, a calendar of events, and an article archive. Subscriptions are free to qualified subscribers.

Cabling Installation and Maintenance Tips and Videos

Cable Installation and Maintenance (CI&M) magazine publishes a book of installation tips and best practices contributed by cabling professionals that all professional installers should own and read. Two more must-haves for cabling professionals are *CI&M*'s *Cable Pulling* video series and their *Installer Tips* video. These may be purchased through *CI&M*'s Web site at www.cable-install.com (click on the Training Resources link).

Newton's Telecom Dictionary by Harry Newton

This 900-page book is a guide to the world of modern data and voice telecommunications terms. It's not easy to keep up with all the terms, acronyms, and concepts today, but this book is a great start. Anyone who owns one will tell you it is indispensable. It is available through most bookstores.

Premises Network Online

This virtual community is designed for people who work with premises cabling. It includes a buyers' guide and allows you to submit an RFQ/RFP, respond to an RFQ/RFP, search for jobs, and purchase used equipment and products in their online marketplace. They can be found at www.premisesnetworks.com.

Building Your Own High-Tech Small Office by Robert Richardson

This book is a great resource for those wanting to run their business in an efficient and high-tech manner. The author discusses everything from Internet connections to office design and software and hardware choices, as well as how to best utilize them. The book is available through most bookstores. The author has developed a Web site to provide ongoing assistance to readers, which can be found at www.smallofficetech.com.

BICSI's *Telecommunications Distribution Methods* and *Cabling Installation Manuals*

The Building Industry Consulting Services International's *Telecommunications Distribution Methods* (TDM) and *Cabling Installation* manuals are great study guides for the RCDD certification and excellent resources for professional cable installers. Discounts are available for BICSI members for these publications on the BICSI Web site at www.bicsi.org.

Understanding the National Electrical Code (3rd Edition) by Mike Holt and Charles Michael Holt

Electricians, engineers, and telecommunications designers need to have a good understanding of the National Electrical Code. This book helps to give you a thorough understanding of the NEC's requirements by explaining the requirements of the NEC's sections in easy-to-understand language. Mike Holt also has a new book called *Technology Wiring—Holt's Illustrated Guide* that explains wiring from the perspective of the NEC. These books are available from almost any bookstore.

TIA/EIA-568-A Commercial Building Telecommunication Cabling Standard

The TIA/EIA-568-A standard is the definitive guide to commercial building cabling. All professional cable designers and installers should own or have access to this standards document. Look for an updated version of the standards near fall 2000. It can be purchased online through Global Engineering Documents at global.ihs.com.

Vendors and Manufacturers

To say that there are a lot of manufacturers and vendors that handle telecommunications and cabling products would be a bit of an understatement. The following is a list of vendors and manufacturers that we have found to provide not only good products, but also good service and information.

The Siemon Company

Telecommunications vendor The Siemon Company has a great Web site, which includes technical references, standards information, an online catalog, white papers, and frequently asked questions. If you visit this site, order their catalog— it is one of the best telecommunications catalogs in the industry. Their site can be found at www.siemon.com.

MilesTek, Inc.

MilesTek has one of the neatest sites and is one of the easiest companies on the Internet to work with for purchasing cabling supplies and tools. They also have a good catalog and helpful people on the ordering side if you are not quite ready for online commerce. They sell cabling supplies, tools, cable, components, connectors, and more. Their site also has good information on standards, cabling, and telecommunications. You can find them on the Internet at www.milestek.com.

IDEAL DataComm

IDEAL DataComm is a leading supplier of cabling and wiring tools and supplies. If you have handled any cabling tools, you have probably used one of theirs. Their Web site has a lot of useful information about the tools that they sell, as well as tips and tricks for premises cabling and electrical wiring. Their customer service is good and the company is very helpful. Their Web site is at www.idealindustries.com.

Ortronics

Manufacturer Ortronics maintains one of our favorite Web sites and catalogs. Ortronics also offers training and a certified installer program. Their catalog is easy to understand and follow. You can find them on the Internet at www.ortronics.com.

Superior Essex

We were surprised to learn that Superior Essex is one of the largest manufacturers of premises, outside plant, and fiber optic cable in the world. They not only manufacture cable labeled as Superior Essex, but also for many other vendors as well. Their Web site has excellent information pertaining to copper and fiber cabling as well as technical specifications. Visit it at www.superioressex.com.

Jensen Tools

Jensen Tools has a huge variety of tools, tool kits, and other products for the computer and telecommunications professional. Visit their Web site at www.jensentools.com and order their catalog.

Lucent SYSTIMAX SCS

To learn more about the Lucent SYSTIMAX SCS (Structured Cabling System), the best place to start is with the source. Lucent designs and installs the SYSTIMAX SCS system to meet and exceed current cabling performance standards; they continue to remain compatible with existing technologies. You can find the SYSTIMAX home page at www.lucent.com/systimax.

Erico

Erico is a leading manufacturer of electrical products, including the CADDY system of fastening and fixing solutions. These products help you to better organize and run cabling. Visit Erico on the Internet at www.erico.com and check out the Fastening and Fixing section of their Web site.

Berk-Tek

Cable manufacturer and supplier Berk-Tek has a great Web site that includes a technical section with standards information, white papers, and industry standards. You can find it at www.berktek.com.

Microtest

Microtest is one of the world's leading manufacturers of cabling testing equipment. Their products include the immensely popular (and easy to use!) Penta-Scanner. Visit them on the Internet at www.microtest.com.

Amp

Amp is the world leader in construction of connectors. Their online catalog has over 100,000 items. They make connectors for many industries including the networking and telecommunications industry. You can find them on the Internet at www.amp.com.

Panduit

Panduit is a leading supplier of telecommunications products and tools. Their Web site offers online ordering and information about their products. Visit them at `www.panduit.com`.

Anixter

Telecommunications product vendor Anixter has a great Web site that includes a lot of relevant information about cabling, standards, and white papers, as well as an online catalog. They can be found on the Internet at `www.anixter.com`.

Registered Communications and Distribution Designer (RCDD) Certification

Certification programs are all the rage in the technology industry. The cabling business is no exception. As with all industry certifications, an organization has to be responsible for the certification program, manage the testing, and set the quality bar. BICSI (Building Industry Consulting Services International) is a professional organization devoted to promoting standards for the design and installation of communications systems. BICSI is instrumental in the provision of guidelines, training, and professional certification of knowledge and experience related to our communication infrastructure.

The breakup and divestiture of the Bell system in 1984 created a void of expertise where communication system design and deployment was concerned. Not only was there no longer a single national entity governing standard practices, many of the old-timers (the ones who really knew what worked—*and why*) left the baby Bells during, and shortly following, the divestiture period.

BICSI recognized the need to acknowledge and certify cabling professionals; it stepped up to fill the void with a two-pronged effort. First, BICSI developed and published the *TDMM* (*Telecommunications Distribution Methods Manual*), a compendium of guidelines, standards, and best practices for the engineering of a communications system. Second, it initiated the RCDD (Registered Communications Distribution Designer) accreditation program to establish a benchmark of expertise for the industry.

As of mid-2000, BICSI has a membership exceeding 17,000 worldwide. Over 5,000 of these members have achieved the professional accreditation of Registered Communications Distribution Designer. The designation of RCDD is not awarded lightly. It takes knowledge, experience, and a lot of hard work to qualify to have those four letters follow your name on your business card and stationery.

Today, the RCDD is a recognized standard of excellence and professionalism within the communications industry. Increasingly, architects and building management consortia specify that an RCDD must perform the design of a building project's low voltage systems: video, security, and communications. Often, the contractor awarded the installation work is required to have an RCDD either on staff or as a direct supervisor of the work performed. In some companies, obtaining your RCDD is a condition of employment if you are in technical sales or technical support. As a result, RCDDs are very much in demand in the job market. All of these things are pretty compelling reasons to become an RCDD if you are serious about working in the field of communications infrastructure.

So, how do you get there? There are three stages:

1. Apply and be accepted as a candidate for the designation of RCDD.

2. Successfully pass the stringent RCDD exam.

3. Maintain your accreditation through continuing membership and education.

Now let's look at what's involved in each stage.

Apply and Be Accepted as a Candidate for the Designation of RCDD

First of all, you must be a member of BICSI before you can apply to become an RCDD. This requires a nominal annual membership fee, currently $100 for an individual. (It should be noted that BICSI is a nonprofit organization and all their fees are very reasonable compared to other professional organizations of the same caliber.)

NOTE   You can find out more about membership in BICSI by visiting their Web site at www.bicsi.org.

Next, you must submit your qualifications to become an RCDD. BICSI doesn't let just anyone sit for the exam. The applicant must be a bona fide member of the industry. This is part of the quality control that elevates the RCDD to an icon of the industry. BICSI requires that you have a minimum of two years of system design experience. You establish this by doing the following:

- Filling out an application, much as if you were applying for employment. You list work experience, educational background, and any awards, accomplishments, or other professional credentials you may have.

- Supplying three letters of reference:

  - One letter from your current employer detailing your involvement in design activities

  - One from a client for whom you have performed design work

- One personal reference touting you as a fine human being and an all-around swell person

- Sending a nonrefundable application fee of $100 and waiting a couple of weeks to see if you are accepted as a candidate to sit for the exam.

NOTE   BICSI members, RCDD candidates, and those who have written letters of reference for colleagues and employees will attest to the fact that BICSI diligently follows up these letters of reference to establish their legitimacy.

Successfully Pass the Stringent RCDD Exam

OK, you've been accepted, now what? Well, this is the hard (some would say *grueling*) part. You have to study for and take the RCDD examination. The RCDD exam consists of 280 multiple choice questions that are selected randomly from a bank of over 2,500 questions. Each copy of the exam is unique. It is given during a strictly proctored 3½-hour session. To be admitted to the test room, you must show a photo ID.

Everything is done using sealed envelopes and a personal test code number that's assigned to you. It is a closed-book test, and no calculators or reference materials are permitted in the test room. You won't be told your score—only that you either passed or failed. These procedures may sound hokey and unnecessary, but in fact, they ensure the integrity of the RCDD title by eliminating the possibility of cheating or favoritism and putting all RCDDs on level ground.

The exam is difficult. It takes a grade of 78 percent to pass, meaning you can miss only 61 of the 280 questions. Only 30 to 40 percent of those who take the test pass the first time. BICSI allows you to retake the test up to three times within one year. If, after that third attempt, you still don't pass, you must wait a full year and then begin the application process again.

The potential test questions all come directly from the *TDMM* (*Telecommunications Distribution Methods Manual*). This is a very important point, and you will fail if you don't take it to heart. *Do not* answer questions from your own experience or based on reference material other than the *TDMM*. The *TDMM* is the bible as far as the RCDD exam is concerned, and *you should only respond to test questions with answers from the* TDMM, regardless of whether or not you agree. RCDDs are convinced that there are two reasons for that 60 to 70 percent first-time failure rate. The first is that people come to the test believing their own experience and know-how should supercede what BICSI teaches in the *TDMM*; the second is that they simply don't study the *TDMM* enough.

For an RCDD candidate with two years of experience and heavy specialization in a few areas of communication system distribution design, BICSI recommends the following study regimen prior to sitting for the exam:

- Study the *TDMM* for 50 hours.

- Attend the five-day BICSI DD102 distribution system design course.

- Attend the 2½-day BICSI DD101 distribution system review course immediately prior to the exam.

NOTE   More information on the BICSI classes can be found on BICSI's Web site at www.bicsi.org.

More extensive experience over a broader range of subjects reduces the number of hours required in study and can eliminate the need for the distribution design courses. However, we recommend the courses to anyone that even slightly doubts their ability to pass the exam. Who knows, even skilled professionals may learn a few new things in the process.

Here's the regimen successful candidates have used in the past. Almost everyone who followed this course of study passed the RCDD test on the first try, which is a pretty good endorsement.

- Study the *TDMM* as much as possible prior to any course work.

- Attend the BICSI DD102 class. (Note: In general, first-time test takers who attend this class as administered by BICSI raise their chances of passing significantly. Some instructor teams have 70 percent or better first-time pass rates for students in their classes.)

- Participate in study groups in the evenings during the DD102 class. Studying and quizzing each other using the *TDMM* or flash cards greatly reinforces the learning and memorization required to pass the exam.

- Purchase and use one of the RCDD practice test packages available from third-party vendors. One such third-party practice exam is from NET CBT (formerly Clark Technology Group); it is computerized test software. They can be found on the Internet at www.netcbt.com. Purchase at least two practice tests. Then, begin testing yourself with one version. Use it over and over, interweaving it with study periods. When you are consistently achieving above 90 percent correct on the first practice test, switch to the other and follow the same procedure. These tests are also a great adjunct to the study group if you use them interactively and answer by panel instead of by individual. Discuss your answers with the group until you all agree why the answer is right or wrong.

- Take the RCDD exam immediately following the DD102 course. There is some controversy over this approach. Some think it is better to wait, let the course material sink in, then take the DD101 as a refresher. Many successful candidates have gone full steam ahead right into the exam and been successful.

TIP

Assuming you're going for broke directly from DD102 into the exam, your brain is packed to bursting with info from the *TDMM*. The most fragile items are the numerous tables that you've memorized on information like the number and size of conduits required to service a building of *x* square feet. These tables don't lend themselves to logical sequence or mnemonic clues. The morning of the exam, you won't want to talk to anyone or have anyone talk to you for fear that you'll lose concentration and these delicate matrices will collapse like a house of cards. Get your test packet, tear it open, and dump your brain onto the back of the test. Then, start the exam.

The exam is offered at each BICSI conference. Three of these are held each year in the U.S., with several others held in other parts of the world. The exam is also offered immediately following BICSI courses such as the DD101 and DD102. In addition, the exam is scheduled periodically in varying locations across the U.S. Finally, special proctoring of the exam can be scheduled for a special-purpose group, such as when a company processes a large number of RCDD candidates at the same time. Usually, this is held in conjunction with a specially scheduled design course as well.

One interesting fact about the exam: BICSI recognizes that neither the *TDMM* nor the exam is absolutely infallible. The *TDMM* has different sections written by different individuals. In a few cases, contradictory information is given. There are also a few buggy questions in the question bank (although BICSI works hard to weed these out).

If you think you've encountered one of these contradictory or erroneous questions, answer it as best you're able but make a note by the question to refer to the back of the test. There, you are allowed to challenge the question by providing an explanation of why you believe the question to be faulty. It's best if you can quote chapter and paragraph numbers for the conflicting or bad info (this is not far-fetched, considering the preparation you'll have done). If you really know your stuff, you will probably catch a buggy question. Though one question probably won't make a difference if you are truly ready to take the test, it could swing the balance if your score is marginal.

The test costs $100 each and every time you take it. This is in addition to the membership fee and RCDD application fee you've already paid.

TIP

Don't rely completely on the practice tests to memorize potential types of questions. Learn the material and concepts and then use the tests to ensure that you are ready. Memorizing test types of questions will only be a disservice to you and the industry.

Maintain Your Accreditation through Continuing Membership and Education

Now that you've passed (congratulations!), you can't just sit back and coast. The world of communications changes very rapidly. BICSI recognizes that for RCDDs to be truly effective in servicing clients, they must keep up with ever-changing standards and best practices.

Your RCDD designation is awarded for a three-year period. During those three years you must maintain your BICSI membership. *Don't let your membership lapse, or you'll have to sit for the exam again.* (Yikes!)

You must also accumulate a minimum of 45 Continuing Education Credits (CECs). You can accomplish this by attending more BICSI or third-party education courses (check with the BICSI office to see if they are sanctioned for CECs) or by attending BICSI's scheduled technical conferences.

A BICSI conference is worth 15 CECs. You must attend at least one during your three-year period as an RCDD. By attending one each year, you accumulate all the CECs you need for renewal of your RCDD accreditation.

A BICSI conference is packed with presentations, workshops, or seminars that will keep you up to date on what's happening in your industry. Virtually everyone has an update on what's happening in the industry standard development committees, such as the committee that works on TIA/EIA 568-A. New developments in areas such as cable performance, connectors, electronics, fiber versus twisted pair, and changes to the NEC are all topics of regular discussion. In addition, information on how to better serve your customers and run your business is often provided. In addition to all this, there are nightly receptions that allow you to network with other industry professionals and review the offerings of vendors who are mainstays of the communications market.

Check Out BICSI and the RCDD Program for Yourself

Visit the BICSI Web site at www.bicsi.org for additional information on the organization and the RCDD program. You can download applications, view membership lists, review presentations made at prior BICSI conferences, read status reports from the TIA working groups involved in cabling standards, and much more.

Home Cabling: Wiring Your Home for Now and the Future

- Home Computing Facts and Trends

- Structured Cabling for the Home

- Picking Equipment for Home Cabling

In case you haven't noticed, you're standing knee-deep in the future of data interchange. High-speed, inexpensive computers, high-bandwidth network technologies, and the just-plain-old-usefulness of the Internet are advancing faster than most of us can assimilate and react to. Corporations, to a large degree, are keeping up when it comes to providing LAN and Internet functionality for their employees.

The home, however, is the last bastion of low-end technology for data exchange. Even the home you just built may only have voice-grade wiring in it—and it may not even support more than one phone line. Category 5 wiring may be all the buzz in new houses above a certain price point, but few contractors know how to properly install and terminate it.

If cable is improperly pulled or terminated, it will be useless for data communications. You can quickly convert Category 5 to Category 1 by stretching it, crimping it, daisy-chaining it, bridge tapping, or using low-quality connectors.

Many homes constructed today simply do not have enough outlets to meet the demands of a modern family. If your home builder wired your home for a typical number of outlets, i.e., one in the master bedroom, one in the kitchen, maybe one in the family room, you won't have enough connection points to take advantage of a number of in-home systems that are rapidly being adopted.

In the past few years, the concept of the "smart home" has begun to emerge. More and more small businesses are being run from homes, and more and more people are working at their homes, requiring them to install more than one personal computer at home and home automation appliances. A home that is wired to support voice, video, and data networking is becoming a valuable asset.

KEY TERM   **SOHO (small office, home office)**   A *SOHO* is a small office or home office. The trend towards having offices at home is driving the need for more sophisticated cabling.

Home Computing Facts and Trends

The growth of the home computer over the past few years is staggering. The growth of the Internet and the use of home computers has far outpaced similar growth patterns of telephone or VCR usage. Here are some facts relating to the use of home computers as of the end of 1999:

- 57 percent of single-family households own PCs.

- 18 percent of single-family households contain two or more PCs.

- 30 percent of single-family households have access to the Internet.

- 30 percent of the workforce works at home at least part-time.

- The "Internet appliance" has arrived. Your TV and refrigerator can now connect directly to the Internet for programming guides, VCR control, and automated shopping.

These trends are just at the beginning of their growth curves, and home networks and smart appliances will be common within five years (probably less, if the rapid adoption of the Internet is any indicator).

In-home networks? Smart appliances? Connection points located conveniently throughout the house? Bah, humbug! Ridiculous frivolities! Oh, yeah? Well, so were home air conditioning, dishwashers, color TV, and cable or satellite TV when they were introduced. Now they are almost necessities for most people in the U.S.

Imagine buying a house and then discovering that you can't install an air conditioner, or that the wiring isn't adequate for running a dishwasher. A similar situation exists for the communication wiring in many homes in the U.S. today when it comes to having a network, multiple phone lines, or even connecting to the Internet at decent speeds via a modem.

Structured Residential Cabling

The FCC has recognized some of the problems associated with residential cabling and, on February 15, 2000, put into effect a requirement that voice and data wiring in new residential structures should be a minimum of Category 3 UTP. However, enforcement will still be an issue. The FCC ruling only addresses part of the problem and doesn't address the need for flexible, centrally controlled access to the wiring in your home.

What's the rest of the answer for residences? Just as in the commercial, corporate world, the answer is structured cabling. A cabling system that is distributed throughout the building, with every connection point leading back to a central location where systems and access to outside services are connected, is what works.

Enter ANSI/TIA/EIA-570-A, or the Residential Telecommunications Cabling Standard. The latest revision was published in October 1999, and it details the requirements for low-voltage cabling systems in single and multitenant residences. Included in the TIA/EIA-570-A standard are definitions for the two grades of residential cabling installations that are shown in Table D.1.

TABLE D.1: Grades of Residential Cabling

Installation Grade	Four-Pair UTP	75-ohm	Fiber Optic
1	Category 3*	RG-6	Not included
2	Category 5**	RG-6	Two-strand multimode optical fiber

*Category 5 cable recommended

**Category 5e cable recommended

For both grades of installation, the following guidelines shall apply to cabling and communication services providers:

- Providers, such as a phone company or CATV (cable TV) company, bring service to the exterior of the house. This is the demarcation point, or the location at which ownership of the infrastructure (wiring and connections) transfers to you, the homeowner.

- From the demarcation point, a cable brings the service into a central distribution device installed inside the residence. The distribution device consists of a cross-connect device of some sort so that incoming service can be transferred to the horizontal wiring that runs to wall outlets. The distribution device provides a flexible method of distributing service to desired locations throughout the house.

- From the distribution device, cables are run to each wall outlet on a one-to-one basis. Outlets are never connected in series (daisy-chained). This is referred to as *star*, or *home-run*, wiring.

- At a minimum, one outlet is required in the kitchen, each bedroom, family/great room, and den/study. In addition, one outlet is required in any wall with an unbroken space of 12 feet or more. Additional outlets should be added so that no point on the floor of the room is more than 25 feet from an outlet. Note that these minimum outlet requirements refer to UTP, coax, and fiber optic cables (if installed.)

- Connecting hardware (plugs, jacks, patch panels, cross-connects, patch cords) shall be at least the same grade as the cable to which they connect, for example, Category 5 cable requires Category 5 or better connectors.

- UTP plugs and jacks shall be eight-position (RJ-45 type), configured to the 568A wiring scheme. Coaxial plugs and jacks shall be F-type connectors, properly sized for the grade and shielding of the coaxial cable used. Fiber optic connectors shall be SC-type in either simplex or duplex configuration.

- Proper labeling of the cables is required, along with documentation that decodes the labeling.

For a Grade 1 installation, you should populate each wall plate with just one cable of each type. For a Grade 2 installation, two cables of each type should be run to each wall plate. We recognize that Grade 2 may seem like overkill *at the present*. But again, break your old ways of thinking. One coax with signals going *to* your entertainment center and one coax with signals *from* your entertainment center means that you can watch a movie in a completely different room from the one in which your VCR or DVD player is playing (from your computer monitor, for instance). Or, you could use a centrally located video switch to route satellite, VCR, CATV, or antenna inbound signals around your house to wherever there is a TV. Likewise, say you've got ADSL coming to your computer via UTP for direct access to the Internet, but you still want to use the modem in your computer for faxing. You need two UTP outlets right there.

Following installation, the cabling system should be tested. At a minimum, continuity tests for opens, shorts, and crosses should be performed. You may want to insist on the UTP and optical fiber cable (if terminated) being tested to transmission performance requirements; further, you may want to assure yourself that your Category 5 or better components will actually deliver Category 5 or better performance.

This appendix is just a short summary of what is contained in the TIA 570-A standard. The standard specifies a great deal of additional detail about cables, installation techniques, electrical grounding and bonding, etc. If you want to read about these details (perhaps you're an insomniac), a copy may be purchased from Global Engineering Documents at global.ihs.com and is currently priced at $65.

Picking Cabling Equipment for Home Cabling

So you've made the decision to move forward with your home-cabling project. One of the decisions you will need to make is what type of equipment you will have to purchase and install. While you can use any structured cabling components in your home, many vendors are now building cabinets, panels, and wall plates that are specifically designed for home use. Manufacturer Ortronics (www.ortronics.com) builds a line of cabling products called In House that is designed with the small office or home office in mind. Figures D.1 and D.2 show two cabinets that can hold specially designed Category 5 patch panels, a hub, and a video patch panel.

FIGURE D.1:

Ortronics' compact-sized In House cabinet

(Photo courtesy of Ortronics)

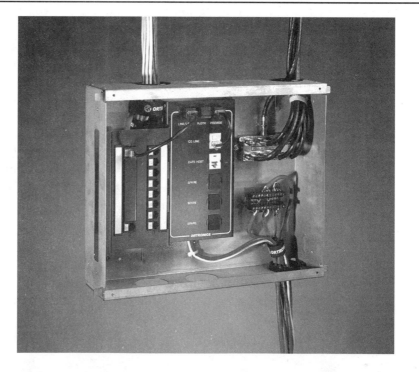

FIGURE D.2:

Ortronics' large-sized
In House cabinet

(Photo courtesy of Ortronics)

Pick a centrally located but out-of-the-way location for your residential cabling cabinet; you probably don't want this cabinet on the wall in your living room. Common locations for residential wiring cabinets include the utility room, laundry room, or garage. This cabinet should ideally be placed close to the termination point of the telephone service, cable TV service, and a power source

In addition to the cabinets, Ortronics also makes a specially designed series of modular faceplates for the In House product family. These modular faceplates (pictured in Figure D.3) offer a variety of modular outlets for RJ-45 connectors, coaxial video, RCA audio/video, S-video, and RJ-25C for voice.

FIGURE D.3:

Different configurations of Ortronics' In House modular faceplate

(Photo courtesy of Ortronics)

> **NOTE** More hints, wiring patterns, and information about residential cabling can be found on David Barnett's Engineering Notebook for Communications Cables at `home1.gte.net/res025bi/index.htm`.

Thinking Forward

Maybe you have looked at the TIA/EIA-570-A standard and are now asking why you may need to put coaxial cable and data cable in every room in the house. After all, you may only have one TV in the family room. But think about other possible services, such as Internet service via cable modem. What about networking using coax? What about delivering VCR output from your entertainment center in the family room to your computer in the study or home office?

It's time to break your old habits of thinking about wiring only being used in traditional ways. The modern idea is to put a universal wiring infrastructure in place so that you can reconfigure at will. This will add value to your home and will make it ready for whatever you want to do in the future.

Builders, as a rule, don't add costs willingly, unless it will clearly allow differentiation or some additional premium to be added to the price of the home. Smart, forward-thinking builders are beginning to install higher-grade wiring, and some are installing structured cabling systems as well. However, it will be up to the consumer to take this trend into the mainstream. It is up to those of us who understand the need and enjoy the technology to demand a structured cabling environment that lets us enjoy it.

INDEX

Note to the Reader: Throughout this index **boldfaced** page numbers indicate primary discussions of a topic. *Italicized* page numbers indicate illustrations.

E

F

G

I

P

Q

R

S

W